HARRAP'S
BOOK OF
BRITISH
DATES

By the same author

Classic Landforms of the Sussex Coast (1982)
The Wilmington Giant: the quest for a lost myth (1983)
The Stonehenge People: an exploration of life in neolithic Britain (1987)
The Knossos Labyrinth: a new view of the 'Palace of Minos' at Knossos (1989)
Minoans: life in bronze age Crete (1990)
Neolithic Britain: new stone age sites of England, Scotland and Wales (1992)

HARRAP'S
BOOK OF
BRITISH
DATES

A comprehensive chronological dictionary
of British dates from prehistoric
times to the present day.

RODNEY CASTLEDEN

HARRAP
London

First published in Great Britain 1991
by HARRAP BOOKS LIMITED
Chelsea House, 26 Market Square,
Bromley, Kent BR1 1NA

ISBN: 0 245-60351-4

Typeset by O'Connor, Parkstone, Poole
Printed and bound in Great Britain by
Mackays of Chatham plc, Chatham, Kent.

For John and Anthea – their sort of book

Preface

The aim of this reference book is to provide as comprehensive and continuous a chronology of Britain's story as can be fitted into a book of manageable length. The middle of 1991 seemed a natural choice for an end-date, since it was then that we had to check proofs and go to press, but it has been less obvious where the book should make its beginning. I feel that, though well-established, the convention of starting with the Roman invasion is an unsatisfactory one, not least because it implies that the native people were doing nothing worthy of notice and that the Romans somehow initiated British culture and history for them. Although written documentation and fine detail began with the Romans, the native story of Britain had been evolving for a long time beforehand. The most natural starting-point seemed to be 8000 BC, the beginning of the present warm stage, or the Flandrian interglacial as it is known to geologists and climatologists. This climatic and cultural watershed was the time when the snows of the Ice Age were in rapid retreat and the landscape as we now see it first appeared and began to be clothed in woodland. By starting this early, we are able to take in the very earliest phase in the long evolution of Stonehenge, still, for many of us, Britain's 'central' monument.

The pre-Roman period is susceptible to dating thanks to refinements in the radiocarbon dating method. With corrected or 'recalibrated' dates, as used in this book, it is possible to achieve an accuracy of within 100 years for dates as old as 2000 BC. The reader should bear in mind that the older the date is, the wider the margin of error becomes.

From the Roman invasion until AD 1000 far greater accuracy is possible, because dated documents exist. Even so, there are inconsistencies among the source documents and sometimes the dates given in the Anglo-Saxon Chronicles are at variance with the archaeological evidence; I have tried to resolve these inconsistencies to the best of my ability, opting always for the dates favoured by recent scholarship.

The book follows Britain's story year by year from the beginning of the interglacial until the present day, listing the major political, dynastic, religious, social, cultural and scientific events — as well as what can only be called Serendipity (see 1754), including such curiosities as the mini-riot caused by the first public appearance of the top hat in 1797. It ranges from the building of Stonehenge to the opening of the Thames Barrier, from

Caractacus to John Major, from 'Sumer is icumen in' to the works of Michael Tippett, from the flooding of the Dover Strait to the 'breakthrough' of the Channel Tunnel. Significant works in the fields of architecture, art, literature and music are listed. Unless otherwise stated, a building is listed in the year of its design, a painting or sculpture in the year of its completion, a book in its year of publication, and a play or a piece of music in its year of first performance.

I hope that this panoramic view of Britain's history will be a useful aid to students of all ages, to researchers, biographers, journalists and creative writers, and that it will come to regarded as a reliable and diverting companion for many a general reader.

Rodney Castleden

Acknowledgements

Thanks are due to my father-in-law, John Dee, for supplying useful dates in the history of transport, and the historian Jeffery Davis for supplying additional information and for his scrupulous checking of the draft text. I should also like to thank Pamela Ruff, Managing Editor at Harrap, for all the care and attention to fine detail which she has put into the book; no author could ask for a more assiduous and sympathetic editor.

Key to icons in text

 Architecture

 Art

 Literature

 Music

BC

8000 The last glaciers in Britain finally melt as the climate becomes warmer. The sea is still about 30m below its AD 1991 level, but rising rapidly. The Straits of Dover and the southern North Sea bed are dry land; people and animals can walk to and from the mainland of Europe. A totem pole is raised on the site of the Stonehenge car park: the place is already a ritual centre of some kind.

6500 The land bridge joining Britain to Europe is flooded, so that Britain becomes an island.

4800 Beginning of agriculture, in small forest clearings.

4070 Flint is mined at Church Hill near Worthing.

3840 A timber trackway, the Sweet Track, is built across the Somerset Levels.

3600 The neolithic enclosure at Maiden Castle is built.

3200 Stonehenge is laid out as an earth circle consisting of an outer ditch and inner bank. It has a round timber building at the centre and a pair of portal stones – of which only the Heel Stone survives – marking the midsummer sunrise. Stone houses are built at Skara Brae, Orkney.

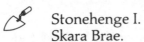 Stonehenge I.
Skara Brae.

3000 Flint mining begins at Grime's Graves in Norfolk.

2700 Silbury Hill near Avebury is built.

Silbury Hill.

2600 Avebury's stone circles are completed at about this time.

Avebury.

2520 A large wooden enclosure is laid out on the site of Dorchester.

 Greyhound Yard, Dorchester.

2300 The neolithic village of Skara Brae is abandoned when a storm engulfs it in sand.

 The Folkton Drums.

2250 85 bluestones are transported from the Preseli Mountains in Wales to Stonehenge, where an unusual double stone circle is begun but not completed.

 Stonehenge II.

2200 The bluestone project at Stonehenge is abandoned. The bluestones are moved off-site so that work can begin on a circle made of larger sarsen stones with running lintels, and a horseshoe arrangement of colossal trilithons. The large sarsens are brought from the hills near Avebury.

 Stonehenge IIIa.

2000 The bluestones are reincorporated into Stonehenge, set as a circle and a horseshoe among the sarsen settings.

 Stonehenge IIIc.

1900 Cairnpapple Hill, Lothian, is laid out as an egg-shaped henge with an arc of 24 standing stones. The hill continues to be a focus for ritual activity until the time of Christ.

1200 Mam Tor, Derbyshire, is occupied; it is one of the highest and oldest hillfort sites to be developed.

1100 Large-scale religious cult activity begins at Flag Fen near Peterborough: for the next 900 years it will be one of the major sacrificial centres of Europe.

450 South Barrule hillfort, Isle of Man, is occupied.

325 Pytheas of Massilia (Marseilles) refers to Ireland and Britain as the Pretanic (or Britannic) Islands: this is thought to be the earliest reference to Britain in documented history.

150   East Anglia, Kent and the Thames Basin are gradually settled from this time on by Belgic people from northern France. Maiden Castle is refortified, apparently against the Belgae.

100   Danebury and other hillforts of southern England are given additional defences because of the threat from Belgic tribes to the east.

55   The Roman Invasion of Britain (55 BC - 45 AD) begins with Julius Caesar's first (reconnaissance) expedition to Britain.

54   Julius Caesar's second expedition, with 800 ships, 5 legions and 2000 cavalry. Cassivellaunus, King of the Catuvellauni, is elected overall war leader in command of a huge confederate Celtic army raised to meet the Roman threat. Caesar crosses the Thames to strike at Cassivellaunus. Cassivellaunus defends the oppidum of Ravensburgh Castle (Hexton, Hertfordshire) against Caesar's forces, but the British army disintegrates.

   The Snettisham gold torcs.

44   Julius Caesar is murdered in Rome.

27   Octavian becomes Emperor, taking the title Augustus; renewed plans for the Roman conquest of Britain come to nothing.

20   Tincommius becomes King of the Atrebates, whose territory centres on Hampshire; it is possible that Tincommius was a Romanizing influence.

   The Waterloo Bridge helmet.

10   Tincommius, King of the Atrebates, is deposed by his own tribesmen. He flees to Rome and is succeeded by his brother Epillus.

8   Camulodunum (Colchester), the capital of the Trinovantes tribe, is captured by the neighbouring (Hertfordshire) Catuvellauni tribe under their leader Tasciovanus, although this conquest is short-lived.

6   Addedomarus, King of the Trinovantes, reclaims his capital.

1   Epillus is deposed and takes refuge in Kent; he is succeeded as King of the Atrebates by Verica.

AD

1   Addedomarus, King of the Trinovantes, dies and is probably buried in the Lexden Tumulus at Colchester; he is succeeded by Dubnovellaunus.

     Lexden Tumulus, Colchester.
Broch of Mousa, Shetland.

     Desborough and Birdlip mirrors.

9   Tasciovanus, King of the Catuvellauni, is succeeded by his son Cunobelinus, who recaptures Camulodunum.

10   Cunobelinus reigns over much of south-east England from his headquarters at Camulodunum, as a tributary ally of the Roman emperors.

20   Epillus, ex-King of the Atrebates, is driven out of his Kentish refuge by Cunobelinus.

     The Battersea shield.

40   Cunobelinus dies and is succeeded by his sons Togodumnus and Caractacus.

41   The invasion of Britain planned by the Emperor Gaius (Caligula) comes to nothing; the expedition peters out in shell-collecting on the French beaches.

42   Verica is deposed and exiled; he is the third successive King of the Atrebates to be ousted.

43   The Romans invade Britain under Aulus Plautius, on the orders of the Emperor Claudius. Waves of defensive activity, including the refortification of hillforts like Mount Caburn, spread through England. Nevertheless, 11 kings throw in their lot with Rome straight away.

44   In the campaign of 43-44, the Romans, under Vespasian, attack and slight over 20 hillforts in southern England. This is the probable date of the massacres at Maiden Castle and Spettisbury and the ballista attack on Hod Hill in Dorset. The Catuvellauni, Trinovantes and Cantiaci, forming a confederation, probably switched their headquarters from Verulamium (St Albans) where there were no defensive earthworks to Camulodunum (Colchester) where there were defences.

47 Roman armies now occupy Britain as far west as the Severn and as far north as the Trent. The Roman military zone is extended to include Devon and Cornwall. The conquest of Britain is progressing so easily and rapidly that a tendency towards Romanization even before the invasion seems likely.

48 British resistance to the Roman occupation nevertheless continues in the territories of the Catuvellauni and Trinovantes, led by the war-leader, Caractacus (correctly Caratacus). Midsummer Hill fort is burnt down by Ostorius Scapula when he attacks the Decangi tribe. Sutton Walls hillfort is similarly attacked and its occupants are massacred.

49 Caractacus continues his guerilla war into Wales. The Romans found Colchester.

50 Caractacus is finally defeated in battle; he flees to the Brigantes. At the large hillfort of Stanwick in North Yorkshire, Venutius prepares his Brigantian supporters for revolt against the Romans. At about this time the Romans found London.

51 Caractacus is handed over to the Romans by Cartimandua, Queen of the Brigantes, and taken to Rome as a prisoner.

58 Quintus Veranius arrives in Britain with new orders to conquer the whole island, a significant expansion of Rome's ambition.

60 Boudicca's East Anglian revolt against Rome begins. A Roman force occupies Sudbrook Camp in Gwent, using it as a base from which the Silures tribe may be subdued.

61 Colchester, St Albans and London are sacked by the Iceni under their queen, Boudicca. The suppression of the Druids in Britain.

62 Boudicca is defeated; she escapes from the field of battle and commits suicide by taking poison.

70 The British Governor Petillius Cerialis attacks Venutius and his followers at Stanwick. The Brigantes are unable to withstand the Roman onslaught.

76 The Emperor Hadrian is born.

78   Gnaeus Julius Agricola's campaigns to subdue northern Britain begin.

80   Scotland, as far north as the Forth and Clyde, is conquered by Roman forces.

84   The final, decisive defeat of the British at Mons Graupius, on the Moray Firth. The British, under the Caledonian war-leader Calgacus, suffer 10,000 casualties. Calgacus tells them just before the battle that they are 'the last men on earth, the last of the free'. Agricola's campaign against the tribes of Scotland is complete.

100

100   At about this time Roman forces temporarily lose control of Scotland; the northern frontier is for a time marked by the Tyne-Solway line.

117   Hadrian becomes Emperor.

121   Hadrian visits Britain and personally surveys the line of the frontier wall which he planned, and which is named after him.

122   Beginning of the building work on Hadrian's Wall (Tyne-Solway) under the supervision of Aulus Platorius Nepos.

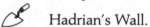 Hadrian's Wall.

138   Emperor Hadrian dies.

140   The Antonine advance into Scotland.

142   Building of the Antonine Wall (Forth-Clyde) under the supervision of Quintus Lollius Urbicus.

 Antonine Wall.

163   Hadrian's Wall is restored.

193   Septimius Severus becomes Emperor, and Clodius Albinus is proclaimed governor of Britain.

196   Clodius Albinus withdraws forces from Britain in his attempt to become Emperor; as a result, the northern frontier of Britain is overrun.

200

208   Emperor Septimius Severus visits Britain himself, to oversee the re-conquest of Scotland.

211   Septimius Severus dies at Eboracum (York).

274   Britain is taken back under central government, and ruled direct from Rome.

287   Carausius, a senior Roman officer charged with clearing the English Channel of pirates, attempts to found an independent 'Empire of Britain'. For a time Britain is under the rule of a local emperor.

293   Carausius loses his foothold on the European mainland when the siege of Boulogne ends. Carausius is deposed and then murdered by Allectus, one of his own men.

296   Constantius Chlorus, Caesar in the West, resumes the conquest of Britain, arriving with a force of Roman troops.

297   Allectus is defeated, and the 'Empire of Britain' comes to an end.

300

304   St Alban is executed at Verulamium; a Roman legionary, he sheltered the Christian Amphibalus and was converted by him. Amphibalus is caught by the Romans four miles away, on Watling Street, and he too is executed.

306   Constantine the Great proclaims himself Emperor at Eboracum (York), and then leaves Britain to fight for his throne. Campaign of Constantius I in Scotland.

343   The Emperor Constans crosses the Channel to Britain, possibly to quell unrest in the north.

360   The Mildenhall Treasure is buried, probably by the family of the Roman general Lupicinus following his arrest.

363   Five years of instability begin, with repeated attacks from Saxons.

364 A large-scale 'barbarian' raid.

367 The great barbarian invasion; the Romans in Britain are successfully attacked by Picts, Scots and Saxons.

369 Roman authority is restored in Britain by Theodosius.

382 Magnus Maximus, the military commander of Britain, wins a victory over the Picts.

383 Magnus Maximus revolts against Rome's authority.

388 The fall of Magnus Maximus.

401 The Roman legions begin to leave Britain. Local defence forces are created. South Cadbury Castle is reoccupied, remaining an important centre for 200 years to come.

406 The usurper Constantine III withdraws Roman forces from Britain to support his claims. This event probably marks the end of the Roman military occupation of Britain.

409 The Saxons renew their attacks on Britain. The British rebel against Constantine III's administration, breaking with Roman rule. From now on, Britain is free of Roman rule.

410 Rome is sacked by the Goths under their leader Alaric. The Emperor Honorius tells the Britons that they must organize their own defence.

418 The Romans gather all the gold-hoards in Britain; some are taken to Gaul and some are buried in Britain.

429 The Roman control of Britain continues to diminish, although the Christian Church maintains close links with Rome until 455. St Germanus, a prominent Gallo-Roman bishop, visits Britain to combat heresy, debating publicly at Verulamium with British leaders.

430 Palladius is sent by Pope Celestine to preach Christian baptism to the Scots.

446 The Britons make a last appeal to Rome to send troops to defend them, but the Romans refuse to help because of their war with the Huns. The Britons also appeal to the Angles.

448 Angles under Hengist and Horsa are invited to Britain by King Vortigern to help defend the country against its enemies.

455 Hengist and Horsa turn against King Vortigern at Aylesford in Kent: Horsa is killed.

456 Hengist and his son Aesc lead a battle against the Britons at Crayford in Kent, killing four companies and putting the rest to flight.

477 The Saxon Aelle and his three sons, Cymen, Wlencing and Cissa, sail to Sussex in three ships, landing at Selsey and killing many Britons.

485 Aelle and his men fight against the Britons at the Battle of Mearcredesburna (Seaford?).

491 A Saxon force under Aelle besieges the Roman fort of Anderida (Pevensey), killing all the Britons inside it.

495 Cerdic, a Saxon leader and ancestor of Alfred, arrives in Wessex.

500

501 The Saxons Port, Bieda and Maegla land at Portsmouth and seize land.

515 Battle of Mount Badon: the West Saxon advance is halted by the Britons, perhaps under Arthur as war-leader.

519 Cerdic and his son Cynric gain control of what is to become the kingdom of Wessex; Cerdic becomes King of the West Saxons.

530 Cerdic and Cynric gain control of the Isle of Wight.

534 Cerdic, King of Wessex, dies, succeeded by Cynric, his son or grandson. Cynric gives the Isle of Wight to Stuf and Wihtgar, his kinsmen.

547 Ida becomes King of Bernicia (part of Northumbria). He builds Bamburgh, first enclosing it with a stockade, then with a rampart.

559 Ida, King of Bernicia, dies and is succeeded by Glappa.

560 Ceawlin, great-grandson of Cerdic, becomes King of Wessex on the death of Cynric, his father. Ceawlin organizes a confederation to drive the Britons out of Wessex and becomes second overlord of the Southern English. Ethelbert, later overking, becomes King of Kent on

the death of his father, Eormenric. Glappa, King of Bernicia, dies and is succeeded by Adda.

563   The Irish St Columba founds a monastery on the island of Iona.

568   Ceawlin and Cutha fight against Ethelbert and drive him into Kent. They kill two Kentish princes, Oslac and Cnebba, at Wibbandum (Wimbledon?). Adda, King of Bernicia, dies and is succeeded by Aedilric.

571   Cutha, the brother of King Ceawlin, fights against the Britons at Biedcanford (unidentified), capturing the villages of Limbury, Aylesbury, Benson and Eynsham. Later in the year Cutha dies.

572   Aedliric, King of Bernicia, dies and is succeeded by Theodric.

574   Columba anoints and inaugurates Aidan as King of Dal Riada.

575   Columba accompanies Aidan, King of Scots, to Ireland and plays a prominent part in the council held at Druim Ceata.

577   Battle of Dyrham, at which Cuthwine and Ceawlin fight against the Britons, killing three of their kings, Coinmail, Condidan and Farinmail. The West Saxon advance is resumed. Cuthwine and Ceawlin also capture Gloucester, Bath and Cirencester.

579   Theodric, King of Bernicia, dies and is succeeded by Friduuald.

582   King Penda of Mercia, son of Pybba, is thought to have been born in this year.

585   Friduuald, King of Bernicia, dies and is succeeded by Hussa.

591   There is a bloody battle at Adam's Grave, Alton Priors, and Ceawlin is deposed; he is succeeded as King of Wessex by Ceol. Hussa, King of Bernicia, dies and is succeeded by Ethefrith.

593   Ceawlin, deposed King of Wessex, dies. Aethelfrith, son of Aethelric, succeeds to the kingdom of Northumbria.

596   Pope Gregory instructs Augustine to go to Britain.

597   St Augustine lands in Kent; he has been sent by the Pope to convert Ethelbert, King of Kent and overking of Southern England. St

Columba dies (8 Jun) on Iona; pilgrims begin arriving within days to see his books, stone pillow, pastoral staff and grave. Augustine becomes Archbishop of Canterbury. Ceol, King of Wessex, dies and is succeeded by Ceolwulf.

600

601   Pope Gregory sends Augustine more assistants. Augustine makes Paulinus Bishop of York, reviving the old Romano-British see of York.

604   Augustine consecrates two bishops, Mellitus and Justus, to preach to the East Saxons. Mellitus is given the see of London, Justus the newly-founded see of Rochester. Aethelfrith, King of Northumbria, kills countless Britons at Chester, including 200 priests who came to pray for the British host; the British leader was Scrocmail, who was one of the few to escape.

607   Aethelfrith, King of Northumbria, defeats the Welsh in a great battle at Chester.

611   Ceolwulf, King of Wessex, dies and is succeeded by Cynegils.

612   Oswiu is born, son of Aethelfrith, King of Northumbria.

616   Aethelfrith, King of Northumbria, dies and is succeeded by Edwin, who becomes the fifth overlord of the English. Aethelberht, King of Kent, dies, succeeded by his son Eadbald. Eadbald reverts to paganism, but is converted by Archbishop Laurentius, Augustine's successor. Redwald, King of East Anglia, takes an army through Mercia and defeats the Northumbrians on their own frontier.

617   Aethelfrith, King of Northumbria, is killed by Redwald, King of East Anglia; he is succeeded by Edwin, under whom Northumbrian power and influence increase. Edwin is acknowledged as bretwalda, or overlord.

619   Archbishop Laurentius dies and is buried beside Augustine; he is succeeded by Mellitus as Archbishop of Canterbury, but when Mellitus leaves London the city reverts to paganism.

624   Archbishop Mellitus dies; Honorius becomes Archbishop of Canterbury.

625   Redwald of East Anglia and overlord of England dies and is buried at Sutton Hoo. The famous ship burial uncovered in 1938-9 is thought to be his.

626   Eomer, a West Saxon assassin, fails to kill King Edwin. Edwin promises Paulinus that he will give his newly-born daughter to God if Paulinus will, by prayer, enable him to overthrow the enemy who sent the assassin. Edwin journeys to Wessex and kills a great number of people. Paulinus baptizes Edwin's daughter on Whit Sunday in the wooden church at York.

627   Edwin, King of Northumbria, is baptized at Easter by Paulinus.

632   OCT   [**14**] The allied forces of Penda of Mercia and Cadwallon of North Wales defeat the Northumbrian army at Hatfield. Edwin, King of Northumbria and fifth overlord of the Southern English, is killed in the battle with his son Osfrith; Osric, son of Aelfric, succeeds Edwin. Penda becomes King of Mercia.

633   Osric dies and is succeeded by Oswald.

634   Birinus begins preaching Christianity to the West Saxons under King Cynegils. Wilfrid begins his education at the court of Oswald, King of Northumbria; Oswald becomes overking.

635   Cynegils, King of Wessex, is baptized by Birinus; Oswald, King of Northumbria, stands sponsor for him. Birinus is given the old Roman fort at Dorchester-on-Thames to found his see.

636   Bishop Aidan chooses the island of Lindisfarne as his base, within sight of King Oswald's Bamburgh Castle.

640   JAN   [**20**] Eadbald, King of Kent, dies and is succeeded by his son Earconberht.

641   King Oswald of Northumbria, sixth overlord of the Southern English, is canonized after his death in battle against Penda at Maserfield (Oswestry?). King Oswald is buried at Bardney and is succeeded by Oswy.

643   Cenwalh succeeds to the kingdom of Wessex after Cynegils' death.

644   Archbishop Paulinus dies in Rochester (OCT 10). Oswine, son of Osric, becomes King of Deira, after Northumbria's division into two kingdoms, Deira and Bernicia.

645 Cenwalh, King of Wessex, is driven from his kingdom by King Penda.

648 St Peter's church in Winchester, founded by King Cenwalh, is completed and consecrated.

650 *The Book of Durrow*, the earliest known example of the new Celtic Christian art, dates from about this time.

651 Aug [**20**] Oswine, King of Deira, dies and is succeeded by Ethelwald, son of King Oswald. [**31**] Bishop Aidan dies in the parish church at Bamburgh; at the same moment Cuthbert, a shepherd in the Lammermuir Hills, sees a vision of a host of angels, which he later connects with Aidan's death and interprets as a call to serve God.

653 Sep [**30**]Archbishop Honorius dies.

654 Anna, King of East Anglia, dies and is succeeded by Aethelhere.

Nov [**15**] Oswy, brother of Oswald, destroys Penda's last alliance in the Battle of Winwaed. Penda and 30 other princes and kings are killed, including Aethelhere of East Anglia, who is succeeded by Ethelwold. Oswiu, King of Bernicia, rules Mercia for three years.

655 Oswiu, King of Bernicia, annexes the Kingdom of Deira and becomes overking. Deusdedit becomes Archbishop of Canterbury.

656 King Peada of Mercia is killed and is succeeded by Wulfhere, son of Penda.

657 The monastery at Whitby is founded. Wulfhere, son of Penda, becomes King of Mercia and overlord of the Southern English.

658 King Cenwalh fights with the Britons at Penselwood.

660 The Augustinian monastery at Canterbury is founded. Bishop Aegelbriht leaves the court of King Cenwalh to receive the bishopric of Paris.

661 Wulfhere, son of Penda, attacks the Isle of Wight and gives the island over to Ethelwold, King of Sussex.

663 Oswiu, King of Northumbria, holds the Synod of Whitby, to resolve the dispute over the date of Easter; Roman Christianity prevails over Celtic Christianity in England.

MAY   [**3**] Eclipse of the sun. Plague sweeps Britain. Bishop Tuda dies. Earconberht, King of Kent, dies and is succeeded by his son Egbert I. Ethelwold, King of East Anglia, dies and is succeeded by Aldwulf. Archbishop Deusdedit dies.

667   Oswiu and Ecgbryht send the priest Wigheard to Rome to be consecrated there as Archbishop of Canterbury, but he dies on arriving in Rome.

668   Pope Vitalianus consecrates Theodorus as Archbishop of Canterbury and sends him to Britain. Theodorus introduces a strictly Roman parochial system and a centralized episcopal system, which will later become a model for the secular state. There is also a revival of Greco-Roman culture.

669   St Wilfrid, the great art patron, is reinstalled as Bishop of Northumbria. St Chad resigns from the bishopric of Lindisfarne to make way for Wilfrid: Wilfrid chooses York as the centre of his diocese.

670   FEB   [**15**] The death of King Oswiu ends the Northumbrian supremacy: he is succeeded by Egfrith.

672   Cenwalh, King of Wessex, dies and is succeeded by his Queen, Seaxburg, for a year. St Chad dies. A synod at Hertford establishes guidelines for the government of the Church.

673   Aescwine succeeds to the throne of Wessex. The Venerable Bede is born; his *Ecclesiastical History of the English Nation* is the main source of information about preceding centuries. St Ethelthryth founds the monastery at Ely. Etheldreda, daughter of Anna, King of East Anglia, founds the convent at Ely.

    JUL   [**4**] Egbert I, King of Kent, dies.

674   The bishopric of Winchester is founded. Building work begins on Hexham Abbey under Wilfrid's direction, using stones from the Roman camp at Corbridge. Wulfhere, King of Mercia, dies and is succeeded by Ethelred, son of Penda.

    Hexham Abbey Crypt.

678   AUG   A comet appears, shining for three months like a sunbeam. Bishop Wilfrid is driven from his bishopric by King Egfrith: he sets out for Rome by way of the Netherlands.

679 Queen Etheldreda dies of cancer of the throat.

680 Wilfrid tells Pope Agatho of the founding of the monastery of Peterborough; the Pope sends a deed for the monastery back to Ethelred. Wilfrid returns with vestments and ornaments for his new church at Hexham. Theodorus, Archbishop of Canterbury, presides over a synod at Hatfield. Hilda, Abbess of Whitby, dies.

Wilfrid's Chair in Hexham Abbey.

685 A 'bloody rain' (probably coloured by Saharan dust) falls on Britain. Centwine, King of Wessex, is deposed and is succeeded by Ceadwalla. The Battle of Nectansmere ends Northumbrian dominance in England. At York, Theodorus consecrates Cuthbert as Bishop of Hexham, at the command of Egfrith.

FEB [6] Hlothere, King of Kent, dies and is succeeded by his son Eadric.

MAY [20] King Egfrith is killed with many of his men; he is succeeded by his brother Aldfrith.

686 Eadric, King of Kent, dies and is succeeded by Oswini.

687 Caedwalla, King of Wessex, launches a second attack on Kent, where his brother Mul is burnt to death.

MAR [20] St Cuthbert dies on Farne Island.

688 Caedwalla abdicates and goes to Rome. Ine becomes King of Wessex, establishing his line as kings of the 'West Saxons', in control of Dorset, Wiltshire and Hampshire. Ine draws up the earliest substantial code of British laws to survive. In Rome, Caedwalla is baptized Peter by Pope Sergius; seven nights later he dies in his baptismal robes and is buried in St Peter's.

690 Archbishop Theodorus, the last Roman archbishop, dies and is buried at Canterbury. Wihtred, son of King Egbert I, becomes King of Kent.

692 JUL [1] Brihtwold, Abbot of Reculver, is chosen archbishop; he is the first English Archbishop of Canterbury.

693 JUN [29] Brihtwold is enthroned as archbishop.

694 The people of Kent confer with Ine, offering to pay compensation for killing Mul.

695 Abbess Sexburga, St Etheldreda's sister, transfers the saint's body to a shrine in the abbey church at Ely.

697 The Mercians kill Osthryth, Ethelred's queen and daughter of Oswy, King of Northumbria.

698 *The Lindisfarne Gospels* are written and illuminated at about this time.

 Bewcastle Cross, Cumbria.

700

704 Cenred becomes King of Mercia in place of Ethelred, who abdicates and becomes a monk. Aldfrith, King of Northumbria, dies and is succeeded by Eadwulf.

709 His mother murdered and his father a monk, Ceolred becomes King of Mercia. Cenred and Offa journey to Rome, Cenred remaining in Rome until his death. Bishop Wilfrid dies at Oundle and is buried at Ripon.

710 Acca, Wilfrid's chaplain, receives Wilfrid's bishopric. Ine and Nun wage war against Geraint, the Welsh king.

713 Aldwulf, King of East Anglia, dies and is succeeded by Alfwold.

714 St Guthlac dies at his hermitage in the Fens.

715 Ine, King of Wessex, and Ceolred, King of Mercia, fight at Adam's Grave.

716 Osred, King of Northumbria, is killed and is succeeded by Cenred. Ceolred, King of Mercia, dies and is buried at Lichfield; he is succeeded by Ethelbald. Ethelred, ex-King of Mercia, dies. Crowland Abbey is founded on the site of St Guthlac's hermitage.

718 Ine's brother Ingild dies; their sister Cuthburg founds the religious community at Wimborne. Cenred, King of Northumbria, dies and is succeeded by Osric, son of King Aldfrith.

721 The kindly John, Archbishop of York, dies in retirement at Beverley.

722   Queen Ethelburg destroys Taunton, which the King of Wessex built.

725   Wihtred, King of Kent, dies after ruling for 34 years, succeeded by his son, Ethelbert II. Ine fights with the South Saxons.

726   Ine, King of Wessex, dies in Rome and is succeeded by Aethelheard.

729   Two comets appear.

      MAY   [**9**] Osric, King of Northumbria, dies and is succeeded by Ceolwulf.

731   Archbishop Beorhtweald dies; Tatwine succeeds him as Archbishop of Canterbury.

          Bede: *Ecclesiastical History of the English People.*

734   JUL   Archbishop Tatwine dies.

735   The death of Bede marks the close of a golden age of Northumbrian art and learning. Nothelm becomes Archbishop of Canterbury.

740   Aethelheard, King of Wessex, dies and is succeeded by Cuthred. Cuthbert succeeds Nothelm as Archbishop of Canterbury.

741   York is burnt down.

743   Ethelbald, King of Mercia, and Cuthred, King of Wessex, fight the Welsh.

744   There are many shooting stars.

746   The First Council of Clofesho (Brixworth?) begins.

747   The Council of Clofesho ends.

748   Cynric, atheling of Wessex, is killed. Eadbriht, King of Kent, dies and is succeeded by Ethelbriht.

749   Alfwold, King of East Anglia, dies; his kingdom is divided among Hun, Beonna and Alberht.

752   Cuthred, King of Wessex, fights with Ethelbald, King of Mercia, and puts him to flight.

756   Cuthred, King of Wessex, dies and is succeeded by Sigeberht. Canterbury is burnt. Ethelbald, King of Mercia and overlord of the Southern English, is killed at Seckington and buried at Repton.

757 Offa seizes the kingdom of Mercia, uniting most of England under his rule; Offa governs England south of the Humber and his son-in-law rules Northumbria. Offa becomes overlord of the Southern English, assuming the title 'rex totius Anglorum patriae'. Sigeberht, King of Wessex, is deposed and killed, and is succeeded by Cynewulf.

758 Edbriht, King of Northumbria, becomes a monk and is succeeded by his son Osulf, who is killed by his own household.

760 Archbishop Cuthbert dies.

761 Moll Ethelwold becomes King of Northumbria. Breguwine becomes Archbishop of Canterbury.

762 Ethelbert of Kent dies and is succeeded by his son Eardwulf.

763 A hard winter.

764 Ceolwulf, King of Northumbria, dies. Breguwine is succeeded by Jaenbeorht as Archbishop of Canterbury.

765 Alhred becomes King of Northumbria.

774 At Easter, the Northumbrians drive their king, Alhred, from York, taking Ethelred I, son of Moll, as their lord.

776 Mercian and Kentish forces meet in battle at Otford in Kent. Strange adders are seen in Sussex.

779 Cynewulf, King of Wessex, and Offa, King of Mercia, fight near Benson (in Oxfordshire): Offa takes the town.

Offa's Dyke.

780 Ethelberht, Archbishop of York, dies and is succeeded by Eanbald. Bishop Ealhmund of Hexham dies, succeeded by Rilberht. Bishop Cynewulf of Lindisfarne resigns and is succeeded by Higbald.

782 The death of Waerburh, Ceolred's queen.

783 Cyneheard kills Cynewulf, King of Wessex, and is himself killed; Brihtric becomes King of Wessex.

787 A contentious synod is held at Chelsea. The first Viking raids. King Offa has his son Egfrith solemnly consecrated as King of the Mercians.

789 Brihtric, King of Wessex, takes Offa's daughter Eadburg for his wife. A dispute arises between Offa and Charlemagne; as a result, Frankish ports are closed to English merchants. The first three ships of the Danes come to England.

790 Osred, King of Northumbria, is betrayed and driven out of his kingdom and is succeeded by Ethelred.

792 King Offa, who lives at Sutton Walls near Hereford, has Ethelbert, King of East Anglia, beheaded. Ethelbert is a suitor for the hand of Offa's daughter Alfrida, and later Offa is stricken with remorse; this leads him to order a tomb for Ethelbert housed in a church, which eventually becomes the Saxon cathedral of Saints Mary and Ethelbert. Jaenbeorht, Archbishop of Canterbury, dies.

793 Athelheard becomes Archbishop of Canterbury. Offa founds St Albans Abbey as a monastery. There are unusual weather phenomena: whirlwinds, lightning storms and 'fiery dragons in the sky' (aurora borealis?): there is also famine. 'Heathen men' ravage and destroy the church at Lindisfarne; this is the earliest report of a Viking raid. King Osred of Northumbria returns from exile, only to be taken and killed: he is buried at Tynemouth. Vikings ransack Egfrith's monastery at Jarrow, but many are later drowned when their ships break up in bad weather; some survivors manage to swim ashore, but they are killed by Northumbrians at Tynemouth.

795 Viking raid on Iona.

796 Eadbert becomes King of Kent. Osbald accedes to the Northumbrian throne but is deposed after a reign of only 27 days, succeeded by Eadwulf, who is crowned on May 26.

JUL   [**29**] Offa, King of Mercia, dies: his death marks the end of Mercian dominance in England.

DEC   [**17**] Offa's son and successor Egfrith dies and is succeeded by Cenwulf.

798 Cenwulf, King of Mercia, ravages Kent, stamping out the attempted Kentish coup against him. The Kentish King Eadbert is taken to Mercia, where his eyes are put out and his hands cut off; the Kentish dynasty is ended, and Cenwulf governs Kent through his brother Cuthred.

800

800 Three Viking raids on Iona are reported at about this time: 68 monks are killed by Vikings at Martyrs' Bay.

802 Brihtric, King of Wessex, dies and is succeeded by Egbert.

803 Higbald, Bishop of Lindisfarne, dies and is succeeded by Egbert.

805 Archbishop Athelheard dies.

806 Wulfred becomes Archbishop of Canterbury. Eardwulf, King of Northumbria, is deposed and expelled, and succeeded by Elfwald.

807 Cuthred, King of Kent, dies; his successor is unknown.

808 Elfwald, King of Northumbria, dies and is succeeded by Eanred, son of King Eardwulf.

814 Archbishop Wulfred journeys to Rome with Wigbriht, bishop of Essex.

815 Wulfred returns to Kent with the Pope's blessing. Egbert, King of Wessex, ravages Cornwall.

821 Cenwulf, King of Mercia, dies and is succeeded by Ceolwulf. Cenwulf's seven-year-old son is murdered and buried beside his father at Winchcombe Abbey in Gloucestershire.

823 Ceolwulf, King of Mercia, is deposed and expelled, and succeeded by Beornwulf.

825 Battle of Ellandun, Wiltshire: Egbert of Wessex defeats the Mercians under Ceolwulf and Wessex becomes the dominant kingdom in England, with suzerainty over Kent, Sussex and Essex. The men of Cornwall fight the men of Devon at Galford. The East Angles kill Beornwulf, King of the Mercians; he is succeeded by Ludecan. Vikings burst into the church on Iona, killing the bishop and several monks, then setting fire to the buildings. Baldred, King of Kent, is deposed and expelled by Egbert, King of Wessex; from now on Kent, Sussex and Essex are to be ruled by the kings of the West Saxons, initially under Egbert's son Ethelwulf as sub-king.

827 Ludecan, King of Mercia, is killed together with his five ealdormen; he is succeeded by Wiglaf. King Egbert conquers Mercia, controlling all England south of the Humber. He is the eighth king to achieve this; the others were Aelle, King of Sussex; Ceawlin, King of Wessex; Aethelbryht, King of Kent; Redwald, King of East Anglia; Edwin, Oswald and Oswy, Kings of Northumbria. Egbert leads his troops against the Northumbrians, who offer him submission and a treaty, which he accepts.

830 The deposed Wiglaf again becomes King of Mercia. King Egbert leads his troops into North Wales and subdues it.

832 Archbishop Wulfred dies; Feologild becomes Archbishop of Canterbury.

833 Ceolnoth becomes Archbishop of Canterbury.

835 The Danes begin to raid the Kentish coast.

836 Egbert's forces are defeated by an army of 25 shiploads of Danes at Carhampton in Somerset.

838 A large force of Danes arrives by sea in Cornwall. Egbert defeats the Danes and their Cornish allies at Hingston Down, putting them to flight.

839 Egbert, King of Wessex, dies after reigning for 37 years; he is succeeded by his son Athelstan as sub-king of Kent, Essex, Sussex and Surrey, and by his son Ethelwulf as King of Wessex. The Pictish king is killed by Danes.

840 In this year the Danes are reported as landing and wintering on the coasts of Britain. Ealdorman Wulfheard fights against 37 ship-companies of Danes at Southampton, and succeeds in beating them off. Ealdorman Aethelhun fights the Danes at Portland: Aethelhun is killed and the Danes hold the field. Wiglaf, King of Mercia, dies and is succeeded by Beorhtwulf. At about this time the Stone of Destiny is removed, probably from Iona, to Scone Abbey by King Kenelm II.

841 Ealdorman Herebryht is killed by Danes, and many of the people of Romney Marsh with him. The same Danish force is responsible for killing many more people in Kent, East Anglia and Lincolnshire. The Danes found Dublin as a trading station and power base in Ireland.

Eanred, King of Northumbria, dies and is succeeded by his son Ethelred II.

842   The Danes kill many in London and Rochester.

844   Kenneth MacAlpin becomes King of Picts as well as Scots, forming the Kingdom of Alban.

845   A Saxon force consisting of men from Somerset under ealdorman Eanulf and men from Dorset under ealdorman Osric meets a Danish army in battle at the mouth of the River Parrett: the Danes are defeated.

849   King Alfred is born, the fifth son of Ethelwulf, at Wantage. Wystan, heir to the Mercian throne, is murdered by his godfather.

850   Ethelred II, King of Northumbria, dies and is succeeded by Osbert.

851   Danes overwinter in southern England. 350 shiploads of Danes sail into the Thames estuary and sack London. The Danes pillage Canterbury and put to flight King Beorhtwulf of Mercia and his troops. After this they advance into Surrey, where they are met by West Saxon troops under Ethelwulf and his son Ethelbald; a great battle follows resulting in a major Saxon victory. Later in the year Athelstan fights a sea battle with the Danes off Sandwich, capturing nine ships and scattering the rest.

852   Beorhtwulf, King of Mercia, dies and is succeeded by Burgred.

853   Alfred visits Rome and is honoured by the Pope. With the aid of King Ethelwulf, King Burgred of Mercia defeats the Welsh. On Thanet, the men of Kent under Ealhere and the men of Surrey under Hutha fight against the Danes; many are killed on both sides, including the two ealdormen. King Burgred of Mercia marries King Ethelwulf's daughter.

855   Alfred makes a state visit to Rome with his father, King Ethelwulf: they remain in Rome for 12 months. The Danes spend their first winter on the Isle of Sheppey. Edmund becomes King of East Anglia.

856   On his return journey from Rome, Ethelwulf marries Judith, the daughter of Charles the Bold, King of the Franks.

858   JAN   [**13**] Ethelwulf, King of Wessex, dies and is succeeded by his son Ethelbald, who has been his co-ruler for three years and who marries his stepmother, Judith.

860   Ethelbald, King of Wessex, dies and is buried at Sherborne; he is succeeded by his brother Ethelbert. The Danes attack Winchester.

863   Aelle becomes King of Northumbria.

865   Ethelbert, King of Wessex, dies and is buried at Sherborne; he is succeeded by his brother Ethelred. The Danish force remains in Thanet and makes peace with the Kentish; the Kentish promise them payment for the truce, but the Danes steal out at night and ravage eastern Kent. The Danish 'Great Army' under the command of Halfdan and Ivarr the Boneless lands on the coast of East Anglia.

866   The 'Great Army' of Danes moves across England.

867   The 'Great Army' takes control of York and ravages Northumbria and Mercia. Alfred marries Elswitha of Mercia. Aelle, King of Northumbria, is murdered by Ragnar Lothbrok; Egbert I is set up as a puppet king by the Danes.

868   Alfred goes with his elder brother King Ethelred in an attempt to dislodge the Vikings from Nottingham.

869   The Great Army descends again on East Anglia.

870   Archbishop Ceolnoth dies and is succeeded by Ethelred as Archbishop of Canterbury.

       Nov   [20] The Danes murder Edmund, King of East Anglia, when he refuses to become their subject; he is succeeded by Oswald, the last English king of East Anglia. The Danes move further south and penetrate up the Thames valley as far as Reading, camping there in readiness for an invasion of Wessex.

871   Battle of Ashdown: King Ethelred of Wessex and Alfred, his younger brother, lead the Wessex armies to victory over the Danes under Kings Bagsac and Halfdan. King Ethelred dies in April of his battle wounds and is succeeded by Alfred as King of Wessex.

872   The Danes occupy London. Egbert I, the puppet king of Northumbria, is driven out.

873   The Danish occupation of north-east England continues. Ricsige becomes King of Northumbria.

874   Mercia falls to the Danes and Burgred, King of Mercia, is driven out; he goes to Rome, where he dies. Burgred is succeeded by Ceolwulf II.

875   The Danes make renewed attacks on the east coast of England. The monks of Lindisfarne put the bones of St Aidan and the head of St Oswald into St Cuthbert's coffin and set off, with the *Lindisfarne Gospels*, to wander about Northumbria and Galloway for the next eight years. The Danes under their leaders Guthrum, Oscytel and Anund turn south and attack Wessex. The Viking kingdom of York is founded by Halfdan.

876   Ricsige, King of Northumbria, dies and is succeeded by Egbert II.

877   A Danish fleet of 120 ships is wrecked at Peveril Point, Swanage.

878   The Danes agree to depart from Exeter and Wareham, but this turns out to be a piece of deception. Guthrum makes a surprise attack on Alfred at Chippenham; Alfred takes refuge at Athelney. Battle of Edington: Alfred, leading troops from all over southern England, succeeds in defeating the Danish forces under Guthrum. Egbert II, King of Northumbria north of the Tyne, dies; he is the last recorded king of Northumbria.

879   Treaty of Wedmore, between Alfred and Guthrum; Guthrum is baptized, and Alfred cedes England north of Watling Street to the Danes.

880   Shaftesbury Abbey is founded. The Viking army settles on the land in East Anglia under their leader Guthrum, who assumes the name Athelstan at his baptism.

883   The monks of Lindisfarne settle at Chester-le-Street. Mercia is now ruled by ealdorman Ethelred, who acknowledges the overlordship of Alfred, King of Wessex.

886   Alfred takes and and occupies London. A treaty with Guthrum formally recognizes the Danelaw, the area of eastern England between Thames and Tees under Viking control; the line of Watling Street from London to Chester is taken as the frontier. Alfred begins to learn Latin.

889   Archbishop Ethelred dies.

890   Plegmund becomes Archbishop of Canterbury. Guthrum dies, possibly succeeded by Eric as ruler of the Danish kingdom of East Anglia.

892 A large Viking force under Haesten invades England, landing in the Thames estuary, but it has only a limited success.

893 At about this time, Pope Formosus (891-6) writes to the Archbishop of Canterbury complaining that 'the abominable rites of the pagans' have been revived in Britain: 'we were minded to cut you off from the body of the Church'.

896 Haesten's Viking invasion force disperses.

899 OCT [26] Alfred the Great dies and is succeeded by Edward the Elder, his son, as King of Wessex.

900

900 JUN [8] Coronation of Edward the Elder.

902 Eric, ruler of the Danish kingdom of East Anglia, dies at the Battle of the Holme.

903 Monks receive what they believe to be the body of King Edmund, who was murdered in 870, and bury the remains at Beodricsworth (later renamed Bury St Edmunds).

910 Asser, bishop of Sherborne, dies. The reconquest of the Danelaw begins.

914 Archbishop Plegmund dies, succeeded by Athelhelm as Archbishop of Canterbury.

917 Aethelflaed, King Edward the Elder's sister, takes Derby; the northern frontier of England now runs from the Wash to the Dee estuary.

918 Edward conquers East Anglia and southern England and receives the 'submissions' of the Welsh kings of Dyfed and Gwynedd.

919 Ragnald becomes ruler of the Viking kingdom of York; in the same year he acknowledges the overlordship of Edward the Elder.

920 Edward the Elder now rules England and Scotland as far north as the Forth and Clyde.

921   Edmund, the son of King Edward and Eadgifu, is born.

923   The King of Scots makes his submission to King Edward. Athelhelm dies and Wulfhelm becomes Archbishop of Canterbury.

924   Jul   [17] King Edward the Elder dies and is succeeded by his son Athelstan.

926   Athelstan compels Welsh, Danish and Scots under-kings to renew the oaths of allegiance they made to his father.

927   The effective northern frontier of England is marked by the River Tees. Athelstan establishes direct rule over the Danes of York.

937   The Battle of Brunanburh, regarded as Athelstan's crowning victory; his English army defeats a combined force of Danes, Scots and Welsh. The West Saxon kings now have clear control over England.

939   Oct   [27] King Athelstan of Wessex dies and is succeeded by his half-brother Edmund I.

940   Dunstan begins the refoundation of Glastonbury as a monastic house.

942   Wulfhelm dies and is succeeded by Oda as Archbishop of Canterbury.

943   Edgar, son of King Edmund and Aelfgifu, is born.

945   Edmund suppresses a Danish rebellion in Mercia and Northumbria and forms a loose alliance with Malcolm, King of Scots.

946   May   [26] King Edmund I is murdered by the outlaw Leofa in his hall at Pucklechurch in Gloucestershire; he is succeeded by his brother Edred.

947   York once again falls to the Danes, under Eric Bloodaxe.

948   Eric Bloodaxe establishes himself as King of York, but is driven out in the same year.

952   The Danes drive Anlaf Sihtricson out of York, and take Eric Bloodaxe back as their leader.

954   King Edred invades Northumbria, driving Eric Bloodaxe out of York. King Eric and his household make for Solway Firth, but they are

ambushed and killed in the Stainmore Pass in the Pennines. England is formally and permanently unified from this time onwards.

955   King Edred dies and is succeeded by Edwig the All-Fair, his nephew.

957   Edwig's brother Edgar leads a rebellion against him and is proclaimed King of Mercia. Dunstan becomes Bishop of London.

958   Oda dies, succeeded by Alfsige as Archbishop of Canterbury; Alfsige also dies, succeeded by Beorhtelm, who is deposed.

959   Edwig dies, succeeded by Edgar the Peaceable, who reunites England. Dunstan leads the movement for monastic reform.

960   Dunstan becomes Archbishop of Canterbury.

965   Westminster Abbey is founded.

966   Crowland Abbey is founded at about this time.

973   Edgar's supremacy as Emperor of Britain is asserted by a solemn coronation by Dunstan at Bath on May 11. The antiphon 'Zadok the Priest' is sung — as it has been at all subsequent coronations. Edgar sails with his fleet to Chester to meet eight British or Welsh sub-kings, who swear fealty to him and row him on the River Dee while Edgar holds the rudder.

975   Jul   [**8**] Edgar the Peaceable dies and is succeeded by his 13-year-old son, Edward the Martyr.

979   Mar   [**18**] King Edward the Martyr is murdered at Corfe Castle; he is succeeded by Ethelred II (the Unready or Ill-advised). Edward is revered as a martyr.

980   From this year, there are increasing numbers of Danish raids. They succeed because of Ethelred's inability to unite the English. Anlaf, King of the Danes in the area round Dublin, abdicates and goes to live as a penitent on Iona.

986   Danes raid Iona, killing the abbot and six monks on the White Sands.

988   Dunstan dies and is succeeded by Athelgar as Archbishop of Canterbury.

990 Athelgar dies and is succeeded by Sigeric Serio as Archbishop of Canterbury.

991 Battle of Maldon: Byrhtnoth of Essex is defeated by the Danes; this is the first Danish victory over the English for 100 years. There are renewed Viking raids on England. 10,000 pounds of silver are paid as Danegeld.

994 The Danish king Sweyn (or Sven) leads an attack on England. Archbishop Sigeric dies.

995 The Lindisfarne community, driven south by the Danes, resettles in Durham, building 'a little church of wands and branches'. Aelfric becomes Archbishop of Canterbury.

997 Another Viking raid.

1000

1002 Ethelred marries Emma, daughter of Richard Duke of Normandy. Massacre of St Brice's Day: Ethelred, motivated by fear and suspicion, attempts to exterminate the Danes in England. The Danes in Oxford take refuge in St Frideswide's minster church, but the citizens burn it down. Among the casualties are Gunhild, Sweyn's sister, and her family.

1003 King Sweyn leads an invasion of England, prompted by the massacre of Danes. After landing on the East Anglian coast, Sweyn sacks Norwich.

1004 Oxford Cathedral (begun).

1005 King Sweyn leaves England, returning to Denmark. Lanfranc, Archbishop of Canterbury, is born. Alphege becomes Archbishop of Canterbury.

1006 King Sweyn returns, leading his army through Berkshire, Hampshire and Wiltshire.

1009 80 ships of the new English fleet are burnt through the treachery of an English captain. A Danish army lands, led by Hemming and Thorkill the Tall.

1010 Thorkill's force burns Oxford and then moves across into East Anglia.

1012 The Danes raid Kent, burning Canterbury Cathedral; Archbishop Alphege is taken prisoner by the Danes and held at Greeenwich.

APR [**19**] During a drunken feast, the Danes murder Alphege. Thorkill, disgusted by his troops' brutality in murdering Alphege, changes sides and brings 45 ships into Ethelred's service.

1013 King Sweyn lands at Sandwich in Kent and establishes his rule over all England. The men of the Danelaw welcome a Danish king and accept Sweyn almost immediately. King Ethelred flees to Normandy. King Sweyn (Forkbeard) sails in triumph up the River Trent to Gainsborough, where he receives the submission of the Northumbrians, the men of Lindsey, and the Danish settlers of north-east Mercia. Lyfing becomes Archbishop of Canterbury.

1014 Battle of Clontarf: Brian Boru, the Irish king, defeats Danish raiders decisively. From this time on, the Danes settle to peaceable trading with the Irish. King Sweyn dies and Ethelred is restored, but the Danish army in England elect Cnut (also spelt Canute) as their king.

1016 Ethelred ravages the old kingdom of Lindsey (part of Lincolnshire), for its complicity in the Danish invasions.

APR [**23**] Ethelred dies and is succeeded by his son Edmund II, Ironside. Edmund and Cnut fight for the kingdom. Edmund comes to an agreement with Cnut whereby he secures Wessex and leaves Cnut in possession of the rest of England.

NOV [**30**] Edmund is murdered, probably at the instigation of Edric Streona. Cnut, son of Sweyn Forkbeard, becomes King of England.

1017 Cnut I divides England into four earldoms. Edric Streona is executed and succeeded as ruler of Mercia by Leofric. Gloucester Abbey is founded.

1018 The Oxford assembly accepts Cnut as king. Buckfast Abbey is founded.

1020 Bury St Edmunds Abbey is founded. Lyfing dies, succeeded by Athelnoth as Archbishop of Canterbury.

1022 Harold Godwinson is born.

1025 At about this time King Cnut's sister runs a lucrative white slave trade, selling English girls to Scandinavia.

1027 William the Conqueror is born in Normandy. Cnut makes a pilgrimage to Rome, demonstrating his alliance with the Church.

1028 In addition to his existing kingdoms, Cnut becomes King of Norway, including Greenland, Orkney, Shetland, Hebrides, Isle of Man; he is now in effect head of a huge Scandinavian empire.

1031 Cnut travels to Scotland and compels Malcolm, King of Scots, to acknowledge his overlordship.

1032 A new stone abbey is dedicated at Bury St Edmunds, on Cnut's orders.

1033 St Anselm is born. The bones of St Alphege are transferred by Cnut from St Paul's Cathedral to Canterbury Cathedral.

1034 Nov   [**25**] Malcolm II of Scotland dies and is succeeded by Duncan I.

1035 William becomes Duke of Normandy.

Nov   [**12**] Cnut I dies at the age of 40, and his empire disintegrates. Harold I, Cnut's son by Aelgifu of Northampton, becomes Regent of England while his half-brother delays in Denmark. England splits once more into the old pattern of Northumbria and Mercia against Wessex.

1036 Alfred and Edward, the sons of Ethelred, return to England from Normandy. On Harold's orders, Alfred is seized and savagely blinded: he dies at Ely. Edward returns to the safety of Normandy.

1037 Archbishop John, who died in 721, is canonized; his body is reburied in a gold-plated shrine at Beverley Minster. The Witan makes Harold I, Cnut's illegitimate son, king.

1038 Eadsige becomes Archbishop of Canterbury.

1040 Mar   [**17**] Harold I dies and is succeeded by Harthacnut (or Cnut II), the son of Cnut by Emma.
Aug   [**14**] Macbeth murders Duncan, King of Scotland: Macbeth himself becomes king.

1041 The men of Worcester murder Harthacnut's tax collectors. Danes burn the monastery at Worcester; Bishop Wulfstan begins rebuilding on a larger scale. Edward the Confessor resides with King Harthacnut, who seems to regard Edward as his successor.

1042 JUN [**8**] Harthacnut dies and Edward the Confessor, son of Ethelred the Unready, becomes King of England; the English line of kings is restored.

1043 APR [**3**] Edward the Confessor is crowned.

1045 JAN [**23**] King Edward marries Edith, daughter of Earl Godwin.

1051 Duke William of Normandy visits England. Edward welcomes him and promises the English succession to him, during a quarrel with Edward's father-in-law, Earl Godwin, over the King's preference for Norman courtiers. Godwin is exiled. Robert Champert of Jumièges becomes Archbishop of Canterbury.

1052 Westminster Abbey is founded by Edward the Confessor. Earl Godwin dies, choking on a crust at a banquet, and is succeeded by his son Harold; Harold, now leader of the army, is in favour with the King. Archbishop Robert is expelled: Stigand becomes Archbishop of Canterbury as well as Bishop of Winchester.

1054 Malcolm III succeeds to the Scottish throne.

1055 Siward, Earl of Northumberland, dies; Harold's untrustworthy brother Tostig is elevated to the earldom in his place.

1056 Harold Godwinson wages a campaign against Griffith ap Llewellyn, the ruler of Wales.

1057 AUG [**15**] Macbeth, King of Scots, dies and is succeeded by his stepson Lulach. Leofric, Earl of Mercia, dies and is succeeded by his son Aelfgar, who surrenders the earldom of East Anglia. East Anglia is bestowed on Harold's brother Gurth. Another of Harold's brothers, Leofwine, is given an earldom made up of the counties north and south of London.

1058 A Norwegian expedition against England is repulsed.

MAR [**17**] Lulach, King of Scots, dies and is succeeded by Malcolm III (Canmore), the son of Duncan I.

1060 Waltham Abbey is completed and consecrated.

1062 Aelfgar, Earl of Mercia, dies and is succeeded by his young son Edwin.

1063 Harold Godwinson wages his second campaign against the aggressions of Griffith ap Llewellyn, King of North Wales. Griffith is killed by his own men.

1064 Harold is shipwrecked on the Normandy coast and falls by chance into the hands of Duke William; he is apparently forced to swear an oath promising William the English Crown.

1065 Nov Northumbria rebels against Earl Tostig, who is forced into exile: he becomes Harold's enemy because Harold does not support him.

Westminster Abbey (completed)

1066 Jan [5] Edward the Confessor dies; Harold Godwinson, Earl of Wessex, is chosen by the Witan to succeed him the next day.

Sep [25] Tostig invades Northumbria with a Norwegian army. Battle of Stamford Bridge: Harold's English army defeats an army led by Harold Hardrada, King of Norway, and Tostig, the English king's brother.

Sep [28] William Duke of Normandy disembarks in Pevensey Bay. Harold begins the march south to meet him.

Oct [14] Battle of Hastings: the English lose the battle partly because they leave their strong position on the crest of a ridge, and partly because they are exhausted by Stamford Bridge and the long march south. The Witan chooses Edgar Atheling, grandson of Edmund Ironside, as king. William circles London and approaches from the north. At Berkhamsted, Edgar and other Saxon notables meet William and offer him the Crown.

Dec [25] William is crowned King in Westminster Abbey.

1067 William is absent in Normandy from February to December. Battle Abbey is founded to commemorate his victory. The Saxon cathedral at Canterbury is burnt down. A rebellion against William in Kent, led by Eustace of Boulogne, is easily suppressed.

The White Tower, London (begun).
Battle Abbey, Sussex.

1068 Henry I is born, son of William I and Matilda.

1069 Rebellion against the Norman invasion breaks out in Mercia and Northumbria; William's troops devastate the north in retaliation.

1070 Council at Winchester summoned and presided over by the King: Stigand is deposed and Lanfranc becomes Archbishop of Canterbury.

     Canterbury Cathedral (the Norman cathedral).

1071 Revolt of Hereward the Wake in the Fens.

1072 William extends his conquest to Scotland. St Margaret orders the abbey on Iona to be rebuilt. A Council at Winchester settles the controversy over the primacy of Canterbury. The Normans capture Ely.

1077   St Albans Cathedral (begun).

1078   Old Sarum Cathedral (begun).

1079 Robert of Normandy rebels against his father in an attempt to gain possession of Normandy for himself. He is defeated by his father, the Conqueror, and reconciled to him.

     Winchester Cathedral (rebuilding begun).
     Hereford Cathedral (begun).

1080 Pope Gregory VII demands that William should do him homage as his vassal, but William refuses on the grounds that it has not been offered by any of his predecessors.

     York Minster (present structure begun).

1082   Rochester Cathedral (completed).

1083 William's queen, Matilda of Flanders, dies.

     Ely Cathedral (present structure begun).

1086 The Domesday Book is compiled.

1087 SEP   [9] William the Conqueror dies at Rouen, as a result of injuries sustained in a horse-riding accident. [26] Coronation of William II of England.

1088 Rebellion in support of Robert Curthose.

1089 MAY [**28**] Archbishop Lanfranc dies: the archbishopric remains vacant for four years.

Worcester Cathedral (begun).

1090 William II wages war on his brother Robert in Normandy.

1091 Malcolm III of Scotland invades England, but is horrified at the English army that confronts him: he readily agrees to offer William homage and acknowledge him as overlord. William is absent from England from February to August. In the Treaty of Caen, William II and Robert of Normandy agree terms: whichever survives will succeed to the dominions of his brother.

Chichester Cathedral (begun).

1092 Lincoln and Chester Cathedrals (begun).
Tewkesbury Abbey (begun).

1093 Anselm becomes Archbishop of Canterbury.

NOV [**13**] Malcolm III of Scotland dies, succeeded by Donald Bane, his brother. Queen Margaret, widow of Malcolm III, dies.

Durham Cathedral (begun).

1094 Rebellions by the Welsh and by the English barons. William II is absent March-December.

MAY King Donald Bane is deposed and Duncan II, son of King Malcolm, becomes King of Scots.
NOV [**12**] Duncan II dies and Donald Bane is reinstated.

1095 William II calls a council at Rockingham to settle the dispute between himself and Anselm. To William's consternation Anselm appeals to Rome, arguing that he may not be tried in a secular court.

1096 William II is absent in France from September. The First Crusade begins.

Norwich Cathedral (completed).
Canterbury Cathedral Crypt (begun).

1097 King Donald Bane of Scotland is deposed; with William's intervention he is succeeded by Edgar, son of Malcolm III. Archbishop Anselm, frustrated by powerlessness, seeks to confer with the Pope; he sails from Dover, leaving the Canterbury estates in the King's hands.

   Westminster Hall.

1098 William II is absent from England all year.

1099 The First Crusade ends. William returns to England in April, absent again June–September.

1100

1100 AUG [2] William II dies in a New Forest hunting accident. Henry I becomes King of England, taking possession immediately of the treasury at Winchester. [5] Henry I is crowned at Westminster Abbey.

1101 JUL Duke Robert of Normandy lands at Portsmouth; many barons flock to his side, but Henry I is also strongly supported. Negotiation at Alton results in Robert's withdrawal on a pension of £2000 a year, on condition that he renounces his claim to the English throne.

1102 Henry I orders Edward the Confessor's tomb to be opened, and the rumour that the body has not decayed is found to be true. Bishop Gundulf of Rochester is strongly rebuked by Abbot Crispin for trying to pull out some tufts of hair from King Edward's white beard, which he wanted to take home as a relic.

1104 The bones of St Cuthbert are buried in the still-incomplete Durham Cathedral.

1106 Battle of Tinchebrai: Henry I acquires Normandy and captures his brother Robert, who remains a captive for the rest of his life in Cardiff Castle.

   Southwark Cathedral (begun).
   Tiverton Castle (begun).

1107 JAN [8] King Edgar of Scotland dies and is succeeded by his brother Alexander I.

1108   Southwell Minster (begun).

1109 APR [**21**] Archbishop Anselm dies, and his archbishopric remains vacant for five years.

1112 Exeter Cathedral (begun).

1113 Hexham Abbey (begun).

The Gloucester Candlestick.

1114 Ralph, Bishop of Rochester, becomes Archbishop of Canterbury.

1117 Magnus (St Magnus), Earl of Orkney, is murdered on the island of Egilsay in Orkney.

Peterborough Cathedral (begun).

1118 Henry I spends the whole year in Normandy, fighting the forces of the French King, the Count of Anjou and the Count of Flanders; while he is overseas, England is governed by a vice-regal committee. Henry's queen, Matilda, dies.

DEC [**21**] Thomas Becket is born at a house in Cheapside.

1119 The Order of Knights Templars is founded.

1120 The wreck of the *White Ship*; William, the heir to the English throne and Henry I's only legitimate son, is drowned.

Llandaff and Bangor Cathedrals (begun).

1122 Archbishop Ralph of Canterbury dies. Henry I remarries, with the aim of producing a new heir, but the marriage proves childless.

1123 William of Corbeil becomes Archbishop of Canterbury.

1124 APR [**25**] Alexander I dies; his brother David I succeeds to the Scottish throne.

1125 Edgar the Atheling, grandson of the Saxon king Edmund II (Ironside) dies.

1128 Henry I's only surviving legitimate child, Matilda, is married to the 14-year-old Geoffrey Plantagenet. Henry compels the English barons to swear to receive Matilda as their queen on his death.

1131 Henry I again insists that his barons swear to recognize Matilda as his successor.

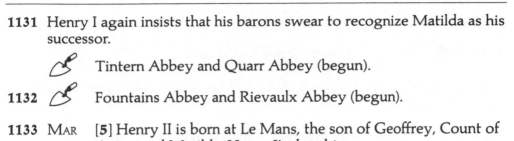 Tintern Abbey and Quarr Abbey (begun).

1132 Fountains Abbey and Rievaulx Abbey (begun).

1133 MAR [5] Henry II is born at Le Mans, the son of Geoffrey, Count of Anjou and Matilda, Henry I's daughter.

Durham Cathedral (completed).

1134 Duke Robert of Normandy dies.

1135 DEC [1] Henry I dies near Rouen. [22] Coronation of King Stephen, followed by civil war between supporters of Stephen and supporters of Matilda. The Scots invade England.

Buildwas Abbey (begun).

1136 William of Corbeil, Archbishop of Canterbury, dies. The King's castle at Norwich is attacked and captured by the Earl of Norfolk.

Geoffrey of Monmouth: *History of the Kings of Britain.*

1137 The Earl of Gloucester, an illegitimate son of Henry I, begins plotting on his half-sister Matilda's behalf.

1138 Battle of the Standard: Thurston, Archbishop of York, organizes an English army to resist the attack of David, the Scots' king, who tries to invade England. It is a resounding English victory. Archbishop Thurston carries with him into battle the banner of St John of Beverley, together with those of St Cuthbert, St Peter of York and St Wilfrid, 'all suspended from one pole like the mast of a ship. The pole was stepped in a four-wheeled cart, on which the bishop stood'.

1139 Theobald of Bec becomes Archbishop of Canterbury. Matilda lands in England, openly supported now by the Earl of Gloucester; the civil war between Stephen and Matilda continues.

1140 St William of Norwich, a 12-year-old skinner's apprentice, is murdered; the citizens of Norwich assume that he has been sacrificed by Jews, which starts a wave of anti-Semitism in England and France.

1141 FEB Battle of Lincoln: Stephen is captured and later exchanged for Robert, Earl of Gloucester. The civil war is resumed.

1143 William the Lion, King of Scots, is born.

1145 🛠 Jervaulx Abbey, Yorkshire (begun).

1147 Matilda's main supporter, Robert of Gloucester, dies. The Second Crusade begins.

1148 Disheartened, Matilda leaves England never to return.

1149 Northumbria is ceded to David, King of Scots. The Second Crusade ends.

1151 King Stephen's wife Matilda dies. Count Geoffrey of Anjou dies, succeeded by Henry, who for a time is diverted from English affairs to deal with his estates in France.

1152 Henry of Anjou, later Henry II, marries Eleanor of Aquitaine, following her divorce from Louis VII. King Stephen's son Eustace dies. Geoffrey of Monmouth, author of *History of the Kings of Britain*, dies.

1153 William, son of Henry of Anjou and Eleanor, is born. Henry invades England to claim his inheritance, and is promised the English succession in the Treaties of Wallingford, Winchester and Westminster.

1154 Oct   [**10**] Roger of Pont L'Eveque becomes Archbishop of York. [**24**] King Stephen dies and is buried at Faversham.

Dec   [**4**] Nicholas Breakspear becomes the first and only English pope – Adrian IV. [**8**] Henry of Anjou arrives in England. [**19**] Henry II of Anjou is crowned King and immediately appoints Thomas Becket his chancellor, apparently on Archbishop Theobald's recommendation. The founding of the House of Plantagenet (Angevin) (1154-1399).

📝 *Anglo-Saxon Chronicle* (completed).

1155 Feb   [**28**] Henry, son of Henry II, is born. The composer Berbart de Ventadorn visits England. The beginning of Henry II's struggle to reduce clerical encroachment on the Royal Courts.

1156 Prince William dies. Matilda, third child and first daughter of Henry II, is born.

1157 SEP [8] Richard I, Duke of Aquitaine, is born at Oxford, the son of Henry II and Eleanor of Aquitaine. Henry regains Northumbria from King David of Scotland.

1158 SEP [23] Geoffrey, Duke of Brittany, is born, the son of Henry II and Eleanor of Aquitaine.

1159 SEP [1] Pope Adrian IV, Nicholas Breakspear, dies.

1161 Eleanor, the sixth child of Henry II, is born.

APR [18] Theobald of Bec, Archbishop of Canterbury, dies

1162 JUN [3] Henry II appoints his Chancellor, Thomas Becket, as Archbishop of Canterbury.

1163 OCT [13] The remains of Edward the Confessor are translated to a new shrine built at Henry II's orders. The still-undecayed body is carried to the new tomb by Archbishop Thomas Becket, Henry II and the Abbot of Westminster.

1164 JAN [13] Council of Clarendon: Henry II obtains ratification for a code based on the practices of Henry I, 'The Constitutions of Clarendon'. Thomas Becket, supported by his bishops, rejects the Constitutions because they limit the power and freedom of the Church. The rift between King and Archbishop widens.

OCT [6] Council of Northampton: this develops into a trial at which Becket is pronounced guilty of feudal disobedience: in fear of his life, Becket rides away to Grantham in the middle of the night.

NOV [2] Becket leaves England and goes into voluntary exile.

1165 OCT Joan, Henry II's seventh child, is born. The Welsh revolt.
DEC [9] Malcolm IV of Scotland dies, succeeded by his brother William the Lion.

1166 Assize of Clarendon: Henry II orders an enquiry into all the crimes committed since the beginning of his reign.

1167 Oxford University is founded at about this time. The Empress Matilda dies.

DEC [24] King John is born at Beaumont Palace in Oxford, the last child of Henry II and Eleanor of Aquitaine.

1168 Princess Matilda marries Henry the Lion, Duke of Saxony.

1169 The dispossessed King of Leinster seeks help in recovering his Crown. Strongbow, Earl of Pembroke, invades Ireland with a small force of Norman adventurers; this is the beginning of Anglo-Norman rule in Ireland.

1170 JUN   [**14**] Coronation of the young king, Prince Henry; he uses the style 'King of the English' and is actually referred to by some chroniclers as 'Henry III'.

DEC   [**2**] Thomas Becket returns to Canterbury from his exile. [**29**] Thomas Becket is murdered in Canterbury Cathedral by four of Henry II's knights, Reginald Fitzurse, William de Tracy, Hugh de Morville and Richard le Breton – on Henry II's orders.

1171 Benedict, the custodian of Thomas Becket's shrine in the crypt at Canterbury, records 14 miraculous cures among the pilgrims approaching the shrine; a cult begins. Strongbow becomes King of Leinster, which arouses Henry II's suspicions. Henry embarks in person on the conquest of Ireland, landing at Waterford and meeting no opposition.

1173 Rebellion against Henry II: William the Lion, King of Scots, invades the north of England. Henry resorts, for the only time in England, to the use of mercenary troops in the suppression of this feudal revolt.

St Magnus' Cathedral, Kirkwall (begun).

1174 APR   [**7**] Richard of Dover becomes Archbishop of Canterbury.

SEP   [**4**] The Choir of Canterbury Cathedral is gutted by fire. The rebuilding of the Choir marks the first appearance in England of the pointed arch. William the Lion is taken prisoner at Alnwick.

Wells Cathedral (begun).
William of Sens: Canterbury Cathedral Choir.

1176 Princess Eleanor marries Alphonso VIII, King of Castile. Assize of Northampton: England is divided into six circuits, each with its own itinerant justices.

Old London Bridge, the first stone bridge over the Thames.

1177 A great fire destroys much of Rochester in Kent. A monk steals the bones of St Petroc from Bodmin Priory and takes them to Brittany; Henry II instigates a search for them and they are returned.

1178 Jun [**18**] A violent explosion is seen on the moon; later astronomers calculate that this may have been the meteor impact that created the crater known as Giordano Bruno.

1180 St David's Cathedral, Dyfed (begun).
Dorchester Abbey in Oxfordshire (begun).

1181 The Assize of Arms: a major reorganization of the English militias.

1183 Death of the young king, Prince Henry, of a fever.

1184 Glastonbury Abbey is badly damaged by fire; rapid rebuilding begins at once.

Dec [**16**] Baldwin becomes Archbishop of Canterbury.

1185 Lincoln Cathedral is destroyed by an earthquake.

William of Sens: Canterbury Cathedral Choir (completed).

1186 The rebuilding of Lincoln and Chichester Cathedrals begins. A great fire sweeps through Chester. Aaron the Jew dies at Lincoln, leaving a fabulous fortune which is seized by the King.

Aug [**19**] Prince Geoffrey, Henry II's third son, dies at a tournament.

Lady Chapel at Glastonbury.

1188 Jul [**10**] Henry II leaves England for the last time.

1189 Princess Matilda, Henry II's daughter, dies.

Jul [**6**] Henry II dies at Chinon, succeeded by his son Richard I, Coeur de Lion.
Aug [**29**] Prince John marries Isabella of Gloucester.
Sep [**3**] Coronation of Richard I in Westminster Abbey. The Third Crusade is launched, led by Frederick Barbarossa, Philip Augustus of France and Richard I of England.

1190 Jul Richard I leaves for the crusade; William Longchamp, Bishop of Ely, is appointed Justiciar.

1191 A Glastonbury monk sees a vision of the coffin of Arthur and Guinevere buried between two pyramids in the Glastonbury burial ground.

MAY   [**12**] Richard I marries Berengaria of Navarre. Acre is captured by the crusaders.

1192 The Third Crusade ends without regaining Jerusalem. Richard I is seized and held to ransom in Austria on his return journey.

1193 Hubert Walter becomes Archbishop of Canterbury.

1194 At a cost of 100,000 marks, Richard I is ransomed and released.

MAR   Richard returns to England.

APR   [**16**] King Richard I takes a bath. The Judicial Inquiry: a questionnaire is sent to all local jurors to assess how local government is working.

1198 AUG   [**24**] Alexander II, King of Scotland, is born, the son of William I and Ermengarde. The New Fiscal Assessment: Hubert Walter reintroduces the idea of a land tax, based on 100-acre units of arable land, but the scheme is not fully worked out or applied.

1199 APR   [**6**] Richard I dies from a crossbow wound received while besieging Chaluz Castle.

MAY   [**27**] John becomes King of England. Establishment of Chancery Rolls.

1200

1200 MAY   Treaty of Le Goulet: the French king recognizes John's French possessions, in return for which John surrenders the Vexin, pays 20,000 marks, and acknowledges King Philip as his overlord in France.

1202 Queen Eleanor, widow of Henry II, dies.

1204 England loses Normandy to France when Philip II of France calls King John to account for the murder of Arthur, John's nephew. Beaulieu Abbey is founded.

1205 On the death of Archbishop Hubert, the Canterbury monks fail to agree on a successor: some favour Reginald, others John de Grey. They appeal to Rome to settle the dispute.

1207 Pope Innocent III sets aside both Canterbury candidates.

JUN [**12**] Stephen Langton becomes Archbishop of Canterbury. King John makes a pilgrimage, in great state, to the shrines of Saints Oswald and Wulfstan at Worcester.

OCT [**1**] Henry III, the son of King John, is born at Winchester.

1208 Simon de Montfort is born. King John refuses to allow Stephen Langton, elected Archbishop of Canterbury in Rome, into England; the Pope, Innocent III, places England under interdict.

1209 Cambridge University is founded at about this time.

JAN [**5**] Prince Richard, son of King John, is born. Pope Innocent III excommunicates King John and declares him deposed.

1210 Llewellyn's revolt in Wales.

JUL [**22**] Joan, daughter of King John, is born.

1213 MAY Pope Innocent III authorizes the French King Philip to prepare an invasion to enforce John's deposition. John surrenders to this pressure, accepting the Pope as overlord, and the interdict is lifted. A great fire destroys Southwark.

AUG Stephen Langton summons a select meeting of barons and prelates in St Paul's to discuss a formula that will provide redress for grievances without open conflict.

1214 Isabella, daughter of King John, is born. Roger Bacon is born at about this time. Battle of Bouvines, in which the French are victorious; this is followed by open rebellion against King John in England. At Bury St Edmunds the barons swear to compel John to grant a charter of rights and liberties, by force if necessary.

DEC [**4**] William the Lion, King of Scotland, dies, succeeded by his son Alexander II.

1215 Eleanor, daughter of King John, is born. At Brackley the barons assemble and restate their demands before advancing to London to confront the King.

JUN [**15**] Magna Carta: King John is compelled by his barons and prelates to sign the Great Charter at Runnymede.

1216 The barons invite King Philip's son Louis to take the English throne. Many of the barons desert John for Louis. John prepares to march on

London, but while crossing the Nene estuary he loses his treasure when a rising tide cuts off his baggage train. There are French raids on the south coast of England.

OCT   [**19**] King John dies unexpectedly at Newark, of a fever, and is succeeded by Henry III. [**28**] Coronation of Henry III; the Earl of Pembroke is appointed Governor during the King's minority.

1217 MAY   Battle of Lincoln.
AUG   Battle of Dover. The French under Louis, later Louis VIII, are driven out of England. Treaty of Lambeth: Louis is able to exact reasonable terms for himself and his supporters before withdrawing to France.

1219 MAY   Earl of Pembroke dies, leaving the direction of the Great Council of magnates to Hubert de Burgh, Peter des Roches, Bishop of Winchester and the new papal legate, Pandulf.

1220 JUL   [**7**] In Canterbury Cathedral, Henry III and a host of bishops, abbots, lords and ladies witness the translation of St Thomas; Archbishop Stephen Langton carries the bones of Thomas Becket up from the old shrine in the crypt to a magnificent new shrine in the newly-built Trinity Chapel.

Salisbury Cathedral (begun).

1221 Dominican and Franciscan friars begin arriving in England.

JUN   [**19**] Princess Joan, King John's daughter, marries Alexander II of Scotland.

1224 Eleanor, daughter of King John, marries William Marshal, Earl of Pembroke. An important Great Council of magnates is convened, when the King is declared formally of age.

JUL   [**19**] The foundation stone of Elgin Cathedral is laid.

1225 Thomas Aquinas is born.

1228 JUL   [**9**] Stephen Langton, Archbishop of Canterbury, dies.

1229 JUN   [**10**] Richard Grant becomes Archbishop of Canterbury.

1230 Queen Berengaria of Navarre, Richard the Lionheart's widow, dies.

Peel Cathedral, Isle of Man (begun).

 Bartolomew Anglicus: *On the Properties of Things* (a popular encyclopaedia).

1232 Hubert de Burgh falls from favour. Lacock Abbey, Wiltshire, is founded.

1234 APR [**2**] Edmund Rich becomes Archbishop of Canterbury.

1235 JUN [**11**] Isabella, daughter of King John, marries Emperor Frederick II. Matthew Paris, monk of St Albans and a friend of Henry III, begins compiling the *Historia Maior*, covering world history; in the section dealing with the years 1235-59, he succeeds in producing a work of original research in which he glorifies England and all things English.

 Matthew Paris: *Historia Maior* (begun).

1236 JAN [**20**] Henry III marries Eleanor of Provence.

1238 JAN Eleanor, daughter of King John and widow of the Earl of Pembroke, marries Simon de Montfort, Earl of Leicester.

1239 JUN [**17**] Edward I is born at Westminster.

1240 Edmund, Archbishop of Canterbury, dies. Llewellyn ap Iorworth, who united Wales and won independence from both the English kings and the Marcher lords, dies; his wife, Joan, was an illegitimate daughter of King John: she predeceased him in 1237.

SEP [**29**] Margaret, daughter of Henry III, is born. At about this time the great council begins to be called 'Parliament'. Knights of the Shire are summoned sometimes to share in its discussions, but its membership and specific functions are far from precisely defined at this stage.

1242 JUN [**25**] Beatrice, daughter of Henry III, is born. Henry III launches an expensive and unsuccessful war to regain the lost English possessions in France.

1245 JAN [**15**] Boniface of Savoy becomes Archbishop of Canterbury. [**16**] Edmund 'Crouchback', son of Henry III, is born.

 Westminster Abbey (rebuilding begun).

1246 Queen Isabella, King John's widow, dies.

1249 University College, Oxford, is founded.

    JUL   [8] Alexander II of Scotland dies, succeeded by his son Alexander III.

1250   'Sumer is icumen in' (written at about this time).

1252 DEC   [26] Margaret, daughter of Henry III of England, marries Alexander III of Scotland.

1254 Henry III accepts the Pope's offer of the throne of Sicily. Prince Edward, later to be Edward I, marries Eleanor of Castile.

1255 A child is found drowned in a cesspool in Lincoln; 'Little St Hugh' is assumed to be a child-sacrifice, a victim of the Jewish community, and canonized, reinforcing the 'blood libel' against the Jews.

1257 JAN   [13] Prince Richard, King John's second son, is elected King of the Romans.

1258 The Provisions of Oxford; the barons under Simon de Montfort force reforms on Henry III: his favourites are to be expelled from England and a committee of 24 appointed to reform the government.

    MAY   In the Treaty of Paris Henry III renounces those provinces in France that he has already lost, and becomes vassal of the French king for fiefs in the south-west of France that are still left to him.

    SEP   [20] Consecration of the newly-completed Salisbury Cathedral.

1259 Matthew Paris, chronicler and miniaturist, dies.

1260 Beatrice, daughter of Henry III, marries John de Dreux, later Duke of Brittany.

1261 The Pope absolves Henry III from his oath to keep the Provisions of Oxford.

    York Minster (begun).

1264 MAY   Battle of Lewes: Simon de Montfort's troops defeat those of Henry III and Prince Edward. Henry III is captured and Simon's party becomes England's rulers.

Jun   Eleanor, daughter of Prince Edward, is born. Simon de Montfort proposes a new form of government, the Forma Regiminis, by which a Council of Nine would be appointed to advise the King in his choice of ministers.

1265 Simon de Montfort's Parliament; burgesses are called as representatives of certain boroughs for the first time.

Aug   [**4**] Battle of Evesham: defeat, death and dismemberment of Simon de Montfort. The battle is the first recorded occasion when a British commander – in this case Prince Edward – exploits an inferior position by taking on one at a time, and defeating, sections of a divided enemy force.

Oct   [**26**] Edmund 'Crouchback' is created Earl of Leicester.

1266 Dictum of Kenilworth, restoring Henry III's full authority and annulling the Provisions of Oxford. The Isle of Man and Hebrides are ceded to the Kingdom of Scotland by Norway.

Jun   [**10**] John, son of Prince Edward, is born.

   Roger Bacon: *Opus Maius*.

1267 Treaty of Montgomery: Henry III recognizes Llewellyn ap Gruffyd as Prince of Wales.

Jun   [**30**] Edmund 'Crouchback' is created Earl of Lancaster.

1268 Balliol College, Oxford, is founded.

Oct   [**13**] Edward the Confessor's body is translated to an even more magnificent new shrine, built at Henry III's orders.

1270 Elgin Cathedral is burnt.

1272 Prince Richard, King of the Romans, dies. William Wallace, the Scottish patriot, is born.

Nov   [**16**] Henry III dies at Westminster, succeeded by his eldest son, Edward I. Edward is in Sicily as the time of his father's death, and stays abroad until August 1274; the country is ruled by regents during this time: Walter Giffard, Archbishop of York, Roger Mortimer and Robert Burnel.

1274 JUL   [**11**] Robert Bruce is born at Turnberry in Ayrshire.
      AUG   [**2**] Edward I arrives back in England.

1275 SEP   [**11**] Margaret, daughter of Edward I, is born.

      Lichfield Cathedral (begun).

1276 First Welsh War begins.

1277 Roger Bacon is imprisoned for heresy. The Welsh War ends.

1279 Statute of Mortmain: the Church is forbidden to inherit any lay person's property without royal licence.

      FEB   [**19**] John Pecham becomes Archbishop of Canterbury.

1282 Rebellion in Wales against English rule. Llewellyn is killed. Edward I succeeds in conquering Wales. Llewellyn's brother Dafydd is captured, tried and executed as a traitor.

1284 The completion of Edward I's conquest of Wales. The Statute of Wales is enacted at Rhuddlan; Wales is formally annexed to England and henceforth subject to the same laws.

      APR   [**25**] Edward II is born at Caernarvon Castle, the third son of Edward I. Peterhouse at Cambridge is founded.

1285 Statute of Winchester: the completion of Henry II's Assize of Arms, providing also for the appointment of Justices of the Peace.

1286 MAR   [**19**] Alexander III, King of Scotland, dies after a fall from his horse, and he is succeeded by Margaret, 'Maid of Norway', the daughter of Eric II of Norway, and Margaret the daughter of Alexander III. Edward I leaves England for Gascony.

1289 Edward I returns from Gascony.

1290 Queen Eleanor of Castile, Edward I's wife, dies. John Schorne becomes rector of North Marston, Buckinghamshire, achieving fame as an exorcist and miracle worker. Statute of Quia Emptores, intended to preserve the rights of lords over their tenants, but in fact it becomes the means of ending tenure by means of knight service.

      JUL   [**8**] Margaret, Edward I's daughter, marries John, Duke of Brabant.

SEP   [**26**] Margaret, Queen of Scotland, 'Maid of Norway', dies at the age of seven in Orkney on her way to marry the six-year-old Edward of Caernarvon, which would have united the Crowns of England and Scotland. The first Scottish interregnum begins. Edward I begins his attempt to rule Scotland. Until now the Jews have been protected by kings as important sources of loans; but public opinion has turned against the Jews, and certain Italian houses are ready to finance royal loans instead. Expulsion of Jews from England.

NOV   [**1**] Massacre of Jews at York Castle.

1291 Queen Eleanor, Henry III's widow, dies. Edward asserts his overlordship of Scotland, persuading the Scots to place the principal Scottish castles in his hands.

1292 NOV   [**17**] The first interregnum in Scotland comes to an end. John Balliol succeeds to the Scottish throne, selected out of 13 competitors by Edward I.

1293 MAY   An Anglo-Gascon fleet defeats a larger Norman-French fleet off the coast of Brittany, and then sacks La Rochelle.

1294 Roger Bacon, the founder of experimental science, dies.

MAY   War with France begins.

SEP   [**12**] Rebellion breaks out again in Wales. [**12**] Robert Winchelsey becomes Archbishop of Canterbury.

1295 The Earl of Warwick's troops defeat those of the principal Welsh leader, Madog ap Llewellyn, breaking the back of the Welsh rebellion. The 'Model Parliament' of Edward I; two knights and two burgesses are called from each shire to vote taxes for him.

OCT   [**23**] Franco-Scottish alliance.

1296 MAR   John Balliol, the Scots' king, sends his defiance to Edward I and renounces his homage. Edward musters a large army at Newcastle in readiness for an invasion of Scotland.

APR   [**27**] Edward I's advance guard defeats the Scottish host at Dunbar.

JUL   [**10**] John Balliol abdicates, forfeiting the throne for contumacy. Edward I takes the government of Scotland into his own hands in the second interregnum; he also, in a symbolic act, takes the Stone of Destiny from the Abbey at

Scone to Westminster Abbey. Edward comes into conflict with the Church.

1297 The rights of the English Parliament to approve taxes and customs dues are confirmed, and also the right to initiate legislation.

AUG [**22**] Edward I sails for Flanders.
SEP [**11**] Battle of Stirling Bridge; Scots troops under William Wallace defeat the English.
OCT [**10**] In Edward I's absence overseas, his regent and council come to terms with opposition leaders. Edward achieves nothing in Flanders, and makes a truce with King Philip IV.

1298 Battle of Falkirk; Edward I's troops defeat Wallace's.

1299 King Edward I of England marries Margaret of France. In Scotland, John Comyn is placed at the head of a Regency for his absent uncle John Balliol.

1300

1300 The English Law Courts are organized into three parts: the King's Bench, the Court of Common Pleas and the Court of the Exchequer.

1301 FEB [**7**] Edward of Caernarvon and Earl of Chester, later to become Edward II, is created Prince of Wales.

 The Coronation Chair.

1302 NOV [**14**] Humphrey, son of Edward I, is born.

1303 John Comyn and his army defeat an English army at Roslin. In retaliation, Edward I for the third time reduces Scotland, and then makes a treaty with Comyn. The Carta Mercatoria grants merchants full freedom of trade and safe conduct, in return for customs dues.

 Glastonbury Abbey (largely rebuilt).

1304 Scotland formally submits to Edward I.

1305 AUG [**3**] William Wallace, the Scots patriot and army commander, is betrayed. Sir John Menteith and 60 men surprise Wallace in his sleep at Robroystoun, capture him and take him to Carlisle.

Wallace is given a show trial by the English. [**23**] Wallace is executed in London by hanging, drawing and quartering.

SEP   An ordinance of Edward I sets out the planned shape of Scotland's future goverment.

1306 FEB   [**10**] Robert Bruce meets John Comyn in the church at Dumfries and kills him: his motive is not known.

MAR   [**25**] The second interregnum in Scotland ends. Robert Bruce is crowned King of Scotland; a revolt against Edward I begins.

APR   [**5**] Furious that his plan for Scotland has been circumvented, Edward I appoints Aymer de Valence as his personal lieutenant in Scotland.

JUN   Valence defeats Bruce at the Battle of Methven: many of those captured are afterwards executed. Bruce becomes a fugitive.

1307 MAY   Bruce defeats Valence at Loudon Hill.

JUL   [**7**] Edward I dies in the arms of his attendants at Burgh-on-Sands near Carlisle, during the march north to Scotland. [**8**] Edward I is succeeded by his son Edward II. Piers Gaveston, a Gascon knight previously banished by Edward I, is recalled by Edward and created Earl of Cornwall.

1308 The death of Duns Scotus.

JAN   [**10**] The Templars are suppressed in Britain. [**25**] Edward II marries Isabella, the daughter of Philip IV of France. While Edward II is in France, Piers Gaveston, Earl of Cornwall, is Regent.

FEB   [**25**] Coronation of Edward II.

MAR   In Parliament the earls demand that the King banish Gaveston. Gaveston leaves for the Lieutenancy of Ireland. In Scotland, Robert Bruce consolidates his position against his Scottish rivals.

1309 Robert Bruce holds his first Parliament at St Andrews.

1310 Edward II leads an English army into Scotland, but to no effect. Parliament appoints Lords Ordainers, 21 bishops and peers, to reform the government and regulate the King's household.

1311 Robert Bruce leads raids across the English border.

1312 Robert Bruce attacks Durham and Hexham. Piers Gaveston, the King's favourite, is recalled, seized by the Earl of Warwick and murdered.

Nov   [**13**] Edward III is born at Windsor Castle, the son of Edward II. [**24**] The King's new son is created Earl of Chester.

1313   Walter Reynolds becomes Archbishop of Canterbury.

Apr   John Balliol, the ex-King of Scotland, dies.

1314   The war between England and Scotland begins again. The Buckinghamshire miracle-worker, John Schorne, dies; pilgrims flock to his tomb at North Marston.

Jun   [**24**] Battle of Bannockburn: the victory of Robert Bruce's army over Edward II's much larger army secures Scotland's independence. Edward II escapes with difficulty to Dunbar and then sails to Berwick. Heavy rains ruin the grain harvests, causing a famine.

1315   Great famine, resulting from a second poor harvest. The Scots raid County Durham and lay siege to the city of Durham.

1316 Aug   John, son of Edward II, is born. The food shortage continues.

1317   Food shortage continues: prices remain high.

1318 Apr   The Scots take Berwick and threaten to conquer the whole of northern England.

Aug   The Treaty of Leake: the English magnates succeed in imposing a programme of reform on the royal household, appointing a formal council.

1319   A truce is agreed between England and Scotland.

1320   Hugh Despenser and his son rise in favour at Edward II's court.

1321 Jan   The Despensers put their castles into a state of defence.

Apr   Civil war breaks out in England.

May   [**24**]The Earl of Lancaster calls an assembly of the chief magnates of northern England; they promise to act together to preserve the peace and defend the realm.

Aug   [**19**] Parliament passes formal judgement on the Despensers; they are sentenced to total forfeiture and banishment.

1322   The English-Scottish truce expires, and Scots cross the border to raid northern England as far south as Preston.

FEB — Thomas, Earl of Lancaster, is denounced as a rebel.

MAR — [**16**] Edward II defeats his opponents at Boroughbridge. [**22**] Edward II orders the execution of the Earl of Lancaster at Pontefract. This is the first time a summary sentence of death and forfeiture for high treason has ever been passed on a peer of the realm.

MAY — [**2**] Statute of York, revoking the earlier Ordinances.

Alan of Walsingham: Octagon Lantern, Ely Cathedral.

1323 MAY — [**30**] A 13-year truce is agreed between England and Scotland at Bishopthorpe.

1324 William of Wykeham is born.

York Minster.

1325 Queen Isabella, Edward II's wife, crosses to France on a pretext; once there, she refuses to return to Edward's court unless he will get rid of the Despensers.

1326 SEP — [**25**] Queen Isabella, Roger Mortimer and Prince Edward land at Orwell in Suffolk and assume royal power. The Despensers are captured and hanged.

OCT — [**26**] Edward, the King's son, is proclaimed Keeper of the Realm.

Clare College, Cambridge.
Oriel College, Oxford.

1327 The Treaty of Corbeil re-establishes the 'auld alliance' of France and Scotland.

JAN — [**13**] A group of bishops and magnates takes an oath at the Guildhall in London to uphold the Queen's cause. [**15**] The Archbishop of Canterbury announces in Westminster Hall that the King is deposed. [**16**] Edward II is kept as a prisoner. [**20**] Edward II agrees to abdicate at Kenilworth. [**25**] He is succeeded by his son, Edward III. During the summer two attempts are made to rescue the ex-king.

SEP — [**21**] Edward II is secretly murdered in Berkeley Castle on Mortimer's orders.

1328 Treaty of Northampton formally recognizes Robert Bruce as Scotland's ruler and Scotland as an independent kingdom.

JAN [**24**] Edward III of England marries Philippa, daughter of William I, Count of Hainault.

JUN [**5**] Simon Mepham becomes Archbishop of Canterbury.

1329 Edward III crosses to Amiens to pay homage to Philip IV of France.

JUN [**7**] Robert Bruce, King of Scotland, dies of leprosy at Cardross Castle, succeeded by his five-year-old son David II.

1330 JUN [**15**] Edward of Woodstock, the Black Prince, is born.

OCT [**19**] The 18-year-old Edward III enters Nottingham Castle by a subterranean passage and surprises and arrests Roger Mortimer. [**20**] Edward III takes the reins of England's government, assuming personal rule for the first time since his accession. Edward keeps his mother, Isabella, imprisoned at Castle Rising in Norfolk for the remainder of her life.

NOV [**29**] Roger Mortimer is hanged as a traitor at Tyburn.

1331 Edward III confirms in writing that it was *liege* homage that he swore to Philip IV in 1329. Edward crosses to France in disguise to discuss with Philip at Pont St Maxence the terms of a lasting peace between England and France.

SEP [**24**] Edward Balliol is enthroned at Scone as King of Scotland.

1332 The first record of the English Parliament dividing into two Houses, Lords and Commoners.

JUN [**16**] Isabella, daughter of Edward III, is born.

DEC [**19**] Edward Balliol is surprised at Annan by the Earl of Moray and Sir Archibald Douglas, supporters of David Bruce, and he flees for his life.

1333 MAR [**18**] Edward the Black Prince is created Earl of Chester.

MAY Edward III blockades Berwick.

JUL [**19**] Battle of Halidon Hill; the Scottish army is defeated by Edward III, demonstrating for the first time the full potential of the English longbow. Edward supports the cause of Edward Balliol and places him on the Scottish throne.

NOV [**26**] John Stratford becomes Archbishop of Canterbury.

1334 Edward III leads an army into Scotland. David II, newly installed as the Scottish king, is offered refuge by the French.

JUN   [**19**] Edward Balliol offers homage to Edward III at Newcastle.

1335 Edward III puts the English Channel ports into a state of defence, anticipating a French intervention in the planned English invasion of Scotland. The French support David Bruce.

JUL   The Archbishop of Rouen declares that 6000 French troops will be sent to help the Scots.

1336 Edward III invades Scotland again. Philip IV's Mediterranean crusading armada appears in the English Channel; there is fighting between English and French at sea.

1337 Edward III leads a smaller army into Scotland, but returns because of fears of an invasion by the French. The beginning of the Hundred Years War between England and France, prompted by rumours that a French fleet has been sighted, preparing to sail to Scotland.

OCT   [**7**] Edward III describes himself as King of France and England, reopening the question of the French succession and making it clear that he is not prepared to compromise.

DEC   Edward III agrees to suspend hostilities against the French until March, at the request of papal representatives.

1338 MAY   [**6**] After a French attack on Portsmouth and the Isle of Wight, Edward III announces that the December truce is no longer binding; the Hundred Years War now begins in earnest. Edward forms an alliance with Flanders.

NOV   [**29**] Lionel, son of Edward III, is born.

1339 Edward III invades France for the first time, without success.

1340 JAN   [**26**] At Ghent, Edward solemnly assumes the arms and title of King of France, mainly to regularize the position of Flemish towns, which have allied themselves to the English cause.

MAR   John of Gaunt (Ghent), Edward III's son, is born.

JUN   Battle of Sluys; Edward III defeats a superior French fleet of 200 ships. Much of the fighting is hand-to-hand, from the castle on one ship to that on another. England loses Edinburgh to the Scots.

SEP   Edward agrees to a one-year truce with France, at Esplechin.

NOV   [**30**] Edward returns to England. Geoffrey Chaucer is born.

🎨   The Luttrell Psalter.

1341 The Trial of Peers: in a clash between Edward III and Archbishop John Stratford the King accuses Stratford of wasting the King's money. The Lords demand that henceforth a peer may only be tried by his Peers in Parliament; Edward III agrees.

Penshurst Place, Kent (begun).

1342 JUN [**30**] Edmund of Langley, son of Edward III, is born.
SEP [**20**] John of Gaunt is created Earl of Richmond.

1343 A truce is declared between England and France.

1344 Peace conference at Avignon, presided over by Pope Clement. The English bid for sovereignty over Gascony, but the conference ends without a settlement.

1346 JUL Edward III decides to lead an army into France on a second campaign, sailing from Portchester, and creating his son a knight.
AUG [**26**] Battle of Crecy; Edward III leads an army of dismounted men-at-arms and archers to destroy a French army of mounted men-at-arms under King Philip: it is the first use of the English longbow in continental warfare.
SEP [**4**] Edward and his army begin the siege of Calais. Battle of Neville's Cross; the Scots attack northern England and are beaten near Durham. King David II of Scotland is taken prisoner.

1347 AUG [**4**] Calais surrenders to the English. In celebration, the first English gold coin is minted: Calais is shortly to become an English colony.
SEP A new truce between England and France is declared at Calais, with England in a position of strength.

1348 The Order of the Garter is founded, to encourage chivalry and military adventure. Black Death in England: the first outbreak of the plague.

1349 Black Death sweeps England.

JUL Black Death reaches its peak. [**19**] Thomas Bradwardine becomes Archbishop of Canterbury.
AUG [**25**] Thomas Bradwardine dies.
DEC [**20**] Simon Islip becomes Archbishop of Canterbury.

Gloucester Cathedral East Window (at about this time).

1350 Owen Glendower is born. Black Death reaches Scotland.

 The Cloud of Unknowing.
Sir Gawain and the Green Knight (at about this time).

1351 First Statute of Labourers; the English Parliament attempts to freeze wages. Statute of Provisors; this recognizes the King as 'patron paramount' of the English Church, as a check against papal control.

1352 First Statute of Treason; this makes the position of the magnates more secure by giving treason a narrower definition, involving an 'open act' aimed at compassing the King's death.

1354 Treaty of Guines; mediated terms are proposed for a peace between England and France based on Edward renouncing his claim to the French throne, in return for which he will receive in full sovereignty Poitou, Aquitaine, Anjou, Maine, Touraine and Calais, yet the treaty is never ratified. Edward refuses to renounce his claim.

1355 JAN   Thomas of Woodstock, son of Edward III, is born.

1356 The Third English Campaign in France.

SEP   [**18**] Cardinal Talleyrand's mediation between Henry of Lancaster and King John fails. [**19**]Battle of Poitiers; Edward the Black Prince defeats the French largely because the French foot soldiers are sent up a hill against the English archers. The Black Prince captures the French king, John II. The victory leads to the Treaty of Bretigny of 1360.

1358 Queen Isabella, Edward II's widow, dies.

1360 Treaty of Bretigny, ending the first stage of the Hundred Years War. Edward III makes great territorial gains in France and appears content with the settlement. King John, the French monarch, is to be freed on payment of a huge ransom of three million gold crowns. Henry Yevele becomes disposer of the King's works of masonry at Westminster Palace and the Tower.

APR   [**14**] 'Black Monday': reported as 'so full dark of mist and hail and so bitter cold that many men died on their horsebacks with the cold'.

1361 Second major outbreak of plague, lasting until 1362.

1362 Wool Staple established at Calais. English becomes the official language in Parliament and the Law Courts instead of French.

William Langland: *Piers Plowman.*

1364 King John of France, unable to raise his ransom, dies a prisoner in London.

1365 JUL [**27**] Isabella, Edward III's daughter, marries Enguerrand de Courcy, later Earl of Bedford.

1366 APR Henry IV, son of John of Gaunt and Blanche, is born.
NOV Simon Langham becomes Archbishop of Canterbury.

1367 Civil war breaks out in Castile. England and France support rival candidates for the Castilian throne, leading to renewed hostilities between England and France. The Black Prince leads an expedition to Spain to support Pedro the Cruel in his attempt to regain the Castilian throne.

JAN [**6**] Richard II is born at Bordeaux.

Jean of Liège: Queen Philippa, marble effigy from life.

1368 OCT [**17**] Lionel, Duke of Clarence, dies.

1369 Fourth Campaign in France: Charles V renews the Hundred Years War with a series of damaging raids on the Channel coast of England. Queen Philippa, Edward III's wife, dies. The third outbreak of plague in Britain.

JAN William Whittlesey becomes Archbishop of Canterbury.

Geoffrey Chaucer: *The Boke of the Duchesse.*

1370 Massacre at Limoges; the Black Prince brutally puts 3000 inhabitants of Limoges to death for deserting the English cause. His health permanently broken, the Black Prince has to resign his command in Aquitaine and return to England.

1371 Popular discontent, largely with the failure of the war in France, is voiced in the English Parliament.

FEB [**22**] King David II of Scotland dies, succeeded by Robert II.

Sep   John of Gaunt marries Constance, daughter of Pedro the Cruel, and assumes the title King of Castile and Leon.

1372 The Castilian fleet destroys at sea an English force on its way to Aquitaine. The Black Prince returns from France.

1373 John of Gaunt leads a large army from Calais to the borders of Burgundy.

1375 Treaty of Bruges; a year-long truce between England and France.

Jun   [**5**] Simon Sudbury becomes Archbishop of Canterbury.

1376 The 'Good Parliament' meets, complaining of illegal profiteering, bribery and waste by named individuals, in particular Lord Latimer, the King's Chamberlain, and Alice Perrers, the King's mistress; this is the first instance of impeachment in English history. The Treaty of Bruges is renewed for another year.

Jun   [**8**] Edward, the Black Prince, dies.

1377 The Spring Parliament grants a poll tax of 4d per head on the whole population between the ages of 12 and 60.

Jun   [**21**] Edward III dies, succeeded by his ten-year-old grandson Richard II; no regent or chief councillor is appointed. [**24**] The Treaty of Bruges expires and the war between England and France resumes with England ill-prepared.

Jul   [**16**] Coronation of Richard II of England; Thomas of Woodstock is created Earl of Buckingham. There are French raids on the Channel coast; Rye and Portsmouth are sacked. Robin Hood is mentioned for the first time.

1378 John of Gaunt besieges St Malo without success. There are further French raids on the Channel coast, especially in Cornwall.

    Canterbury Cathedral Nave (begun).

1379 The Spring Parliament grants another poll tax, this time graded by rank, from 10 marks for the Duke of Lancaster down to 4d for a labouring man. New College is founded by William of Wykeham.

1380 The Spring Parliament agrees to another poll tax, this time one shilling a head for the entire male population, three times the 1377 tax; the tax is to be collected in two instalments, in January and June,

1381. The announcement leads to demonstrations of anger across England. There are more French raids on the Channel coast; Gravesend and Winchelsea are burned.

John Wycliff: English translation of the Bible.

1381 JAN The first instalment of the poll tax comes in and it is plain that large-scale evasion has taken place, so the Government decides to collect the second instalment straight away.

MAY Poll-tax collectors are set upon and expelled from some towns.

JUN [**4**] The Peasants' Revolt begins; rebels attack Dartford. [**6**]Rebels besiege Rochester. [**7**] Rebels enter Maidstone and choose Wat Tyler as their chief. [**10**] Rebels enter Canterbury under Tyler's leadership. [**12**] Essex rebels reach Mile End and Kentish rebels reach Blackheath. [**13**] The Essex and Kentish rebels enter London; the King withdraws to the safety of the Tower; the rebels ransack John of Gaunt's palace. [**14**] Richard II rides to Mile End to parley with rebels, who demand the abolition of serfdom and limitation of rents, and for the heads of Chancellor Sudbury, Treasurer Hales, John of Gaunt and others. Richard agrees to all but the executions. Meanwhile, Kentishmen are breaking into the Tower and beheading Sudbury and Hales. The deaths of the Treasurer and Chancellor, who is also Archbishop of Canterbury, are followed by a general massacre of Flemings in the City of London. [**15**] Richard II summons the Kentish rebels to Smithfield; Tyler meets the King, grows insolent and abusive, and is killed by Mayor Walworth.

OCT [**23**] William Courtenay becomes Archbishop of Canterbury.

1382 John Wycliff, after surviving the heresy trials of 1377-8 thanks to John of Gaunt's intervention, is finally condemned. The Statute de Heretico Comburendo forbids unlicenced preaching and allows obdurate heretics to be burned; this is aimed at suppressing the Lollards.

JAN [**20**] Richard II marries Anne of Bohemia, the daughter of Charles VI of France.

1384 John Wycliff, critic of the Pope's supremacy and infallibility, has a stroke at Mass and dies. The Lollards are expelled from Oxford.

Geoffrey Chaucer: *House of Fame*.

1385 Richard II leads an army into Scotland as far as Edinburgh, but fails to bring the Scots into battle. Joan of Kent, the Black Prince's widow and Richard II's mother, dies.

AUG [**6**] Edmund of Langley and Thomas of Woodstock, sons of Edward III, are created Duke of York and Duke of Gloucester.

Geoffrey Chaucer: *Troilus and Criseyde.*

1386 The Council of Eleven is appointed; the King is compelled to entrust the government of England to a Council of Eleven headed by the Duke of Gloucester. A large French army gathers at Sluys and an invasion of England seems imminent, but the army disbands.

JUL John of Gaunt sails for Galicia and is away for four years. The Autumn Parliament demands the dismissal and impeachment of Pole. Pole is sentenced to forfeiture of a large part of his estates and to imprisonment 'at the King's pleasure'.

1387 Richard II leaves Westminster taking with him a rival council to the Council of Eleven, or commission council.

SEP [**16**] Henry V is born at Monmouth Castle, the son of Henry IV and Mary Bohun.
NOV [**17**] The commission council appears before the King, 'appealing' (or requesting the arrest of) five of his favourites.

1388 The 'Merciless Parliament' meets; the appelant lords (Gloucester, Arundel, Warwick, Derby and Nottingham) appear arm in arm and dressed in cloth of gold, to impeach the King's favourites, de Vere, de la Pole (Earl of Suffolk) and others for high treason.

1389 Richard II, now 23, declares himself of age, dismisses his protectors and assumes authority.

MAY A three-year truce is arranged between England and France. John of Gaunt returns to England untainted, in the King's eyes, by the events of the previous year.

1390 The fourth outbreak of plague in Britain. Elgin Cathedral is burnt again.

APR [**19**] Robert II, King of Scotland, dies, succeeded by Robert III, his son. John of Gaunt, already Duke of Lancaster and King of Castile and Leon, is created Duke of Aquitaine.

Geoffrey Chaucer: *The Canterbury Tales* (at about this time).

1392 An English deputation led by John of Gaunt is received in Amiens by Charles VI; terms for a final peace settlement are discussed.

1393 Richard II orders a cycle of sculptures to decorate the remodelled Westminster Hall. William of Wykeham founds Winchester College.

1394 Richard II grants Chaucer a pension of £20 a year for life. Richard leads an expedition to Ireland (ending in 1395).

JUN [**17**] Anne of Bohemia, Richard II's wife, dies.

1396 Anglo-French Treaty.

MAR [**12**] Richard II marries Isabella, daughter of Charles VI of France.

Nicholas Broker & Godfrey Prest: *Richard II* (gilt effigy made for Westminster Abbey).

1397 Richard II makes himself an absolute monarch; the 'tyranny' begins. Richard Whittington, a wealthy merchant, becomes mayor of London.

JAN [**11**] Thomas Arundel becomes Archbishop of Canterbury, but is later transferred to St Andrews.
SEP [**9**] Thomas of Woodstock, Duke of Gloucester, is put to death at Calais at the instigation of his nephew Richard II. Other Lords Appellant also suffer; Arundel is beheaded and Warwick is imprisoned for life.

1398 Roger Walden becomes Archbishop of Canterbury.

JAN Parliament at Shrewsbury: all the acts of the Merciless Parliament are annulled. [**30**] Bolingbroke appears before the King in Parliament with allegations of treason against Mowbray. Investigations reveal no evidence.
SEP [**16**] Mowbray and Bolingbroke are ordered to fight a judicial duel at Coventry to settle the matter; the King intercedes and banishes them both.

1399 FEB [**3**] John of Gaunt dies. Richard extends Bolingbroke's banishment from ten years to life and takes the whole of his inheritance into his own hands.

MAY Richard II goes to Ireland, giving the exiled Henry Bolingbroke the opportunity to return to England .

JUL Bolingbroke returns to England to claim his father's estates.

AUG [**10**] At Conway, Richard is assured that his throne will not be in jeopardy, so long as he restores Bolingbroke's estates to him; Richard agrees to these terms. [**19**] At Chester, Richard becomes a captive of Henry Bolingbroke, Duke of Lancaster, until his death.

SEP [**29**] Richard II becomes the second British monarch to abdicate. [**30**] Henry Bolingbroke is chosen by Parliament to succeed Richard, as Henry IV.

OCT [**13**] Coronation of Henry IV, the first Lancastrian king of England; founding of the House of Lancaster (1399-1461). [**15**] His son, later Henry V, is created Prince of Wales. [**19**] Archbishop Walden is deprived of his office, and Thomas Arundel is restored as Archbishop of Canterbury.

1400

1400 Rebellion of the Earls of Huntingdon, Kent, Rutland and Salisbury, to restore Richard to the throne; it is soon suppressed and Kent, Salisbury and Huntingdon are executed.

FEB [**10**] Richard II disappears while imprisoned in Pontefract Castle; it is presumed that he is murdered at about this date. His corpse is shortly afterwards displayed in London to prove that he is dead.

SEP [**16**] The Owen Glendower revolt in Wales; Welsh landowners proclaim him Prince of Wales and there are attacks on the English in Flint and Denbigh. A punitive expedition to North Wales is launched by Henry IV.

OCT [**25**] Geoffrey Chaucer, poet and story-teller, dies.

1401 Persecution of the Lollards; a new act permitting the burning of heretics is passed. William Sawtre, sometime Rector of Lynn, is burnt by royal command for preaching Lollard doctrines; he is the first to be executed for Lollard heresy.

Westminster Hall remodelled (fabric by Henry Yevele, hammerbeam roof by Hugh Herland).

1402 Rumours circulate that Richard is still alive somewhere in Wales or Scotland. A Scottish force led by the Duke of Albany invades

England. On its way home it is heavily defeated by the Percies at Homildon Hill; many Scottish noblemen are taken prisoner.

Aug   [1] Edmund of Langley, Duke of York, dies.

1403 Rebellion of the Percies; Henry IV owes the Percies £20,000, so the Percies ally themselves with Owen Glendower, the Mortimers and the Scottish Earl Douglas.

Jul   [12] Henry IV hears the news that his former supporters the Percies are in revolt against him. [21] Battle of Shrewsbury; advancing towards Wales to join Glendower, Henry Hotspur is defeated and killed. The Prince of Wales is wounded in the face. Northumberland submits and is pardoned with a fine.

1404 William of Wykeham dies. The French form an alliance with Owen Glendower.

1405 Rebellion against Henry IV in North Wales, and a second rebellion led by Northumberland together with Archbishop Scrope and Mowbray; the Northumberland rebellion is in favour of Edmund Mortimer, Earl of March, who is Henry IV's prisoner. French forces join Glendower's in his great raid into England.

Apr   Northumberland makes a Treaty of Partition with Glendower and Sir Edmund Mortimer.
May   Prince Henry's force routs the Welsh near Usk; Owen's son Griffith is captured. Northumberland's rebellion is suppressed; Northumberland escapes to Scotland, but Archbishop Scrope and Mowbray are captured and executed. From this time on, Henry IV is often ill; his eldest son Prince Henry gradually assumes a dominating influence in the government.

1406 James, the Scottish King's son, is captured at sea by the English and held captive.

Apr   [4] Robert III, King of Scotland, dies; his successor, James, is still held by the English, so a Regency is assumed by the Duke of Albany. Richard Whittington is again Mayor of London.

1407 Plague strikes England for the fifth time.

1408 Northumberland's third rebellion against Henry IV.

Feb   At the Battle of Bramham Moor, the Earl of Northumberland is defeated, captured and executed. John Gower, the last of the

Anglo-Norman poets, dies; he wrote in both Latin and French and later, perhaps as a result of Chaucer's influence, in English.

1409 Prince Henry, by virtue of his father's illness, is effective president of the King's Council.

SEP [**13**] Queen Isabella, widow of Richard II, dies.

The North Bar (a brick city gate), Beverley.

1410 Owen Glendower's revolt ends.

1411 Canterbury Cathedral Nave (completed).
Guildhall, London (begun).

1412 JUN Henry IV suspects the Prince of Wales of plotting to usurp the throne.

JUL [**9**] Henry IV's second surviving son, Thomas, is created Duke of Clarence and Earl of Aumale.

1413 John Wycliff's writings are condemned by Pope John.

MAR [**20**] Henry IV dies of a stroke as he prays at Edward the Confessor's Shrine in the Jerusalem Chamber at Westminster Abbey, it having been prophesied that he would die in Jerusalem. His elder son, Henry V, succeeds to the English throne. [**21**] Henry V has James of Scotland put in the Tower as a precaution.

JUL Sir John Oldcastle, the King's friend, is found to be an obdurate heretic, arrested and condemned to be executed. Henry V requests a stay of execution so that he can reason with Oldcastle.

OCT [**19**] Oldcastle escapes from the Tower.

DEC Richard II's body is taken from Langley and reburied at Westminster.

1414 JAN [**9**] Lollards attempt to capture Henry V and seize the City of London, but the King's troops arrest them in St Giles' Field as they approach the city gates. [**13**] About 40 of the insurgents are hanged, though Sir John Oldcastle, the probable organizer, escapes.

MAY [**30**] Henry Chichele becomes Archbishop of Canterbury.

DEC The Commons plead with Henry V to negotiate a peaceful settlement instead of resorting to arms against France.

The Wilton Diptych (painted at about this time).

1415 Apr [**16**] At a great council meeting the Chancellor, Bishop Beaufort, announces that Henry V has decided to cross the Channel to recover his heritage; in his absence England will be governed by the Duke of Bedford.

Jul [**31**] A Lollard Plot to assassinate the King at Portchester on his way to embark for France is exposed. The conspirators (Richard, Earl of Cambridge, Lord Scrope and Sir Thomas Grey) favour Edmund Mortimer, Earl of March, as king. Grey is executed at once.

Aug [**5**] Cambridge and Scrope are executed at Southampton after trial by their peers. [**11**] Henry V sails with his army from Southampton. Hostilities between England and France are resumed in the second stage of the Hundred Years War.

Sep [**22**] Henry succeeds in taking Harfleur after a five-week siege; he needs to secure this port for his conquest of Normandy.

Oct [**25**] Battle of Agincourt; 20 miles inland from Boulogne, Henry V defeats a French army three times the size of his own, mounted and heavily armed, with a force of only 6000 men, mostly archers.

Nov [**23**] Henry V's triumphant return to London.

1416 Owen Glendower dies. Henry V makes a pilgrimage to St Winifrede's Well at Shrewsbury.

May [**1**] Emperor Sigismund arrives in England to try to arrange an alliance between England, France and the Empire.

Aug [**15**] Treaty of Canterbury agreed between Henry V and Sigismund, a friendship treaty by which the Emperor promises England military support.

1417 Sir John Oldcastle is finally run to earth in Herefordshire, hung in chains and executed by burning.

Feb There is widespread rearmament in England (gathering goose-feathers for arrow flights).

Jul [**23**] English troops embark once more for France.

Sep [**4**] Henry V is victorious at the Battle of Caen. [**11**] Henry V takes Pontoise.

1418 Jan [**20**] The English army takes Louviers.

Jul [**21**] The English army takes Compiègne. [**30**] The Siege of Rouen begins.

SEP   Cherbourg falls to English forces under Gloucester and Huntingdon. The Duke of Brittany tries unsuccessfully to bring the warring parties together to find a peace formula.

NOV   Inconclusive discussions between the English and French leaders at Alençon.

1419 Richard Whittington is Mayor of London for the third time.

JAN   [**19**] The long siege of Rouen ends; Henry starves the inhabitants into submission. Remaining resistance to Henry V in Normandy crumbles. [**20**] Henry V enters Rouen.

FEB   [**5**] Mantes surrenders to the English. [**8**] Dieppe surrenders to the English.

MAY   [**30**] Henry V meets Duke John of Burgundy at Meulan and falls in love with the Princess Catherine.

JUL   [**31**] Gisors and Pontoise fall to the English.

DEC   [**25**] A formal treaty is agreed between England and France.

1420 APR   [**9**] Treaty of Troyes; English claims to the French throne are recognized and Henry undertakes to marry a French princess; the English conquest of Normandy is complete.

JUN   [**2**] Henry V marries Catherine de Valois, daughter of Charles VI of France, in Troyes Cathedral.

NOV   [**18**] Henry V takes Melun after a siege.

DEC   [**1**] Henry makes a triumphal entry into Paris.

1421 FEB   [**1**] Henry V and Catherine land at Dover to an enthusiastic welcome; the barons of the Cinque Ports wade into the sea to carry them in on their shoulders. [**23**] Coronation of Catherine, followed by a royal tour of the kingdom that includes a visit to the shrine of St John of Beverley.

MAR   [**22**] Thomas, Duke of Clarence, is killed at Beaugé by the French.

JUN-AUG A revival of French resistance causes Henry V to return to France.

DEC   [**6**] Henry VI, the only child of Henry V, is born at Windsor.

1422 William Caxton is born.

MAY   [**2**] Meaux falls to the English army under Henry V.

AUG   [**31**] Henry V dies at Vincennes of dysentery, succeeded by his nine-month-old son, Henry VI. John, Duke of Bedford, acts as Protector of England and Regent in France during the King's minority; the claim of the Duke of Gloucester to the Regency is resisted. Under Bedford, the third stage of the Hundred Years War begins. The Paston letters, a remarkable collection of correspondence of a middle-class English family, begin in this year (and go on until 1509).

📝 Thomas Walsingham: *Historia Anglicana.*

1423 Richard Whittington dies. In prison, King James of Scotland writes his *Kingis Quair.* The Duke of Bedford marries Anne, sister of Philip the Good, strengthening England's alliance with Burgundy.

AUG [**23**] Battle of Verneuil; English and Burgundian forces defeat Franco-Scottish forces.

1424 James I returns to Scotland after his captivity in England. The Cambridge University Library now consists of 122 volumes.

1425 The Parliament of Bats: members are forbidden to carry arms, so they carry sticks and bats instead.

SEP Henry Beaufort, Bishop of Winchester, gathers troops in London; England is close to civil war.
OCT [**30**] There is a skirmish at London bridge between Beaufort's supporters and those of his rival, the Duke of Gloucester; Archbishop Chichele intervenes and arranges a truce.

1426 A reconciliation between Beaufort and Gloucester is organized by a committee of peers.

MAR [**13**] After attempting to explain his conduct in a speech, Beaufort resigns as Chancellor and prepares to leave the country.

1427 Beaufort, now a Cardinal, leaves England for Bohemia as a legate for the Roman Curia.

1428 Richard Neville, Earl of Salisbury and Warwick, is born. English forces under Salisbury lay siege to Orléans, the key to the southern provinces of France; Salisbury himself is killed by a cannon-ball. Beaufort returns to England with a legatine commission to preach against the Hussites. There is a dispute in East Anglia between the Duke of Norfolk and the Earl of Huntingdon; serious rioting results.

1429 The Battle of Herrings; the French make an unsuccessful attack on Sir John Fastolf's convoy; he is carrying supplies of fish to those under siege.

APR   [**28**] Joan of Arc drives the English force away from Orléans. Joan's leadership saves Orléans and France from the English. At Pataye, Joan of Arc defeats Talbot and captures him.

JUL   [**17**] The French Dauphin is crowned Charles VII.

NOV   [**5**] Coronation of Henry VI of England.

1430 Joan of Arc is captured by the Burgundians at Compiègne and sold to the English.

JAN   [**5**] Philippa, daughter of Henry IV, marries King Eric IX of Denmark.

APR   [**23**] Henry VI, a boy of eight, goes to France for two years; during his absence, Humphrey, Duke of Gloucester, is Regent.

OCT   [**16**] James II of Scotland is born, the son of James I and Joan Beaufort.

1431 A Lollard rising is planned in England, but does not take place. Henry VI is crowned in Paris.

MAY   [**30**] Joan of Arc is burnt as a witch at Rouen, by the English.

1432 FEB   Henry VI returns to England.

1433 Henry VI makes a pilgrimage to Bury St Edmunds, where the monks present him with an illustrated *Life of St Edmund*.

John Lydgate: *Life of St Edmund*.

1435 AUG   Congress of Arras begins. The French offer to cede Normandy and Guienne if Henry VI will renounce his claim to the French throne.

SEP   [**6**] The English reject the terms offered by the French and the peace conference ends inconclusively. [**15**] John, Duke of Bedford, dies.

1436 The French army takes Paris.

1437 English troops under John, Lord Talbot, take Pontoise from the French and threaten Paris. Catherine of Valois, Henry V's queen, dies. All Souls College, Oxford, is founded.

FEB   [**21**] James I of Scotland is murdered, succeeded by his son, James II.

NOV   [**12**] Henry VI is declared to be of age.

1439 A peace conference at Calais ends in failure.

1440 Oct [**11**] Eton College is founded by Henry VI.

1441 King's College, Cambridge, is founded by Henry VI. English troops under York and Talbot make significant gains in Normandy, breaking the French siege of Pontoise, but lack of money and reinforcements make it impossible for them to consolidate these successes.

Oct The Duchess of Gloucester is tried for traffic in sorcery and dealing with sorcerers. She admits the charges are true, but denies plotting to destroy the King by sorcery. She is sentenced to public penance followed by life imprisonment. The Duke of Gloucester's political influence is negligible from now on.

1442 It becomes clear that the English possessions in Calais, Normandy and Guienne may all be lost to the French.

Apr [**28**] Edward IV is born at Rouen, the son of Richard, Duke of York.

Sudeley Castle, Glos.

1443 Apr [**12**] Archbishop Henry Chichele dies. A decision is made to send an expedition to Guienne.
Jun [**25**] John Stafford becomes Archbishop of Canterbury.

1444 May It is agreed that Henry VI will marry Margaret of Anjou, in return for a two-year truce., the Truce of Tours.

1445 The French indicate that the cession of Maine to France would form the basis of a peace settlement.

Apr [**23**] Henry VI marries Margaret of Anjou.
Dec [**22**] Henry VI promises in a personal letter to Charles VII to deliver Maine to France.

1446 There is widespread anger in England and among the English in France, that Maine is to be ceded to France. The Duke of Suffolk is blamed, though it is really the King's fault.

London Guildhall (complete).
King's College, Cambridge (complete).

1447 FEB   The Spring Parliament is summoned to Bury. [**18**] Humphrey, Duke of Gloucester, arrives at Bury and is arrested and confined, apparently at Suffolk's instigation. [**23**] Gloucester dies; he may have been murdered or have died of heart failure brought on by the shock of arrest. It is widely assumed that he has been murdered on Suffolk's orders.

1449 The French overrun Normandy, partly because of the Duke of Suffolk's miscalculations; Normandy is finally lost to the French.

1450 Jack Cade's rebellion against Henry VI's government; the rebels demand the blood of the traitors who have lost the French possessions.

FEB   [**7**] The Commons in Parliament impeach the Duke of Suffolk for mismanaging the war and for fraud. Henry VI intervenes to save Suffolk's life by banishing him from England for five years.

MAR   Sir Thomas Kyriel lands at Cherbourg with a force of 3000 men.

APR   [**15**] Kyriel's troops are virtually annihilated by the French.

MAY   [**1**] Suffolk embarks for France, but his ship is run down in the Channel by another ship, the *Nicholas of the Tower*, and Suffolk is captured.

MAY   [**2**] The captain of the *Nicholas* orders Suffolk to be beheaded over one of the ship's boats.

JUN   The French close in on Somerset's troops at Caen.

JUL   [**1**] Somerset surrenders Caen. [**4**] Cade's rebels are in control of London. [**5**] There is fierce fighting on London Bridge between Cade's rebels and Lord Scales' troops; the rebels are dispersed after they are offered free pardons.

AUG   Cherbourg is lost to the French, leaving the whole of Normandy under French control and exposing the south coast of England to attack by the French. Morale collapses in England.

1451 The French take Guienne.

JAN   [**7**] Glasgow University is founded.

SEP   The Earl of Devon lays siege to his old enemy Lord Bonville in Taunton Castle.

1452 MAY   James III of Scotland is born.

SEP   [**6**] John Kempe becomes Archbishop of Canterbury.

OCT   [**2**] Richard III is born at Fotheringhay Castle.

1453 John Dunstable, composer, dies. The French overrun Gascony. The Battle of Chatillon; the final English defeat in France and the end of the Hundred Years War; the English withdraw entirely from France, except for the Channel Islands and Calais, which they retain. The Battle of Heworth, between the followers of the Nevilles and the Percies; this is the first skirmish leading to the Wars of the Roses.

AUG   Henry VI loses his senses and his memory, the first attack of a periodic mental disorder.

OCT   [**13**] Edward, son of Henry VI, is born and created Duke of Cornwall.

DEC   Somerset is arrested and put in the Tower, probably for his own safety.

1454 MAR   [**15**] Prince Edward is created Prince of Wales. [**27**] York is named Protector during the King's insanity, and chief of the council.

AUG   [**22**] Thomas Bourchier becomes Archbishop of Canterbury.

DEC   Henry VI recovers his sanity.

1455 FEB   Somerset is released from the Tower; York is dismissed from his Protectorship.

MAY   [**22**] First Battle of St Albans, marking the beginning of the Wars of the Roses, a struggle between the Dukes of York and Lancaster for the throne of England. Yorkist troops under the Duke of York and the Earls of Salisbury and Warwick break into the town, defeat the royal army and capture the wounded Henry VI; Somerset, the Earl of Northumberland and Lord Clifford die in action, although only 120 men altogether are killed.

1457 JAN   [**28**] Henry VII is born at Pembroke Castle, the son of Edmund Tudor, Earl of Richmond and Margaret Beaufort.

MAR   Henry VI attempts to reconcile the two sides in the civil war, but the reconciliation is a matter of form only.

AUG   The French raid the port of Sandwich.

1459 Queen Margaret prepares for war, raising troops in Cheshire.

SEP   [**23**] Battle of Blore Heath; Salisbury defeats a Lancastrian force. Bills of Attainder are passed against the Duke of York and his supporters.

OCT   [**12**] Battle of Ludford Bridge at Ludlow; the Yorkists are routed by Lancastrian forces headed by Henry VI.

[**13**] Richard, Duke of York, and his son the Earl of Rutland escape to Wales and then to Ireland; Salisbury, Warwick and the Earl of March flee to Calais.

Nov [**20**] Parliament of Devils meets at Coventry; an Act of Attainder convicts York, the Nevilles and their supporters, and legalizes the seizure of their lands.

1460 Jul [**10**] Battle of Northampton; the Yorkists win and Henry VI is again taken prisoner by the Yorkist lords; he is taken to London in royal state.

Aug [**3**] King James II of Scotland dies, succeeded by James III, his eldest son.

Oct [**6**] The Duke of York arrives back in England. [**10**] York arrives with his army in London. [**16**] York's counsel submits to Parliament York's claim to the throne, now publicly mentioned for the first time. [**25**] The Lords' Act of Accord: Henry VI should retain the Crown for his lifetime, but then York and his heirs are to succeed; Henry VI agrees.

Dec [**9**] York and Salisbury set off for the north, pursued by the Lancastrians. The poet John Skelton is born.

1461 Feb [**2**] Battle of Mortimer's Cross; the Yorkists are victorious, capturing Owen Tudor and other Lancastrian lords. Owen Tudor is beheaded. Queen Margaret advances south, with promises of aid from Scotland and France. [**17**] Second Battle of St Albans; Queen Margaret defeats the Earl of Warwick and releases her husband, Henry VI, from captivity by the Yorkist lords.

Mar [**4**] Henry VI is deposed, succeeded by Edward, Earl of March, the late Duke of York's son, as Edward IV; the founding of the House of York (1461-85). Edward sets off for the North, seeking Margaret's army. [**29**] Battle of Towton; the Yorkists win a particularly bloody battle between the largest armies ever to have met on an English battlefield: 28,000 men die. The outcome of the battle confirms Edward's position.

Jun [**28**] Coronation of Edward IV.

The Croxton Play of the Sacrament.

1462 Norway surrenders the Shetlands to the kingdom of Scotland.

Oct Queen Margaret sails to north-east England from Boulogne with 800 French troops.

1463 Henry Beaufort, Duke of Somerset, changes sides again, deserting Edward IV and rejoining Henry VI in Scotland.

1464 Another outbreak of plague in Britain.

APR [**23**] Robert Fayrfax, composer, is born.
MAY [**1**] Edward IV secretly marries Elizabeth Woodville at Grafton Regis. Somerset is captured and executed after a skirmish at Hexham.
JUN [**1**] Edward IV successfully negotiates a 15-year truce with Scotland, depriving the Lancastrians of a Scottish refuge. As a result, Henry VI becomes a fugitive.

1465 MAY Queen Elizabeth's Coronation.
JUL Henry VI is captured by Edward IV and kept prisoner until 1470.
DEC France declares war on England, although no action is taken.

 John Norreys: Ockwells Manor House, Berkshire.

1466 Princess Elizabeth, daughter of Edward IV, is born.

1468 Norway surrenders the Orkneys to the kingdom of Scotland.

1469 Rebellion of Richard, Earl of Warwick, and George, Duke of Clarence, against Edward IV.

JUL [**11**] Clarence marries Isabella Neville at Calais. [**26**] Battle of Edgecote; Warwick's forces defeat Edward IV. Edward IV is imprisoned by Warwick until the end of September, but then released. Warwick and Edward IV are reconciled.

1470 Rebellion breaks out against royal tax-gatherers in Lincolnshire, led by Sir Robert Wells. Edward IV defeats the rebels nears Empingham in a battle known as 'Lose Coat Field'.

MAY [**5**] Edward IV summons Warwick and Clarence. They realize that Edward knows of their treachery and escape to France, where they join Queen Margaret after a reconciliation effected by Louis XI; Warwick becomes a Lancastrian.
SEP [**13**] Warwick, Clarence and Queen Margaret return to England and dethrone Edward IV. Edward escapes from Lynn to the Netherlands.
OCT [**3**] Return and re-crowning of Henry VI.
NOV [**2**] Edward V, the son of Edward IV, is born.

1471 Londoners deride the spectacle of Henry VI being brought out in procession in an old blue velvet gown.

MAR   [**14**] Edward IV returns to England.

APR   [**11**] Henry VI is deposed again. [**14**] Battle of Barnet; the Lancastrians are defeated and Warwick, 'the Kingmaker', is killed trying to escape from the battlefield.

MAY   [**4**] Battle of Tewkesbury; Prince Edward, the son of Henry VI and Queen Margaret, is stabbed to death by Clarence and Gloucester after the battle. The Lancastrians are crushed. [**21**] The deposed king, Henry VI, who has been Edward IV's prisoner since April 11, is murdered in the Tower; Edward IV marches into London in triumph.

JUN   [**26**] Edward IV's son Edward is created Prince of Wales. Sir Thomas Malory dies. St Wilfrid's remains are transferred to a large shrine in York Minster.

1472 JUL   [**12**] Richard, Duke of Gloucester, marries Anne Neville, daughter of Richard, Earl of Warwick.

1473 Edward, Richard Duke of Gloucester's son, is born.

MAR   [**17**] James IV of Scotland is born.

AUG   [**17**] Edward IV's son Richard is born.

1474 MAY   [**28**] Edward IV's son Richard is created Duke of York. William Caxton prints the first book in English, *The Recuyell of the Historyes of Troye*, in Bruges.

1475 Edward IV makes an alliance with the Duke of Burgundy against Louis XI, reviving the old claim to the French throne. John Schorne's body is transferred to St George's Chapel, Windsor. Clarence quarrels with his brothers, the Duke of Gloucester and the King, over property.

JUL   [**4**] Edward IV begins a military expedition to France.

AUG   [**29**] The Anglo-French Treaty of Pecquigny; Louis is to pay a yearly pension to Edward and a ransom for Queen Margaret.

1476 William Caxton sets up his printing press at Westminster.

1477 FEB   Richard, Edward IV's son, is created Duke of Norfolk. In the summer, John Stacey and Thomas Burdett are executed for trying to kill the King by necromancy. The Duke of Clarence protests their innocence before the council at Westminster, confirming in the King's mind his untrustworthiness; Clarence is placed in custody.

Nov [18] William Caxton publishes the first book dated in England, *The Sayings of the Philosophers.*

The Dictes or Sayings of the Philosophers.

1478 Jan The Duke of Clarence is attainted by Parliament, found guilty of high treason and sentenced to death.

Feb [7] Sir Thomas More, statesman and philosopher, is born in London. [15] Edward, Richard Duke of Gloucester's son, is created Earl of Salisbury. [18] Clarence is secretly executed in the Tower.

1479 An outbreak of plague.

John Lydgate: *The Temple of Glass.*

1480 Caxton prints *The Chronicles of England.*

Pattyndenne, Kent (built at about this time).
Ightham Mote, Kent.

1482 Aug [25] Margaret of Anjou, widow of Henry VI, dies.

Oxburgh Hall, Norfolk.

1483 Louis XI breaks off the marriage contract made by the Treaty of Pecquigny. Edward IV prepares to invade France again.

Apr [9] Edward IV dies suddenly and unexpectedly at the age of 40, succeeded by his 12-year-old son Edward V. [29] The Dukes of Gloucester and Buckingham join forces at Northampton. [30] Gloucester takes possession of Edward V at Stony Stratford as his Protector, and exercises effective control from this time on.

May Richard, Duke of Gloucester, arrives in London with Edward V and is recognized as Protector of the Realm.

Jun [16] Edward V and his brother are held in the Tower. [22] Bishop Stillington declares that the two boys are technically bastards, invalidating Edward's claim to the throne. [25] Edward V is deposed. [26] Accession of Richard III; his son Edward is created Duke of Cornwall.

Aug [24] Prince Edward is created Prince of Wales; the Princes in the Tower are probably murdered at about this time.

Oct   Rebellion of Henry, Duke of Buckingham.

St George's Chapel, Windsor.
William Orchard: Divinity School, Oxford.

1484 Mar   [**1**] Elizabeth Woodville, Edward V's mother, is persuaded to come out of sanctuary.

Apr   [**9**] Richard III's son Edward dies.

Aug   Richard III orders the body of Henry VI to be removed from Chertsey Abbey to St George's Chapel, Windsor; the King's body is well preserved, although the face is 'somewhat sunken, with a more meagre appearance than ordinary'.

John Lydgate: *The Life of Our Lady*.

1485 James III of Scotland recovers Dunbar Castle.

Mar   [**16**] Anne Neville, Richard III's queen, dies.

Aug   [**7**] Henry Tudor lands at Milford Haven with 1800 French troops. [**22**] Battle of Bosworth Field; Richard III is killed and his army defeated, largely because sections of his army under the treacherous Stanley brothers defect during the battle. Henry Tudor, the victor, becomes Henry VII.

Oct   [**31**] Coronation of Henry VII; the founding of the House of Tudor (1485-1603).

Dec   [**16**] Catherine of Aragon, the first wife of Henry VIII, is born, the daughter of Ferdinand and Isabella.

Thomas Malory: *Morte d'Arthur* (published posthumously by Caxton).

1486 Jan   [**18**] Henry VII marries Elizabeth, the daughter of Edward IV, uniting Yorkist and Lancastrian claims in his own dynasty.

Mar   An attempted rising in North Yorkshire is led by Lord Lovell. It collapses as the King travels north to deal with it; Lovel flees abroad.

Jul   [**14**] Queen Margaret, wife of James III of Scotland, dies. [**16**] Henry VII announces that the Princes in the Tower were murdered by Richard III.

Sep   [**19**] Henry VII's son Arthur is born and created Duke of Cornwall.

Dec   [**6**] John Morton becomes Archbishop of Canterbury.

Juliana Berners: *Book of St Albans*.

1487 Henry VII founds the court subsequently known as the Court of the Star Chamber.

MAY [**5**] A party of Yorkists with German troops lands at Dublin. [**24**] Lambert Simnel, an impostor, is supported by the Lord Deputy of Ireland, Lord Kildare, and crowned in Dublin as Edward V.

JUN [**16**] Battle of Stoke; Simnel's rising is crushed by the King's forces.

J. leGrand: *The Book of Good Manners.*

1488 JUN [**11**] Battle of Sauchieburn; King James III of Scotland is defeated and afterwards murdered, succeeded by his son, James IV.

Duke Humphrey's Library, Oxford.

1489 In Scotland, rebellions by Lennox in the west and Forbes in the east are suppressed by James IV. Thomas Cranmer, Archbishop of Canterbury, is born at Aslockton. The Treaty of Medina del Campo is agreed between Henry VII and Ferdinand of Aragon.

NOV [**29**] Henry VII's daughter Margaret is born; Arthur is created Prince of Wales.

1490 The Scottish alliance with France is renewed; Scotland is now bound to attack England in the event of an English-French war.

1491 William Caxton, who established the first printing press in London and published nearly 80 books, dies. Charles VIII of France annexes Brittany by compelling Anne, Duchess of Brittany, to marry him. Henry VII opposes this and lays siege to Boulogne. Perkin Warbeck arrives in Cork, calling himself Richard, Duke of York.

JUN [**28**] Henry VIII is born at Greenwich, the son of Henry VII and Elizabeth of York.

DEC [**21**] Truce between England and Scotland declared at Coldstream.

1492 JUN [**8**] Queen Elizabeth Woodville, widow of Edward IV, dies.

NOV By the Treaty of Etaples, Henry agrees to withdraw from Boulogne on promise of a payment of £149,000.

1493 Margaret, Duchess of Burgundy, receives Warbeck as her nephew, calling him the 'White Rose of England'.

1494 Sir William Stanley and other noblemen are arrested, charged with complicity in the Warbeck plot and executed.

DEC Poynings' Law (the Statute of Drogheda) is passed by Sir Edward Poynings, the King's Deputy in Ireland; the law states that no Irish Parliament shall be held and no legislation made without the consent of the English Parliament. The University of Aberdeen is founded.

1495 William Tyndale is born.

AUG Warbeck fails to take Waterford.
Nov Perkin Warbeck arrives in Stirling.

1496 Jesus College, Cambridge, is founded. John Colet begins to lecture at Oxford. Mary Tudor, daughter of Henry VII, is born. Henry VII issues a patent to John Cabot's syndicate, giving him permission to annexe and trade with any lands hitherto unknown on his voyage of exploration. Perkin Warbeck is warmly received at the court of James IV of Scotland; James gives Warbeck Lady Catherine Gordon in marriage.

SEP James IV crosses the English Border accompanied by troops and Perkin Warbeck, but the raid is unsuccessful. Magnus Intercursus; this treaty between Henry VII and Philip of Burgundy encourages the export of wool to the Netherlands but forbids the entry of rebels against Henry into Philip's domains.

J. Stanbridge: *Vocabula.*

1497 The Cabots reach Nova Scotia and return with reports that lead to the development of the Newfoundland fisheries. Rebellion in Cornwall; the Cornish object to paying taxes for a war against Scotland. 15,000 rebels march on London, camping at Blackheath. Many desert; the remaining rebels are beaten by the King's troops and the leaders executed.

JUL [6] Warbeck leaves Scotland. James IV fails to take Norham Castle; a truce is negotiated. [26] Warbeck lands in Cork. Landing in Cornwall, he fails to take Exeter and flees to Beaulieu Abbey where he is captured.

Bell Harry (central tower), Canterbury Cathedral.

1498 A war between England and Scotland is narrowly averted. Perkin Warbeck escapes, but is recaptured.

1499 An epidemic of plague sweeps across Scotland.

FEB   [**22**] Henry VII's son Edmund Tudor is born (dies 1500).
JUL   The truce between England and Scotland is renewed at
      Stirling.
NOV   [**23**] Perkin Warbeck is hanged in the Tower of London. The
      Earl of Warwick is also executed, and with his death the male
      line of Edward IV becomes extinct.

1500

1500 Wynkyn de Worde sets up his printing press in Fleet Street, London;
          this is the beginning of a long connection between Fleet Street and
          printing.

SEP   [**15**] John Morton, Archbishop of Canterbury, dies.

1501 Negotiations are made for the marriage of James IV of Scotland to
          Margaret Tudor. A spectacular pageant is staged to greet Catherine
          of Aragon's arrival in London.

AUG   [**2**] Henry Deane becomes Archbishop of Canterbury.
NOV   [**14**] Arthur, Prince of Wales, marries Catherine of Aragon,
      forming a major diplomatic link between England and Spain
      against France.

Gawain Douglas: *Palace of Honour.*

1502 Margaret, Countess of Richmond (Henry VII's mother), founds
          divinity professorships at the Universities of Oxford and Cambridge.
          James IV of Scotland marries Margaret, Henry VII's daughter.

APR   [**2**] Arthur, Prince of Wales, dies; Catherine of Aragon is
      espoused to Arthur's 11-year-old brother Henry, after papal
      dispensation is obtained.

William Vertue: Henry VII's Chapel, Westminster Abbey.

1503 Sir Thomas Wyatt is born. Queen Elizabeth, Henry VII's wife, dies in
          childbirth: the King is heart-broken.

FEB   [**15**] Archbishop Deane dies.

1504 Henry VII places guilds and companies under state supervision. Coins
          are minted bearing an accurate likeness of the King.

JAN   [**24**] William Warham becomes Archbishop of Canterbury.

FEB   [**18**] Prince Henry, who became Duke of Cornwall on his brother Arthur's death, is created Prince of Wales and Earl of Chester.

1505 Henry VII grants a new charter to the Merchant Adventurers Company which holds an export monopoly in English cloth to Germany and the Low Countries. Thomas Tallis, composer, is born. Christ's College, Cambridge, is founded. The Prince of Wales' engagement to Catherine of Aragon is broken off.

APR   James IV of Scotland threatens to declare war on England.

    Michael Sittow: *Henry VII.*

1506 By the Treaty of Windsor, Henry Prince of Wales is engaged to Margaret of Austria, the daughter of Archduke Philip. Philip extradited the Yorkist pretender to the English throne, Edmund Earl of Suffolk, from the Tyrol; Edmund is subsequently imprisoned in the Tower of London.

1507 London is ravaged by an epidemic of 'sweating sickness', an infectious disease similar to the plague.

1508 James IV declines to give Henry VII of England an undertaking not to renew his alliance with France. Archbishop Warham opens the tomb of St Dunstan at Canterbury. In a leaden case he finds the saint's bones and a lead plate inscribed with Dunstan's name. Warham triumphantly writes to Abbot Bere of Glastonbury of his discovery, instructing him to abandon all claim to his , Bere's, obviously fake 'Dunstan' relics. The first book to be printed in Scotland is produced: it is a volume of Chaucer.

   John Wastell: Fan Vault, King's College Chapel, Cambridge.

1509 Sebastian Cabot leads an expedition to search for the North-West Passage to Asia, but turns back in Hudson Bay when confronted by ice. Erasmus visits England for the third time and lectures at Cambridge.

APR   [**21**] Henry VII dies at Richmond; his death is greeted wth feasting, dancing and general rejoicing. He is succeeded by his 17-year-old son, Henry VIII.

JUN   [**11**] Henry VIII marries Catherine of Aragon. [**24**] Coronation of Henry VIII.

Brasenose College, Oxford.
St John's College, Cambridge.

 Erasmus: *In Praise of Folly* (dedicated to Thomas More).

1510 John Colet founds St Paul's School, London. Erasmus becomes Professor of Greek at Cambridge. Richard Empson and Edmund Dudley are executed for alleged treason; they were Henry VII's extortionate tax-gatherers and House of Commons speakers, and their execution was a calculated bid for popularity. *Everyman*, the morality play, is performed for the first time.

 Everyman.

1511 Henry VIII joins the Holy League against the French and begins large-scale reforms of the Royal Navy. The Scottish warship *Great Michael* is built. All men under the age of 40 are required to possess bows and arrows, and practise archery.

1512 Henry VIII claims the French throne. Scotland renews its alliance and England finds itself at war with both France and Scotland. English troops are sent, unsuccessfully, into Spain. For the first time in the English Royal Navy double-decked warships are used; they displace one thousand tons and are armed with 70 guns. An Act of Parliament is passed removing benefit of clergy for many serious crimes. Physicians and surgeons are required to obtain licences from the Bishop of London in order to practise in London. Parliament forbids the importing of foreign caps into England.

APR [**10**] Queen Margaret of Scotland gives birth to a son, James V.

DEC Bitter anti-clerical feelings in London result in the arrest of Richard Hunne on heresy charges and his murder in prison.

 Erasmus: *De Ratione Studii et Instituendi Pueros.*

1513 The Scots renew their alliance with France and invade England.

SEP [**9**] Battle of Flodden Field; King James IV of Scotland is defeated and killed by English troops under Thomas Howard, Earl of Surrey, and thousands of Scots are slaughtered in the battle. James is succeeded by his son, James V, with Queen Margaret as his guardian. The Scottish Navy is sold to France. Henry VIII withdraws from the Holy League. Edmund, Earl of Suffolk, is executed.

1514 England makes peace with Scotland and France. Mary Tudor, Henry VIII's sister, marries Louis XII of France; Louis dies three months later and Mary then marries the Duke of Suffolk. Thomas Wolsey becomes Archbishop of York and orders work to begin on Hampton Court Palace.

AUG   Queen Margaret Tudor, Regent of Scotland, marries Archibald Douglas, Earl of Angus. John Colet and Erasmus visit and describe the Shrine of St Thomas at Canterbury; Erasmus leaves Cambridge and returns to the Continent. Fresh green peas become a fashionable ingredient in the English diet.

1515   Laws are passed against the enclosure of common land. Richard Kidderminster, Abbot of Winchcombe, and Dr Henry Standish debate the independence of the English Church. The 300-foot spire of Louth Church is completed at a cost of £305.

MAY   The Duke of Albany captures the young James V and makes himself Protector of Scotland.
SEP   [**30**] Albany forces Margaret Tudor, the Queen Regent, to flee to England.
DEC   [**24**] Thomas Wolsey becomes Lord Chancellor of England and a cardinal.

King's College, Cambridge (completed).
Hampton Court Palace (begun).

John Skelton: *Magnificence.*
Alexander Barclay: *Eclogues* (earliest pastoral poems in English).

1516   FEB   [**18**] Queen Mary I (Mary Tudor) is born at Greenwich Palace, the daughter of Henry VIII and Catherine of Aragon.

Erasmus: *New Testament, Latin Translation.*
Thomas More: *Utopia.*

1517   The Duke of Albany goes to France and Queen Margaret returns to Scotland. 'Evil May Day' riots in London are brutally suppressed; on Wolsey's orders 60 rioters are hanged. Wolsey is made papal legate to England. The galley *Virgin Mary* is launched, with Henry VIII acting the role of the ship's master, blowing a large whistle 'almost as loud as a trumpet'. A printing press is set up for the first time in Oxford.

1518   The Peace of London is devised by Wolsey between England, France, the Pope, Maximilian I and Spain; now that he is papal legate

Wolsey's authority exceeds that of the Archbishop of Canterbury. Authorized by Henry VIII, Thomas Linacre founds a college of physicians. Another epidemic of 'sweating sickness' sweeps England, killing large numbers in the towns. Queen Margaret of Scotland quarrels with her husband Angus.

 Torrigiano: *Effigy of Henry VII.*

1519 Henry VIII becomes a candidate in the election of a Holy Roman Emperor; his secretary, Richard Pace, is sent to Germany to represent him. The King's illegitimate son, Henry Fitzroy, is born. Queen Margaret of Scotland forms an alliance with the Earl of Arran, the enemy of her husband Angus. The Royal Exchange in London is founded by Thomas Gresham, a merchant.

 St George's Chapel, Windsor (completed).
Henry VII's Chapel, Westminster (completed).
Lord Marney: Layer Marney Towers, Essex (begun). [Only the gatehouse was completed.]

 John Skelton: *Colin Clout.*

1520 Henry VIII journeys to Otford Palace, then on to Canterbury, Dover and France for the 'Field of the Cloth of Gold', a diplomatic meeting with the French King Francis I; the result is an Anglo-French commercial treaty, agreed at Dover and Canterbury. Bowling lanes are built in Whitehall at the King's orders. A printing press is set up at Cambridge. A religious discussion group sympathetic to Church reform meets regularly at the White Horse tavern in Cambridge; among its members are Thomas Cranmer, Hugh Latimer, John Firth and Miles Coverdale.

NOV [19] The Duke of Albany returns to Scotland.

 Robert Fayrfax: *Music for the Field of the Cloth of Gold.*

1521 Henry VIII and Wolsey attempt to set up a National Company to promote trade and discovery, but are prevented by obstruction from the London Livery Companies. Pope Leo X confers the title 'Defender of the Faith' on Henry VIII. Henry orders the execution of Edward Stafford, Duke of Buckingham, on trumped-up charges of disloyalty.

MAY In London many foreign Lutheran books are ceremoniously burned in front of Cardinal Wolsey.
OCT [24] Robert Fayrfax, composer, dies.

 Henry VII: *The Golden Book* (a refutation of Luther).
Major: *History of Scotland.*

Alexander Barclay: *The Introductory to Write and Pronounce French* (the first French grammar).

1522 England declares war on France and Scotland. The Holy Roman Emperor Charles V visits Henry VIII in England and signs the Treaty of Windsor; the two monarchs agree to invade France. Wolsey faces increasing opposition and criticism as his power increases. Hugh Aston, composer, dies.

1523 Sir Thomas More is elected Speaker of the House of Commons, after Parliament meets at Blackfriars. Parliament rebels against Henry VIII's demands for extra funds and he is forced to abandon his request.

APR   An English army under Dorset invades Scotland.
SEP   The Duke of Albany returns to Scotland from France.

Anthony Fitzherbert: *Book of Husbandry*
John Skelton: *Why come ye not to Court?*

1524 Queen Margaret governs Scotland in alliance with the Earl of Arran, her husband having left Scotland for France in 1522. English courtiers feast on turkeys brought from South America. William Tyndale leaves England for Germany.

OCT   [**20**] Thomas Linacre, physician to Henry VII and Henry VIII, dies.

1525 Wolsey founds Cardinal College, Oxford, and completes the suppression of 29 religious houses, transferring their revenues to his new college. Wolsey concludes a peace agreement with France. Hops are introduced into England from Artois. Wolsey is forced to abandon his Amicable Loan, which is in effect a tax without Parliamentary approval. Henry Fitzroy, the King's illegitimate son, is created Duke of Richmond and Somerset.

Hampton Court Palace (completed). [New wings added 1531-6.]

William Tyndale: The New Testament (in English).

1526 The Earl of Kildare, who rules Ireland, is committed to the Tower; he is replaced by Sir William Skeffington. The authorities in England try to prevent Tyndale's Bible being distributed. The portrait painter Hans Holbein come to England.

Hans Holbein: *Sir Thomas More and his Family.*

Hector Boece: *History of Scotland.*

1527 Copies of William Tyndale's English translation of the New
Testament are publicly burnt in St Paul's Cathedral. The Royal
Divorce crisis begins, as Henry VIII appeals to the Pope for
permission to divorce Catherine of Aragon. Henry's sister Margaret
divorces Angus, and secretly marries Henry Stuart, Lord Methven. Sir
Hugh Willoughby sets sail to try to discover a North-East Passage to
China; he gets little support from the King, who prefers to spend his
money strengthening the Royal Navy. John Dee, scholar and
alchemist, is born.

 Hans Holbein: *Sir Thomas More.*

1528 England and France are at war with Spain. In Scotland, Angus falls
from power and the Scottish Reformation begins. The Scots under
James V conclude a five-year truce with England. Wolsey dissolves 22
religious houses to provide funds for the foundation of several
colleges. Wolsey has several men prosecuted for distributing copies
of the Tyndale testament. Kentish weavers riot when the English
staple for wool moves from Antwerp to Calais. The first outbreak of
plague occurs this year.

1529 English Church reforms begin; Henry VIII summons the Reformation
Parliament. The Peace of Cambrai is signed. Cardinal Wolsey fails to
procure for Henry a divorce from Catherine of Aragon; he is stripped
of his property and most of his official positions, but remains
Archbishop of York. After the fall of Wolsey, Sir Thomas More
succeeds him as Lord Chancellor. Kildare is released from the Tower
and returns to Ireland. Another epidemic of 'sweating sickness'
sweeps through England.

1530 22 abbots sign a petition to the Pope in support of the Royal Divorce;
royal agents tour European universities seeking the support of
scholars for the 'illegality' of Henry's marriage, in the hope that this
will persuade the Pope. The King orders a Commission to examine
the need for an English Bible; its report is favourable to the idea.
Wolsey is accused of treason and summoned to London.

Nov　[**29**] Wolsey dies at Market Harborough on his way from York
to London.

1531 The appearance of Halley's Comet causes widespread panic. The
English clergy recognize Henry VIII as Supreme Head of the English

Church. John Hilsey and George Browne 'visit' all the friaries in the country; the Houses of Observant Friars are closed. Thomas Cromwell, formerly an agent of Wolsey's, joins the Privy Council. The building of sewers in London is to be regulated by law.

 Sir Thomas Elyot: *The Governor.*

1532 The Act of Annates. Henry VIII steadily whittles away papal authority in England in his determination to divorce Catherine of Aragon and marry Anne Boleyn; as a result, More resigns as Chancellor. Anne Boleyn is created Marquess of Pembroke. Skeffington is succeeded by Kildare as Lord Deputy in Ireland and there is increasing disorder. Holbein decides to settle permanently in England. Thomas Cromwell takes charge of the machinery of government.

AUG   [**22**] Archbishop Warham dies.

 St James' Palace, London (begun).

1533 The truce between England and Scotland is renewed. The Act of Appeals proclaims Henry VIII's new imperial status.

JAN   [**25**] Henry VIII marries Anne Boleyn in secret at Whitehall.
MAR   [**30**] Thomas Cranmer becomes Archbishop of Canterbury.
MAY   [**23**] The King's marriage to Catherine of Aragon is formally annulled. [**28**] The King's marriage to Anne Boleyn is declared valid. [**31**] Coronation of Anne Boleyn at Westminster; the crowds who watch are sullen and quiet.
JUN   [**24**] Mary, the King's sister, dies.

 Holbein: *The Ambassadors; Derick Born.*

 Thomas Elyot: *Pasquil the Playne.*
John Heywood: *A Merry Play between the Pardoner and the Friar.*

1534 The Act of Supremacy; Henry VIII formally asserts control over the English Church, severing ties with Rome. The First Act of Succession; the succession to the English throne is to lie with the heirs of Henry VIII and Queen Anne, and it is treason to dispute that succession. The Treason Act; the definition of treason is extended to include verbal attacks on the King. The Act in Restraint of Annates; the King is empowered to appoint bishops. The Dispensations Act; requests from clerics to hold more than one living are to be submitted to the Archbishop of Canterbury, not the Pope. The Act for the Submission of the Clergy; all measures of Convocation are to be submitted to the King for approval, and the ultimate appeal in any ecclesiastical disputes is to lie with the Crown. Cranmer invites several bishops and scholars to correct and modify Tyndale's Bible, but nothing worthwhile comes of this initiative. In Antwerp, Miles Coverdale starts work on his own translation of the Bible into English. English farmers are forbidden by law to own more than 2000 sheep. The manufacturing of woollen cloth begins in Worcester. A peace treaty is signed between England and Scotland.

MAR   The King's marriage to Catherine of Aragon is 'utterly dissolved' by Act of Parliament.
APR   Elizabeth Barton, the 'Nun of Kent' who denounced the King's divorce, is arrested and hanged at Tyburn.
NOV   Anne Boleyn bears Henry VIII a son, but he dies in infancy.

 Polydore Vergil: *Anglica Historia.*

1535 Thomas Cromwell is appointed Vicar General by Henry VIII and begins to put into effect his plan for the seizure of the Church's wealth; the visitation of all religious houses begins. The execution of Prior Houghton and other Carthusian monks for resistance. Miles Coverdale's Bible in English is printed in Zürich. Henry VIII authorizes the printing of Coverdale's complete English Bible in London, by the printer James Nicholson. Lectures in civil law are substituted for those in canon law in English universities.

JUL   [6] Sir Thomas More is executed on Tower Hill for treason; John Fisher is also executed.

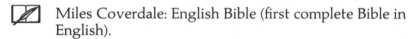 Miles Coverdale: English Bible (first complete Bible in English).

1536 Parliament passes an Act for the Dissolution of the Smaller Monasteries, those with an annual income of less than £200, instigated by Henry VIII and Thomas Cromwell. Suppression of Robert Aske's Catholic rebellion. The Union of England and Wales. William Tyndale, the English Protestant and translator of the New Testament from Greek into English, is lured out of his safe house at Vilvorde and burnt at the stake as a heretic. Holbein is appointed Court painter to Henry VIII.

JAN   [1] Lord Leonard Grey succeeds Skeffington as Lord Deputy in Ireland. [8] Catherine of Aragon dies at Kimbolton Palace.
MAY   [17] The King's marriage to Anne Boleyn is declared invalid.

[**19**] Anne Boleyn is executed. [**30**] Henry VIII marries Jane Seymour in the Queen's Chapel, Whitehall, only eleven days after his previous wife's execution.

Jul [**22**] The Duke of Richmond, the King's illegitimate son, dies aged 27.

Oct [**1**] The Pilgrimage of Grace begins at Louth; as a result of this rebellion against religious innovations 216 people are hanged.

 Holbein: *Jane Seymour.*

1537 Robert Aske, the leader of the Yorkshire rebels in the Pilgrimage of Grace, is executed at York for treason. More Carthusian monks are executed. Coverdale's Bible is given a royal licence by Henry VIII.

Jan [**1**] James V of Scotland marries Madeleine, the daughter of Francis I of France.

May [**19**] James V returns to Scotland.

Jul [**7**] Madeleine dies.

Oct [**12**] Edward VI is born at Hampton Court Palace. [**24**] His mother, Queen Jane Seymour, dies.

 Holbein: *Henry VIII;* Privy Chamber Fresco of the Tudor Dynasty.

1538 James V of Scotland marries Mary of Guise. The surrender of the friaries. Thomas Becket's shrine at Canterbury is destroyed during an orgy of anti-papal iconoclasm.

Sep [**5**] Cromwell's Injunctions to the Clergy, instructing them to keep parish registers of weddings, baptisms and burials.

 Nonesuch Palace, Surrey (begun).

 Holbein: *Christina of Milan.*

 Sir Thomas Elyot: *Dictionary.*
Sir David Lyndsay: *The Complaint and Testament of a Popinjay.*

1539 Parliament passes an Act for the Dissolution of the Greater Monasteries; the remaining monasteries and abbeys are dissolved. Thomas Beche, Abbot of Colchester, Hugh Cook, Abbot of Reading, and Richard Whiting, Abbot of Glastonbury, are executed for treason. The Act of Six Articles sets out the points of Catholic doctrine that are still to be followed; instigated by Henry VIII, it is an attempt to stem the growing influence of English Protestants. Lady Glammis and her second husband Lord Lyon are accused of attempting to poison James V. Lady Glammis is burnt alive on the Castle Hill at Edinburgh; the next day her husband falls to his death from the rock while trying to escape. Their accuser, William Lyon, confesses to the King that they are innocent, but he is too late to save their lives.

APR   The 'Great Bible', in English, appears with Royal Approval.

[image]   Sir Thomas Elyot: *The Castle of Health.*

1540 Robert Barnes, one of the first English Lutherans, is arrested and burnt for heresy at Smithfield.

JAN   [1] Henry VIII meets Anne of Cleves for the first time. [6] Henry VIII marries Anne of Cleves. [25] Edmund Campion, English Jesuit and martyr, is born.

FEB   [9] The first recorded horse-race meeting in Britain takes place; it is held at the Roodeye Field, now the Roodee, at Chester.

JUL   [9] The King's marriage to Anne of Cleves is annulled and Cromwell is condemned for treason by a Bill of Attainder. [28] Thomas Cromwell is executed, largely for organizing the King's marriage to Anne of Cleves.

AUG   [8] Henry VIII marries Catherine Howard.

[image]   Robert Strode: Parnham House, Dorset.
Ingatestone Hall in Essex is built at about this time.

1541 The Reformation begins in Scotland, led by John Knox. There is increasing friction between English and Scots in the Borders. James V of Scotland agrees to meet Henry VIII at York, but fails to turn up. Sir Thomas Wyatt dies. Henry VIII is elected King of Ireland and head of the Irish Church by the Irish Parliament; Wales is granted representation in the English Parliament.

OCT   [18] Margaret, daughter of Henry VII, dies as the widow of James IV of Scotland.

1542 Ireland is formally declared to be a kingdom. Henry VIII's Second War with Scotland, precipitated by frequent border raids by the Scots. The Duke of Norfolk's army invades Scotland. The Battle of Solway Moss; the English army is victorious over the Scots, even though the Scots outnumber the English 3:1.

FEB   [13] Queen Catherine Howard is executed on Tower Green; two of her alleged lovers, Thomas Culpepper and Francis Dereham, have already been executed.

MAR   [28] Margaret Davy is boiled alive for committing murder by poisoning. All Englishmen between the ages of 17 and 60 are required to possess bows and arrows.

AUG [**24**] The Scots defeat Sir Robert Bowes' troops at Hadden Rigg in the Borders.

DEC [**8**] Mary Stuart, later Queen of Scots, is born at Linlithgow Palace, the daughter of James V. [**14**] Demoralized by his crushing defeat at Solway Moss, James V of Scotland dies, succeeded by Mary, daughter of James V by his second marriage to Mary of Lorraine.

1543 An Act for the Advancement of True Religion is passed, forbidding the labouring classes to read scripture. William Byrd, composer, is born. Hans Holbein, painter, dies. England is at war with France because of the 'secret' Franco-Scottish alliance; Henry VIII and Charles V form an alliance against France.

JUL The Treaties of Greenwich are signed by the English and Scots, providing for the engagement of Mary, Queen of Scots, to Prince Edward Tudor. [**12**] Henry VIII marries Catherine Parr, his sixth wife, the widow of Lord Latimer.

DEC [**11**] The Scottish Parliament repudiates the Treaties of Greenwich and renew the alliance with France.

1544 An Act of Parliament releases the King from his debts. Henry VIII crosses to Calais to campaign with the Emperor Charles V against France. The English invasion of Scotland; English forces under Edward Seymour and John Dudley capture Leith and leave Edinburgh in flames. Henry VIII secretly promises to make Matthew, Earl of Lennox, Governor of Scotland if Scotland is defeated. Princess Mary and Princess Elizabeth are recognized by Parliament as heirs, after Prince Edward, to the English throne.

 Master John: *Mary I.*

1545 FEB [**25**] English forces are defeated by the Scots at Ancrum Moor. Parliament meets to raise funds for the war against Scotland. A French fleet enters the Solent; French troops land on the Isle of Wight. Treport in Normandy is set on fire by an English fleet under Lord Lisle. The sale of monastic lands encourages the rise of the middle classes, but inflation hits the poorest classes.

JUL [**19**] The warship *Mary Rose* suddenly heels over and sinks in the Solent; 700 men are drowned as Henry watches from Southsea Castle.

Thomas Cranmer: *The King's Primer.*
Roger Ascham: *Toxophilus.*

1546 The Peace of Ardres: Anglo-French hostilities end. The first book in Welsh is printed (*Yng Lhyvyr hwnn*). Henry VIII falls dangerously ill with syphilis and cirrhosis and nominates a Council of Regency for his heir. The population of England tops four million; thousands of people are close to starvation after a succession of poor harvests.

MAY   [**29**] Cardinal Beaton is murdered.
JUL   Anne Askew is burnt at the stake at Smithfield for the heresy of attacking the Mass.

 Gerlach Flicke: *Cranmer.*

1547 The Vagrant Act; an able-bodied vagrant may be adjudged by two magistrates to anyone wanting him as a slave, branded with a 'V' and kept in slavery for two years. The miniaturist Nicholas Hilliard is born.

JAN   [**21**] The Earl of Surrey, poet and soldier, is executed. [**28**] Henry VIII dies at Whitehall Palace at the age of 55. [**31**] Earl of Hertford becomes Lord Protector in the name of the new boy king, Edward VI.
FEB   [**16**] Earl of Hertford is created Duke of Somerset. [**25**] Coronation of the nine-year-old Edward VI at Westminster Abbey.
JUL   The town of St Andrews is captured by the Scottish Regent, Arran. In the war between the English and the Scots, the English seek to enforce the Marriage Treaty of 1543, which would unite the two kingdoms.
SEP   [**10**] Battle of Pinkie; English troops under the Duke of Somerset defeat the Scottish army, capture Edinburgh, and crush resistance to Edward VI.

 Thomas Cranmer: *Book of Homilies.*
W. Baldwin: *Moral Philosophy.*

1548 The heresy laws in England are abolished. All craft guilds are abolished except for the London Guilds which are powerful and resist abolition.

JUN   6000 French troops land at Leith and Mary Stuart, aged six and engaged to the Dauphin, is taken to France.
AUG   [**13**] Mary Stuart arrives in France.
SEP   [**5**] Catherine Parr, former queen of Henry VIII and now wife of Lord Seymour, dies in childbirth at Sudeley Castle near Cheltenham.

John Bale: *Kynge Johan* (first historical drama in English).
Edward Hall: *Chronicle*.

1549 A rebellion in Devon and Cornwall, caused by widespread dislike of Protestant reforms, is suppressed by Lord Russell.

Jun [**9**] An Act of Uniformity, authorizing the first English Book of Common Prayer, compiled by Thomas Cranmer.

Jul [**12**] Kett's Rebellion in Norfolk is prompted by economic grievances — antipathy towards the enclosure movement in particular. The rebels capture Norwich and set up a commonwealth on Mousehold Heath; they are later routed by the Earl of Warwick's troops at the Battle of Dussindale, and the leaders hanged. Thomas, Lord Seymour of Sudeley, brother of Protector Somerset, is executed for treason.

Oct [**10**] The Duke of Somerset is deprived of office as Lord Protector and imprisoned in the Tower; his fall from power is due to failures in the Scottish war, the execution of his own brother for treason, and his generally overbearing conduct. The Earl of Warwick rules England as Protector.

 John Cheke: *The Hurt of Sedition*.
Thomas Cranmer: *The Book of Common Prayer*.

1550 The Duke of Somerset is released from the Tower, but plots to regain his former authority. The Duke of Northumberland, formerly Earl of Warwick, fears Somerset's influence and causes him to be arrested and condemned to death for treason.

 Robert Smythson: Longleat House, Wiltshire (begun).

 Hans Eworth: *Sir John Luttrell*.

 Robert Crowley: *Way to Wealth*.
John Marbeck: *Concordance*.

1551 Thomas Cranmer's 42 Articles, the basis of Anglican Protestantism, are published. The first civil divorce is granted on the grounds of adultery. The theodolite is invented by Leonard Digges. Stephen Gardiner, Bishop of Winchester, is deposed. Miles Coverdale becomes Bishop of Exeter.

 Leonard Digges: *Pantometria*.
W. Turner: *A New Herbal*.

1552 Second Act of Uniformity, authorizing the Second Protestant Prayer Book of Edward VI, which dismantles the Mass. Christ's Hospital in

London is founded by Edward VI. Books of geography and astronomy are burnt in England because of fears that they may be used for magic. The poet Edmund Spenser is born.

JAN   Edward Seymour, Duke of Somerset, is executed.

1553 Sir Hugh Willoughby and Richard Chancellor try to find the North-East Passage to Asia. Willoughby discovers Novaya Zemlya and later dies on the Kola Peninsula. Chancellor reaches Archangel and journeys overland to Moscow, where negotiations lead to the founding of the Muscovy Company. Thomas Cromwell becomes Lord Chancellor.

MAY   [**21**] Lady Jane Grey marries Lord Guildford Dudley, son of the Duke of Northumberland.
JUL   [**6**] Edward VI dies of tuberculosis at Greenwich. [**9**] Lady Jane Grey is proclaimed Queen by the Duke of Northumberland, who had earlier persuaded the dying King to will the throne to her. Northumberland fails to secure Mary, the rightful heir, because the army will not support him; Mary escapes to East Anglia and then returns to London with her supporters. As she arrives in London, she is acclaimed as Queen by the people. [**19**] Lady Jane Grey is deposed, succeeded by Mary I. The Royal Supremacy is retained by Mary, but by an Act of Repeal many other Acts are revoked, such as the 1549 and 1552 Acts of Uniformity; the Mass, holy-days and celibate clergy are all revived. Miles Coverdale is deprived of his bishopric.
AUG   [**22**] Northumberland is executed.

 Sawston Hall, Cambridge.

 T. Geminus: *Anatomy.*
Christopher Tye: *The Acts of the Apostles.*

1554 The Corn Law of 1436 is re-enacted by the English Parliament in a vain effort to relieve serious food shortages.

JAN   Wyatt's Rebellion; Sir Thomas Wyatt raises a rebel army of 4000 in Kent, in opposition to Queen Mary's impending marriage. Wyatt surrenders on the outskirts of London, is arrested and executed. Princess Elizabeth is suspected of complicity in Wyatt's Rebellion and sent to the Tower.
FEB   [**12**] Lady Jane Grey, who was Queen of England for only nine days, is executed on Tower Green for high treason.

Jul   [**25**] Mary I marries Philip King of Naples and Jerusalem (who is to become King Philip II of Spain in Jan 1556); the English Parliament will not allow Philip to be crowned King of England. A reconciliation is negotiated between England and the Pope, and the Pope once again becomes head of the English Church. John Knox flees to Geneva.

Nov   A Second Act of Repeal removes all anti-papal measures passed since 1529.

    Antonio Mor: *Mary I.*

1555 The persecution of Protestants begins in Britain. A Commission headed by Bishop Gardiner opens at Southwark for the trial of heretics: transubstantiation and the Pope's supremacy are the key issues. Mary appoints a committee to consider the re-foundation of certain religious houses, and monasteries at Greenwich, Smithfield, Sheen, Syon and Kings Langley are reopened. Princess Elizabeth is released from the Tower. The Muscovy Company is founded. Famine sweeps Britain.

Feb   [**9**] John Hooper, Bishop of Gloucester, is burned at the stake in Gloucester for heresy, under the newly-revived laws.

Oct   [**16**] Hugh Latimer, Bishop of Worcester, and Nicholas Ridley, Bishop of London, are burned at the stake for heresy outside the town ditch in Oxford.

Nov   Bishop Gardiner dies.

Dec   [**11**] Archbishop Cranmer is deprived of his office. John Knox returns to Scotland. Polydore Vergil, scholar, dies.

1556 Richard Chancellor dies when his ship is wrecked off Scotland. Stephen Borough tries to find the North-East Passage, and reaches the Kara Sea. The writer Nicholas Udall dies. The Benedictine house at Westminster is re-founded.

Mar   [**21**] Thomas Cranmer, the first Protestant Archbishop of Canterbury (in 1533), is burned at the stake at Oxford, condemned both as traitor and heretic. [**22**] Reginald Pole becomes Archbishop of Canterbury after his predecessor's execution.

Jul   Knox leaves Scotland for Geneva.

    William Cecil (Lord Burghley): Burghley House, Stamford (begun).

    Robert Recorde: *The Castle of Knowledge* (navigational guide).

1557 Philip II visits England and persuades Mary to declare war on France.

JUL [**16**] Anne of Cleves, the fourth wife of Henry VIII, dies in retirement in Lewes.

AUG [**10**] Battle of St Quentin; English and Spanish armies are victorious over the French. An English whale fishery is established at Spitzbergen. The explorer Sebastian Cabot dies. The first English play to be censored, *The Sack-Full of Newes*, is put on at Aldgate in London and promptly suppressed. The composer William Morley is born.

William Whittingham: *The Geneva Testament* (the first English Testament to be divided into verses).
Robert Recorde: *Whetstone of Witte* (treatise on algebra).
Thomas More: *A History of King Richard III*.

1558 Thomas Gresham, the English financier, proposes reforms in currency based on the assumption, 'Gresham's Law', that bad money drives good money out of circulation.

JAN [**7**] Calais is lost to the French; this is regarded in England as a national disaster.

APR The last of the Scottish Protestant martyrs, Walter Milne, is burned to death. [**24**] Mary Stuart marries the Dauphin, later Francis II of France.

SEP [**1**] Protestant riot in Edinburgh.

NOV [**17**] Mary I dies at St James's Palace, succeeded by Elizabeth I, her half-sister. Elizabeth keeps Mary's council, adding Sir William Cecil, later Lord Burghley; Sir Francis Walsingham is her private secretary. [**18**] Cardinal Pole dies. After the accession of Elizabeth, English Protestants begin to return from Switzerland, as more favourable conditions for them prevail in England.

John Knox: *The First Blast of the Trumpet against the Monstrous Regiment of Women*.

1559 Elizabeth suppresses the re-founded religious houses. A Royal Injunction is issued, to the effect that a Bible must be available in every church. Act of Supremacy; Elizabeth I becomes Supreme Governor of the English Church. Act of Uniformity; this orders the use of the 1552 Prayer Book, leading to a religious settlement in England. Mary, Queen of Scots, assumes the title Queen of England and Scotland when her husband Francis II succeeds to the French throne.

JAN   [**15**] Coronation of Elizabeth I.
APR   [**2**] Treaty of Cateau-Cambrésis between France and England;
       Calais is to be ceded to England in eight years' time.
MAY   John Knox preaches an inflammatory sermon at Perth, inciting
       the Protestant lords to rise in rebellion; they capture
       Edinburgh and sack religious houses.
JUN   [**10**] The Queen Regent of Scotland dies.
DEC   [**17**] Matthew Parker becomes Archbishop of Canterbury.

 Little Moreton Hall, Cheshire (begun).

 Thomas Sackville: *Mirror for Magistrates.*
J. Aylmer: *An Harbour for Faithful Subjects.*

1560 Eric XIV succeeds to the Swedish throne and courts Elizabeth I,
unsuccessfully. The Church of Scotland is founded. Westminster
School is founded. Puritanism begins in England. Elizabeth I orders
the subjugation of Shane O'Neill, who has become the most powerful
man in Ireland. Mary, Queen of Scots', claim to the English throne is
repudiated; Francis II of France dies and Mary is widowed.

JAN   Treaty of Berwick, between Elizabeth I and the Scottish
       reformers. French troops are besieged at Leith.
JUL   [**6**] Treaty of Edinburgh between England, France and
       Scotland; French troops are to be withdrawn from Scotland
       and France's interference in Scottish affairs is to end.

 Whittingham, Gilby & Sampson: *Geneva Bible* (first to be
divided into verses).

1561 John Knox's *Book of Discipline* establishes a church constitution in
Scotland. St Paul's Cathedral in London suffers serious fire damage.

JAN   [**22**] Francis Bacon is born at York House in the Strand.
AUG   [**19**] Mary, Queen of Scots, returns to Scotland.

 Thomas Sackville and Thomas Norton: *Gorboduc* (earliest
known English tragedy).

1562 John Hawkins, a naval commander, takes 300 African slaves from a
Portuguese slave ship bound for Brazil; this is the beginning of British
participation in the slave trade. Milled coins are introduced for the
first time in England. The Earl of Tyrone leads two unsuccessful
rebellions in Ireland. The first conservatory in Britain is built by
William Cecil to protect his sub-tropical plants from the English
weather. Treaty of Hampton Court, signed by Elizabeth I and Louis I

de Bourbon, the Huguenot leader; it calls for English troops to occupy Dieppe and Le Havre.

JAN   [6] Shane O'Neill appears in London to make submission to Queen Elizabeth.

 Hans Eworth: *Margaret Audley, Duchess of Norfolk.*

 John Jewel: *Apology of the Church of England.*

1563 English soldiers at Le Havre catch the plague and bring it back to England, where it kills 20,000 people in London alone. The 39 Articles of Anglican belief define the Elizabethan Church Settlement. The Statute of Apprentices empowers Justices of the Peace to determine wage levels. The composer William Byrd becomes organist at Lincoln Cathedral. The composers John Bull and John Dowland are born.

 A Booke in English metre of the great Marchante Man called Dives Pragmaticus, very preaty for Children to read (first children's book).
John Foxe: *Acts and Monuments* (known as *Book of Martyrs*).

1564 The Peace of Troyes ends the war between England and France; England renounces its claim to Calais in exchange for a substantial payment. An English trading centre is established at Emden. Elizabeth I involves herself in the slave trade by lending John Hawkins a ship in return for a share of the profits.

FEB   [6] The poet and dramatist Christopher Marlowe is born at Canterbury.
APR   [23] William Shakespeare is born.

1565 The Royal College of Physicians in London is officially permitted to carry out human dissections. The Royal Exchange in London is founded. Tobacco and sweet potatoes are introduced into Britain. The manufacture of pencils begins in England.

JUL   [29] Mary, Queen of Scots, marries her cousin Lord Darnley at her private chapel in Holyroodhouse. [30] Heralds proclaim Darnley as Henry, King of Scots, but without Parliament's agreement.

1566 Archbishop Parker's 'Advertisements' demand religious conformity. David Rizzio, Italian private secretary to Mary, Queen of Scots, is murdered in Holyroodhouse on the orders of her husband, Lord Darnley.

JUN   [**19**] James VI of Scotland is born in Edinburgh, the son of Henry Stewart, Lord Darnley, and Mary, Queen of Scots.

J. Alday: *Theatrum Mundi.*
Nicholas Udall: *Ralph Roister-Doister* (first performed c.1553).

1567 Rugby School is founded by Laurence Sheriff. The writer Thomas Nashe is born.

JAN   Thomas Campion, physician, composer and poet, is born.

FEB   [**10**] Lord Darnley, second husband of Mary, Queen of Scots, is murdered in the early hours of the morning at a house near Edinburgh called Kirk o' Field. There is an explosion, which wrecks the house, but Darnley's corpse is found some distance away; he has apparently been strangled while trying to escape. Lord Bothwell, the probable murderer, pretends to abduct Mary.

MAY   [**15**] Mary, Queen of Scots, marries Bothwell.

JUN   [**15**] Mary surrenders at Carberry Hill. [**16**] Mary is imprisoned at Loch Leven Castle. [**24**] Mary, Queen of Scots, is deposed, abdicating under pressure in favour of her son, James VI. The Earl of Moray is named Regent.

1568 John Hawkins is defeated and his slave-trading voyages come to an end. Adventurers from Devon attempt to settle in Munster, Ireland. Twenty years of conflict between Catholic and Protestant Churches begin. Elizabeth I's tutor, Roger Ascham, dies.

MAY   [**2**] Mary, Queen of Scots, escapes from Loch Leven. [**13**] Mary and her supporters lose the Battle of Langside. [**16**] Mary sails across the Solway Firth to England. [**19**] Mary is captured and imprisoned at Carlisle Castle. [**28**] Mary receives Sir Francis Knollys and Lord Scrope and urges her right of access to Queen Elizabeth.

JUN   [**8**] Elizabeth I writes to Mary, assuring her safety and saying that it would be one of her 'highest worldly pleasures' to receive her, once she was acquitted of the crime of her husband's murder.

1569 A public lottery is held in London to help pay for repairs to the port. The Revolt of the Desmonds in Ireland. Miles Coverdale, translator of the Bible, dies. Rebellion in England of the Northern (Catholic) Earls, led by the Earls of Northumberland and Westmorland in an abortive attempt to restore Catholic worship and release Mary,

Queen of Scots, from captivity. They ransack Durham Cathedral, but flee to Scotland when faced with Elizabeth's army.

 Monogrammist HE: *Elizabeth I and the Three Goddesses.*

1570 Thomas Cartwright, Professor of Divinity at Cambridge, compares the Elizabethan Church unfavourably with the early Church, and is subsequently dismissed.

JAN [**23**] The Earl of Moray, the Scottish Regent, is assassinated by the Hamiltons, resulting in a civil war with Mary's supporters. [**27**] The Earl of Lennox is proclaimed Regent.

FEB Queen Elizabeth is anathametized and declared deposed by Pope Pius V. As a result, Catholics come under suspicion as possible traitors.

 Joris Hoefnagel: *Marriage Feast at Bermondsey.*
Nicholas Hilliard: *Elizabeth I.*

 Roger Ascham: *The Schoolmaster.*

1571 Harrow School and Jesus College, Oxford, are founded. Roberto di Ridolfi, a Florentine, plots with Philip II, the Duke of Alva and the Pope to marry Mary, Queen of Scots, to the Duke of Norfolk, depose Queen Elizabeth and restore Catholicism to England. The plot is exposed; the Duke of Norfolk and the Earl of Westmorland are later executed.

JAN [**23**] The Royal Exchange in London is opened as a bankers' meeting house.

APR [**7**] The Archbishop of St Andrews is hanged for complicity in the Earl of Moray's murder.

SEP [**4**] The Scottish Regent, the Earl of Lennox, dies, succeeded by the Earl of Mar.

 R. Edwards: *Damon and Pithias.*

1572 The Society of Antiquaries in London is founded. The Duke of Norfolk and Earl of Northumberland are executed for treason. Lord Burghley becomes Lord High Treasurer.

JUN [**11**] The poet and dramatist Ben Jonson is born at Westminster.

OCT The Scottish Regent, the Earl of Mar, dies.

NOV [**24**] The Earl of Morton is elected Scottish Regent; John Knox dies.

1573 The composer Christopher Tye dies; the composer John Wilbye is born. John Donne, poet, is born. The Revolt of the Desmonds in Ireland is crushed. Fighting in Scotland ends with the Pacification of Perth. Edinburgh Castle later surrenders to an English army, finally freeing Elizabeth I from all threats from Scotland; support for Mary in Scotland collapses. Sir Francis Drake captures a huge shipment of Spanish silver in Panama.

JUL   [**15**] The architect Inigo Jones is born in London.

 George Gower: *Sir Thomas and Lady Kytson.*

1575 Parliament guarantees freedom from arrest to its members and their servants. Elizabeth I grants Thomas Tallis and William Byrd a music-publishing monopoly.

MAR   [**5**] William Oughtred, mathematician and inventor of the slide rule, is born at Eton.
MAY   [**17**] Archbishop Parker dies.
JUL   [**7**] English troops are defeated by Scots in a skirmish at Redswire in the Borders.

 George Gascoigne: *Princely Pleasures at the Court of Kenilworth.*
Turberville: *Book of Falconrie.*
William Stevenson or John Still: *Gammer Gurton's Needle.*

1576 Peter Wentworth, a Puritan MP, alleges that the Queen is curbing free speech in the Commons, and is sent to prison for saying so. The Theatre in Shoreditch is the first purpose-built theatre in Britain. Martin Frobisher discovers Frobisher Bay in Canada.

FEB   [**15**] Edmund Grindal becomes Archbishop of Canterbury.
DEC   The Queen instructs Grindal to suppress all prophesyings, but he refuses to comply on the grounds that this will exclude Puritans from the Church; he offers to resign.

 Buckland Abbey, near Plymouth, Devon (rebuilt).

 W. Lambarde: *A Perambulation of Kent.*

1577 At the 'Black Assize' in Oxford, all those in court, including the judge and jury, die of typhus carried by the prisoners. Sir Thomas Gresham establishes by will the first British institute for teaching science, which is later to become the Royal Society. London's second playhouse, The Curtain, opens in Finsbury.

JUN   Archbishop Grindal is suspended for continuing to oppose the Queen on the matter of prophesyings.

DEC   [**13**] Francis Drake begins his voyage round the world in the *Golden Hind*, embarking from Plymouth.

Parham Park, Sussex (begun).
Thomas Clease: Churche's Mansion, Cheshire.

Nicholas Hilliard: *Portrait of the Artist, aged 30.*
Cornelius Ketel: *Sir Martin Frosbisher.*

Raphael Holinshed: *Chronicles of England, Scotland and Ireland.*

1578   Sir Humphrey Gilbert is granted a patent to settle North America.

MAR   [**12**] James VI of Scotland assumes personal rule when the Regent, the Earl of Morton, resigns.

APR   [**1**] William Harvey, discoverer of the circulation of the blood, is born at Folkestone.

John Lyly: *Euphues, The Anatomy of Wit.*
Thomas Dekker: *Canaans Calamitie.*

1579   The English Eastland Company is chartered to trade with Scandinavia and the Baltic States. The first Englishman to settle in India, Father Thomas Stephens, settles in Goa. The Duke of Anjou lands in England to propose marriage to Queen Elizabeth. There is a new outbreak of the Desmond revolt in Ireland; Munster is laid waste by the fighting.

JUN   [**17**] Francis Drake claims 'Nova Albion' (California) in the name of Queen Elizabeth, according to a brass plaque discovered near the Golden Gate Bridge.

Thomas North: *Plutarch's Lives* (translated).
John Lyly: *Euphues and his England.*
Edmund Spenser: *Shepherd's Calendar.*

1580   New building in London is prohibited to prevent the city from growing any larger.

APR   [**6**] An earth tremor kills two people in London and damages Old St Paul's Cathedral. In the summer a Jesuit mission in England is begun by Edmund Campion and Robert Parsons.

SEP   [**26**] Drake and his crew return to Plymouth in the *Golden Hind* at the end of the world voyage.

Robert Smythson: Wollaton Hall, Notts (begun).
Robert Smythson: Longleat, Wiltshire (completed).
Scone Palace, Perth, Scotland.

1581 In England, fears spread that a Jesuit invasion is imminent. Converts to Roman Catholicism in Britain are subject by law to the penalties for high treason. Edmund Campion's *Decem Rationes* is secretly printed at Stonor Park in Oxfordshire. The *Ark Royal* is built for Sir Walter Raleigh, as *Ark Raleigh*, and then sold to the Queen as a flagship. Sedan chairs come into general use in Britain.

JAN [4] Archbishop Ussher is born.
APR [4] Francis Drake is knighted on the *Golden Hind* at Deptford.
JUN [2] The Earl of Morton is executed for his part in Lord Darnley's murder.
DEC Edmund Campion is executed.

 Nicholas Hilliard: *Portrait of Drake.*

 Sir Philip Sidney: *Defence of Poesy.*

1582 Sir Humphrey Gilbert's expedition reaches Newfoundland. 30,000 people die in Munster, mainly of starvation. Edinburgh University is founded. London's first waterworks are installed, pumping water to private houses for the first time.

AUG [22] The Raid of Ruthven; James VI of Scotland is kidnapped by Protestant nobles to separate him from the influence of his Catholic favourites.
NOV [27] William Shakespeare marries Anne Hathaway at the age of 18.

 Edmund Campion: *Decem Rationes.*
Richard Hakluyt: *Divers Voyages Touching the Discovery of America.*
Sir Philip Sidney: *Astrophil and Stella.*

1583 Sir Walter Raleigh goes to Virginia. Gerald Earl of Desmond dies; the Plantation (or colonization) of Munster begins. The composer Orlando Gibbons is born. Francis Throckmorton leads a conspiracy to overthrow Queen Elizabeth and free Mary Stuart; Throckmorton's plot is discovered and he is executed.

JUN [27] James VI escapes from his abducters and hides in St Andrews.
JUL [6] Archbishop Grindal dies.

SEP [**9**] Sir Humphrey Gilbert, the explorer, is drowned during his voyage home; his ship, *The Squirrel*, sinks off the Azores drowning all on board. [**23**] John Whitgift becomes Archbishop of Canterbury.

Breamore House, Hampshire.

Sir Thomas Smith: *The Manner of Government of England*. Philip Stubbes: *Anatomy of Abuses*.

1584 Walter Raleigh founds a colony on Roanoke Island and is knighted for his services. With Parliamentary approval, an Association of noblemen is formed to 'pursue to the death anyone plotting against the Queen': it is even signed by Mary.

MAY [**4**] The Earl of Gowrie, one of the instigators of the Raid of Ruthven, is beheaded at Stirling.

John Knox: *History of the Reformation of Religion within the Realm of Scotland* (Books 1-3).

1585 The English intervene in the Spanish-Dutch War: Drake attacks Spanish ports and English ships in other Spanish ports are confiscated. John Davis discovers the Davis Strait between Greenland and Canada. William Shakespeare leaves Stratford for London. The composer Thomas Tallis dies. John Schorne's bones are removed to an unknown place from his tomb in St George's Chapel, Windsor. Dr William Parry is tried for alleged treason and subsequently executed. James VI signs a peace pact with England.

NOV Secretary Fenton visits Munster and devises a scheme to repopulate the province.

1586 The Virginia settlers choose to return to England with Drake rather than stay in America. In York, Margaret Clitheroe is pressed to death for hiding priests. The Babington Plot to kill the Queen is uncovered by Sir Francis Walsingham; Francis Babington and his fellow conspirators are executed. Mary Stuart is clearly implicated in the plot, but her sentence is postponed. Thomas Cavendish leaves Plymouth to sail round the world, becoming the second British commander to do so. John Ford, playwright, is born in Devon.

JUL [**28**] The first potatoes arrive in Britain, brought from Colombia to Plymouth by Sir Thomas Harriot.
SEP [**22**] Battle of Zutphen; Anglo-Dutch victory.
OCT Sir Philip Sidney dies of battle wounds after the Battle of Zutphen.

📓 William Camden: *Britannia*.

1587 Sir Francis Drake makes further raids on Spanish shipping.

FEB [**8**] Mary, Queen of Scots, is executed at Fotheringhay Castle after nearly 19 years in prison. She is executed for her implication in the Babington Plot to overthrow Queen Elizabeth and restore Roman Catholicism in England.

APR [**18**] John Foxe, author of *The Book of Martyrs*, dies.

🔨 Shipton Hall, Shropshire.
Burghley House, Northamptonshire (begun).

📓 Christopher Marlowe: *Tamburlaine the Great*.

1588 31 Catholic priests are executed during the year. Robert Dudley, Earl of Leicester, dies. Timothy Bright publishes the first shorthand manual, *An Arte of Shorte, Swifte and Secrete Writing by Character*.

MAY [**19**] The Catholic invasion fleet, the Spanish Armada, sets sail from Lisbon.

JUL [**29**] The Spanish Armada is defeated by an English fleet under Howard and Drake, off Plymouth. The defeat of the Armada opens the world to English trade and colonization.

🔨 Montacute House, Somerset (begun).

🎨 George Gower: *Elizabeth I, Armada Portrait*.
Nicholas Hilliard: *Young Man Among Roses*.

📓 William Allen: *Admonition* (urging rebellion).
Christopher Marlowe: *Dr Faustus*.
William Morgan: *Welsh Bible*.

🎵 William Byrd: *Psalms, sonnets and songs of sadness and piety*.

1589 The stocking frame, the first knitting machine, is invented by William Lee. John Harington invents, designs and instals the world's first flushing water closet at his house at Kelston near Bath; he calls it 'Ajax'. A Commission is appointed to examine the progress of the Munster colonization project.

APR The Portugal Expedition; Drake fails in an attempt to capture Lisbon with 150 ships and 18,000 men.

AUG [**20**] James VI of Scotland marries Anne of Denmark.

📓 Richard Hakluyt: *The Principal Navigations, Voyages and Discoveries of the English Nation*.

1590 APR [**6**] Sir Francis Walsingham, diplomat and creator of Elizabeth I's secret service, dies.

MAY [**1**] James VI of Scotland returns to Leith.

Robert Smythson: Hardwick Hall, Derbyshire (begun).

William Seger: *Robert Devereux, Earl of Essex.*

Sir Philip Sidney: *Arcadia.*
Edmund Spenser: *The Faerie Queene*, Books 1-3.
Christopher Marlowe: *The Jew of Malta.*

1591 Trinity College, Dublin, is founded. The composer Thomas Whythorne dies. Sir Christopher Hatton, Lord Chancellor and favourite of the Queen, dies. Sir Richard Grenville, the naval commander, is killed when his ship, the *Revenge*, is sunk by a large Spanish squadron in a battle off the Azores.

Cannongate Tolbooth, Edinburgh.

Shakespeare: *Henry VI.*

William Byrd: *My Ladye Nevells Booke* (anthology compiled and copied out by John Baldwyn).

1592 Queen Elizabeth visits Kelston, tries the 'Ajax' flushing lavatory, likes it and orders one for herself. John Davis, the English explorer, discovers the Falkland Islands. Sir John Burrows captures the Portuguese galleon *Madre de Dios* with its £800,000 cargo. Plague in London kills 15,000 people. John Jenkins, composer, is born.

FEB [**7**] The Earl of Moray is murdered by the Earl of Huntly.

Gheeraerts: *Elizabeth I, Ditchley Portrait* (at about this time).

1593 London's theatres close for a year because of the plague. Admiral Sir Richard Hawkins recommends drinking orange and lemon juice as a way of preventing scurvy in the Navy. George Herbert, writer, is born.

MAY [**30**] Christopher Marlowe, poet and playwright, is murdered in mysterious circumstances in a pub brawl at Deptford; he is 29.

AUG [**9**] Izaak Walton, author, is born at Stafford.

R. Bancroft: *Dangerous Positions and Proceedings.*
Shakespeare: *Venus and Adonis; Richard III; Comedy of Errors.*

1594 The first of five consecutive bad harvests starts an economic recession. The Scottish Highlanders under the Earl of Argyl are defeated by the Earl of Huntly. Hugh O'Neill, Earl of Tyrone, leads a rising in Ulster, appealing to Spain for help. Martin Frobisher is killed while helping an Anglo-French force to recapture the port of Brest from the Spanish. The London theatres re-open.

FEB [**19**] Henry, son of James VI of Scotland, is born.

 Thomas Kyd: *The Spanish Tragedy.*
Robert Parsons: *A Conference about the next succession the Crowne of Ingland.*
Thomas Nashe: *The Unfortunate Traveller.*
Shakespeare: *The Rape of Lucrece; Titus Andronicus; Taming of the Shrew.*

1595 Raleigh explores 300 miles of the Orinoco with four ships and 100 men, in his search for El Dorado. Attempts by Sir John Norris, commander of the English forces in Ireland, fail to stamp out the Tyrone revolt. The University of Cambridge is divided over the issue of predestination; the Queen intervenes, calling a halt to the discussion. Londoners riot for bread. The bow is finally abandoned by the English army as a weapon of war.

AUG Expedition to the West Indies; Richard Hawkins and Francis Drake leave on their last voyage to the Spanish Main. The expedition is a failure and both Drake and Hawkins die during the voyage.

 Shakespeare: *Two Gentlemen of Verona; Love's Labour's Lost.*
Edmund Spenser: *Amoretti.*

1596 The Pacification of Ireland is signed, but the Earl of Tyrone refuses to abide by it. Cadiz is sacked by the English; the Spanish capture Calais. Tomatoes are introduced into Britain, where they are grown initially as ornamental plants. Bartholomew Steere and 20 others are executed in Oxford for planning a rebellion.

JAN [**28**] Sir Francis Drake dies of dysentery on board his ship and is buried at sea.

 Shakespeare: *A Midsummer Night's Dream.*
Edmund Spenser: *The Faerie Queene,* Books 4-6.

1597 A second Armada leaves for Britain, but is scattered by storms. Hammocks are authorized by the Admiralty for use on Royal Naval vessels. Sentences of transportation for criminals are prescribed by Act of Parliament. Several Acts are passed which try to deal with problems of poverty and social distress: the Act against the Decay of Towns and Houses, the Act for the Maintenance of Husbandry and Tillage, the Act for the Relief of the Poor.

SEP   Nine people are reported to have died 'for want in the streets' in Newcastle.
OCT   16 more die in the streets in Newcastle.

Robert Smythson: Hardwick Hall, Derbyshire (completed).

Shakespeare: *Sonnets; Romeo and Juliet; Richard II; King John; The Merchant of Venice.*
Thomas Deloney: *Jack of Newbury.*
James VI of Scotland: *Demonologie.*

Thomas Morley: *Plaine and Easie Introduction to Practicall Musicke.*
John Dowland: *First Booke of Songs.*

1598 The Poor Law Act: Parliament provides for the founding of workhouses and the punishment of beggars. Parliament votes to levy increased taxation to pay for the Spanish War. William Cecil, Lord Burghley, dies. The Bodleian Library at Oxford is founded by Sir Thomas Bodley.

AUG   [**14**] Battle of the Yellow Ford; English forces are defeated.
SEP   Francis Bacon is arrested for debt.

Shakespeare: *Henry IV.*
Ben Jonson: *Every Man in His Humour.*
Thomas Deloney: *The Gentle Craft.*
Emanuel Forde: *Parismus.*

1599 The Earl of Tyrone leads a rebellion against English rule. Robert Devereux, Earl of Essex, is appointed Lord Lieutenant in Ireland. The Globe Theatre is opened in Southwark; it is owned by the actors themselves.

MAR   [**22**] Sir Anthony van Dyck, Court painter to Charles I, is born at Antwerp.
APR   [**25**] Oliver Cromwell is born at Huntingdon, the son of Robert Cromwell and Elizabeth Steward.

SEP   [8] Essex signs a truce with the Irish rebel leader, the Earl of Tyrone, after being defeated at Arklow. [28] Essex returns to England without leave.

NOV   Essex is arrested and banished.

Montacute House, Somerset (completed).

Shakespeare: *Julius Caesar.*
Richard Hakluyt: *Map of North America.*

1600

1600   The Earl of Essex is tried for his actions in Ireland and deprived of his offices. Will Kemp morris-dances all the way from London to Norwich. William Gilbert discovers the earth's magnetism. The Queen grants a charter establishing the East India Company.

JAN   The Earl of Tyrone and his men invade Munster; Mountjoy succeeds Essex as Deputy.

AUG   [5] Gowrie and Ruthven conspire to murder James VI; both are killed.

Robert Smythson: Doddington Hall, Lincolnshire.

Shakespeare: *Henry V; As You Like It; Much Ado About Nothing.*
Ben Jonson: *Every Man out of his Humour.*
Thomas Dekker: *The Shoemaker's Holiday.*
William Gilbert: *De Magnete.*

1601   Monopolies are abolished. The Poor Law Act: a codification of all the previous Tudor Poor Laws. Elizabeth's 'Golden Speech' to Parliament, in which she reviews England's achievements during her reign. Two fleets from Spain arrive to help the Irish in their rebellion against English rule. The writer Thomas Nashe dies.

FEB   [8] The Earl of Essex's Rebellion. [25] The Earl of Essex is executed.

Shakespeare: *Twelfth Night; Troilus and Cressida.*
John Donne: *The Progress of the Soule.*

Thomas Morley: *Triumphs of Oriana.*

1602   English forces under the command of Lord Mountjoy capture an invading Spanish army in Ireland. The Jesuits are ordered to leave

England. The composer Thomas Morley dies; the composer William Lawes is born.

 Shakespeare: *The Merry Wives of Windsor.*
Thomas Dekker: *Satir-mastix.*
Ben Jonson: *Poetaster.*

1603 MAR [**24**] Elizabeth I dies at Richmond Palace aged 69. [**31**] Accession of James VI of Scotland as James I of England, uniting the kingdoms of England and Scotland.

APR [**5**] King James leaves Scotland for England. [**28**] Elizabeth I's funeral in Westminster Abbey.

MAY [**7**] James enters London.

JUL [**25**] Coronation of James I. Sir Walter Raleigh is suspected of leading a plot (the Main Plot) to dethrone James I; he is tried for treason and imprisoned in the Tower. Plague becomes widespread in Britain. Puritans present the Millenary Petition to James I, objecting to pluralities, non-residence and non-preaching ministers. Cobham's Plot to dethrone James I and place Arabella Stuart on the throne results in Cobham's imprisonment.

 Bernard Janssen (or Johnson): Audley End House. Essex (begun).

 John de Critz: *Earl of Southampton.*

 Shakespeare: *Hamlet; All's Well That Ends Well.*
Dod and Cleaver: *Exposition of the Ten Commandments*
John Davies: *Microcosmos.*

Thomas Robinson: *Schoole of Musicke.*

1604 Treaty of London: Peace between Britain and Spain. A commercial treaty with France is signed.

JAN [**14**] The Hampton Court Conference meets to discuss Church reforms, based on the Millenary Petition. James I disappoints the Puritans and fails to resolve religious conflicts, but the conference does lead to the production of the Authorized Version of the Bible.

FEB [**29**] Archbishop Whitgift dies.

DEC [**10**] Richard Bancroft becomes Archbishop of Canterbury.

 Shakespeare: *Othello; Measure for Measure.*
Thomas Dekker: *Magnificent Entertainment; The Honest Whore.*
Robert Cawdrey: *Table Alphabetical* (The first dictionary)

1605 The first railway in Britain is constructed, a pit-head track built by Sir Francis Willoughby at Wollaton in Nottinghamshire. The Butchers' and Shipwrights' Companies are incorporated in London.

Nov [5] The Gunpowder Plot. Failing to gain religious toleration from James, Catholics plan to destroy King and Parliament; the plot fails when 36 barrels of gunpowder are discovered in the cellars of the Houses of Parliament. This is the last major Catholic conspiracy. Some of the conspirators, including Robert Catesby, are killed at Holbeach House; others, including Guy Fawkes, are captured and tortured.

 Knole, Kent (begun).

 Shakespeare: *King Lear.*
Francis Bacon: *Advancement of Learning.*

1606 Impositions (taxes) are levied at English ports as part of the Royal Prerogative. The Virginia Company is formed and granted a Royal Charter: 120 colonists set off for Virginia. Sir William Davenant, writer, is born.

Jan [31] Guy Fawkes and his fellow-conspirators are executed by being hanged, drawn and quartered.
Apr [12] The Union Jack is adopted as the English flag.

 John Thorpe: Holland House, London.

 Shakespeare: *Macbeth; Antony and Cleopatra.*
Ben Jonson: *Volpone.*
Robert Burton: *Philosophaster* (written).
Thomas Dekker: *The Seven Deadly Sinnes of London.*
John Ford: *Fames Memoriall; Honor Triumphant.*

1607 King James's plan to unite the kingdoms of England and Scotland fails; the English Parliament rejects the proposed union. Nevertheless, the courts confirm the common citizenship of English and Scottish subjects born after James's accession to the English throne.

May [13] Virginia is re-colonized; Jamestown is founded by Captain John Smith.

 John Thorpe: Hatfield House, Hertfordshire (begun).

 Francis Beaumont & John Fletcher: *The Knight of the Burning Pestle.*
Shakespeare: *Timon of Athens.*
Thomas Middleton: *Michaelmas Terme.*

> Edward Sharpham: *Cupid's Whirligig.*
> Edward Topsell: *The Historie of Four-Footed Beastes.*
> Cyril Tourneur: *The Revenger's Tragedy.*
> Thomas Heywood: *A Woman Killed with Kindness.*
> Richard Johnson: *The Most Pleasant History of Tom a Lincoln.*

1608 The first municipal library is opened in Norwich: it contains mainly theological books. The Royal Blackheath Golf Club is founded in London. John Dee, Queen Elizabeth I's astrologer, dies in extreme poverty.

DEC [**9**] The poet John Milton is born at Cheapside in London.

 Shakespeare: *Coriolanus.*
Thomas Dekker: *The Dead Tearme; Lanthorne of Delight.*

1609 Rebellion of the Northern Earls in Ireland; beginning of the Planting of Ulster by Scots and English Protestants. James I encourages the colonization of North America. A regular financial grant to the King is discussed in Parliament but not agreed. James I appoints Justices of the Peace to prevent feuding in the Scottish Border country.

 Shakespeare: *Sonnets* (completed).
Ben Jonson: *Masque of Queens.*
Thomas Dekker: *The Guls Horne-Booke.*

Thomas Weelkes: *Ayeres.*
Pammelia (first published book of catches, rounds and canons).
Deuteromelia (more catches and rounds including, for the first time in print, 'Three Blind Mice').

1610 Arabella Stuart, Pretender to the throne, is imprisoned in the Tower for marrying William Seymour, Earl of Hertford. The Great Contract between King and Commons is drafted by the younger Cecil; the King offers to give up some of his feudal rights in return for an annual allowance of £200,000, but the Commons reject the proposal. Henry, the King's son, is created Prince of Wales and Earl of Chester. Archbishop Bancroft dies.

 Burton Agnes Hall, near Bridlington, Humberside (completed).

 Shakespeare: *Cymbeline.*
John Donne: *Pseudo-Martyr.*
Ben Jonson: *The Alchemist.*

1611 Colonization of Ulster by English and Scottish colonists; the confiscated estates of rebel lords are shared out among the immigrants. The Authorized Version of the Bible appears, probably the only great literary work ever to have been produced by a committee. The Order of Baronets is instituted by James I to raise money. James I dissolves Parliament for the first time.

APR   [9] George Abbot becomes Archbishop of Canterbury.

 John Thorpe: Hatfield House, Hertfordshire (completed).

 Gheeraerts: *Frances, Duchess of Richmond.*

 Cyril Tourneur: *The Atheist's Tragedy.*
Ben Jonson: *Catiline his Conspiracy.*
Thomas Middleton & Thomas Dekker: *The Roaring Girl.*
Shakespeare: *Winter's Tale; The Tempest.*
Francis Beaumont & John Fletcher: *Philaster.*
Ben Jonson & Inigo Jones: *Oberon Faery Prince* (masque).
Thomas Heywood: *The Golden Age.*
Authorized Version of the Bible.

 Parthenia (first printed virginals music by Byrd, Bull, Gibbons).
Melismata (collection of part-songs).

1612   Robert Cecil, Lord Salisbury, dies. Robert Carr, Viscount Rochester, becomes the King's chief minister in his place. A flag is flown at half mast to signify a death for the first time, as a tribute to the master of the *Heartsease*, who dies while searching for the North-West Passage. The two last people to be burnt for heresy are Bartholomew Legate and Richard Wightman of Lichfield.

JAN   [17] Thomas Fairfax, commander of the Parliamentary army in the Civil War, is born.
NOV   [6] Prince Henry, James's promising elder son, dies.

 Isaac Oliver: *Henry, Prince of Wales.*

 John Webster: *The White Devil.*

1613   Sir Thomas Overbury, poet and courtier, is sent the Tower for disrespect to the King. He has circulated a poem entitled *A Wife*, which is interpreted as an attack on Lady Essex, whom the King's favourite Robert Carr wished to marry. Overbury dies slowly, poisoned with copper sulphate by Lady Essex's agents.

 Shakespeare: *Henry VIII.*
Francis Beaumont & John Fletcher: *Knight of the Burning Pestle.*
George Withers: *Abuses Stript and Whipt.*
Thomas Dekker: *A Strange Horse Race.*

Richard Johnson: *Look on me, London.*
Thomas Middleton: *The Triumphs of Truth.*
Samuel Purchas: *Purchas his Pilgrimage.*

1614 George Villiers is introduced to James I in an attempt to win the King away from Robert Carr. The scandal surrounding Sir Thomas Overbury's death is made public. Carr and Lady Essex are disgraced and her agents are hanged. The first logarithm tables are published by John Napier.

APR-JUN Second Parliament of James I; its 300 new members include John Pym, Thomas Wentworth and John Eliot.
JUN [**7**] James I dissolves the 'Addled' Parliament, which has disputed non-stop with the King over impositions and produced no legislation. For seven years after this James I calls no Parliament.

 John Webster: *The Duchess of Malfi.* [First performed 1623.]
Sir Walter Raleigh: *The History of the World.*
Ben Jonson: *Bartholomew Fayre.*
John Napier: *Mirifici Logarithmorum Canonis Descriptio.*

1615 A monopoly for the export of British cloth is granted to the Merchant Adventurers. Firewood becomes increasingly scarce and expensive; cheap coal becomes a popular substitute for the first time. Coin-in-the-slot vending machines for loose tobacco are introduced into taverns. Lady Arabella Stuart dies in the Tower.

AUG [**28**] The singer and composer John Baldwin dies.

 Nicholas Stone: The Bodley Monument, Oxford.

 Chapman: *Iliad* and *Odyssey* (translation completed).
Thomas Tomkis: *Albumazar.*
William Camden: *Annals.*

1616 James I begins selling peerages to raise money. Raleigh is released from the Tower on parole to search for El Dorado. Charles is created Prince of Wales. William Baffin discovers and names Baffin Bay while searching for the North-West Passage. The dramatist Francis Beaumont dies.

APR [**23**] William Shakespeare dies.
NOV [**23**] Richard Hakluyt dies.

Bernard Janssen: Audley End, Essex (completed).
Inigo Jones: The Queen's House, Greenwich (begun).

 Peter Oliver: *Richard Sackville, Earl of Dorset.*

1617 Francis Bacon is made Keeper of the Great Seal of England. James I travels to Scotland to meet the Scottish Parliament. One-way streets for traffic control are introduced in London by an Act of Common Council. George Villiers, the King's new favourite, is created Earl of Buckingham. Thomas Weelkes, composer, is dismissed as choirmaster at Chichester for persistent drunkenness.

APR [4] The mathematician John Napier dies.

1618 Francis Bacon is created Lord Chancellor. Suffolk is dismissed. A dredger is invented by Captain John Gilbert. Sir Peter Lely, painter, is born.

OCT [29] Sir Walter Raleigh, explorer, adventurer and courtier, is executed at Whitehall, ostensibly for treason, but in fact for attacking Spaniards in South America. The Banqueting House, Whitehall, destroyed by fire (rebuilt 1619-22).

 Thomas Holt: Bodleian Library, Oxford.

 Nathaniel Field: *Amends for Ladies.*

1619 Dulwich College is founded.

JAN [7] Nicholas Hilliard, the miniature portrait painter, dies.

Inigo Jones: The Banqueting House, Whitehall (rebuilding begins).

Francis Beaumont & John Fletcher: *A King and No King.*

Francis Tregian: *Fitzwilliam Virginal Book* (compiled in prison).

1620 Negotiations are under way with Spain to arrange a marriage between Prince Charles and the Infanta Maria. The Duke of Buckingham digs at the centre of Stonehenge.

FEB Thomas Campion, writer, dies.
SEP [16] The Pilgrim Fathers sail in the *Mayflower* under Captain Myles Standish.
OCT [31] John Evelyn, diarist, is born.
DEC [21] The Pilgrim Fathers land at Plymouth, Massachusetts and settle in New England.

Quenby Hall, Leicestershire.
Haughley Park, Suffolk.

Francis Quarles: *A Feast of Worms.*
Francis Bacon: *Novum Organum Scientiarum.*
James I: *The Works of the Most High and Mightie Prince, James, King of Great Britain, France and Ireland.*
Thomas Dekker: *Dekker, his Dreame.*
John Ford: *A Line of Life.*

1621 There is friction between the House of Commons and James I over the proposed marriage of Charles, Prince of Wales, to the Spanish Infanta. This leads to a declaration (December) of Parliamentary rights by the Commons called 'the Great Protestation'. Robert Cromwell, the first son of Oliver Cromwell, is born. John Donne becomes Dean of St Paul's and begins to compose his famous sermons. The poet Henry Vaughan is born.

JAN-FEB Third Parliament of James I.
MAR　[**31**] The poet Andrew Marvell is born.
MAY　[**3**] Bacon is charged with accepting bribes for granting monopoly patents. impeached, fined £40,000 and banned from Parliament and Court; the King later pardons him and remits the fine.
JUN　[**2**] The first issue of the British newspaper, *The Corante*, is published.

Peter Oliver: *Charles I when Prince of Wales.*

Richard Johnson: *The History of Tom Thumbe.*
Peter Heylin: *Microcosmus.*
Robert Burton: *Anatomy of Melancholy.*
Thomas Dekker: *Greevous Grones for the Poore.*

1622 Prince Charles and Buckingham set off in secret for Spain to woo the King of Spain's daughter. Oliver Cromwell, second son of Oliver Cromwell, is born. The Archbishop of Canterbury, George Abbot, accidentally kills a gamekeeper; a commission of enquiry into the incident cannot agree on a conclusion, so he remains in office. Enraged by the Great Protestation, James I dissolves Parliament. John Pym, Sir Edward Cole, John Selden and the Earl of Southampton are arrested for criticizing the King's policy. William Oughtred invents the slide rule.

Inigo Jones: Banqueting House, Whitehall (completed).

Francis Bacon: *Historia Naturalis et Experimentalis*.
Michael Drayton: *Polyolbion*. [First part published 1612.]
John Reynolds: *The Triumph of God's Revenge against the crying
and execrable sinne of Murther*.

1623 Prince Charles and Buckingham arrive in Madrid in disguise, but the
Infanta does not like Charles and the King of Spain expects him to
become a Catholic. The port of Gloucester is founded. A patents law
comes into force, protecting inventors. The historian William Camden
and the composer William Byrd die.

OCT Prince Charles returns to England, rebuffed and angry. George
Villiers becomes the Duke of Buckingham.
NOV Thomas Weelkes, composer, dies.

 Inigo Jones: The Queen's Chapel, St James's Palace.

 Shakespeare: *Comedies, Histories and Tragedies* ('First Folio').

1624 James I's Fourth Parliament (February-March). In spite of its anger,
Parliament refuses to declare war on Spain; nevertheless, supplies are
voted for increased defence. Monopolies are declared illegal. The
English are driven out of the Spice Islands by the Dutch. The Dutch
settle in New Amsterdam (later to become New York). An
Anglo-French Treaty is signed, providing for Prince Charles's
marriage to Henrietta Maria, daughter of Henry IV of France. The
first working submarine, built by the Dutch physicist Cornelius
Drebbel, travels underwater in the River Thames for two hours,
propelled by 12 oarsmen. Lionel Cranfield, the Lord Treasurer, is
impeached for bribery and dismissed.

 Herbert of Cherbury: *De Veritate*.
Thomas Heywood: *The Captives*.
Ben Jonson: *The Fortunate Isles*.
Captain John Smith: *The General History of Virginia*.
Francis Quarles: *Job Militant*.

1625 England, Denmark and France form an alliance against the Hapsburgs.
An Anglo-Dutch alliance against Spain is formed by the Treaty of
Southampton. John Fletcher, dramatist, dies.

MAR [27] James I dies at Theobalds Park, Cheshunt, succeeded by
his son Charles I. Mytens is appointed Court painter.
MAY [1] Charles I marries, by proxy, the 16-year-old Henrietta
Maria, sister of Louis XIII of France.

JUN [**5**] Orlando Gibbons, composer, dies suddenly while waiting to officiate at Charles I's marriage service. The Black Death kills 41,000 people in London alone; Charles I's First Parliament adjourns to Oxford for safety. Parliament grants additional funds to continue the war with Spain. A tobacco tax is levied.

John Donne: *The First Sermon preached to King Charles.*
Francis Bacon: *Essays.*
Philip Massinger: *A New Way to Pay Old Debts.*

1626 FEB-JUN Charles I's Second Parliament is convened. Buckingham is impeached; Sir John Eliot leads the attack, denouncing Buckingham as 'the canker in the King's treasure'. Digges and Eliot are sent to the Tower for conducting the impeachment, and the Commons refuse to continue with business until Digges and Eliot are released. Charles obliges, but dissolves the Parliament. Charles offers knighthoods for sale, to raise funds independently of Parliament. The composer John Dowland dies.

MAR [**12**] John Aubrey, antiquary, is born.
APR [**9**] Francis Bacon, philosopher and statesman, dies in London as Lord Verulam.
OCT [**4**] Richard Cromwell is born, the third son of Oliver Cromwell.

Samuel Purchas: *Hakluytus Posthumus.*

1627 England declares war on France, largely because of a personality clash between Buckingham and Richelieu. Charles sends the Duke of Buckingham with a fleet in an abortive attempt to help the French Huguenots defend La Rochelle. Robert Boyle, scientist, is born.

JUL [**2**] Thomas Middleton, dramatist, dies.

Francis Bacon: *New Atlantis.*

1628 John Bunyan, writer, is born. Harvey publishes his work on the circulation of blood.

JAN [**20**] Henry, fourth son of Oliver Cromwell, is born.
MAR [**12**] John Bull, composer and organist, dies. Oliver Cromwell enters Charles I's Third Parliament. A Petition of Right (Pym and Wentworth) requests that no one should be compelled to pay a loan, benevolence or tax without Parliament's consent

and that no subject should be imprisoned without cause shown: the King accepts these proposals.

JUL [5] Michael Cavendish, composer, dies.

AUG [23] The Duke of Buckingham is murdered; Wentworth deserts the popular party and becomes the King's chief adviser.

 Braemar Castle (built at about this time).

 William Harvey: *Exercitatio Anatomica de Motu Cordis et Sanguinis in Animalibus.*
Francis Fletcher: *The World Encompassed by Sir Francis Drake.*

1629 Rubens, now in England, is knighted. The colony of Massachusetts is founded in America. Charles I meets opposition in the House of Commons; resolutions by Sir John Eliot are read criticizing illegal taxation and royal intolerance.

MAR [5] Charles has Eliot and eight other members arrested and begins Personal Rule, advised by Laud and Wentworth. [10] Parliament is dissolved for 11 years. Charles raises money by various means, including fines imposed by the Star Chamber and sales of monopolies.

NOV Eliot dies in the Tower.

 Daniel Mytens: *James, Duke of Hamilton.*

 William Davenant: *The Tragedy of Albovine.*
John Parkinson: *A Garden of all sorts of pleasant flowers which our English ayre will permit to be noursed up.*
John Ford: *The Lovers' Melancholy.*

1630 Large-scale emigration to Massachusetts begins. The English gentry is forced to contribute large sums to the Crown by an extortionate method called Distraint of Knighthood. Sash windows are used for the first time, installed by Inigo Jones at Raynham Hall in Norfolk.

MAY [29] Charles II is born at St James's Palace.

 Stratfield Saye, Hampshire (at about this time).
Glamis Castle, Tayside, Scotland (rebuilding begins).

 William Davenant: *The Cruel Brother.*
John Donne: *Death's Duell.*

1631 The British settlement of St Kitts marks the start of colonization in the Leeward Islands. William Oughtred introduces the multiplication sign (x).

MAR [**31**] The poet John Donne dies.
AUG [**9**] John Dryden, poet, is born at Aldwincle in Northamptonshire.
NOV [**4**] Mary, daughter of Charles I, is born.

Kew Palace, Surrey.

Nicholas Stone: Effigy of John Donne.

William Oughtred: *Clavis Mathematica.*

1632 Anthony van Dyck is appointed Court painter to Charles I. Sir Francis Windebank becomes Secretary of State. The colonies of Maryland and Antigua are founded. George Herbert, writer, dies.

AUG [**29**] John Locke, philosopher, is born.
OCT [**20**] Sir Christopher Wren, architect, is born.

William Rowley: *A New Wonder: A Woman Never Vexed.*

1633 William Prynne's book *Historio-mastix*, denouncing the theatre, is the first book to be publicly burnt by the hangman; Prynne himself is sentenced to lose his ears. A sawmill powered by wind is built in London. Bananas appear in British shops for the first time, in the window of Thomas Johnson in London. Charles I is crowned in Edinburgh.

FEB [**23**] Samuel Pepys, diarist, is born in Fleet Street.
JUL Thomas Wentworth, Earl of Strafford, takes up his post as Lord Deputy of Ireland; he proceeds to subdue Ireland ruthlessly.
AUG [**4**] Archbishop Abbot dies.
SEP [**19**] William Laud becomes Archbishop of Canterbury.
OCT [**14**] James II is born at St James's Palace, the son of Charles I and Henrietta Maria.

William Rowley: *All's Lost by Lust.*
John Donne: *Poems.*
Fulke Greville: *Certaine Learned and Elegant Workes.*
George Herbert: *The Temple.*
William Rowley: *A Match at Midnight.*
John Ford: *'Tis Pity She's a Whore.*

1634 Charles I attempts during the next three years to raise taxes without Parliament. Ship Money is introduced, a tax on seaports and maritime counties, ostensibly to raise a fleet for defence. Covent Garden Market is opened in London. Milton's masque *Comus* is performed at Ludlow Castle. Sir Julius Vermuyden, the Dutch engineer, drains the Fens.

 Bateman's, Sussex.

 Rubens: Painted ceiling, Banqueting House, Whitehall.
Nicholas Stone: Lyttleton Monument, Oxford.

 John Ford: *The Chronicle Historie of Perkin Warbeck*.
John Milton: *Comus*.
William Davenant and Inigo Jones: *The Temple of Love*.

1635 Ship Money is now exacted from inland towns too. Charles I makes Archbishop Spottiswoode Chancellor of Scotland. A public postal service between London and Edinburgh is established; the rates are 2d-8d. A speed limit of 3 mph is imposed on hackney coaches in London. The colony of Rhode Island is founded in America.

JUL   [**18**] Robert Hooke, physicist, is born.

 Rousham Park, Oxfordshire, built at about this time (remodelled by William Kent 1738-40).

 Sir Anthony van Dyck: *Charles I*.

 Robert Herrick: *King Oberon's Feast*.
Thomas Heywood: *The Hierarchie of the Blessed Angells*.
Francis Quarles: *Emblemes*.

1636 The colony of Connecticut is founded in America. William Juxon, Bishop of London, is appointed Lord High Treasurer. William Gascoigne invents the micrometer.

 Isaac de Caux: Wilton House, near Salisbury (begun).

 Sir Anthony van Dyck: *Charles I in Three Positions*.

 Thomas Dekker: *The Wonder of a Kingdome*.

1637 Ship Money is declared by the legislature to be a legal form of tax. John Hampden refuses to pay Ship Money, but judgement is given against him. On Laud's advice, Charles tries to force the English Liturgy onto the Scottish Church. The Scots resist by organizing Four Tables or committees to oppose the measure.

James Shirley: *The Lady of Pleasure.*

1638 The Solemn League and Covenant is widely signed in Scotland as a show of solidarity in defence of the reformed religion; Charles threatens to impose his will on Scotland by force. The Covenanters form an army under Alexander Leslie. Torture is abolished in Britain.

NOV   A general assembly at Glasgow abolishes episcopacy in Scotland and gives final form to the Scottish Kirk.

Thomas Grumbold: Clare College quad, Cambridge (begun); Clare Bridge (begun).

John Ford: *The Fancies Chaste and Noble.*
Bishop John Wilkins: *The Discovery of a World in the Moon.*

1639 Charles moves against the Scots to force them to reinstate the bishops they evicted last year. The Covenanters rise up against the alleged introduction of 'Popery'. Charles charges them with seeking to overturn royal power. The Covenanters capture Edinburgh, Stirling and Dumbarton; the First Bishops' War.

MAY   Robert Cromwell, eldest son of Oliver Cromwell, dies aged 18.
JUN   Charles I comes to terms with the Scots, signing the Pacification of Berwick. The transit of Venus is accurately predicted and observed by Jeremiah Horrocks.
JUL   [8] Henry, son of Charles I, is born.

Richard Zouche: *The Sophister.*

1640 Charles I makes Thomas Wentworth Earl of Strafford and chief adviser. William Wycherley and Thomas Shadwell, dramatists, are born. The first stagecoach lines are opened, with coaching houses at regular intervals.

JAN   [25] Robert Burton, clergyman, scholar and author, dies.
APR–MAY
      Charles I summons his Fourth or Short Parliament.
AUG   The Second Bishops' War; Scottish forces cross the Tweed and enter Newcastle and Durham. [28] English forces are defeated by the Scots at Newburn.
OCT   [26] Treaty of Ripon; Charles I agrees to pay the Scottish army £850 a day until a permanent settlement can be reached. Charles summons a Great Council of Peers at York but, fearful of acting independently of the Commons, it recommends calling another Parliament.

Nov Giles Farnaby, composer, dies. [3] The Fifth or Long Parliament begins. Royal prerogatives are abolished; Strafford and Laud are impeached; Leyton, Prynne and other victims of the Star Chamber are released.

🖉 Thomas Hobbes: *Elements of Law* (written).

1641 The first cotton factories are opened in Manchester. Mary, Charles I's daughter, marries William II, Prince of Orange. Thomas Dekker, the prolific dramatist, dies.

Mar The trial of the King's minister, Thomas Wentworth, Earl of Strafford.
May [12] Execution of Strafford. [15] Triennial Act; every Parliament is to be dissolved after three years and only dissolved with its own consent.
Jul The Courts of the Star Chamber and High Commission are abolished.
Oct 30,000 rebelling Protestants in Ulster are massacred. The Marquis of Montrose plots the seizure of the Earl of Argyle, the Presbyterian leader. The Montrose plot seems to implicate Charles I himself, who virtually surrenders control to Argyle and the Presbyterians.
Dec [9] Sir Anthony van Dyck, Flemish Court painter to Charles I, dies at his studio in Blackfriars.

🖉 Shackerley Marmion: *The Antiquary.*
Sir Robert Naunton: *Fragmenta Regalia.*
Thomas Heywood: *The Life of Merlin.*

1642 Thomas Shadwell, writer, is born near Grantham. Income tax and property tax are introduced.

Jan [3] Charles I orders the impeachment of five members of Parliament for treasonable correspondence with the Scots during the recent troubles; the Commons refuse to order the arrests. [4] Charles I enters the Commons Chamber in person in an attempt to arrest the Five Members (Hollis, Hampden, Strode, Haselrigg and Pym), but fails because they are in hiding. The Commons follow the Five Members to the Guildhall, where they are secure in the protection of the citizens of London. [10] Charles I withdraws from London. The Commons, emboldened, prepare Bills excluding bishops from the House of Lords and giving Parliament control of the army.

MAR Charles I, now in York, refuses to give assent to the Bills.
JUN Parliament makes a final appeal to the King to assent to the Militia Bill, but he refuses.
JUL Parliament appoints a committee of public safety and puts Essex in charge of an army of 24,000; King and Parliament prepare for war. The theatres close, and remain closed until 1660.
AUG [**22**] Charles I raises his standard at Nottingham, opening the military phase of the Great Rebellion; the outbreak of the English Civil War.
OCT [**23**] In the First Campaign, the first general engagement is the Battle of Edgehill, which has no clear outcome.
NOV [**12**] Charles I marches on London, but is beaten back at Turnham Green.
DEC [**25**] Isaac Newton, scientist, is born.

Thomas Browne: *Religio Medici.*
Thomas Hobbes: *De Cive.*

1643 In the Second Campaign of the Civil War, the King's armies prosper. Royalist victories include the Battles of Chalgrove Field, Atherton Moor and Roundway Down, and the sacking of Bristol by Prince Rupert. Parliamentary victories include Bradford, Gainsborough, Grantham and Winceby. The English Parliament agrees to the Solemn League and Covenant, securing the services of the Scottish army. Scots Covenanters invade England on the Parliamentary side.

APR [**27**] Skirmish at Reading in Essex.
JUN [**18**] Skirmish at Chalgrove Field, in which Hampden is mortally wounded.
JUL [**25**] Prince Rupert captures Bristol.
SEP Essex's Parliamentary troops relieve Gloucester. [**20**] The First Battle of Newbury is indecisive.

William Dobson: *Endymion Porter* (painted at about this time).

William Davenant: *The Unfortunate Loves.*

1644 Isaac Fuller's now-lost altarpiece is described by John Evelyn as 'too full of nakeds for a chapel'. John Milton opposes censorship. The 'Clubmen' risings of armed neutrals become a threat to both sides in the Third Campaign of the Civil War. The Queen flees to France. The Self-Denying Ordinance is passed by the Commons; this removes all MPs except Cromwell from Military commands.

JAN Charles I calls a Royalist Parliament at Oxford. [**25**] Royalists are defeated at the Battle of Nantwich.

FEB [**15**] Parliamentarians form a joint committee of the two kingdoms of England and Scotland.

MAR Oliver, Cromwell's second son, dies aged 22.

APR Fairfax's Parliamentary troops besiege York.

JUL [**1**] Prince Rupert raises the siege of York. [**2**] Battle of Marston Moor; Parliament wins the decisive battle of the Civil War.

AUG Montrose enters Scotland in disguise and raises the Highland clans in support of Charles I.

SEP [**1**] Battle of Tippamuir; Royalist Highlanders defeat the Covenanters.

OCT [**14**] William Penn, the founder of Pennsylvania, is born. [**27**] The Second Battle of Newbury is indecisive; after it, Charles escapes to Oxford.

 Isaac Fuller: Altarpiece, All Souls College, Oxford.

 John Knox: *History of the Reformation of Religion within the Realm of Scotland* (Books 4-5).
John Milton: *Areopagitica*.

1645 The composer William Lawes dies. Wallpaper is used for the first time as a cheap substitute for tapestry.

JAN [**10**] William Laud, Archbishop of Canterbury from 1633, is beheaded on Tower Hill for treason; he is not replaced until 1660.

FEB [**2**] Battle of Inverlochy: Royalist Highlanders are victorious over Covenanters.

APR [**3**] The Self-Denying Ordinance is passed by the House of Lords, with the intention of removing faint-hearted generals from their posts. All MPs except Cromwell are required to resign their commissions within 40 days. Fairfax supersedes Essex as captain-general.

MAY [**1**] Battle of Auldcarn; Royalists defeat Covenanters.

JUN [**14**] Battle of Naseby; the main Royalist army is crushed, effectively terminating the war. [**18**] The Royalist town of Leicester falls to Parliamentarian troops.

JUL [**2**] Battle of Alford; Royalists defeat Covenanters. [**23**] Bridgewater, another Royalist town, falls to the Parliamentarians.

SEP [**13**] Battle of Philiphaugh; Montrose's army supporting Charles in Scotland is destroyed by General Leslie's troops. Montrose escapes to the Continent.

Edmund Waller: *Poems.*

1646 Jeremiah Rich, the first shorthand teacher, starts shorthand classes in London.

MAY [**5**] Charles I surrenders to the Scots at Newark, bringing the military phase of the Civil War to an end.

JUL The King is presented with Parliament's Newcastle Propositions, demanding that he relinquish control of the army to Parliament for 20 years and agree to religious reforms favouring Protestants. Charles cannot accept them and makes an abortive attempt to escape from captivity.

AUG [**19**] The astronomer John Flamsteed is born.

Henry Vaughan: *Poems.*
Richard Crawshaw: *Steps to the Temple.*
Sir John Suckling: *Fragmenta Aurea.*

1647 Parliament votes to disband most of the army, but the army refuses to comply. Radical movements criticize Parliamentary tyranny. The writer, the Earl of Rochester, and the composer, Pelham Humfrey, are born.

JAN [**30**] At Newcastle, the Scots agree to hand Charles I over to the English Parliament for £400,000.

JUN [**4**] At Holmby House in Northamptonshire, Charles I is seized by the army. On the same day, Cromwell flees from Parliament to rejoin the army at Triptow Heath. [**10**] From St Albans, the army submits to Parliament a 'humble representation', asking for the exclusion of 11 members of whom it disapproves; about 100 MPs flee to the army.

AUG [**6**] The army enters London, forcing Parliament to take back the members who left in June.

OCT The Agreement of the People, the Leveller constitution, is debated in the Army Council at Putney.

NOV [**11**] Charles I flees from Hampton Court to the Isle of Wight; he is once again detained and imprisoned at Carisbrooke Castle. He signs a secret treaty with the Scots, who promise to restore him by force.

DEC [**24**] Parliament presents the King with four Bills to sign, one giving Parliament control of the army for 20 years, one requiring all declarations against Parliament to be recalled, one excluding all the Peers created by Charles from sitting in the House of Lords, one allowing the two Houses to adjourn at their own pleasure.

Francis Beaumont and John Fletcher: *Comedies and Tragedies.*

1648 The Levellers, a Puritan group, demand an egalitarian and republican society.

JAN [**15**] Parliament renounces allegiance to the King and votes to have no further communication with him. The Scots now join Charles I in a Second Civil War.

MAR The army returns to London, pressing for the King to be brought to trial; the King is brought from Hurst Castle to Whitehall.

AUG [**17-20**] Battle of Preston; a Scottish army under the Duke of Hamilton invades England in support of Charles I, but is beaten back by Cromwell.

DEC [**1**] Charles is once again seized by the army. [**6-7**] Pride's Purge; Colonel Pride forcibly excludes 96 Presbyterian members from Parliament, which is known from this time on as the Rump Parliament, consisting of only 60 members. [**13**] The Rump decides to discontinue the reopened negotiations with the King and instead bring him to trial.

Robert Herrick: *Hesperides.*
John Gauden: *Eikon Basilike: the Portraicture of his sacred maiestie in his solitude and sufferings.*

1649 The Royal Navy takes delivery of its first frigate, the *Constant Warwick*. John Aubrey draws attention for the first time to the megalithic monument at Avebury.

JAN [**20**] An Army Council draws up a temporary Instrument of Government. [**20-27**] Trial of Charles I: no defence witnesses are called. [**30**] Charles I is executed on a scaffold outside the Banqueting House of Whitehall Palace; the executioner is Richard Brandon.

FEB [**5**] The Scots proclaim Charles II King in Edinburgh; the Irish under Ormond also rise in Charles II's favour. [**9**] Charles I's funeral and burial in the Garter Chapel at St George's, Windsor.

MAR [**16**] The monarchy and the House of Lords are abolished. Parliament sets up a Commonwealth run by a Council of State with Bradshaw as President and Milton as Latin Secretary. The Levellers claim their 'Agreement of People' as the basis for a new constitution; they are defeated at Burford and their leaders arrested and executed.

APR [**9**] The Duke of Monmouth, son of Charles II and Lucy Walter, is born at Rotterdam.

SEP   [**12**] The storming of Drogheda by Ireton's army marks the conclusion of the reconquest of Ireland.

Inigo Jones and John Webb: Wilton House, Wiltshire (rebuilt after a fire destroyed the original house in 1647).

Richard Lovelace: *Lucasta*.
John Lilburne: *England's New Chaines Discovered*.

1650 FEB   [**2**] Nell Gwyn, barmaid, actress and mistress of Charles II, is born. The Marquis of Montrose returns to Scotland.

APR   [**27**] Battle of Corbiesdale; Montrose is defeated and captured.

MAY   [**14**] Parliament votes in favour of the death penalty for adultery, but the law is never implemented. [**21**] Montrose is executed at Edinburgh. [**26**] The Duke of Marlborough is born at Ashe in Devon as John Churchill.

JUN   [**24**] Charles II lands in Scotland, takes the covenant and is proclaimed King.

SEP   [**3**] Battle of Dunbar; Cromwell's army invades Scotland and succeeds in defeating a Scottish army twice its size.

OCT   George Fox, in court on a charge of preaching illegally, urges the judge, Gervase Bennet, to 'tremble at the word of the Lord'; the judge replies that the only quaker in the court is Fox himself, and the nickname sticks.

NOV   [**4**] William III is born at The Hague, the posthumous son of William II of Orange and Mary Stuart, daughter of Charles I.

Sir Roger Pratt: Coleshill, Berkshire (begun).

Thomas Hobbes: *Human Nature*.
Henry Vaughan: *Silex Scintillans*.

John Playford: *The English Dancing Master*.

1651 The first edition of *Mercurius Scoticus*, the first Scottish newspaper, appears. All courts in Britain now begin recording their proceedings in English.

JAN   [**1**] Charles II is crowned King of Scotland at Scone Palace. Afterwards, Charles marches south into England.

AUG   [**2**] Cromwell's army takes Perth.

SEP   [**3**] Battle of Worcester; Charles II's supporters are defeated and Charles makes his escape to France.

OCT   [**9**] First Navigation Act; aimed at the growing Dutch threat, this measure gives British shipping a monopoly of foreign trade and also helps to precipitate an Anglo-Dutch War.

John Milton: *The Life and Reign of King Charles.*
Sir Henry Wotton: *Reliquiae Wottonianae.*
Thomas Hobbes: *Leviathan.*
Sir William Davenant: *Gondibert.*

1652 The first tea reaches Britain: a small amount is found on a captured Dutch ship and brought home. A Perpetuation Bill is introduced in an attempt to make all existing MPs members for life. The writer Nahum Tate is born.

FEB   Act of Indemnity and Oblivion; this deals with the return of confiscated Royalist estates in an attempt to reconcile Royalists.

MAR   [3] Thomas Otway, dramatist, is born. [29] 'Black Monday': a total eclipse of the sun causes widespread apprehension and disturbance.

MAY   Battle of the Downs; the English fleet scores a victory over the Dutch before war is formally declared.

JUN   [21] The architect Inigo Jones dies.

JUL   [8] The First Anglo-Dutch War begins.

AUG   Act of Settlement for Ireland.

 Sir Roger Pratt: Coleshill, Berkshire (completed).

 Gerrard Winstanley: *Law of Freedom.*

1653 Thomas Durfey, writer, is born.

FEB   [18] In the Anglo-Dutch War, an English fleet under Blake and Monk defeats a Dutch fleet under Van Trump off Portland.

APR   [20] Cromwell dissolves the Rump Parliament and becomes head of state, setting up a council of 10 members and a nominated Parliament of 140 members.

JUL   The 'Bare-Bones Parliament' meets. [31] Battle of the Texel; the English under Monk are victorious, and Admiral Van Trump is killed in action.

DEC   [12] Cromwellian MPs resign their powers to Cromwell. [16] Cromwell sets up a Protectorate with a Council of State and himself as Lord Protector.

 William Rowley and Thomas Middleton: *The Changeling.*
Izaak Walton: *The Compleat Angler.*
Nicholas Culpeper: *The English Physician Enlarged.*

1654 Surveyors are empowered by an Act of Parliament to assess the inhabitants of each parish, hire labour and carts, and mend the highways; this leads to rapid improvements in the roads and the speed of travel. A treaty of commerce between England and Sweden is signed. The formal Union of Ireland and Scotland with England and Wales is arranged, with free trade and representation at Westminster. The First Protectorate Parliament meets, including MPs from the three kingdoms.

APR   [**5**] The Treaty of Westminster ends the First Anglo-Dutch War.

SEP   [**3**] The Republican party headed by Vane opposes Cromwell in Parliament, calling into question the legality of 'the Instrument' and the pre-eminence of Cromwell himself. [**12**] Cromwell orders an exclusion of members.

1655 Under Cromwell's 'Western Design', the Caribbean is to become an arena for British ambition. Charles II is expelled from France following an Anglo-French treaty directed against Spain.

JAN   Parliament votes that the office of Protector should be elective not hereditary. [**22**] Cromwell turns to the idea of military rule, dissolving Parliament. Major-generals are appointed to supervise the eleven military districts of England.

MAR–   A Royalist insurrection in the West Country (Colonel John
MAY   Penruddock's Rising is a complete failure, ending in Penruddock's execution).

John Webb: Lamport Hall, Northamptonshire (begun).

Thomas Hobbes: *In Corpore.*
Roger Boyle: *Parthenissa.*

1656 Letters posted in London are delivered in Winchester the next day. *The Siege of Rhodes*, the first English opera, is produced, with words by William Davenant and music by Locke, Lawes, Crooke, Colman and Hudson.

MAR   [**21**] James Ussher, retired Archbishop of Armagh, dies at Reigate.

MAY   An English expedition led by Penn and Venables to capture Jamaica causes Spain to declare war on Britain. [**30**] The regiment of Grenadier Guards is founded.

SEP   [**9**] Blake captures Spanish treasure ships off Cadiz. [**17**] The Second Protectorate Parliament meets.

James Harrington: *Oceana.*
John Bunyan: *Some Gospel Truths Opened.*
Thomas Hobbes: *Liberty, Necessity and Chance.*
Davenant, Locke and others: *The Siege of Rhodes.*

1657 Cromwell founds Durham University.

JAN   Sindercombe's Plot to assassinate Cromwell is discovered.

MAR   Parliament's 'Humble Petition and Advice' offers Cromwell the title 'King' and the right to name his successor.

MAY   [8] Cromwell rejects the title 'King', but elects to nominate the members of his own House of Lords.

JUN   [3] William Harvey, physician and anatomist, dies.

AUG   [7] Robert Blake, one of the greatest naval commanders, dies as his ship sails into Plymouth.

 William Allen: *Killing no Murder.*

1658 Cromwell's Third and Last Protectorate Parliament assembles in its reconstructed form, with a second house of 60 members, although only one of these actually takes his seat. Cromwell dissolves this Parliament after only 16 days, ruling for the rest of his life without Parliament. France joins Britain against Spain.

JUN   [4] Allied Anglo-French troops defeat a Spanish force at the Dunes and capture Dunkirk.

SEP   [3] Cromwell dies of pneumonia in Whitehall. He is succeeded as Protector by his son Richard. Cromwell is buried in Westminster Abbey, his effigy wearing a crown and holding an orb and sceptre.

 John Bunyan: *A Few Sighs from Hell.*
William Davenant: *The Cruelty of Spaniards in Peru.*
Thomas Browne: *Urn Burial.*

1659 Henry Purcell, composer, is born.

JAN   [27] Richard Cromwell's Parliament meets; a new dispute between Parliament and army quickly develops.

FEB   [16] The first cheque known to have been drawn on a British bank is written today.

APR   [22] Richard Cromwell dissolves his Protectorate Parliament.

MAY   [7] The Rump Parliament is restored. [24] The Rump induces Richard Cromwell to abdicate as Protector.

OCT   The Rump is expelled by the army and a military committee of safety is appointed; another military dictatorship seems imminent.

DEC   [**26**] Reaction against military coups results in a restoration of the Rump Parliament.

John Dryden: *Heroic Stanzas* (on Cromwell's death).
Thomas Hobbes: *De Homine.*

1660 The war with Spain ends. Robert Boyle invents the air pump.

JAN   [**1**] Samuel Pepys begins his diary.

FEB   [**3**] General Monk arrives in London from Scotland and assumes control of the Government. [**21**] Monk re-establishes the Long Parliament.

MAR   [**16**] The Long Parliament finally dissolves itself. [**28**] George I is born at Osnabruck Castle in Hanover.

APR   [**4**] Charles II issues the Declaration of Breda, promising a lawful Parliamentary settlement, a general pardon to all except those named by Parliament (the regicide judges), and a measure of religious liberty. [**25**] Monk summons a Convention Parliament to consider the Declaration.

MAY   [**1**] The Convention Parliament resolves to restore the monarchy with limited powers and invites Charles II to return. [**8**] The formal restoration of the monarchy in England, when Charles II is proclaimed King. [**25**] Charles II returns to England. [**29**] Charles enters London amid great rejoicing: it is his thirtieth birthday. Ten regicides are executed. The bodies of Cromwell, Bradshaw and Ireton are dragged from Westminster Abbey, hanged at Tyburn and buried beneath the gallows. The theatres reopen. An actress plays Desdemona in *Othello*: the first appearance of an actress in the English theatre. The Royal Society is founded.

JUN   [**30**] William Oughtred, mathematician, dies.

OCT   [**2**] The army is disbanded except for about 5,000 men.

DEC   [**24**] Mary, Charles I's daughter and wife of William II of Orange, dies. [**29**] The Convention Parliament is disbanded.

Forde Abbey, Dorset (remodelling completed – originally built 1150).

Peter Lely: *Anne Hyde, Duchess of York.*

John Dryden: *Astraea redux.*
Richard Allestree: *The Whole Duty of Man.*
Nathaniel Ingelo: *Bentivolio and Urania.*

1661 The architect Nicholas Hawksmoor and the novelist Daniel Defoe are born. Matthew Locke is appointed Court composer by Charles II. The first London playhouse with a proscenium arch, Lincoln's Inn Fields Theatre, opens with *Hamlet*.

APR [**16**] Charles Montagu, founder of the Bank of England, is born. [**19**] Postmarks are introduced by the Post Office. [**23**] Coronation of Charles II.

MAY [**1**] The tallest and longest-standing maypole in England is erected in the Strand to a fanfare of trumpets and drums: it is 130 feet high. [**8**] Charles II's First Parliament, the 'Cavalier Parliament', meets. It establishes the Anglican Church and enacts a series of repressive measures that will later be known as the Clarendon Code. All Acts of Cromwell's Parliaments are annulled. According to the Treason Act it is now treason merely to plan rebellion: no open act is required.

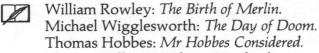 Robert Boyle: *The Sceptical Chymist*.
William Rowley and John Webster: *A Cure for a Cuckold*.

1662 Tea-drinking is introduced to Court by the Queen. Britain sells Dunkirk to France for £400,000. Quakers Act: severe penalties are imposed on Quakers meeting for worship. Licensing Act: new books on theology are to be vetted by the Church. The Act of Settlement authorizes Justices to send any newcomer who might become a charge on the rates back to his last address.

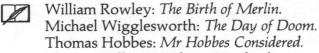 William Rowley: *The Birth of Merlin*.
Michael Wigglesworth: *The Day of Doom*.
Thomas Hobbes: *Mr Hobbes Considered*.
Thomas Fuller: *Worthies of England*.

1663 The first theatre in Drury Lane is built. Turnpike tolls are levied for the first time. The first gold guinea is minted. Sheerness Royal Naval Dockyard is established. Samuel Pepys begins to use one of the newly-invented fountain pens to write his diary. A Hearth Tax is introduced. It becomes apparent that the Clarendon Code is restricting religious freedom.

FEB [**24**] John Milton marries for the third time.
AUG [**31**] Gilbert Sheldon becomes Archbishop of Canterbury.

Christopher Wren: Pembroke College Chapel, Cambridge.

Samuel Butler: *Hudibras*.
Sir Samuel Tuke: *The Adventures of Five Hours*.

1664 The colony of New Jersey is founded in America. The British Government protests to the Dutch that the island of Pulo Run has still not been handed over: calls for war with Holland are restrained by Charles II, who fears the cost.

JAN   Sir John Vanbrugh, architect and dramatist, is born.

MAY   The Conventicle Act discriminates against nonconformists by forbidding meetings of more than five people for worship unless they are Anglican.

Christopher Wren: Sheldonian Theatre, Oxford.
Hugh May: Eltham Lodge, Kent.

Sir George Etherege: *The Comical Revenge, or Love in a Tub.*

1665 Isaac Newton conceives the idea of gravitation after watching an apple fall in his garden. Robert Hooke discovers living cells in plants. Christopher Wren meets the architect Bernini in Paris.

FEB   [6] Queen Anne is born at St James's Palace: she is the second daughter of the Duke of York by his first wife, Anne Hyde.

MAR   The Second Dutch War begins after a Swedish ship carrying ships' masts to England is captured by the Dutch.

JUN   [3] The Duke of York defeats a Dutch fleet off Lowestoft; the Dutch Admiral Opdam is killed in the action and 16 of his ships are sunk. [7] The Great Plague is first reported in London: it is an exceptionally hot day. 70,000 people are to die by October. Plague forces the Cavalier Parliament to meet for its fifth session in Oxford.

OCT   The Five Mile Act drives ejected dissenting clergymen from the towns.

NOV   [16] The *London Gazette* is first published.

William Winde; Ashdown House, Oxfordshire.

John Dryden: *The Indian Emperor.*
John Bunyan: *The Resurrection.*
Royal Society: *Philosophical Transactions, Vol 1.*

1666 Isaac Newton propounds integral calculus.

JAN   France declares war on Britain.

JUL   [25] Off the North Foreland, a British fleet under Albemarle is defeated by De Ruyter and De Witt. Growing debts and the Dutch blockade of Newcastle colliers cause Charles II and Clarendon to open negotiations for peace, using Sweden as negotiator.

SEP [2] The Great Fire of London breaks out in Pudding Lane in the bakehouse of Thomas Farriner. The splendid medieval St Paul's Cathedral and a large area of central London are burnt. [6] The Great Fire burns itself out. Pratt, May and Wren are appointed to rebuild the city of London.

NOV [28] A revolt of Scottish Covenanters is ruthlessly crushed in the Battle of Pentland Hills.

DEC The Great Plague comes to an end.

Francis Barlow: *Aesop's Fables* (illustrations).

John Dryden: *Annus Mirabilis.*

1667 Robert Hooke proposes systematic weather recording, marking the start of meteorology.

JUN A Dutch fleet under De Ruyter enters the Medway estuary and tows away the British flagship, the *Royal Charles*, and sinks six other ships. The incident produces near-panic throughout the country.

JUL [21] The Second Anglo-Dutch War ends with the Treaty of Breda. Britain gives up her claim to Pulo Run, but retains New Amsterdam.

AUG The Lord Chancellor, Clarendon, falls from power, a scapegoat for the Cavalier Parliament's many unpopular measures. Parliament begins the process of impeachment, so Clarendon leaves for France. Parliament sentences him to perpetual banishment. The Cabal Ministry, a kind of Cabinet, is formed (Clifford, Arlington, Buckingham, Ashley and Lauderdale).

NOV [30] The satirist Jonathan Swift is born in Dublin.

John Milton: *Paradise Lost.*
Bishop Sprat: *History of the Royal Society.*

1668 Isaac Newton builds the first reflecting telescope. The East India Company takes control of Bombay.

JAN [13] A Triple Alliance (Britain, Holland and Sweden) is formed to check the power of Louis XIV.

APR [7] Sir William Davenant, writer, dies. [13] John Dryden is appointed first Poet Laureate.

Christopher Wren: Emmanuel College, Cambridge.

Thomas Shadwell: *The Sullen Lovers.*
John Dryden: *Essay of Dramatic Poesy.*

Sir George Etherege: *She Would if She Could.*
Henry Neville: *The Isle of Pines.*

 Sir Charles Sedley: *The Mulberry-Garden.*

1669 The Yeomen Warders of the Tower of London are nicknamed
'Beefeaters' because of their reputation for eating large daily rations
of beef.

MAY [**31**] Samuel Pepys' diary comes to an end.

 John Worlidge: *Systema Agriculturae.*
William Penn: *No Cross, No Crown.*
John Dryden: *Conquest of Granada.*

1670 The colonies of North and South Carolina are founded in America.
The rebuilding of London's churches begins, under Christopher
Wren's direction; 87 destroyed churches are to be replaced, in due
course, with 51. James Fitzjames, natural son of James Duke of York,
is born.

FEB [**10**] The dramatist William Congreve is born.
JUN [**1**] The two Treaties of Dover (one secret, one public)
between Charles II and Louis XIV. Charles II secretly agrees to
declare his conversion to Catholicism and subsequently to
restore it to Britain, in return for two ports on the mouth of
the River Scheldt. Charles II does not announce his
conversion, to Louis' annoyance, although the Duke of York
does.

1671 John Evelyn discovers the woodcarver Grinling Gibbons and
introduces him to Charles II and Christopher Wren. Sir Henry
Morgan, sometime buccaneer, is appointed Deputy Governor of
Jamaica by Charles II.

MAR [**31**] Anne Hyde, Duchess of York, dies.
MAY [**9**] Captain Thomas Blood, disguised as a clergyman, attempts
to steal the Crown Jewels from the Tower of London.
NOV [**12**] Thomas Fairfax, general and leader of the Parliamentary
army in the Civil War, dies.

 Lady Wilbraham: Weston Park, Staffordshire (begun).
Sir William Bruce (architect) and Robert Mylne (builder):
Palace of Holyroodhouse, Edinburgh.

 John Bushnell: *Charles I.*

Thomas Shadwell: *The Humourists.*
Aphra Behn: *The Forc'd Marriage.*
John Milton: *Paradise Regained; Samson Agonistes.*
William Wycherley: *Love in a Wood.*

1672 Newton reads his new theory about light and colours to the Royal Society. The composer William Young dies.

MAR Charles II issues his Declaration of Indulgence, permitting freedom of worship and assuming the right to cancel all penal legislation against both Protestants and Catholics. [17] The Third Anglo-Dutch War begins, because Charles II is bound under the secret provisions of the Treaty of Dover to support Louis XIV.

MAY [28] A naval battle between English and Dutch fleets in Southwold Bay is indecisive.

 Christopher Wren: St Stephen, Walbrook (begun).

 Thomas Shadwell: *The Miser.*
William Wycherley: *The Gentleman Dancing Master.*
George Villiers: *The Rehearsal.*

1673 The Dutch successfully fend off an Anglo-French attempt to invade Holland. Christopher Wren is knighted. Dentists fit the first metal dental fillings. The Earl of Clarendon dies in exile, lonely and ill-rewarded.

FEB The Test Act deprives Catholics and nonformists of public office; two members of the Cabal are forced to resign as a result.

MAR [23] Henry Cromwell, fourth son of Oliver Cromwell, dies aged 45.

NOV [21] James Duke of York marries Maria d'Este of Modena.

DEC The Cabal ministry disintegrates under Parliamentary opposition. Louis XIV send Charles £500,000 to stop him making a separate peace with the Dutch, to no avail.

 Edward Pierce: Bust of Sir Christopher Wren.

 Elkanah Settle: *The Empress of Morocco.*
John Dryden: *Amboyna; Marriage à la Mode.*

1674 The composer Pelham Humfrey dies. The painter Godfrey Kneller settles in Britain. There is agitation throughout Britain to exclude the Duke of York from the succession because of his known Catholic leanings and his new Catholic wife.

FEB   [**19**] The Treaty of Westminster ends the Third Dutch War; the Dutch agree to pay an indemnity of £180,000 and to salute British ships from Cape Finisterre to Norway. New Amsterdam becomes British by formal treaty and is renamed New York.

NOV   [**8**] The poet John Milton dies at Chalfont St Giles, Buckinghamshire.

 William Wycherley: *The Country Wife.*

1675 John Ogilby's *Britannia* is published: this is the first road book based on an actual survey of the British road system. Charles II receives a bribe of 500,000 crowns from Louis XIV, enabling him to prorogue Parliament for 15 months. Corpuscular theory of light (Isaac Newton).

JUN   [**21**] Work on Sir Christopher Wren's new St Paul's Cathedral begins. [Foundation stone laid.]

AUG   [**10**] The Royal Observatory at Greenwich is founded.

Sir Christopher Wren: Royal Observatory, Greenwich.
Sir Christopher Wren: St Peter's, Cornhill, London (begun).

Sir Peter Lely: *Nell Gwyn.*
Caius Cibber: *Raving Madness* and *Melancholy Madness.*

Thomas Otway: *Alcibiades.*
John Bunyan: *Instruction for the Ignorant.*
Andrew Marvell: *Dialogue between Two Horses.*
John Dryden: *Aurengzebe.*
Thomas Shadwell: *The Libertine.*
Nathaniel Lee: *Nero.*

Mathew Locke: *Psyche* (earliest surviving British opera).

1676 Robert Hooke devises the universal joint to help manoeuvre astronomical instruments. William Sherwin develops a fast-dyeing process for calico. Observance of the Sabbath Day gains legal protection. Thomas Tompion is appointed clockmaker for the new Royal Observatory. An influenza epidemic sweeps across Britain.

AUG   [**26**] Sir Robert Walpole, the first British Prime Minister, is born at Houghton Hall in Norfolk.

The Monument, London (completed).
Sir Christopher Wren: Trinity College Library, Cambridge (begun).

William Wycherley: *The Plain Dealer.*
Thomas Mace: *Musical Grammarian.*
Thomas Otway: *Don Carlos.*
Sir George Etherege: *The Man of Mode.*
Thomas Durfey: *Madam Fickle; Siege of Memphis.*

1677 Edmund Halley observes the transit of Venus.

Nov [4] In London, William III marries his 15-year-old cousin Princess Mary, eldest daughter of James Duke of York and Anne Hyde.

 Sir Christopher Wren: St Martin, Ludgate, London (begun).

 Thomas Durfey: *A Fond Husband.*
Aphra Behn: *The Debauchee.*
Nathaniel Lee: *The Rival Queens.*
Thomas Otway: *The Cheats of Scapin.*
Samuel Pepys: *The Portugal History.*
Andrew Marvell: *Account of the Growth of Popery.*

1678 The poet Andrew Marvell and the composer John Jenkins die. The composer William Croft is born. Charles II bows to pressure of public opinion, by concluding an alliance with the Dutch against the French. There are eclipses of the sun and moon, and the Devil is reputedly sighted in Scotland; a credulous and hysterical mood grips the country.

Jan [27] William Sancroft becomes Archbishop of Canterbury.
Aug The 'Popish Plot' concocted by Israel Tonge and Titus Oates is whipped up by Danby, the Lord High Treasurer. Tonge reveals that in April Catholic conspirators plotted to kill the King. Some 35 Catholics are executed as a result of this fraud.
Nov A Disabling Act disqualifies Catholics from sitting in Parliament, the Duke of York excepted: this act is not to be repealed until 1829. [21] Lord Chief Justice Scroggs brutally condemns a Catholic banker, William Staley, to death for 'speaking treason'.
Dec Danby is impeached on a charge of criminal correspondence with France and dismissed from office.

 Sir Godfrey Kneller: *James, Duke of Monmouth.*

 Thomas Durfey: *The Fool Turn'd Critic; Trick for Trick.*
Aphra Behn: *Sir Patient Fancy.*
Edward Cocker: *Cocker's Arithmetick.*

John Bunyan: *The Pilgrim's Progress*, Part 1.
John Dryden: *All for Love.*
Nathaniel Wanley: *The Wonders of the Little World.*

1679 Robert Hooke's law of elasticity.

JAN [24] The Cavalier Parliament is dissolved.

MAR [6] The Third Parliament of Charles II begins. Danby's impeachment peters out, but he remains in the Tower. The Scottish Convenanters rebel against the repressive measures of Lauderdale.

MAY [3] Archbishop Sharpe is pulled from his coach near St Andrews and murdered. [22] Samuel Pepys is committed to the Tower on a charge of treason. [27] The Habeas Corpus Act defines the procedure for ensuring speedy trials: when asked, judges must issue a writ ordering a gaoler to bring a prisoner before a court and show why he or she has been imprisoned.

JUN [1] Battle of Drumclog: Claverhouse is defeated by Covenanters led by Balfour. [22] Battle of Bothwell Bridge; the Scottish Covenanters are suppressed by the Duke of Monmouth's troops. The Bill of Exclusion, designed to exclude James Duke of York from the line of succession, is drafted.

 Gilbert Burnet: *History of the English Reformation.*
Lee and Dryden: *Oedipus King of Thebes.*
Edmund Halley: *Catalogue of the Southern Stars.*
Aphra Behn: *The Feign'd Curtizans.*
Thomas Durfey: *Squire Oldsapp.*

1680 Lord Shaftesbury organizes nationwide petitions to exclude the Duke of York from the succession; the petitioners become known as Whigs and their opponents, the Abhorrers, become the Tories. The Penny Post is instituted in London. The colony of New Hampshire is founded in America. The writer the Earl of Rochester dies. Henry Purcell is appointed organist at Westminster Abbey. The Cameronians, a group of Scottish field-preachers, renounce their allegiance to Charles II, for which their leaders, Cameron and Cargill, are killed.

MAR Pepys is released from the Tower.
MAY [27] The Third Parliament of Charles II is dissolved.
AUG [24] Captain Blood, the Irish adventurer, dies.
SEP [25] Samuel Butler dies.
OCT [21] The Fourth Parliament of Charles II begins.

Nov [**30**] The painter Sir Peter Lely dies.

Sir Christopher Wren: St Mary-le-Bow, London.
Sir Christopher Wren: St Clement Danes, London.

Sir William Temple: *Miscellanea*.
John Bunyan: *The Life and Death of Mr Badman*.
Thomas Otway: *The Orphan of China*.
Sir Robert Filmer: *Patriarcha*.

Henry Purcell: *Dido and Aeneas*.

1681 The colony of Pennsylvania is founded. The Test Act, designed to repress Presbyterians, causes 80 bishops to resign. Oliver Plunket, Archbishop of Armagh, is put to death at Tyburn (Plunket is canonized in 1975). Lord Shaftesbury is prosecuted for treason, but a grand jury rejects the charge; Shaftesbury nevertheless leaves for Holland.

Mar [**21**] Charles II's Fifth or Oxford Parliament. Charles II rejects the Exclusion Bill when it is introduced and dissolves Parliament; he offers to install William III of Orange as a regent for James as a compromise and begins to rule without Parliament.

Dec The trial and condemnation of Argyle, who leaves the country.

Sir Christopher Wren: Tom Tower, Christ Church, Oxford.

Thomas Durfey: *Sir Barnaby Whig*.
Aphra Behn: *The Rover*.
Andrew Marvell: *Miscellaneous Poems* (posthumous).
John Dryden: *Absalom and Achitophel*.
Thomas Otway: *The Soldier's Fortune*.

1682 Edmund Halley, the Astronomer Royal, observes a bright comet, checks his records and realizes that it has returned every 76 years — and that it was this same comet that was seen shortly before the Battle of Hastings; it has become known as Halley's Comet. Elias Ashmole founds a museum in Oxford. French Protestants are excluded from employment in the Civil Service and the King's Household.

Nov [**21**] George (later George I) marries Sophia Dorothea, the daughter of George Duke of Luneburg-Celle.

Sir Christopher Wren: Royal Hospital, Chelsea (begun).

 Thomas Shadwell: *The Medal of John Bayes.*
John Ray: *Historia generalis plantarum.*
John Dryden: *MacFlecknoe.*
Thomas Durfey: *The Royalist.*
John Bunyan: *The Holy War.*
Thomas Otway: *Venice Preserved.*

1683 Newton explains the connection between tides and gravitation. The last wild boar in Britain is killed. The Rye House Plot, a Whig plot to assassinate Charles II, is discovered. Two of the leaders of the conspiracy, Lord William Russell and Algernon Sydney, are executed: another, Essex, commits suicide; Monmouth, the King's natural son, is pardoned.

JUN   [**6**] The first museum in Britain, the Ashmolean Museum in Oxford, is opened to the public by its owner, Elias Ashmole.
JUL   [**28**] Anne, daughter of James Duke of York, marries Prince George of Denmark.
OCT   There is a rain of small toads on the village of Acle in Norfolk.
[**30**] George II, the only son of George I, is born at Hanover.
DEC   [**15**] Izaak Walton, author of *The Compleat Angler*, dies at Winchester aged 90.

 Alexander Oldys: *The London Jilt.*
Benjamin Keach: *The Travels of True Godliness.*
William Penn: *General Description of Pennsylvania.*
John Bunyan: *Greatness of the Soul.*

1684 Robert Hooke invents the heliograph. The first attempt is made to light the streets of London. The Duke of Monmouth, who, as well as being the illegitimate son of Charles II, is the exclusionist candidate for the throne, is banished to Holland in the aftermath of the Rye House Plot. The Duke of York is restored to his former offices.

 Sir Christopher Wren: Trinity College Library, Cambridge (completed).

 Thomas Durfey: *The Malcontent.*
Aphra Behn: *Adventures of the Black Lady.*
John Bunyan: *The Pilgrim's Progress*, Part 2.
Thomas Burnet: *Theory of Earth.*
Thomas Otway: *The Atheist.*

1685 Titus Oates is found guilty of perjury and sentenced to life imprisonment. Dangerfield, another of the informers in the Popish Plot, is flogged to death; it is the last time this cruel and unusual type of punishment is given in Britain.

FEB [2] Charles II has an apoplectic fit. [6] Charles II dies, succeeded by his brother as James II of England and VII of Scotland. [23] George Frederick Handel is born at Halle.

MAY [19] The Parliament of James II opens. Danby is released from the Tower.

JUN Argyle lands in Scotland, but cannot raise the support of the Covenanters. [30] Argyle is captured and executed. Monmouth lands at Lyme Regis and is proclaimed King at Taunton.

JUL [6] Battle of Sedgemoor, the last formal battle to be fought on English soil; Monmouth's Protestant rebellion is crushed. [15] The Duke of Monmouth is beheaded with five axe-strokes on Tower Hill: Jack Ketch bungles another execution. Judge Jeffreys conducts the 'Bloody Assizes', sentencing 320 of Monmouth's supporters to death and 840 to be sold into slavery. Jeffreys is later appointed Lord Chancellor.

 William Talman and Thomas Archer: Chatsworth House, Derbyshire (begun about this time).
Honington Hall, Warwickshire.
William Stanton: Belton House, Lincolnshire (begun).

John Dryden: *Albion and Albinus.*
Aphra Behn: *The Unfortunate Lady.*
Thomas Durfey: *Advice to the Ladies of London.*

1686 Edmund Halley draws the first meteorological map, using it to explain monsoon and trade winds. The writer Allan Ramsay is born. James II challenges the validity of the Test Act; the test case of Sir Edward Hales results in the readmission of Catholics into the army. James II visits St Winifrid's Well at Shrewsbury, a holy well which his wife has had restored.

Grinling Gibbons: Statue of James II.
John Riley: *Bridget Holmes.*

Richard Blome: *Gentleman's Recreation.*
Thomas Durfey: *A Commonwealth of Women.*

1687 James II expels the Fellows of Magdalen College, Oxford, because they will not appoint a Catholic, Dr Parker, as their President. James II creates his natural son, James Fitzjames, Duke of Berwick. Admiral Herbert is dismissed and a Catholic, Admiral Strickland, is given command of the fleet. Laws of gravitation and motion – Isaac Newton.

APR [1] James II's Declaration of Liberty of Conscience; although professing toleration for all religions, this measure favours Catholics.

NOV [13] Nell Gwyn, who had two sons by Charles II, dies in London at the age of 37.

William Stanton: Belton House, Lincolnshire (completed).
Sir Christopher Wren: Kensington Palace, London (begun).

John Dryden: *The Hind and the Panther.*
Isaac Newton: *Philosophia Naturalis Principia Mathematica.*
Aphra Behn: *The Emperor of the Moon.*

1688 APR James II's Second Declaration of Liberty of Conscience, which is to be read out in churches. Seven bishops including Archbishop Sancroft petition the King to be excused from reading the Declaration.

MAY [21] The poet Alexander Pope is born.

JUN [10] The 'Glorious Revolution' begins when a son, James Stuart (the Old Pretender), is born to James II, opening up the prospect of a succession of Catholic Kings. [29-30] The Seven Bishops are tried and acquitted.

JUL [7] Whig and Tory leaders invite the King's son-in-law, William III of Orange, to save Britain from Catholicism. In alarm, James reinstates the Fellows of Magdalen College.

SEP [30] William of Orange accepts the invitation.

NOV [5] William of Orange lands at Torbay.

DEC [10] The Queen and the baby Prince James are sent to France. [11] James II drops the Great Seal into the Thames and attempts to escape. He is stopped at Sheerness and brought back to London, but his reign is legally over and an interregnum begins. [19] William enters London. [22] James finally succeeds in escaping to France. [24] The Lords in London assume executive functions for the duration of the interregnum.

Thomas Shadwell: *The Squire of Alsatia.*
Aphra Behn: *Oroonoko.*
Lord Halifax: *The Lady's New Year's Gift.*

1689	JAN	[**22-27**] The Convention Parliament is summoned on the advice of the House of Lords. [**28**] The Commons declare that James II has tried to subvert the constitution and can be considered to have abdicated. Although the Lords disagree on the use of the word 'abdicate', there is agreement between the two Houses that the Crown should be offered to Mary and the regency to William. William rejects this offer.

FEB [**13**] Parliament offers the Crown to William and Mary jointly. A Declaration accompanies Parliament's new offer; making or suspending laws without Parliament's consent is illegal; it is lawful to petition the sovereign; maintaining an army without Parliament's consent is illegal; election of MPs must be free; Parliament should meet frequently. [**22**] The Convention Parliament is transformed into a regular Parliament.

MAR A Scottish Convention Parliament orders the proclamation of William and Mary as sovereigns. [**14**] James lands in Ireland with a few followers. [**24**] James enters Dublin. Tyrconnel raises a rebellion in James's favour. The Protestants in the north of Ireland declare for William, taking refuge in Derry.

APR [**11**] William III and Mary II become joint sovereigns of Great Britain, Mary exercising the royal power during William's absences abroad. They are crowned by the Bishop of London, because the Archbishop of Canterbury refuses to do it. [**16**] Mrs Aphra Behn, the writer, dies. [**18**] Judge Jeffreys dies in the Tower. [**20**] Derry is besieged by a Catholic army led by James. [**24**] Toleration Act, establishing permanent freedom of worship.

MAY [**7**] War breaks out with France. In Scotland, Claverhouse (Viscount Dundee) raises his standard in support of James among the Highlanders.

JUL [**24**] Anne (later Queen Anne) gives birth to a son, William. [**27**] Battle of Killicrankie; Dundee defeats the Whig General Mackay but is himself killed in the battle. The Highland revolt peters out.

DEC [**16**] Bill of Rights, a Parliamentary enactment of the earlier Declaration of Rights, summarizing the liberties established by the 'Glorious Revolution', and asserting that no Catholic may become sovereign.

Aphra Behn: *The Lucky Mistake.*
John Selden: *Table Talk.*
William Sherlock: *A Practical Discourse Concerning Death.*
John Locke: *On Civil Government.*

1690 There are fears of a French invasion.

FEB [**1**] Archbishop Sancroft is deprived of his office.

JUN [**30**] Battle of Beachy Head; the French are victorious over Anglo-Dutch forces under Herbert. The English Admiral Lord Torrington is court-martialled and acquitted, but dismissed the service. William goes to Ireland.

JUL [**1**] Battle of the Boyne; at Oldbridge near Drogheda William's army defeats James II's army. James flees to Waterford and then to France.

AUG James's supporters, led by Sarsfield, still resist in Limerick.

William Talman: Uppark House, Sussex.

John Locke: *Two Treatises of Government; Human Understanding.*
Thomas Shadwell: *The Amorous Bigot.*

Henry Purcell and Thomas Durfey: *The Yorkshire Feast Song.*

1691 A new East India Company is established. William III subdues the south of Ireland and the Irish rebels retreat west of the Shannon.

JAN [**13**] George Fox, founder of the Society of Friends, the 'Quakers', dies in London.

MAY [**31**] John Tillotson becomes Archbishop of Canterbury.

JUL [**12**] Battle of Aughrim: Sarsfield and the French St Ruth are defeated by William's forces under Ginkel.

OCT [**3**] Limerick is besieged and taken by William; James II's Irish and French supporters surrender on conditions (the Treaty of Limerick) which are later not fulfilled by the Irish Parliament, which is predominantly Protestant. William nevertheless makes the agreement in good faith and returns to England. William calls on all the Scottish Highland chiefs to take the oath of allegiance before the end of the year; Ian MacDonald of Glencoe fails to do so. Lloyd's Coffee House becomes an office for maritime insurance.

DEC [**30**] Robert Boyle, scientist, dies.

Drumlanrig Castle, Dumfries and Galloway.
Sir Christopher Wren: Royal Hospital, Chelsea (completed: the first Chelsea Pensioners arrive in 1692).

Thomas Durfey: *Wit for Money.*
Thomas Southerne: *Sir Anthony Love.*

Henry Purcell and John Dryden: *King Arthur.*

1692   The writer Thomas Shadwell dies.

JAN   [6] Ian MacDonald takes the oath of allegiance, but knowledge of this is suppressed by William's agent, the Master of Stair.

FEB   [13] Massacre of Glencoe. The MacDonalds are treacherously massacred by the Campbells, their traditional enemies. Sir John Dalrymple wishes to make an example of the MacDonalds and orders the Campbells to kill every member of the MacDonald clan under the age of 70. Dalrymple is later forced to resign. Louis XIV and James II contemplate an invasion of England, amassing a fleet at Brest and an army of 30,000 in Normandy.

MAY   [19] Battle of the Cap de la Hogue; a large French fleet is destroyed by a British fleet under Russell.

JUN   [28] Louisa Maria Theresa, daughter of James II, is born.

Thomas Durfey: *The Marriage Hater Matched.*
William Congreve: *Incognita.*
Nehemiah Grew: *Anatomy of Plants.*
Thomas Southerne: *The Wives' Excuse.*

Henry Purcell: *Hail, Bright Celia; The Fairy Queen.*

1693   JAN   Britain's National Debt begins when William III borrows £1 million at 10% to pay for the war with France. William's forces are defeated at Landen.

Thomas Southerne: *The Maid's Last Prayer.*
Thomas Durfey: *The Richmond Heiress.*
William Congreve: *The Old Bachelor; The Double Dealer.*
John Locke: *Ideas on Education.*
William Penn: *Essay on the Present and Future Peace of Europe* (proposing federation).

1694   The composers Henry Carey and Joseph Gibbs are born. The tax on salt is doubled. The Royal Navy bombards Le Havre, Dieppe and Dunkirk, but is repulsed at Brest. This last failure is blamed on John Churchill, who supports James II and who may have betrayed military secrets to France. Greenwich Hospital is founded by Queen Mary. The Licensing Act runs out, which frees the press from censorship.

JUL   [27] The Bank of England is founded by Montagu, the Chancellor of the Exchequer, to carry out all the monetary business of the Government and to obtain interest on the Government's money.

DEC   [**22**] Triennial Act, requiring a new Parliament to be elected every third year. [**28**] Mary II dies of smallpox; after this William III reigns alone.

Thomas Sydenham: *Whole Works.*

Henry Purcell: *Jubilate; Come, ye sons of art, away.*

1695 British troops recapture Namur. The composer Maurice Greene is born. The poet Henry Vaughan dies. Isaac Newton becomes master of the Mint. The first public drinking fountain in Britain is built in Hammersmith by Sir Samuel Morland.

JAN   [**16**] Thomas Tenison becomes Archbishop of Canterbury.
NOV   [**1**] The Bank of Scotland is founded. [**21**] The composer Henry Purcell dies of tuberculosis in London at the age of 36. [**22**] William III's Third Parliament begins.

William Congreve: *Love for Love.*

Henry Purcell: *Indian Queen.*

1696 Henry Winstanley begins work on the first Eddystone Lighthouse. The Assassination Plot to murder the King near Turnham Green is discovered; Sir George Barclay and Sir John Fenwick are among the conspirators. The Second Treason Act; this entitles the accused to have a copy of the indictment and a list of the jurors a few days before the trial; it also entitles the accused to have the aid of counsel. The Habeas Corpus Act is suspended in the aftermath of the Assassination Plot. The Board of Trade is founded. The Window Tax is introduced; this influences domestic architecture for at least 50 years.

John Aubrey: *Miscellanies.*
Thomas Southerne: *Oroonoko, a tragedy.*

1697 Whitehall Palace is burnt down. The Royal African Company has its trading monopoly withdrawn by Parliament. Sir John Fenwick is tried for high treason. One of the two witnesses required by the Second Treason Act absconds, so the trial ends. Nevertheless, a Bill of Attainder is passed against Fenwick enabling his execution.

JUN   John Aubrey, antiquary, dies.
SEP   [**20**] Treaty of Ryswyck between William III and Louis XIV; William is internationally acknowledged as the King of England and Anne as his successor.

Nov　[**10**] The painter William Hogarth is born at Smithfield, London.

Dec　[**2**] The consecration and formal reopening of the rebuilt St Paul's Cathedral.

William Congreve: *The Mourning Bride.*
John Vanbrugh: *The Provok'd Wife; The Relapse.*

John Blow: *I was glad* (anthem for consecration of St Paul's).
Jeremiah Clarke: *Alexander's Feast; The World in the Moon.*

1698 Newton calculates the speed of sound. Thomas Savery patents his heat-operated vacuum pump for emptying tin and coal mines of water, but it is not strong enough to cope. The slave trade across the Atlantic from Africa is officially sanctioned for British merchants by Parliament. The London Stock Exchange is founded. White's Club opens in London, with the opening of Mrs White's chocolate house: it soon becomes the headquarters of the Tory Party.

Dec　[**6**] The Fourth Parliament of William III opens.

Edward Ward: *The London Spy.*
Revd Jeremy Collier: *A short view of the Immorality and Profaneness of the English Stage.*

1699 With Admiralty backing, William Dampier explores the west coast of Australia in the *Roebuck*. The Darien scheme; some Scots colonists attempt to found a settlement on the Isthmus of Darien with the idea of trading with both East and West Indies. The scheme fails for lack of support and opposition from the East India Company. Billingsgate Market opens in London. William III becomes increasingly unpopular because of his grants of English land to his Dutch favourites and several blatantly anti-Catholic measures.

Feb　Disbanding Act; this reduces the army to 7000 men.
May　Shrewsbury, Montagu and Russell resign their offices.

Richard Bentley: *Phalaria.*
John Toland: *Amyntor, or a defence of Milton's life.*
George Farquhar: *Love and a Bottle.*

1700

1700 William Dampier explores New Guinea.

MAY [**1**] John Dryden, Poet Laureate for over 20 years, dies in London.

JUL [**30**] William Duke of Gloucester dies aged 11. He is the only surviving child of (Queen) Anne; as a result the succession to the throne passes to the Electress Sophia of Hanover.

Sir John Vanbrugh: Castle Howard, North Yorkshire (begun). Gunby Hall, Lincolnshire.

Sir Godfrey Kneller: *Matthew Prior.*

William Congreve: *The Way of the World.*
Nicholas Rowe: *The Ambitious Stepmother.*
Thomas Southerne: *The Fate of Capua.*

1701 Britain, Holland, Savoy and the Emperor Leopold form a Grand Alliance. Jethro Tull invents the first practical seed drill at about this time. Henry Playford, the music publisher, opens a series of weekly concerts in Oxford.

FEB [**6**] William III's Fifth Parliament begins.

MAY [**8**] 'Captain' William Kidd, the pirate, is tried at the Old Bailey. [**23**] Kidd is hanged at Execution Dock; he is hanged three times, because the rope breaks twice.

JUN [**12**] The Act of Settlement settles the royal succession on the Protestant descendants of Sophia of Hanover.

SEP [**17**] Ex-King James II dies after a stroke at St Germain in France; his son James Edward (the Old Pretender) is proclaimed King of Great Britain and Ireland by Louis XIV.

DEC [**30**] William III's Sixth Parliament begins. Attainder of James Edward, the 'pretender' Prince of Wales.

Hanbury Hall, Hereford and Worcester.

George Farquhar: *Sir Harry Wildair.*
Thomas Durfey: *The Bath.*

1702 The colony of Delaware is founded in America.

MAR [**8**] William III dies after falling from his horse at Hampton Court. Anne, his sister-in-law, succeeds. A combined Whig-Tory Ministry takes the Government, under Churchill and Godolphin. [**11**] The first English daily newspaper, the *Daily Courant*, is published by E. Mallet. [**23**] Coronation of Queen Anne. Lord Cornbury, governor-general of America, opens the New York Assembly on the Queen's behalf — dressed as the Queen, which causes great consternation. The

Queen is under the influence of her favourite, Sarah Churchill. Her husband, John Churchill, becomes captain-general of England's land forces. In a successful campaign, he captures Kaiserworth, Venloo and Liege; as a reward he is created Duke of Marlborough.

Oct Sir George Rooke, commanding an English fleet, is repulsed at Cadiz but captures a Spanish treasure fleet in Vigo Bay. The Queen gives her approval to horse-racing and sweepstakes. [**20**] First Parliament of Queen Anne begins.

 Dewlish House, Dorset.
William Talman: Drayton House, Leicestershire.

 Sir Godfrey Kneller: *Portrait of Newton.*

 Congreve and Weldon: *The Judgement of Paris* (masque).
George Farquhar: *The Inconstant.*
Nicholas Rowe: *Tamerlane.*
Sir John Vanbrugh: *The False Friend.*
John Weaver: *The Tavern Bilkers* (first British pantomime ballet).

1703 Marlborough's troops capture Bonn, Huy, Limoges and Guelders. England is devastated by a hurricane-force storm; the Eddystone lighthouse is completely destroyed.

Mar [**3**] The scientist Robert Hooke dies.
May [**26**] Samuel Pepys dies at Clapham.
Jun [**17**] The evangelist John Wesley is born at Epworth.
Jul Daniel Defoe is sentenced to a fine, the pillory and imprisonment for libelling the Church; he is wreathed with flowers in the pillory, but then sent to Newgate prison.
Dec [**27**] The Methuen or Port Wine Treaty is signed by England and Portugal; this gives preference to the import of Portuguese wines into England: in return, English woollen goods are admitted into Portugal.

 Sir Christopher Wren: St Bride's, Fleet Street, London (steeple erected).

 Nicholas Rowe: *The Fair Penitent.*
Colley Cibber: *She Would and She Would Not.*

1704 After a quarrel, Alexander Selkirk, first mate on a ship in the Pacific, is put ashore on the uninhabited island of Juan Fernandez, at his own request. Selkirk is to be marooned for four years before being rescued. Jeremiah Clarke becomes the Chapel Royal organist. Beau Nash becomes master of ceremonies at Bath.

JUL   [**24**] Capture of Gibraltar from the Spanish by Admiral Sir George Rooke and Sir Cloudesley Shovel.

AUG   Defoe is released from prison. [**13**] Battle of Blenheim; a major Anglo-Austrian victory under Marlborough and Prince Eugene against French and Bavarian armies.

William Talman: Dyrham Park, Avon.
Orangery, Kensington Palace.

Thomas Durfey: *Tales Tragical and Comical.*
Daniel Defoe: *Review* (first issue of periodical).
Jonathan Swift: *A Tale of a Tub.*
Joseph Trapp: *Abra-Mule, or Love and Empire.*
Nicholas Rowe: *The Biter.*
Isaac Newton: *Opticks.*

Handel: *St John Passion.*

1705 Edmund Halley correctly predicts the return of the comet that now bears his name. Isaac Newton is knighted.

JUL   [**13**] Titus Oates, the conspirator who fabricated a Catholic plot to assassinate Charles II, dies.

AUG   [**22**] George (later George II) marries Caroline, daughter of John Margrave of Brandenburg-Anspach.

OCT   [**4**] Lord Peterborough captures Barcelona.

Sir John Vanbrugh and Nicholas Hawksmoor: Blenheim Palace (begun).

Sir John Vanbrugh: *The Confederacy.*

Handel: *Almira.*

1706 The merchant Thomas Twining opens Tom's Coffee House in London and starts a major tea importing business. Work begins on the second Eddystone Lighthouse. Parliament creates the first Turnpike Trust, empowering local gentry to take over a certain length of road from the parish, and to improve and maintain it by charging tolls. The Earl of Galway and the Allies enter Madrid.

FEB   [**27**] John Evelyn, diarist for the last 65 years of his life, dies at Wotton near Dorking.

MAY   [**23**] Battle of Ramillies, near Louvain in Belgium; the Spanish and French are defeated by allied British, Dutch and Danish armies under Marlborough. The Spanish Empire in Europe is dismantled.

Nov [**17**] Sophia Dorothea, daughter of George I, marries Prince Frederick William of Prussia.

Thomas Durfey: *Wonders in the Sun.*
George Farquhar: *The Recruiting Officer.*
Nicholas Rowe: *Ulysses.*
Sir John Vanbrugh: *The Mistake.*

1707 Jan [**20**] Frederick, eldest son of George II, is born.

Apr George Farquhar, dramatist, dies. [**22**] The novelist Henry Fielding is born at Sharpham Park, Glastonbury.

May [**1**] Act for the Union of England and Scotland. The English and Scottish Parliaments are united at Westminster; Scotland is to send 16 elective peers to the House of Lords and 45 members to the Commons. The Union Jack (Crosses of St George and St Andrew) is adopted as the national flag. The two countries are nevertheless to retain their own independent legal systems and Churches.

Oct [**23**] The First Parliament of Great Britain begins; in reality, it is the Second Parliament of Queen Anne revived by proclamation. From this time on, parliaments cease to be numbered officially by reigns.

Dec [**1**] The composer Jeremiah Clarke commits suicide. [**18**] The evangelist and hymn writer Charles Wesley is born at Epworth in Lincolnshire.

George Farquhar: *The Beaux' Strategem.*
Isaac Watts: *Hymns and Spiritual Songs.*
Colley Cibber: *The Double Gallant.*

Handel: *Rodrigo; Nero.*

1708 Lord Cornbury, the transvestite governor-general of America, is finally recalled to England in debt. Thomas Newcomen patents his steam engine for pumping water out of mines; although this is effective, it is expensive to run because it uses a lot of fuel. New figures of Gog and Magog at the London Guildhall replace those destroyed in the Great Fire. New and old East India Companies are amalgamated as the United East India Company, becoming the most influential power on the coasts of India.

Mar The Old Pretender, James Edward, lands in Scotland from France in a short and unsuccessful attempt to regain the British throne for the Stuarts. The French fleet sent to assist him is beaten by Admiral Byng. Robert Walpole is appointed Secretary of War.

JUL   [**11**] Battle of Oudenarde in west Belgium; the Duke of
       Marlborough's troops are victorious over the French led by
       Vendome. Marlborough also captures Lille after a four-month
       siege.
NOV   [**15**] William Pitt the Elder is born at Westminster.

    Thomas Durfey: *The French Pride Abated.*
    Joseph Addison: *The Present State of the War.*

1709 Alexander Selkirk is rescued from his desert island; his story forms the
          basis of Defoe's *Robinson Crusoe.* High-quality and low-cost iron is
          produced by Abraham Darby, an iron worker at Coalbrookdale in
          Shropshire; the iron ore is smelted with coke and moulded in sand.
          The new process leads to the mass production of iron. Francis
          Hawksbee makes the first accurate observation of capillary action in
          glass tubes. Postage rates are regulated by mileage.

    Thomas Durfey: *The Old Mode and the New.*
    Richard Steele: *The Tatler* (periodical first published).
    Mrs Manley: *The New Atlantis.*
    William Dampier: *A New Voyage Round the World.*

    Handel: *Agrippina.*

1710 The composer William Boyce is born. Handel comes to Britain; in
          London he writes *Rinaldo* in 14 days. A Tory government under
          Harley and St John replaces the Whig-Tory government, reducing
          British involvement in the European war.

FEB-   Impeachment of Dr Henry Sacheverell, a hot-headed political
MAR   preacher who attacked the Whigs. Sacheverell is found guilty,
       sentenced to abstain from preaching for three years and his
       sermon to be burnt by the public hangman; there is great
       public support for Sacheverell and a strong Tory reaction
       generally to the impeachment.
MAR   [**12**] Thomas Arne, composer of 'Rule Britannia', is born in
       London.

    Thomas Archer: Birmingham Cathedral (begun).
    Sir Christopher Wren: St Paul's Cathedral (exterior
    completed). [Reopened 1697.]

    Bishop Berkeley: *A Treatise concerning the Principles of Human
    Knowledge.*

    Handel: *Rinaldo.*

1711 The tuning fork is invented by John Shore, trumpeter at the Chapel Royal. Sir Godfrey Kneller founds the Academy of Painting in St Martins Lane, London. Lord Cornbury is made a Privy Councillor. The South Sea Company is incorporated by Parliament. Occasional Conformity Act; this stops the practice by which dissenters qualify for state office by taking the Anglican Communion on rare occasions. Landed Property Qualifications Act; this measure is an attempt by landowners to exclude merchants, financiers and industrialists from Parliament. It is not successfully enforced but not repealed until 1866.

MAR   [1] *The Spectator* is first published, succeeding *The Tatler* as the great British review.

AUG   [7] The first Royal Ascot horse-race meeting takes place, attended by Queen Anne.

Thomas Archer: St John, Smith Square, London.

Alexander Pope: *Essay on Criticism.*
John Gay: *The Present State of Wit.*
Steele and Addison: *The Spectator* (first issue).
James Puckle: *The Club.*
Lord Shaftesbury: *Characteristics of Men, Manners, Opinions, Times.*

1712 Thomas Newcomen develops the first piston-operated steam-engine at Tipton. The last witch trial and execution for witchcraft take place in England. Rob Roy becomes an outlaw after the chief of the Macgregor clan evicts him from his lands for debt. Robert Walpole is expelled from the Commons and sent to the Tower on charges of corruption and bribery while in the Navy Office.

JUL   [12] Richard Cromwell, sometime Lord Protector, dies at the age of 86.

Sir John Vanbrugh: Castle Howard (exterior completed: interiors completed by 1759).

Ambrose Philips: *The Distrest Mother.*
John Arbuthnot: *The History of John Bull.*

1713 The tall north-west flanking stone of the Cove at Avebury is taken down and destroyed. Robert Brydges, friend of Charles II, drowns in a lake while trying to save his dog. Roger Cotes produces a revised edition of Newton's *Principia*. The South Sea Company takes over the whole of the National Debt at 8% interest. Lord Bolingbroke plots for the accession of the Old Pretender. Spain gives Britain the exclusive right to supply the Spanish colonies with slaves for the next 30 years.

APR   [**11**] Treaty of Utrecht; this establishes the terms of peace with Louis XIV's France: Gibraltar and Minorca are formally ceded to Britain. [**22**] Daniel Defoe is prosecuted for libel, imprisoned and immediately pardoned.

NOV   [**24**] The writer and cleric Laurence Sterne is born at Clonmel in Tipperary. The painter Allan Ramsay is born.

    Joseph Addison: *Cato.*
    John Gay: *Rural Sports; The Wife of Bath.*
    Alexander Pope: *Windsor Forest.*

1714 The Board of Longitude offers a prize of £20,000 for the discovery of a North-West Passage to the Far East. The Schism Act aims at restoring the Church's educational monopoly and destroying nonconformist schools.

FEB   [**16**] The Fifth Parliament of Queen Anne, the Fourth of Great Britain, opens.

AUG   [**1**] Queen Anne dies; the German Prince George Louis of Hanover succeeds as George I under the 1701 Act of Settlement: he speaks no English. A Whig Ministry is formed under Townsend, Stanhope and Walpole.

SEP   [**18**] George I lands in England. [**27**] George I's son (later George II) is created Prince of Wales.

DEC   William Congreve is appointed Secretary for Jamaica.

    Colen Campbell: Wanstead House, near London.
    James Gibbs: St Mary-le-Strand, London.

    Alexander Pope: *The Rape of the Lock.*
    Nicholas Rowe: *The Tragedy of Jane Shore.*
    Thomas Durfey: *Court Gallantry.*

1715 Robert Walpole becomes Chancellor of the Exchequer. Nicholas Rowe is appointed Poet Laureate. Andrew Becker invents the first practical diving suit and demonstrates it in the Thames. The Riot Act is passed.

MAR   [**17**] A new Parliament meets, with a large Whig majority. It impeaches Oxford (Harley), Bolingbroke (St John) and Ormond for surrendering British honour and interests under the terms of the Treaty of Utrecht. Ormond and Bolingbroke manage to escape to France, but Oxford is caught and sent to the Tower.

NOV   A Jacobite Rising (the '15') is suppressed at Preston and Sheriffmuir. Some Jacobite supporters are able to escape to

France, others are captured and executed, Derwentwater and Kenmure among them. The Rebellion, organized by the Earl of Mar, aims at overthrowing the Hanoverian succession and installing the 'Old Pretender'.

DEC [**14**] Archbishop Tenison dies. [**22**] James Stuart, the 'Old Pretender', lands at Peterhead but is forced to return to France straight away with the Earl of Mar.

Thomas Archer: Birmingham Cathedral (completed).

Alexander Pope: *The Temple of Fame.*
Colen Campbell: *Vitruvius Britannicus.*
Colley Cibber: *Hob, or the Country Wake.*
John Gay: *What-d'ye-Call-it.*
Nicholas Rowe: *Lady Jane Grey.*

Handel: *Water Music.*

1716 The first central-heating system in Britain, a hot water system in a greenhouse, is installed by Swedish engineer Martin Triewald. Mineral waters are discovered at Cheltenham, and the town is soon transformed into a popular spa. Nicholas Hawksmoor, one of the two architects to the Commission for Fifty New Churches, begins work on St Mary Woolnoth, considered by some to be his finest church. The Royal Regiment of Artillery is founded. The Septennial Act prolongs the life of a Parliament from three to seven years: this is a response to the unsettled political situation. Treaty of Westminster; Britain and Austria become allies in a mutual defence pact. Britain signs a similar treaty with France.

JAN [**16**] William Wake becomes Archbishop of Canterbury. The Jacobite troops are dispersed.
FEB [**24**] The leaders of the Jacobite rising captured at Preston are executed. The Pretender himself escapes.
DEC [**26**] Thomas Gray, poet, is born in London.

Nicholas Hawksmoor: St Mary Woolnoth, London (begun).

John Gay: *Court Poems.*
Colley Cibber: *Venus and Adonis.*
Alexander Pope: *The Worms.*

Handel: *Brockes Passion.*

1717 The Strand maypole is taken down to be used by Sir Isaac Newton as a support for his new telescope. The composer Handel stays at Canons in Edgware, the seat of the Duke of Chandos. The value of the golden guinea is fixed at 21 shillings.

JAN   [4] A Triple Alliance is concluded between Britain, France and
        Holland to uphold the Treaty of Utrecht; the Old Pretender
        has to leave France. Robert Walpole resigns and Lord
        Stanhope becomes First Lord of the Treasury.
FEB   [19] The actor David Garrick is born at Hereford.
MAR   [8] Abraham Darby, the first ironmaster to use coke to smelt
        iron, dies at Worcester.
JUN   [24] The first Freemasons' Lodge is inaugurated, in London.

Sir James Thornhill: *Scenes from the Life of St Paul*, Dome of St
Paul's Cathedral.

1718 Thomas Lombe patents a machine to make thrown silk. A
        machine-gun is patented by lawyer James Puckle. The Society of
        Antiquaries is founded. Lord Stanhope becomes Secretary of State.
        Lady Mary Wortley Montagu introduces inoculation against
        smallpox.

JAN   The Occasional Conformity and Schism Acts are repealed.
JUL   [30] William Penn, the English Quaker leader and founder of
        the American state of Pennsylvania, dies.
AUG   [2] A Quadruple Alliance is formed by England, France,
        Holland and Austria against Spain, after Spain seizes Sicily and
        raises the spectre of another European war. Admiral Byng is
        sent with a fleet to defend Sicily. In a sea battle off Cape
        Passaro, he completely destroys the Spanish fleet.
NOV   [22] Edward Teach, the English pirate known as 'Blackbeard',
        is killed off the coast of North Carolina.

1719 Spanish troops invading Scotland in support of the Jacobites are
        defeated at Glenshiel. The Peerage Bill, aimed at restricting the House
        of Lords, is rejected by the Commons.

JUN   [17] Joseph Addison, the writer, dies at Holland House,
        London.
DEC   [31] John Flamsteed, the first Astronomer Royal, for whom
        Charles II built the Greenwich Royal Observatory, dies, his
        catalogue of stars for ships' navigators still incomplete after 40
        years of work.

Thomas Southerne: *The Spartan Dame*.
Thomas Durfey: *Wit and Mirth*.
Daniel Defoe: *Robinson Crusoe*.
Colley Cibber: *Love in a Riddle*.

Handel: *Acis and Galatea*.

1720 Handel becomes director of the Royal Academy of Music in London. Ralph Allen of Bath is granted a monopoly of the country (non-London) posts; he establishes a postal system using post-boys on horseback. Walpole and Townsend are recalled to office, Townsend as President of the Privy Council.

JAN   The 'South Sea Bubble' bursts; many investors are ruined after speculating in the stock of the South Sea Company. The Quadruple Alliance makes peace with Spain.

Colen Campbell: Stourhead, Wiltshire (begun about this time)
Sir John Vanbrugh: Blenheim Palace, Oxfordshire (completed).
Sir John Vanbrugh: Seaton Delaval, Northumberland (begun).

Giles Jacob: *The Poetical Register.*
Mrs Manley: *The Power of Love in Seven Novels.*
Mrs Haywood: *Love in Excess.*
Alexander Pope: *Iliad* (verse translation).
Daniel Defoe: *Captain Singleton.*

Handel: *Chandos Anthems* (at about this time).
Handel and Pope: *Haman and Mordecai* (masque).

1721 The compensator pendulum for clocks is invented by George Graham. The directors of the collapsed South Sea Company are prosecuted. The writer Tobias Smollett is born.

APR   [3] Sir Robert Walpole becomes the first British Prime Minister; he is also First Lord of the Treasury and Chancellor of the Exchequer. Walpole's policy of maintaining a permanent National Debt brings prosperity. [15] William Augustus, son of George II, is born.
AUG   [3] The woodcarver Grinling Gibbons dies.

Daniel Defoe: *Moll Flanders.*

1722 The Atterbury Plot: Francis Atterbury, Bishop of Rochester and a leading Jacobite, is arrested for alleged conspiracy in a plot to seize the King, the Tower and the Bank of England in order to restore the Old Pretender. The Habeas Corpus Act is suspended. Workhouse Test Act, for the care and housing of the needy.

JUN   [16] The Duke of Marlborough, Britain's most successful military commander, dies at Windsor.

Sir John Vanbrugh: Grimsthorpe, Lincolnshire.
James Gibbs: St Martin-in-the-Fields, London (begun).

Mrs Haywood: *Secret History of Cleonia.*
Samuel Richardson: *Guide Book* (for the Grand Tour).
Daniel Defoe: *Colonel Jack; Journal of the Plague Year.*

1723 The young William Stukeley and his patron Lord Winchelsea dance a minuet on top of one of the Stonehenge trilithons. Wood's Halfpence; Wood, an English ironmaster, is given a patent by Walpole to issue copper coinage in Ireland. Dean Swift of Dublin writes against the coinage, stirring up popular feeling in Ireland to the extent that Walpole has to withdraw it. Francis Atterbury is sentenced to banishment for life for his part in the plot to overthrow the King. Treaty of Charlotteburg between Britain and Prussia; George I's grandson will eventually marry a Prussian princess and Prince Frederick of Prussia will marry the Prince of Wales' daughter. Walpole reduces the duty on tea.

FEB [**22**] Mary, daughter of George II, is born. [**25**] Sir Christopher Wren dies in London at the age of 91. [**26**] The prolific playwright Thomas Durfey dies.
JUN [**5**] Adam Smith, economist and philosopher, is born at Kirkcaldy.
JUL [**16**] The painter Sir Joshua Reynolds is born near Plymouth, Devon.

Colen Campbell: Mereworth, Kent.
Nicholas Hawksmoor: Christ Church, Spitalfields, London.
James Lamb: Lamb House, Rye, Kent.
Francis Smith: Chicheley, Buckinghamshire.

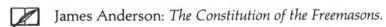 James Anderson: *The Constitution of the Freemasons.*

Handel: *Ottone.*

1724 The Three Choirs Festival is founded. Longman's, one of the oldest surviving publishing house in Britain, is founded. The Sanctuary, a megalithic monument near Avebury, is destroyed by farmers. John Carteret, the King's favourite, is sent to Ireland as Lord Lieutenant, clearing the way for his cabinet rivals, Walpole and Townsend.

JUN [**8**] The civil engineer John Smeaton is born.
AUG [**24**] The painter George Stubbs is born at Liverpool.
NOV [**16**] Jack Sheppard, the notorious highwayman, is hanged at Tyburn.
DEC [**12**] Admiral Samuel Hood is born at Thorncombe in Devon.

John Gay: *The Captives.*
George Cheyne: *An Essay on Health and Long Life.*
Daniel Defoe: *Roxana.*

Handel: *Flavio; Giulio Cesare.*

1725 Guy's hospital is founded. Lord Bolingbroke is given permission to return to England and take possession of his estates. George I revives the Military Order of the Bath. Stereotyping invented by William Ged.

SEP [3] Treaty of Hanover between Britain, France and Prussia.
[29] Robert Clive, soldier and administrator, is born.

Richard Boyle (Lord Burlington) and William Kent: Chiswick House, London.
Finchcocks, Kent.

Allan Ramsay: *The Gentle Shepherd.*

1726 Stephen Hales, a clergyman and physicist, measures blood-pressure for the first time. John Harrison, a clockmaker, invents the gridiron pendulum. Handel becomes a British citizen. Lloyd's List, a record of shipping data and news, is published for the first time in London. General George Wade builds 250 miles of military road in Scotland. The first circulating library in Britain is established in Edinburgh by Allan Ramsay. War breaks out between Britain and Spain. The writer Charles Burney is born. William Augustus, George II's son, is created Duke of Cumberland.

MAR [7] The writer and musician Charles Burney is born. [8] Admiral Richard Howe is born. [26] Sir John Vanbrugh, dramatist and architect of Blenheim Palace, dies of a quinsy in London.

James Gibbs: St Martin-in-the-Fields, London (completed).

Jonathan Swift: *Gulliver's Travels.*
Alexander Pope: *Odyssey* (verse translation).
Eliza Haywood: *Memoirs of a Certain Island adjacent to the Kingdom of Utopia.*
Thomas Southerne: *Money the Mistress.*

Handel: *Alessandro.*

1727 The first railway bridge, the Tanfield Arch, is built by Ralph Wood over a colliery railway at Cawsey Dell. William Kent publishes Inigo

Jones' architectural designs. War between Britain and Spain over Gibraltar begins. Britain for the first time employs mercenaries from Hesse to fight in battle. The composer William Croft dies. First Indemnity Act for Nonconformists.

JAN [2] General James Wolfe is born at Westerham.
MAR [20] Sir Isaac Newton dies in London.
MAY [14] Thomas Gainsborough, painter, is baptized at Sudbury, Suffolk.
JUN [11] George I dies of apoplexy on his way to Hanover, in the room where he was born at the castle at Osnabruck. He is succeeded by his 44-year-old son, George II.
OCT [11] Coronation of George II. [17] John Wilkes, the political agitator, is born at Clerkenwell. Sir Spencer Compton is briefly appointed Prime Minister by George II, but he is so incompetent that Walpole is quickly recalled.

William Adam: Hopetoun House, near Edinburgh – façade.

John Dyer: *Grongar Hill.*

Handel: *Scipione; Zadok the Priest.*

1728 The architect and designer Robert Adam is born. Colley Cibber becomes manager of Drury Lane Theatre. The Siege of Gibraltar is lifted by Spain after 14 months. The Anglo-Spanish War ends with the Convention of Prado. Publication of Parliamentary debates is declared to be a breach of privilege. The governor of the Fleet Prison, Thomas Bainbridge, is accused of brutality to the inmates and a Parliamentary inquiry into his conduct is opened.

JAN [29] The first performance of *The Beggar's Opera.*
OCT [28] The explorer Captain James Cook is born at Marton, Yorkshire.
NOV [10] The poet, novelist and dramatist Oliver Goldsmith is born.

Roger Morris: Clearwell Castle, Gloucestershire.

Henry Fielding: *Love in Several Masques.*
Ephraim Chambers: *Cyclopaedia.*

Handel: *Riccardo Primo.*
John Pepusch and John Gay: *The Beggar's Opera.*

1729 James Bradley, the astronomer, detects stellar aberrations, the apparent shift in position of stars caused by the Earth's movement;

this is the first definitive confirmation of Copernicus' theory that the Earth revolves around the sun. The Methodist movement begins in Oxford. The dramatist William Congreve dies.

JAN [**12**] The statesman Edmund Burke is born in Dublin.

AUG [**5**] Thomas Newcomen, who invented the first steam-engine in 1705, dies.

NOV [**9**] Treaty of Seville between Britain and Spain; by this treaty, Britain retains Gibraltar.

DEC Samuel Johnson leaves Pembroke College, Oxford after only one year.

Sir John Vanbrugh: Seaton Delaval, Northumberland (completed).

Alexander Pope: *Dunciad*.
Jonathan Swift: *A Modest Proposal*.

Henry Carey: *The Contrivances* (ballad opera).

1730 The mathematician John Hadley invents the reflecting quadrant. The Serpentine is created in Hyde Park.

MAY [**15**] Townsend resigns from the Government after a quarrel with Walpole, and becomes an agricultural pioneer, devising a four-crop rotation system.

JUL [**12**] Josiah Wedgwood is born at Burslem, Staffordshire.

Henry Fielding: *Rape upon Rape; Tom Thumb*.

1731 The first lightship, *The Nore*, is anchored in the Thames estuary. George Lillo writes the first serious play in which the leading characters are not all from the upper classes. 10 Downing Street becomes the Prime Minister's official residence. Captain Jenkins of the English ship *Rebecca* loses an ear in a skirmish with Spanish coastguards; this incident is to be used in eight years' time as a pretext for war with Spain.

MAR [**16**] Treaty of Vienna, between Britain, Spain, Austria and Holland; the Ostend East India Company, Britain's main colonial trading rival in cotton and spices, is dissolved.

APR [**26**] The novelist and author of *Robinson Crusoe*, Daniel Defoe, dies.

OCT [**10**] Henry Cavendish, the discoverer of hydrogen, is born at Nice.

NOV [**15**] The poet William Cowper is born at Berkhamsted.

George Lillo: *The London Merchant*.

1732 The Academy of Ancient Music is founded in London. A threshing machine is invented by Michael Menzies. The first sedative, the 'Dover sedative powder', is invented by Captain Thomas Dover. The colony of Georgia is founded: the last of the 'Thirteen Colonies' which make up English East Coast America.

APR [**13**] The Tory Prime Minister Lord North is born.

JUN [**10**] Handel's masque *Acis and Galatea* is performed in public for the first time at the King's Theatre, London.

DEC [**4**] The poet and playwright John Gay dies. [**6**] Warren Hastings, the first Governor-General of India, is born. [**7**] Covent Garden Opera House is opened. [**23**] Sir Richard Arkwright, inventor of mechanical spinning processes in the cotton industry, is born at Preston, the last of 13 children.

Edward Shepherd: First Covent Garden Theatre, London (completed).

Henry Fielding: *The Lottery; The Modern Husband; The Debauchees.*

Handel and Gay: *Acis and Galatea.*
Handel: *Esther* (first English oratorio).

1733 John Kay invents the flying shuttle, the first of the great textile inventions. Britain prohibits trade between her American and West Indian colonies by the Molasses Act; this measure leads to widespread smuggling. Walpole's attempt to introduce excise duty instead of 'customs' levied at ports only (on wine and tobacco) brings great unrest. The Tories are too weak to overthrow Walpole, but the Excise Bill is withdrawn.

MAR [**13**] Joseph Priestley, the scientist who later discovers oxygen, is born at Leeds.

George Lambert: *Extensive landscape with four gentlemen on a hillside.*

Henry Fielding: *The Miser.*
Stephen Hales: *Haemostaticks.*
Jethro Tull: *The New Horse-Hoeing Husbandry.*

Handel: *Deborah.*
Thomas Arne: *Rosamund.*

1734 A Trade Treaty between Britain and Russia is signed. The Dilettanti Society is founded in London, to encourage travel for the collection of classical antiquities. George II's daughter Marie Anne marries the Prince of Orange-Nassau. James Fitzjames, the Duke of Berwick, dies; he was the illegitimate son of James II.

 Nicholas Hawksmoor: All Souls College, Oxford (completed).

 Charles Johnson: *A General History of the Lives and Adventures of the Most Famous Highwaymen, Murderers, etc.*
Henry Fielding: *Don Quixote in England.*

1735 William Pitt becomes MP for Old Sarum, a 'rotten borough' with so few constituents that election is in the gift of the landowner. John Harrison invents the ship's chronometer.

JUL [9] Samuel Johnson marries Mrs Porter.
SEP [14] Robert Haikes, founder of the Sunday School system, is born.

 William Kent, Lord Burlington and Thomas Coke (Lord Leicester): Holkham Hall, Norfolk (begun).
James Paine: Nostrell Priory, Yorks (begun). (Interiors by Robert Adam.)
John Wood the Elder: Prior Park, Bath (begun).

 William Hogarth: *The Rake's Progress* (engravings published).

Handel: *Ariodante; Serse.*

1736 The tenor voice first displaces the castrato in a leading operatic role when John Beard sings at Covent Garden. The witchcraft statutes are repealed in England. John and Charles Wesley return from Georgia and begin their evangelical mission in England. George Whitefield, their collaborator, is ordained. The architect Nicholas Hawksmoor dies. The Porteous Riots take place in Edinburgh when a smuggler is hanged for theft. Captain Porteous orders his Town Guard to fire on the rioting mob. He is found guilty of murder, reprieved and finally lynched on a barber's pole in Grassmarket.

JAN [19] The engineer and inventor James Watt is born at Greenock.
FEB [19] The first performance, at Covent Garden, of *Alexander's Feast*, with words by Dryden and music by Handel.

Handel and Dryden: *Alexander's Feast.*
Thomas Arne: *Tom Thumb the Great; Love and Glory.*

1737 The portrait painter Joseph Nolleken is born in Soho. Queen Caroline dies, weakening Walpole's authority, which relied partly on favour at Court. Frederick Prince of Wales quarrels with his father, siding with the anti-Walpole faction. The opposition party supported by the Prince of Wales calls itself 'The Patriots'. The Licensing Act subjects all plays to censorship by the Lord Chamberlain.

JAN [24] Archbishop Wake dies. [29] The political thinker Thomas Paine is born at Thetford.

FEB [28] John Potter, Bishop of Oxford, becomes Archbishop of Canterbury.

MAR Samuel Johnson goes to London, taking one of his pupils, David Garrick, with him.

APR [27] Edward Gibbon, historian, is born at Putney.

James Gibbs: Radcliffe Camera, Oxford (begun).

Henry Fielding: *Eurydice; Tumbledown Dick.*

1738 The first spinning-machines are patented in England, although invented by a Swiss physicist, Lewis Paul. The House of Lords is invaded by a bevy of peeresses, led by the Duchess of Queensberry, in the middle of a debate.

MAY [24] George III is born in lodgings at St James's Square in London.

NOV [15] Sir William Herschel, astronomer and discoverer of the planet Uranus in 1781, is born at Hanover.

The Octagon, Studley Royal, Yorkshire.

1739 John Wesley begins his life-long crusade as an open-air preacher. Walpole gives in to the demand for war with Spain, although he personally opposes it; the War of Jenkins' Ear begins, partly because of the right claimed and exercised by the Spanish of searching all British vessels while at sea, and partly also because of the resulting acts of violence done to British sailors by the Spanish.

APR [7] Dick Turpin, the notorious highwayman, is hanged at York for murder, cattle-stealing, smuggling and holding up stage-coaches.

NOV [22] Admiral Vernon captures the Spanish base of Porto Bello.

George Dance the Elder: Mansion House, London.

John Mottley: *Joe Miller's Jests.*

Handel: *Saul; Ode for St Cecilia's Day; Israel in Egypt.*
Henry Carey: *Nancy, or the Parting Lovers.*

1740 Benjamin Huntsman invents the crucible method of making steel from scrap iron. Admiral Edward Vernon issues the naval rum ration diluted with water; he is known as 'Old Grog' because of his grogram coat, and the weakened tot also becomes known as 'grog'. Vernon and Wentworth make an unsuccessful attack on Cartagena. David Garrick becomes manager of Drury Lane Theatre.

MAY [8] George II's daughter Mary marries Frederick, who later is to become Landgrave of Hesse-Cassel.

OCT [29] James Boswell, diarist and biographer, is born at Edinburgh.

NOV [4] The hymn writer Augustus Toplady is born at Farnham.

 William Hogarth: *Captain Coram*.

 William Stukeley: *Stonehenge, A Temple Restor'd to the British Druids*.
David Hume: *A Treatise of Human Nature*.
Samuel Richardson: *Pamela*.
Colley Cibber: *An Apology for the Life of Mr Colley Cibber*.

 Thomas Arne: 'Rule Britannia'.

1741 David Garrick makes his first appearance on the London stage, in *Richard III*. The Royal Military Academy at Woolwich is founded. Walpole is attacked by his critics, but an attempt to have him dismissed fails. Highways Act, to improve the roads.

FEB [21] The agricultural pioneer Jethro Tull dies near Hungerford.

 Henry Fielding: *Shamela*.
David Garrick: *The Lying Varlet*.
Batty Langley: *Gothic Architecture Restored and Improved*.

 Handel: *Deidamia*.
Thomas Arne: *An Hospital for Fools; The Blind Beggar of Bethnal Green*.

1742 Cotton factories are set up in Birmingham and Northampton. Britain forms an alliance with Prussia. Support for Austria in the War of Austrian Succession and opposition to the war with Spain lead to the fall of Walpole.

FEB [26] Walpole is succeeded by John Lord Carteret as Prime Minister.

APR [13] The first performance of Handel's *Messiah* in Dublin: the climax of Handel's popularity.

Henry Fielding: *Joseph Andrews.*
William Shenstone: *The School-Mistress.*
Edward Young: *The Complaint.*

 Handel: *Messiah.*

1743 The composer Henry Carey dies.

APR [**24**] Edmund Cartwright, inventor of the power loom, is born at Marnham.
JUN [**16**] Battle of Dettingen, the last battle in which a British monarch commands an army on the field of battle; George III defeats the French.
AUG [**16**] Jack Broughton, the champion pugilist, assembles the earliest code of boxing rules for the prize-ring. [**27**] The Whig Henry Pelham becomes Prime Minister.
OCT [**27**] George II's daughter Louisa marries Prince Frederick, later King of Denmark.

 Colley Cibber: *The Egotist.*
Henry Fielding: *Jonathan Wild.*
William Stukeley: *Avebury, a Temple of the British Druids.*

1744 George Anson arrives back in Britain after a successful four-year circumnavigation of the world. In retaliation for Dettingen, the French send a fleet led by Charles Edward, the Old Pretender's son, to invade Britain; a storm scatters the fleet. The words and music of the first stanza and the original second stanza of the National Anthem first appear in print. Robert Clive arrives in Madras as an employee of the East India Company. War between Britain and France continues intermittently in Europe, India, North America and the West Indies from now until 1815. In a Cabinet reshuffle, John Carteret, who is accused of favouring Hanoverian against British interests, loses his position as Secretary of State; he is replaced by Henry Pelham.

MAY [**30**] The poet Alexander Pope dies at Twickenham.

 Roger Morris: Inverary Castle, Scotland (begun).

 Joseph Highmore: Illustrations to Richardson's *Pamela.*
William Hogarth: *Marriage à la Mode.*
John Wootton: *The Beaufort Hunt.*

 Mark Akenside: *The Pleasures of Imagination.*
Sarah Fielding: *The Adventures of David Simple.*

A Little Pretty Pocket-Book published by John Newbery (possibly the author). [One of the first English children's books intended for amusement as well as instruction.]

Handel: *Joseph and His Brethren: Hercules.*

1745 The agriculturalist Robert Bakewell produces the Leicester breed of sheep, with twice the amount of meat compared with earlier breeds. The composer Charles Dibden is born.

MAR [**18**] Sir Robert Walpole, Prime Minister from 1721 to 1742, dies in London.

MAY [**11**] Battle of Fontenoy; the British army under the Duke of Cumberland is defeated by the French under Marshal Saxe.

JUL [**25**] The Young Pretender, Charles Edward, lands in Scotland.

AUG [**19**] Intent on claiming the throne, Prince Charles Edward raises his father's standard at Glenfinnan.

SEP [**11**] 2000 Jacobites enter Edinburgh. [**21**] Battle of Prestonpans; Bonnie Prince Charlie's Jacobite army gains a victory over English forces led by Sir John Cope. Charles leads his army into England, vainly hoping for popular English support and decides to return to Scotland. [**28**] The first known performance of the National Anthem, 'God Save the King', at Drury Lane Theatre.

OCT [**19**] The satirist Jonathan Swift dies aged 77.

DEC [**18**] Jacobite victory at Penrith.

Allan Ramsay: *The Painter's Wife.*
William Hogarth: *Self-Portrait; Shortly After the Marriage* (*Marriage à la Mode* series).

Colley Cibber: *Papal Tyranny in the Reign of King John.*

Handel: *Belshazzar.*
Thomas Arne: 'The National Anthem'.

1746 John Roebuck invents a process for manufacturing sulphuric acid, used to bleach textiles, on an industrial scale. Canaletto arrives in London. Pelham resigns his ministry when George II refuses to accept William Pitt; he eventually forces the King's hand, returning to office with Pitt as Paymaster of the Forces.

JAN [**17**] Battle of Falkirk; Charles defeats General Hawley's troops.

APR [**16**] Battle of Culloden; the Jacobites are finally annihilated by a Hanoverian force under the Duke of Cumberland, and attempts by the Stuarts to regain the British throne are ended. Culloden is the last battle fought on Scottish soil. Now a fugitive, Charles roams the Scottish Highlands during the summer. The Highlanders are disarmed and forbidden to wear their tartans; the hereditary jurisdiction of the Highland chiefs over their clans is abolished.

SEP   [**20**] Prince Charles Edward escapes capture by dressing as a girl and sailing to France on the French ship *L'Heureux*.

 Handel: *Judas Maccabeus* (tribute to Cumberland's Culloden victory).

1747 Under David Garrick's management, audiences are removed from the stage of the Drury Lane Theatre and the orchestra is brought down from the gallery. James Bradley discovers that the Earth's axis is variable. Simon Fraser, Lord Lovat, is beheaded for supporting the Jacobite rising. A Carriage Tax is imposed by Parliament. Horace Walpole acquires a villa (Strawberry Hill) at Twickenham; with his striking alterations, it is to become the stimulus for the Gothic revival in domestic architecture. The Duke of Cumberland's forces are defeated by a French army at Lauffeld. Britain, Holland and Russia sign the Convention of St Petersburg.

OCT   [**10**] John Potter, Archbishop of Canterbury, dies.
NOV   [**10**] The Fourth Parliament of George II opens. [**24**] Thomas Herring, Archbishop of York, becomes Archbishop of Canterbury.

 Hugh Walpole: Strawberry Hill, Twickenham.

 Hannah Glasse: *The Art of Cookery*.
David Garrick: *Miss in her Teens*.

1748 John Palmer of Bath persuades the Government to accept the idea of a Mail-Coach service, protected against highwaymen by armed guards. Treaty of Aix-la-Chapelle.

FEB   [**15**] Jeremy Bentham is born.
NOV   [**25**] The hymn writer Isaac Watts dies.

 Allan Ramsay: *Norman MacLeod of MacLeod*.
Thomas Gainsborough: *Mr and Mrs Robert Andrews*.

 Lord Anson: *Voyage Round the World*.
Samuel Richardson: *Clarissa Harlowe*.
Tobias Smollett: *Roderick Random*.

Handel: *Joshua; Solomon.*

1749 There are serious riots at Bedminster, Bristol, against turnpike tolls. Consolidation Act, authorizing the reorganization of the Royal Navy.

JAN [**24**] The Whig statesman and orator Charles James Fox is born in London.

APR [**27**] Handel's *Music for the Royal Fireworks* is first performed in Green Park, London.

MAY [**17**] Edward Jenner, vaccination pioneer, is born at Berkeley vicarage.

Charles Wesley: *Hymns and Sacred Poems.*
John Cleland: *Fanny Hill.*
Henry Fielding: *Tom Jones.*

Handel: *Royal Fireworks Music; Susanna.*

1750 In India, Robert Clive captures and defends Arcot. Jonas Hanway is the first *man* to use an umbrella in public; he suffers jeers and catcalls in the streets of London. Britain surrenders the Asiento, a monopoly of selling black slaves to the Spanish colonies, for £100,000. The interest on the National Debt is reduced to 3%; from this time on, the Bank of England assumes responsibility for the debt. The bounty on whales is increased to £2 a ton to encourage greater participation in the whaling industry. Iron Act; this is designed to prevent American colonists from manufacturing their own iron products. One of the stones (Stone 14) at Stonehenge falls over.

MAR [**2**] Earth tremor in London.

APR [**2**] Earth tremor in Warrington.

AUG [**23**] Earth tremor at Spalding.

SEP [**26**] Lord Collingwood, Nelson's second-in-command at Trafalgar, is born at Newcastle. [**30**] Earth tremor at Northampton.

John Smart: *On the Eternity of the Supreme Being.*

Handel: *Theodora.*

1751 Clive holds Arcot against the French with a force of only 500; by doing so, he establishes British control over southern India.

MAR [**20**] The Prince of Wales, Frederick Lewis, dies after being hit by a cricket ball; he had lived in a state of perpetual enmity towards his parents after being dismissed from Court in 1737.

Oct [**30**] The dramatist Richard Brinsley Sheridan is born in Dublin.

Arthur Devis: *The James Family.*
William Hogarth: *Gin Lane.*

Eliza Haywood: *History of Miss Betty Thoughtless.*
Henry Fielding: *Amelia.*
Tobias Smollett: *Peregrine Pickle.*
Thomas Gray: *An Elegy Wrote in a Country Churchyard.*

Handel: *Jeptha.*

1752 Robert Clive relieves the siege of Trichinopoly. Government by a regular cabinet comprising the heads of the main administrative departments is adopted.

Jan [**1**] Officially 'New Year's Day' for the first time; until now the year officially began on March 25.
Jun [**13**] The novelist and diarist Frances (Fanny) Burney is born at King's Lynn.
Sep [**14**] Britain belatedly adopts the Gregorian calendar introduced by Pope Gregory XIII in 1582. The Gregorian calendar is adopted by the British Parliament at the instigation of Lord Chesterfield. The changeover results in a loss adjustment of 11 days, losing the 11 days September 3-13 inclusive. There is widespread protest from people who innocently believe that their lives have been shortened: 'Give us back our eleven days!'
Nov [**20**] The poet Thomas Chatterton is born.

Charlotte Lennox: *The Adventures of Arabella.*

John Stanley: *Jeptha.*

1753 James Lind, a Scottish doctor, advocates the use of citrus fruits as a cure for scurvy. The Jewish Naturalization Act faces so much opposition that it is repealed. A Land Tax of two shillings in the pound is imposed throughout England and Wales. The Marriage Act is introduced by the Earl of Hardwicke, with the intention of putting an end to clandestine marriages solemnized without a licence; it states that banns of marriage must be published in the parish church where the parties live for three successive Sundays, and that no licence should be granted to a minor. The Broad Wheels Act fixes nine inches as the minimum width for wheels except for those of light vehicles. The intention of this act is to reduce damage to road surfaces; in fact, instead of causing ruts, broad wheels grind the whole road surface to powder.

JAN   [**11**] Sir Hans Sloane dies. The British Museum is begun with the Government purchase of Sloane's collection of antiquities.

SEP   [**10**] John Soane, architect of the Bank of England, is born.

DEC   [**3**] Samuel Crompton, inventor of the spinning mule which substituted machinery for hand work in the cotton industry, is born at Firwood near Bolton.

Sir Joshua Reynolds: *Commodore Keppel.*
Richard Wilson: *Rome from the Villa Madonna.*

Tobias Smollett: *Ferdinand, Count Fathom.*
William Hogarth: *The Analysis of Beauty.*

1754   The first iron rolling-mill is established at Fareham. The Scottish chemist Joseph Black discovers carbonic gas. Henry Pelham dies and is succeeded by Thomas Pelham, Duke of Newcastle, as Prime Minister.

JAN   [**28**] In a letter to a friend written after reading a fairy-tale, Horace Walpole coins the word 'serendipity' to describe the Three Princes of Serendip's happy knack of making discoveries entirely by accident.

AUG   [**5**] James Gibbs, the architect who designed St Martin-in-the-Fields, dies. [**21**] William Murdock, who will invent coal-gas lighting in 1792, is born at Auchinleck.

SEP   [**9**] William Bligh, Captain of the *Bounty*, is born at Plymouth.

OCT   [**8**] The author Henry Fielding dies.

John Wood, father and son: The Circus, Bath.

Samuel Richardson: *Sir Charles Grandison.*
Thomas Chippendale: *Gentleman and Cabinet Maker's Director.*

1755   Joseph Black demonstrates the difference between lime and magnesium. Henry Fox, originally Pitt's ally but later his rival, is manoeuvred into the Cabinet by the Duke of Newcastle, becoming Secretary of State and leader of the House of Commons; he succeeds in having Pitt dismissed from the Pay Office. The composer Maurice Green dies. The artist John Flaxman is born.

Samuel Johnson: *A Dictionary of the English Language.*

Thomas Arne: *Eliza; Britannia.*
John Smith: *The Fairies.*

1756 Joseph Black discovers carbon dioxide. General Braddock is sent by the British Government to assist American colonists against the French; he is defeated and killed at Fort Duquesne. Britain and Prussia become allies; Britain declares war on France. The Seven Years War begins; Britain becomes involved because she is competing with France for colonies in India and America. Highland regiments serve for the first time in this war. Minorca is taken from the British by a large French fleet; Admiral John Byng is sent to the rescue, but he withdraws to Gibraltar. Outcry at the loss of Minorca and inept handling of the war leads to the fall of Newcastle's ministry.

JUN [**20**] The Black Hole of Calcutta; the suffocation of many British subjects imprisoned by Surarjak Dowlah, the Nawab of Bengal, in the tiny guardroom at Fort William: only 23 survive out of 146 people imprisoned overnight. Clive is sent from Madras to punish the Nawab; he retakes Calcutta and forces the Nawab to sign a peace treaty.

NOV [**16**] Newcastle is succeeded by William Cavendish, Duke of Devonshire, as First Lord of the Treasury. William Pitt is Secretary of State and quickly becomes the main influence in the British Government.

 Thomas Hudson: *George Frederick Handel.*
Sir Joshua Reynolds: *Mrs Francis Beckford.*

Edmund Burke: *A Vindication of Natural Society.*

 John Smith: *The Tempest.*

1757 The Duke of Cumberland's forces are defeated in two engagements at Hastenbeck and Klosterseven.

MAR [**13**] Archbishop Herring dies. [**14**] Admiral John Byng is shot by firing squad on the quarter deck of the *Monarque*, after being court-martialled for failing to relieve the island of Minorca.

APR [**29**] Matthew Hutton, Archbishop of York, becomes Archbishop of Canterbury.

JUN [**22**] Captain George Vancouver, explorer of the Pacific coast of North America, is born at King's Lynn. [**23**] Battle of Plassey in Bengal; Clive conquers the Indian forces, securing Bengal for Britain and laying the foundations of the British Empire in India.

JUL   [**2**] The Duke of Newcastle becomes First Lord of the Treasury and Prime Minister again; Pitt continues as Secretary of State.

AUG   [**9**] Thomas Telford, engineer of roads, canals and bridges, is born at Westerkirk.

NOV   [**28**] The poet, artist and visionary William Blake is born in London.

DEC   [**11**] The organist and composer Charles Wesley is born. [**12**] Colley Cibber dies.

Edmund Burke: *The Sublime and the Beautiful.*

1758 Jedediah Strutt invents a ribbing machine for manufacturing stockings. The first blast furnace is installed by John Wilkinson, an ironmaster at Bilston. John Bird invents the sextant. Fort Duquesne is taken from the French by a mixed force of Americans and Scots under Generals Washington and Forbes; they rename the captured town 'Pittsburgh'. The Duke of Cumberland is recalled after several defeats and replaced as commander of British-Hanoverian forces by Duke Ferdinand of Brunswick.

MAR   [**13**] The return of Halley's Comet, as predicted by Edmund Halley in 1682. [**19**] Archbishop Hutton dies.

APR   [**21**] Thomas Secker, Bishop of Oxford, becomes Archbishop of Canterbury.

SEP   [**29**] Horatio Nelson is born at Burnham Thorpe rectory, Norfolk.

David Hume: *An Enquiry Concerning Human Understanding.*

Thomas Arne: *The Temple of Dullness; King Pepin's Campaign.* John Smith: *Paradise Lost.*

1759 James Brindley designs the Worsley-Manchester Canal; this is the first true dead-water canal and marks the beginning of a new form of transport in Britain. General Wolfe is appointed by Pitt to take command of the British army in Canada and drive the French out. It is the 'Year of Victories' or Annus Mirabilis for Britain, with victories at Quebec, Minden, Lagos and Quiberon Bay. Horace Walpole says, 'one is forced to ask every morning what victory there is for fear of missing one'.

JAN   [**12**] Anne, daughter of George II and wife of Prince William IV of Orange, dies. [**15**] The British Museum at Montague House in Bloomsbury is opened to the public. [**25**] The poet Robert Burns is born at Alloway, Ayrshire.

APR [**14**] The death of Handel at the age of 74.

MAY [**28**] William Pitt the Younger is born at Hayes.

JUL [**23**] Work begins on the building of HMS *Victory* at Chatham.

AUG [**24**] William Wilberforce, campaigner against slavery, is born at Hull.

SEP [**13**] General Wolfe dies in battle on the Plains of Abraham near Quebec, defeating the French forces under Montcalm. [**14**] Montcalm dies from his wounds. [**18**] The British capture Quebec from the French, virtually ensuring British supremacy in Canada.

NOV [**20**] Naval Battle of Quiberon Bay; Admiral Hawke's first fleet destroys the French invasion fleet under Admiral Conflans.

John Carr: Harewood House, West Yorkshire.
Nicholas Hawksmoor: Queen's College, Oxford.
James Paine and Robert Adam: Kedleston Hall, Derbyshire (completed).
Sir John Vanbrugh: Castle Howard, Yorkshire (interiors completed).

Samuel Johnson: *Rasselas*.
Adam Smith: *The Theory of Moral Sentiments*.

1760 Josiah Wedgwood establishes his pottery works at Etruria in Staffordshire. Dr Johnson writes his final weekly piece for the Idler column of the *Universal Chronicle*. Thomas Braidwood of Edinburgh opens the first school specially for the deaf and dumb. The Botanical Gardens at Kew are opened. Portsmouth Dockyard is burnt out. In India, Colonel Eyre Coote's troops defeat the French at Wandewash and take Madras; this marks the end of French power in India.

MAY [**5**] The hangman's drop is used for the first time at Tyburn for the execution of Earl Ferrers.

OCT [**25**] George II dies suddenly, at 8 a.m., aged 76. He is succeeded by his grandson, George III.

John Stanley: *Zimri*.
Thomas Arne: *The Prophetess*.
John Smith: *The Enchanter*.

1761 The British capture Belle Isle and Dominica. In India, Pondicherry is captured from the French. The German painter Johann Zoffany settles in England.

JUN [**7**] John Rennie, civil engineer, is born.

JUL [4] Samuel Richardson, novelist, dies. [17] The Bridgewater Canal (Worsley-Manchester) is opened.

SEP [8] George III marries Charlotte, daughter of Charles Duke of Mecklenburg-Strelitz. [22] Coronation of George III.

OCT [5] Fall of William Pitt. Pitt fears the close alliance of France and Spain under the Family Compact and wants to declare war on Spain; he is not supported by his colleagues, and resigns. Newcastle is Prime Minister in the new Cabinet.

Robert Adam: Osterley Park House, Middlesex (changes to Jacobean house begun).

Roubiliac: The Nightingale Monument, Westminster Abbey.

Frances Sheridan: *Memoirs of Miss Sidney Biddulph.*
Tobias Smollett: *Sir Lancelot Greaves.*
Charles Churchill: *The Rosciad.*

Thomas Arne: *The Death of Abel; Judith.*
John Stanley: *The Shepherd's Wedding.*

1762 John Nash, architect, dandy and leader of fashion, is born. Cast iron is converted into malleable iron at the Carron Ironworks in Scotland.

JAN Britain declares war on Spain, capturing Havana, Manila, Martinique, St Lucia, St Vincent, Grenada. British forces under General Burgoyne drive the Spanish out of Portugal.

MAY [26] The Duke of Newcastle is succeeded as Prime Minister by the King's friend John Stewart, Earl of Bute.

AUG [12] King George IV is born at St James's Palace. [19] The new prince is created Prince of Wales.

Robert Adam: Syon House interior, Brentford, Middlesex (begun).

Sir Joshua Reynolds: *Garrick between Tragedy and Comedy.*
Allan Ramsay: *George III.*

John Hall-Stevenson: *Crazy Tales.*
William Falconer: *The Shipwreck.*
Stuart and Revett: *The Antiquities of Athens.*

Thomas Arne: *Artaxerxes.*

1763 The painter George Morland is born. The scientific instrument maker at Glasgow University, James Watt, is given a model of the Newcomen engine to repair ; it sets him thinking about ways of devising a more efficient steam-engine. Pontiac's conspiracy; the Red Indian attempt to destroy British power in America fails.

FEB   [**10**] Treaty of Paris, between Britain, France and Spain, by which Canada is ceded to Britain, along with Cape Breton, Nova Scotia, Minorca, Tobago, St Vincent, Grenada, Dominica, Senegal and Florida; the British make great colonial gains by this treaty.

MAR   [**9**] William Cobbett, political journalist, is born at Farnham.

APR   [**16**] The Earl of Bute is forced to resign; he is succeeded as Prime Minister by Charles Grenville. [**23**] John Wilkes, a radical MP, is expelled from the House of Commons and outlawed for writing scurrilous articles attacking both King and Government in his newspaper, the *North Briton*. He is later released on grounds of Parliamentary privilege.

AUG   [**16**] Frederick, the second son of George III, is born.

Sir Joshua Reynolds: *Portrait of Nelly O'Brien.*

Lady Wortley Montagu: *Letters.*
Frances Sheridan: *The Discovery.*
Christopher Smart: *Song to David.*

1764 Numbered houses appear for the first time in London. James Hargreaves invents the spinning-jenny. Sugar Act; Britain hopes to recover revenue from the American colonies, but this arouses much local opposition. Tension increases between the American colonists and the British Government, because of the British assumption that colonies exist for the benefit of the founding country. Mozart meets Carl Philipp Emanuel Bach in London.

JUL   [**9**] The authoress Ann Radcliffe is born.

OCT   [**26**] The painter William Hogarth dies in London.

James Ridley: *The Tales of the Genii.*
Thomas Reid: *An Inquiry into the Human Mind.*
Samuel Foote: *The Liar.*

John Smith: *Jehoshaphat.*

1765 The steam-engine with separate condenser is invented by James Watt. Nelson's flagship, HMS *Victory*, is launched at Chatham. Robert Clive reforms the Indian administration; the British rule Bengal and Bihar, maintaining a puppet Mogul emperor. Regency Bill; this is drawn up by Grenville's ministry as a result of the King's worsening mental condition. The Queen's name is deliberately omitted from the list of regents, and this so angers the King that Grenville is forced to resign.

JUL   [**13**] Grenville is succeeded as Prime Minister by the Marquis of Rockingham. The American Stamp Act, the taxation of legal documents as a way of getting the colonies to help pay for the troops maintained for their protection, angers the American colonists.

JUL   [**27**] William Augustus, Duke of Cumberland, son of George II, dies.

Johann Zoffany: *David Garrick in the 'Provok'd Wife'*.
Sir Joshua Reynolds: *Lady Sarah Bunbury*.
Thomas Gainsborough: *Mary, Countess of Howe*.

Horace Walpole: *The Castle of Otranto*.

Thomas Arne: *Love in a Village; The Birth of Hercules*.

1766 Henry Cavendish discovers hydrogen, making the development of the balloon possible. John Byron takes the Falklands for Britain, unaware that de Bougainville has already claimed the islands for France.

JAN   David Hume brings Rousseau to England. [**1**] James Stuart, son of James II, dies in Rome.

FEB   [**17**] The economist Thomas Malthus is born. [**24**] The composer Samuel Wesley is born. Rockingham repeals the Stamp Act, but the Declaratory Act reaffirms the right of the British Parliament to tax the colonies. George III dismisses Rockingham and Pitt is created Earl of Chatham.

JUL   [**30**] Pitt becomes Prime Minister, but illness prevents him from attending the House so the Government is controlled by the Duke of Grafton.

SEP   [**6**] John Dalton, chemist and physician, is born at Eaglesfield. [**29**] Charlotte, daughter of George III, is born.

DEC   [**5**] Christie's, the London auctioneers, hold their first sale. [**29**] Charles Macintosh, inventor of waterproof fabrics, is born in Glasgow.

Oliver Goldsmith: *The Vicar of Wakefield*.
Richard Cumberland: *The Fool of Quality*.
George Stubbs: *The Anatomy of the Horse*.
Thomas Amory: *The Life of John Buncle, Esquire*.
David Garrick and G. Colman: *The Clandestine Marriage*.

1767 Robert Clive leaves India for England for the last time, leaving disorder behind him. Revenue Act; the Chancellor of the Exchequer,

Charles Townshend, taxes American imports of tea, glass, paper and lead to help pay for the defence and government of the American colonies. Townshend dies and is succeeded by Lord North as Chancellor of the Exchequer.

Nov [2] George III's fourth son, Edward, is born.
Dec The Duke of Grafton becomes Prime Minister.

John Wood the Younger: Royal Crescent, Bath.
Robert Adam: Kenwood House, London.

Alexander Runciman; *King Lear in the Storm.*
Joseph Wright of Derby: *An Experiment on a Bird in an Air Pump* (painted at about this time).

Thomas Mawe: *Every Man his own Gardener.*
Laurence Sterne: *Tristram Shandy.*
Joseph Priestley: *The History and Present State of Electricity.*
Neville Maskelyne: *Nautical Almanac.*

1768 William Brodie of Edinburgh begins his long career in crime, copying some bank keys and stealing £800; he escapes suspicion by being a pillar of the establishment. Richard Arkwright invents the water frame, a water-powered machine for spinning cotton into strong thread. Lord Shelburne resigns from the Cabinet in protest against Townshend's taxes on American imports. John Wilkes is elected MP for Middlesex; he then waives his Parliamentary privilege and is sentenced to two years' imprisonment and fined £1000 for his offences of 1763. The St George's Fields Riots; a mob tries to rescue John Wilkes.

Mar [18] Laurence Sterne, writer and cleric, dies in poverty in London.
May [10] George III's Second Parliament opens. [25] Beginning of Captain Cook's first voyage of exploration.
Aug [3] Archbishop Secker dies.
Oct [14] The Duke of Grafton becomes Prime Minister.
Nov [8] George III's daughter Augusta is born.
Dec [10] The Royal Academy of Arts is founded, with Sir Joshua Reynolds as its first President. [22] The landscape painter John Crome is born at Norwich.

Adam brothers: The Adelphi, London (begun).
George Dance the Younger: Newgate Prison, London.

Laurence Sterne: *Sentimental Journey.*
Oliver Goldsmith: *The Good-Natured Man.*
Encyclopaedia Britannica (first edition)

1769 James Watt's steam-engine is patented. Watt forms a partnership with John Roebuck, founder of the Carron Iron Works; they build a full-sized trial engine — which does not work. Richard Arkwright builds a spinning mill, using the newly invented water frame, a water-powered spinning machine. Venetian blinds are patented in London by Edward Bevan. The 'Letters of Junius', anonymous attacks on the Duke of Grafton, Lord Mansfield and other members of the Government, begin to appear in the *Daily Advertiser*; no one ever discovers who wrote them, but the author is believed to be Sir Philip Francis. The portrait painter Thomas Lawrence is born.

APR [29] The Duke of Wellington is born in Dublin.
JUN [18] Lord Castlereagh is born, also in Ireland.
OCT [7] Captain Cook reaches New Zealand.

Old Blackfriars Bridge, London.

Laurence Sterne: *The History of a Good Warm Watch-Coat.*

1770 The Falklands Islands Crisis; the conflict between Spanish and British interests in the islands is resolved by French intervention — for the time being. The Duke of Grafton faces increasing opposition from the colonies and from sympathizers with John Wilkes; his ministry is finally overthrown by George III and Lord North.

JAN [28] Lord North, Earl of Guildford, becomes Prime Minister. To conciliate the American colonists, North abolishes all the import duties except the one on tea; this is retained in order to establish the British right to tax Americans.
MAR [5] Boston massacre; British troops fire into a crowd, killing five; the incident leads to the War of Independence. [11] William Huskisson, Tory politician, is born.
APR [7] William Wordsworth is born at Cockermouth, Cumberland. [11] George Canning, Tory Prime Minister, is born. [24] Thomas Chatterton leaves Bristol for London. [28] Captain James Cook discovers the east coast of Australia, claiming it for Britain; he lands at Botany Bay.
MAY [22] George III's daughter Elizabeth is born.
AUG [23] The poet Thomas Chatterton commits suicide.
NOV [14] James Bruce discovers the source of the Blue Nile, Lake Tana.

John Carr: Constable Burton, North Yorkshire.
William and Robert Adam: Mellerstain, Gordon, Borders.
Robert Adam: Pulteney Bridge, Bath (begun).
Castle Ward, County Down.

George Stubbs: *White Horse Frightened by a Lion.*
Thomas Gainsborough: *Blue Boy.*
Richard Wilson: *Snowdon from Llyn Nantil.*

 Edmund Burke: *Thoughts on the Present Discontents.*
Thomas Chatterton: *Elegy on William Beckford.*
Oliver Goldsmith: *The Deserted Village.*

1771 Spain cedes the uninhabited Falkland Islands to Britain. Captain Cook returns home after his first Pacific expedition. The Secret Debates Dispute; the Commons attempt to arrest a printer, Brass Crosby, for publishing reports of their debates. The City authorities support Crosby and a quarrel ensues between the Commons and the Aldermen. The Commons finally agree to allow debates to be reported.

APR [**13**] Richard Trevithick, designer of steam-engines, is born at Illogan near Redruth.
MAY [**14**] Robert Owen, industrialist and social reformer, is born at Newtown in Wales.
JUN [**5**] George III's son Ernest Augustus is born.
JUL [**30**] The poet Thomas Gray dies.
AUG [**15**] The novelist Sir Walter Scott is born in Edinburgh.
SEP [**10**] Mungo Park, surgeon and West African explorer, is born at Foulshiels near Selkirk. [**17**] Tobias Smollett, the novelist, dies at Leghorn in Italy.

 Benjamin West: *The Death of General Wolfe.*

 Richard Cumberland: *The West Indian.*
Henry Mackenzie: *The Man of Feeling.*
Tobias Smollett: *The Expedition of Humphrey Clinker.*
George Vertue: *Anecdotes of Painting in England.*

1772 Daniel Rutherford discovers nitrogen. Warren Hastings becomes Governor of Bengal. Captain James Cook leaves on his second voyage of exploration. Royal Marriage Act, preventing undesirable marriages of descendants of George II.

APR [**19**] The economist David Ricardo is born.
SEP [**30**] James Brindley, who built the Bridgewater, Grand Trunk and Manchester Canals, dies at Turnhurst in Staffordshire.
OCT [**21**] The poet Samuel Taylor Coleridge is born at Ottery St Mary, Devon.

Sir James Clerk: Rossdhu, Strathclyde.

 Johann Zoffany: *The Academicians of the Royal Academy.*
Nathaniel Dance: *Lord Clive.*

 Horace Walpole: *Description of the Villa at Strawberry Hill.*

 Thomas Arne: *Squire Badger; The Fairy Prince.*

1773 Warren Hastings prepares for his campaign against the Mahrathas by forming an alliance with the state of Oudh. Clive defends his former conduct in India in the House of Commons. Act for the Regulation of India, introduced by Lord North to give the Crown direct control over the East India Company; the administration of Bengal is vested in the Governor-General, Warren Hastings. Samuel Johnson goes on a tour of Scotland with Boswell. Josiah Wedgwood sets up a new pottery at Etruria.

JAN   [**17**] Captain Cook's *Resolution* becomes the first ship ever to cross the Antarctic Circle. [**27**] George III's son Augustus is born.

DEC   [**16**] The Boston Tea Party, promoted by protest against Britain taxation. A group of radical colonists disguised as Indians board British ships and empty their cargoes of tea into the sea. The British Government declares the port of Boston closed and takes away the colony's charter.

 John Carr: Assize Court, York.

 David Garrick: *Albumazar.*
Oliver Goldsmith: *She Stoops to Conquer.*
James and Robert Adam: *Works in Architecture, Volume 1.*

1774 Joseph Priestley discovers oxygen. John Wilkinson, ironmaster, patents a cannon-borer that will allow accurate boring of cylinders for steam-engines. John Wilkes is elected Lord Mayor of London. American colonists regard the closure of Boston intolerable. Congress at Philadelphia, at which the American Declaration of Independence is set out. The importation of goods is prohibited.

FEB   [**24**] George III's son Adolphus is born.
APR   [**4**] Oliver Goldsmith dies in London.
AUG   [**12**] The Poet Laureate Robert Southey is born at Bristol.
NOV   [**22**] Robert Clive, soldier and administrator, commits suicide.

 Lord Chesterfield: *Letters* [to his son] (posthumous).
Oliver Goldsmith: *A History of the Earth.*

Samuel Wesley: *Ruth.*
John Smith: *The Redemption.*
John Stanley: *The Fall of Egypt.*

1775 Watt and Boulton work in partnership at the Soho Engineering
Works, Birmingham. Alexander Cummings takes out a patent for the
flushing water closet similar to Harington's 'Ajax' of 1589. In India,
the British gain control of Ghazipur (part of the Ganges valley). Pitt's
Bill to conciliate the American colonists is rejected.

JAN [**17**] First performance of Sheridan's *The Rivals* at Covent
Garden.
FEB [**10**] Charles Lamb, essayist, is born.
APR [**23**] The painter Joseph Mallord William Turner is born at
Covent Garden. The American War of Independence begins,
10 miles from Boston, with skirmishes at Lexington and
Concord. In the Battle of Lexington British troops are defeated
by a group of American settlers led by George Washington.
MAY Representatives from all the American colonies meet at the
Philadelphia Congress and set up an army under George
Washington's leadership. The Duke of Grafton resigns
because he opposes the war; the Earl of Dartmouth replaces
him as Lord Privy Seal.
AUG [**6**] The Irish nationalist leader Daniel O'Connell is born.
DEC [**16**] The novelist Jane Austen is born at Steventon in
Hampshire, the seventh of the Rector's eight children.

John Wood the Younger: Royal Crescent, Bath, Avon
(completed).

Thomas Gainsborough: *Portrait of the Hon. Mrs Graham.*
Nathaniel Hone: *The Conjurer.*
Sir Joshua Reynolds: *Miss Jane Bowles.*

David Garrick: *The Fairies.*
Samuel Johnson: *A Journey to the Western Isles of Scotland.*

1776 Britains recruits 29,000 Hessian mercenaries for the American War. A
submarine is used unsuccessfully against British ships in New York
Harbour; it is the first time a submarine is used in warfare. British
troops under General Howe are forced to leave Boston. For the first
time a motion is put before the Commons to abolish slavery in Britain
and the British colonies; it is proposed by David Hartley.

MAR [**24**] John Harrison, watchmaker and inventor of the
chronometer, dies.

APR　[**25**] George III's daughter Mary is born.

JUN　[**11**] The artist John Constable is born.

JUL　[**4**] American Congress draws up and passes the Declaration of Independence. [**11**] Captain Cook sails from Plymouth in the *Resolution*, accompanied by the *Discovery*, on his third and last expedition.

Sir William Chambers: Somerset House (begun).
James Wyatt: The Radcliffe Observatory, Oxford (begun).
[Designed by Henry Keene and completed by Wyatt.]

Jeremy Bentham: *A Fragment on the Government*.
Henry Brooke: *The Fool of Quality*.
Edward Gibbon: *Decline and Fall of the Roman Empire* (begins).
Sir John Hawkins: *General History of the Science and Practice of Music*.
Charles Burney: *History of Music*.
Adam Smith: *The Wealth of Nations*.

1777 The Habeas Corpus Act is suspended. Tailors in Birmingham form a co-operative workshop, to provide work for men on strike. Battle of Saratoga; General Burgoyne is hemmed in by American troops and forced to surrender to the Americans under General Horatio Gates.

JAN　[**3**] Battle of Princeton: Washington defeats British forces under Lord Cornwallis.

SEP　[**11**] Battle of Brandywine Creek; British troops under General Howe defeat George Washington, but fail to follow up this major success.

NOV　[**3**] George III's daughter Sophia is born.

Robert Adam: Culzean Castle, Scotland (begun).
Samuel Wyatt: Doddington Hall, Cheshire (begun).

Richard Sheridan: *The School for Scandal*.
Thomas Chatterton: *Poems supposed to have been written at Bristol, by Thomas Rowley and others, in the fifteenth century*.
James Cook: *A Voyage Towards the South Pole and Round the World*.
Joseph Priestley: *Experiments and observations on different kinds of air*.

1778 France and Holland form a military alliance with the American colonists. In retaliation, Britain declares war on France. Dominica is captured by the French for use as a naval base; the British counter-action is to capture St Lucia from the the French. In India, Warren Hastings captures Chandernagore from the French and Sir Hector Munro captures Pondicherry. Lord North's plan for conciliating the Americans, the Reconciliation Bill, is rejected. Roman Catholic Relief Act; this relaxation of the penal laws against Catholics reflects the Government's confidence.

MAR [5] The composer Thomas Arne dies.
APR [22] James Hargreaves, who invented the spinning-jenny, dies at Nottingham.
MAY [11] William Pitt the Elder, Earl of Chatham, dies at Hayes.
JUN [7] George 'Beau' Brummell, leader of fashion, is born in London.
AUG [14] Augustus Toplady, author of the hymn 'Rock of Ages', dies.
DEC [17] Sir Humphry Davy, scientist and inventor, is born at Penzance.

Joseph Nollekens: *Venus chiding Cupid*.
Sir Joshua Reynolds: *The Marlborough Family*.

Fanny Burney: *Evelina*.
Sir Joshua Reynolds: *Seven Discourses delivered in the Royal Academy*.
Clara Reeve: *The Old English Baron*.

1779 Spain joins France and declares war on Britain; the great Franco-Spanish siege of Gibraltar begins. The British capture Senegal. French forces capture St Vincent and Grenada. The Irish raise a Protestant Volunteer Movement, 40,000 strong, to defend Ireland in the event of a French invasion; Britain ends restrictions on Irish trade. Samuel Crompton invents the spinning-mule, introducing an era of mass production in the British textile industry.

JAN [20] The actor and theatre manager David Garrick dies.
FEB [7] The composer William Boyce dies. [14] Captain Cook is stabbed to death by natives at Kealakekua Bay in the Hawaiian Islands.
MAR [15] Lord Melbourne, Prime Minister, is born in London as William Lamb.
SEP [23] John Paul Jones on the *Bonhomme Richard* defeats the British ship *Serapis* in an engagement off Flamborough Head.

John Carr: Royal Crescent, Buxton, Derbyshire (begun).
Abraham Darby III: The Iron Bridge, Coalbrookdale, Shropshire [First iron bridge.].

Sir Joshua Reynolds: *Jane, Countess of Harington.*

 Samuel Wesley: *The Death of Abel.*

1780 A petitioning movement begins in Yorkshire, spreading across the whole country; the complaint is that taxes are too high and the Government is wasting money. Britain declares war on Holland because of Holland's support for the American colonists. Russia, Sweden and Denmark enter an alliance, the Armed Neutrality, to prevent the British from exercising their old 'right' of searching vessels at sea. The Irish MP Henry Grattan demands Home Rule for Ireland; Lord North grants Ireland the right to trade freely with the colonies, but this small concession does not satisfy the Irish.

JAN [16] Battle of Cape St Vincent; Admiral Rodney destroys all but four ships of the Spanish fleet and succeeds in temporarily lifting the siege of Gibraltar.

MAR [26] The first Sunday newspaper, the *British Gazette and Sunday Monitor*, appears.

MAY [4] The first Derby (three-year-olds over a distance of 1½ miles) is run at Epsom; it is won by 'Diomed'. [21] Elizabeth Fry, the prison reformer, is born at Norwich.

JUN [2] The Lord George Gordon Riots break out in London: anti-Catholic demonstrations.

 Robert Adam: Osterley Park, Middlesex (alterations completed).

Jeremy Bentham: *Introduction to the Principles of Morals and Legislation.*
George Crabbe: *The Candidate.*

1781 Dr James Graham, an eccentric Edinburgh physician, offers childless London couples the chance to solve their problems by spending a night on his 'Celestial Bed' at £500 a time; these and other bizarre treatments become a craze in Fashionable London. Warren Hastings deposes the Rajah of Benares for refusing to contribute to war expenses. The first noticeable effects of the Industrial Revolution are felt, with the sudden growth of the cotton industry. A British plan to seize the Cape of Good Hope is thwarted by the French. William Pitt the Younger enters Parliament.

MAR [13] Sir William Herschel discovers the planet Uranus; at first he names it Georgium Sidus, in honour of George III.

JUN [8] George Stephenson, the builder of the 'Rocket', is born at Wylam-on-Tyne.

SEP   [5] Battle of Chesapeake Bay, between French and British fleets off the Atlantic coast of America.

OCT   [19] Lord Cornwallis surrenders with 7000 men to General Washington at Yorktown in Virginia, marking the end of the fighting in the American War of Independence.

Henry Holland: Berrington Hall, Hereford and Worcester.
Abraham Darby: Iron Bridge, Coalbrookdale (completed).

Joseph Wright of Derby: *Sir Brooke Boothby.*

Samuel Johnson: *Lives of the English Poets.*
Edward Gibbon: *Decline and Fall of the Roman Empire, Vol. 6.*

1782 James Watt invents the double-acting rotary steam-engine, a much more powerful engine than his earlier invention. Josiah Wedgwood becomes the first manufacturer to install a steam-engine in his factory. The painter Richard Wilson dies. Grenville travels to Paris to negotiate for peace in the American War of Independence with Benjamin Franklin and the Count of Vergennes. Henry Grattan makes his Irish Declaration of Rights, demanding legislative freedom for Ireland. Fox introduces the Repeal of Ireland Bill which grants Ireland legislative independence and removes the power of British Parliaments to control Irish Parliaments. Lord North wants to end the American War as soon as possible, is opposed by George III, and resigns.

MAR   [27] The Whig Marquis of Rockingham becomes Prime Minister again.

JUL   [4] Rockingham dies and is succeeded by the Whig William Petty, Earl of Shelburne (Marquis of Lansdowne).

AUG   [29] HMS *Royal George*, a 100-ton battleship, sinks at anchor at Spithead; over 900 lives are lost as the ship turns turtle, including that of Admiral Kempenfelt.

NOV   [30] Preliminary Treaty of Paris; the United States (i.e. the Anglo-American colonies), Great Britain, France, Spain and Holland recognize the independence of the 13 United States; Britain is to surrender Tobago and Senegal to France.

Sir Robert Taylor: North front of Heveningham Hall, Suffolk (interior remodelled later by James Wyatt).

Henry Fuseli: *The Nightmare.*

Frances Burney: *Cecilia.*
William Cowper: *Poems.*

1783 FEB **[6]** Lancelot 'Capability' Brown, the landscape gardener, dies.

APR **[2]** Lord Shelburne resigns after being censured over the peace preliminaries with America and is succeeded as Prime Minister by William Bentinck, Duke of Portland. **[26]** After the death of Archbishop Frederick Cornwallis, John Moore, Bishop of Bangor, becomes Archbishop of Canterbury.

MAY **[22]** William Sturgeon, inventor of the first working electromagnet, is born at Whittington.

JUN **[17]** Samuel Johnson is paralyzed by a stroke.

SEP **[3]** Treaty of Versailles; American independence is formally recognized. Britain is to pay a war indemnity of £10 million. The Treaty also provides for Britain ceding Tobago, St Lucia, Senegal, Pondicherry and Chandernagore to France in exchange for Grenada, Dominica, St Vincent, Nevis, Montserrat, St Kitts and the Gambia; Britain is to relinquish Florida and Minorca to Spain in exchange for Providence, the Bahamas and Gibraltar.

DEC **[7]** William Pitt the Younger becomes Britain's youngest Prime Minister at the age of 24.

George Crabbe: *The Village*.

1784 Shrapnel, invented by Lt Henry Shrapnel, is first tested at Stirling. Warren Hastings makes an effective peace with the Mahrathas; Margalore, a strategic shipbuilding base, is ceded to Britain. Pitt reduces the duties on tea and spirits.

AUG **[2]** The first specially constructed Royal Mail coach runs, from Bristol to London. **[13]** East India Act; the company is placed under a Board of Control to manage its revenues and administration.

OCT **[20]** Lord Palmerston is born at Westminster, as Henry Temple.

DEC **[13]** Dr Samuel Johnson, writer and lexicographer, dies.

Sir Joshua Reynolds: *Mrs Siddons as the Tragic Muse*.

Charles Macklin: *Love à la Mode*.

Samuel Wesley; *First Symphony*.

1785 Edmund Cartwright invents the power loom, which mechanizes weaving, and paves the way to mass production in the textile industry. The English Channel is successfully crossed by balloon for the first time. Jean-Pierre Blanchard and Dr John Jeffries, his American backer, launch from Dover but begin to lose height prematurely six miles from the French coast. They jettison everything, including their clothes, in order to make landfall in France. James Hutton's *Theory of the Earth* lays the foundation of modern geology and geomorphology; it is based on a uniformitarian view of earth processes and proposes a very great age for the earth. Learning of Pitt's East India Act, Warren Hastings resigns and returns to Britain. Supported by Fox, Pitt proposes a scheme for parliamentary reform, but it is rejected by the Commons.

AUG [**15**] Thomas de Quincey, the writer, is born.
OCT [**18**] The essayist Thomas Love Peacock is born.

Thomas Baldwin: Pulteney Street, Bath.
John Soane: Chillington Hall, Staffordshire.

Thomas Gainsborough: *Mrs Siddons; The Morning Walk.*

James Hutton: *The Theory of the Earth.*
Elizabeth Inchbold: *Appearance is Against Them.*
William Cowper: *The Task.*
Francis Grose: *Dictionary of the Vulgar Tongue.*

1786 An economic boom begins, based on the growth of the coal-mining and cotton industries; industrial towns begin to grow rapidly in the Midlands and North of England, and in the Scottish Lowlands. Charles Cornwallis becomes Governor-General of India. The Rajah of Kedah cedes Penang to Britain. Anglo-French commercial treaty; duty is reduced on English clothes, cotton and iron goods, and on French soap, wines and olive oil. William Brodie's criminal career comes to an end with an abortive raid on the headquarters of the Scottish Customs and Excise; Brodie escapes to Amsterdam, but is extradited to stand trial in Edinburgh.

OCT [**31**] George II's daughter Amelia dies.

Thomas Baldwin and John Palmer: The Pump Room and Colonnade, Bath.

Elizabeth Inchbold: *I'll tell you what.*
Robert Burns: *Poems.*
William Beckford: *Vathek.*
William Herschel: *Catalogue of Nebulae.*
Hester Lynch Piozzi: *Anecdotes of the late Samuel Johnson.*

1787 The Association for the Abolition of the Slave Trade is founded, mainly by the Quakers. Warren Hastings is impeached for alleged irregularities during his administration in India; the attack on him is led by Burke, Fox and Philip Francis.

 James Barry: *King Lear weeping over the body of Cordelia.*

1788 Sierra Leone becomes a British refuge settlement for black waifs and ex-slaves. Andrew Meikle patents the threshing machine he has invented. George III shows signs of insanity; the Commons debate the possibility of a regency, but the King recovers. The seven-year-long trial of Warren Hastings begins; there are 22 charges of cruelty, oppression and robbery towards the princes of India. The composer Joseph Gibbs dies.

JAN [22] George Gordon, Lord Byron, is born in London. [26] The first consignment of English convicts arrives at Botany Bay; the founding of the penal colony there marks the beginning of the colonization of Australia. [31] Prince Charles Edward, the Young Pretender and leader of the Jacobite Rebellion aimed at deposing George II, dies in Rome.
FEB [5] Sir Robert Peel is born at Bury in Lancashire, the son of a cotton millionaire.
MAR [29] The evangelist Charles Wesley dies.
AUG [2] The painter Thomas Gainsborough dies.
SEP [30] Lord Raglan, the Field Marshal responsible for the disastrous Charge of the Light Brigade, is born at Badminton.
OCT [1] William Brodie is hanged at Edinburgh; his career inspires Robert Louis Stevenson to write *The Strange Case of Dr Jekyll and Mr Hyde.*

 Sir Joshua Reynolds: *Lord Heathfield.*

 Elizabeth Inchbold: *Such Things Are.*
The Times, first edition (Jan 1).

1789 The Scottish explorer Sir Alexander Mackenzie discovers the River Mackenzie in North America (named for him).

APR [28] The mutiny on the *Bounty,* in the Friendly Islands; Captain Bligh and 17 others are set adrift in an open boat, eventually reaching Timor.
MAR [20] William, George III's third son, is created Duke of Clarence.
JUL [14] The outbreak of the French Revolution sends shock waves through Britain. Coleridge, at 16, writes his first truly original poem, *The Fall of the Bastille.*

Robert Adam: Edinburgh University.

 Thomas Lawrence: *Portrait of Queen Charlotte*.

 Ann Radcliffe: *The Castles of Athlin and Dunbayne*.
William Blake: *Songs of Innocence*.
Gilbert White: *The Natural History and Antiquities of Selborne*.
Charles Burney: *General History*, 4th and final volume.
William Bowles: *Fourteen Sonnets*.

1790 Crompton's Mule, until now a cottage spinning machine, is harnessed to water power for the first time by William Kelly, the manager of the New Lanark Mills; the machine's use spreads very rapidly. A stone coffin containing a boy's skeleton is discovered at Lincoln, beneath the shrine of Little St Hugh. Turner exhibits his first watercolour at the Royal Academy. Sir Joshua Reynolds delivers the last of his 'Discourses on Art'. James Watt applies his flyball governor to regulate the speed of a steam-engine. An election returns Pitt's Government with an increased majority.

JAN [**30**] The first purpose-built lifeboat, called *The Original*, is launched at South Shields.
MAR [**5**] Flora Macdonald, the Jacobite heroine who helped Prince Charles Edward to escape from the island of Benbecula, dies.
JUL [**11**] William Wordsworth and his friend Robert Jones set off on their walking tour of France and Switzerland. [**17**] The economist Adam Smith dies in Edinburgh.

 James Wyatt: Castle Combe, Northern Ireland.

 Thomas Bewick: *A General History of Quadrupeds* (illustrated).

 Ann Radcliffe: *A Sicilian Romance*.
William Blake: *Marriage of Heaven and Hell*.
William Bligh: *A Narrative of the Mutiny on Board HMS Bounty*.
Charlotte Smith: *Ethelinda*.
Edmund Burke: *Reflections on the Revolution in France*.
James Boswell: *Conversation between George III and Samuel Johnson*.

1791 Indiarubber cloth is patented by Samuel Peel. Joseph Priestley's house in Birmingham is burnt down by a mob in protest at his support for the French Revolution. The Royal Navy is expanded because of Russian hostility in the Black Sea. In Ireland, the Society of United Irishmen is formed; its aim is to persuade the French to invade Ireland, throw off English rule and set up a republic. William Wilberforce proposes a Parliamentary motion for the abolition of slavery; the motion is carried.

MAR [2] John Wesley, evangelist and founder of the Methodist Movement, dies in London aged 87.

SEP [22] The chemist and physicist Michael Faraday is born at Newington Butts.

NOV [26] The poet Wordsworth sails from Brighton for France, where he is to visit the National Assembly in Paris.

DEC [4] The Sunday newspaper *The Observer* is published for the first time.

 Robert Adam: Charlotte Square, Edinburgh.

 George Morland: *Inside a Stable.*

 William Blake: *French Revolution.*
Jeremy Bentham: *Panopticon.*
Ann Radcliffe: *The Romance of the Forest.*
James Boswell: *The Life of Samuel Johnson, LL.D.*
Thomas Paine: *Rights of Man.*

1792 Coal gas is used for the first time for lighting. The London Corresponding Society is founded by artisans to campaign for electoral reform.

FEB [23] Sir Joshua Reynolds, the first President of the Royal Academy, dies in London; he is succeeded as President by Benjamin West.

MAR [3] The architect and designer Robert Adam dies. [7] The astronomer Sir John Herschel is born at Slough.

MAY [24] Admiral Lord Rodney dies at Hanover Square in London.

JUL [10] The novelist Frederick Marryat is born.

AUG [3] Sir Richard Arkwright, inventor of the mechanical spinning process, dies. [4] The poet Percy Bysshe Shelley is born at Warnham. [5] Lord North, Tory Prime Minister 1770-82, dies.

OCT [28] John Smeaton, designer of the third Eddystone Lighthouse, dies.

NOV [19] A Decree published by the French Convention offers help 'to all those nations who desire to overthrow their kings'; this is seen as provocative.

 Joseph Nollekens: *Portrait Bust of Charles James Fox.*
Francis Wheatley: *Cries of London.*

Thomas Holcroft: *The Road to Ruin.*
Mary Wollstonecraft: *Vindication of the Rights of Women.*
Thomas Malton: *A Picturesque Tour through the Cities of London and Westminster.*

1793 FEB [1] The French Republic declares war on Britain. The Government takes action against agitation by drafting the Traitorous Correspondence Bill. Exchequer bills are issued by Pitt to help finance the war with France. The British economy enters a depression.

APR [15] The first Bank of England £5 notes are issued.

NOV [1] Lord George Gordon, the anti-Catholic agitator and leader of the 'Gordon Riots' in 1780, dies in Newgate Prison.

Cruciform building at Milford, Derbyshire (early use of cast-iron columns).

Thomas Banks: Penelope Boothby Tomb.

 Charlotte Smith: *The Old Manor House.*
William Blake: *Gates of Paradise; Vision of the Daughters of Albion.*
William Godwin: *Political Justice and its Influence on General Virtue and Happiness.*

1794 Haydn visits London for the second time. The Habeas Corpus Act is suspended.

JAN [16] The historian Edward Gibbon dies.

MAY The trial of Hardy, Horn Tooke and Thelwall on charges of high treason begins.

JUN The poet Coleridge leaves Cambridge without taking a degree. [1] Battle of Brest, the 'Glorious First of June'; Lord Howe gains a resounding victory over the French fleet.

NOV Jay's Treaty between Britain and the United States.

DEC Hardy, Horn Tooke and Thelwall are acquitted.

William Godwin: *Caleb Williams.*
Ann Radcliffe: *The Mysteries of Udolpho.*
William Blake: *Songs of Experience.*

1795 The Speenhamland system of outdoor relief is adopted, making up wages to equal the cost of subsistence. Holland joins France, so Britain is force to declare war on Holland. The British take Ceylon (Sri Lanka) from the Dutch. The Cape of Good Hope is also captured by the British. Mungo Park explores the upper reaches of the Gambia river and the Niger. Joseph Bramah invents the hydraulic press. Warren Hastings is acquitted after a trial lasting seven years.

JAN   Raisley Calvert dies, leaving Wordsworth £900 – enough to enable him to write. [3] Josiah Wedgwood, the creator of blue jasper ware, dies.

APR   [8] George (later George IV) marries Caroline, daughter of Charles Duke of Brunswick-Wolfenbuttel.

MAY   [19] James Boswell, biographer of Dr Johnson, dies. [23] Sir Charles Barry, co-architect of the Palace of Westminster, is born.

JUN   [13] Thomas Arnold, educationalist, is born at Cowes.

DEC   [3] Sir Rowland Hill, pioneer in postal services, is born at Kidderminster. [4] The historian Thomas Carlyle is born at Ecclefechan.

William Blake: *Elohim Creating Adam.*
John Flaxman: Mansfield Monument, Westminster Abbey.

Ann Radcliffe: *A Journey through Holland.*
William Blake: *The Song of Los.*

1796 A 27-year-old engineer, William Smith, proves from his own fieldwork that the geological succession is the same throughout England and Wales, an important concept which opens the prospect of devising a history of the Earth. The violin is introduced into India by the British; Indian musicians absorb the new instrument into their own music. Through Swiss mediators, Pitt initiates secret but unsuccessful negotiations with France.

JAN   [7] The Prince of Wales' daughter Charlotte is born.

APR   [2] The first and only performance of *Vortigern and Rowena* at the Drury Lane Theatre; this 'long-lost play by Shakespeare' is a hoax, written by the 17-year-old William Henry Ireland.

MAY   [14] Edward Jenner successfully proves the vaccination theory, laying the foundations for modern immunology and leading directly to the eradication of smallpox in Britain.

SEP   [17] Opening of Parliament.

DEC   An attempted invasion of Ireland by the French under General Hoche fails when the French fleet is scattered by a storm.

Rowland Burdon: Sunderland Bridge.
Benyon, Bage & Marshall's flax-spinning mill at Ditherington (revolutionary design using cast-iron columns and cast-iron beams).

James Wyatt: Fonthill Abbey, Wiltshire (begun).

Robert Southey: *Joan of Arc.*
Matthew Lewis: *The Monk.*
Erasmus Darwin: *Zoonomia, or the Laws of Organic Life.*
Regina Roche: *Children of the Abbey.*
Fanny Burney: *Camilla.*

1797 The top hat is worn in public for the first time, by James Hetherington in London, drawing a huge disorderly crowd. Hetherington is arrested and charged with causing a breach of the peace, having 'appeared on the public highway wearing a tall structure of shining lustre and calculated to disturb timid people'.

JAN [**3**] One of the Stonehenge trilithons (stones 57 and 58) falls down, causing an earth tremor felt half a mile away.

FEB [**12**] The last invasion of Britain; 1400 French troops under the command of the Irish-American General Tate land in Dyfed; they later surrender to British soldiers. [**14**] Battle of Cape St Vincent; British forces under Admiral Sir John Jervis and Commodore Nelson defeat the Spanish fleet. [**26**] £1 notes are first issued by the Bank of England, and the first copper pennies are minted.

APR [**15**] Sailors mutiny at Spithead off Portsmouth.

MAY [**18**] George III's daughter Charlotte marries Prince Frederick of Wurtemberg. [**23**] The Nore Mutiny, led by Richard Parker, against bad food and inadequate pay begins.

JUN [**5**] Coleridge walks to Racedown Lodge in Dorset to meet the Wordsworths for the first time. He characteristically jumps over a gate and runs down through a field of corn to meet Dorothy; it is the beginning of an important creative relationship. [**30**] The collapse of the Nore Mutiny.

JUL [**9**] The politician and writer Edmund Burke dies.

AUG [**11**] A secret Home Office report records that Coleridge and the Wordsworths are suspected of being enemy agents because of their strange behaviour, wandering about the countryside with camp-stools and making detailed observations about the landscape. [**30**] Mary Shelley, author of *Frankenstein*, is born.

OCT Coleridge writes *Kubla Khan* at Ash Farm near Culbone. [**11**] Battle of Camperdown off the Dutch coast; the British under Admiral Duncan are victorious over a Dutch fleet challenging Britain's naval supremacy.

DEC   [**26**] John Wilkes, radical politician and agitator for the freedom of the press, dies.

    Ann Radcliffe: *The Italian.*
William Wilberforce: *Practical View of the Prevailing Religious Systems of Professed Christians ... contrasted with Real Christianity.*
Thomas Bewick: *A History of British Birds*, Volume 1.
Sir Frederick Morton: *The State of the Poor.*

1798 Henry Cavendish, chemist and physicist, determines the mean density of the Earth. The Romantic movement begins with the publication of *Lyrical Ballads* by Wordsworth and Coleridge. The vault and coffin of Henry VI come to light in St George's Chapel, Windsor. Lord Stanhope constructs the first printing press with an iron frame. Pitt increases the tax on newspapers. Richard Wellesley, elder brother of the Duke of Wellington, becomes Governor-General of India. A Second Coalition against France is formed by an Anglo-Russian Alliance.

MAR   [**23**] Coleridge completes *The Rime of the Ancient Mariner* and takes it to show Wordsworth.
JUN   [**21**] In the Irish Rebellion, stimulated by the spread of republicanism, the rebels are defeated at Vinegar Hill near Wexford by General Lake's troops.
AUG   [**1**] Battle of the Nile: Nelson destroys 11 out of 13 French battleships which have convoyed Napoleon to Egypt, thus effectively trapping the French army in the Middle East.

    Sawrey Gilpin: *Horses Frightened by a Thunderstorm.*

    Matthew Lewis: *The Castle Spectre.*
Wordsworth and Coleridge: *Lyrical Ballads* (including *The Rime of the Ancient Mariner* and *Tintern Abbey*).
John Cary: *New Itinerary.*
Thomas Malthus: *An Essay on the principle of Population as it affects the future improvement of society.*

1799 A peace offer by France is rejected by Britain and Austria. The Duke of York, commanding the British army in Holland, ignominiously surrenders to the French at Alkmaar. The British assume control of the Carnatic (southern India) after Tipu Sahib, the last ruler of Mysore, is killed in battle. The rebellion of the United Irishmen is suppressed. Combination Laws make trade unions illegal.

JAN [9] William Pitt the Younger introduces income tax, at two shillings in the pound on incomes over £200, to raise money for the war with France.

APR [24] George III's sons Edward and Ernest are created Dukes of Kent and Cumberland.

MAY [23] The poet Thomas Hood is born.

AUG [5] Admiral Richard Howe dies.

DEC [27] William and Dorothy Wordsworth move to Dove Cottage in the Lake District.

John Frere and George Canning: *Poetry of the Anti-Jacobin.*
Mungo Park: *Travels in the interior districts of Africa.*

1800

1800 Sir William Herschel discovers infra-red rays in sunlight. The Royal College of Surgeons is founded in London. The Armed Neutrality of the North; an alliance between Russia, Denmark, Sweden and Prussia to counter the British right of search on the high seas, and to keep the British out of the Baltic. Malta is captured by the British. Henry Maudslay invents the lathe.

FEB [11] The pioneer photographer William Fox Talbot is born at Evershot.

APR [4] 'Galloping Dick' the highwayman is hanged at Aylesbury.
[25] The poet William Cowper dies at East Dereham.

MAY [15] James Hatfield attempts to assassinate George III at the theatre in Drury Lane.

Maria Edgeworth: *Castle Rackrent.*
Sydney Smith: *Six Sermons.*

1801 William Cunnington excavates the Boles long barrow at Heytesbury and finds a large block of bluestone in it, showing that bluestones were being imported from Wales well before the building of Stonehenge. Health and Morals of Apprentices Act; this forbids children under nine from working and restricts the working day of older children to 12 hours in the daytime only.

JAN [1] Act of Union of Great Britain and Ireland becomes effective. The name of the newly-constituted state is to be the United Kingdom. Ireland is to send four spiritual lords, 28 temporal peers elected for life from the Irish peerage, and 100 Commons MPs to Westminster. The Churches are to be united into one Protestant Episcopal Church.

FEB [3] Pitt proposes to include concessions to Catholics in the plans for the Union: the King objects, and Pitt resigns after 17 years in office. [21] Cardinal Newman is born.

MAR [17] Pitt is succeeded as Prime Minister by the Tory Henry Addington, Viscount Sidmouth.

APR [2] Battle of Copenhagen; Nelson, who is second in command on board the *Elephant*, puts a telescope to his blind eye and in consequence does not see Admiral Hyde Parker's signal to break off the naval engagement. The Danish fleet is destroyed and the Northern League against Britain is shattered. [28] Lord Shaftesbury, one of the great Victorian social reformers, is born in London as Anthony Cooper.

JUN [29] The results of Britain's first-ever census are published.

AUG [3] Sir Joseph Paxton, architect of the Crystal Palace, is born at Milton Bryant near Woburn.

NOV [27] George III's sons Augustus and Adolphus are created Dukes of Sussex and Cambridge.

DEC [24] Richard Trevithick's steam carriage, the first steam-powered vehicle to run on British roads, is given its first outing in spite of outspoken warnings from James Watt that the high pressure involved will cause the boiler to explode. [27] Trevithick takes some friends out to a pub in his steam carriage, leaving the boiler fire burning, and emerges from the pub to find the carriage a smoking wreck.

 James Wyatt: Belvoir Castle, Leicestershire.

 Francis Barrett: *The Magus.*
James Hogg: *Scottish Pastorals.*
Lewis, Scott and Southey: *Tales of Wonder.*

1802 Madame Tussaud arrives in Britain with her waxworks collection. Thomas Telford begins building roads in the Scottish Highlands. It is proposed for the first time to link Britain and France with a Channel Tunnel; the French engineer Albert Mathieu visualizes horse-drawn coaches passing through a candle-lit tunnel. Wars in the Deccan lead to the supremacy of the British East India Company in India. Ceylon becomes a Crown colony.

FEB [6] Sir Charles Wheatstone, pioneer of telegraphy, is born at Gloucester.

MAR [7] The painter Sir Edwin Landseer is born in London. [27] Peace of Amiens, between Britain and France; Britain returns most of the gains made during the Revolutionary Wars, except for Ceylon and Trinidad: Malta is returned to the Knights of St John.

SEP   [**28**] William Cunnington digs at the centre of Stonehenge.

NOV   [**15**] The portrait artist George Romney dies at Kendal.

 William Atkinson: Scone Palace, Perthshire.

 John Debrett: *Debrett's Correct Peerage.*
William Wordsworth: *Westminster Bridge.*

 Samuel Wesley: *Fourth Symphony.*

1803 John Dalton, physicist and chemist, introduces the atomic theory. John Horrocks of Stockport installs the first power looms made wholly of metal; this is a decisive development in the mechanization of the textile industry. John Crome founds the Norwich Society. The philosopher Arthur Schopenhauer arrives as a very young boy to attend Nelson House School, Wimbledon; the experience turns him against Christianity for life. Britain refuses to evacuate Malta until Napoleon gives up Piedmont, Piacenza and parts of Switzerland. Napoleon assembles a huge fleet at Boulogne and an army of 150,000 at Dunkirk in preparation for the invasion of Britain. British forces capture Tobago and St Lucia from France. Robert Emmet's rebellion in Ireland is encouraged by Napoleon; Lord Kilwarden is murdered in Dublin.

MAR   [**3**] The Duke of Bridgewater, pioneer of the canal network, dies.

MAY   [**16**] Britain is again at war with France. [**25**] Lord Lytton is born.

 Maria Edgeworth: *Belinda.*
Thomas Chatterton: *Collected Poems* (posthumous).

1804 William Wollaston isolates palladium from platinum. Richard Trevithick builds the first steam train to haul a load successfully. Urged on by Napoleon (now Emperor), Spain declares war on Britain.

FEB   [**6**] Joseph Priestley, discoverer of oxygen, dies at Northumberland in Pennsylvania.

APR   [**30**] Shrapnel is used in warfare for the first time, by the British against the Dutch in Surinam.

MAR   [**10**] Lord Sidmouth resigns and is succeeded by the Tory William Pitt as Prime Minister.

JUN   [**3**] Richard Cobden, economist and politician, is born at Heyshott.

DEC   [**21**] Benjamin Disraeli is born in Theobald's Road, London.

Thomas Bewick: *A History of British Birds*, Volume 2.
William Blake: *Jerusalem; Milton.*
William Wordsworth: *Intimations of Immortality.*
Thomas Love Peacock: *The Monks of St Mark.*

1805 The painter Samuel Palmer is born. Arthur Wellesley is recalled from India and briefly replaced by Lord Cornwallis as Governor-General.

FEB   [**4**] The writer Harrison Ainsworth is born. [**5**] The *Earl of Abergavenny*, a large and well-known East Indiaman, is wrecked in a gale off Portland Bill. The poet Wordsworth's brother, Captain John Wordsworth, is drowned along with 300 others; the sinking is felt to be a national disaster. [**21**] After the death of Archbishop John Moore, Charles Sutton, Bishop of Norwich, becomes Archbishop of Canterbury.

JUN   [**4**] The first 'Trooping the Colour' ceremony takes place, at Horse Guards Parade in London.

OCT   Lord Byron goes to Cambridge. [**21**] Battle of Trafalgar: Nelson's great victory over a joint French-Spanish fleet off the coast of Portugal. Nelson himself is killed in the action.

DEC   [**2**] Battle of Austerlitz; Napoleon's victory stuns Pitt.

Thomas Telford: iron aquaduct over Ellesmere Canal.

John Sell Cotman: *Greta Bridge.*
J. M. W. Turner: *The Shipwreck.*

Elizabeth Inchbald: *To Marry or Not to Marry.*
William Hazlitt: *The Principles of Human Actions.*
William Wordsworth: *The Prelude.*
Walter Scott: *The Lay of the Last Minstrel.*

1806 Rear-Admiral Sir Francis Beaufort designs the wind strength scale named after him.

JAN   [**9**] The funeral and burial of Lord Nelson at St Paul's Cathedral. [**23**] William Pitt the Younger, Tory statesman and twice Prime Minister, dies at Putney.

FEB   [**11**] William Lord Grenville succeeds as Prime Minister, leading a Whig Coalition Government.

MAR   [**6**] Elizabeth Barrett Browning, poetess and wife of Robert Browning, is born at Coxhoe Hall, Durham.

APR   [**9**] The engineer Isambard Kingdom Brunel is born at Portsmouth.

Jul [**10**] The painter George Stubbs dies aged 81.

Sep [**13**] Charles James Fox, the Foreign Secretary, dies at Chiswick.

Oct [**7**] Ralph Wedgwood, the inventor of carbon paper, secures a patent for his invention. [**22**] Thomas Sheraton, furniture designer and cabinet-maker, dies. Food prices rise and the textile industry declines as a result of Napoleon's 'Continental System', which is in effect an economic blockade.

Maria Rundell: *Family Receipt Book.*

1807 At the extravagant Gothic Revival masterpiece of Fonthill Abbey in Wiltshire (designed by James Wyatt), the 270 feet high central tower collapses. The Geological Society of London is founded. Lord Byron has his first volume of poetry, *Hours of Idleness*, published while he is still an undergraduate. Gas lighting is first introduced in London; by 1820, much of the city will be gas lit. The Slave trade is abolished throughout the British Empire. Grenville rejects Catholic Emancipation, and his 'Ministry of All the Talents' falls as a result.

Mar [**31**] Grenville is succeeded as Prime Minister by the Tory Duke of Portland.

Matthew Lewis: *The Wood Demon.*
Thomas Moore: *Irish Melodies.*
Charles and Mary Lamb: *Tales from Shakespeare.*
William Wordsworth: *Poems in Two Volumes.*
Lord Byron: *Hours of Idleness.*
James Beresford: *The Miseries of Human Life.*
James Hogg: *The Shepherd's Guide.*

1808 The French occupy Spain; there is a Spanish rising. The Peninsular War begins.

Aug [**21**] British troops under Wellington defeat the French.

Sep William Cunnington excavates the Bush Barrow near Stonehenge and finds a spectacularly rich burial of an Early Bronze Age chief; Sir Richard Colt-Hoare misses the dig because he has a migraine. [**19**] Covent Garden Theatre burns down.

Nov [**22**] The pioneer travel agent Thomas Cook is born at Melbourne in Derbyshire.

James Wyatt: Ashridge Park, Hertfordshire.
Sir John Soane: Bank of England (completed).
William Porden: The Dome, Royal Pavilion, Brighton.

Matthew Lewis: *Romantic Tales.*

1809 Humphry Davy invents the arc lamp. Lord Chatham, William Pitt's elder brother, commands the Walcheren Expedition, which fails to capture Antwerp. George Canning, the Foreign Secretary, tries to remove Lord Castlereagh from the War Office because of the Walcheren fiasco; they fight a duel over it and Canning is wounded.

JAN [**16**] Battle of Corunna; Sir John Moore is killed in action.

FEB [**12**] Charles Darwin is born at Shrewsbury.

MAR [**31**] The scholar and poet Edward Fitzgerald is born.

JUN [**8**] Thomas Paine, radical political activist and author of *Rights of Man*, dies in poverty in New York.

JUL [**28**] Battle of Talavera in the Peninsular War comes to an end; Wellesley is victorious over Soult. Wellesley is rewarded with the title Duke of Wellington.

AUG [**6**] Alfred Tennyson, poet, is born at Somersby rectory, Lincolnshire. [**18**] Matthew Boulton, James Watt's partner, dies in Soho.

OCT [**4**] The Duke of Portland resigns owing to ill health; the Tory Spencer Perceval becomes Prime Minister.

DEC [**29**] William Ewart Gladstone, four times Prime Minister, is born at Liverpool.

 Lord Byron: *English Bards and Scotch Reviewers.*

1810 John Metcalfe, known as 'Blind Jack of Knaresborough', dies. In spite of his disability he has constructed 180 miles of turnpike road, mostly in Lancashire and Yorkshire, doing the survey work himself by tapping his way across the moors with a stick; he pioneered side drains along the road edges and the cambered surface. George III loses his sanity entirely and remains insane until his death. William Cobbett is sent to prison for libel. Wellington forces a large French army into retreat at Torres Vedras near Lisbon. Guadeloupe, the last remaining French colony in the West Indies, is captured by the British.

FEB [**9**] Robert Coates makes his stage début as Romeo in Bath. His performance is so appalling that he becomes a cult figure overnight; he goes on to be a major success in London. [**24**] Henry Cavendish, who discovered the properties of hydrogen and other gases, dies.

APR [**24**] William Cunnington leaves a bottle of port under the Slaughter Stone at Stonehenge.

SEP [**29**] The novelist Elizabeth Gaskell is born in Chelsea.

John Linnell Bond: Waterloo Bridge, London.
Daniel Alexander: Maidstone Prison, Kent.
Sir Robert Smirke: Eastnor Castle, Herefordshire (begun).
William Wilkins: Grange Park, Hampshire.

 John Flaxman: The Nelson Monument, St Paul's.

 Sir Walter Scott: *The Lady of the Lake.*
George Crabbe: *The Borough.*
Jane Porter: *The Scottish Chiefs.*
Robert Southey: *The Curse of Kehama.*
Ann and Jane Taylor: *Hymns for Infant Minds* (including 'Twinkle, Twinkle, Little Star').
David Ricardo: *The High Price of Bullion, a proof of the depreciation of Bank Notes.*

1811 The Prince Regent gives a lavish banquet at Carlton House. Along the length of the main table, 200 feet, runs an artificial stream flowing from a silver fountain at its head. The Prince presides from a plume-backed throne beneath a crown and an illuminated 'GR' cipher. Sir Samuel Romilly contrasts 'the great expense of this entertainment' with 'the misery of the starving weavers of Lancashire and Glasgow'. There are outbreaks of Luddite riots and machine breaking in Nottinghamshire and Yorkshire; unemployed weavers fear the impact of mechanization on their livelihood. Two new music publishing houses are founded in London — Novello and Chappell.

FEB [5] George III is formally declared insane; the Prince of Wales becomes Prince Regent, ruling in his father's place.
MAR [25] The poet Shelley is sent down from Oxford for publishing *The Necessity of Atheism.*
APR [5] Robert Raikes, founder of the Sunday School movement, dies at Gloucester.
JUL [18] The novelist William Makepeace Thackeray is born in Calcutta.
NOV [16] The radical politician John Bright is born at Rochdale.
DEC [14] Byron sees Kemble on the London stage for the first time, and thinks his acting 'glorious'.

 Jane Austen: *Sense and Sensibility.*
Edward Nares: *Thinks-I-to-myself.*
Percy Shelley: *The Necessity of Atheism.*

1812 The food-canning process is invented by Bryan Donkin of London. The Elgin marbles are brought from Athens to Britain. The year of the waltz: the Continent-wide craze for the new dance reaches Britain.

The first meat cannery in Britain is set up at Bermondsey, but the technology is not yet perfected: the cans have to be opened with a hammer and chisel.

JAN [**8**] Two more regiments are called out to control the Luddite rising, which breaks out at various places during the year.

FEB [**7**] The novelist Charles Dickens is born at Portsmouth. [**27**] Lord Byron's maiden speech in the House of Lords is well received; he opposes Lord Liverpool's Frame-Breaking Bill, which seeks to make frame-breaking a capital offence, advising against the hasty introduction of a 'death bill'. Byron becomes a celebrity during the year, following the publication of *Childe Harold*, which achieves unprecedented popularity.

MAY [**10**] The Duchess of Devonshire writes: 'Byron continues to be the great attraction at all parties and suppers . . . He is going back to Naxos, and then the husbands may sleep in peace. I should not be surprised if Caro William (Lady Caroline Lamb) were to go with him'. [**11**] Spencer Perceval, the Tory Prime Minister, is assassinated in the Lobby of the House of Commons by an insane merchant called Francis Bellingham. Lord Liverpool becomes Prime Minister. [**12**] The eccentric poet and artist Edward Lear is born at Highgate.

OCT [**12**] Annabella Milbanke wisely declines Byron's proposal of marriage.

 Thomas Rowlandson: *The Tour of Dr Syntax* (illustrations).
J. M. W. Turner: *Snowstorm: Hannibal and his Army crossing the Alps*.

 Horace and James Smith: *Rejected Addresses*.
Lord Byron: *Childe Harold's Pilgrimage*.
Samuel Rogers: *Poems*.
Thomas Peacock: *The Philosophy of Melancholy*.

1813 The architect James Wyatt is killed when a coach he is travelling in overturns near Marlborough. Robert Southey is appointed Poet Laureate. The Royal Philharmonic Society is founded in London. The last gold guinea coins are minted. The East India Company's monopoly is abolished in India. Parliament abandons the Catholic Relief Bill. Brewster's law (polarization of light) – Sir David Brewster.

JAN [**4**] Isaac Pitman, pioneer of phonetic shorthand, is born in Trowbridge. [**19**] Sir Henry Bessemer, inventor of a method for converting iron into steel, is born at Charlton.

FEB [**3**] The writer Leigh Hunt begins two years in prison (Surrey Gaol) for describing the Prince Regent as 'a corpulent man of

50, a violator of his word, a libertine over head and ears in disgrace, a despiser of domestic ties, the companion of gamblers and demireps, a man who has just closed half a century without one single claim on the gratitude of his country'.

MAR [**19**] The explorer and missionary David Livingstone is born at Blantyre.

JUN [**21**] Wellington defeats the French at Vitoria.

OCT [**16-19**] The Fourth Coalition (Britain, Russia, Prussia, Sweden, Austria) closes in on Napoleon, forcing him back to Leipzig where he is heavily defeated in the 'Battle of the Nations'.

DEC [**29**] Alexander Parkes, the chemist who will later invent celluloid, is born at Birmingham.

 Sir Henry Raeburn: *The MacNab* (painted at about this time).

 Lord Byron: *The Giaour.*
Jane Austen: *Pride and Prejudice.*
Robert Owen: *A New View of Society.*
Percy Shelley: *Queen Mab.*
Robert Southey: *The Life of Nelson.*
James Hogg: *The Queen's Wake.*

1814 George Stephenson builds his first steam locomotive.

JAN [**14**] Britain makes peace with Denmark, restoring all conquests except Heligoland.

MAR [**9**] Treaties of Chaumont, between the Allies, and arranged by Lord Castlereagh who has hurried to France to prevent the premature break-up of the Coalition. The treaties provide for continuing the struggle against Napoleon and guard against separate peace agreements. [**10**] Battle of Laon; the Allied forces defeat Napoleon. [**12**] Wellington captures Bordeaux. [**31**] The Allies' victorious entry into Paris; Napoleon is declared deposed in his absence by the French Senate.

APR [**10**] Soult's army is finally defeated by Wellington at Toulouse. [**11**] Napoleon abdicates. [**12**] The writer and composer Charles Burney dies. Byron sees Edmund Kean play Hamlet. [**20**] Louis XVIII, returning to France to claim his throne, makes a triumphal entry into London. The French King has to be lifted out of his carriage to greet the Prince Regent, who is dressed incongruously as a field-marshal.

MAY [**30**] First Peace of Paris, settled mainly by Castlereagh and Metternich; France is to renounce all claims to Germany, Italy, Holland, Switzerland and Malta, but to keep her 1792 borders.

JUN [6] The King of Prussia and Emperor of Russia arrive in London, to scenes of great popular excitement and acclaim. [8] The novelist Charles Reade is born. [22] The first cricket match is played at the Lord's Ground in London. [27] The King of Prussia and Emperor of Russia leave London for home.

JUL [1] The Watier's Masquerade for 1700 guests at Burlington House, held in honour of Wellington's return to England. Byron dresses as a monk, and Lady Caroline Lamb wears green pantaloons; Colonel Armstrong, the Duke of York's aide-de-camp, dresses up as an old lady, fanning himself and cracking outrageous jokes to 'admirers'. [19] Matthew Flinders, the explorer who surveyed and charted the coasts of Australia, dies at the age of 40.

SEP The Congress of Vienna begins (and lasts until June 1815): a conference to negotiate the Resettlement of Europe.

 Sir John Soane: Dulwich Picture Gallery; 13 Lincoln's Inn Fields, London.

 John Constable: *Old Sarum.*

 William Wordsworth: *The Excursion.*
Jane Austen: *Mansfield Park.*
Sir Walter Scott: *Waverley.*
Lord Byron: *The Corsair.*
Matthew Flinders: *A Voyage to Terra Australis.*
Legh Richmond: *The Annals of the Poor.*
Henry Salt: *A Voyage to Abyssinia.*

 John Field: *Nocturnes.*

1815 Sir Humphry Davy invents the miners' safety lamp. William Smith produces the first geological map of England and Wales. The quadrille is danced for the first time in Britain. Corn Law; imports of foreign grain are virtually banned from Britain until home-grown grain reaches a minimum price of 80 shillings a quarter, after which imports will be allowed in duty free. One effect of this measure is to cause even greater hardship to the working class by increasing the price of bread. John Loudon McAdam improves roads by the use of crushed stone and tarmac.

JAN [2] Lord Byron marries Annabella Milbanke, after two refusals; on their wedding night he wakes up shouting, 'Good God! I am surely in Hell!' [15] Emma Hamilton, Nelson's mistress, dies in poverty in Calais.

FEB [3] Leigh Hunt is released from prison. [26] Napoleon escapes from Elba.

APR   [**7**] Byron meets Sir Walter Scott for the first time; Byron gives Scott a silver urn from Greece and Scott gives him in return a Turkish dagger. [**24**] The novelist Anthony Trollope is born.

JUN   [**18**] Battle of Waterloo; in spite of Ney's great cavalry charges, Napoleon's army and political career are ruined: a great victory for Blücher and Wellington. To celebrate Waterloo, Southey and Wordsworth throw a party on the summit of Skiddaw, light a bonfire, roll lighted tar barrels down the mountain, and sing 'God Save The King'. [**22**] Napoleon's second abdication.

NOV   [**20**] Second Peace of Paris; this time France is restricted to her 1790 frontiers, all looted art treasures are to be returned, 700 million francs war indemnity are to be paid, and an Allied army of occupation is to be installed: France is to lose that part of Savoy that she had been allowed to keep in the First Peace. The Quadruple Alliance, between Britain, Austria, Prussia and Russia, is renewed. [**24**] Grace Darling, heroine of the famous 1838 North Sea rescue, is born at Bamburgh.

Henry Hakewill: Holy Trinity Church, Wolverton, Buckinghamshire.
John Nash: Royal Pavilion, Brighton (begun).

James Ward: *Gordale Scar.*
Charles Eastlake: *Napoleon on board the 'Bellerophon'.*
J. M. W. Turner: *Crossing the Brook.*

David Ricardo: *Influence of a Low Price of Corn on the Profits of Stock.*
Sir Walter Scott: *Guy Mannering.*
William Wordsworth: *The White Doe of Rylstone.*

1816   Lord Elgin sells the Elgin marbles to the British Museum. British forces defeat the King of Kandy; Ceylon becomes a British colony. Poverty and distress lead to rising numbers of people emigrating to North America. Britain enters an economic depression following the end of the Napoleonic Wars, contrary to popular expectation; dislocated and impoverished markets in Europe are unable to absorb the stockpiles of British manufactured goods. Thousands of people employed in industry are consequently thrown out of work. Unemployment is swelled further by the demobilization of 400,000 men in the armed services. George Canning joins the Cabinet as President of the Board of Control for India.

JAN   [**15**] Lady Byron leaves her husband, although apparently not because of his affair with his sister Augusta.

MAR The 10% income tax is abolished in an attempt to alleviate distress, but the benefits of this measure are offset by adding duties to many products, and this raises prices. [25] Byron is, as he requested, given first refusal on Napoleon's coronation robes by the French, but he does not take up this offer.

APR [13] William Sterndale Bennett, composer, is born at Sheffield. [21] The novelist Charlotte Brontë is born at Thornton, Yorkshire. [25] Byron sails from Dover into self-imposed exile in Italy.

MAY [2] The Prince Regent's daughter Charlotte marries Prince Leopold of Saxe-Coburg-Saalfeld.

JUN [27] Admiral Samuel Hood dies at Bath aged 91.

DEC [2] The Spa Fields Riot; a crowd gathers to hear an address on Parliamentary reform, and turns violent. [30] The poet Shelley marries Mary Wollstonecroft after his first wife's suicide.

Edward Blore and William Atkinson: Abbotsford, Roxburghshire, Scotland.
St John's Episcopal Chapel, Edinburgh.

Sir Henry Raeburn: *Master Henry Raeburn Inglis.*

Lady Caroline Lamb: *Glenarvon.*
Lord Byron: *The Prisoner of Chillon.*
Jane Austen: *Emma.*
William Cobbett: *Weekly Political Register.*
Sir Walter Scott: *The Antiquary.*
Thomas Love Peacock: *Headlong Hall.*
Humphry Davy: *Practical Hints on the Application of wire-gauze to Lamps for preventing Explosions in Coal Mines.*
David Ricardo: *Proposals for a Secure Currency.*
Percy Shelley: *Alastor.*

1817 In Derbyshire, workers riot in protest at low pay and unemployment. The Habeas Corpus Act is suspended after a secret report to Parliament about an imminent rebellion. The economic slump results in the Blanketeers' March and other disturbances. Shots are fired in an attempt to assassinate the Prince Regent after he opens Parliament. The painter George Frederick Watts is born. The Third Mahratha War begins in India, an Indian rebellion against British rule. The kaleidoscope is invented by Sir David Brewster.

MAR Coercion Acts; these repressive measures suspend the Habeas Corpus Act, extend the 1798 act against seditious meetings, extend to include the Prince Regent in all the safeguards against treason that have hitherto only secured the monarch, and provide for the punishment of all attempts to undermine the loyalty of soldiers and sailors.

JUL [**5**] The first sovereigns are issued. [**18**] The novelist Jane Austen dies in lodgings in College Street, Winchester.

NOV [**6**] The Prince Regent's daughter, Princess Charlotte, dies.

John Rennie: Waterloo Bridge, London (opened).
Sir John Soane: Royal Hospital Stables.

Francis Chantrey: *The Sleeping Children.*
John Constable: *Flatford Mill.*

Stamford Raffles: *The History of Java.*
Samuel Coleridge: *Biographia Literaria.*
Thomas Moore: *Lallah Rookh.*
John Keats: *Poems.*
Sir Walter Scott: *Old Mortality.*
William Hazlitt: *Characters of Shakespeare's Plays.*
Lord Byron: *Manfred.*
Thomas Rickman: *An Attempt to discriminate the Styles of English Architecture.*
David Ricardo: *On the Principles of Political Economy and Taxation.*
Jeremy Bentham: *Plan of Parliamentary Reform.*

1818 The first iron ship is built on the Clyde: the lighter *Vulcan.* The British East India Company effectively controls India. Java is given back to the Dutch.

JUL [**11**] William Duke of Clarence marries Adelaide, daughter of George Duke of Saxe-Meiningen. [**30**] The novelist Emily Brontë is born at Thornton, Yorkshire.

DEC [**24**] The physicist James Joule is born at Salford.

Sir Thomas Lawrence: *The Campaign Leaders* (18 portraits).

Jane Austen: *Northanger Abbey; Persuasion* (posthumous).
John Keats: *Endymion.*
Mary Shelley: *Frankenstein.*
Sir Walter Scott: *The Heart of Midlothian; Rob Roy.*
William Hazlitt: *Lectures on the English Poets.*
James Hogg: *The Brownie of Bodsbeck.*

1819 Britain acquires Singapore through the East India Company; it is administrated by Sir Stamford Raffles. The Factory Act is passed after a campaign by Robert Owen. The 'Six Acts' limit the scope of political meetings, to curb the spread of rioting. The steamship *Savannah* arrives at Liverpool, having crossed the Atlantic mainly under steam power. The painter William Frith is born.

FEB [**8**] The writer, artist and critic John Ruskin is born at Dulwich.

MAR [**11**] Sir Henry Tate, the philanthropist whose money and pictures are to be the foundation of the Tate Gallery, London, is born at Chorley.

APR [**11**] Sir Charles Hallé, pianist, conductor and founder of the Hallé Orchestra, is born in Germany.

MAY [**24**] Queen Victoria is born at Kensington Palace; she is the daughter of Edward Duke of Kent and Mary the daughter of Francis Duke of Saxe-Coburg-Saalfeld.

JUN [**5**] John Adams, astronomer and co-discoverer of the planet Neptune, is born near Launceston. [**12**] The clergyman and author Charles Kingsley is born at Hone vicarage.

AUG [**16**] A radical Parliamentary reform meeting at St Peter's Fields, Manchester, is dispersed by the army; 11 people are killed. The incident is widely referred to as the 'Peterloo' massacre and becomes a symbol of goverment repression. [**19**] James Watt, inventor of the modern steam engine, dies near Birmingham at the age of 83. [**26**] Prince Albert is born at Rosenau in Bavaria.

NOV [**22**] The novelist George Eliot is born near Nuneaton as Marian Evans.

DEC The 'Six Acts'; these increase the penalties for seditious libel, impose a newspaper stamp duty on all periodicals containing news (a blow aimed at the radical press), limit the scope of public meetings, forbid training in the use of weaponry, and empower magistrates to search for and seize arms. The Six Acts greatly increase the Cabinet's unpopularity and increase unrest.

 Thomas Telford: Menai Strait Suspension Bridge.
H. W. and W. Inwood: St Pancras Parish Church, London.

 Thomas (Lord) Macaulay: *Pompeii.*
William Wordsworth: *Peter Bell.*
Percy Shelley: *The Cenci.*
John Keats: *The Eve of St Agnes; Ode to a Nightingale; On a Grecian Urn; On Melancholy; To Psyche.*
Sir Walter Scott: *Ivanhoe.*
Lord Byron: *Mazeppa; Don Juan* (first cantos).
George Crabbe: *Tales of the Hall.*

1820 JAN   [**17**] The novelist Anne Brontë (known as Acton Bell) is born at Thornton, Yorkshire. [**23**] George III's son, Edward Duke of Kent, dies. [**29**] George III dies aged 81, the longest-lived and longest-reigning King of England. The Prince Regent accedes to the throne as George IV. His long-separated wife Caroline returns from the Continent to claim her position as Queen; she is warmly received by the public, who see her as grossly wronged by her husband. George IV nevertheless immediately induces his Cabinet ministers to begin divorce proceedings.

FEB   [**23**] The Cato Street Conspiracy, a plot to assassinate the entire Cabinet with explosives and set up a provisional government, is discovered; the conspiracy is led by Arthur Thistlewood. The Cato Street Conspiracy leads to renewed fears of radicalism and deals a severe blow to the cause of moderate reform.

MAR   [**30**] Anna Sewell, author of *Black Beauty*, is born at Great Yarmouth.

APR   [**10**] The first British settlers arrive in South Africa, landing at Algoa Bay.

MAY   [**12**] The hospital reformer Florence Nightingale is born in Florence.

JUN   [**19**] Sir Joseph Banks, the botanist who accompanied Captain Cook, dies.

JUL   [**5**] Introduction of the Bill of Pains and Penalties, designed to deprive the Queen of her royal title and dissolve the royal marriage. Canning resigns from Lord Liverpool's Cabinet over the treatment of Queen Caroline.

SEP   John Keats, dying of tuberculosis, sails to Italy.

NOV   [**10**] The Bill of Pains and Penalties is dropped by the Government when it sees that it will be heavily defeated in the Commons. The royal marriage fiasco results in a serious decline in the Cabinet's prestige.

 Samuel Brown: Union Bridge, Berwick-on-Tweed (completed). James Savage: St Luke's Church, Chelsea.

 John Constable: *Flatford Mill.*

 Lord Lytton: *Ismael.*
Henry Luttrell: *Advice to Julia.*
John Keats: *Lamia; Isabella; The Eve of St Agnes.*
Percy Shelley: *Prometheus Unbound.*
Charles Maturin: *Melmoth the Wanderer.*

1821 Sir Charles Wheatstone demonstrates that sound reproduction is possible. Famine in Ireland begins, lasting two years. The London Co-operative Wholesale Society is founded. Shortly before her death, Queen Caroline is granted an annuity of £50,000. Work begins on the building of the Stockton-Darlington Railway.

FEB   [**23**] The poet John Keats dies in Rome, aged only 25.
MAR   [**19**] The explorer and writer Sir Richard Burton is born at Torquay.
JUL   [**19**] Coronation of George IV in Westminster Abbey.
OCT   [**4**] The bridge designer John Rennie dies. [**11**] George Williams, founder of the YMCA in 1844, is born at Dulverton.

Sir Jeffry Wyatville: Sidney Sussex College, Cambridge (Tudorized).

William Blake: illustrations to *Jerusalem*.
John Constable: *The Hay Wain*.

Sir Walter Scott: *Kenilworth*.
Michael Faraday: *Principles of the Electric Motor*.
Percy Shelley: *Adonais, an elegy on the death of John Keats*.
Pierce Egan: *Life in London, or the Adventures of Tom and Jerry*.
William Hazlitt: *Table Talk*.
Thomas de Quincey: *Confessions of an English Opium Eater*.

1822 Congress of Verona; the congress system breaks down with Britain's refusal to intervene against revolution. The Royal Academy of Music in London is founded.

FEB   [**16**] Sir Francis Galton, pioneer in eugenics, is born in Birmingham.
JUL   [**8**] The poet Shelley is accidentally drowned off Leghorn in Italy while sailing in his boat *Ariel*.
AUG   [**12**] Lord Castlereagh commits suicide; George Canning replaces him as Foreign Secretary. [**25**] The astronomer Sir William Herschel dies.
OCT   [**20**] The author Thomas Hughes is born at Uffington.
DEC   [**24**] The poet and critic Matthew Arnold is born near Staines.

John Nash: Royal Pavilion, Brighton (completed).
William Atkinson: Abbotsford (completed).
Thomas Rickman: St George's Church, Birmingham.

Edward Bailey: *Eve at the Fountain*.
David Wilkie: *Chelsea pensioners reading the Gazette of the Battle of Waterloo*.

Frederick Marryat: *Suggestions for the Abolition of Impressment.*
Charles Colton: *Lacon, or Many Things in Few Words.*
Sir Walter Scott: *The Pirate; The Fortunes of Nigel; Peveril of the Peak.*
Thomas Peacock: *Maid Marian.*
Percy Shelley: *Hellas.*
Francis Place: *Illustrations and Proofs of the Principles of Population.*
William Wordsworth: *Description of the Scenery of the Lakes.*

1823 Michael Faraday succeeds in liquefying chlorine. Charles Babbage invents a rudimentary calculator. Von Beuth, the Prussian Minister of Commerce, travels in Britain and is impressed by the size and modern construction methods of British factories; many are eight and nine storeys high with thin walls, iron columns and iron beams. The death penalty is abolished for over 100 different crimes. Robert Peel initiates a pioneering prison reform act. Charles Macintosh invents waterproof fabric. The portrait sculptor Joseph Nollekens dies.

JAN   [**3**] Robert Whitehead, inventor of the naval torpedo, is born at Bolton-Le-Moors. [**26**] Edward Jenner, pioneer in vaccination, dies at Berkeley.
FEB   [**7**] The writer Ann Radcliffe dies.
SEP   [**11**] The economist David Ricardo dies.
OCT   [**30**] Edmund Cartwright, inventor of the power loom, dies at Hastings aged 80.
NOV   [**25**] Brighton's Chain Pier is opened.

W. H. Playfair: Royal Scottish Academy, Edinburgh.
Sir Robert Smirke: British Museum, London (begun).
William Wilkins: New Court, Corpus Christi College, Cambridge (begun)
Chain Pier, Brighton.
Sir Charles Barry: St Peter's Church, Brighton.
Thomas Cubitt: Polesden Lacey, Dorking, Surrey.

J. M. W. Turner: *The Bay of Baiae.*

Mrs Sharpe: *Dame Wiggins of Lee and her Seven Wonderful Cats.*
Charles Lamb: *Essays of Elia.*
Sir Walter Scott: *Quentin Durward.*
Isaac D'Israeli: *Curiosities of Literature.*

1824 The painters Constable and Bonington exhibit their work at the so-called 'English Salon' in Paris. The Anglo-Burmese Wars begin, after Burmese aggression; Britain moves towards the annexation of Burma. After a campaign led by Francis Place and Joseph Hume, the Combination Acts which have forbidden trade unions are repealed.

JAN   [**8**] The writer Wilkie Collins is born in London.

FEB   [**10**] Samuel Plimsoll is born at Bristol.

MAR   [**4**] The Royal Naval Lifeboat Institution is founded by Sir William Hillary.

APR   [**19**] Lord Byron dies at sunset of marsh fever at Missolonghi during the Greeks' struggle for independence: he is 36.

JUN   [**26**] The physicist and mathematician Lord Kelvin is born in Belfast as William Thomson.

OCT   [**21**] Portland cement is patented by Joseph Aspdin of Wakefield.

 Lord Byron: *Don Juan.*
Percy Shelley: *Posthumous Poems.*
Sir Walter Scott: *Redgauntlet.*
James Hogg: *Private Memoirs and Confessions of a Justified Sinner.*
George Wells: *Joseph and his Brethren.*

1825 Michael Faraday isolates benzene. Horse-drawn buses appear in London. An act to regulate cotton mills and factories is passed; children under 16 are not allowed to work more than 12 hours a day. The electromagnet is invented by William Sturgeon.

MAY   [**4**] Thomas Huxley is born.

JUN   [**24**] W. H. Smith, the founder of the book-selling chain, is born in London.

SEP   [**27**] The steam locomotive 'Active' pulls the first train 27 miles along the Stockton-Darlington railway line, starting from Shildon: this is the first railway to carry goods and passengers.

Sir Robert Smirke: Post Office, St Martins-le-Strand, London.
Thomas Telford: Menai Straits Suspension Bridge (completed).
Decimus Burton: Hyde Park screen, London.
Thomas Rickman: Ombersley Church, Worcestershire.

Samuel Palmer: *A Valley Thick With Corn.*

James Mill: *Analysis of the Phenomenon of the Human Mind.*
Robert Ward: *Tremaine, or the Man of Refinement.*
Sir Walter Scott: *The Talisman.*

Lord Braybrooke (ed): *Pepys' Diary.*
Charles Wolfe: *The Burial of Sir John Moore.*

 Beethoven: *Ninth Symphony* (first performance in Britain).

1826 The Royal Zoological Society is founded in London by Sir Stamford Raffles. The Burmese War ends with the Treaty of Yandabu. Sir Walter Scott is financially ruined by the collapse of his publisher, Ballantyne & Co.

JUL [**5**] Sir Stamford Raffles, founder of Singapore, dies in London.

 Thomas Rickman: New Court, St John's College, Cambridge (and Bridge of Sighs).
Thomas Telford: Conway Road Suspension Bridge (begun).

 John Constable: *The Cornfield.*

 Richard Whately: *Elements of Logic.*
Benjamin Disraeli: *Vivian Grey.*
Sir Walter Scott: *Woodstock.*

1827 John Walker, a chemist at Stockton-on-Tees, sells his first box of friction matches; unfortunately, he does not bother to take out a patent on his invention. Richard Bright first describes the disease that bears his name. The Treaty of London is signed by Britain, France and Russia to protect the Greeks from Turkish tyranny. A combined British, Russian and French fleet under Admiral Codrington destroys a Turkish-Egyptian fleet in Navarino Bay.

JAN [**5**]Frederick Duke of York, George III's second son, dies.
APR [**2**] The painter William Holman Hunt is born. [**5**] Joseph Lister, surgeon and pioneer of antiseptics, is born. [**10**] Lord Liverpool resigns as Prime Minister after suffering a stroke. [**30**] The Tory George Canning succeeds as Prime Minister.
MAY [**18**] William Corder murders Maria Marten in the Red Barn at Corder Farm, Polstead: her body is not discovered for a year.
JUN [**26**] Samuel Crompton, inventor of the spinning-mule in 1779, dies at Bolton.
JUL [**16**] The potter Josiah Spode dies.
AUG [**8**] George Canning, Prime Minister for only three months, dies at Chiswick. [**31**] Viscount Goderich (Earl of Ripon) succeeds Canning as Prime Minister.

John Nash: Cumberland Terrace, Regent's Park.
James Savage: St James's Church, Bermondsey.
Charles Fowler: Syon House Conservatory.

 Thomas Hood: *The Plea of the Midsummer Fairies.*
Sir Thomas Lauder: *The Wolfe of Badenoch.*
Lady Charlotte Bury: *Flirtation.*
John Clare: *The Shepherd's Calendar.*

1828 The London Protocol is concluded by Britain, France and Russia, recognizing Greek independence. University and King's Colleges, London, are founded. James Nielson first uses a blast furnace. The Australian interior is explored by Charles Sturt.

JAN [**22**] Lord Goderich resigns as Prime Minister; he is succeeded by the Duke of Wellington.

FEB [**12**] The poet and novelist George Meredith is born at Portsmouth.

APR [**27**] Regent's Park in London is opened.

MAY [**9**] The Test Act is repealed. [**12**] The poet and painter Dante Gabriel Rossetti is born in London as Gabriel Charles Dante.

JUL [**15**] A new Corn Law is passed; imports of foreign grain are allowed with duties on a sliding scale, varying with the current price of British corn. [**21**] Archbishop Sutton dies.

AUG [**15**] William Howley, Bishop of London, becomes Archbishop of Canterbury.

OCT [**31**] Sir Joseph Swan, inventor (independently of Edison) of the electric lamp, is born at Sunderland.

 Francis Chantrey: Statue of George IV, Trafalgar Square, London.

 Lord Lytton: *Pelham.*
Sir Walter Scott: *The Fair Maid of Perth.*
J. Curtis: *An Authentic and Faithful History of the Mysterious Murder of Maria Marten in the Red Barn.*
William Cobbett: *A Letter to the Pope.*
Pierce Egan: *Finish to the story of Tom, Jerry and Logic.*

1829 Thomas Graham, a Scottish chemist, formulates his law on the diffusion of gases. Suttee, the Indian practice of sacrificing a widow on her husband's funeral pyre, is declared illegal in British India. The Irish leader Daniel O'Connell MP begins to agitate for repeal of the Act of Union. The Earl of Surrey becomes the first Catholic MP, representing Horsham. The composer Felix Mendelssohn visits the Hebrides.

APR [10] William Booth, founder of the Salvation Army, is born at Nottingham.

MAY [29] Sir Humphry Davy, inventor of the miners' safety lamp in 1815, dies in Geneva.

JUN [8] Sir John Millais, painter, is born at Southampton. [10] The first Oxford and Cambridge University boat race takes place; Oxford wins easily. [19] Sir Robert Peel founds the London Metropolitan Police Force.

JUL [4] The first regular scheduled bus service in Britain is introduced in London by George Shillibeer.

OCT [6] Trials begin at Rainhill near Liverpool for a locomotive for use on the Liverpool and Manchester Railway. The five entrants are 'Rocket', 'Cycloped', 'Sans Pareil', 'Perseverance', 'Novelty'; Stephenson's 'Rocket' is the winner.

Thomas Hamilton: The Royal High School, Edinburgh.
John Nash: St James's Park, London.
Pembroke College, Oxford (Tudorized).
Xavierian Seminary, Brighton (one of the first 'Italian' villas).
Peter Robinson: Swiss Cottage, London.
Decimus Burton: Athenaeum Club, London (begun).

John Constable: *The Leaping Horse; Hadleigh Castle.*
Benjamin Haydon: *Punch and Judy.*

Thomas Hood: *The Epping Hunt.*
Gerald Griffin: *The Collegians.*
Frederick Marryat: *Frank Mildmay.*
Thomas Peacock: *The Misfortunes of Elphin.*
James Hogg: *The Shepherd's Calendar.*

1830 The first major cholera epidemic strikes Britain. The British East India company takes Mysore.

JUN [26] George IV dies, succeeded by his brother as William IV.

SEP [15] The politician William Huskisson is knocked down and killed by Stephenson's 'Rocket' at Parkside; the accident happens when he is attending the opening of the Liverpool and Manchester Railway, the first railway in the world to be built for passenger traffic as well as for freight. It marks the beginning of the railway age.

NOV [16] The Duke of Wellington resigns as Prime Minister. He is succeeded by the Whig Earl Grey, whose liberal Cabinet is determined to make Parliamentary reforms.

DEC [5] The poetess Christina Rossetti is born.

Covent Garden Market, London.
St Dunstan-in-the-West, Fleet Street, London.
Thomas Hamilton: Burns Monument, Calton Hill, Edinburgh.

 George Richmond: *The Eve of Separation.*
Samuel Palmer: *Coming from Evening Church.*
William Etty: *The Storm.*

 Alfred Tennyson: *Poems.*
William Cobbett: *Rural Rides.*
Lord Lytton: *Paul Clifford.*

1831 The Captain Swing riots; rebellion in rural areas of England against the mechanization of agriculture and low pay for farm labourers. Britain and France guarantee the independence of Belgium. Michael Faraday discovers electro-magnetic induction (previously discovered by Joseph Henry but not published).

FEB   [**27**] Captain John Briscoe discovers the continent of Antarctica.
MAR   [**22**] The First Reform Bill is introduced by Lord John Russell and rejected by the Lords.
APR   [**19**] Lord Grey dissolves Parliament, going to the country with the Reform Bill as the main issue. The election result is a Whig triumph.
JUN   [**1**] James Ross finds the North Magnetic Pole and plants a Union Jack there.
AUG   [**7**] Dean Farrar, writer of school stories, is born in Bombay.
SEP   [**8**] Coronation of William IV. [**21**] The Second Reform Bill is passed in the Commons.
OCT   [**8**] The Second Reform Bill is rejected by the Lords. Agitation for reform in the country now turns violent; troops kill or maim 100 people and civil war is narrowly averted.
DEC   [**27**] The Admiralty survey ship *HMS Beagle*, with Charles Darwin on board, sets out from Plymouth on its famous five-year scientific voyage round the world; its findings are to have profound effects on scientific thought.

 John Rennie: New London Bridge (completed).
Hungerford Market, Charing Cross, London.

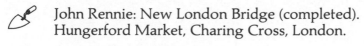 Thomas Peacock: *Crotchet Castle.*
Edward Trelawney: *Adventures of a Younger Son.*
William Cobbett: *Cobbett's Penny Trash.*

1832 A cholera epidemic kills thousands of people in Britain. William Ewart Gladstone enters politics. The Irish Reform Act is passed.

JAN   [**27**] Lewis Carroll (Charles Lutwidge Dodgson) is born at Daresbury.

MAR   [**23**] The Third Reform Bill is passed by the Commons. The Lords demand amendments, which leads to renewed popular agitation. Grey advises the King to create enough liberal peers to pass the measure; William IV refuses, and Grey and his Cabinet resign. Wellington is unable to form an alternative ministry. William IV is forced to recall Grey and promise to appoint the new peers if they are needed.

JUN   [**4**] The threat of a changed composition of the House of Lords is sufficient to force the more reactionary Lords to withdraw, allowing the passage of the Bill. [**6**] Jeremy Bentham dies.

SEP   [**21**] Sir Walter Scott dies at Abbotsford. [**30**] Field Marshal Lord Roberts is born at Cawnpore in India.

William Wilkins: National Gallery, London.

Sir Walter Scott: *Count Robert of Paris; Castle Dangerous.*
Lord Lytton: *Eugene Aram.*

1833 The Tithe War continues in Ireland; the predominantly Catholic Irish resent the enforced payment of tithes to support the Protestant Church, and resort to violence. Britain's sovereignty over the Falkland Islands is proclaimed. The East India Company is granted a renewal of its charter, with the proviso that its monopoly of trade with China and India will end. The first Education Grant of £20,000 for elementary education is passed. The painter and designer Sir Edward Burne-Jones is born. The 'Oxford Movement' in the Anglican Church begins: it involves a belief in a 'catholic', i.e. undivided, Church.

JAN   [**28**] General Gordon is born at Woolwich.

APR   Coercion Bill; this gives the Lord Lieutenant of Ireland unlimited powers to supress public meetings. [**22**] Richard Trevithick, pioneer of steam railway locomotives, dies at Dartford.

JUL   [**29**] William Wilberforce, who played a large part in the abolition of slavery, dies.

AUG   [**2**] Irish Church Temporalities Bill; this attempt to reduce the burden of tithes outrages O'Connell and his followers. [**23**] Slavery is abolished in the British colonies, and compensation totalling £20 million is provided for slave-owners.

[**29**] Factory Act; the first measure of its kind, applied only to the textile industry, but it is the forerunner of a whole string of reforms; it forbids the employment of children under the age of nine, and children under 13 are to have two hours of schooling a day.

SEP [**15**] Tennyson's close friend Arthur Hallam dies suddenly in Vienna at the age of 22.

 Wilberforce Monument, Westminster Abbey.

 Michael Scott: *Tom Cringle's Log.*
Sir Charles Lyell: *The Principles of Geology*, Vol 3 (completed).
Elizabeth Barrett Browning: *Prometheus Bound.*

1834 Michael Faraday discovers electrical self-induction. The colony of Victoria is founded in Australia. The artist James Whistler is born.

JAN Robert Owen sets up the Grand National Consolidated Trades Union, with the aim of organizing a general strike for an eight-hour working day. This results in a Government clamp-down.

MAR [**6**] The novelist and artist George du Maurier is born. [**17**] Kate Greenaway, illustrator of children's books, is born. [**18**] Six Dorset farm workers, the Tolpuddle Martyrs, are sentenced to transportation to Australia for swearing an oath to join a trade union; they formed a lodge of the Grand National. [**24**] The artist, publisher, writer and designer William Morris is born.

APR [**22**] The Quadruple Alliance (Britain, France, Spain and Portugal) is formed to protect Spain and Portugal.

JUL [**2**] Grey resigns as Prime Minister, succeeded by Lord Melbourne. [**25**] The poet Coleridge dies.

AUG [**14**] The New Poor Law (Poor Law Amendment Act) provides workhouses for the destitute; it also takes Poor Law administration away from the old parish authorities and gives it to elected Boards.

SEP [**2**] Thomas Telford, engineer, 'the Colossus of Roads', dies.

OCT [**16**] The Palace of Westminster is burnt down; firemen manage to save Westminster Hall and St Stephen's Chapel.

NOV [**15**] Lord Melbourne resigns as Prime Minister; he is succeeded by Sir Robert Peel.

DEC [**23**] The Hansom cab is patented by the architect Joseph Hansom. Thomas Malthus, the economist, dies. [**27**] Charles Lamb, essayist and friend of Coleridge and Wordsworth, dies.

Lord Lytton: *The Last Days of Pompeii*.
Harrison Ainsworth: *Rockwood*.
Frederick Marryat: *Peter Simple*.

 Tom Cooke: *King Arthur and the Knights of the Round Table*.

1835 British trade with China increases as the East India Company's monopoly ends. 4000 Boers begin the Great Trek in South Africa to find new territory free from British rule. English becomes the official government language in India. The abolition of slavery in the colonies leads to increases in the prices of products. An early computer is invented by Charles Babbage.

JAN   In the General Election, Sir Robert Peel sets out his conception of a new kind of liberal Conservatism in the 'Tamworth Manifesto'; it embodies an acceptance of the 1832 Reform Act and a readiness to proceed with a programme of moderate reforms.

APR   [**18**] The Whig Lord Melbourne becomes Prime Minister again.

MAY   [**13**] John Nash, architect of Regent's Park and Brighton Pavilion, dies on the Isle of Wight. [**16**] Felicia Hemans, the poetess who wrote *The boy stood on the burning deck*, dies in Dublin. [**30**] The poet Alfred Austin is born.

JUN   [**18**] William Cobbett, journalist and reformer, dies near Guildford.

NOV   [**21**] The poet James Hogg dies.

DEC   [**4**] The novelist and satirist Samuel Butler is born.

Anthony Salvin: Harlaxton Manor, Lincolnshire.
Sir Charles Barry and Augustus Pugin: Houses of Parliament.
Harvey Elmes: Fitzwilliam Museum, Cambridge.
Philip Hardwick: Doric Arch at Euston, London.

William Wordsworth: *Extempore Effusion on the Death of James Hogg*.
John Clare: *The Rural Muse*.
William Cobbett: *Cobbett's Opinion of the Whig Ministry*.
Samuel Lover: *The Olympic Picnic*.

Michael Balfe: *The Siege of Rochelle*.

1836 The Tithe Commutation Act orders that tithes should be paid in cash, not in kind. Parliament provides for the systematic registration of births, marriages and deaths. The Chartist Movement starts, when a

Working-men's Association in London sets out its programme for Parliamentary reform in a People's Charter, in effect a petition addressed to Parliament. The Charter demands manhood suffrage, vote by ballot, the abolition of the property qualification for MPs, payment of MPs, equal electoral districts, and annual Parliaments. The working class is rapidly won over to the People's Charter by missionary speakers who tour the country addressing huge public meetings. Screw propeller invented by Sir Francis Smith.

MAR [**2**] The first point-to-point meeting is held, at the Madresfield Estate by the Worcester Hunt.

MAY [**17**] Sir Norman Lockyer, discoverer of helium, is born.

 I. K. Brunel: Clifton Suspension Bridge (702ft span), Avon Gorge (begun). [Work suspended in 1851 and resumed in 1861.]
Scott Monument, Edinburgh.
Wrest Park Orangery, Bedfordshire.
George Basevi: Fitzwilliam Museum, Cambridge (begun).

Robert Owen: *The Book of the New Moral World.*
Charles Dickens: *Pickwick Papers* (begins).
Frederick Marryat: *Mr Midshipman Easy.*

1837 Isaac Pitman invents his system of shorthand. Charles Wheatstone and William Cooke invent the first electric telegraph. Disraeli makes his maiden speech in the House of Commons. The composer Samuel Wesley dies.

JAN [**20**] Sir John Soane, architect, dies in London. [**23**] John Field, composer and inventor of the nocturne, dies.

MAR [**31**] The painter John Constable dies.

APR [**5**] The poet Algernon Swinburne is born. [**20**] Robert Southey writes to Charlotte Brontë, telling her that 'Literature cannot be the business of a woman's life, and it ought not to be'.

JUN [**20**] William IV dies at Windsor, succeeded by Queen Victoria. Hanover now becomes separated from Britain because female succession is forbidden by Salic Law; Ernest Augustus, Duke of Cumberland and son of George III, succeeds as King of Hanover.

JUL [**1**] Registration of births, marriages and deaths begins in Britain. [**13**] Queen Victoria adopts Buckingham Palace as the official royal residence. [**19**] Brunel's 'Great Western' is launched at Bristol. [**20**] Euston Railway Station, the first in London, is opened.

Sir Robert Smirke: British Museum, London.
Anthony Salvin: Scotney Castle, Kent.
Samuel Beazley: St James's Theatre, London.
Augustus Pugin: Scarisbrook Hall, Lancashire.
Sir Charles Barry: Reform Club, Pall Mall, London.

 Sir Edwin Landseer: *The Old Shepherd's Chief Mourner.*
Edward Bailey: Statue of Earl Grey, Newcastle.

 Thomas Peacock: *Paper Money Lyrics.*
Thomas Carlyle: *The French Revolution.*
Robert Browning: *Strafford.*

 Michael Balfe: *Joan of Arc.*

1838 The Chartist Movement grows, especially in the North. War breaks out between the British and the Afghans; the First Afghan War results from British attempts to curb Russian influence. The National Gallery opens.

FEB The first reported attack by Spring-Heeled Jack, who is apparently a sadist wearing a hideous mask and metal claws; he brutally assaults a girl called Jane Alsop in Bow. [6] The actor Sir Henry Irving is born in Somerset as John Henry Brodribb.

APR [8] Regular steamship services between Britain and America start; Brunel's *Great Western* leaves Bristol for New York on her maiden voyage under Captain James Hosken. [22] The *Sirius* reaches Sandy Hook, New York, becoming the first ship to cross the Atlantic entirely under steam power (left Queenstown on April 4).

JUN [28] Coronation of Queen Victoria. [31] Poor Law Bill introduced, designed to extend to Ireland the provisions of the New Poor Law.

SEP [7] The *Forfarshire* is wrecked near the Farne Islands off the Northumberland coast; Grace Darling rescues the crew.

 Sir Charles Barry: Trentham Hall, Staffordshire (rebuilt).
Corn Exchange, Winchester.

 J. M. W. Turner: *The Fighting Temeraire.*

 Charles Dickens: *Oliver Twist.*
Robert Surtees: *Jorrocks' Jaunts and Jollities.*
Thomas Carlyle: *Sartor Resartus.*

Michael Balfe: *Falstaff.*

1839 William Fox Talbot invents photography (simultaneously with the French Daguerre). Kirkpatrick MacMillan of Dumfries invents the first true bicycle. The Peninsula and Oriental Line begins a regular steamship service between Britain and Egypt, to meet East India Company ships coming from the east. The Treaty of London establishes the independence of Belgium.

FEB The first National Convention of Chartists is held in London. [**26**] The first official Grand National Steeplechase is run at Aintree; it is won by Jem Mason on 'Lottery'.

APR [**9**] The Jamaica problem surfaces in British politics. The liberation of slaves creates great difficulties for the planters, who have treated the slaves with brutality. In view of the disorder, Melbourne feels obliged to suspend the Jamaica Constitution for five years, but feels that his own position has become untenable.

MAY [**7**] Melbourne resigns. [**13**] The Charter is presented to Parliament, but it is rejected.

JUN [**12**] Wordsworth receives an honorary doctorate at Oxford. [**14**] The first Henley Regatta takes place.

JUL There are Chartist riots in Birmingham.

OCT [**25**] The first national railway timetable, *Bradshaw's Railway Companion,* is published.

NOV [**3**] The Opium War with China breaks out. [**4**] There is a Chartist riot at Newport, South Wales; the crowd is fired on by constables and 20 people are killed. John Frost, the Chartist leader, is sentenced to transportation.

Augustus Pugin: St Chad's Cathedral, Birmingham.
Harvey Elmes: St George's Hall, Liverpool.
Southampton Railway Station.
Philip Hardwick: Euston Hotel, London.

Thomas Boys: *Picturesque architecture in Paris.*
Frederick Radcliffe: *The Noble Science, a few general ideas on fox-hunting.*
George Reynolds: *Pickwick Abroad.*
Col. Philip Taylor: *Confessions of a Thug.*
Charles Dickens: *Nicholas Nickleby.*

1840 Sir William Grove invents the incandescent electric light. The Botanical Gardens at Kew are opened. The Afghan War ends with the

Afghans surrendering. Treaty of London; Britain, Russia, Prussia and Austria agree to limit Egyptian expansion. Municipal Act; this confers the right to vote on all persons paying at least £10 rent a year.

JAN [**6**] Fanny Burney, novelist, diarist and friend of Dr Johnson, dies. [**10**] The Penny Post is instituted.

FEB [**5**] John Boyd Dunlop, vet and patentee of the pneumatic bicycle tyre, is born at Dreghorn. [**10**] Queen Victoria marries Prince Albert of Saxe-Coburg-Gotha; both are aged 20.

MAR [**30**] Beau Brummell, the Regency dandy, dies at Caen in a pauper lunatic asylum.

APR [**27**] Edward Whymper, mountaineer and the first person to climb the Matterhorn, is born in London.

MAY [**6**] The first adhesive postage stamps (Penny Black and Twopence Blue) are introduced; the first stamp on the first sheet of Penny Blacks is stuck on a letter to George Waterman of Thame, Oxfordshire. [**21**] New Zealand is declared a British Colony.

JUN [**2**] The novelist Thomas Hardy is born at Bockhampton. [**6**] John Stainer, composer, is born. [**10**] Edward Oxford, a servant in a pub, fires two shots at Queen Victoria and Prince Albert as they travel up Constitution Hill in an open carriage: both shots miss. Oxford is sent to a mental hospital, then exiled.

JUL [**4**] Samuel Cunard founds the Cunard Steamship Company, and his first vessel, the *Britannia*, sails on her maiden voyage from Liverpool to Halifax, Nova Scotia.

SEP [**22**] George III's daughter Augusta dies.

NOV [**21**] The first of Queen Victoria's children, Victoria, is born.

Prince's Gate, Knightsbridge.
Christ Church, Streatham.
Joseph Paxton: Chatsworth Conservatory (completed).

Francis Danby: *The Deluge.*
J. M. W. Turner: *The Slave Ship.*

Henry Cockton: *The Life and Adventures of Valentine Fox.*
Pierce Egan: *Robin Hood and Little John* (Penny Dreadful serial).
Harrison Ainsworth: *The Tower of London.*
William Thackeray: *Catherine.*
Matthew Arnold: *Alaric at Rome.*
Thomas Carlyle: *Chartism.*

1841 The Straits Convention; Russia, Britain, France and Austria agree to close the Dardanelles and Bosporus to foreign shipping. The Second

Afghan War begins after Afghans massacre British soldiers. Sir James Clark Ross discovers some of the coastline of Antarctica. The British Pharmaceutical Society is founded.

JAN   [**26**] Britain acquires Hong Kong. [**28**] Sir Henry Stanley, journalist and explorer, is born at Denbigh as John Rowlands.

AUG   [**28**] Lord Melbourne resigns as Prime Minister. [**30**] The Tory Robert Peel becomes Prime Minister again.

NOV   [**9**] Edward VII, second child and eldest son of Queen Victoria, is born at St James's Palace.

DEC   [**4**] Edward is created Prince of Wales.

Charles Cockerell: Ashmolean and Taylorian Building, Oxford.
Sir Gilbert Scott: Protestant Martyrs' Memorial, Oxford.

Frederick Marryat: *Masterman Ready*.
Charles Dickens: *The Old Curiosity Shop; Barnaby Rudge*.
Robert Browning: *Pippa Passes*.
Augustus Pugin: *Contrasts*.
Charles Mackay: *Memoirs of extraordinary popular delusions and the madness of crowds*.
Punch (first edition July 17).

1842 The first railway telegraph system, between Paddington and Slough, comes into service. The Treaty of Nanking ends the Opium Wars and opens Chinese ports to British trade. British forces surrender at Kabul, and are wiped out during their retreat to India. Mudie's lending library opens in London. James Nasmyth invents the steam hammer. Lord Ashley's Mines Act prohibits the employment of child or female labour underground. Peel abolishes the prohibition on meat and cattle imports.

APR   [**12**] – MAY [**12**] The Second National Convention of Chartists; a second petition to Parliament is rejected on May 3.

MAY   [**13**] Sir Arthur Sullivan, composer of operettas, is born at Lambeth. [**30**] John Francis attempts to assassinate the Queen as she drives down Constitution Hill with Prince Albert.

JUN   [**12**] Thomas Arnold, educationalist and reformer, dies aged 46. [**13**] Queen Victoria's first train journey, from Slough to Paddington.

SEP   [**20**] Sir James Dewar, inventor of the vacuum flask, is born at Kincardine-on-Forth.

OCT   [**20**] Grace Darling, who saved the crew of the *Forfarshire*, dies.

NOV   [**12**] The physicist Lord Rayleigh is born at Witham near Maldon.

John Carr and Robert Adam: Harewood House, Leeds.
Sir Jas. Pennethorne: West Wing, Somerset House, London.

 Samuel Lover: *Handy Andy.*
Alfred Tennyson: *Morte d'Arthur; The Lady of Shalott.*
Lord Macaulay: *Lays of Ancient Rome.*
John Wilson: *Recreations of Christopher North.*
Edwin Chadwick: *The Sanitary Conditions of the Labouring Population.*
Illustrated London News (first edition).

1843 In Ireland, Daniel O'Connell persistently demands the repeal of the Union, and his Young Ireland Party causes unrest; O'Connell and his co-agitators are arrested and the situation quietens. Maori revolts against the British break out in New Zealand. The first workers' Co-operative Society is formed: the Pioneers of Rochdale.

MAR [**21**] Robert Southey, Poet Laureate since 1813, dies at Keswick. [**25**] The Thames Tunnel, linking Wapping and Rotherhithe, is formally opened; it is later turned into a tube tunnel.

APR [**6**] William Wordsworth is appointed Poet Laureate. [**15**] Henry James, American novelist, is born in New York. [**21**] Augustus, Duke of Clarence dies. [**25**] The royal yacht *Victoria and Albert* is launched at Pembroke. Queen Victoria's daughter Alice is born.

JUN [**21**] The Royal College of Surgeons is founded.

JUL [**19**] Brunel's *Great Britain*, the first all-metal liner, is launched at Wapping by Prince Albert. [**25**] Charles Macintosh, the chemist who patented waterproof fabric in 1823, dies in Glasgow.

OCT [**1**] The *News of the World* begins publication.

NOV [**3-4**] The 17-foot statue of Lord Nelson is hauled up in two pieces to the top of the column in Trafalgar Square. [**21**] Vulcanized rubber is patented by Thomas Hancock.

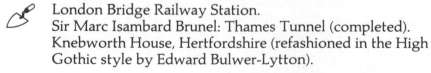 London Bridge Railway Station.
Sir Marc Isambard Brunel: Thames Tunnel (completed).
Knebworth House, Hertfordshire (refashioned in the High Gothic style by Edward Bulwer-Lytton).

Edward Bailey: Statue of Nelson, Trafalgar Square, London.
J. M. W. Turner: *'The Sun of Venice' going to sea.*

John Stuart Mill: *A System of Logic.*
John Ruskin: *Modern Painters*, Volume I.

Charles Dickens: *A Christmas Carol.*
Richard Horne: *Orion.*
Matthew Arnold: *Cromwell.*

1844 Potato famine in Ireland. Railway mania grips the country; massive speculation and investment lead to the building of 5000 miles of track this year and the next. Bank Charter Act; Peel gives the Bank of England a monopoly on printing money, but separates banking and note-issuing into two separate departments.

MAY   [**3**] The theatre impresario Richard D'Oyly Carte is born.
JUL   [**22**] Revd William Spooner, originator of spoonerisms, is born. [**27**] John Dalton, chemist and physicist, dies.
AUG   [**6**] Queen Victoria's son Alfred is born.
OCT   [**23**] Robert Bridges, Poet Laureate, is born at Walmer.
DEC   [**21**] The Rochdale Pioneers open the first co-operative shop, at Toad Lane.

Charles Cockerell: Bank of England, Liverpool.
Sir William Tite: Royal Exchange, London.

Sir Edwin Landseer: *The Challenge.*
J. M. W. Turner: *Rain, Steam and Speed.*

James Rymer: *The Black Monk* (a Penny Blood).
Charles Dickens: *Martin Chuzzlewit.*
William Thackeray: *Barry Lyndon.*
Benjamin Disraeli: *Coningsby.*
Robert Chambers: *Vestiges of the Natural History of Creation.*

Michael Balfe: *The Bohemian Girl.*

1845 Potato famine in Ireland continues. The world's largest telescope is built in Ireland by the Earl of Rosse, an amateur astronomer; it allows a view, for the first time, of galaxies beyond our own. Peel's 'Free Trade' Budget repeals all export duties and many import duties. The Maori rebellion in New Zealand continues. The Anglo-Sikh Wars in northern India result in Britain annexing the Punjab.

FEB   [**7**] The Portland Vase, a unique dark blue carved Roman glass vessel, is smashed by a madman with a stone; it is afterwards restored.
MAR   [**11**] Self-raising flour is patented by Henry Jones of Bristol.
MAY   [**3**] The poet Thomas Hood dies after a long illness.
JUN   [**17**] Richard Barham, author of the *Ingoldsby Legends*, dies.
JUL   [**4**] Thomas Barnardo, founder of homes for destitute children, is born in Dublin. [**26**] The *Great Britain*, Brunel's only

surviving ship, leaves Liverpool on her maiden voyage to
New York.

Oct [12] The social worker and prison reformer Elizabeth Fry dies.

Dec [10] The first pneumatic tyres are patented by Scottish
engineer Robert Thomson.

Charles Cockerell: Bank of England, Manchester.
Prince Albert and Lewis Cubitt: Osborne House, Isle of Wight.
Jesse Hartley: Albert Dock, Liverpool.
W. H. Playfair: National Gallery, Edinburgh.

William Dyce: *The Madonna and Child.*

Sheridan Lefanu: *The Cock and Anchor.*
Richard Cobbold: *The History of Margaret Catchpole.*
Benjamin Disraeli: *Sybil.*
Friedrich Engels: *Situation of the Working Classes in England.*

1846 The continuing famine in Ireland results in mass emigration to the
United States. Defeated by the British, the Sikhs settle for peace under
the Treaty of Lahore. Louis Napoleon escapes from the fortress where
he has been confined and reaches London. Mendelssohn's *Elijah* is
first performed at the Birmingham Festival.

May [15] Customs Law; this measure abolishes duty on all live
animals and nearly every kind of meat, and reduces the duties
on other foods.

Jun [6] Repeal of the Corn Laws; the import duty on corn is fixed
at one shilling a quarter from 1849 onwards, and there is to be
a small protective duty on corn between now and 1849. [27]
Charles Parnell, Irish politician, is born at Avondale in County
Wicklow. [29] Peel's government is overthrown by a revolt
led by Disraeli, who objects to a new coercion Bill for Ireland.
[30] The Whig Lord John Russell becomes Prime Minister.

Sir Charles Barry: The Treasury, Whitehall, London
(remodelled).
Philip Hardwick: The Great Hall, Euston Station, London
(begun).

Richard Redgrave: *The Seamstress.*

Edward Lear: *Book of Nonsense.*
George Reynolds: *Faust* (Penny Dreadful).
Charlotte Brontë: *The Professor* (written; not published until
1857).

Douglas Jerrold: *Mrs Caudle's Curtain Lectures.*
Brontë sisters: *Poems* by Acton, Currer and Ellis Bell.

1847 Famine and the resulting distress continue in Ireland; mass emigration also continues. Factory Act; women and young people 13-18 are prohibited from working more than 10 hours a day. British Museum opens. Dr James Simpson first uses chloroform as an anaesthetic.

JAN   [**14**] Wilson Carlile, founder of the Church Army, is born at Buxton.
FEB   [**27**] The actress Ellen Terry is born at Coventry.
MAR   [**3**] The inventor of the telephone, Alexander Graham Bell, is born in Edinburgh.
MAY   [**7**] Lord Rosebery, Prime Minister, is born. [**15**] The Irish political leader Daniel O'Connell dies at Genoa.
JUN   [**11**] Sir John Franklin, the Arctic explorer, dies in Canada attempting to discover the North-West Passage.

 Sir Gilbert Scott: St John's Church, Holbeck.
William Butterfield: Sessay Church, Yorkshire.
Sir James Pennethorne: Record Office, London, also Stationery Office, Westminster.
Penrith Railway Station.
Sir Charles Barry: Bridgewater House, Green Park, London.
Sidney Smirke: Carlton Club, London (begun).
Sir Robert Smirke: British Museum (completed).

 George Cruikshank: *The Bottle.*

 Elizabeth Barrett Browning: *Sonnets from the Portuguese.*
Anne Brontë: *Agnes Grey.*
Charlotte Brontë: *Jane Eyre.*
Emily Brontë: *Wuthering Heights.*
Frederick Marryat: *Children of the New Forest.*
Benjamin Disraeli: *Tancred.*
James Rymer: *Varney the Vampire* (Penny Blood serial).
George Reynolds: *Wagner the Were-Wolf* (Penny Dreadful serial).
Thomas Prest: *The String of Pearls* (first telling of the Sweeney Todd story).

1848 Huge Chartist meeting on Kennington Common. The Pre-Raphaelite Brotherhood is founded. The Second Sikh War begins. The Public Health Act rules that every new house must have a 'water closet, privy or ash pit'.

FEB   [11] Archbishop Howley dies. [27] The composer Sir Hubert
        Parry is born at Bournemouth.

MAR   [10] John Sumner, Bishop of Chester, becomes Archbishop of
        Canterbury. [18] Queen Victoria's daughter Louise is born.

APR   [22] The surviving members of the crew of the Franklin
        expedition abandon ship. According to later Innuit reports,
        'they fell down and died as they walked'; they are probably
        the victims of lead poisoning.

JUL   [18] The cricketer W. G. Grace is born at Downend near
        Bristol. [25] Arthur Balfour, the Conservative Prime Minister,
        is born in East Lothian.

AUG   [6] The officers and crew of HMS *Daedalus* see a huge sea
        monster in the Atlantic; the incident is reported by Captain
        Peter McQuhae to the Admiralty in October. [9] The author
        Frederick Marryat dies at Langham in Norfolk. [12] George
        Stephenson, the engineer who built the first modern railway in
        1825, dies at Tapton.

NOV   [1] W. H. Smith's first railway bookstall opens, at Euston
        Station in London. [24] Lord Melbourne, twice Prime Minister,
        dies near Welwyn.

DEC   [19] The novelist and poet Emily Brontë dies aged 30.

Charles Cockerell: St George's Hall, Liverpool (completed).
Richard Turner and Decimus Burton: Palm House, Kew.
Perth Railway Station.

George Cruikshank: *The Drunkard's Children.*

John Stuart Mill: *Principles of Political Economy.*
Anne Brontë: *The Tenant of Wildfell Hall.*
William Thackeray: *Vanity Fair.*
Elizabeth Gaskell: *Mary Barton.*
Charles Dickens: *Dombey and Son.*
Albert Smith: *The Struggles and Adventures of Christopher
Tadpole.*

1849 The Sikhs surrender at Rawalpindi after being defeated by British
troops. Thomas Macaulay begins, never to finish, his *History of
England.* Disraeli becomes leader of the Conservative Party. The
Navigation Acts are repealed. William Sterndale Bennett forms the
London Bach Society.

FEB   [13] Lord Randolph Churchill, politician, is born at Blenheim
        Palace.

MAY   [19] William Hamilton attempts to assassinate Queen Victoria.

[**28**] The novelist and poet Anne Brontë dies at Scarborough aged 29.

DEC An anti-semitic crowd in Athens burns the house of a British subject, Don Pacifico, who has a large claim against the Greek government. Lord Palmerston sends a squadron to Piraeus to force a settlement of the claim on Don Pacifico's behalf; the Greeks will not comply. [**2**] Queen Adelaide, widow of William IV, dies. [**12**] Sir Marc Isambard Brunel, builder of the Thames Tunnel, dies aged 80.

 Lewis Vulliamy: Dorchester House, Park Lane, London.
Augustus Pugin: St Augustine's Abbey, Ramsgate (completed).

 John Millais: *Lorenzo and Isabella.*

 Lord Lytton: *King Arthur.*
Dean Hook: *The Nonentity of Romish Saints.*
Charlotte Brontë: *Shirley.*
John Ruskin: *The Seven Lamps of Architecture.*

1850 The first issue of *The Germ*, the Pre-Raphaelite Brotherhood magazine, is published. The railway from London to Edinburgh is completed. Southwark Roman Catholic Cathedral becomes the first Catholic cathedral since the Reformation; the fabric of the building was completed in 1848, as St George's Church, and it becomes a cathedral with the restoration of the Catholic hierarchy.

JAN The British squadron at Piraeus lays an embargo on all Greek ships in the harbour.

APR [**6**] Madame Tussaud, founder of the wax museum, dies aged 90. [**23**] Wordsworth dies of pleurisy at midday at Rydal Mount, Grasmere. [**26**] The Greek government complies with Palmerston's demands.

MAY [**1**] Queen Victoria's son Arthur is born.

JUN [**24**] Lord Kitchener is born near Ballylongford in Ireland. [**29**] Lord Palmerston's 'civis Romanus sum' speech stirs feelings of patriotic pride and nationalism.

JUL [**2**] Sir Robert Peel dies in London as a result of a horse riding accident. [**8**] Adolphus Duke of Cambridge, one of George III's sons, dies.

NOV [**13**] The writer Robert Louis Stevenson is born in Edinburgh. [**19**] Alfred Lord Tennyson is appointed Poet Laureate, a post he will hold until his death in 1892.

DEC [**4**] William Sturgeon, who devised the first electro-magnet, dies at Prestwich.

Robert Stephenson and William Fairbairn: Britannia Railway Bridge, Menai Straits.
Royal Border Bridge, Berwick-on-Tweed.
James Bunning: Billingsgate Market, London.
Sir Joseph Paxton: The Crystal Palace, Hyde Park, London.
Sidney Smirke: Athenaeum Club, London.

 Sir Edwin Landseer: *The Monarch of the Glen.*
Sir John Millais: *Christ in the House of His Parents.*
Ford Madox Brown: *Chaucer at the Court of Edward III.*
Dante Gabriel Rossetti: *The Annunciation.*

 Elizabeth Gaskell: *The Moorland Cottage.*
Frank Smedley: *Frank Farleigh.*
Leigh Hunt: *Autobiography.*
Charles Dickens: *David Copperfield.*
Lord Tennyson: *In Memoriam.*
William Thackeray: *Pendennis.*
Charles Kingsley: *Alton Locke.*
William Wordsworth: *The Prelude* (later version).

1851 Following the Don Pacifico affair, the Queen, aided by her husband and Baron Stockmar, draws up a memorandum demanding that she be kept fully informed and that once she has approved a measure it should not altered. Queen Victoria is increasingly irritated by Palmerston's indiscretions and high-handed behaviour.

FEB Ecclesiastical Titles Bill; this forbids priests and bishops of the Roman Catholic Church to assume titles taken from any place in the United Kingdom. The law remains a dead letter and is repealed in 1871. [1] Mary Shelley, author of *Frankenstein*, dies.

MAR [29] Marble Arch is moved from Buckingham Palace to its present site.

MAY [1] The Great Exhibition at the Crystal Palace in Hyde Park, the first world fair, is opened by Queen Victoria.

SEP [19] William Lever, soap-maker and philanthropist, later Viscount Leverhulme, is born at Bolton.

OCT [15] The Great Exhibition ends.

NOV [13] The telegraph service between London and Paris is opened. [18] The Duke of Cumberland, a son of George III and also King of Hanover, dies.

DEC [**2**] Palmerston expresses approval at Louis Napoleon's *coup d'état*, but without referring back to the Queen. [**5**] The Cabinet, in accordance with the Queen's memorandum, carries on as if the French coup had not occurred. [**19**] The Queen dismisses Palmerston for his discourtesy. The painter J. M. W. Turner dies in a lodging in Chelsea, under the assumed name of Booth.

 Richard Carpenter: Hurstpierpoint College.

 Charles Collins: *Convent Thoughts.*

 John Ruskin: *Pre-Raphaelitism.*
Edward Creasey: *The Fifteen Decisive Battles of the World.*
George Borrow: *Lavengro.*
Charles Kingsley: *Yeast.*
Wilkie Collins: *Rambles beyond Railways.*

1852 Lord Kelvin and W. Rankine invent refrigeration. British forces subdue Burma. Britain recognizes the independence of the Transvaal. Hector Berlioz visits London.

FEB [**14**] The first patient, Eliza Armstrong, is admitted to the Children's Hospital in Great Ormond Street, London. [**20**] Lord John Russell's Government is defeated on a militia bill. [**23**] Lord John Russell resigns. [**27**] The Tory Earl of Derby becomes Prime Minister.

SEP [**12**] Herbert Asquith, Liberal Prime Minister, is born at Morley. [**14**] The Duke of Wellington dies at Walmer Castle aged 83. Augustus Pugin, co-designer of the Houses of Parliament, dies at Ramsgate. [**30**] The composer Charles Stanford is born.

OCT [**2**] Sir William Ramsay, discoverer of inert gases, is born in Glasgow.

NOV [**18**] Funeral of the Duke of Wellington in St Paul's Cathedral.

DEC [**19**] Earl of Derby resigns as Prime Minister. [**28**] A Coalition Ministry led by Lord Aberdeen begins.

 Lewis Cubitt: King's Cross Station.
John Thomas: Somerleyton Hall, Suffolk.
Sir Charles Barry: Houses of Parliament (completed).
Philip Hardwick: Paddington Hotel, London.
Sir Joseph Paxton: Mentmore, Buckinghamshire (begun).

 John Gibson: *Tinted Venus.*

Herbert Spencer: *A Theory of Population.*
William Thackeray: *Henry Esmond.*
Peter Roget: *Thesaurus.*
Lord Tennyson: *Ode on the Death of the Duke of Wellington.*
George Reynolds: *The Necromancer* (Penny Dreadful serial).

1853 The Queen uses chloroform to help her through the birth of her seventh child, Leopold, on April 7; this establishes chloroform as the favoured anaesthetic in Britain.

JUL   [**5**] The colonial administrator Cecil Rhodes is born at Bishop's Stortford.

 Edward Walters: Free Trade Hall, Manchester.
Cuthbert Brodrick (designer): Leeds Town Hall (sculpture by Matthew Noble and John Thomas). [Opened by Queen Victoria in 1859.]

 Charlotte Yonge: *The Heir of Redclyffe.*
John Ruskin: *The Stones of Venice.*
Elizabeth Gaskell: *Cranford; Ruth.*
Charles Dickens: *Bleak House.*
Charlotte Brontë: *Villette.*
Charles Reade: *Peg Woffington.*

1854 The Chartist movement comes to an end. Edwin Chadwick is forcibly retired because he has come to be regarded as a nuisance in his campaign for healthier living conditions. The Northcote-Trevelyan Report introduces reforms in the Civil Service. The Offices of Colonial Secretary and Secretary for War are separated. Sir John Elder invents the compound marine steam-engine.

MAR   [**28**] The Crimean War begins when Britain and France declare war on Russia.
JUN   [**13**] Sir Charles Parsons, engineer and inventor, is born. [**21**] A 20-year-old Irishman, Charles Lucas, wins the first Victoria Cross; on HMS *Hecla* in the Baltic he throws an unexploded Russian bomb over the side.
AUG   [**8**] The Vienna Four Points, agreed by Britain and France; the conditions of peace are to be the guarantees of the preservation of Serbia, free passage through the mouths of the Danube, a revision of the Straits Convention, and abandonment of Russia's claims to a protectorate over the Sultan's Christian subjects. Russia rejects these terms.

SEP   [**14**] Allied French and British troops land in the Crimea. [**20**] Battle of Alma.

OCT   [**16**] Oscar Wilde is born in Dublin. [**17**] The Allies begin bombing Sebastopol; it is the beginning of a long siege. [**25**] The Charge of the Light Brigade, led by Lord Cardigan, takes place in the Battle of Balaklava.

NOV   [**5**] Battle of Inkerman: French and British forces are victorious over the Russians. [**13**] John Peel, the famous hunting squire, dies at Caldbeck in Cumbria.

DEC   [**2**] Austria forms a defensive and offensive alliance with Britain and France.

Richard Carpenter: Lancing College, Sussex.
I. K. Brunel, M. Wyatt and O. Jones: Paddington Station, London.
Sidney Smirke: Reading Room, British Museum, London.
John Ruskin: University Museum, Oxford.

Sir John Millais: *Ophelia.*
Holman Hunt: *The Awakening Conscience; The Light of the World.*

Harrison Ainsworth: *Star Chamber.*
Charles Dickens: *Hard Times.*
Lord Tennyson: *The Charge of the Light Brigade.*
Charles Reade: *White Lies.*
Herbert Spencer: *Over-Legislation.*

1855 David Livingstone discovers the Victoria Falls on the Zambezi. Alexander Parkes patents the first synthetic plastic, later named celluloid. Florence Nightingale initiates nursing reforms during the Crimean War. The Crystal Palace concerts begin. Richard Wagner conducts in London. The Bessemer converter is invented by Sir Henry Bessemer. Robert Bunsen invents the Bunsen burner.

JAN   [**20**] Lord Aberdeen resigns as Prime Minister.

FEB   [**6**] The Whig/Liberal Lord Palmerston becomes Prime Minister. [**9**] Mysterious hoof-prints appear overnight in the snow in Devon; a two-legged hoofed creature appears to have trekked 100 miles over fields, walls and roof-tops; no satisfactory explanation is available.

MAR   [**2**] Tsar Nicholas I dies; his successor Alexander is more disposed to make peace with the Allies, but negotiations break down. [**31**] Charlotte Brontë, author of *Jane Eyre*, dies.

MAY   [**24**] The dramatist Sir Arthur Wing Pinero is born.

JUN [**28**] Lord Raglan, Commander of the Expeditionary Force in the Crimean War, dies. [**29**] The first issue of the *Daily Telegraph* is published.

SEP [**11**] The Russians abandon Sebastopol to the Allies, blowing up their forts as they go.

 Ford Madox Brown: *The Last of England.*

 Elizabeth Gaskell: *North and South.*
Anthony Trollope: *The Warden.*
Charles Kingsley: *Westward Ho!*
William Thackeray: *The Newcomes.*
John Timbs: *Curiosities of London.*

1856 Natal and Tasmania become self-governing British colonies. Lord Dalhousie, Governor-General of India, dethrones the King of Oudh because of his tyranny and annexes his kingdom. The Arrow War breaks out; Britain and France ally against China when a ship flying the British flag, the *Arrow*, is boarded by the Chinese and the crew arrested. 'Big Ben', the clock-tower bell of the Houses of Parliament, is cast at Whitechapel. William Perkin creates mauve, the first artificial dye: it soon appears on textiles.

JAN [**29**] The Victoria Cross, Britain's highest military decoration, is instituted by Queen Victoria.
FEB [**1**] Russia agrees to preliminary peace conditions at Vienna.
MAR [**5**] The second Covent Garden Theatre burns down. [**30**] The Crimean War ends with the Treaty of Paris: Britain, France and Austria guarantee the independence of Turkey and the Black Sea is declared neutral.
JUN [**22**] Rider Haggard, the novelist, is born at Bradenham Hall in Norfolk.
JUL [**26**] George Bernard Shaw, the dramatist and critic, is born in Dublin.
AUG [**15**] Keir Hardie, the Labour leader, is born in Lanarkshire.
DEC [**18**] Sir J. J. Thomson, discoverer of the electron, is born near Manchester. [**23**] The geologist and author Hugh Miller commits suicide.

 John Shaw: Wellington College.
John Baird: The Iron Building, 36 Jamaica Street, Glasgow.

Arthur Hughes: *April Love.*
Holman Hunt: *The Scapegoat.*
Sir John Millais: *Autumn Leaves; The Blind Girl.*

Hugh Miller: *Strange But True.*
Dinah Craik: *John Halifax, Gentleman.*
William Thackeray: *Barry Lyndon.*
Charles Reade: *It is Never Too Late to Mend.*
Charles Kingsley: *The Heroes.*
George Meredith: *The Shaving of Shagpat.*

1857 The Peace of Paris ends the Anglo-Persian War; the Shah recognizes the independence of Afghanistan. A Chinese fleet is destroyed by the Royal Navy; British and French troops take Canton. Charles Hallé founds the Hallé Orchestra in Manchester. Prince Albert is created Prince Consort. The Matrimonial Causes Act establishes divorce courts in England and Wales.

JAN   [**30**] The naval uniform for ratings in the Royal Navy is authorized.

FEB   [**22**] Lord Baden-Powell, founder of the Boy Scout movement, is born in London.

APR   [**14**] Queen Victoria's daughter Beatrice is born. [**30**] Mary Duchess of Gloucester, daughter of George III, dies.

MAY   [**10**] The Indian Mutiny begins. Discontented sepoys mutiny, capture the prison at Meerut and march on Delhi.

JUN   The Siege of Delhi begins, leading eventually to the banishment of Bahadur Shah and the end of the Mogul Empire. [**2**] The composer Edward Elgar is born at Broadheath. [**26**] The first investiture ceremony of VCs is held, in Hyde Park.

JUL   [**15**] Massacre at Cawnpore; a three-week siege at Cawnpore comes to an end when the garrison is offered a safe conduct by the sepoys. All the men are killed as they come out and the women and children are thrown in prison. [**17**] Havelock arrives at Lucknow, butchering the mutineers in retaliation for the Cawnpore massacre.

SEP   [**25**] First Relief of Lucknow by Havelock.

NOV   [**3**] The first attempt to launch the *Great Eastern* is abandoned when a spinning winch handle kills a workman. [**16**] The final Relief of Lucknow by Campbell.

DEC   [**3**] The novelist Joseph Conrad is born in Poland.

Henry Clutton: Quantock Lodge, Somerset.
Alexandra Hotel, London.

Rossetti, Burne-Jones and Morris: Frescoes, Oxford Union (begun).
James Collinson: *The Empty Purse.*

John Inchbold: *Lake of Lucerne.*
Thomas Woolner: Bust of Tennyson.

 Elizabeth Gaskell: *Life of Charlotte Brontë.*
George Borrow: *The Romany Rye.*
Thomas Hughes: *Tom Brown's Schooldays.*
Anthony Trollope: *Barchester Towers.*
Charles Dickens: *Little Dorrit.*
George Eliot: *Scenes of Clerical Life.*
David Livingstone: *Missionary Travels and Researches in Southern Africa.*

1858 Queen Victoria is proclaimed Sovereign of India. Sir Richard Burton and John Speke discover Lake Tanganyika. The property qualification for MPs is removed. The composer Dame Ethel Smyth is born.

JAN [**31**] The *Great Eastern*, 692 feet long, is finally launched at Millwall after three months delay.

MAY [**15**] The present Royal Opera House at Covent Garden (the third) is opened.

JUL [**14**] The suffragette Emmeline Pankhurst is born at Manchester.

AUG [**2**] Government of India Act; the British Government takes complete control over India, the East India Company losing its political powers. [**3**] Lake Victoria is discovered by John Speke. [**5**] The first transatlantic cable is completed (laid by USS *Niagara* and HMS *Agamemnon*) and opened by Queen Victoria and President Buchanan exchanging pleasantries. [**19**] The novelist Edith Nesbit is born.

SEP [**16**] Andrew Bonar Law, Conservative Prime Minister, is born in Canada.

NOV [**17**] The social reformer Robert Owen dies aged 87.

 Henry Clutton: Minley Manor, Hampshire.
Royal Opera House, Covent Garden (rebuilt).
Westminster Palace Hotel, London.

 Alfred Steven: Monument to the Duke of Wellington.
Augustus Egg: *Past and Present.*
Sir Edwin Landseer: Lions, Trafalgar Square.
William Frith: *Derby Day.*

 Lord Tennyson: *Idylls of the King.*
Edward Trelawney: *Recollections of Shelley and Byron.*
Anthony Trollope: *Doctor Thorne.*

Frederic Farrar: *Eric, or Little by Little.*
Robert Ballantyne: *The Coral Island.*
Henry Gray: *Anatomy.*
Charles Reade: *Jack of All Trades.*

Michael Balfe: *The Rose of Castile.*
William Sterndale Bennett: *The May Queen.*

1859 The folk-song collector Cecil Sharp is born.

FEB [**9**] John Lewis, working in a timber yard at Mountain Ash in Glamorgan, is hit by a rainstorm of falling fish. [**21**] George Lansbury, the Labour Party leader, is born near Lowestoft.

MAR [**8**] Kenneth Grahame, author of *The Wind in the Willows*, is born in Edinburgh.

MAY [**2**] Jerome K. Jerome, author, is born at Walsall. [**22**] The novelist Sir Arthur Conan Doyle is born in Edinburgh. [**31**] 'Big Ben' first begins to tell the time.

JUN [**12**] Lord Derby's ministry is defeated on Disraeli's Reform Bill; Derby resigns. [**18**] Lord Palmerston becomes Prime Minister again.

SEP [**15**] Isambard Kingdom Brunel, engineer and innovator, dies at Westminster.

Isambard Brunel: Royal Albert Bridge over River Tamar, Saltash.
Deane and Woodward: Pitt-Rivers Museum, Oxford.
Philip Webb & William Morris: The Red House, Bexley Heath.
William Butterfield: All Saints', Margaret St, London (completed).

George Meredith: *The Ordeal of Richard Feverel.*
Charles Darwin: *On the Origin of Species.*
Charles Dickens: *A Tale of Two Cities.*
William Thackeray: *The Virginians.*
John Stuart Mill: *On Liberty.*
George Eliot: *Adam Bede.*
Samuel Smiles: *Self-Help.*
Charles Reade: *Love me Little, Love me Long.*
Edward Fitzgerald: *Omar Khayyam* (verse translation).

1860 British and French troops enter Peking, ending the Anglo-Chinese War . The Second Maori War begins in New Zealand. The first modern Eisteddfod is held. The painters Walter Sickert and Wilson Steer are born. Robert Burke and William Wills cross Australia from south to north (1860-61). Joseph Lister introduces antiseptic surgery.

Jan [**23**] A Commercial Treaty (the Cobden-Chevalier Treaty) is concluded with France.

May [**9**] The playwright and novelist J. M. Barrie is born at Kirriemuir. [**12**] Sir Charles Barry, co-architect of the new Palace of Westminster, dies.

Jun [**17**] The *Great Eastern* begins its first transatlantic voyage.

Jul [**13**] The last naval execution at the yard-arm takes place today, aboard HMS *Leven* in the River Yangtse; the victim is Marine Private John Dalliger.

Aug [**30**] The first tramway in Britain opens, at Birkenhead.

Oct [**17**] The first professional golf tournament takes place, at Prestwick in Scotland; it is won by Willie Parks.

Dec [**29**] The first sea-going ironclad warship, HMS *Warrior*, is launched.

W. N. Pugin and E. W. Pugin: Scarisbrick Hall, Lancs (remodelled).
Alfred Octavius Edwards & Sir Edwin Lutyens: Grosvenor Hotel, Park Lane, London (begun).

Charles Dodgson: *Plane Algebraical Geometry*.
George Eliot: *The Mill on the Floss*.
Wilkie Collins: *The Woman in White*.
George Meredith: *Evan Harrington*.
Florence Nightingale: *Notes on Nursing: what it is and what it is not*.
John Tyndall: *The Glaciers of the Alps*.
Elizabeth Barrett Browning: *Poems before Congress*.

1861 A British colony is founded in Nigeria, the first true British colony in Africa. The firm of Morris, Marshall, Faulkner & Co is founded as an association of 'fine art workmen'. Daily weather forecasts begin. The Post Office Savings Bank is established. The Royal Academy of Music is founded in London. The singer Dame Nellie Melba is born. Frederick Walton invents Linoleum.

Apr [**22**] Viscount Allenby, army commander, is born at Brackenhurst.

Jun [**19**] Earl Haig, army commander, is born in Edinburgh. [**30**] Elizabeth Barrett Browning dies in Florence.

Dec [**14**] Prince Albert dies of typhoid at Windsor Castle.

G. T. Greene: Iron-framed Boat Store at Sheerness.
J. T. Knowles: Grosvenor Hotel, Buckingham Palace Road, London.

Elizabeth Gaskell: *Lois the Witch.*
Dickens and Wilkie Collins: *A Message from the Sea.*
Mrs Beeton: *Book of Household Management.*
Mrs Henry Wood: *East Lynne.*
George Eliot: *Silas Marner.*
Charles Dickens: *Great Expectations.*
Anthony Trollope: *Framley Parsonage.*
Charles Reade: *The Cloister and the Hearth.*
Francis Palgrave: *The Golden Treasury of English Songs and Lyrics.*
Thomas Hughes: *Tom Brown at Oxford.*

1862 Britain recognizes Zanzibar's independence. The Companies Act introduces limited liability companies. A cotton famine brings starvation and disaster to Lancashire mill-workers.

JAN [**29**] The composer Frederick Delius is born at Bradford.
FEB [**11**] Elizabeth Siddall dies; Dante Gabriel Rossetti, her husband, buries his unpublished manuscript poems in her coffin. [**17**] Edward German (Jones), composer, is born at Whitchurch in Shropshire.
JUL [**1**] Princess Alice marries Prince Louis of Hesse-Darmstadt.
SEP [**6**] John Sumner, Archbishop of Canterbury, dies.
NOV [**26**] Charles Longley, Archbishop of York, becomes Archbishop of Canterbury.

 Sir Gilbert Scott: Preston Town Hall.

 William Frith: *The Railway Station.*
James Whistler: *The White Girl.*

 Edward Viles: *Black Bess* (Penny Dreadful serial).
William Thackeray: *Philip.*
Mary Braddon: *Lady Audley's Secret.*
Wilkie Collins: *No Name.*
Christina Rossetti: *Goblin Market.*
George Borrow: *Wild Wales.*
George Meredith: *Modern Love.*

1863 Henry Clifton Sorby discovers the micro-structure of steel; this leads to the development of metallurgy. Sir Lawrence Alma-Tadema visits Pompeii and begins painting archaeological subjects.

JAN [**10**] The first section of the London Underground is opened to passengers by Mr Gladstone: the Metropolitan Railway Line from Paddington to Farringdon Street. [**17**] David Lloyd George is born at Manchester.

FEB   [**9**] Anthony Hope, author of *The Prisoner of Zenda,* is born in London. [**21**] A new Post Office mailbag service begins, using pneumatic conveyors underneath London's streets.

MAR   [**10**] The Prince of Wales marries Princess Alexandra of Denmark in St George's Chapel, Windsor. [**27**] Sir Henry Royce, car manufacturer, is born at Alwalton.

MAY   [**27**] Broadmoor Asylum for the criminally insane is established at Crowthorne in Berkshire.

OCT   [**16**] Sir Austen Chamberlain, politician, is born in Birmingham.

NOV   [**21**] Sir Arthur Quiller-Couch, writer, is born.

DEC   [**24**] William Makepeace Thackeray, novelist, dies.

George Street: Clifton Chapel, Bristol.
William Burges: St Finbar's Cathedral, Cork.
Meadow Buildings, Christ Church, Oxford.
John Hawkshaw (engineer) and E. H. Barry: Charing Cross Station and Hotel.
Sir George Gilbert Scott: Albert Memorial, London (begun).

George Sala: *The Perfidy of Captain Sly-Boots.*
Elizabeth Gaskell: *A Dark Night's Work.*
Ouida: *Held in Bondage.*
Charles Kingsley: *The Water Babies.*
Charles Reade: *Hard Cash.*
Dante Gabriel Rossetti: *Beata Beatrix.*
Thomas Huxley: *Evidence as to Man's Place in Nature.*

Michael Balfe: *The Armourer of Nantes.*

1864 Octavia Hill begins her work reforming housing in the London slums. James Clerk Maxwell proposes the electromagnetic theory of light.

JAN   [**8**] The Prince of Wales's son Albert is born. [**11**] Charing Cross railway station is formally opened.

APR   [**28**] Britain makes the Ionian Islands over to Greece.

JUN   [**9**] Charles Dickens is involved in a train crash at Staplehurst in Kent; he has to return to his wrecked carriage to retrieve the manuscript of part of *Our Mutual Friend.*

SEP   [**15**] The explorer John Speke dies in a shooting accident.

DEC   [**25**] The first Christmas Day dip in the Serpentine.

Edward Godwin: Congleton Town Hall.
Cannon Street Station.
Clifton Suspension Bridge (completed). [After Brunel's death in 1859 the bridge was completed by Hawkshaw & Barlow.]

George Frederick Watts: *Choosing.*

James Payn: *Lost Sir Massingberd.*
Anthony Trollope: *Can You Forgive Her?*
Sheridan Lefanu: *Uncle Silas.*
George Meredith: *Emilia in England.*
John Henry Newman: *Apology for his life.*
Charles Piazzi Smith: *Our Inheritance in the Great Pyramid.*

1865 Joseph Lister pioneers antiseptic surgery, applying carbolic acid to wounds. The Second Maori War ends.

FEB [**28**] Sir Wilfrid Grenfell, medical missionary, is born.

APR [**2**] Richard Cobden dies.

JUN [**3**] George V is born at Marlborough House in London, son of Edward Prince of Wales and Princess Alexandra. [**8**] Sir Joseph Paxton, architect, landscape gardener and designer of the Crystal Palace, dies. [**13**] William Butler Yeats, poet, is born at Sandymount near Dublin.

JUL The *Great Eastern* leaves Ireland to lay a new cable across the Atlantic. [**2**] William Booth founds the Salvation Army with a revival meeting in Whitechapel. [**5**] The world's first speed limit is imposed in Britain, under the Locomotives and Highways Act, nicknamed the 'Red Flag Act'. [**13**] Edward Whymper becomes the first person to climb the Matterhorn. [**15**] Lord Northcliffe, newspaper proprietor, is born near Dublin. [**25**] Dr James Barry, a retired army surgeon, dies in London aged 73; the post-mortem reveals that he was a woman and had, moreover, probably borne a child.

OCT [**18**] Lord Palmerston, the Prime Minister, dies at Brocket Hall, Welwyn. [**29**] Lord John Russell succeeds him as Prime Minister; Gladstone becomes Leader of the House.

NOV [**12**] The novelist Elizabeth Gaskell dies near Alton.

DEC [**4**] Edith Cavell, nurse and war heroine, is born at Swardeston. [**30**] Rudyard Kipling, story and verse writer, is born in Bombay.

 Anthony Salvin: Thoresby Park, Nottinghamshire.
Peter Ellis: Oriel Chambers, Cork Street, Liverpool.
Bank of Scotland, Glasgow.
Sir Gilbert Scott: Grand Midland Hotel, St Pancras Station (begun). [Iron roof by W. H. Barlow.]
William Burges: Cardiff Castle (modified).

 Ford Madox Brown: *Work.*

George Meredith: *Rhoda Fleming.*
Elizabeth Gaskell: *Hand and Heart; Cousin Phyllis.*

Lewis Carroll: *Alice's Adventures in Wonderland.*
John Ruskin: *Sesame and Lilies.*
Charles Dickens: *Our Mutual Friend.*
John Henry Newman: *The Dream of Gerontius.*
Dinah Craik: *Home Thoughts and Home Scenes.*
David Livingstone: *Expedition to the Zambezi.*

 John Stainer: *Gideon.*

1866 Thomas Barnardo opens his first home for destitute children. A cholera epidemic ravages Britain. The Sanitary Act empowers local authorities to take action in cases of nuisance caused by smoke.

FEB [**24**] Sir Arthur Pearson, newspaper owner, is born at Wookey.
MAR [**29**] John Keble, the clergyman who inspired the Oxford Movement, dies at Hursley.
MAY [**24**] Queen Victoria's son Albert is created Duke of Edinburgh.
JUN [**28**] Lord John Russell is succeeded by the Conservative Earl of Derby as Prime Minister.
JUL [**5**] Queen Victoria's daughter Princess Helena marries Prince Christian of Schleswig-Holstein. [**28**] Beatrix Potter, author and illustrator of children's books, is born in South Kensington.
AUG [**6**] The hymn writer John Neale dies at East Grinstead.
SEP [**21**] The author H. G. Wells is born in Bromley, Kent.
OCT [**12**] Ramsay MacDonald, the Labour Prime Minister, is born at Lossiemouth.

Sir James Pennethorne: University of London building, Burlington Gardens.
Bolton Town Hall.

Christina Rossetti: *The Prince's Progress.*
Wilkie Collins: *Armadale.*
Charles Kingsley: *Hereward the Wake.*
George Eliot: *Felix Holt, the Radical.*
Algernon Swinburne: *Poems and Ballads.*
Frances Burnett: *Little Lord Fauntleroy.*

Sir Arthur Sullivan: *Cello Concerto.*

1867 George Grove and Arthur Sullivan visit Vienna and discover the music for Schubert's *Rosamunde*. Disraeli says, 'we do not, however, live - and I trust it will never be the fate of this country to live - under a democracy'. The London Conference guarantees the neutrality of Luxembourg. The British North America Act establishes the status of

Canada as a British dominion; at this time Russia sells Alaska to the United States.

JAN [**31**] The completed Nelson's Column, with its statue and four lions, is unveiled in Trafalgar Square, London.

FEB [**20**] The Prince of Wales' daughter Louise is born.

APR [**18**] Sir Robert Smirke, the architect who designed the façade of the British Museum, dies.

MAY [**20**] The foundation stone of the Royal Albert Hall is laid. [**26**] Queen Mary, the wife of George V, is born in Kensington Palace.

JUN [**17**] Joseph Lister performs the first operation under antiseptic conditions on his own sister, at Glasgow Infirmary.

JUL [**1**] Canada becomes a British dominion. [**14**] Alfred Nobel first demonstrates dynamite at Merstham Quarry, Redhill. [**24**] The author E. F. Benson is born.

AUG [**3**] Stanley Baldwin, Prime Minister, is born at Bewdley. [**14**] The novelist and playwright John Galsworthy is born in Surrey. [**15**] Second Parliamentary Reform Bill; this measure introduces household suffrage to all house-holders paying rates and to lodgers who pay at least £10 a year in rent. [**25**] Michael Faraday, scientist and inventor, dies at Hampton Court.

 Alfred Waterhouse: Balliol College, Oxford.
Lieut-Colonel H. Y. D. Scott: Royal Albert Hall, London.

 Sir Edward Poynter: *Israel in Egypt.*

 Sheridan Lefanu: *The Tenants of Malory.*
Walter Bagehot: *The English Constitution.*
Anthony Trollope: *The Last Chronicle of Barset.*
Ouida: *Under Two Flags.*
Arthur Sketchley: *Mrs Brown's Visit to the Paris Exhibition.*
Herbert Spencer: *The Principles of Biology.*

 Sir Arthur Sullivan: *Cox and Box.*

1868 The Third Maori War begins in New Zealand. Sir Charles Napier makes a dash across Abyssinia to rescue British captives. The Trades Union Congress is founded. Sir William Ramsay discovers helium.

FEB [**27**] Lord Derby resigns as Prime Minister due to ill health. [**29**] The Conservative Benjamin Disraeli becomes Prime Minister.

MAR [**28**] The Earl of Cardigan, who led the disastrous cavalry charge at the Battle of Balaklava in 1854, dies.

APR [**10**] The film actor George Arliss is born in London as George Andrews.

MAY [**26**] The last public execution in Britain takes place outside Newgate Prison; Michael Barrett, the hanged man, had murdered 12 people with a bomb.

JUN [**2**] The first Trades Union Congress opens in Manchester.

JUL [**6**] The Prince of Wales' daughter Victoria is born.

AUG [**7**] The composer Granville Bantock is born.

OCT [**21**] Sir Ernest Swinton, one of the inventors of the military tank, is born in India.

NOV Disraeli is defeated in a General Election.

DEC [**9**] W. E. Gladstone (Liberal) becomes Prime Minister for the first time.

Alfred Waterhouse: Manchester Town Hall.
William Butterfield: Keble College, Oxford.
G. E. Street: London Law Courts, Fleet Street.
Philip Webb: No 19 Lincoln's Inn Fields, London.

William Morris: *The Earthly Paradise.*
Wilkie Collins: *The Moonstone.*
Robert Browning: *The Ring and the Book.*
Robert Louis Stevenson: *The Charity Bazaar.*

1869 A College for Women, afterwards called Girton College, is founded at Cambridge. Mahatma Gandhi is born. The science of eugenics is founded by the explorer and scientist Sir Francis Galton. Gladstone becomes committed to disestablishing the Anglican Church in Ireland, where the nationalist movement is gaining in strength.

MAR [**3**] Sir Henry Wood, conductor and founder of the Promenade Concerts, is born in London. [**18**] Neville Chamberlain, Conservative Prime Minister, is born in Birmingham. [**29**] The architect Edwin Lutyens is born in London.

JUL [**26**] The Irish Episcopal Church is to be disestablished as from January 1, 1871.

OCT Elizabeth Siddal's coffin is dug up and opened so that Rossetti, who has changed his mind about the poems interred there, can retrieve them.

NOV [**16**] The opening of the Suez Canal revolutionizes communication between Britain and India. [**26**] The Prince of Wales' daughter Maud is born.

Sheridan Lefanu: *The Wyvern Mystery.*
Thomas Hughes: *Alfred the Great.*

Francis Galton: *Hereditary Genius.*
Matthew Arnold: *Culture and Beauty.*
John Stuart Mill: *The Subjection of Women.*
Anthony Trollope: *Phineas Finn.*
Robert Browning: *The Ring and the Book.*
R. D. Blackmore: *Lorna Doone.*
William Gilbert: *The 'Bab' Ballads.*
A. Austin: *A Vindication of Lord Byron.*

1870 The painters Monet and Pissarro take refuge in England; Tissot and
Alma-Tadema also come to England. Married Women's Property Act;
this measure extends the rights of women to property in marriage.

FEB   [12] The music hall singer Marie Lloyd is born as Matilda
        Wood.
APR   [4] Peace Preservation Act; the Government increases its
        powers of repression to meet agrarian outrages, particularly in
        Ireland but also in England.
JUN   [9] Charles Dickens dies at Godshill near Rochester.
JUL   [27] The writer Hilaire Belloc is born at St Cloud near Paris.
AUG   [9] Education Act; this provides for compulsory primary
        education in Britain, with the option of two types of school,
        voluntary (= independent) and board (= local authority)
        schools.
OCT   [1] The postcard is officially introduced, together with a
        halfpenny postage stamp. [24] The aurora borealis, the
        northern lights, is seen in southern England; it appears in a
        rare arch shape.

Sir Gilbert Scott: Glasgow University, Scotland.
J. L. Pearson: St Augustine's, Kilburn.
Alfred Waterhouse: Eaton Hall, Cheshire.
A. J. Humbert: Sandringham, Norfolk.

Sir John Millais: *Autumn Leaves.*

Charles Reade: *Put yourself in his place.*
Charles Dickens: *Edwin Drood.*
Cobham Brewer: *Dictionary of Phrase and Fable.*
Benjamin Disraeli: *Lothar.*
Dante Gabriel Rossetti: *Poems.*
Alfred Wallace: *Contributions to the Theory of Natural Selection.*

1871 Britain annexes the diamond mines at Kimberley in South Africa. The
first catering services are provided on British trains.

JAN   [**17**] David Earl Beatty, the First World War admiral, is born at Nantwich. [**26**] The Rugby Football Union is founded.

MAR   [**21**] Princess Louise marries John Marquis of Lorne, later Duke of Argyll. [**27**] The first Rugby International is played at Edinburgh: Scotland defeats England.

MAY   [**11**] Sir John Herschel, astronomer and pioneer of celestial photography, dies. [**29**] Today, Whit Monday, is Britain's first Bank Holiday.

JUN   University Tests Act; this measure allows students at Oxford and Cambridge to gain degrees and fellowships without subscribing to any religious tests or requirements. [**29**] Trades Unions are legalized.

NOV   [**2**] Systematic photographing of convicted prisoners begins. [**10**] Stanley meets Livingstone at Ujiji on the shore of Lake Tanganyika; Livingstone is not aware that he is 'lost'.

DEC   [**14**] George Hudson, the 'Railway King', dies.

William Burges: Skelton Church, Yorkshire.
Basil Champneys: Newnham College, Cambridge.

James Whistler: *The Artist's Mother.*
Frank Holl: *No Tidings from the Sea.*

George Meredith: *Harry Richmond.*
Thomas Hardy: *Desperate Remedies.*
Charles Darwin: *The Descent of Man.*
Lord Redesdale: *Tales of Old Japan.*
Lewis Carroll: *Through the Looking-Glass.*

Henry Smart: *King Rene's Daughter.*
William Gilbert and Arthur Sullivan: *Thespis.*

1872 The expedition of HMS *Challenger* to study marine life and physiography in the Atlantic, Pacific and Indian Oceans; this marks the foundation of the science of oceanography. Lord Kelvin invents a machine for taking depth soundings at sea; this makes possible the detailed mapping of seabed features and opens the way to the discovery of the Mid-Atlantic Ridge. The Earl of Mayo, Viceroy of India, is assassinated. The National Agricultural Labourers' Union is founded by Joseph Arch, with the aim of getting better working conditions and pay for farm workers. Third Class passengers are now carried on all trains. The Ballot Act introduces the secret ballot in Britain. Scottish Education Act.

MAR   [**16**] The first English FA Cup Final takes place; Wanderers (ex-public school and university men) beat the Royal

Engineers 1-0 at the Oval. [**31**] Arthur Griffith, President of the Irish Free State, is born.

MAY [**18**] The mathematician and philosopher Bertrand Russell is born. [**31**] The illustrator and humorist Heath Robinson is born.

JUL [**12**] Lord Birkenhead, Conservative politician and law reformer, is born as Frederick Smith.

AUG [**24**] The writer and caricaturist Max Beerbohm is born.

SEP [**25**] The theatrical impresario and producer C. B. Cochran is born at Lindfield.

OCT [**12**] The composer Ralph Vaughan Williams is born at Down Ampney.

Ernest George: Rousdon, Devon.
Edward Walters: Burlington House façade, Piccadilly.
William Butterfield: Rugby School Chapel.
Norman Shaw: New Zealand Chambers, Leadenhall Street; Grims Dyke, Harrow Weald.
Sir George Gilbert Scott: Albert Memorial, London (completed).

Briton Riviere: *Daniel in the Lions' Den.*

Christina Rossetti: *Sing Song.*
Samuel Butler: *Erewhon.*
Dinah Craik: *Adventures of a Brownie.*
Thomas Hardy: *Under the Greenwood Tree.*

1873 The Second Ashanti War breaks out in West Africa, in what is now Ghana. Refrigeration goes into industrial production. The first sleeping cars are provided on trains.

JAN [**9**] Napoleon III dies in exile at Chislehurst.

FEB The Irish Universities Bill, which seeks to unite Irish colleges into a single university open to Protestants and Catholics alike, is defeated in Parliament; Gladstone resigns. Disraeli is not prepared to take office with a minority administration, so Gladstone returns as Prime Minister. Judicature Act; Gladstone introduces major reforms to the law courts, consolidating the three common law courts into one supreme court of judicature, to consist of two main divisions: the High Court of Justice (Queen's Bench; Chancery; Probate, Divorce and Admiralty) and the Court of Appeal. [**7**] The journalist and author Sheridan Lefanu dies.

MAR [**13**] The Scottish Football Association is formed.

APR   [**25**] Walter de la Mare, poet and novelist, is born at Charlton.

MAY   [**1**] David Livingstone, the explorer and missionary, is found dead at Chitambo, kneeling in prayer by his bed. [**9**] Howard Carter, the discoverer of Tutankhamun's tomb, is born at Swaffham.

OCT   [**1**] Sir Edwin Landseer, painter, dies in London.

Alfred Waterhouse: Natural History Museum, South Kensington (begun).

Walter Bagehot: *Physics and Politics.*
Charles Reade: *A Simpleton.*
Anthony Trollope: *The Eustace Diamonds.*
Robert Bridges: *Poems.*
Sheridan Lefanu: *Willing to Die.*
Thomas Hardy: *A Pair of Blue Eyes.*

Henry Smart: *Jacob.*
Sir Arthur Sullivan: *The Light of the World.*

1874   The Second Ashanti War ends. The Gold Coast (later to be called Ghana) becomes a British colony. Fiji is annexed by Britain. The Prince of Wales visits France. Agricultural workers strike for higher pay in eastern England.

JAN   [**25**] The writer William Somerset Maugham is born in Paris.

FEB   [**15**] The explorer Sir Ernest Shackleton is born at Kilkee in County Clare. [**20**] Benjamin Disraeli succeeds Gladstone as Prime Minister. [**23**] The game of lawn tennis is patented by Major Walter Wingfield under the extraordinary name of 'Sphairistike'.

APR   [**18**] David Livingstone is buried in Westminster Abbey.

MAY   [**24**] Prince Arthur is created Duke of Connaught. [**29**] G. K. Chesterton, writer, is born at Kensington.

SEP   [**21**] The composer Gustav Holst is born at Cheltenham as Gustavus von Holst.

NOV   [**30**] Sir Winston Churchill is born at Blenheim Palace, Oxfordshire.

W. H. Barlow: St Pancras Station Shed, London.

Luke Fildes: *Applicants for Admission to a Casual Ward.*
James Whistler: *The Falling Rocket.*

Thomas Hardy: *Far From the Madding Crowd.*
Anthony Trollope: *Phineas Redux.*

1875 The agricultural depression deepens; the plight of the agricultural workers worsens, with significantly lower pay than the average factory worker. Peaceful picketing is allowed by legislation, and trade disputes are freed from charges of conspiracy. The Public Health Act codifies sanitary laws. The Artisans' Dwellings Act is designed to combat slum housing.

JAN   [**23**] The writer Charles Kingsley dies in London.
APR   [**1**] *The Times* becomes the first newspaper to publish a daily weather chart. The thriller writer Edgar Wallace is born at Greenwich.
AUG   [**15**] Samuel Coleridge-Taylor, composer, is born. [**25**] Captain Matthew Webb becomes the first to swim the English Channel; he takes 22 hours, using the breaststroke. [**26**] The politician and novelist John Buchan is born at Perth.
NOV   [**25**] On his own initiative, Disraeli negotiates and buys a decisive portion of the Suez Canal shares, gaining a controlling interest for Britain; Parliament afterwards gratefully ratifies his action.

William Burges: Castell Coch, Glamorgan.
Sir Thomas Jackson: Hertford College Chapel, Oxford.

Gerard Manley Hopkins: *The Windhover*.
Anthony Trollope: *The Way We Live Now*.
Helen Mathers: *Comin' Thro' the Rye*.

William Gilbert and Arthur Sullivan: *Trial by Jury*.

1876 The telephone is invented by Scottish-born Alexander Graham Bell. The art critic John Ruskin makes an outspoken denunciation of Whistler's *The Falling Rocket*; as a result, Whistler brings a libel action against Ruskin. Massacres of Christians in Turkish-occupied Bulgaria provoke anti-Turkish reaction in Britain. The Purcell Society is formed. The painter Gwen John is born. The Merchant Shipping Act is designed to prevent overloading and the use of unseaworthy vessels; this important measure results from the efforts of Samuel Plimsoll, 'the sailor's friend'.

JAN   [**29**] The composer Havergal Brian is born.
MAR   [**25**] The first Scotland v. Wales football international is played at Glasgow: Scotland wins.
APR   Royal Titles Bill. This measure declaring the Queen Empress of India flatters the Queen and proves to be very popular in India. Opposition to the new title as 'un-English' is met by the promise that it will not be used in Britain.

Aug   Disraeli is created Earl of Beaconsfield. Charles Stanford and
       Hubert Parry see the first production of Wagner's 'Ring' cycle
       at Bayreuth.

 Sir Thomas Jackson: Examination Schools, Oxford.

 Richard Jefferies: *Suez-cide.*
       George Eliot: *Daniel Deronda.*
       George Meredith: *Beauchamp's Career.*
       Anthony Trollope: *The Prime Minister.*
       Thomas Hardy: *The Hand of Ethelberta.*
       Sir Lewis Morris: *The Epic of Hades.*

1877 The Transvaal is annexed to the British Empire. The first shipment of
      frozen meat from Argentina reaches Britain, a landmark in
      international trade. Sir Henry Stanley traces the River Congo (Zaire).

Jan   [1] Queen Victoria is declared Empress of India.
Mar   [15] The first cricket Test Match takes place, when Australia
       play England at Melbourne - and win. [24] The only dead-heat
       in the history of the Oxford-Cambridge Boat Race takes place.
May   Richard Wagner is in London to conduct six concerts of his
       music at the Royal Albert Hall. He stays in Bayswater, and
       meets Browning, George Eliot, Queen Victoria and the Prince
       of Wales.
Jun   [24] The Ambulance Association, later to become St John's
       Ambulance Brigade, is formed.
Jul   [19] The first men's Wimbledon tennis final takes place: it is
       won by Spencer Gore.
Sep   [17] The pioneer of photography, William Fox Talbot, dies at
       Lacock Abbey, Wiltshire.
Oct   [10] Lord Nuffield, the car manufacturer, is born.
Nov   [13] There is a demonstration by socialist marchers, including
       Annie Besant, in Trafalgar Square; there are violent clashes
       with mounted police and guardsmen.

 Norman Shaw: Old Swan House, Chelsea Embankment,
       London.

James Whistler: *Nocturne in Black and Gold.*

Anna Sewell: *Black Beauty.*
       William Russell: *The Wreck of the 'Grosvenor'.*
       William Morris: *Sigurd the Volsung.*
       Sir Arthur Pinero: *Two Can Play at That Game.*
       Charles Reade: *A Woman Hater.*

1878 H. J. Lawson invents the modern safety bicycle. Joseph Swan demonstrates the first reliable filament electric lamp. David Edward Hughes invents the microphone. Muybridge begins to publish his famous multiple exposure photographs of people and animals in motion. John Ruskin loses the libel action brought against him by Whistler, who is awarded damages of one farthing. The Criminal Investigation Department of Scotland Yard is established. Lord Derby resigns as Foreign Minister and is succeeded by Lord Salisbury. Factory and Workshop Act. The Second Afghan War begins; Britain tries to secure her position in India by stopping Russian expansion into Afghanistan.

JAN [**4**] The painter Augustus John is born at Tenby. [**14**] The newly-invented telephone is demonstrated to Queen Victoria at Osborne House. [**23**] The composer Rutland Boughton is born at Aylesbury.

APR [**25**] The author Anna Sewell dies.

JUN [**1**] The Poet Laureate John Masefield is born at Ledbury.

JUL [**12**] Turkey cedes Cyprus to Britain.

SEP [**12**] 'Cleopatra's Needle', an ancient Egyptian obelisk in red granite and made originally for Thothmes III in 1460 BC, is re-erected on the Thames Embankment.

OCT [**14**] The first football match played under floodlights takes place at Sheffield.

John Pearson: Truro Cathedral, Cornwall.
Edward Godwin: White House, Tite Street, Chelsea, London.
Thomas Bouch: Tay Bridge.

William Yeames: *'And when did you last see your father?'.*

Thomas Hardy: *The Return of the Native.*
Robert Louis Stevenson: *An Inland Voyage.*

John Stainer: *The Daughter of Jairus.*
Gilbert and Sullivan: *HMS Pinafore.*

1879 The Zulu War; Britain declares war on Cetewayo, the Zulu leader. The British are defeated at Isandhlwana, but win at Ulundi and succeed in capturing Cetewayo. The frontier between India and Afghanistan is fixed by the Treaty of Gandamak. Charles Parnell mobilizes the Irish nationalists and aims to reform the Irish Land Law. The severe agricultural depression in Britain continues. The painter Matthew Smith is born.

JAN [**1**] The novelist E. M. Forster is born in London. [**18**] The first England v. Wales football international is played at the Oval:

England win. [22] Battle of Rorke's Drift; a handful of British soldiers under Lieutenants Chard and Bromhead heroically and successfully resist a huge Zulu army.

FEB [26] The composer John Ireland is born.

APR [29] The conductor Sir Thomas Beecham is born at St Helens.

MAY [19] Lady Astor, the first woman to sit in the House of Commons, is born in Virginia. [25] The newspaper proprietor Lord Beaverbrook is born in Canada as Max Aitken.

AUG [27] Sir Rowland Hill, the pioneer of the postal service, dies.

SEP [18] Blackpool's first annual illumination begins.

DEC [4] The Irish composer Hamilton Harty is born. [28] The Tay Bridge disaster; the railway bridge designed by Thomas Bouch collapses, carrying the Edinburgh-Dundee train and its passengers down into the Firth of Tay. About 90 people are killed. [30] The first performance of *The Pirates of Penzance* takes place at Torquay.

 Alfred Waterhouse: Prudential Building, Holborn, London.

 Anthony Trollope: *Thackeray.*
Robert Louis Stevenson: *Travels with a Donkey.*
Arthur Pinero: *Daisy's Escape.*
Samuel Butler: *Evolution, old and new.*
George Meredith: *The Egoist.*

 Gilbert and Sullivan: *The Pirates of Penzance.*
Charles Stanford: *Service in B flat.*

1880 The Second Afghan War ends. The Transvaal is declared a republic. Parliament ends the confusion over time conflicts resulting from each town using 'sun' time, by ordering the whole country to set its clocks by Greenwich Mean Time. Relief of Distress Act for Ireland.

JAN [15] The first telephone directory is published by the London Telephone company: it contains 255 entries.

FEB [2] The first frozen meat arrives in Britain from Australia aboard the SS *Strathleven.*

APR [23] Disraeli is succeeded as Prime Minister by Gladstone (Gladstone's second ministry). Charles Bradlaugh, a newly-elected MP, refuses to take the oath on the grounds that he is an atheist; he asks to affirm instead, but this is not accepted.

SEP [6] The first cricket Test Match to be played in Britain takes place between England and Australia at the Oval. [13] The first Employers' Liability Act provides compensation for

workers for injuries that are not their own fault. [**22**] The
suffragette Christabel Pankhurst is born.

Nov [**10**] The sculptor Jacob Epstein is born in New York.
Dec [**22**] The novelist George Eliot dies at Chelsea.

Philip Webb: Clouds, East Knoyle, Wiltshire.
Peter Paul Pugin: Cardiff Roman Catholic Cathedral.
John Crawley: Portsmouth Cathedral.

Arthur Pinero: *The Money-Spinner.*
R. D. Blackmore: *Mary Anerley.*
Anthony Trollope: *The Duke's Children.*
Thomas Hardy: *The Trumpet-Major.*
Samuel Butler: *Unconscious Memory.*

Sir Hubert Parry: *Prometheus Unbound.*

1881 At Folkestone, work on the Channel Tunnel begins but stops again
after only 879 yards. A Smoke Abatement Committee is formed in
reaction to the increasing nuisance from factory chimneys in British
towns and cities. The Affirmation Bill, designed to allow Charles
Bradlaugh to take his seat in the Commons, is defeated for the first
time. The Land Act is designed to meet Irish demands for fair rents
and fixity of tenure, but it proves unpopular with both landlords and
tenants. Flogging is abolished in the army and Navy. The Savoy
Theatre in London is opened. The painter Samuel Palmer dies. British
troops are defeated by Boers at Majuba; the independence of the
Transvaal is recognized at the Treaty of Pretoria.

Jan [**1**] Postal orders are issued for the first time.
Feb [**5**] The historian Thomas Carlyle dies at 5 Cheyne Row,
Chelsea.
Mar [**9**] Ernest Bevin, Labour politician, is born at Winsford.
Apr [**19**] Benjamin Disraeli dies; the date becomes known as
'Primrose Day' from his liking for the flower.
May [**24**] Queen Victoria's son Prince Leopold is created Duke of
Albany. [**28**] There is a very severe thunderstorm at
Worcester, with a heavy fall of hailstones and periwinkles.
Jul [**26**] The writer George Borrow dies.
Aug [**6**] Sir Alexander Fleming, discoverer of penicillin, is born.
Oct [**13**] Parnell and others are sent to Kilmainham Gaol for
inciting Irishmen to intimidate tenants who are trying to take
legitimate advantage of the Land Act. [**14**] Fishing disaster at
Eyemouth in south-east Scotland; 189 haddock fishermen die
in a storm after being lured out to the fishing grounds by fair

weather in the morning. [**15**] The writer P. G. Wodehouse is born at Guildford, Surrey.

 Alfred Waterhouse: St Paul's School, Hammersmith.

 Sir Lawrence Alma-Tadema: *In the Tepidarium.*

 Richard Jefferies: *Wood Magic.*
Tit-Bits (first edition).
Thomas Hardy: *A Laodicean.*
Henry James: *The Portrait of a Lady*
Joseph Shorthouse: *John Inglesant.*
Charles Darwin: *The Formation of Vegetable Mould through the Action of Worms.*

 Sir Charles Stanford: *The Veiled Prophet of Khorassan.*
Gilbert and Sullivan: *Patience.*

1882 British forces bombard Alexandria; the French withdraw and Egypt becomes a British colony. Queen Victoria gives Epping Forest to the nation. The Primrose League is founded. Wagner's 'Ring', in the Leipzig production, is given for the first time in Britain at Her Majesty's Theatre in London under the baton of Anton Seidl. The painter Wyndham Lewis is born.

JAN [**18**] A. A. Milne, creator of 'Winnie the Pooh', is born at St John's Wood. [**25**] The novelist Virginia Woolf is born in London.

FEB [**2**] James Joyce, writer, is born in Dublin. [**15**] The first shipment of frozen meat from New Zealand arrives in Britain aboard SS *Dunedin.* [**25**] The first Wales-Ireland football international takes place at Wrexham: Wales win.

MAR [**2**] R. MacLean makes an attempt to assassinate Queen Victoria at Windsor. [**4**] The first electric tramcars are seen in London.

APR [**19**] Charles Darwin dies. [**24**] Lord Dowding, responsible for victory in the Battle of Britain, is born at Moffat.

MAY [**2**] Charles Parnell is released when he agrees in the 'Kilmainham Treaty' to stop 'boycotting'. [**6**] Lord Frederick Cavendish, Irish Secretary, and Thomas Burke, Under-Secretary, are murdered in Phoenix Park by Fenians; Parnell dissociates himself from the killings.

JUL Prevention of Crimes Act; limited to three years, this measure suspends trial by jury and gives the police unlimited powers of search. Irish extremists resort to a campaign of terrorism.

SEP [**14**] British troops occupy Cairo.

Oct [**14**] Eamon de Valera, Prime Minister and President of the Irish Republic, is born in New York. [**24**] The actress Sybil Thorndike is born at Gainsborough.

Dec [**1**] Archbishop Tait dies. [**6**] The novelist Anthony Trollope dies in London. [**16**] The cricketer Jack Hobbs is born at Cambridge.

George Street: London Law Courts, Fleet Street (completed).

 William Stott: *The Ferry.*

 Anthony Trollope: *Lord Palmerston.*

Gilbert and Sullivan: *Iolanthe.*

1883 Sir Joseph Swan produces the first synthetic fibre. Britain occupies Egypt. British forces begin evacuating the Sudan. The Royal College of Music is opened under the direction of George Grove. The Corrupt and Illegal Practices Act limits spending by political parties and individuals in general elections. The Affirmation Bill is defeated in Parliament a second time.

Jan [**3**] Clement Attlee, Labour Prime Minister, is born at Putney. [**17**] Compton Mackenzie, writer, is born at West Hartlepool as Edward Compton.

Mar [**3**] Edward Benson, Bishop of Truro, becomes Archbishop of Canterbury. [**14**] The social and political philosopher, Karl Marx, dies in London.

Jun [**14**] The poet Edward Fitzgerald dies in Suffolk.

Aug [**1**] Parcel post is introduced. [**27**] The eruption of Krakatoa between Sumatra and Java causes spectacular red sunsets in Britain for several weeks.

Sep [**18**] Lord Berners, composer, painter and writer, is born.

Oct [**4**] The Boys' Brigade is founded in Glasgow by Sir William Smith.

Nov [**8**] The composer Arnold Bax is born.

Briton Riviere: *The Gadarene Swine.*
William Orchardson: *The Marriage of Convenience.*
William Morris: The Honeysuckle Chintz (fabric pattern).

Robert Louis Stevenson: *Treasure Island.*
Anthony Trollope: *Autobiography.*
Olive Schreiner: *The Story of an African Farm.*
Sir Arthur Pinero: *The Rector; The Rocket.*
Charles Reade: *Readiana.*

1884 Sir Charles Parsons devises his steam turbine, which revolutionizes steam engineering. Friese-Green invents the cine camera. There is a rising against the British in the Sudan, led by a charismatic leader, the Mahdi. General Gordon is sent to Khartoum to rescue the Egyptian garrison; Gordon himself is trapped and besieged at Khartoum, and an expedition headed by Wolseley is sent to rescue Gordon. The Greenwich Meridian is adopted internationally as the prime meridian, from which longitude is to be measured. The Fabian Society is formed.

JAN [**28**] The first Ireland v. Scotland football international takes place at Belfast: Scotland win.

MAR [**13**] Sir Hugh Walpole, novelist, is born at Auckland, New Zealand. [**28**] Leopold, Duke of Albany dies. [**30**] Sean O'Casey, playwright, is born.

APR [**5**] John Wisden, cricketer and compiler of Wisden record books, dies in London. [**11**] The novelist Charles Reade dies.

APR [**22**] An earthquake in the Colchester area kills four people.

JUN [**14**] The singer John McCormack is born at Athlone.

DEC The Franchise Act (or Third Parliamentary Reform Act) opens the franchise to almost all adult males, although domestic servants, bachelors living with their parents, and those of no fixed address are not to be given the vote. This measure adds two million voters, four times the number added in 1832.

 Sir Edward Burne-Jones: *King Cophetua and the Beggar-Maid.*

 Sir Charles Stanford: *The Canterbury Pilgrims; Savonarola.*

1885 The Third Anglo-Burmese War; Burma is formally annexed by Britain. Bechuanaland in southern Africa becomes a British colony. The first public labour exchanges are established. The office of Secretary of State for Scotland is created. Sir James Dewar invents the vacuum flask.

JAN [**26**] The Mahdi takes Khartoum; General Gordon is killed by a spear flung by a Muslim soldier.

MAR [**11**] Sir Malcolm Campbell, racing driver, is born at Chislehurst. [**26**] The composer Julius Harrison is born. The first cremation in Britain in modern times takes place at Woking Crematorium.

JUN [**9**] Gladstone resigns after a hostile amendment to his budget. [**24**] The Conservative Robert Cecil, Lord Salisbury, becomes Prime Minister.

JUL [**12**] The composer George Butterworth is born.

AUG The Ashbourne Act provides a £5 million fund for low-interest loans to Irish tenants, enabling them to buy their holdings.

SEP [**11**] The poet and novelist D. H. Lawrence is born at Eastwood.

DEC Gladstone is converted to the idea of Home Rule for Ireland.

John Lavery: *The Tennis Party.*
Henry Scott Tuke: *Lying on the Beach.*

Christina Rossetti: *Time Flies.*
Sir Arthur Pinero: *Mayfair.*
Sir Rider Haggard: *King Solomon's Mines.*
George Meredith: *Diana of the Crossways.*
Lord Tennyson: *Idylls of the King.*
Revd Edward Hardy: *How to be Happy Though Married.*

Gilbert and Sullivan: *The Mikado.*

1886 Upper Burma is annexed by Britain. Kenya becomes a British colony. Gold is discovered in the Transvaal. The Severn Tunnel is opened.

JAN Charles Bradlaugh takes the oath and his seat as an MP. [**1**] Edwin Bartlett dies, apparently poisoned with chloroform; his wife Adelaide is later acquitted of his murder, but under grave suspicion. She disappears after the trial. [**20**] The Mersey Railway Tunnel is formally opened by the Prince of Wales.

FEB [**1**] Lord Salisbury resigns. [**12**] Gladstone becomes Prime Minister for the third time.

MAR [**10**] The first Cruft's Dog Show is held in London.

APR The first Home Rule Bill is introduced.

JUL The Home Rule Bill is defeated in the Commons, leading to a call for a General Election. [**23**] Sir Arthur Brown, the aviator who will co-pilot the first transatlantic flight, is born in Glasgow. [**26**] Gladstone is succeeded as Prime Minister by the Conservative Lord Salisbury, after the failure of the Home Rule Bill.

AUG [**22**] The composer Eric Coates is born.

NOV [**8**] Fred Archer, the champion jockey, shoots himself at his house in Newmarket at the age of 29.

Norman Shaw: New Scotland Yard, London (begun).
Sir Thomas Jackson: Brasenose College front quad.
Portsmouth Guild Hall.

Sir John Millais: *Bubbles.*
George Frederick Watts: *Hope.*

Marie Corelli: *A Romance of Two Worlds.*
John Davidson: *Bruce, a drama.*
Dinah Craik: *King Arthur.*
Thomas Hardy: *The Mayor of Casterbridge.*
Robert Louis Stevenson: *Kidnapped; Dr Jekyll and Mr Hyde.*
Henry James: *The Bostonians.*
James Froude: *Oceana, or England and her colonies.*

1887 Zululand is annexed by Britain. Baluchistan is united with India.

JAN   [**1**] Queen Victoria is proclaimed Empress of India in Delhi.
[**22**] Sir Joseph Whitworth, the engineer who standardized screw threads, dies at Monte Carlo.
JUN   [**21**] Queen Victoria's Jubilee celebrations.
AUG   [**3**] The poet Rupert Brooke is born at Rugby. [**14**] The writer Richard Jefferies dies.
SEP   [**26**] Barnes Wallis, inventor and designer of aircraft and specialized bombs, is born.
NOV   [**1**] The artist L. S. Lowry is born at Rusholme. [**17**] Viscount Montgomery, army commander in the Second World War, is born in Kensington. [**23**] Boris Karloff, the film actor, is born at Dulwich as William Pratt.

Second Tay Bridge, Scotland (opened June 20).
W. H. Lever (plan) and William Owen (architect): Port Sunlight.

Sir Arthur Pinero: *Dandy Dick.*
Sir Arthur Quiller-Couch: *Dead Man's Rock.*
Conan Doyle: *A Study in Scarlet* (first Sherlock Holmes story).
Thomas Hardy: *The Woodlanders.*
Sir Rider Haggard: *She.*
Fergus Hume: *The Mystery of a Hansom Cab.*
Talbot Reed: *The Fifth Form at St Dominic's.*

John Stainer: *The Crucifixion; St Mary Magdalene.*
Frederick Delius: *Florida Suite* (written).
Sir Hubert Parry: *Blest Pair of Sirens.*

1888 North Borneo, Brunei and Sarawak are established as British protectorates. John Boyd Dunlop invents an improved pneumatic tyre with a rubber outer casing and an air-filled inner tube inflated through a valve: the first modern inflatable tyre. The *Great Eastern* is broken up on Merseyside. The Miners' Federation of Great Britain is founded, a landmark in the development of trade-unionism. The Local Government Act sets up County Councils. The Affirmation Act is finally established, thanks to the efforts of Charles Bradlaugh; it removes the last remaining religious disability for membership of the House of Commons.

JAN [3] The politician Herbert Morrison is born at Lambeth.

FEB [8] Dame Edith Evans, actress, is born in London.

MAR [22] The English Football League is formed.

APR [15] The writer Matthew Arnold dies suddenly at Liverpool.

MAY [31] Naval Defence Act, designed to meet the growing sea-power of France and Russia.

AUG [7] A Whitechapel prostitute, Martha Tabram, is murdered with 29 stab wounds; no one is arrested for the crime. [13] John Logie Baird, inventor of television, is born at Helensburgh. [15] T. E. Lawrence (of Arabia) is born at Tremadoc. [31] Mary Ann Nicholls is murdered at Whitechapel by Jack the Ripper.

SEP [8] Annie Chapman is murdered by Jack the Ripper. [26] The poet T. S. Eliot is born at St Louis in Missouri. [29]The Central News Agency receives the 'Dear Boss' letter from Jack the Ripper (first use of the name); during the following night prostitutes Elizabeth Stride and Catherine Eddowes are murdered. There is widespread panic in the East End of London.

NOV [9] Mary Kelly, the last of Jack the Ripper's victims, is murdered.

DEC [23] The film magnate J. Arthur Rank is born at Hull. [31] The body of Montague Druitt, a prominent suspect in the Ripper murder inquiry, is found floating in the Thames.

Thomas Colcutt: Imperial Institute, London.
Basil Champneys: Mansfield College, Oxford.

John Waterhouse: *The Lady of Shalott.*
Frank Bramley: *A Hopeless Dawn.*

Sir Arthur Quiller-Couch: *Troy Town.*
Henry James: *The Aspern Papers.*
Oscar Wilde: *The Happy Prince.*
Robert Louis Stevenson: *The Black Arrow.*
Rudyard Kipling: *Plain Tales from the Hills.*

Sir Arthur Pinero: *The Weaker Sex.*
Sir Rider Haggard: *Alan Quatermain.*

 Sir Hubert Parry: *Judith.*
Gilbert and Sullivan: *The Yeoman of the Guard.*

1889 Sir Frederick Abel invents cordite. The London County Council is formed. The Board of Agriculture is created. The Socialist battle song, 'The Red Flag', is written in London following the dock strike. The painter Paul Nash is born.

MAR [**27**] John Bright, the reformer who worked with Richard Cobden for the repeal of the Corn Laws, dies.
APR [**8**] The conductor Sir Adrian Boult is born at Chester. [**16**] Charlie Chaplin is born at Kennington in London. [**24**] The Labour politician Sir Stafford Cripps is born.
JUL [**4**] The police are alerted to the use of 19 Cleveland Street, London as a homosexual brothel; the names of several aristocrats, including that of Lord Arthur Somerset, are drawn into the scandal.
AUG [**7**] Florence Maybrick is condemned to death for poisoning her husband; the sentence is later commuted to life imprisonment. [**15**] The London dock strike begins.
SEP [**16**] The dock strike ends. [**23**] The novelist Wilkie Collins dies in London.
OCT [**11**] James Joule, who established the first law of thermodynamics, dies.
NOV [**10**] The character actor Claude Rains is born in London.
DEC [**12**] The poet Robert Browning dies in Venice.

 Gabriel Destailleur: Waddesdon Manor, Buckinghamshire.

 S. Forbes: *The Health of the Bride.*
George Henry: *A Galloway Landscape.*

 Sir Arthur Quiller-Couch: *The Splendid Spur.*
Jerome K. Jerome: *Three Men in a Boat.*
George Gissing: *The Nether World.*
H. G. Wells: *The War of the Worlds.*
Robert Louis Stevenson: *The Master of Ballantrae.*
Sir Arthur Pinero: *The Profligate.*

 Gilbert and Sullivan: *The Gondoliers.*
'The Red Flag' (song).

1890 The United States overtakes Britain in steel production. The City and South London Line is the first deep underground railway line in London. Free elementary (= junior) education is established. Charles Parnell is cited in a divorce case and forced to resign. The painter David Bomberg is born. The publication of Sir James Frazer's *The Golden Bough* is a landmark in the development of anthropology and psychology.

FEB   [**25**] The pianist Dame Myra Hess is born in London.

MAR   [**4**] The Forth Bridge, the longest bridge (so far) in Britain, is opened by the Prince of Wales.

MAY   [**7**] James Nasmyth, inventor of the first steam hammer, dies. [**17**] The first comic paper, *Comic Cuts*, is published. [**24**] The Prince of Wales' son Albert is created Duke of Clarence.

JUN   [**16**] Stan Laurel, comedian, is born at Ulverston as Arthur Stanley Jefferson.

JUL   [**21**] Battersea Bridge is opened by Lord Rosebery.

AUG   [**11**] Cardinal Newman, leader of the Oxford Movement, dies at Edgbaston aged 89.

SEP   [**15**] Agatha Christie, crime writer, is born. [**24**] The writer and MP A. P. Herbert is born.

OCT   [**1**] The entertainer Stanley Holloway is born in London. [**20**] Sir Richard Burton, explorer and writer, dies; his wife Isabel builds a bonfire of his unpublished manuscripts, some 28 complete works including his private journal, thus destroying a large body of scholarship.

Sir Benjamin Baker and Sir John Fowler: Forth Railway Bridge, Scotland.
Norman Shaw: Bryanston House, Dorset.
Edgar Wood: Halecroft, Cheshire.
Sir Arthur Blomfield: Southwark Cathedral (rebuilt).
E. W. Mountford: Sheffield Town Hall.

Sir Arthur Pinero: *The Cabinet Minister.*
Henry Stanley: *In Darkest Africa.*
Sir James Frazer: *The Golden Bough.*
Marie Corelli: *Wormwood.*

Sir Edward Elgar: *Froissart Overture.*

1891 Joseph Chamberlain becomes leader of the Liberal Unionists in the Commons. The Liberal Party advocates Irish Home Rule, the disestablishment of the Welsh Church, 3-year Parliaments, and reform of the House of Lords. The Public Health (London) Act seeks to control factory chimney emissions in the capital. Oscar Wilde's *Picture of Dorian Gray* typifies the brilliant decadence of the 1890s. The painter Stanley Spencer is born.

FEB [9] Film star Ronald Colman is born at Richmond, Surrey.
AUG [2] The composer Sir Arthur Bliss is born.
OCT [6] Charles Stewart Parnell, Irish politician, dies at Brighton. W. H. Smith, the newsagent and bookseller, dies. [8] The first street collection for charity takes place in Manchester, for Lifeboat Day. [20] Sir James Chadwick, discoverer of the neutron, is born in Manchester.

 J. M. Barrie: *The Little Minister.*
Thomas Hardy: *Tess of the d'Urbervilles.*
Sir Arthur Conan Doyle: *The White Company.*
Rudyard Kipling: *Barrack Room Ballads.*
Oscar Wilde: *The Picture of Dorian Gray.*
George Gissing: *New Grub Street.*
Sir Arthur Quiller-Couch: *The Blue Pavilions.*

1892 Charles Cross and E. Bevan produce viscose, which leads to the manufacture of rayon. The socialist leader Keir Hardie becomes the first Labour MP.

JAN [14] The eldest son of the Prince of Wales, Albert Duke of Clarence, dies.
APR [13] Sir Arthur Harris, wartime bomber commander, is born. [19] Producer-Director Herbert Wilcox is born in Cork, Ireland.
MAY Oscar Wilde falls in love with Lord Alfred Douglas. [11] The actress Margaret Rutherford is born. [23] Broad gauge railway tracks are finally abandoned in Britain. [24] The second son of the Prince of Wales, George, is created Duke of York.
JUL [18] The pioneer travel agent Thomas Cook dies.
OCT [6] Lord Tennyson, Poet Laureate for the last 42 years, dies at Aldworth in Surrey.
NOV [6] The aviator Sir John Alcock is born at Manchester.

Philip Webb: Standen, Sussex.
Sir Alfred Gilbert: Eros (unusual use of aluminium), Piccadilly Circus, London. [Unveiled 1893 by the Duke of Westminster.]
Henry T. Hare: Oxford Town Hall.

Frederick Leighton: *Garden of the Hesperides.*
Roderic O'Conor: *Still Life with Bottles.*
Philip Wilson Steer: *The Beach at Boulogne.*

Marie Corelli: *The Soul of Lilith.*
Israel Zangwill: *Children of the Ghetto.*
George and Weedon Grossmith: *The Diary of a Nobody.*
Sir Arthur Quiller-Couch: *I Saw Three Ships.*
Sir Arthur Conan Doyle: *The Adventures of Sherlock Holmes.*
Sir Rider Haggard: *Nada the Lily.*

Granville Bantock: *Caedmar.*
Frederick Delius: *Irmelin.*
Sir Charles Stanford: *Mass.*

1893 Natal is granted self-government. The Imperial Institute in South Kensington is founded. The Liverpool Overhead Railway is opened, the first such railway to run on electricity from its inception. The painter Ivon Hitchens is born.

JAN The Independent Labour Party is formed under the chairmanship of Keir Hardie.
FEB [**4**] The first stretch of the Liverpool Overhead Railway (Alexandra Dock to Herculaneum Dock) is opened by Lord Salisbury. [**13**] The second Home Rule Bill is introduced.
APR [**24**] Film actor Leslie Howard is born in London.
JUN [**13**] Dorothy Sayers, academic and writer of detective novels, is born at Oxford. [**22**] HMS *Victoria*, the Royal Navy's flagship, is rammed and sunk by HMS *Camperdown* as a result of a misunderstood order.
JUL [**6**] George V marries Princess Mary of Teck.
SEP [**1**] The second Home Rule Bill passes its third Commons reading. [**8**] The Home Rule Bill is rejected by the Lords. [**16**] The film producer Sir Alexander Korda is born in Hungary.
OCT [**28**] The Royal Navy's first destroyer, HMS *Havoc*, goes on its trials.

T. E. Knightley: Queen's Hall, London.
Perrycroft, Malverns.

Aubrey Beardsley: *Siegfried; Morte D'Arthur.*

Sir Arthur Pinero: *The Amazons.*
Robert Louis Stevenson: *Catriona.*
Oscar Wilde: *Salome; Lady Windermere's Fan.*
E. F. Benson: *Dodo.*
Beatrice Harraden: *Ships that Pass in the Night.*
Sir Max Beerbohm: *The Iron Pirate.*
William Butler Yeats: *The Celtic Twilight.*

1894 Uganda becomes a British protectorate. Aubrey Beardsley becomes art editor of *The Yellow Book*. Argon is discovered by Sir William Ramsay and Baron Rayleigh.

JAN [**1**] The Manchester Ship Canal is opened to traffic.

FEB [**10**] Harold Macmillan, Lord Stockton, Conservative Prime Minister, is born in London.

MAR [**3**] Gladstone resigns after splitting his party over Irish Home Rule; he is succeeded by Lord Rosebery as Prime Minister.

MAY [**6**] The aviator Sir Alan Cobham is born.

JUN [**23**] Edward VIII is born at Richmond. There is a pit disaster at Cilfynydd in South Wales with the loss of 286 lives. [**30**] Tower Bridge is officially opened.

AUG [**2**] Death duties are introduced.

SEP [**13**] The author J. B. Priestley is born at Bradford. [**28**] The first branch of Marks and Spencer (Penny Bazaar) opens at Cheetham Hill in Manchester. [**30**] The composer Peter Warlock is born as Philip Heseltine.

DEC [**3**] Robert Louis Stevenson, author of *Treasure Island*, dies on the island of Samoa in the Pacific.

C. F. A. Voysey: 14 South Parade, Bedford Park, Chiswick.
C. H. Townsend: Bishopsgate Institute, London.
Sir Horace Jones: Tower Bridge, London.

1895 Uganda becomes a British colony. The National Trust is founded; the first property to be taken into care is the Clergy House, Alfriston. Work begins on Westminster (Roman Catholic) Cathedral, designed by John Bentley; it is the last great building in Britain to be constructed in brick without steel reinforcement.

JAN [**24**] The Conservative Party leader Randolph Churchill dies.

MAR [**15**] Bridget Clary, aged 27, is burned to death for witchcraft at Battyradhen in County Tipperary.

APR [**26**] Oscar Wilde's first trial opens. [**29**] The conductor Sir Malcolm Sargent is born.

MAY [**15**] Joseph Whitaker, the publisher who founded *Whitaker's Almanack*, dies. [**24**] The first stage knighthood is awarded, to Henry Irving. [**25**] Oscar Wilde's second trial ends; he is sentenced to two years' hard labour.

JUN [**25**] The Liberal Lord Rosebery resigns, to be succeeded by the Conservative Lord Salisbury as Prime Minister (third ministry).

OCT [**6**] The Promenade Concerts are founded by Sir Henry Wood. [**15**] The first motor show takes place, at the Agricultural Show Ground at Tunbridge Wells.

DEC [**1**] The writer Henry Williamson is born. [**14**] George VI, the second son of George V, is born at Sandringham in Norfolk. [**29**] The Jameson Raid into the Boer colony of Transvaal in support of the Uitlanders, the European settlers; Sir Leander Starr Jameson's attack on the Boers is unsuccessful.

John Francis Bentley: Westminster (Roman Catholic) Cathedral, London.
Charles Rennie Mackintosh: Glasgow Herald Building.

Sir Arthur Pinero: *The Second Mrs Tanqueray*.
Oscar Wilde: *The Importance of Being Earnest*.
George Meredith: *The Amazing Marriage*.
Joseph Conrad: *Almayer's Folly*.
H. G. Wells: *The Time Machine*.
Grant Allen: *The Woman who Did*.
Marie Corelli: *The Sorrows of Satan*.

1896 William Ramsay discovers helium. Cecil Rhodes relinquishes the premiership of Cape Colony. Anglo-Egyptian forces under General Kitchener begin the reconquest of the Sudan. Tsar Nicholas II visits London.

JAN [**3**] The Kruger Telegram; Kaiser Wilhelm sends a telegram to President Kruger of the Transvaal congratulating him on defeating the raiders led by Jameson. This leads to an outburst of indignation and anti-German feeling in Britain. [**19**] Sir Michael Balcon, film producer, is born in Birmingham.
MAR [**22**] Thomas Hughes, author of *Tom Brown's Schooldays*, dies.
MAY [**4**] The *Daily Mail* is founded by Lord Northcliffe.
JUN [**19**] Bessie Wallis Warfield, later Duchess of Windsor, is born in Pennsylvania.
JUL [**19**] The novelist A. J. Cronin is born at Cardross.
AUG [**13**] Sir John Millais, painter, dies.
OCT [**3**] The artist, designer and craftsman William Morris dies. [**11**] Archbishop Benson dies while staying with Gladstone at Hawarden.
NOV [**16**] Sir Oswald Mosley, leader of the Fascist movement in Britain, is born.
DEC [**22**] Frederick Temple, Bishop of London, becomes Archbishop of Canterbury.

Charles Rennie Mackintosh: Glasgow School of Art (begun).
Sir Edwin Lutyens: Munstead Wood, Surrey.

John Waterhouse: *Hylas and the nymphs*.
Sir Edward Burne-Jones: illustrations for Kelmscott 'Chaucer'.

Sir Arthur Conan Doyle: *Rodney Stone.*
R. D. Blackmore: *Tales from the Telling House.*
A. E. Housman: *A Shropshire Lad.*
Thomas Hardy: *Jude the Obscure.*
H. G. Wells: *The Island of Dr Moreau.*
Henry Newbolt: *Drake's Drum.*
William Morris: *The Well at the World's End.*
Frederick Farrar: *The Young Man Master of Himself.*
The Savoy Magazine (first issue).

 Sir Edward Elgar: *Enigma Variations.*

1897 Sir J. J. Thomson discovers the electron. Ronald Ross demonstrates that malaria is transmitted by the mosquito. The first all-corridor train runs from London to Glasgow.

JAN [**8**] The novelist Dennis Wheatley is born. [**12**] Sir Isaac Pitman dies in Somerset.

MAR [**17**] Bob Fitzsimmons becomes the only British-born boxer to win the world heavyweight boxing title.

APR [**25**] George V's daughter Mary is born.

MAY [**19**] Oscar Wilde is released from Pentonville Prison. [**22**] The Blackwall Tunnel under the Thames is officially opened by the Prince of Wales. [**27**] Sir John Cockcroft, nuclear physicist, is born.

JUN [**12**] Sir Anthony Eden, Lord Avon, the Conservative Prime Minister, is born at Bishop Auckland. Leon Goossens, oboist, is born in Liverpool.

JUN [**22**] Queen Victoria's Diamond Jubilee celebrations coincide with the peak of Britain's imperialist ambitions.

AUG [**10**] The Automobile Club of Great Britain, later to become the R.A.C., is founded. [**11**] Enid Blyton, writer of children's books, is born at Dulwich.

SEP [**10**] George Smith, a London taxi-driver, is convicted of drunken driving; he is the first motorist to be so convicted.

NOV [**15**] The Labour Party leader Aneurin Bevan is born at Tredegar.

 Tate Gallery, London (completed).
H. V. Lanchester and Edwin Rickards: Cardiff City Hall and Law Courts.
Mary Watts: Watts Memorial Chapel, Compton.

 Ernest Dowson: *The Pierrot of the Minute.*
H. G. Wells: *The Invisible Man.*
Henry James: *The Spoils of Poynton; What Maisie Knew.*

Vincent O'Sullivan: *The Houses of Sin.*
Bram Stoker: *Dracula.*
Thomas Hardy: *The Well-Beloved.*
Joseph Conrad: *The Nigger of the Narcissus.*
Dorothy Wordsworth: *Journals* (posthumous).
Ouida: *The Altruist.*

 Samuel Butler: *Ulysses.*
Sir Hubert Parry: *Symphonic Variations.*
Alexander Mackenzie: *Scottish Piano Concerto.*

1898 The Folksong Society is formed. The painter Sir Edward Burne-Jones dies. John P. Holland invents the submarine.

JAN [**9**] The entertainer Gracie Fields is born at Rochdale. [**14**] Lewis Carroll dies at Guildford.

MAY [**19**] William Ewart Gladstone, four times Prime Minister, dies at Hawarden Castle in North Wales aged 88.

JUN [**9**] Hong Kong's New Territories are leased by Britain from China for 99 years.

JUL [**30**] The sculptor Henry Moore is born at Castleford.

AUG [**13**] Alfred Hitchcock, film producer, is born at Leytonstone.

SEP [**2**] Battle of Omdurman; Kitchener's Anglo-Egyptian forces defeat the Khalifa's army, winning back the Sudan for Egypt. [**19**] Kitchener reaches Fashoda and finds the French under Major Marchand in occupation. [**24**] Sir Howard Florey, pioneer of penicillin production, is born in Australia.

 C. F. A. Voysey: Broadleys, Lake Windermere.

 George Bernard Shaw: *The Perfect Wagnerite.*
Joseph Conrad: *Tales of Unrest.*
Henry James: *The Turn of the Screw.*
Arnold Bennett: *A Man from the North.*
G. W. Steevens: *With Kitchener to Khartoum.*
Oscar Wilde: *The Ballad of Reading Gaol.*
Anthony Hope: *Rupert of Hentzau.*

 Sir Edward Elgar: *Caractacus.*
Samuel Coleridge-Taylor: *Hiawatha.*
Gustav Holst: *The Idea.*
Sir Arthur Sullivan: *The Beauty Stone.*

1899 The Coal Smoke Abatement Society is founded. Rutherford identifies alpha and beta rays. The Board of Education and the London Borough Councils are created.

JAN   [**19**] The Anglo-Egyptian Convention establishes what becomes known as Anglo-Egyptian Sudan.

MAR   [**5**] The composer Patrick Hadley is born. [**21**] A Convention between Britain and France confirms that France is excluded from the Sudan and Egypt.

JUL   [**1**] Charles Laughton, actor, is born.

AUG   [**27**] The novelist C. S. Forester is born in Cairo.

SEP   [**29**] Billy Butlin, the holiday camp owner, is born in South Africa.

OCT   [**10**] The Boer War begins between the British and the republics of the Orange Free State and the Transvaal.

NOV   [**2**] The Siege of Ladysmith in west Natal begins; British troops are surrounded by Transvaal forces. [**24**] Sir Reginald Wingate's forces pursue and kill the Khalifa in the Sudan.

DEC   [**2**] The conductor Sir John Barbirolli is born in London. [**5**] Sir Henry Tate, philanthropist and founder of the Tate Gallery, dies aged 80. [**10**] Sir Noel Coward, actor, playwright, songwriter, is born at Teddington.

C. H. Townsend: Whitechapel Art Gallery.
Sir Edwin Lutyens: Tigbourne Court, Surrey.
Palace Pier, Brighton.

William Rothenstein: *Augustus John.*
Sir George Clausen: *Harvesters cutting up sheaves.*

Sir Arthur Pinero: *The Gay Lord Quex.*
Col. D. Streamer: *Ruthless Rhymes for Heartless Homes.*
Edith Nesbit: *The Story of the Treasure Seekers.*
Mary Cholmondley: *Red Pottage.*
Somerville and Ross: *Some Experiences of an Irish R.M.*
E. F. Benson: *Mammon & CO.*

Sir Edward Elgar: *Sea Pictures.*

1900

1900   The Dunlop Rubber Company produces its first pneumatic motor tyre. Sir Patrick Manson identifies the anopheles mosquito as the carrier of malaria. The British Labour Party is founded by combining the Independent Labour Party, the Fabian Society and the Trade Unions.

JAN   [**3**] The new royal yacht *Victoria and Albert* capsizes as it embarks. [**6**] General White repels an attack by the Boers on

Ladysmith. [**9**] In the influenza epidemic in London people are dying at the rate of 50 a day. [**10**] Field Marshal Lord Roberts arrives in Cape Town to take command of the British forces in South Africa. [**20**] The artist and writer John Ruskin dies at Coniston. The novelist R. D. Blackmore also dies. [**24**] Battle of Spion Kop; Sir Redvers Buller's troops are repulsed with severe losses. [**28**] The composer Michael Head is born.

FEB [**12**] A meeting at Mile End to protest against the Boer War ends in uproar. [**15**] The Relief of Kimberley. The Hippodrome Theatre in Charing Cross Road opens. [**28**] Relief of Ladysmith by Sir Redvers Buller's troops.

MAR [**8**] Queen Victoria makes a rare visit to London, greeted by an enthusiastic welcome from the public. [**23**] Sir Arthur Evans begins his historic dig at Knossos. [**31**] George V's son Henry is created Duke of Gloucester.

APR [**4**] The Prince of Wales escapes unhurt when a boy fires a gun at him twice in Brussels, apparently in protest at the Boer War.

MAY [**17**]Relief of Mafeking after a Boer siege lasting 217 days. 26,000 women and children die in concentration camps set up by the British for Boer civilians. [**22**] The age limit for boys working in coal mines is raised from 12 to 13.

JUN [**25**] Earl Louis Mountbatten is born at Frogmore, Isle of Wight.

JUL [**22**] 11 people die when the *Campania* runs down a smaller vessel in the Thames estuary.

AUG [**4**] Queen Elizabeth, the Queen Mother, is born in Hertfordshire as Lady Elizabeth Bowes Lyon.

SEP [**1**] General Roberts annexes the Boer republic of Transvaal. [**2**] There are demonstrations in Dublin against British rule. [**3**] There is an outbreak of bubonic plague in Glasgow. [**9**] James Hilton, author of *Lost Horizon*, is born at Leigh in Lancashire.

OCT [**3**] Sir Edward Elgar's *Dream of Gerontius* is first performed at Birmingham.

NOV [**22**]The composer Sir Arthur Sullivan dies. [**30**] The poet and dramatist Oscar Wilde dies in poverty in Paris as Sebastian Melmoth.

DEC [**11**] Lord Roberts leaves South Africa to return to England. [**22**] The composer Alan Bush is born. [**30**] 50 people die as gales sweep across Britain. [**31**] At Stonehenge, Stone 22 and its lintel fall down.

C. F. A. Voysey: The Orchard, Chorleywood.
E. W. Mountford: Central Criminal Courts, Old Bailey, London.

Gwen John: *Self-portrait.*

 Winston Churchill: *Savrola.*
H. G. Wells: *Love and Mr Lewisham.*
Joseph Conrad: *Lord Jim.*
Ernest Smith: *The Wallet of Kai Lung.*
Marie Corelli: *Boy; The Greatest Queen in the World.*

 Sir Edward Elgar: *The Dream of Gerontius.*
'I'm only a bird in a gilded cage' (song).
'Goodbye, Dolly Gray' (song).

1901 J. Langley demonstrates the effect of adrenalin in speeding up the heart rate. The composer Edmund Rubbra is born. The vacuum cleaner is invented by Cecil Booth.

JAN [1] The six states and two territories are federated to form the Commonwealth of Australia. [8] 12 retailers are prosecuted for selling beer containing arsenic. [22] Queen Victoria dies at Osborne House aged 81, the longest reigning monarch and longest lived of all British monarchs. [27] Edward VII, the new King, makes his nephew the Kaiser a Field Marshal in the British army.

FEB [2] Queen Victoria's funeral. [15] Edward VII resigns as Grand Master of Freemasons.

MAR [23] Reports that Boers are starving in British concentration camps begin to leak out.

APR [3] Richard D'Oyly Carte, impresario responsible for staging the Gilbert and Sullivan operettas, dies. [4] The liner *Celtic* is launched at Belfast. [21] Lillie Langtry opens as Marie Antoinette in *A Royal Necklace* at the Imperial Theatre. [30] The game of ping pong is created by James Gibb.

MAY [13] Lord Salisbury speaks out against the idea of Irish Home Rule. [15] The Admiralty decides to build three huge battleships. [16] Britain's first diesel submarine, *D1*, is launched at Barrow.

JUN [17] David Lloyd George denounces the high death rate among Boer women and children in the prison camps in South Africa. [26] The liner *Lusitania* is wrecked off Newfoundland: 350 are rescued.

JUL [9] The novelist Barbara Cartland is born. [22] The British Congress on Tuberculosis begins.

AUG [1] The Commons vote an extra £12 million for naval and war budgets.

SEP [15]The yachtsman Sir Francis Chichester is born at Barnstaple. [18] A torpedo boat sinks at Grimsby, drowning

59 people. [**26**] An outbreak of smallpox begins to spread.

OCT   [**2**] The first Royal Navy submarine, *Holland I*, is launched at Barrow. [**6**] Sir Henry Irving and Ellen Terry leave for a US tour. [**25**] Joseph Chamberlain gives an anti-German speech and defends the Boer camps.

NOV   [**6**] Kate Greenaway, illustrator, dies. [**9**] Edward VII's eldest surviving son George is created Prince of Wales. [**12**] 200 people are killed in gales. [**15**] The death rate in refugee camps for Boer families continues to rise, partly due to a measles epidemic; charges of neglect and brutality are rejected by an official report.

DEC   [**12**] The first transatlantic wireless (radio) signal, the letter S, is sent from Poldhu in Cornwall and received by Marconi at St John's in Newfoundland. [**18**] Lloyd George is forced to leave a pro-Boer meeting as a riot breaks out.

Charles Rennie Mackintosh: Windy Hill, Kilmacolm.
Sir Edwin Lutyens: The Deanery, Sonning.
Giles Gilbert Scott: Liverpool Cathedral.
Harrods, Knightsbridge, London.

Luke Fildes: *The Village Wedding.*
Sir William Rothenstein: *An interior.*

Matthew Shiel: *The Purple Cloud.*
George Douglas: *The House with the Green Shutters.*
Rudyard Kipling: *Kim.*
H. G. Wells: *The First Men in the Moon.*
Daily Express (first issue April 24).
Ouida: *Street Dust.*

Sir Edward Elgar: *Cockaigne Overture; Pomp and Circumstance* Nos 1 and 2 (containing the 'Land of Hope and Glory' tune).
Sir Charles Stanford: *Much Ado About Nothing.*

1902 Ernest Rutherford proposes the disintegration theory to explain radio-activity. Sinn Fein (Ourselves Alone) is founded by the Irish republican Arthur Griffith to promote the cause of Home Rule for Ireland. Sir Ronald Ross is awarded the Nobel Prize for Physiology and Medicine.

JAN   [**28**] The census shows that London's population has reached 6.5 million. [**30**] Anglo-Japanese Alliance formed. [**31**] The number of smallpox victims in London rises to 2273.

FEB   [**13**] The Government refuses to allow a German committee to visit the South African concentration camps. [**14**] In a speech,

Lord Rosebery declares that he will never give Ireland its independence.

MAR [**26**] Cecil Rhodes dies. [**28**] The actress Dame Flora Robson is born. [**29**] The composer Sir William Walton is born at Oldham.

APR [**1**] The treadmill is abolished in prisons. [**20**] The actor Sir Donald Wolfit is born at Newark-on-Trent.

MAY [**24**] Empire Day is celebrated for the first time. [**29**] Lord Rosebery opens the London School of Economics. [**31**] The Treaty of Vereeniging ends the Boer War; the Transvaal and Orange Free State accept British sovereignty and Britain provides £3 million to repair war damage.

JUN [**10**] Ellen Terry and Beerbohm Tree open in *The Merry Wives of Windsor* at His Majesty's Theatre. [**18**] The novelist Samuel Butler dies. [**23**] Edward VII founds the Order of Merit. [**30**] Lillie Langtry marries the MP Ian Malcolm.

JUL [**7**] Joseph Chamberlain is involved in a hansom cab accident: he suffers a deep head wound. [**12**] The Conservative Arthur Balfour becomes Prime Minister. Lord Kitchener returns to London from South Africa: he is given a triumphal welcome.

AUG [**9**] Coronation of Edward VII, which has been delayed six weeks by the King's appendicitis operation.

SEP [**13**] The first conviction on fingerprint evidence is secured by the Metropolitan Police, in a case against Harry Jackson. [**19**] Stanley Spencer makes a 30 mile flight in an airship of his own design.

OCT [**16**] The first Borstal Institution opens, at Borstal near Rochester.

NOV [**8**] The Kaiser arrives in London in an attempt to improve Anglo-German relations.

DEC [**9**] The Conservative politician R. A. Butler is born in India. [**19**] The actor Sir Ralph Richardson is born at Cheltenham. [**20**] George VI, son of George V, is born. [**22**] Archbishop Temple dies.

 H. V. Lanchester & Edwin Rickards: Deptford Town Hall.
C. H. Townsend: Horniman Museum, London (completed).
G. W. J. Neatby: Harrods' Food Hall.

 John Singer Sargent: *The Acheson Sisters.*

 Arthur Mason: *The Four Feathers.*
Hilaire Belloc: *The Path to Rome.*
Arnold Bennett: *Anna of the Five Towns.*
Rudyard Kipling: *Just So Stories.*
Joseph Conrad: *The Heart of Darkness.*

J. M. Barrie: *The Admirable Crichton.*
Beatrix Potter: *The Tale of Peter Rabbit.*
Sir Arthur Conan Doyle: *The Hound of the Baskervilles.*
Michael Fairless: *The Roadmender.*

Edward German: *Merrie England.*
Sir Edward Elgar: *Coronation Ode.*

1903 Letchworth, the first garden city, is begun, to designs by Parker and Unwin.

JAN   [**10**] The sculptor Barbara Hepworth is born at Wakefield. [**27**] 51 people die in a fire at a mental hospital at Colney Hatch.

FEB   [**6**] Randall Davidson, Bishop of Winchester, becomes Archbishop of Canterbury. [**21**] It rains 'blood' in southern England; the rain is coloured by dust from the Sahara. [**24**] A British field force marches on the 'Mad' Mullah from Obbiah on the Indian Ocean.

MAR   [**22**] Dean Farrar, clergyman and author of *Eric, or Little by Little*, dies. [**29**] A regular news service begins between New York and London using Marconi's wireless.

APR   [**23**] The Government reveals that the Boer and Boxer Wars cost one-third of the United Kingdom's annual budget.

MAY   [**1**] Edward VII arrives in Paris on a goodwill visit. [**5**] Foreign Secretary Lord Lansdowne declares that the Persian Gulf is the western frontier of India. [**12**] The actor Wilfrid Hyde White and the composer Sir Lennox Berkeley are born. [**29**] The comedian Bob Hope is born at Eltham as Leslie Townes Hope.

JUN   [**18**] 16 people die in an explosion at Woolwich Arsenal. [**25**] The novelist George Orwell is born at Motihari in Bengal as Eric Blair. [**29**] The Government protests to Belgium about atrocities in the Congo.

JUL   [**1**] The aviator Amy Johnson is born at Hull. [**2**] Sir Alec Douglas-Home, Conservative Prime Minister, is born. King Olav V of Norway is born at Sandringham. [**3**] Britain and Japan demand that Russia evacuates Manchuria. [**7**] The current birth rate, if continued, will result in a population standstill in 18 years. [**20**] The Government announces that larger numbers of troops will be sent to India.

AUG   [**22**] Lord Salisbury, Prime Minister four times, dies. [**24**] The painter Graham Sutherland is born. [**25**] A Royal Commission into the Boer War criticizes poor campaign planning and reveals that 100,000 British lives were lost.

SEP   [**1**] Imports of sugar from Denmark, Russia and Argentina are banned as part of an imperial preference policy. [**8**] The TUC opposes the Government's tariff policy. [**10**] A great storm in southern England causes widespread damage.

Oct [**5**] Austen Chamberlain becomes Chancellor in a reshuffle following Joseph Chamberlain's resignation. [**10**] Mrs Pankhurst founds the Woman's Social and Political Union, to continue her campaign for votes for women with more extreme action. [**12**] The shipbuilders Cammell and Laird are to amalgamate. [**23**] HMS *Victory* is rammed by a modern battleship causing severe damage. [**28**] The novelist Evelyn Waugh is born.

Nov [**20**] The New Zealand government approves the UK preferential trade agreement.

Dec [**8**] The philosopher Herbert Spencer dies. [**15**] The Australian government approves the preferential trade agreement.

Charles Rennie Mackintosh: Hill House, Helensburgh.
Sir Aston Webb: St Michael's Court, Caius College, Cambridge.

Walter Sickert: *Mamma Mia Poveretta.*

Joseph Conrad: *Typhoon.*
Henry James: *The Ambassadors.*
Samuel Butler: *The Way of All Flesh.*
G. E. Moore: *Principia Ethica.*
George Bernard Shaw: *Man and Superman.*
Erskine Childers: *The Riddle of the Sands.*
Bertrand Russell: *Principles of Mathematics.*
Daily Mirror (first issue November l).

Gustav Holst: *Indra.*

1904 The governments of France and Britain sign the Anglo-French Entente ('Entente Cordiale'), ending the long-standing friction over territorial claims in Africa. The Abbey Theatre, Dublin opens. The London Symphony Orchestra gives its first concert. The painter George Frederick Watts dies. Lord Rayleigh is awarded the Nobel Prize for Physics and Sir William Ramsay that for Chemistry. Sir John Fleming devises the first electron tube (the Diode valve).

Jan [**1**] Earl Russell has the first motor vehicle registration plate in Britain, Al, for his Napier. [**13**] The composer Richard Addinsell is born. [**14**] Sir Cecil Beaton, photographer and designer, is born in London. [**18**] The film actor Cary Grant is born in Bristol as Archibald Leach.

Feb [**1**] Britain agrees with France to remain neutral in the event of a war between Japan and Russia. [**3**] John Redmond, Irish

Nationalist, renews the call for Home Rule for Ireland. [**29**] It is revealed that the colonies would prefer metric weights and measures to imperial.

MAR [**12**] The first mainline electric train in Britain runs from Liverpool to Southport. [**29**] Edward VII opens Richmond Park to the public.

APR [**1**] Henry Royce's firm makes its first car. [**14**] The first attempts at talking pictures are made at the Fulham Theatre. The actor Sir John Gielgud is born in London. [**27**] The Poet Laureate C. Day Lewis is born at Sligo.

MAY [**4**] Charles Rolls and Henry Royce form a car manufacturing company. [**9**] Sir Henry Morton Stanley, journalist and explorer, dies in London. He regretted his greeting to Livingstone in 1871, because he was met with 'Mr Stanley, I presume?' wherever he went. [**26**] The entertainer George Formby is born. [**30**] A strike by 3000 London cab drivers begins.

JUN [**9**] Commons debate on the alleged Belgian atrocities in the Congo. [**28**] The steamship *Norge* is wrecked off Ireland: 700 Scandinavian emigrants die in the disaster.

JUL [**5**] Edward Elgar is knighted, following the success of the Elgar Festival at Covent Garden in March.

AUG [**3**] A British force under Younghusband takes Lhasa in Tibet. [**4**] The first Atlantic weather forecast is received by wireless. [**16**] The British Government protests to Russia about the sinking of neutral merchant shipping. [**25**] The first ocean-going turbine steamship, the *Victorian*, is launched at Belfast. [**26**] The author Christopher Isherwood is born.

SEP [**7**] Treaty with Tibet signed in Lhasa. [**17**] Sir Frederick Ashton, founder of the Royal Ballet, is born. [**19**] British pressure succeeds in making Leopold, King of the Belgians, set up a commission of inquiry into the atrocity allegations.

OCT [**2**] Graham Greene, novelist, is born at Berkhamsted. [**10**] Actress Anna Neagle is born in London as Marjorie Robertson. [**22**] The Russian Baltic fleet attacks and sinks two Hull trawlers on the Dogger Bank. They claim they believed they were Japanese torpedo boats, but there is widespread indignation in Britain; only French diplomatic intervention stops the Dogger Bank Incident escalating into war. [**27**] Royal Navy ships surround Russian ships in the North Sea.

NOV [**17**] The first under-water voyage of a submarine is made, crossing the Solent. [**29**] There is a dramatic increase in the numbers of people receiving poor relief: 800,000 in England and Wales. 250,000 are reduced to living in workhouses.

DEC [**24**] The Coliseum opens in London.

Charles Mewès & Arthur Davis: Ritz Hotel, London.
Charles Rennie Mackintosh: Cranston Tearoom, Sauchiehall Street, Glasgow.

Gwen John: *Dorelia by Lamplight.*
George Frederick Watts: *Physical energy.*

George Bernard Shaw: *Candida.*
W. H. Hudson: *Green Mansions.*
Joseph Conrad: *Nostromo.*
J. M. Barrie: *Peter Pan.*
Frederick Rolfe: *Hadrian VII.*

Frederick Delius: *Koanga.*
Sir Edward Elgar: *In the South.*

1905 The sculptor Jacob Epstein settles in London. The composer Alan Rawsthorne is born.

JAN [**2**] The composer Sir Michael Tippett is born in London. [**11**] Transatlantic liner tickets are costing more: it now costs £6 to cross to America third class. [**25**] The Cullinan Diamond, the largest ever found, is discovered in the Premier Diamond Mine; it is later presented to Edward VII. [**26**] Cardinal Heenan, Roman Catholic Archbishop of Westminster, is born.

FEB [**11**] Frenchmen land at Crystal Palace in a balloon after crossing the Channel. [**17**] Outbreak of typhus in East London.

MAR [**1**] Spending on the Navy is to treble. [**10**] 32 die in a pit disaster in South Wales. [**15**] 23 die in severe storms off Land's End. [**18**] The film actor Robert Donat is born in Manchester. In a Royal Command Performance of Shaw's *John Bull's Other Island*, Edward VII laughs so much he breaks his chair. [**31**] *The Return of Sherlock Holmes* is published by popular demand.

APR [**1**] The *Victorian* arrives in Halifax, Nova Scotia at the end of her maiden voyage.

MAY [**12**] A Bill to give women the vote is 'talked out': the Bill fails.

JUN [**15**] The film actor James Robertson Justice is born. [**26**] The Automobile Association is founded.

JUL [**1**] The Colonial Office considers a plan to resettle Britain's surplus population in various parts of the Empire. [**10**] Puccini's *Madame Butterfly* is given its first UK performance at Covent Garden. [**11**] 124 miners die in a Glamorgan pit disaster. [**12**] George V's son John is born.

Aug [1] Field Marshal Lord Roberts alleges that the British armed services are worse prepared now than they were at the beginning of the Boer War.

Sep [11] Published figures show that rural lunacy is on the increase; this is attributed to the tedium of life in the country. [19] Britain and Germany hold simultaneous war manoeuvres. Thomas Barnardo, founder of children's homes, dies.

Oct [13] Sir Henry Irving dies at Bradford from a heart attack outside his hotel. [25] Lord Rosebery calls for a future Liberal government to challenge the power of the House of Lords.

Nov [7] The composer William Alwyn is born in Northampton. [12] Queen Alexandra launches an appeal for the unemployed. [14] Robert Whitehead, who invented the naval torpedo in 1866, dies in Berkshire. [22] The world's largest turbine-powered liner, the *Carmania*, leaves Liverpool on her maiden voyage. [26] Emlyn Williams, actor, playwright, screenwriter, is born.

Dec [3] British troops quell a riot at Georgetown in British Guyana. [5] The roof of Charing Cross Station collapses. [14] The trades unions call for universal suffrage, an eight-hour working day and old-age pensions. [23] The final heat of the earliest known beauty contest in Britain takes place at Newcastle-upon-Tyne.

 Norman Shaw: Piccadilly Hotel, London; The New Quadrant, Regent Street, London.

 Philip Wilson Steer: *Chepstow Castle.*
Maxwell Armfield: *The Tunnel.*

 Edgar Wallace: *The Four Just Men.*
Captain Robert Scott: *The Voyage of the Discovery.*
William Holman Hunt: *Pre-Raphaelitism.*
H. G. Wells: *Kipps.*
Oscar Wilde: *De Profundis.*
E. M. Forster: *Where Angels Fear to Tread.*
Baroness Orczy: *The Scarlet Pimpernel.*
Sir Arthur Conan Doyle: *The Return of Sherlock Holmes.*

 Sir Edward Elgar: *Introduction and Allegro; Pomp and Circumstance No 3.*

1906 Sir Joseph Thomson is awarded the Nobel Prize for Physics.

Jan [22] A tram accident in Liverpool kills 30.
Feb [1] The Government drops its plan to build a faster motor

road from London to Brighton. [7] The General Election results in a Liberal landslide (Liberal 399, Conservative 156, Labour 29) and significant gains for Labour. [8] A march of unemployed people from the Midlands to London meets with an unsympathetic reception. [10] HMS *Dreadnought* is launched; the revolutionary new battleship design marks the start of a desperate naval arms race between Britain and Germany.

MAR   [14] Parliament approves old-age pensions in principle.

APR   [6] Sir John Betjeman, Poet Laureate, is born in London. [9] Hugh Gaitskell, Labour Party leader, is born. [13] The playwright Samuel Beckett is born. [17] The Labour Party calls for votes for women. [22] Delius's amanuensis Eric Fenby is born. [24] The Nazi collaborator William Joyce, 'Lord Haw-Haw', is born in Brooklyn. [27] China agrees reluctantly to allow the British to control access to Tibet.

MAY   [6] British soldiers kill 60 Zulus at Durban.

JUN   [7] The liner *Lusitania* is launched, the largest and fastest passenger liner in the world. [12] Ellen Terry celebrates 50 years on the stage. 322 British ships are involved in naval exercises, making mock attacks on British ports. [23] A deputation demanding votes for women meets the Prime Minister.

JUL   [3] George Sanders, film actor, is born in Russia to British parents. [7] Britain's first hot-air balloon race. [12] Ten Londoners on a day trip to Brighton are killed in a bus crash. [15] A Commons select committee proposes the introduction of school meals. [23] 1000 Zulu rebels surrender to British troops in South Africa.

AUG   [8] Churchill and others protest at the excessive noise made by vehicle traffic. [9] The Boer War Commission reports that corruption and incompetence in the conduct of the war cost over £1 million. [15] Edward VII visits the Kaiser; discussions about the naval situation are fruitless.

SEP   [20] The liner *Mauretania* is launched. [22] Thousands in London help in the recapture of the Life Guards' escaped mascot, a bear.

OCT   [1] In sea trials, *Dreadnought* makes a record speed of 21 knots. [24] Eleven suffragettes are sent to prison after causing disturbances in Parliament.

NOV   [6] Sylvia Pankhurst, a prominent suffragette, is released from prison.

DEC   [15] The Piccadilly Line of the London Underground is opened. [30] The film director Carol Reed is born at Putney.

Vauxhall Bridge over the Thames (opened May 26).
Sir Edwin Lutyens: Heathcote, Ilkley, Yorkshire.

 Charles Conder: *Newquay*.
John Strudwick: *When Apples were Golden*.

 George Bernard Shaw: *The Doctor's Dilemma*.
Angela Brazil: *The Fortunes of Philippa*.
John Galsworthy: *The Man of Property*.
Winston Churchill: *Lord Randolph Churchill*.
Upton Sinclair: *The Jungle*.
Keble Howard: *The Smiths of Surbiton*.
John Bull (first issue).

 Vaughan Williams: *Norfolk Rhapsodies; English Hymnal* (edited).
Sir Edward Elgar: *The Kingdom*.
Dame Ethel Smyth: *The Wreckers*.

1907 Rudyard Kipling is awarded the Nobel Prize for Literature.

FEB [**15**] James Thompson, the laziest man in the world, is forced to get out of bed after 29 years and go for help when his 80-year-old mother becomes too ill to look after him. [**27**] The Central Criminal Court is opened on the site of Newgate Prison. [**28**] The Government is to spend less on the Navy this year, but still orders three more dreadnoughts. [**21**] The poet W. H. Auden is born.

MAR [**8**] Keir Hardie's Women's Enfranchisement Bill is defeated. [**16**] HMS *Indomitable*, the world's largest cruiser, is launched on the Clyde. [**21**] The Prime Minister opposes the Channel Tunnel Bill. [**25**] The Channel Tunnel Bill is defeated because of War Office opposition and lack of popular support.

MAY [**13**] The novelist Dame Daphne du Maurier is born. [**22**] Sir Laurence Olivier (Lord Olivier), actor, director and producer, is born at Dorking. [**28**] The first Isle of Man motor cycle TT Race is held.

JUN [**14**] The Government announces its plan to curb the power of the House of Lords.

JUL [**6**] The Brooklands motor racing track near Weybridge opens. [**27**] The dreadnought HMS *Bellerophon* is launched at Portsmouth. [**29**] The first Boy Scout camp begins as an experiment on Brownsea Island in Dorset.

AUG [**13**] The architect Sir Basil Spence is born.

SEP [**10**] Britain's first military airship flies successfully at Farnborough. [**13**] The *Lusitania* arrives in New York after a record Atlantic crossing, averaging 23 knots.

OCT [**9**] The Conservative politician Lord Hailsham is born as Quintin Hogg. [**26**] The Territorial Army is founded by the Secretary of State for War, Richard Haldane.

NOV [**15**] The German Kaiser is awarded an honorary degree at Oxford. [**22**] The liner *Mauretania* arrives in New York at the end of her maiden voyage. [**27**] Florence Nightingale is awarded the Order of Merit.

DEC [**12**] Dinizulu, the King of the Zulus, surrenders to the British; the Zulu rebellion was triggered off by the imposition of a poll tax. [**17**] Lord Kelvin, physicist and inventor, dies. [**22**] Dame Peggy Ashcroft, actress, is born at Croydon, London.

Charles Holden: Bristol Library.
F. L. Pearson: Hever Castle, Kent (alterations completed).
J. R. Scott: Waterloo Station façade (opened 1922).

Muirhead Bone: The British Museum Reading Room, London.

Joseph Conrad: *The Secret Agent*.
Edmund Gosse: *Father and Son*.
J. M. Synge: *The Playboy of the Western World*.
E. M. Forster: *The Longest Journey*.
Maud Diver: *Captain Desmond, VC*.

Frederick Delius: *A Village Romeo and Juliet; Brigg Fair*.
Frank Bridge: *Isabella*.
Gustav Holst: *A Somerset Rhapsody*.
Sir Edward Elgar: *Pomp and Circumstance No 4*.
Vaughan Williams: *Towards the Unknown Region*.

1908 JAN [**12**] Prices of transatlantic liner tickets fall sharply, thanks to competition between the Cunard and White Star companies. [**26**] The first boy scout troop is registered (First Glasgow).

FEB [**11**] Explorer Sir Vivian Fuchs is born in Kent. [**13**] Dentist Arthur Hyne is sent down for seven years for bigamy: he has five wives. [**22**] The actor Sir John Mills is born at Felixstowe.

MAR [**5**] Sir Rex Harrison, actor, is born in Liverpool as Reginald Carey. [**20**] Sir Michael Redgrave, actor, is born at Bristol. [**21**] Sir John Hare proposes a National Theatre as a memorial to Shakespeare. [**25**] Sir David Lean, film director, is born at Croydon.

APR [**2**] HMS *Tiger* and HMS *Berwick* collide off the Isle of Wight; the *Tiger* sinks, drowning 35 men. [**7**] Sir Henry Campbell-Bannerman resigns due to ill health and the Liberal H. H. Asquith becomes Prime Minister, quickly introducing legislation to provide old-age pensions for those over 70. [**22**] Sir Henry Campbell-Bannerman, Liberal Prime Minister, dies.

MAY   [**28**] Ian Fleming, novelist and creator of James Bond, is born.

JUN   [**10**] Invalid and Old Age Pensions Act passed: non-contributory pensions for the over-70s. [**21**] A crowd of 200,000 in Hyde Park demonstrates for votes for women.

JUL   [**10**] A new British torpedo is announced, with a four mile range and a speed of four knots. [**16**] Fire breaks out at the Moorgate tube station. [**17**] The first criminal appeal, against a murder conviction, is turned down at the Central Criminal Court.

AUG   [**6**] The Admiralty announces that the battleships the Germans are building will be the most heavily armed in the world. [**14**] An airship blows up in London: one person is killed. [**31**] W. G. Grace retires from cricket, after scoring over 54,000 runs in first-class cricket.

SEP   [**12**] Winston Churchill marries Clementine Hozier. [**24**] 'Pensions Day': elderly people apply for their pensions [**29**] Film actress Greer Garson is born in County Down, Ireland.

OCT   [**1**] A penny post to the USA starts. [**16**] The first aeroplane flight in Britain takes place at Farnborough. The new harbour at Dover is opened, as part of the national defence system. [**31**] An indiscreet interview given by the Kaiser to the *Daily Telegraph* astonishes both British and Germans.

NOV   [**9**] Britain's first woman mayor, Elizabeth Garrett Anderson, is elected at Aldeburgh.

Selfridges store, Oxford Street, London. [Originally Selfridge & Co. Ltd – founded by Harry Gordon Selfridge.]

John Singer Sargent: *Mosquito nets*.
C. F. Voysey: *Stags and Trees linen pattern*.

Alfred Noyes: *Drake*.
Sir Oliver Lodge: *Man and the Universe*.
Arnold Bennett: *The Old Wives' Tale*.
W. H. Davies: *The Autobiography of a Super-Tramp*.
Kenneth Grahame: *The Wind in the Willows*.
G. K. Chesterton: *Orthodoxy*.
E. M. Forster: *A Room with a View*.
J. M Barrie: *What Every Woman Knows*.
Henry de Vere Stacpoole: *The Blue Lagoon*.

Frederick Delius: *In a Summer Garden*.
Sir Edward Elgar: *First Symphony; Wand of Youth*.
Gustav Holst: *Savitri*.

1909 The first Rolls-Royce Silver Ghost is tested. The painter William Frith dies. The painter Francis Bacon is born.

JAN [1] Old Age Pensions become payable to people aged 70 and over. [14] Churchill describes Britain as 'the best country in the world for rich men'. [24] Film actress Ann Todd is born.

FEB [8] The Government announces that the Navy is to have six more dreadnoughts. [24] Colour films are shown for the first time, in Brighton. [28] The poet Stephen Spender is born.

MAR [15] Selfridges opens in Oxford Street; it is the city's first big department store.

APR [5] The Aerial League of the British Empire is founded, to promote British supremacy in the air. [9] The first closed-top double-decker bus is introduced, at Widnes. [10] The poet Algernon Swinburne dies.

MAY [15] The actor James Mason is born in Huddersfield, Yorkshire.

JUN [13] Shackleton arrives back in Britain after his Antarctic expedition. [26] Edward VII opens the Victoria and Albert Museum. [29] Suffragettes are arrested in Westminster.

JUL [27] MPs give the South African Union Bill its second reading, but deplore the fact that it denies the black population the right to vote.

AUG [16] The Conservative leader Arthur Balfour argues that giving equal rights to South African blacks would undermine white civilization. [20] Wells, Arnold Bennett, Conrad and Thomas Hardy speak out against the Lord Chamberlain's powers to censor stage plays.

SEP [4] The first Boy Scout rally takes place, at Crystal Palace. [14] The naturalist Sir Peter Scott is born. [28] It is admitted in the Commons that some imprisoned suffragettes have been force-fed.

NOV [5] The first Woolworths store opens in Britain. [30] The House of Lords rejects Lloyd George's 'People's Budget' over land value duties; this precipitates a major constitutional crisis over the roles of the two Houses. Lloyd George asks, 'should 500 men, ordinary men chosen accidentally from among the unemployed, override the judgement of millions of people who are engaged in the industry which makes the wealth of this country?'

DEC [3] Edward VII dissolves Parliament; the taxes on beer, spirits and tobacco are lifted because no Budget has been passed.

François Espinasse: Michelin House, Fulham Road, London. Charles Rennie Mackintosh: Glasgow School of Art, Scotland (completed).

 Duncan Grant: *Portrait of James Strachey.*

 Herbert Strang: *Lord of the Sea.*
Ernest Shackleton: *The Heart of the Antarctic.*
George Bernard Shaw: *Press Cuttings.*
Florence Barclay: *The Rosary.*
H. G. Wells: *Tono-Bungay.*

 Arnold Bax: *In the Faery Hills.*
Vaughan Williams: *The Wasps; On Wenlock Edge.*
Frederick Delius: *A Mass of Life.*

1910 The Argentine tango becomes popular in Britain.

JAN   A General Election is fought on the issues of the Budget, the veto power of the Lords and the Home Rule Bill; the Liberals are returned. [18] The first sighting of Halley's Comet on its 1910 visit; its next appearance will be in 1986. [31] Dr Hawley Crippen poisons his wife Cora in Camden Town.

FEB   The officers of HMS *Dreadnought* are hoaxed; a quartet of Abyssinian princes piped aboard and shown round the ship turn out to be Guy Ridley, Anthony Buxton, Duncan Grant and Virginia Woolf in disguise. [1] The first 80 Labour Exchanges are opened; they are flooded by people looking for work. [20] Hurricane-force winds cause severe damage. [21] Douglas Bader, fighter pilot, is born.

MAR   [22] Nicholas Monsarrat, writer of sea stories, is born in Liverpool.

APR   [4] The first Commons reading of a Bill to abolish the House of Lords' power of veto.

MAY   [6] Edward VII dies from pneumonia; he is succeeded by George V. [10] The Commons pass resolutions that the Lords may not veto a money bill and that any other measure may be passed if it has come before the Commons three times even if vetoed by the Lords twice. [20] The last broad gauge train in Britain runs from Paddington to Penzance; from now on all main lines are standard gauge. [21] Edward VII's funeral. [31] The Girl Guides are founded.

JUN   [4] Christopher Cockerell, inventor of the amphibious hovercraft, is born at Cambridge. [15] Captain Scott sets out on his ill-fated expedition to the South Pole. [22] Sir John

(Lord) Hunt, leader of the successful Everest expedition, is born. [23] George V's son Edward is created Prince of Wales.

JUL [12] Charles Rolls, aviator and co-founder of Rolls-Royce, dies in an air crash at Bournemouth. [14] Cora Crippen's remains are discovered in the cellar at her home; the police hunt for Crippen begins.

AUG [13] Florence Nightingale dies aged 90.

SEP [7] William Holman Hunt, painter, dies. [17] A London doctor says that if lunacy goes on increasing at its current rate the sane will be outnumbered by the insane within 40 years. [20] The huge White Star liner *Olympic*, sister-ship of the *Titanic*, is launched at Belfast. [22] Crippen is convicted of murder and condemned to death.

NOV [8] 'Manet and the Post-Impressionists' exhibition opens in London: organized by Roger Fry, it proves to be a major influence on British painters. [11] Asquith asks George V if he will create enough peers to allow the passage of the Lords' Reform Bill. [16] Sir Edward Carson warns that Ulster (Northern Ireland) will fight the proposals for Irish Home Rule. [23] Dr Crippen is hanged at Pentonville. [28] Parliament is dissolved in preparation for the second General Election of the year.

DEC [20] The General Election is a dead heat (Liberals 272, Conservatives 272): Asquith continues as Prime Minister. [22] The Hulton Colliery disaster: 350 miners lose their lives.

 W. Burn, M. Hadfield and C. Buckler: Arundel Castle (completed).

 James Innes: *The Waterfall*.
Augustus John: *Dorelia with Three Children at Martigues*.
Gwen John: *Girl with Bare Shoulders*.
Sir William Orpen: *Homage to Manet*.

 H. G. Wells: *The History of Mr Polly*.
John Buchan: *Prester John*.
Arnold Bennett: *Clayhanger*.
E. M. Forster: *Howards End*.
John Galsworthy: *Justice*.
George Bernard Shaw: *Pygmalion*.
Jeffery Farnol: *The Broad Highway*.

 Arnold Bax: *Enchanted Summer*.
Vaughan Williams: *A Sea Symphony; Fantasia Concertante on a Theme of Thomas Tallis*.

Gustav Holst: *Beni Mora Suite.*
Sir Edward Elgar: *Violin Concerto.*

1911 Ernest Rutherford demonstrates that the atom has a nuclear structure. Charles Wilson produces the first cloud-chamber photographs of sub-atomic particles.

JAN [**1**] Leon Beron, a Russian Jew, is found murdered on Clapham Common; a link with anarchists is suspected. [**3**] The Sidney Street Siege; three anarchists suspected of killing three policemen engage in a gun battle with 1000 soldiers and police in the East End of London. The house catches fire and two of the anarchists are burnt to death. [**17**] Sir Francis Galton, pioneer on heredity, dies. [**30**] At the Beron inquest Stinie Morrison is accused of wilful murder.

FEB [**1**] Edward Mylius is sentenced to one year in prison for accusing George V of polygamy. HMS *Thunderer,* the last battleship to be built on the Thames, is launched. [**4**] Rolls Royce adopt the 'Spirit of Ecstasy' statuette. [**23**] A schoolgirl in a playground in Bradford is lifted 20 feet off the ground by a freak gust of wind; she falls to the ground and is killed.

MAR [**2**] The Lords' Veto Bill (Parliamentary Bill) passes its second Commons reading. [**9**] The Government announces that five more British battleships are to be built. [**15**] Stinie Morrison is sentenced to death for Beron's murder.

APR [**4**] The Duke of Marlborough and other former pupils bemoan the abolition of birching at Eton. [**12**] Morrison's sentence is commuted to life imprisonment.

MAY [**4**] The first British airship is wrecked at Aldershot. [**12**] The Festival of Empire opens at Crystal Palace. [**15**] George V and his visiting cousin the Kaiser reassert their friendship. The Parliamentary Bill is again passed by the Commons. [**29**] Sir William Gilbert, writer of operettas in collaboration with Sir Arthur Sullivan, dies of a heart attack in his swimming-pool. [**31**] The White Star liner *Titanic* is launched at the Harland and Wolff shipyard in Belfast.

JUN [**10**] The playwright Terence Rattigan is born. [**17**] Women demanding the vote march through London to a meeting at the Albert Hall. [**20**] Leeds introduces the first trolley-bus service in Britain. [**22**] Coronation of George V. Liverpool's Liver clock, 'Great George', begins telling the time.

JUL [**1**] The Shops Act provides a half-day holiday for shop workers. [**11**] Liverpool's Gladstone Dock is opened by George V. [**20**] The Parliamentary Bill is passed by the Lords, but with amendments unacceptable to Asquith, who threatens to create enough peers to carry the Bill in its unaltered form. [**22**] George V guarantees to create the number of Liberal peers Asquith requires.

AUG [**8**] National strike of railwaymen, dockers and carters; Manchester and other cities are brought close to famine. [**10**] The Lords pass the Parliamentary Bill unamended (= Parliamentary Act). The Commons for the first time vote MPs a salary, set at £400 a year. [**18**] Official Secrets Act. [**23**] There are violent anti-semitic riots in Wales. [**28**] A heat-wave sends the death rate up; London becomes one of the unhealthiest cities in Europe with a death rate of 19 per 1000.

SEP [**5**] The TUC condemns the use of troops in the recent strikes. [**23**] Carson again rejects any possibility of Home Rule.

OCT [**6**] The Labour politician Barbara Castle is born. [**9**] The Navy's biggest battleship, HMS *King George V*, is launched at Southampton.

NOV [**2**] 6000 London cab drivers go on strike. [**8**] Arthur Balfour, leader of the Conservative and Unionist Party, resigns.

DEC National Insurance Act; this covers ill health and unemployment benefits for all with incomes below £150, and marks the beginning of the Welfare State. [**12**] George V is crowned Emperor of India and founds the city of New Delhi.

Harry Fairhurst: York House, Manchester.
Sir Aston Webb: Victoria Memorial, The Mall, London; Admiralty Arch, London.

Sir Frank Brangwyn: *Fisherwomen.*
Henry Lamb: *Portrait of Edie McNeill.*
Vanessa Bell: *Studland Beach.*

Rupert Brooke: *Poems.*
Joseph Conrad: *Under Western Eyes.*
Sir Max Beerbohm: *Zuleika Dobson.*
G. K. Chesterton: *The Innocence of Father Brown.*
Oliver Onions: *Widdershins.*
Arnold Bennett: *Hilda Lessways.*
D. H. Lawrence: *The White Peacock.*

Sir Edward Elgar: *Second Symphony.*
Frank Bridge: *The Sea.*
Frederick Delius: *Fennimore and Gerda* (completed); *On Hearing the First Cuckoo in Spring.*
'I'm 21 today' (song).

1912 JAN [**1**] The National Telephone Company is taken over by the Post Office. [**3**] The Cabinet is reported to be divided over votes for women. [**18**] Scott reaches the South Pole only to find that Amundsen has beaten him by 35 days.

FEB [**10**] Lord Lister, pioneer of antiseptic surgery, dies at Walmer aged 84. [**26**] 2000 coal miners go on strike in Derbyshire.

MAR [**1**] Suffragettes smash shop windows in London's West End. [**4**] 96 are arrested after a suffragette raid on the House of Commons. [**5**] The police raid the offices of the Women's Social and Political Union. [**7**] The first non-stop aeroplane flight from Paris to London.

MAR [**17**] Lawrence Oates dies heroically during the return journey from the South Pole with Scott: it is his 32nd birthday. [**27**] The Labour Prime Minister James Callaghan is born at Portsmouth. The Coal Miners Act establishes the principle of a minimum wage. [**28**] The Women's Enfranchisement Bill is defeated on its second Commons reading. [**29**] Captain Scott dies in his tent in Antarctica.

APR [**1**] Asquith introduces the third Home Rule Bill. [**9**] 240,000 people demonstrate against Home Rule in Belfast. [**10**] Troops are called out to quell riots in Wigan. [**14**] The *Titanic*, steaming too fast through a sea littered with icebergs, hits one and sinks in the early hours of 15 April on her maiden voyage: 1500 lives are lost. [**17**] A total eclipse of the sun is seen in London. [**20**] Bram Stoker, author of *Dracula*, dies. [**22**] The contralto Kathleen Ferrier is born at Higher Walton.

MAY [**9**] The Home Rule Bill passes its second Commons reading. [**29**] 100,000 dockers are now out on strike in London.

JUN [**12**] John Seely succeeds Haldane as War Secretary. [**16**] Conservative politician Enoch Powell is born. [**25**] Asquith is attacked in the Commons over the force-feeding of imprisoned suffragettes. [**28**] The suffragettes start a new window-smashing campaign at Post Offices and Labour Exchanges.

JUL [**3**] The Board of Trade inquiry into the *Titanic* disaster finds Captain Smith guilty of negligence. [**12**] Second reading of the Franchise Bill, which will give all men over 21 the vote. [**22**] Battleships are to be withdrawn from the Mediterranean and placed on patrol in the North Sea; spending on both ships and sailors is to be increased. [**23**] Film actor Michael Wilding is born at Westcliff-on-Sea.

AUG [**20**] William Booth, founder of the Salvation Army, dies aged 83.

SEP [**4**] The first tube collision occurs in London: 22 are injured.

[**28**] A week of rallies and speeches in Ulster ends with the signing of a covenant to defeat Home Rule.

OCT [**12**] HMS *Iron Duke*, the world's largest and most powerful battleship, is launched.

NOV [**5**] A British Censor of Films is appointed. [**25**] The writer Francis Durbridge is born.

DEC [**6**] Prince Louis Battenberg and Sir John Jellicoe become First and Second Sea Lords. [**18**] The discovery of Piltdown man in Sussex is announced by Charles Dawson; that it is a hoax is not to be discovered until 1953.

Sir Giles Gilbert Scott: County Hall, London.

Charles Ginner: *The Circus.*
Duncan Grant: *The Queen of Sheba.*
Jacob Epstein: Monument to Oscar Wilde.

H. H. Munro: *The Unbearable Bassington.*
Ethel M. Dell: *The Way of an Eagle.*
Sir Compton Mackenzie: *Carnival.*
James Stephens: *The Crock of Gold.*
George & Weedon Grossmith: *The Diary of a Nobody.*

Frederick Delius: *Summer Night on the River.*
George Butterworth: *A Shropshire Lad.*
John Ireland: *Greater Love Hath No Man.*
Jack Judge and Harry Williams: 'Tipperary' (song written for a bet in a pub in Stalybridge).

1913 Carson forms the Ulster Volunteers, a private army to resist Home Rule by force. Atomic number invented by Henry Mosely. The geiger counter is invented by Hans Geiger.

JAN [**1**] Film censorship starts. [**7**] The Government introduces proportional representation into its Home Rule proposals to protect the interests of Protestants. [**15**] The first sickness, unemployment and maternity benefits are introduced. [**16**] The Home Rule Bill passes its second Commons reading.

FEB [**3**] Stravinsky's *Petroushka* is performed in Britain for the first time. [**5**] Sylvia Pankhurst goes to prison. [**10**] The bodies of Scott and his two companions are found in their tent in Antarctica. [**13**] Stravinsky's *Firebird* is performed in Britain for the first time. [**19**] A suffragette bomb destroys Lloyd George's house. [**24**] Emmeline Pankhurst is arrested and charged in connection with the Lloyd George bombing.

APR [**3**] Emmeline Pankhurst is sentenced to three years for inciting her supporters to place explosives at Lloyd George's house.

MAY [**7**] A suffragette bomb is found in St Paul's. [**15**] The Home Secretary bans public meetings by suffragettes. [**20**] The first Chelsea Flower Show opens. [**21**] The world's largest liner, the *Aquitania*, is launched on the Clyde. [**25**] The broadcaster Richard Dimbleby is born.

JUN [**2**] Alfred Austin, Poet Laureate, dies. [**4**] Emily Davidson, a suffragette, is trampled when she throws herself under the King's horse, 'Anmer', at Tattenham Corner, Epsom. [**8**] Emily Davidson dies of her injuries. [**10**] A misadventure verdict is returned on Emily Davidson's death.

JUL [**7**] The Home Rule Bill is passed for a second time by the Commons. [**8**] Sylvia Pankhurst is sentenced to three months in prison. [**12**] The Craigavon meeting; 150,000 Ulstermen pledge to resist Home Rule by force. [**15**] The House of Lords rejects the Home Rule Bill a second time. [**16**] Robert Bridges is appointed Poet Laureate. [**23**] The Labour Party leader Michael Foot is born. [**29**] The Liberal Party leader Jo Grimond is born. [**31**] Lloyd George says that the Lords must be abolished.

AUG [**14**] The actor Herbert Wilson dies in hospital after he is shot on stage. [**31**] The astronomer Sir Bernard Lovell is born.

SEP [**7**] The actor-manager Sir Anthony Quayle is born.

OCT [**14**] 439 are killed in a pit disaster at Senghenydd in Glamorgan. [**16**] The world's first oil-powered battleship, HMS *Queen Elizabeth*, is launched.

NOV [**5**] The film and stage actress Vivien Leigh is born at Darjeeling as Vivian Hartley. [**22**] The composer Benjamin Britten (Lord Britten) is born at Lowestoft.

DEC [**4**] Emmeline Pankhurst is arrested on her return from the USA. [**15**] The battlecruiser HMS *Tiger* is launched on the Clyde. [**18**] Lord Plymouth gives money to allow the Crystal Palace to be bought for the nation.

Sir Edwin Lutyens: Government Buildings, New Delhi.
Sir Aston Webb: Buckingham Palace façade (redesigned and heightened).

Stanley Spencer: *Zacharias and Elizabeth*.
Walter Sickert: *Ennui*.
Jacob Epstein: *Rock Drill*.
William Roberts: *The Return of Ulysses*.

Arthur Ward: *The Mystery of Dr Fu-Manchu*.
John Squires: *Steps to Parnassus*.
John Oxenham: *Bees in Amber*.

D. H. Lawrence: *Sons and Lovers*.
Joseph Conrad: *Chance*.
James Elroy Flecker: *The Golden Journey to Samarkand*.

Vaughan Williams: *London Symphony*.
George Butterworth: *The Banks of Green Willow*.
Percy Grainger: *Shepherd's Hey*.
John Ireland: *The Forgotten Rite*.

1914 The Welsh Disestablishment Act disestablishes the Welsh Church. Sir Ernest Shackleton sets off on his epic Antarctic expedition. The poet Dylan Thomas is born. Sir Ernest Swinton invents the tank.

JAN [1] Lloyd George calls the arms build-up in Western Europe 'organized insanity'. [5] Vanessa Bell, Roger Fry and Duncan Grant open a London exhibition of their work following their break from Cubism. [7] Joseph Chamberlain decides to retire from politics. [8] Doctors at the Middlesex Hospital successfully treat cancer with radium.

FEB [2] The Cub Scouts are founded at Robertsbridge in Sussex. The first UK performance of Wagner's *Parsifal* takes place. [4] Suffragettes burn two Scottish mansions. [10] Thomas Hardy marries Eva Dugdale.

MAR [5] The Irish Home Rule Bill is reintroduced in the Commons. [8] Sylvia Pankhurst is rearrested. [9] Asquith offers a compromise on Home Rule; electors in Ulster may vote to be excluded from an independent Ireland for six years. [10] Mary Richardson, a suffragette, damages the *Rokeby Venus* with a cleaver at the National Gallery in protest against 'the Government's destruction of Miss Pankhurst'.

APR [2] The actor Sir Alec Guinness is born at Marylebone, London. [17] Yarmouth Pier is damaged by a suffragette bomb.

MAY [15] The Commons reject the idea of a Scottish Home Rule Bill. [25] The Irish Home Rule Bill passes its final Commons stage, without separate provisions for Ulster. [27] Sir Joseph Swan, inventor, dies aged 85.

JUN [4] Railway and mine workers join builders on strike: now two million British workers are on strike. [10] Sylvia Pankhurst is arrested for the eighth time. [14] A severe thunderstorm in London brings ten centimetres of rain in three hours. [23] Asquith's March 9 compromise is introduced in the Lords.

JUL [8] The Government agrees to accept the Lords' amendment to the Home Rule Bill excluding Ulster. [30] The Home Rule process is shelved in the fate of the growing European crisis.

AUG [**2**] The Royal Navy is mobilized after the Kaiser declares war on Russia. [**3**] The Government warns Germany that Britain will honour the 1839 Treaty of London guaranteeing Belgian neutrality. [**4**] German troops invade Belgium; Britain declares war on Germany. [**17**] A British Expeditionary Force of 70,000 men lands in France. [**23**] Battle of Mons, the first engagement between British and German forces; the British are defeated and pull back.

SEP [**5-12**] Battle of the Marne; the British and French armies advance. [**8**] Home Rule Act, to come into force at the end of the war. [**15**] Commons passes a suspending bill to delay the operation of the Home Rule Act for one year. [**16**] Trench warfare begins on the Aisne salient. [**22**] Three British cruisers are sunk by one U-boat; 1500 men are lost as the *Cressy*, *Aboukir* and *Hogue* sink. [**23**] British planes bomb Zeppelin sheds at Dusseldorf.

OCT [**4**] The first German bomb falls on London. [**12**] Start of the First Battle of Ypres (lasts until 11 November). [**30**] Lord Fisher succeeds Prince Louis as First Sea Lord.

NOV [**1**] Battle of Coronel; the German cruisers *Scharnhorst* and *Gneisenau* sink the British cruisers *Monmouth* and *Good Hope*. [**5**] Britain declares war against Turkey; Cyprus is annexed to Britain. [**14**] Lord Roberts, the Boer War commander, dies while visiting troops in the field in France. [**17**] Lloyd George announces that income tax will double in 1915 to pay for the war, which is currently costing £1 million a day. [**26**] HMS *Bulwark* blows up at Sheerness, killing 700 people.

DEC [**11**] The Royal Flying Corps adopts the roundel for easy aircraft identification. [**16**] Scarborough and Whitby are shelled from the sea; over 100 people are killed. [**29**] The first Zeppelin appears over the British coast.

A. D. Smith and Cecil Brewer: Heal's, Tottenham Court Road, London.

Walter Bayes: *The Underworld.*
Henry Lamb: *Lytton Strachey.*
David Bomberg: *The Mud Bath.*
Stanley Spencer: *Mending Cowls, Cobham.*
Wyndham Lewis: *Red Duet.*

Robert Tressall: *The Ragged-Trousered Philanthropist.*
Laurence Binyon: *The Winnowing Fan.*
E. M. Forster: *Maurice* (written; published 1971).

James Joyce: *The Dubliners* (short stories).
Sir Compton Mackenzie: *Sinister Street*.
Bertrand Russell: *Our Knowledge of the External World*.
Clive Bell: *Art*.

 Rutland Boughton: *The Immortal Hour*.
Vaughan Williams: *Hugh the Drover; The Lark Ascending* (written).
'Keep the Home Fires Burning' (song).

1915 The Munitions of War Act forbids strikes in key industries without permission from the Government's arbitration body. Sir William H. Bragg and William L. Bragg are awarded the Nobel Prize for Physics.

JAN [1] The Military Cross is introduced and awarded for the first time. A German submarine sinks HMS *Formidable*. [19] The first air-raid casualties are inflicted in Britain when bombs are dropped on King's Lynn and Great Yarmouth by the German L3 Zeppelin. [24] A British squadron (HMS *Lion, Tiger* and *Princess Royal*) shells and sinks the *Blücher*, a huge German battlecruiser on its way to shell Yarmouth.

FEB [1] Passport photographs are required for the first time. [4] UK casualties to date total 104,000 dead. [18] The Germans begin a sea blockade of Britain. Shackleton's *Endurance* becomes stuck in pack-ice. [26] Armaments workers on the Clyde strike for more pay.

MAR [1] Britain begins to blockade Germany. [11] HMS *Bayano* is sunk off Scotland: 200 die.

APR [7] George V offers to abstain from alcohol to encourage armaments workers to abstain, in the belief that alcohol consumption slows down production. [22] Britain launches a spring offensive at Ypres; there are heavy casualties in the Second Battle of Ypres (lasting until May 25): the Germans use chlorine gas. [23] The poet Rupert Brooke dies of blood poisoning on Skyros, on his way to the Dardanelles. [25] The first landing of British, Australian and New Zealand troops on the Gallipoli peninsula meets bitter and determined resistance from the Turks.

MAY [1] There is widespread resentment among workers at the new anti-alcohol measures. [3] The war is now costing Britain £2 million a day. [7] The liner *Lusitania* is sunk, torpedoed by a German submarine off the Old Head of Kinsale with a loss of 1198 lives. [9-25] Battle of Aubers Ridge (Second Battle of Artois); the French advance three miles at great cost. [22] The worst-ever train disaster in Britain: a triple collision at Quintins Hill near Gretna Green kills 227 - 200 of them Scots Guards on their way to war. The shocked and dishevelled survivors are later mistaken for German prisoners-of-war and stoned by civilians. [26] A Coalition Government is formed. [27] HM Auxiliary Ship *Irene* explodes at Sheerness: 270 die. [31] The first air raids on London take place.

JUN [6] The Kaiser promises that in future the German navy will not attack passenger vessels. [28] A German submarine sinks the passenger liner *Armenia* off Cornwall.

JUL [3] The war is now costing Britain £3 million a day. [15] 200,000 Welsh miners strike for improved wages.

AUG [19] A German submarine sinks the British liner *Arabic:* 44 are missing. [31] The Welsh miners go back to work.

SEP [18] The Kaiser gives renewed assurances that passenger vessels will not be attacked. [21] Stonehenge is sold by auction for £6,600; a Mr Chubb buys it as a present for his wife. [26] Keir Hardie, founder of the Labour Party, dies.

OCT [12] Edith Cavell, a nurse, is executed by a German firing squad for helping Allied prisoners to escape. [23] The cricketer W. G. Grace dies. [28] George V falls off his horse while inspecting troops in France, but suffers only bruises.

NOV [1] Actor Michael Denison is born.[9] British war casualties now total 510,000. [21] Shackleton's *Endurance* is crushed and sunk by pack-ice; Shackleton and his team drift on a disintegrating ice floe for the next four months.

DEC [8] Battle of the Falkland Islands; a British squadron under Admiral Sturdee defeats a German attack, sinking four out of the five German ships; Admiral von Spee and his two sons are killed in the action. [15] Sir John French is replaced as Commander of British forces on the Western Front by Sir Douglas Haig. [20] British troops withdraw from Anzac and Suvla after 25,000 men are killed and 76,000 wounded. [30] HMS *Natal* blows up and sinks in Cromarty Firth as a result of sabotage: 350 die.

Christopher Nevinson: *Returning to the Trenches.*
Wyndham Lewis: *The Crowd.*
Ambrose Mc Evoy: *Silver and Grey.*
Vanessa Bell: *Portrait of Mrs Hutchinson.*

Virginia Woolf: *The Voyage Out.*
Rupert Brooke: *1914 and other Poems.*
Joseph Conrad: *Victory.*

D. H. Lawrence: *The Rainbow.*
W. Somerset Maugham: *Of Human Bondage.*
John Buchan: *The Thirty-Nine Steps.*
Arnold Bennett: *These Twain.*

Granville Bantock: *Hebridean Symphony.*
Sir Edward Elgar: *The Starlight Express.*

1916 JAN   [**6**] The Commons vote in favour of conscription, although the Home Secretary Sir John Simon resigns over the issue; single men are to be conscripted first. [**8**] The Evacuation of Gallipoli is completed. [**29**] Tanks are given their first trials at Hatfield.

FEB   [**19**] National Saving Certificates go on sale. [**21**] Opening of the Battle of Verdun; the Germans launch a massive offensive that goes on until December, with enormous losses on both sides. [**28**] The novelist Henry James dies at Rye.

MAR   [**2**] The Military Service Act, enabling conscription. [**11**] Sir Harold Wilson, Labour Prime Minister, is born at Huddersfield.

APR   [**9**] Shackleton and his crew leave the ice floe, taking to the sea in small boats. [**12**] Shackleton and his crew reach Elephant Island. [**24**] The Sinn Fein Rebellion in Ireland; Irish Nationalists seize the Post Office in Dublin and proclaim a provisional government. The Easter Rising lasts five days; 14 of the rebel leaders are later executed. Roger Casement is arrested after landing in Ireland from a German submarine. [**25**] The first Anzac Day commemorates the Gallipoli landings last year.

MAY   [**8**] The Commons back William Willett's Daylight Saving plan to put the clocks forward one hour in summer. [**10**] Shackleton reaches South Georgia. [**21**] Daylight Saving is introduced. [**31**] Battle of Jutland; there are heavy British losses in this large-scale naval battle and the result is inconclusive, though the Germans afterwards retreat.

JUN   [**5**] Lord Kitchener is drowned off the Orkney coast when HMS *Hampshire* hits a mine. [**29**] Sir Roger Casement is found guilty and sentenced to death in Dublin.

JUL   [**1**] - NOV [**13**] Battle of the Somme; the largest and bloodiest engagement on the Western Front, in which 420,000 British soldiers are killed in a fruitless attempt to relieve the French: only 10 miles are gained from the Germans. [**6**] Lloyd George becomes War Secretary after Kitchener's death. [**9**] Edward Heath, Conservative Prime Minister, is born at Broadstairs.

[**23**] Sir William Ramsay, chemist and discoverer of argon, helium, neon, krypton and xenon, dies at High Wycombe.

AUG [**3**] Sir Roger Casement, Irish Nationalist, is hanged in London for treason. [**5**] The composer George Butterworth is killed in action at Pozières. [**30**] Shackleton's crew are rescued from Elephant Island, after a remarkable Antarctic expedition.

SEP [**15**] Tanks designed by Sir Ernest Swinton are used in action for the first time by the British army in the Somme offensive. Margaret Lockwood, film actress, is born in Karachi, Pakistan to British parents. [**28**] Actor Peter Finch is born in London as William Mitchell. [**29**] The film actor Trevor Howard is born in Cliftonville.

NOV [**24**] Sir Hiram Maxim, the Anglo-American inventor of the machine-gun, dies in London.

DEC [**7**] A Coalition Government led by the Liberals is formed; Lloyd George, as Prime Minister, forms a War Cabinet.

 Edgar Wood: Royd House, Hale.

Mark Gertler: *The Merry-go-round.*
Dame Laura Knight: *On the Cliff.*
Sir Matthew Smith: *Nude, Fitzroy Street, No 1.*

Thomas Burke: *Limehouse Nights.*
James Joyce: *Portrait of the Artist as a Young Man.*
D. H. Lawrence: *Women in Love.*
John Buchan: *Greenmantle.*
H. G. Wells: *Mr Britling sees it Through.*

Gustav Holst: *The Planets; Savitri.*
Sir Arnold Bax: *The Garden of Fand.*
'Take me back to dear old Blighty' (song).
'If you were the only girl in the world' (song).

1917 Charles Barkla is awarded the Nobel Prize for Physics.

JAN [**1**] Britain and Germany agree to exchange all internees over the age of 45. [**25**] HMS *Laurentic* hits a mine in the Atlantic: 350 die.

FEB [**1**] Unrestricted submarine warfare begins. [**2**] Bread rationing starts. [**25**] The passenger liner *Laconia* is torpedoed: 30 passengers die. The writer Anthony Burgess is born.

MAR [**8**] A Government Commission on the Dardanelles Campaign blames Kitchener in part for its failure. [**11**] British troops occupy Baghdad. [**20**] The singer Vera Lynn is born in London. [**29**] Lloyd George announces a plan to introduce a Bill enabling married women over 30 the vote.

APR [**9-14**] Battle of Arras. [**14**] Valerie Hobson, actress, is born in Larne, New Zealand.

JUN [**7**] The British take Messines Ridge. Haig launches a new Flanders offensive. [**19**] Large Commons majority in favour of giving wives over 30 the vote. [**26**] The Royal Family decide to drop German titles; the family name of Saxe-Coburg-Gotha becomes Windsor, and Battenberg becomes Mountbatten.

JUL [**24**] MPs are alarmed to discover that the war is costing Britain £7 million a day. [**31**] The Third Battle of Ypres begins.

AUG [**4**] Captain Noel Chavasse of the Royal Army Medical Corps, the second of only three people ever to be awarded a bar to the Victoria Cross, dies of his wounds. [**7**] There is a heated debate in the House of Lords over the alleged sale of titles. [**20**] Over 100 people die in an air raid on Sheppey and Thanet. [**30**] The Labour statesman Denis Healey is born.

OCT [**4**] British victory on Passchendaele Ridge. [**5**] 'Chequers' is given to the nation as the official residence of the Prime Minister.

NOV [**6**] Passchendaele is captured by the British. [**8**] The Balfour Declaration recognizes Palestine as 'a national home' for the Jews, and gives official British support to the founding of a Jewish state. [**13**] Bankers call for the decimalization of British currency. [**26**] Sir Leander Jameson, colonial administrator and leader of the notorious Jameson Raid into the Transvaal, dies.

DEC [**3**] The Government refuses to recognize the Bolshevik regime in Russia. [**17**] Elizabeth Garrett Anderson, the first woman doctor, dies.

 Sir William Nicholson: *Portrait of Walter Greaves.*

 Alec Waugh: *The Loom of Youth.*
Norman Douglas: *South Wind.*
W. Somerset Maugham: *The Moon and Sixpence.*
T. S. Eliot: *Prufrock and other observations.*

 Sir Arnold Bax: *November Woods.*
Gustav Holst: *The Hymn of Jesus.*
'Goodbye-ee' (song).

1918 Anti-tetanus vaccinations are used extensively among the troops, and the success of this treatment does a great deal to popularize vaccination among civilians. Britain is hit by a worldwide influenza epidemic; at its height, it causes 3000 deaths per week in London alone. Education Act; this fixes the school-leaving age at 14, resulting in the perpetuation of very large classes, many of them with over 60 pupils.

JAN   [**30**] The House of Commons rejects the Lords' recommendation for proportional representation.

FEB   [**6**] Representation of the People Act, giving men over 21 and, for the first time, women over 30 the right to vote.

MAR   [**7**] Bonar Law asks the Commons for another war loan of £600 million. [**21**] A German offensive against the British is opened on the Somme.

APR   [**1**] The Royal Air Force is formed by amalgamating the Royal Flying Corps and Royal Naval Air Service. [**9-25**] Second German offensive on the Somme. [**18**] Military Service Act; the maximum conscription age is raised to 50, and is extended to include Ireland for the first time. [**23**] The British raid Zeebrugge and Ostend, with the intention of bottling up the two submarine bases.

MAY   [**9**] HMS *Vindictive* is sunk in Ostend harbour.

JUN   [**18**] The Government asks for a further war loan of £500 million. An Allied counter-attack on the Western Front begins. [**19**] General rationing begins. [**20**] After protests, the Government abandons Irish conscription.

AUG   [**8**] British, Canadian and Australian troops attack the Germans near Amiens: the Germans retreat.

SEP   [**15**] Mr C. Chubb presents Stonehenge to the nation. [**26**] A general Allied offensive on the Western Front begins; the Germans are fighting now only to cover their retreat.

OCT   [**7**] The composer Sir Hubert Parry dies. [**15**] Britain's first oil well is sunk at Hardstoft in Derbyshire. [**23**] The Commons vote in favour of allowing women to become MPs.

NOV   [**4**] The poet Wilfrid Owen is killed in action, trying to get his men across the Sambre Canal. [**9**] The Germans sign the Armistice. [**11**] The German army surrenders to Marshal Foch. [**14-15**] Widespread celebrations in Britain. [**21**] The German High Seas Fleet is handed over to the British for internment at Scapa Flow.

DEC   [**14**] Women vote for the first time in a General Election.

Sir William Orpen: *Dead Germans in a Trench.*
John Nash: *The Cornfield.*
Paul Nash: *We are making a new world.*
S. J. Peploe: *Still life with Japanese background.*

Lytton Strachey: *Eminent Victorians.*
Wilfrid Owen: *Smile, smile, smile* (written in September).

Gerard Manley Hopkins: *Poems.*
Marie Stopes: *Married Love.*
Valentine Williams: *The Man with the Club Foot.*

Sir Hubert Parry: *An English Suite* (written).

1919 The Irish Republican Army is founded by Michael Collins to fight against Britain until a united Republic of Ireland is established: a long campaign of bombing and guerilla warfare begins. At St Magnus' Cathedral, Kirkwall, the bones of Saints Magnus and Rognavald are discovered secreted within the Norman piers of the Cathedral; St Magnus was murdered in 1117. The Paris Peace Conference (Britain, France, Italy, USA) discusses terms for the Treaty of Versailles. Ernest Rutherford discovers the proton.

JAN [1] 200 sailors returning home from the war drown when the *Stornoway* sinks off Scotland.

FEB [3] London tube workers strike for shorter hours.

MAR [10] The Government is reported to favour the idea of a Channel Tunnel. [29] The Kaiser threatens suicide rather than submit to a trial.

APR [5] Eamon de Valera is elected president of Sinn Fein. [24] Edward Prince of Wales is to become a freemason.

MAY [12] The first post-war performance at Covent Garden (*La Bohème*). [18] The ballet dancer Dame Margot Fonteyn is born at Reigate as Margaret Hookham.

JUN [21] The German fleet (72 ships) is scuttled in Scapa Flow on the orders of Rear-Admiral von Reuter. [23] The Government's Coal Commission recommends nationalizing the coal industry. [28] The peace treaty with Germany is signed at Versailles. [30] The physicist Lord Rayleigh dies at Witham, Essex.

JUL [6] The British airship 'R34' arrives in New York from Scotland (starting July 2), becoming the first airship to cross the Atlantic. [9] The Government decides to raise the price of coal. [18] Edwin Lutyens' war memorial, the Cenotaph, is unveiled. [22] The Commons vote to ratify the terms of the Treaty of Versailles.

AUG [3-4] There are riots in Liverpool during the police strike. [29] The daily air service between London and Paris begins.

SEP [10] The TUC favours nationalizing the coal industry.

OCT [10] Teachers ask for their salaries, still at their pre-war level, to be doubled.

NOV [12] Pilots Smith and Ross set out from Hounslow on the first aeroplane flight to Australia.

DEC [**1**] Nancy, Lady Astor, MP for Portsmouth (Sutton), becomes the first woman to take her seat in the House of Commons. [**13**] Smith and Ross reach Darwin in Australia. [**18**] Sir John Alcock, aviator, dies of injuries received in an aeroplane accident. [**23**] Sex Disqualification Removal Act; the professions are now opened to women.

Louis de Soissons: Welwyn Garden City.
Sir Edwin Lutyens: The Cenotaph, Whitehall, London.

Augustus John: *Marchesa Casati.*
Ethelbert White: *The Tunnel.*
Edward Wadsworth: *Dazzle Ships in Dry Dock at Liverpool.*
Sir Stanley Spencer: *Travoys Arriving with Wounded.*

Hugh Walpole: *Jeremy.*
Max Beerbohm: *Seven Men.*
J. M. Keynes: *The Economic Consequences of the Peace.*
Ronald Firbank: *Valmouth.*
John Buchan: *Mr Standfast.*
Daisy Ashford: *The Young Visiters* [sic].
Bruce Cummings: *The Journal of a Disappointed Man.*

Frederick Delius: *Violin Concerto.*
Sir Edward Elgar: *Cello Concerto.*
Sir Arnold Bax: *Tintagel.*
'Don't dilly-dally on the way' (song).
'I'm forever blowing bubbles' (song).

1920 Irish Republicans begin an assassination campaign against British soldiers; in reprisal, the Black and Tans open fire on innocent spectators at a football match. The Road Fund is established; licence money collected from motorists is to be used for road building and maintenance, although this fund is later to be 'raided' by successive Chancellors of the Exchequer. The Coal Mines Act limits the profits of private pit-owners and sets up a welfare fund for the miners. Unemployment Insurance Act; this gives financial assistance for up to 15 weeks to unemployed people who contribute regularly to the scheme.

FEB [**5**] The Germans refuse to hand over alleged war criminals to the Allies. The Royal Air Force College at Cranwell opens.
MAR [**26**] A magistrate is dragged from a train and murdered in Ireland: it is the 29th political murder in Ireland this year. [**29**] Sir William Robertson attains the rank of Field Marshal, and becomes the only private ever to have risen to that rank.

APR [**13**] 300,000 workers strike in protests against British treatment of Sinn Fein prisoners. [**14**] 89 Sinn Fein hunger strikers are released from Dublin Prison.

MAY [**30**] 20 people drown in serious flooding in Lincolnshire.

JUN [**4**] Prince George (George VI) is created Duke of York.

JUL [**1**] Germany surrenders her largest airship 'L71', to Britain. [**8**] British troop set up roadblocks outside Dublin. [**13**] The LCC bans the employment of foreigners in council jobs.

AUG [**3**] The novelist P. D. James (Baroness James) is born.

SEP The politician Victor Grayson mysteriously disappears, never to be seen again. [**5**] The composer Peter Racine Fricker is born. [**11**] A motor-cycle speed record of 100 mph is set at Brooklands. [**22**] The Metropolitan 'Flying Squad' is formed.

OCT [**7**] The first 100 women are admitted to Oxford to take degrees. [**16**] The coal miners go on strike. [**17**] Michael Fitzgerald is the first Irish hunger striker to die. [**28**] Sylvia Pankhurst is sent to prison for six months after urging people to loot the docks.

NOV [**10**] The body of an unknown British soldier arrives in London for burial in Westminster Abbey. [**11**] The politician Roy Jenkins (Lord Jenkins) is born at Abersychan. [**20**] Actress Dulcie Gray is born. [**29**] The IRA kills 15 army cadets amid escalating violence.

DEC [**3**] Rudyard Kipling wins £2 damages from a medical firm that has used part of his poem *If* in its advertising campaign.

Sir Edwin Lutyens: Britannic House, Finsbury Circus, London (begun).

William Strang: *The Harlequin Hat.*
William Roberts: *The Cinema.*
Sir William Orpen: *The Signing of the Peace Treaty at Versailles.*

Gilbert Frankau: *Peter Jackson, Cigar Merchant.*
Roger Fry: *Vision and Design.*
Agatha Christie: *The Mysterious Affair at Styles.*
John Galsworthy: *In Chancery.*
E. F. Benson: *Queen Lucia.*
Freeman Wills Croft: *The Cook.*
Edith Hull: *The Sheik.*
Wilfrid Owen: *Poems.*

E. J. Moeran: *Ludlow Town.*

1921 Railways Act; over 100 lines amalgamate into four large companies (LMS, LNER, GWR and SR) in the interests of efficiency. The first Everest Reconnaissance Expedition is led by Lt Col Howard-Bury. Frederick Soddy is awarded the Nobel Prize for Chemistry.

JAN [**3**] Airships 'R-36' and '37' are completed; they are capable of carrying 50 passengers. [**8**] Lloyd George becomes the first Prime Minister to occupy 'Chequers', the house given to the nation by Lord Lee of Fareham. [**20**] Six policemen in Ireland are killed by the IRA. The British submarine 'K5' sinks in the Channel: 56 are drowned. [**22**] British tanks and troops seal off parts of Dublin in an attempt to catch the gunmen.

FEB [**16**] Eight Sinn Fein supporters are shot dead in a gun battle with British soldiers.

MAR [**11**] Queen Mary becomes the first woman to be awarded an Oxford degree. [**17**] Marie Stopes opens her first birth control clinic in Holloway. [**31**] The jockey Sir Gordon Richards rides 'Gay Lord' at Leicester, the first of his 4870 winners. Churchill promises that Britain will abide by the Balfour Declaration to create a Jewish homeland in Palestine.

APR [**3**] Coal rationing becomes necessary because of the miners' strike. [**15**] Railway and transport unions decide not to strike in support of the coal miners. [**27**] The Allies claim £6650 million compensation from Germany for damage done during the war; the Germans reluctantly agree, but it will put a great strain on Germany's war-damaged economy.

JUN [**10**] Prince Philip is born on Corfu. [**12**] Postmen stop collecting and delivering mail on Sundays.

JUL [**12**] de Valera comes to London to discuss the Irish crisis with Lloyd George.

AUG [**14**] de Valera rejects Lloyd George's offer of Dominion status for Ireland.

OCT [**2**] Robert Runcie, Archbishop of Canterbury, is born.

OCT [**21**] The composer Malcolm Arnold is born. [**23**] John Boyd Dunlop, inventor of the pneumatic tyre, dies.

NOV [**11**] The British Legion holds its first Poppy Day.

DEC [**6**] The Irish Free State is established by peace treaty with Britain; six of the nine counties of Ulster are given limited self-government as the province of 'Northern Ireland'. [**25**] Gandhi's organized mass boycott of the Prince of Wales as he arrives in Calcutta is successful.

Regent Cinema, Brighton.
Southwark Bridge.

Lytton Strachey: *Queen Victoria*.
Aldous Huxley: *Crome Yellow*.
John Galsworthy: *To Let*.
D. H. Lawrence: *The Lost Girl*.
George Bernard Shaw: *Back to Methuselah*.
Sheila Kaye-Smith: *Joanna Godden*.

 E. J. Moeran: *In the Mountain Country*.
Vaughan Williams: *Third Symphony*.
Peter Warlock: *The Curlew*.

1922 'Oxford bags' are in fashion. The Transport and General Workers Union is formed. Archibald Hill (British) and Otto Meyerhof (German) are awarded the Nobel Prize for Physiology and Medicine.

JAN There are many deaths from influenza. [5] Sir Ernest Shackleton, explorer, dies on South Georgia.

FEB [28] The British protectorate over Egypt comes to an end.

MAR [8] There are 100 mph winds along the south coast. [31] The Irish Free State Bill receives the Royal Assent today.

APR [13] The author John Braine is born at Bradford. [16] The poet and novelist Sir Kingsley Amis is born in London.

MAY [11] The British radio station '2LO' is opened at Marconi House in the Strand. [29] The MP Horatio Bottomley is sentenced to seven years in prison for his Victory Bonds fraud.

JUN [12] The Mallory expedition succeeds in climbing to within 3,200 feet of the summit of Everest.

AUG [22] The Irish politician and revolutionary Michael Collins is assassinated by republican extremists in an ambush between Bandon and Macroom.

OCT [7] Marie Lloyd, the music hall entertainer, dies after collapsing on the stage of the Alhambra Theatre. As unemployment grows in the North, trade unionists and socialists in Glasgow organize the first Hunger March to London. [18] The BBC is formed. [23] Bonar Law becomes Prime Minister.

NOV [1] Radio licences costing ten shillings a year are introduced. [5] Howard Carter discovers the tomb of King Tutankhamun in Egypt. [9] Sir William Horwood, the Metropolitan Police Commissioner, is poisoned by arsenic-filled chocolates. [25] Carter opens the inner tomb of Tutankhamun and sees 'wonderful things'.

DEC [6] Trial of Edith Thompson and Frederick Bywaters for the murder of Percy Thompson begins. [17] The last British troops leave the Irish Republic. [23] The BBC starts broadcasting a daily news programme.

Robert Bevan: Adelaide Road, London.
J. R. Scott: Waterloo Station, London (completed).
E. T. & E. S. Hall: Liberty's, Regent Street, London.

Ernest Raymond: *Tell England.*
Rebecca West: *The Judge.*
Richmal Crompton: *Just William.*
Katherine Mansfield: *The Garden Party* (short stories).
James Joyce: *Ulysses.*
D. H. Lawrence: *Aaron's Rod.*
T. S. Eliot: *The Waste Land.*
Ludwig Wittgenstein: *Tractatus.*
Edith Sitwell: *Façade.*
David Garnett: *Lady into Fox.*

Sir Arnold Bax: *First Symphony.*
Rutland Boughton: *Alkestis; The Round Table.*
Vaughan Williams: *Classical Symphony.*
Sir Arthur Bliss: *A Colour Symphony.*
Gerald Finzi: *String Quartet.*

1923 Sir Frederick Banting (Canadian) and John MacLeod (British) are awarded the Nobel Prize for Physiology and Medicine. W. B. Yeats receives the Nobel Prize for Literature.

JAN [**1**] Re-grouping of British railways according to the Railways Act. [**9**] Edith Evans is hanged for murder, even though she shouted 'Oh, don't' as her lover stabbed her husband; Bywaters, the lover, is hanged at the same time. The New Zealand writer Katherine Mansfield dies.

FEB [**9**] The playwright Brendan Behan is born in Dublin. [**17**] Lord Caernarvon 'officially' opens the inner tomb of Tutankhamun.

MAR [**27**] The astronomer and broadcaster Patrick Moore is born at Pinner. [**27**] Sir James Dewar, inventor, dies aged 80.

APR [**16**] Stanley Baldwin's Budget cuts income tax by sixpence. [**26**] The Duke of York, later to become George VI, marries Lady Elizabeth Bowes-Lyon (the Queen Mother) in Westminster Abbey.

MAY [**8**] Jack Hobbs scores his one hundredth century in first class cricket. [**21**] Stanley Baldwin becomes Prime Minister following Bonar Law's resignation on being told he has an incurable throat cancer.

JUL [**18**] Matrimonial Causes Act, allowing wives to divorce adulterous husbands. [**31**] Housing Act, providing subsidies for house building.

AUG [**29**] Sir Richard Attenborough, film actor and producer, is born at Cambridge.

SEP [**11**] The actor Alan Badel is born at Rusholme, Manchester.

OCT [**1**] Britain agrees to the creation of an autonomous Southern Rhodesian (Zimbabwe) government. [**4**] Five men are rescued from a flooding pit at Redding near Falkirk after being trapped for ten days. [**30**] Andrew Bonar Law, Conservative Prime Minister, dies.

DEC [**13**] Lord Alfred Douglas is sentenced to six months in prison for libelling Winston Churchill. [**31**] The chimes of Big Ben are broadcast for the first time.

Philip Gibbs: *The Middle of the Road.*
Joseph Conrad: *The Rover.*
Aldous Huxley: *Antic Hay.*
D. H. Lawrence: *Sea and Sardinia.*
Winston Churchill: *The World Crisis.*
George Bernard Shaw: *Saint Joan.*
Dorothy Sayers: *Whose Body?*
P. G. Wodehouse: *Leave it to Psmith; The Inimitable Jeeves.*
Radio Times (first issue).

Sir William Walton: *Façade.*
Gustav Holst: *The Perfect Fool.*
Peter Warlock: *Serenade for Strings.*

1924 Work begins on the trunk road system. Ampleforth Abbey is founded. Agricultural Wages Act; this sets up county boards to fix wage rates, but some farmers lay off workers rather than pay the higher wages.

JAN [**10**] Submarine 'L-34' sinks off Weymouth: all 43 on board die. [**22**] The first Labour Government is formed under Ramsay MacDonald, following the December 6 election.

FEB [**1**] The Labour Government formally recognizes the Communist regime in Russia. [**5**] The BBC time pips are broadcast for the first time. [**16**] The dock strike begins.

MAR [**30**] Sir Charles Stanford, composer, dies.

APR [**23**] The Empire Exhibition opens at Wembley Stadium.

MAY [**4**] Sir Edward Elgar is appointed Master of the King's Musick. The author Edith Nesbit dies.

JUN [**8**] On the third Everest Expedition, Mallory and Irvine are lost somewhere above 8450m; it is generally believed that they did not reach the summit.

JUL [**30**] Eric Liddell sets a new 400m running record at the Paris Olympics.

AUG [3] The novelist Joseph Conrad dies. [8] Commercial treaty with Russia. [15] Robert Bolt, playwright and screenwriter, is born in Sale. [16] The British Government agrees to withdraw British troops from of the Ruhr.

OCT [7] The Labour Party resists a move from the Communist Party to affiliate. [29] The Conservatives win the General Election by a large majority after a press story about the Zinoviev letter (October 25) urging British Communists to whip up revolution in Britain.

NOV [1] de Valera is sentenced to one month in prison for entering Ulster illegally. [7] The second Baldwin Ministry begins. [21] The treaties made with Russia during the previous government are repudiated.

Sir Giles Gilbert Scott: Memorial Court, Clare College, Cambridge.
E. T. and E. S. Hall: Liberty's Annexe.

Matthew Smith: *Couleur de rose.*

Miles Malleson: *The Fanatics.*
Roy Campbell: *The Flaming Terrapin.*
E. M. Forster: *A Passage to India.*
Rose Macaulay: *Orphan Island.*
Ronald Firbank: *Prancing Nigger.*
John Galsworthy: *The White Monkey.*
Michael Arlen: *The Green Hat.*
P. C. Wren: *Beau Geste.*
Mary Webb: *Precious Bane.*
A. A. Milne: *When We Were Very Young.*
Osbert Sitwell: *Triple Fugue.*

Granville Bantock: *The Seal Woman.*
Rutland Boughton: *The Queen of Cornwall.*
Vaughan Williams: *Hugh the Drover* (completed in 1914).

1925 John Logie Baird invents a working television system. George Bernard Shaw is awarded the Nobel Prize for Literature.

MAR [12] Britain rejects the Geneva Protocol. [14] The poet John Wain is born. [18] Fire destroys two floors of Madame Tussaud's waxworks museum, London. [20] Lord Curzon dies.

APR [22] The actor George Cole is born in London.

MAY [1] Cyprus becomes a British colony.

MAY [7] Lord Leverhulme (William Lever), manufacturer, dies. [13] Gold Bullion Standard Act; Churchill introduces this return to the Gold Standard. [14] The novelist Sir Rider Haggard dies. The composer Tristram Cary is born. [22] General Sir John

French dies. [**28**] The Home Secretary orders all known 'subversives' to be barred from entering the country.

JUN [**13**] The opening night of Noel Coward's *Hay Fever*. [**11**] The first murder in the air takes place, when a London gem dealer is thrown out of a plane.

AUG [**7**] Summer Time Act; changing clocks in the summer is made a permanent institution.

SEP [**8**] The comedy actor Peter Sellers is born at Southsea. [**9**] The TUC votes against the amalgamation of all trade unions.

OCT [**6**] The Archbishop of Canterbury blames low church attendance on poor preaching and outdated clergy. [**13**] Margaret Thatcher, Conservative Prime Minister, is born in Grantham as Margaret Roberts.

NOV [**10**] The actor Richard Burton is born at Pontrhydfen, Wales as Richard Jenkins. [**12**] The submarine 'M-1' is lost in the Channel: all 68 men on board die. [**20**] Queen Alexandra, widow of Edward VII, dies.

DEC [**3**] The Irish boundary agreement is signed, fixing the border between Northern Ireland and the Irish Free State.

 Odeon Cinema, Kensington, London.

 Jacob Epstein: W. H. Hudson Memorial.
Sir Alfred Munnings: *Their Majesties Return from Ascot.*

 Sean O'Casey: *Juno and the Paycock.*
Virginia Woolf: *Mrs Dalloway.*
P. G. Wodehouse: *Carry on, Jeeves.*
Dame Ivy Compton-Burnett: *Pastors and Masters.*
Noel Coward: *Hay Fever; The Vortex.*
Ezra Pound: *A Draft of Cantos.*
Lowell Thomas: *With Lawrence in Arabia.*
Warwick Deeping: *Sorrell & Son.*

 Sir William Walton: *Viola Concerto; Portsmouth Point* (composed).
Vaughan Williams: *Violin Concerto* (composed).
Gustav Holst: *At the Boar's Head.*

1926 The Hadow Committee's Report on Education recommends raising the school-leaving age to 15 and dividing children at the age of 11 by means of testing.

JAN [**5**] The first widows' pensions are paid out. [**27**] John Logie Baird gives the first public demonstration of television to members of the Royal Institution in his workshop in Soho. [**30**] The British occupation of the Rhineland ends as troops move out.

MAR   [**5**] Four paintings by Constable are stolen from the Royal Academy. [**6**] The Shakespeare Memorial Theatre at Stratford is destroyed by fire. [**24**] The Miners' Federation refuses to accept the Royal Commission's proposals to cut wage levels and abolish the minimum wage.

APR   [**6**] The Northern Ireland politician Ian Paisley is born. [**7**] The Hon. Violet Gibson attempts to assassinate Mussolini, but the bullet only grazes his nose. [**21**] Queen Elizabeth II is born at 17 Bruton Street in London, the daughter of the Duke and Duchess of York.

MAY   [**1**] The coal miners go on strike; the TUC calls for a General Strike in their support. [**2**] The trade union leader Clive Jenkins is born. [**3**] The General Strike begins. [**8**] The naturalist and broadcaster Sir David Attenborough is born. [**12**] The General Strike ends; the TUC backs down, saying that the Government is better prepared for a long conflict than the strikers. [**20**] The miners, feeling betrayed by the unions, vote to stay out on strike.

JUN   [**8**] Dame Nellie Melba gives her farewell performance at Covent Garden.

AUG   [**3**] London's first traffic lights come into use at Piccadilly Circus. [**6**] Actor Frank Finlay is born in Farnworth, Lancs. [**9**] Southern Railway decides to convert from steam to electric by 1928. [**21**] Riots break out among the striking coal miners.

OCT   [**5**] Most of the miners return to work. [**15**] There is a clash between police and striking miners near Port Talbot. [**19**] The Imperial Conference begins.

NOV   [**2**] The formation of Imperial Chemical Industries is announced. [**18**] The Imperial Conference ends with a declaration that Britain and her dominions are of equal political status and in no way subordinate to one another. [**20**] The British Empire is renamed the British Commonwealth.

DEC   [**3**] The novelist Agatha Christie disappears from her London home. [**14**] Agatha Christie is found in a Harrogate Hotel, apparently having lost her memory; she never accounts for the eleven lost days.

Sir Giles Gilbert Scott: telephone booth Model No 2 (for a long time the standard phone box).
Sir Edwin Lutyens: Britannic House, Finsbury Circus, London (completed).
Alfred Octavius Edwards & Sir Edwin Lutyens: Grosvenor House, Park Lane, London (completed).

Sir Gerald Kelly: *James.*

Sylvia Warner: *Lolly Willowes.*
Vita Sackville-West: *The Land.*
A. N. Whitehead: *Science and the Modern World.*
T. E. Lawrence: *Seven Pillars of Wisdom.*
R. H. Tawney: *Religion and the Rise of Capitalism.*
Agatha Christie: *The Murder of Roger Ackroyd.*
D. H. Lawrence: *The Plumed Serpent.*
John Galsworthy: *The Silver Spoon.*
A. A. Milne: *Winnie-the-Pooh.*
H. E. Bates: *The Two Sisters.*
Lord Birkenhead: *Famous Trials of History.*

 Granville Bantock: *A Pagan Symphony.*
Lord Berners: *The Triumph of Neptune.*
Sir Arthur Bliss: *Introduction and Allegro.*
Gustav Holst: *The Golden Gorse.*

1927 The Unemployment Insurance Act extends the benefit period. Arthur Crompton (American) and Charles T. W. Wilson (British) are awarded the Nobel Prize for Physics.

JAN   The newly-founded British Broadcasting Corporation (formerly Company) broadcasts its first programme.

FEB   [**4**] Malcolm Campbell breaks the world land speed record on Pendine Sands (174 mph). [**8**] Sir Stanley Baker (actor) is born at Ferndale, Wales.

MAR   [**29**] Henry Segrave breaks the world land speed record in Florida (203 mph).

JUN   [**14**] Jerome K. Jerome, author of *Three Men in a Boat*, dies. [**20**] There is a fight between Communists and Fascists in Hyde Park. [**28**] Trade Disputes and Trade Union Act; this measure makes sympathy strikes and lock-outs illegal, and forbids the use of union funds for political purposes.

JUL   [**6**] The Church of England approves revisions to the Book of Common Prayer.

OCT   A newspaper article about the Oscar Slater case (1909) includes an interview with a witness; Ramsay MacDonald, the Prime Minister, orders Slater's release after 18 years of wrongful imprisonment. Slater receives £6000 compensation from the Scottish Office.

NOV   [**5**] The first automatic traffic lights begin working, at the Prince Square crossroads in Wolverhampton. [**8**] The comedian Ken Dodd is born in Liverpool. [**12**] The first veteran car rally from London to Brighton takes place, sponsored by the *Daily Sketch*. [**22**] 200 unemployed Welsh miners march to London but fail to meet Stanley Baldwin.

Dec [**25**] A white Christmas.

Curtis Brown: Westminster Bank, Piccadilly, London.
Elizabeth Scott: Shakespeare Memorial Theatre, Stratford.
(New theatre after a fire destroyed the former one in 1927.
Opened in 1932.)
Curtis Brown: Barclays Bank, Piccadilly.

L. S. Lowry: *The Arrest.*
Philip de Laszlo: *The Countess of Mansfield.*
Stanley Spencer: *The Resurrection* (begun).

Henry Williamson: *Tarka the Otter.*
E. F. Benson: *Lucia in London.*
Ronald Firbank: *Concerning the Eccentricities of Cardinal Pirelli.*

Frank Bridge: *Enter Spring.*
Constant Lambert: *The Rio Grande.*

1928 Owen Richardson is awarded the Nobel Prize for Physics.

Jan [**5**] The first Old Age Pensions, of ten shillings a week are
drawn. [**6**] The Thames bursts its banks, flooding London: four
drown. [**11**] The poet and novelist Thomas Hardy dies aged
87. [**29**] Earl Haig, the First World War army commander, dies.

Feb [**15**] Herbert Henry Asquith, Prime Minister 1908-16, dies.
[**22**] The entertainer Bruce Forsyth is born.

Mar [**4**] Alan Sillitoe, writer, is born at Nottingham. [**19**] The
Revised Book of Common Prayer is published.

May [**7**] The voting age for women is brought down from 30 to 21.

Jun [**14**] The suffragette Emmeline Pankhurst dies. [**28**] Sir Cyril
Smith, Liberal politician, is born at Rochdale.

Jul [**3**] The world's first colour television pictures are tramsmitted
by John Logie Baird at the Baird Studios in London. [**21**] The
actress Ellen Terry dies aged 81.

Aug [**1**] The Morris Minor appears. [**19**] Lord Haldane, who
founded the Territorial Army, dies.

Nov [**12**] Archbishop Davidson resigns. [**22**] The first £1 and 10
shilling notes come into circulation. [**23**] The King's illness is
made public. [**30**] Cosmo Gordon Lang, Archbishop of York,
becomes Archbishop of Canterbury.

Dec [**20**] A treaty is concluded with China, recognizing the
Nanking government, in return for which China abolishes
coast and interior duties.

Bradshaw, Gass and Hope: Lewisham Town Hall (Gothic
façade added).
Tyne Bridge, Newcastle.

Raymond Hood: National Radiator Building, Great Marlborough Street, London.

 Mark Gertler: *Supper.*

 John van Druten: *Young Woodley.*
Siegfried Sassoon: *Memoirs of a Fox-hunting Man.*
Radclyffe Hall: *The Well of Loneliness.*
Edmund Blunden: *Undertones of War.*
John Galsworthy: *Swan Song.*
Wyndham Lewis: *The Childermass.*
Aldous Huxley: *Point Counterpoint.*
Evelyn Waugh: *Decline and Fall.*
D. H. Lawrence: *Lady Chatterley's Lover.*
A. A. Milne: *The House at Pooh Corner.*
Dorothy Sayers: *Lord Peter Views the Body.*

 Granville Bantock: *The Pilgrim's Progress.*
Gustav Holst: *Egdon Heath.*

1929 Local Government Act; the de-rating of farms and farm buildings is designed to help farmers. Christian Eijkman (Dutch) and Sir Frederick Hopkins (British) are awarded the Nobel Prize for Physiology and Medicine. Arthur Harden (British) and Hans von Euler-Chelpin (German/Swedish) are awarded the Nobel Prize for Chemistry.

JAN [**31**] The actress Jean Simmons is born in London.
FEB [**4**] The first 'Green Belt' area is approved near Hendon. [**8**] de Valera is sentenced to a month in prison for illegal entry into Northern Ireland. [**12**] The actress Lillie Langtry dies in Monte Carlo.
MAR [**23**] Roger Bannister, the first athlete to run a mile in under four minutes, is born at Harrow. [**29**] Jeremy Thorpe, Liberal Party leader, is born.
MAY [**21**] Lord Rosebery, Prime Minister, dies. [**30**] Labour wins the General Election (Labour 288, Conservatives 260).
JUN [**7**] Ramsay MacDonald forms Britain's second Labour Government.
JUL The police seize 12 of D. H. Lawrence's paintings on show in a Mayfair gallery, after receiving complaints about their obscenity. [**31**] The World Boy Scouts' Jamboree opens at Arrowe Park, Birkenhead.
AUG [**6**] Britain and Egypt agree a draft treaty for the evacuation of British troops from Egypt, except for the Suez Canal zone. [**11**] The Welsh composer Alun Hoddinott is born.
SEP [**25**] The comedian Ronnie Barker is born at Bedford. [**28**] Ramsay MacDonald begins a visit to the USA and Canada.

OCT [1] Diplomatic relations with Soviet Russia are resumed. [14] The 'R101' airship flies on its first trial from Cardington across London. [26] It is announced that all London buses will be painted red; trials with red-and-yellow proved unpopular. [28] The London Stock Exchange feels the first shock waves from the Wall Street Crash; shares fall sharply.

NOV [1] Ramsay MacDonald returns to Britain.

DEC [2] Britain's first 22 public phone boxes come into service in London. [5] 94 mph winds sweep across Britain, killing 26 people. [12] The actor and playwright John Osborne is born.

Sir Giles Gilbert Scott: Battersea Power Station (begun; completed 1933).
O. P. Bernard: Art Deco Lobby, Strand Palace Hotel.

Ben Nicholson: *Still Life* (jug and playing cards).
Sir John Lavery: *The Chess Players.*
David Jones: *The Terrace.*
Henry Moore: *Reclining Figure.*

Noël Coward: *Bittersweet.*
E. F. Benson: *Paying Guests.*
Graham Greene: *The Man Within.*
John Powys: *Wolf Solent.*
Richard Hughes: *A High Wind in Jamaica.*
J. B. Priestley: *The Good Companions.*
Robert Graves: *Goodbye to All That.*
R. C. Sherriff: *Journey's End.*
Robert Bridges: *The Testament of Beauty.*

Vaughan Williams: *Sir John in Love.*
E. J. Moeran: *Seven Poems of James Joyce.*
Sir Edward Elgar: *Violin Concerto.*

1930 Sir Frank Whittle invents the jet engine.

JAN [15] Ramsay MacDonald advocates that the world powers abolish battleships.

FEB [25] A Bill to abolish blasphemy as a legal offence is dropped.

MAR [2] The poet and novelist D. H. Lawrence dies of tuberculosis. [7] The Earl of Snowdon, ex-husband of Princess Margaret, is born as Antony Armstrong-Jones. [14] The Government Channel Tunnel Committee approves the building of a Channel Tunnel. [19] Arthur Balfour, Conservative Prime Minister 1902-5, dies aged 81.

APR [1] Robert Bridges, Poet Laureate, dies.

MAY [5] Amy Johnson takes off from Croydon on her solo flight to Australia, arriving on May 24. [9] John Masefield is appointed Poet Laureate. [25] Randall Davidson, retired Archbishop of Canterbury, dies. [29] The BBC Symphony Orchestra is founded under Sir Adrian Boult.

JUN [1] Toscanini conducts at the Albert Hall. [5] The Government rejects proposals for a Channel Tunnel. [11] The luxury liner *Empress of India* is launched at Clydebank by the Prince of Wales. [13] Sir Henry Segrave is killed when his speed-boat crashes at nearly 100 mph on Lake Windermere. [30] Britain formally recognizes Iraq as an independent state.

JUL [7] Sir Arthur Conan Doyle, creator of Sherlock Holmes, dies. [17] A Labour MP seizes the mace in the House of Commons, causing uproar. [28] The airship 'R-101' starts its maiden flight across the Atlantic.

AUG [17] Ted Hughes, Poet Laureate, is born. [21] Princess Margaret is born at Glamis Castle. [29] William Spooner, the creator of spoonerisms, dies.

SEP [29] George Bernard Shaw declines the offer of a peerage. [30] The politician Lord Birkenhead dies.

OCT [5] The 'R-101' is destroyed when it crashes at Beauvais in France on its first flight to India; 48 lives are lost, including that of the Air Minister, Lord Thomson. The loss of the 'R-101' marks the end of British interest in airships. [10] The Tyne Bridge at Newcastle is opened. The playwright Harold Pinter is born.

NOV [10] Four elephants run amok in the Lord Mayor's Show, injuring 30 people.

DEC [7] Mosley's manifesto advocating a programme of public works is published. Sir Yehudi Menuhin (aged 13) plays at the Albert Hall. [15] A Commons Select Committee recommends ending the death penalty.

Sir Edwin Lutyens: Castle Drogo (completed).
Dorchester Hotel, Park Lane, London.

Henry Tonks: *Sodales, Mr Steer and Mr Sickert*.
Sir Matthew Smith: *Jeune femme*.
Dame Ethel Walker: *The Waterfall*.
Jacob Epstein: *Genesis*.

Wyndham Lewis: *The Apes of God*.
Arthur Ransome: *Swallows and Amazons*.
J. B. Priestley: *Angel Pavement*.

W. Somerset Maugham: *Cakes and Ale.*
Evelyn Waugh: *Vile Bodies.*
Maynard Keynes: *Treatise on Money.*
Noël Coward: *Private Lives.*
Rudolf Besier: *The Barretts of Wimpole Street.*
Sellar and Yeatman: *1066 and All That.*
Francis Yeats-Brown: *Bengal Lancer.*

Sir Arnold Bax: *Overture to a Picaresque Comedy.*
Sir Arthur Bliss: *Morning Heroes.*
Sir Edward Elgar: *Pomp and Circumstance No 5.*

1931 JAN [**1**] Road Traffic Act comes into force; it introduces traffic police and compulsory third-party insurance for motorists. [**6**] The new Sadler's Wells Theatre opens in London. [**20**] Julia Wallace is murdered at her home in Wolverton Crescent, Anfield, Liverpool; police suspect her husband, but Herbert Wallace claims as his alibi that he was lured out of the house to meet a man called Qualtrough. [**21**] The Bill to raise the school-leaving age to 15 is defeated in the Commons. [**26**] Churchill resigns from Baldwin's shadow cabinet over Indian policy, a proposed federation with limited self-government.

FEB [**2**] Herbert Wallace is charged with murder. [**5**] Malcolm Campbell breaks the world land speed record at Daytona Sands (245 mph). [**11**] Sir Charles Parsons, inventor of the first practical steam turbine in 1884, dies at Kingston in Surrey. [**28**] Sir Oswald Mosley forms his New Party.

MAR [**27**] The novelist Arnold Bennett dies of typhoid; he drank water from a carafe in a Paris hotel in order to show that it was safe.

APR [**14**] The first Highway Code is issued. [**22**] The trial of Herbert Wallace starts; he is found guilty but acquitted on appeal. The real murderer, the mysterious 'Qualtrough', who is believed to have died in in April 1980, was never brought to trial. [**30**] Mosley's New Party splits the Labour vote, letting in the Conservative candidate in the Ashton-under-Lyne by-election.

JUN [**2**] George V creates no new peers in his Birthday Honours List. [**7**] Violent earth tremors are felt throughout Britain.

JUL [**6**] The census result shows that the population of the United Kingdom (44.8 million) is almost at a standstill.

AUG [**24**] The Labour Government is defeated and replaced by an all-party Coalition or National Government led by Ramsay MacDonald.

SEP [**7**] George V decides to take a £50,000 pay cut for the duration of the economic crisis. [**20**] Sterling is taken off the Gold Standard; the pound falls dramatically in value from 4.86 to 3.49 dollars.

OCT [**2**] After two nights of rioting in Glasgow in protest against the Government's emergency measures, 49 people are arrested. [**27**] A second General Election results in a National Government landslide, with Ramsay MacDonald continuing as Prime Minister.

DEC [**11**] Statute of Westminster, recognizing the independence of the British Commonwealth.

Sir Giles Gilbert Scott: Wolfson Building, Lady Margaret Hall, Oxford.
Joseph Emberton: Royal Corinthina Yacht Club, Burnham-on-Crouch.

Eric Gill: *The Sower.*
Barbara Hepworth: *Figure in Sycamore.*

E. F. Benson: *Mapp and Lucia.*
Anthony Powell: *Afternoon Men.*
Virginia Woolf: *The Waves.*
Dame Ivy Compton-Burnett: *Men and Wives.*
Vita Sackville-West: *All Passion Spent.*
A. J. Cronin: *Hatter's Castle.*

Vaughan Williams: *Piano Concerto; Job.*
Sir William Walton: *Belshazzar's Feast.*

1932 Sir James Chadwick discovers a new sub-atomic particle, the neutron. The new Shakespeare Memorial Theatre opens in Stratford-on-Avon. The London Philharmonic Orchestra is founded by Sir Thomas Beecham. Unemployment reaches 2.75 million; the Trade Unions organize the largest ever hunger march on London, protesting against the means-testing of unemployment benefits. John Galsworthy is awarded the Nobel Prize for Literature.

JAN [**25**] Dartmoor Prison riot; the prison governor's life is saved by a man who has been reprieved from hanging. [**27**] The submarine 'M2' sinks; 50 die.

FEB [**4**] A 10% tariff is imposed on all imports, with concessions for those from the Empire. [**27**] The film actress Elizabeth Taylor is born in London. [**29**] Protective Tariffs Acts; these trade-restrictive measures include a new 'corn law' giving British farmers a guaranteed price for their wheat.

MAR [**31**] Revd. Harold Davidson, Rector of Stiffkey, is charged with immoral behaviour with teenage girls.

APR [**24**] A mass trespass on Kinderscout to establish a public right of access results in five arrests. [**26**] Motor Traffic Act: drivers who kill may be found guilty of manslaughter.

MAY [**9**] Piccadilly in London is lit by electricity for the first time. [**11**] After Ireland's threat to abolish the Loyal Oath to the King, the British Government warns that she may lose her tariff preference. [**19**] A Bill abolishing the Loyal Oath becomes law in Dublin.

JUN [**12**] The Rector of Stiffkey tries to grab the Bible from a stand-in clergyman during a service.

JUL [**6**] Kenneth Grahame, author of *The Wind in the Willows*, dies. [**8**] The Rector of Stiffkey is found guilty of disreputable association with women.

AUG [**10**] The composer Alexander Goehr is born.

OCT [**1**] Richard Harris, actor, is born in Limerick. [**30**] Ralph Reader presents the first Gang Show at the Scala Theatre, London.

DEC [**25**] George V makes the first Royal Christmas Day broadcast to the Empire. [**30**] The London-Brighton railway line is electrified.

Sir Owen Williams: Daily Express Building, Fleet Street; Boots Factory.
Elizabeth Scott: Shakespeare Memorial Theatre (completed).
V. Myers and W. Hart: Broadcasting House, London.

Ben Nicholson: *At the Chat Botté*.
Eric Gill: *Prospero and Ariel*.

Evelyn Waugh: *Black Mischief*.
Aldous Huxley: *Brave New World*.
E. F. Benson: *Secret Lives*.
Stella Gibbons: *Cold Comfort Farm*.
John Powys: *A Glastonbury Romance*.
Graham Greene: *Stamboul Train*.

Sir Arnold Bax: *Cello Concerto*.
Frank Bridge: *The Christmas Rose*.
Vaughan Williams: *Riders to the Sea*.
E. J. Moeran: *Lonely Waters*.

1933 'A London surgeon' takes, and publishes in the *Daily Mail*, the first photograph of the Loch Ness Monster; this starts an ongoing interest in the contents of the lake. Paul Dirac (British) and Erwin Schrödinger (Austrian) are awarded the Nobel Prize for Physics.

JAN [12] The writer Compton Mackenzie is fined for revealing in *Greek Memories* the identity of British Secret Servicemen in the First World War. [18] The botanist and conservationist David Bellamy is born. [31] The novelist John Galsworthy dies.

FEB [9] The 'King and Country' debate at the Oxford Union; the motion is 'that this house would in no circumstances fight for King and Country'.

MAR [14] The film actor Michael Caine is born (as Maurice Micklewhite). [22] The car manufacturer Sir Frederick Henry Royce dies.

MAY [23] Actress Joan Collins is born in London. [24] The TUC calls for a boycott of Germany to protest at Hitler's regime.

JUL [15] The musician Sir Julian Bream is born. [20] 30,000 Jews take part in a Hyde Park March to protest against Nazi anti-semitism. [23] The World Monetary and Economic Conference ends in London without any agreement. Its failure leads the British Government to extend its policy of economic nationalism; free trade is finally abandoned and people are encouraged to 'buy British'.

AUG [14] Richard Hardy complains that the English language is becoming polluted by fashions for such words as 'definitely, frightfully, absolutely, awfully and priceless'. [21] The singer Dame Janet Baker is born.

SEP · [10] Forest fires accompany the long drought.

OCT [15] Mosley and his Fascist sympathizers are stoned in Manchester.

DEC [17] For this day only members of the public are allowed to walk through the newly completed Mersey Road Tunnel.

Sir Giles Gilbert Scott: Cambridge University Library.
C. Holden: Senate House, London University.
Basil Champneys: Somerville College, Oxford.

Sir Stanley Spencer: *Portrait of Patricia Preece.*

Herbert Read: *Art Now.*
Winston Churchill: *Marlborough.*
Ernest Newman: *The Life of Richard Wagner.*
Vera Brittain: *Testament of Youth.*
George Orwell: *Down and Out in Paris and London.*

1934 The Glyndebourne Operatic Festival is founded. Schoolchildren are to be given half a pint of milk a day as part of a national policy of improving nutrition. The Government grants a subsidy to Cunard-White Star to enable the firm to complete the liner *Queen*

Mary. The Unemployment Assistance Board is founded; extended benefits are to be means-tested, a very unpopular development. A speed limit of 30 mph is reintroduced in built-up areas, owing to the large number of accidents.

Jan [**16**] Churchill says in a broadcast that Britain has never been so defenceless as it is now. [**21**]There is a large rally of the British Union of Fascists in Birmingham.

Feb [**17**] Actor Alan Bates is born. [**20**] Anthony Eden has a friendly meeting with Hitler. [**23**] The composer Sir Edward Elgar dies at Worcester.

Mar [**26**] Driving tests are introduced.

Apr [**27**] Britain and France warn Germany not to default on war reparations payments.

May [**3**] H. G. Wells stands by his earlier prediction that there will be another world war by 1940. [**25**] The composer Gustav Holst dies.

Jun [**10**] The composer Frederick Delius dies.

Jul [**15**] The composer Sir Harrison Birtwistle is born at Accrington. [**18**] The Mersey Road Tunnel is opened by George V.

Sep [**8**] Sir Peter Maxwell Davies, composer, is born. [**9**] Police separate Fascists and anti-Fascists in a London march. [**22**] The Gresford pit disaster in North Wales; 265 miners are killed. [**26**] The liner *Queen Mary* is launched at John Brown's yard at Clydebank.

Oct [**10**] Prince George, George V's son, is created Duke of Kent.

Nov [**30**] The Flying Scotsman reaches a record speed of 97 mph.

Nov [**9**] Actress Dame Judi Dench is born. [**28**] Actress Dame Maggie Smith is born.

Berthold Lubetkin: Penguin Pool, London Zoo.
Wandsworth Town Hall.

Edward Burra: *The Serpent's Eggs.*
William Coldstream: *The Studio.*
Henry Moore: *Two Forms.*

Arnold Toynbee: *A Study of History.*
Robert Graves: *I, Claudius.*
James Hilton: *Goodbye, Mr Chips.*
Evelyn Waugh: *A Handful of Dust.*
Graham Greene: *It's a Battlefield.*

Benjamin Britten: *Simple Symphony*
Vaughan Williams: *Fourth Symphony.*

Rutland Boughton: *The Lily Maid.*
Sir Arnold Bax: *Sixth Symphony.*

1935 A prototype of the Spitfire is built. The first Penguin paperback books are produced by Allen Lane. Eric Shipton leads an expedition to survey the Everest region. Sir James Chadwick is awarded the Nobel Prize for Physics.

FEB [**26**] RADAR (Radio Detection And Ranging) is first demonstrated, in secret, by Robert Watson-Watt at Daventry.

MAR [**7**] Malcolm Campbell sets a new world land speed record (276 mph). [**24**] George Stoner murders Francis Rattenbury, his mistress's husband.

APR [**15**] Chamberlain claims that Britain has '80% recovered' from the Depression. [**19**] Dudley Moore, comedian, musician and composer, is born in London.

MAY [**4**] Leicester Square tube station opens. [**6**] George V's Silver Jubilee prompts a national demonstration of loyalty and patriotism. [**22**] The RAF is to be trebled in size within two years, to make sure that the British air force equals Germany's.

JUN [**7**] Stanley Baldwin succeeds Ramsay MacDonald following a General Election precipitated by MacDonald's resignation for health reasons; a Conservative-led National Government is formed. [**18**] Anglo-German naval agreement; Germany is to have no more than 35% of Britain's tonnage; this in turn leads to a distinct cooling in relations between Britain and France.

AUG [**2**] Government of India Act; a step towards self-government.

OCT [**8**] Clement Attlee becomes Labour Party leader. [**20**] The ex-Labour leader Arthur Henderson dies. 11 are killed in a 92 mph wind.

NOV [**20**] Lord Jellicoe, Admiral of the Fleet in the First World War, dies.

Eric Mendelsohn and Serge Chermayeff: De la Warr Pavilion, Bexhill, Sussex.

Walter Sickert: *Sir Alec Martin.*
Wyndham Lewis: *Portrait of Edith Sitwell.*
Ben Nicholson: *White Relief.*
Paul Nash: *Equivalents for the Megaliths.*

T. E. Lawrence: *Seven Pillars of Wisdom.*
E. F. Benson: *Lucia's Progress.*
Dame Ivy Compton-Burnett: *A House and its Head.*
Christopher Isherwood: *Mr Norris Changes Trains.*

T. S. Eliot: *Murder in the Cathedral.*
Elizabeth Bowen: *The House in Paris.*
Graham Greene: *England Made Me.*

Sir William Walton: *First Symphony.*
Sir Lennox Berkeley: *Jonah.*
Sir Michael Tippett: *First String Quartet.*

1936 Sir Henry Dale (British) and Otto Loewi (German/Austrian) are awarded the Nobel Prize for Physiology and Medicine.

JAN [11] Arthur Scargill, National Union of Mineworkers leader, is born. [18] The writer Rudyard Kipling dies. [20] George V dies at Sandringham aged 70; he is succeeded by his son as Edward VIII.

FEB [11] Dame Laura Knight becomes the first woman to be admitted to membership of the Royal Academy.

MAR [29] The composer Richard Rodney Bennett is born.

APR [30] The Government announces its plan to build 38 warships.

MAY [9] Actress Glenda Jackson is born. The actor Albert Finney is born in Salford. [18] Jasmine Bligh and Elizabeth Cowell become the BBC's first women announcers. [27] The first open prison in Britain, New Hall near Wakefield, is opened. The *Queen Mary* sails on her maiden voyage.

JUN [3] Emperor Haile Selassie arrives in London in exile. [6] Gatwick Airport opens. [11] Leslie Mitchell is to be the first television announcer. [14] The author G. K. Chesterton dies.

JUL [14] Britain starts mass-producing gas masks. [16] George McMahon, a journalist, makes an attempt to assassinate Edward VIII. [24] The 'Speaking Clock' is introduced by the Post Office at the suggestion of Eugene Wender. [31] Education Act, raising the school-leaving age to 15.

AUG [21] The first television broadcast from Alexandra Palace.

SEP [30] The Pinewood Film Studios open.

OCT [5] The Jarrow Hunger March begins. [11] There are violent clashes in the East End of London between Mosleyite Fascists and their opponents: 80 people are injured. [12] The London-Paris through-train service opens. [16] Lord Beaverbrook calls on the King in order to come to an agreement about press silence on the King's relationship with Mrs Simpson.

NOV [11] Baldwin refuses to meet the Jarrow marchers. [18] Edward VIII visits South Wales, sees several thousands of unemployed men and says, 'something must be done'.

DEC [10] Edward VIII abdicates after a reign of 325 days; his younger brother, the Duke of York, becomes George VI.

Sir Edward Maufe: Guildford Cathedral.
Slater, Crabtree and Moberly: Peter Jones Store, Sloane Square, London.
Erno Goldfinger: Hill Pasture, Essex.

 Sir Stanley Spencer: *Double-nude portrait.*
Walter Sickert: *Edward VIII.*
Paul Nash: *Encounter in the Afternoon.*

 A. J. Ayer: *Language, Truth and Logic.*
F. R. Leavis: *Revaluation.*
Graham Greene: *A Gun for Sale.*
Daphne du Maurier: *Jamaica Inn.*
J. M. Keynes: *General Theory of Employment, Interest and Money.*
Eric Fenby: *Delius as I knew him.*

 John Ireland: *A London Overtune.*
Vaughan Williams: *The Poisoned Kiss.*
Benjamin Britten: *Our Hunting Fathers.*

1937 Walter Haworth (British) and Paul Karrer (Swiss) are awarded the Nobel Prize for Chemistry. Sir George Thomson (British) and Clinton Davidson (American) are awarded the Nobel Prize for Physics.

JAN [1] Public Order Act comes into force; the Government is determined to end the British Union of Fascists' provocative marches. [2] Anglo-Italian Mediterranean Agreement; this is intended to reduce the dangerous level of friction between Britain and Italy in the Mediterranean. [3] Britain makes a formal protest to France about the shelling of the *Blackhill* in the Bay of Biscay. [10] The Government bans volunteers from fighting in Spain, introducing a two-year prison sentence for offenders. [18] Horse-drawn traffic is banned from a large area of the West End of London.

FEB [4] The German ambassador von Ribbentrop gives George VI a Nazi salute.

MAR [16] Sir Austen Chamberlain, Conservative politician, dies.

APR [1] London's Green Belt is proposed. [13] HMS *Ark Royal* is launched.

MAY [12] Coronation of George VI (the BBC's first outside television broadcast). [14] Viscount Allenby, army commander in Palestine in the First World War, dies. [28] Following Baldwin's resignation, a Coalition Government under Neville Chamberlain is formed: a Conservative-led National Government.

JUN   [**3**] The Duke of Windsor (ex-King Edward VIII) marries Mrs Wallis Simpson at Monts in France. [**19**] Sir James Barrie, creator of 'Peter Pan', dies. [**29**] Italy and Germany oppose Anglo-French patrols round the coasts of Spain.

JUL   [**1**] The '999' emergency telephone service comes into operation. [**8**] The Peel Report proposes dividing Palestine into Jewish and Arab states, but Parliament will not agree to it. [**9**] The painter David Hockney is born. [**28**] The ex-Rector of Stiffkey is mauled by a lion at Skegness.

SEP   [**10**] The TUC votes in favour of re-armament.

OCT   [**10**] Sir Oswald Mosley is hit by a stone and knocked unconscious at a rally in Liverpool. [**14**] The first Motor Show opens at Earls Court. [**19**] Lord Rutherford, the founder of atomic theory, dies at Cambridge. [**22**] The Duke and Duchess of Windsor meet Hitler in Berlin, on something approaching a state visit.

NOV   [**9**] Ramsay MacDonald, Labour Prime Minister, dies at sea while on a cruise. [**17**] Lord Halifax arrives in Berlin for talks with Hitler on the Sudeten Germans; this is the first step in the appeasement policy.

DEC   [**29**] The new Irish Constitution comes into force; the Republic is to be called Eire. [**31**] Actor Anthony Hopkins is born.

Sir John Burnet: Senate House, London University.

Tristram Hillier: *La Route des Alpes.*
Sir Roland Penrose: *Portrait of Valentine.*

Ernest Rutherford: *The Newer Alchemy.*
Dame Ivy Compton-Burnett: *Daughters and Sons.*
J. R. R. Tolkien: *The Hobbit.*
George Orwell: *The Road to Wigan Pier.*
P. G. Wodehouse: *Summer Moonshine.*

Vaughan Williams: *Fourth Symphony.*
Benjamin Britten: *Variations on a Theme of Frank Bridge.*
William Walton: *Crown Imperial.*
Frederick Delius: *Florida Suite* (written in 1887).

1938 JAN   [**8**] Sigmund Freud arrives in London to escape persecution.

FEB   [**14**] The British naval base at Singapore opens. [**17**] John Logie Baird demonstrates a prototype colour television. [**20**] The Foreign Secretary, Sir Anthony Eden, resigns in protest against Chamberlain's determination to try to obtain agreement with Italy without waiting for a settlement over Spain.

MAR [**30**] £11 million are to be spent on new RAF airfields. [**31**] Sir David Steel, Liberal Party leader, is born. Sir Edwin Lutyens' plan for a National Theatre is made public.

APR [**1**] Britain and the US abandon the London naval treaty to allow them to build battleships. [**16**] Anglo-Italian Agreement; this measure, which Chamberlain has been working towards, is to come into force as soon as Italian 'volunteers' are withdrawn from Spain.

MAY [**9**] Scotland Yard announce that they are to use police dogs. [**16**] The Women's Voluntary Service is founded by the Marchioness of Reading.

JUN [**2**] Regent's Park Children's Zoo is opened by Robert and Edward Kennedy. [**9**] The Government signs a contract to buy 400 planes from the USA.

JUL [**7**] Augustus John opens a London exhibition of art banned in Germany. [**15**] The Government orders 1000 spitfire fighters. [**28**] The liner *Mauretania* is launched at Birkenhead.

SEP The German-Czechoslovakia Crisis begins. [**15**] Chamberlain visits Hitler at Berchtesgaden concerning Czechoslovakia. [**22**] Chamberlain meets Hitler again, at Godesberg. [**27**] The liner *Queen Elizabeth* is launched at Clydebank by the Queen Mother. [**28**] The British Navy is mobilized. [**29**] Chamberlain meets Hitler, Mussolini and Daladier at Munich; the Munich Agreement is a guarantee to Czechoslovakia against further aggression.

OCT [**4**] Hitler's troops invade the Sudetenland.

NOV [**2**] The Anglo-Italian Agreement is ratified. [**9**] The British Government calls a conference on the future of Palestine.

DEC [**1**] A national register for war service is opened, initially on a voluntary basis, as a preliminary to war. [**2**] 206 German Jewish schoolchildren arrive in Britain as refugees. [**21**] The Government allocates £200,000 to the building of air-raid shelters.

Paul Nash: *Night Landscape.*
Graham Sutherland: *Sun Setting between Hills.*
John Armstrong: *Heaviness of Sleep.*
Ceri Richards: *The Variable Costerwoman.*
Wyndham Lewis: *T. S. Eliot.*
Henry Moore: *Reclining Figure.*

Daphne du Maurier: *Rebecca.*
Evelyn Waugh: *Scoop.*
Elizabeth Bowen: *The Death of the Heart.*

Graham Greene: *Brighton Rock.*
Samuel Beckett: *Murphy.*

 Sir Arnold Bax: *Violin Concerto.*
Vaughan Williams: *Serenade to Music.*

1939 George Bernard Shaw wins an Academy Award for his screen adaptation of *Pygmalion.* The IRA begin a bombing campaign in mainland Britain; a bomb in Coventry kills five passers-by.

JAN [**11**] Chamberlain and Lord Haldane visit Mussolini to discuss recognition of the Franco regime. [**25**] Sir Stafford Cripps is expelled from the Labour Party. [**28**] The poet W. B. Yeats dies.

FEB [**3**] The police hunt for IRA extremists after bombs explode at London tube stations. [**27**] Britain recognizes Franco's government. Borley Rectory, reputed to be Britain's most haunted house, is burnt to the ground. [**28**] Hitler denounces the Anglo-German Naval Treaty and the Polish Non-Aggression Treaty.

MAR [**2**] Howard Carter, discoverer of Tutankhamun's tomb in 1922, dies. [**17**] Talks on Palestine end in failure. Chamberlain denounces Hitler. [**26**] The first commercial oil deposit is found in Britain at Eakring in Nottinghamshire.

APR [**5**] HMS *Illustrious,* Britain's largest aircraft carrier, is launched. [**6**] Britain, Poland and France sign a mutual assistance pact in case of attack. [**25**] The Budget allocates £1.3 billion to defence. [**27**] Conscription of 20-21 year old men is introduced. [**28**] Hitler tears up the 1934 naval treaty with Britain.

MAY [**3**] British farmers are urged by the Government to plough up pasture to increase food production. [**11**] Chamberlain warns Hitler that if the Germans use force in Danzig it will mean war. [**17**] George VI and Queen Elizabeth begin a short visit to North America in an attempt to strengthen Anglo-Saxon solidarity. [**19**] The TUC decides not to oppose the Government's conscription plans. [**25**] An Anglo-Polish treaty is signed in London. Actor and director Sir Ian McKellen is born.

JUN [**1**] The submarine *Thetis* sinks during trials in Liverpool Bay, with the loss of 99 lives.

JUL [**10**] Chamberlain reaffirms Britain's pledge to stand by Poland.

AUG [**22**] Britain and France again reaffirm their pledge to Poland. [**23**] The German-Soviet Pact is signed by von Ribbentrop. [**25**] Movable treasures are taken to safety from London's museums and galleries. [**28**] The Admiralty declares the Baltic and Mediterranean closed to British Merchant Shipping.

SEP [**1**] The German army invades Poland. The BBC radio 'Home Service' (later to become Radio 4) begins broadcasting. [**1-4**] Evacuation schemes are put into action in England and Wales; 1.2 million people are moved. [**2**] Military service for all British men between ages of 18 and 41 becomes compulsory. [**3**] At 11 am war is declared between Britain and Germany as from 5 pm; this marks the beginning of the Second World War. [**4**] A German submarine sinks the British liner *Athenia* off the Irish coast. The RAF raid the entrance to the Kiel Canal and bomb German warships. [**6**] First German air raid on Britain. [**11**] British troops land in France. [**18**] HMS *Courageous* is sunk in the Atlantic: 500 men die. [**23**] Sigmund Freud, the founder of modern psychology and psychoanalysis, dies in Hampstead aged 83.

OCT [**1**] 250,000 more conscripts are called up. [**14**] The battleship *Royal Oak* is torpedoed at anchor in Scapa Flow; 810 men are killed.

NOV [**13**] The first German bombs fall on British soil, in the Shetlands.

DEC [**13**] Battle of the River Plate; the German warship *Admiral Graf Spee* is engaged by HMS *Exeter*, *Ajax* and *Achilles*. [**18**] The *Admiral Graf Spee* is scuttled by her crew at the mouth of Montevideo harbour.

Walter Gropius and Maxwell Fry: Impington Village College, near Cambridge.

Paul Nash: *Monster field*.
Graham Sutherland: *Entrance to a Lane*.

Anthony Powell: *What's Become of Waring?*
Joyce Cary: *Mister Johnson*.
James Joyce: *Finnegan's Wake*.
Christopher Isherwood: *Goodbye to Berlin*.
Dame Ivy Compton-Burnett: *A Family and a Fortune*.
Graham Greene: *The Confidential Agent*.
T. S. Eliot: *The Family Reunion*.
E. F. Benson: *Trouble for Lucia*.
Flann O'Brien: *At Swim Two Birds*.

Benjamin Britten: *Young Apollo; Les Illuminations*.
Sir Michael Tippett: *Concerto for Double String Orchestra*.
Sir Arnold Bax: *Seventh Symphony*.

1940 Sir Howard Florey devises an important new process that will enable the large-scale production of penicillin; clinical trials begin.

JAN   [3]Unity Mitford, who tried to befriend Hitler, returns to England after her unsuccessful suicide attempt. [8] Rationing of butter, bacon and sugar is introduced.

FEB   [11] The novelist John Buchan dies. [6] 299 British prisoners are rescued from the German ship *Altmark* in Norwegian waters.

MAR   [11] Meat rationing starts. [12] British ships are to be fitted with a device to protect them against magnetic mines. [29] Metal strips are put into banknotes for the first time as a defence against forgery.

APR   [14] Actress Julie Christie is born. [15] British troops arrive in Norway. The politician and writer Jeffrey Archer is born.

MAY   [2] British troops withdraw from Norway. [10] Belgium, Luxembourg and the Netherlands are invaded by German troops; British troops cross into Belgium. Neville Chamberlain resigns as Prime Minister, and a National Government is formed under the leadership of Winston Churchill. [13] Churchill gives his 'Blood, toil, tears and sweat' speech. The Dutch Queen Wilhelmina arrives in London at the beginning of her exile. [22] Emergency Powers Act. [27] The Belgian army surrenders to the Germans; British forces begin to withdraw from Belgium and northern France. Dunkirk; the British Expeditionary Force and the First French Army are cut off near Dunkirk. 335,490 men are evacuated from the beach by 299 British warships and 420 small boats under continual German attack; the withdrawal takes a week (May 17-June 4). [31] Mosley is interned at Brixton Prison.

JUN   [4] Churchill makes his famous 'We shall fight them on the beaches' speech in the Commons. Later the same day, actor Norman Shelley reads the speech on the radio, impersonating Churchill's voice. [5] The Government bans strikes. Hitler declares a war of total annihilation against his enemies. [10] Italy declares war on Britain and France. [16] Churchill proposes a union of France and Britain. [17] The troopship *Lancastria* is sunk off St Nazaire with the loss of 2500 lives.

JUL   [1] The Channel Islands are occupied by German troops. [10] The British Union of Fascists becomes a banned organization.

AUG   [17] The German blockade of British waters begins. [22] Sir Oliver Lodge, pioneer of wireless telegraphy, dies. [25] The RAF begins night bombing in Germany. [30] Sir J. J. Thomson, discoverer of the electron, dies.

SEP [6] London experiences the largest air attack since the start of the war and is severely damaged. [15] The Battle of Britain ends with victory for Britain; the Germans lose 1,733 aircraft and the British 915. Because the Germans' air supremacy is broken they are now unable to invade Britain; it is a turning-point in the war. [23] The George Cross, the highest civilian award for acts of courage, is instituted.

OCT [9] The musician John Lennon is born in Liverpool. Churchill is elected leader of the Conservative Party. [10] A German bomb destroys the high altar of St Paul's Cathedral. [19] Actor Michael Gambon is born.

NOV [9] Neville Chamberlain, Conservative Prime Minister 1937-40, dies of cancer. [14] A massive German attack on Coventry destroys the cathedral. [7] The sculptor and engraver Eric Gill dies. [20] A Luftwaffe raid on Birmingham. [29] Air raid on Liverpool.

DEC [2] Bristol is heavily bombed. Britain invades Libya. [22] Sir Anthony Eden becomes Foreign Secretary again. [29] The City of London is badly burned by incendiary bombs; the Guildhall and eight of Wren's churches are destroyed.

Edward Wadsworth: *Bronze ballet.*
Eric Ravilious: *Submarines in Dry Dock.*
Merlyn Evans: *The Chess Players.*
Lawrence Gowing: *Julia Strachey.*
Edward Burra: *Wake.*

E. F. Benson: *Final Edition.*
T. S. Eliot: *East Coker.*
Graham Greene: *The Power and the Glory.*
C. P. Snow: *Strangers and Brothers.*
Arthur Koestler: *Darkness at Noon.*

Benjamin Britten: *Sinfonia da Requiem.*

1941 JAN [5] Amy Johnson dies in plane crash in the Thames Estuary; officially she has 'disappeared', but it will emerge in years to come that she has been shot down by mistake by the British. [7] British troops capture Tobruk airport. [8] Lord Baden Powell, founder of the Boy Scout movement, dies. [10] British bases on Malta are bombed. [13] The novelist James Joyce dies in Zürich.

FEB [1] The RAF raids Tripoli. [5] The war is costing Britain £11 million a day. [7] British and Commonwealth troops take Benghazi. [18] Churchill's Government receives a unanimous vote of confidence in Parliament. [**27**] Jeremy (Paddy) Ashdown, leader of the Liberal Democrats, is born.

MAR [**4**] The British raid the Lofoten Islands. [**28**] The Battle of Cape Matapan; the Italian fleet is mostly destroyed by the British off the south coast of Greece. Virginia Woolf, novelist, drowns herself in the Sussex Ouse at Rodmell.

APR [**3**] British-led troops evacuate Benghazi as Rommel advances. [**7**] A War Budget raises income tax to a record 50%. [**27**] The Germans capture Athens.

MAY [**2**] British and Commonwealth troops complete their evacuation of Greece. [**5**] Haile Selassie returns to Ethiopia from exile in Britain after his country is liberated by British forces. [**10**] Rudolf Hess lands by parachute in Scotland. [**11**] In a severe bombing raid on London the Chamber of the House of Commons is destroyed. [**12**] The Commons meet for the first time in the House of Lords. [**15**] The first jet-propelled aircraft, designed by Frank Whittle, flies for the first time. [**20**] Crete is invaded by German troops. [**24**] HMS *Hood* is sunk 13 miles off the Greenland coast: only three out of the crew of 1421 survive the disaster. [**27**] The German battleship *Bismarck* is sunk. British forces withdraw from Crete. [**31**] The first shipments of food arrive from the USA.

JUN [**2**] Clothes rationing begins. [**7**] The RAF reveals for the first time that radar has been used to locate enemy bombers.

JUL [**11**] Sir Arthur Evans, who excavated Knossos, dies.

AUG [**14**] The Atlantic Charter; this is a joint US and UK declaration of peace aims. [**24**] Churchill promises the US aid if the US becomes involved in a war with Japan. [**25**] British and Russian troops enter Iran and set up a new regime that will be sympathetic to their interests.

OCT [**16**] The composer Derek Bourgeois is born.

NOV [**6**] The counter-tenor James Bowman is born. [**14**] The aircraft carrier *Ark Royal* is sunk near Gibraltar. [**18**] The Battle of Libya begins: the Eighth Army's first offensive in North Africa. [**24**] HMS *Dunedin* is torpedoed. [**25**] HMS *Barham* is sunk.

DEC [**8**] The United States declares war on Japan. Britain declares war on German puppet regimes in Finland, Romania and Hungary. [**9**] British forces in Tobruk are relieved. [**10**] HMS *Repulse* and *Prince of Wales* are sunk off Malaya by Japanese aircraft action. [**11**] Germany and Italy declare war on the US. [**25**] Hong Kong surrenders to the Japanese.

 Sir Giles Gilbert Scott: New Bodleian Library, Oxford.

Edward Burra: *Soldiers at Rye.*
Paul Nash: *Totes Meer.*

T. S. Eliot: *Burnt Norton.*
Daphne du Maurier: *Frenchman's Creek.*
Noel Coward: *Blithe Spirit.*

Benjamin Britten: *Paul Bunyan* (composed but not performed).
Sir Michael Tippett: *A Child of Our Time* (composed).
'White Cliffs of Dover' (song).

1942 The painters Philip Steer and Walter Sickert die. The Beveridge
Report on Social Insurance and Allied Services recommends state
social insurance 'from the cradle to the grave', and forms the basis of
post-war social legislation.

JAN [**19**] The entertainer Michael Crawford is born at Salisbury as
Michael Dumble-Smith. [**9**] The first edition of 'Desert Island
Discs' is broadcast, with Roy Plomley in the chair.

FEB [**9**] Soap is rationed. [**12**] The German raiders *Scharnhorst,
Gneisenau* and *Prinz Eugen* escape through the English Channel.
[**15**] The British naval base of Singapore is surrendered to the
Japanese.

MAR [**28**] Neil Kinnock, Labour Party leader, is born. The RAF
begins its terror bombing campaign with an attack on Lubeck.
[**29**] Stafford Cripps meets Gandhi in Delhi and offers him a
British plan for full Indian independence after the war. [**31**]
Archbishop Lang retires.

APR [**15**] Malta is awarded the George Cross for heroism during
German and Italian bombardments. [**17**] William Temple,
Archbishop of York, becomes Archbishop of Canterbury. [**18**]
Lord Mountbatten is put in charge of combined Allied
operations in South-East Asia. [**25**] Princess Elizabeth registers
for war service.

MAY [**7**] Madagascar is invaded by British troops to forestall the
Japanese. [**30**] Thousand-bomber raid on Cologne. Churchill
and Molotov agree a 20-year mutual aid treaty.

JUN [**3**] The Government announces that it will take over the coal
mines. [**9**] The US and UK agree to pool all food and
production resources in order to ensure victory. [**18**] Paul
McCartney, musician, is born in Liverpool. [**20**] Tobruk is
captured by the Germans.

JUL [**16**] The RAF makes its first daylight raid on the Ruhr.

AUG [**6**] Montgomery becomes commander of the Eighth Army.
[**11**] HMS *Eagle, Manchester* and *Cairo* are lost in Malta

convoy action. [**12**] Churchill begins a four-day visit to Moscow, to discuss with Stalin the establishment of a second front in Europe. [**19**] The Dieppe Raid, called 'Operation Jubilee'; there are unexpectedly heavy casualties. [**25**] George, Duke of Kent, is killed in action.

Sep [**6**] Two Belfast policemen are shot dead by the IRA.

Oct [**2**] The British cruiser *Curaçao* collides with the liner *Queen Mary* off the coast of Donegal and sinks immediately with the loss of 338 lives. [**10**] Following German action, in chaining 2500 Allied prisoners after the Dieppe Raid, British camps are now chaining up German prisoners-of-war. [**23**] Battle of El Alamein; the Allied offensive opens in Egypt. The German Afrika Corps is only 80 miles from Alexandria; British and Commonwealth troops under Montgomery and Alexander counter-attack and break the German forces. [**31**] The Germans bomb Canterbury as a reprisal for the bombing of Cologne.

Nov [**4**] Rommel's army is in full retreat. [**7**] Allied invasion of North Africa, with Eisenhower in command. [**10**] Churchill's 'end of the beginning' speech on the Alamein victory. [**13**] Tobruk is recaptured by the Allies.

 Sir Giles Gilbert Scott: Waterloo Bridge (new bridge).

 Jacob Epstein: *Jacob and the Angel.*

 Richard Hillary: *The Last Enemy.*
Evelyn Waugh: *Put Out More Flags.*
T. S. Eliot: *Little Gidding.*

 Benjamin Britten: *Hymn to St Cecilia; A Ceremony of Carols.*
Sir Michael Tippett: *Second String Quartet.*
'We'll Meet Again' (song).

1943 Mulberry harbours are constructed. Daily expenditure on the war, in Britain alone, is estimated at £14 million.

Jan [**14**] The Casablanca Conference (until January 24) between Roosevelt and Churchill. [**23**] Allied troops recapture Tripoli. [**27**] After the Casablanca Conference it is announced that plans have been made for an Allied offensive in Europe that will secure the Axis powers' unconditional surrender.

Feb [**12**] Lord Nuffield founds the Nuffield Foundation with a gift of £10 million.

MAR [**2**] The RAF bombs Berlin. [**3**] 178 people are killed in an accident at the Bethnal Green air raid shelter. [**6**] Heavy bombing raid on Essen.

APR RAF bombers raid Stuttgart.

MAY [**3**] It becomes compulsory for British women of 18-45 to do part-time work. [**7**] Tunis and Bizerta are captured by the Allies. [**12**] German resistance in Tunisia ends. Churchill visits Washington to discuss the preparation of a second front in Europe and to promise British assistance in the war against Japan. [**16**] The Mohne, Sorpe and Eder dams in the Ruhr are breached by the RAF, using special bouncing bombs invented by Sir Barnes Wallis. [**27**] The entertainer Cilla Black is born in Liverpool.

JUN [**1**] The actor Leslie Howard is killed when his plane is shot down over the Bay of Biscay. [**21**] Sir Michael Tippett is sentenced to three months in prison at Oxted for refusing to do military service.

JUL [**10**] The Allies invade Sicily. [**16**] A White Paper recommends raising the school-leaving age again, to 16.

AUG [**13**] The Allies bomb Rome, Milan and Turin. [**7**] Sicily is secured by the Allied forces.

SEP [**3**] Allies invade the Italian mainland. [**7**] Italy surrenders to the Allies. [**21**] The Patronal Festival of St Matthew's, Northampton, organized by Canon Walter Hussey; first performance of Britten's *Rejoice in the Lamb* and Tippett's *Fanfare*. [**23**] The German battleship *Tirpitz* is seriously damaged and disabled.

NOV [**20**] Mosley is released from prison, but is to remain under house arrest. [**22**] The Labour Party protests against Mosley's release. [**25**] Bomber Harris undertakes to bomb Berlin 'until the heart of Nazi Germany ceases to beat'. [**28**] Churchill, Roosevelt and Stalin meet in Teheran to discuss the question of a second front against the Axis.

DEC [**22**] Beatrix Potter, writer of children's stories, dies. [**6**] The last German battleship, *Scharnhorst*, is sunk.

John Piper: *Gordale Scar.*
Ivon Hitchens: *Flower group.*
Victor Pasmore: *Evening, Hammersmith.*

Herbert Read: *Education through Art.*
Graham Greene: *The Ministry of Fear.*

Vaughan Williams: *Fifth Symphony.*
Benjamin Britten: *Rejoice in the Lamb; Serenade.*
Sir Michael Tippett: *Boyhood's End; Fanfare No 1.*

1944 Education Act, introduced by R. A. Butler, raises the school-leaving age to 15, in effect implementing a report of 1926.

JAN [**1**] The architect Sir Edwin Lutyens dies. [**22**] The Allies land at Anzio.

MAR [**10**] The Education Minister R. A. Butler lifts the ban on women teachers marrying. [**11**] The Prime Minister of Eire, de Valera, refuses to comply with the American request to close the German and Japanese embassies in Dublin, to prevent the possible transmission of military intelligence through their agents. Britain suspends all travel between Britain and Eire. [**15**] The ancient monastery at Monte Cassino in Italy is destroyed by the Allies. [**19**] Tippett's *A Child of Our Time* is first performed. [**24**] Orde Wingate is killed in a plane crash in Assam.

APR [**6**] From today income tax may be paid by the PAYE scheme. [**30**] The first pre-fabricated houses go on show in London.

MAY [**9**] The composer Dame Ethel Smyth dies. [**19**] 50 Allied officers are shot after escaping from a German prison camp.

JUN [**4**] Allied forces enter Rome. [**6**] D-Day; the invasion of Europe by a huge invasion fleet crossing the English Channel. [**9**] There is heavy fighting near Caen. [**12**] The first V-1 bomb falls on Britain.

JUL [**3**] The evacuation of children from London begins as a response to the V-1 bombing. [**9**] Caen is captured by the Allies.

AUG [**12**] PLUTO (Pipe-Line Under the Ocean) is operational from today, supplying petrol to the Allied forces in France; it runs southwards from Shanklin. [**19**] The conductor Sir Henry Wood dies at Hitchin. [**23**] The liberation of Paris. [**31**] Montgomery is made a Field Marshal.

SEP [**4**] Brussels and Antwerp are taken by the Allies. [**8**] The first V-2 bomb falls on Britain. [**9**] John Haigh batters Donald McSwann to death in Pimlico and dissolves his body in acid. Shortly afterwards he murders McSwann's parents; strangely, their disappearance is not noticed until Haigh confesses to their murder several years later. [**13**] The artist Heath Robinson dies. [**17**] Allied air-borne troops land near Arnhem.

OCT [**5**] British troops land on the mainland of Greece. [**14**] Athens is taken by the Allies.

NOV [**12**] The battleship *Tirpitz* is sunk in Tromso Fjord by Lancaster bombers. [**30**] The largest and last of the British battleships, HMS *Vanguard*, is launched.

Ceri Richards: *Cycle of Nature.*
Paul Nash: *Landscape of the Vernal Equinox.*
Francis Bacon: *Three Studies for a Crucifixion.*
Henry Moore: *Madonna and Child* (the Northampton Madonna).

 T. S. Eliot: *Four Quartets.*
L. P. Hartley: *The Shrimp and the Anemone.*
Joyce Cary: *The Horse's Mouth.*
Cyril Connolly: *The Unquiet Grave.*
G. M. Trevelyan: *English Social History.*
H. E. Bates: *Fair Stood the Wind for France.*
W. Somerset Maugham: *The Razor's Edge.*

 Sir William Walton: Music for *Henry V* (Olivier's film).
Patrick Hadley: *The Hills.*
Sir Michael Tippett: *First Symphony* (composed).
'Mairzy Doats' (song).

1945 Sir Alexander Fleming, Sir Howard Florey and Ernst Chain are awarded the Nobel Prize for Physiology and Medicine.

FEB [2] Geoffrey Fisher, Bishop of London, becomes Archbishop of Canterbury. [4] Beginning of the Yalta Conference in Crimea between Stalin, Roosevelt and Churchill (ends February 11). [12] Yalta statement: the Allies have concerted plans for Germany's final defeat. [14] The bombing of Dresden; this is one of the most destructive and controversial bombing raids of the war in which around 100,000 civilians die in the firestorms which engulf the city.

MAR [6] Cologne is captured by the Allies. [7] Allied troops cross the Rhine by way of the Ludendorff Bridge at Remagen. [11] The Krupps factory is destroyed. [26] David Lloyd George, Liberal Prime Minister 1916-22, dies aged 82. [27] The last V-2 bomb lands at Orpington in Kent; since September 1944 over a thousand of these 'Vengeance' weapons have been launched against Britain.

APR [15] British troops liberate Belsen concentration camp. [23] The black-out in London comes to an end. [28] Mussolini is shot. [30] Hitler commits suicide.

MAY [3] Rangoon is captured by the British. [4] German troops in north-west Germany surrender. [7] The German Provisional Government under Admiral Doenitz surrenders unconditionally. [8] The end of the Second World War against Germany is officially declared.

Jun [**15**] Family allowances are introduced: five shillings a week per child after the first child.

Jul [**26**] Labour win the General Election with a majority of 173 seats; Clement Attlee, the new Prime Minister, embarks on a programme of nationalization and social reform. The UK, US and China demand that Japan surrenders unconditionally; the demand is ignored.

Aug [**6**] The atomic bomb is used for the first time; four square miles of Hiroshima are laid waste and over 50,000 civilians are killed. [**9**] A second atom bomb is dropped on Nagasaki. [**14**] Japan surrenders to the Allies on the one condition that the Emperor will remain head of state. The secret of radar is disclosed for the first time. [**26**] Following some criticism of the severity of the Dresden bombing, it is announced that Sir Arthur 'Bomber' Harris is to retire. [**30**] Hong Kong is reoccupied by the British.

Sep [**2**] Victory over Japan is celebrated in Britain, and the final end of the Second World War. [**16**] The singer Count John McCormack dies.

Nov [**20**] The Nuremberg War Trials begin.

L. S. Lowry: *Deserted Mill.*
Victor Pasmore: *The Jewish model.*
Michael Ayrton: *Entrance to a Wood.*
John Minton: *Sunflowers.*

Evelyn Waugh: *Brideshead Revisited.*
George Orwell: *Animal Farm.*
Osbert Sitwell: *Left Hand, Right Hand.*

Edmund Rubbra: *Canterbury Mass.*
Benjamin Britten: *Peter Grimes.*
Sir Michael Tippett: *First Symphony* (performed).

1946 The Bank of England is nationalized, although in effect it remains substantially independent of Government. The coal industry is also nationalized; the National Coal Board is to take over all mines. The Inland Transport Act nationalizes railways, road transport, docks and harbours.

Jan [**3**] William Joyce, 'Lord Haw Haw', is hanged for treason. [**22**] Pit owners protest at the Government's plan to nationalize the mines.

Mar [**1**] The Bank of England passes to public ownership. [**5**] Churchill gives a speech at Fulton, Missouri in which he refers to the 'iron curtain' for the first time; it is the first public acknowledgement that the Cold War has begun. [**9**] The Burnden Park disaster at Bolton; 33 people are killed and 400 injured as crush-barriers give way before the FA Cup match. [**22**] Jordan becomes an independent kingdom, having been until now under British protection.

APR [**2**] The Royal Military Academy is established at Sandhurst, after being at Woolwich since 1741. [**21**] The economist Lord Keynes dies.

JUN [**1**] The first television licences, costing £2, are issued. [**14**] The inventor of television, John Baird, dies aged 58. [**17**] The Allies decide not to put Hirohito on trial as a war criminal.

JUL [**13**] The US House of Representatives approves a loan to Britain. [**22**] Bread rationing begins in Britain. The British Headquarters in Jerusalem are blown up.

AUG [**1**] Peace Conference opens in Paris. [**13**] The writer H. G. Wells dies.

SEP [**29**] The BBC's Third Programme, later to become Radio 3, begins.

OCT [**16**] The death sentences on Nazi criminals convicted at Nuremberg are carried out; Goering succeeds in committing suicide just before his execution.

NOV The National Health Service Act, guided though Parliament by the Minister of Health Aneurin Bevan, is to become operative in 1948; it institutes free diagnosis and treatment, both by general practitioners and in hospitals. [**10**] George VI unveils an additional inscription on the Cenotaph – '1939-1945'.

Chamberlin, Powell and Bon: New Hall, Cambridge.
James Stirling: Faculty of History Building, Cambridge.

Barbara Hepworth: *Pelagos*.
Graham Sutherland: *Crucifixion*.
Robert MacBryde: *Performing Clown*.

Bertrand Russell: *The History of Western Philosophy*.
Terence Rattigan: *The Winslow Boy*.
Mervyn Peake: *Titus Groan*.

Benjamin Britten: *The Rape of Lucretia; Young Person's Guide to the Orchestra*.
Alan Bush: *The Press Gang*.
Sir Michael Tippett: *Third String Quartet*.

1947 The Edinburgh Festival is founded. The India Independence Act is rushed through Parliament; it establishes a mainly Hindu India and a

Muslim Pakistan. The 550 private electricity generating companies are nationalized. Sir Edward Appleton is awarded the Nobel Prize for Physics and Sir Robert Robinson the Nobel Prize for Chemistry.

JAN [1] The nationalization of the coal industry becomes effective. [8] The steel works close through lack of coal. There are food shortages as a result of the hauliers' strike.

FEB [2] The RAF begins evacuating Britons from Palestine. [20] Lord Mountbatten is appointed last Viceroy of India. In Britain, very cold weather combined with fuel shortages threaten to damage the economy.

MAR [6] 15 towns are cut off by deep snow. [15] The worst floods ever recorded in Britain follow the thaw; two million sheep are drowned.

APR [1] The school-leaving age is raised to 15. [24] The Government bans the use of coal and gas until September.

JUN [5] Beginning of 'Marshall Aid'. [22] George VI issues a proclamation renouncing the title 'Emperor of India', in anticipation of the statutory changes in India's status. [28] The statue of Eros returns to Piccadilly Circus.

AUG [10] Attlee makes a radio broadcast pleading for a wartime-style national effort to cope with the economic crisis. [15] The first British atomic reactor is opened at Harwell. India becomes independent.

SEP [30] The Government asks women to wear shorter skirts, to save cloth.

OCT [24] 31 people die in a train crash at Croydon. [26] Berwick train crash: 21 die.

NOV [14] Three people are killed in secret rocket tests in Buckinghamshire. [19] Prince Philip is created Duke of Edinburgh. [20] Princess Elizabeth (Elizabeth II) marries Prince Philip, son of Prince Andrew of Greece, in Westminster Abbey.

DEC [14] Stanley Baldwin, Earl Baldwin of Bewdley, three times Prime Minister, dies.

Sir Giles Gilbert Scott: Bankside Power Station, London.
Sir Frederick Gibberd: Harlow New Town.

Anne Redpath: *Pinks.*

C. P. Snow: *The Light and the Dark.*
Dame Ivy Compton-Burnett: *Manservant and Maidservant.*
L. P. Hartley: *Eustace and Hilda.*
Malcolm Lowry: *Under the Volcano.*

Vaughan Williams: *Sixth Symphony.*
Benjamin Britten: *Albert Herring.*
'Maybe it's because I'm a Londoner' (song).

1948 London hosts the first post-war Olympic Games; 59 countries take part. The railways are nationalized; the British Transport Commission takes control of most forms of transport, and the four railway groups are combined to form British Railways. Patrick M. S. Blackett is awarded the Nobel Prize for Physics; T. S. Eliot that for Literature.

JAN [3] Attlee denounces the USSR's 'new imperialism'. [4] Burma becomes independent. [30] Gandhi is assassinated in New Delhi.

FEB [4] Ceylon Independence Act: Ceylon (Sri Lanka) becomes a self-governing Dominion within the Commonwealth, having been a Crown Colony since 1802. [16] Britain warns Argentina to keep off the Falklands, as the Argentine navy conducts sabre-rattling exercises in the area. [28] The last British troops leave India.

MAR [22] The composer Andrew Lloyd Webber is born.

APR [1] The British electricity industry is nationalized. [5] The first European Aid shipments leave the USA.

MAY [14] The British mandate for Palestine ends: Jews proclaim the new state of Israel. [29] The composer Michael Berkeley is born.

JUN [7] Over half of the doctors in Britain agree to join the National Health Service.

JUL [1] The Berlin Airlift: American, French and British zones of Berlin are supplied by air. The first Oxfam shop opens, in Oxford. [4] Two passenger planes collide over Middlesex, killing 39 people. [13] It is revealed that the coal industry lost £23 million in its first year of nationalization. [29] Bread rationing comes to an end.

AUG [8] Twelve people die in 70 mph winds.

SEP [22] Captain Mark Phillips, later to marry Princess Anne, is born at Tewkesbury.

OCT [4] The pioneer aviator Sir Arthur Brown dies. [12] The first Morris Minor comes off the production line at Cowley, Oxford.

NOV [14] Princess Elizabeth gives birth to a son, Prince Charles Philip Arthur George. [30] Severe fog in London causes three train crashes.

DEC [21] The Republic of Ireland Bill is signed in Dublin. [31] Sir Malcolm Campbell, holder of the world land and water speed records, dies.

L. S. Lowry: *The Industrial City.*
Josef Herman: *Tired Miner.*
Lucien Freud: *Girl with Roses.*
Graham Sutherland: *The Crucifixion.*

 Christopher Fry: *The Lady's Not for Burning.*

 Vaughan Williams: *Scott of the Antarctic* (film score).
Sir Michael Tippett: *Suite for the Birthday of Prince Charles.*

1949 The samba, a Brazilian dance, becomes popular this year. Three major Ealing Studios comedy films appear: *Passport to Pimlico*, *Whisky Galore* and *Kind Hearts and Coronets*. The frigate HMS *Amethyst*, trapped for 14 weeks by Communist forces in the Yangtze River, makes its escape to open sea under cover of darkness. The House of Lords' power to delay legislation is reduced to one year.

JAN [9] The comedian Tommy Handley dies. [20] Attlee sets up a Royal Commission on capital punishment. [29] The British Government recognizes Israel.

FEB [23] Sir David Lean's film *Oliver Twist* is denounced in Berlin as anti-semitic.

MAR [1] After a series of accidents, Tudor IV airliners are banned from carrying passengers. [15] Clothes rationing comes to an end. [25] Sir Laurence Olivier's film of *Hamlet* wins five Oscars.

APR [1] The National Parks Bill is approved by Parliament. [18] Eire is now officially to be called the Republic of Ireland, and its independence from Britain is re-asserted by leaving the Commonwealth. [30] Sir Alfred Munnings, the retiring President of the Royal Academy, makes a violent attack on recent developments in art as 'silly daubs'.

MAY [1] The Gas Industry is nationalized. [3] A ten-power conference in London leads to the formation of the Council of Europe. [9] Britain's first launderette opens in Bayswater. [12] The Berlin blockade is lifted.

JUL [1] The London Docks come to a halt as the dockers go on strike. [12] 12,000 dockers are now out on strike. [27] The Lords vote in favour of admitting women who are peeresses in their own right to sit in the House of Lords. [29] The BBC televises its first weather forecast.

AUG [10] John Haigh, the acid bath murderer, is hanged. [19] A British European Airways DC-3 crashes in Yorkshire, killing 24 people. [24] The North Atlantic Treaty comes into force.

SEP [**11**] The milk ration is reduced to 2½ pints a week. [**18**] The milk ration is reduced to 2 pints a week. The pound is devalued by 30%.

OCT [**12**] Lord Boyd-Orr is awarded the Nobel Peace Prize for his work in helping the starving Third World.

NOV [**29**] Parliament Act, restricting the Lords' delaying abilities.

Graham Sutherland: *Portrait of Somerset Maugham.*
Jacob Epstein: *Lazarus.*
Victor Pasmore: *Triangular Motif.*

Christopher Fry: *The Lady's Not for Burning.*
C. P. Snow: *Time of Hope.*
Elizabeth Bowen: *The Heat of the Day.*
Kenneth Clarke: *Landscape into Art.*
Gilbert Ryle: *The Concept of Mind.*
George Orwell: *Nineteen Eighty-Four.*

Benjamin Britten: *Spring Symphony.*
Vaughan Williams: *The Pilgrim's Progress.*
Sir Arnold Bax: *Cello Concerto.*
Sir Arthur Bliss: *The Olympians.*
Gerald Finzi: *Introit.*

1950 Christopher Cockerell begins experimenting with the hovercraft idea. Excavations at Stonehenge by Stone, Atkinson and Piggott produce the first radiocarbon date for the monument, which proves to be unexpectedly old (around 2200 BC for the stones). Sir Fred Hoyle proposes his theory of the continuous creation of matter ('steady state'). Cecil Frank Powell is awarded the Nobel Prize for Physics; Bertrand Russell that for Literature.

JAN [**6**] Britain officially recognizes the Communist regime in China. [**12**] The submarine *Truculent* sinks after a Thames collision with the Swedish tanker *Divina*; 65 men die. [**21**] The author George Orwell dies.

FEB [**23**] The General Election returns are televised for the first time; Labour is returned, but with a reduced majority. [**26**] The music hall entertainer Sir Harry Lauder dies aged 79.

MAR [**12**] In the Cardiff air crash (a Tudor V plane) 80 people are killed.

APR [**4**] At Liverpool, the liner *Franconia* is found to be stuffed with smuggled nylon stockings with an estimated black market value of £80,000.

MAY [**26**] Petrol rationing ends. [**29**] 'The Archers' radio serial, created by Godfrey Baseley, is broadcast for the first time.

JUN   [**30**] It is revealed that the National Coal Board made a profit of £9.5 million in 1949.

JUL   [**7**] The first Farnborough Air Display takes place. [**15**] Churchill warns of the danger of a Third World War. [**26**] The British Government decides to send troops to Korea.

AUG   [**15**] Princess Anne is born at Clarence House, London.

SEP   [**6**] British troops are in action in Korea. [**7**] Attlee rejects a request from Quintin Hogg, who has just succeeded to the title Lord Hailsham, to sit in the House of Commons as an MP. [**9**] Soap rationing ends. [**28**] The Cresswell pit disaster; fire kills 80 miners.

OCT   [**4**] Three generations of the Bowler family attend celebrations marking the centenary of the bowler hat.

NOV   [**2**] The dramatist and critic George Bernard Shaw dies at Ayot St Lawrence aged 94. [**16**] King Farouk of Egypt demands the immediate evacuation of British troops from the Suez Canal. [**25**] The Coronation Stone, the Stone of Destiny, is stolen from Westminster Abbey by Scottish Nationalists. [**28**] The Peak District is designated as Britain's first National Park.

 Kenneth Armitage: *People in the wind.*

 Ernst Gombrich: *The Story of Art.*
Mervyn Peake: *Gormenghast.*
Graham Greene: *The Third Man.*
T.S. Eliot: *The Cocktail Party.*

 'I've got a lovely bunch of coconuts' (song).

1951 Eric Shipton leads a reconnaissance expedition to Mount Everest, climbing the Khumbu Icefall and preparing the way for the first ascent in two years' time. The first smokeless zone in Britain is established in Coventry. Sir John Cockcroft and Ernest Walton are awarded the Nobel Prize for Physics.

JAN   [**1**] The steel industry is nationalized.

MAR   [**6**] The actor and composer Ivor Novello dies in London. [**24**] The Oxford and Cambridge Boat Race has to be called off when the Oxford boat sinks.

APR   [**5**] The Government approves in principle the withdrawal of British troops from the Suez Canal zone. [**11**] The Stone of Destiny is found at Forfar in Scotland. [**13**] The Stone of Destiny is returned to Westminster Abbey. [**14**] The politician Ernest Bevin dies. [**16**] The submarine *Affray* sinks in the English Channel with the loss of 75 lives. [**19**] The first 'Miss World' contest takes place at the Lyceum Ballroom; Miss

Sweden is the winner. [**29**] The philosopher Ludwig Wittgenstein dies.

MAY [**3**] The Festival of Britain is opened by George VI from the steps of St Paul's Cathedral. [**25**] Foreign Office officials Guy Burgess and Donald Maclean disappear; they have defected to Russia.

JUN [**7**] George VI is too ill to attend, so Princess Elizabeth stands in for her sick father at the Trooping the Colour ceremony.

AUG [**15**] Sir Basil Spence wins the competition to design a new Coventry Cathedral. Dartmoor is designated a National Park. [**21**] The composer Constant Lambert dies.

SEP [**6**] 12 million gallons of petrol are lost in a big oil fire at Avonmouth. [**10**] There are anti-British riots in Egypt. [**14**] Fawley oil refinery is opened. [**23**] The King has an operation to remove his left lung.

OCT [**3**] The first British atom bomb tests take place in the Pacific. [**15**] The first Party Political television broadcast is given, by Lord Samuel for the Liberal Party. [**19**] British troops take control of key points on the Suez Canal. [**21**] Four British warships dock at Port Said, at the northern entrance to the Suez Canal. [**22**] Britain's arms exports to Egypt cease. [**26**] The General Election is won by the Conservatives, with Winston Churchill as Prime Minister. [**31**] Zebra crossings are introduced.

NOV [**5**] Clement Attlee is awarded the Order of Merit. [**20**] The evacuation of British army families from Egypt begins.

DEC [**27**] The cargo ship *Flying Enterprise* capsizes in heavy seas in the English Channel.

Sir Robert Matthew and Sir Leslie Martin: Royal Festival Hall, South Bank, London.

Keith Vaughan: *Leaping Figure.*
Lucien Freud: *Girl with a White Dog.*
John Craxton: *Four Herdsmen.*
Claude Rogers: *Miss Lynn.*
Reg Butler: *The Birdcage.*

Anthony Powell: *A Question of Upbringing.*
Jacquetta Hawkes: *A Land.*
C. P. Snow: *The Masters.*
Graham Greene: *The End of the Affair.*

Benjamin Britten: *Billy Budd.*
Alan Bush: *Wat Tyler.*

1952 London smog kills 4000 people. Archer Martin and Richard Synge are awarded the Nobel Prize for Chemistry.

JAN [**10**] The freighter *Flying Enterprise* sinks off Falmouth; her captain, Kurt Carlsen, stays on board until just minutes before she sinks, refusing offers of rescue. [**25**] British troops capture the police headquarters of Ismailia; 46 Egyptians are killed in this action. [**31**] Princess Elizabeth and Prince Philip leave London on the first stage of their Commonwealth Tour.

FEB [**4**] The Government offers farmers £5 an acre to plough up grassland for crops. [**6**] George VI dies of cancer at Sandringham aged 56. He is succeeded by his eldest daughter as Elizabeth II, although she does not know of her accession for two days. [**8**] The Queen hears of her accession at the Treetops Hotel in Kenya. [**15**] The funeral of George VI at Windsor. [**21**] Identity cards are abolished.

APR [**21**] The Labour politician Sir Stafford Cripps dies in Switzerland.

MAY [**5**] Elizabeth II takes up residence at Buckingham Palace.

JUL [**6**] The last London tram runs for the last time.

AUG [**16**] Severe localized thunderstorms in Somerset and North Devon swell the rivers, bringing devastation to the town of Lynmouth; 31 people are killed in the Lynmouth disaster.

SEP [**6**] A de Havilland 110 fighter disintegrates at the Farnborough Air Show, killing 28 people.

OCT [**8**] The Harrow train disaster, in which 112 are killed and 200 injured.

NOV [**14**] Charts for pop single records are published for the first time in Britain, in the *New Musical Express*. [**25**] Agatha Christie's *The Mousetrap* begins its record-breaking run at the Ambassador's Theatre, London. 2000 Kikuyu are rounded up in Kenya as the Mau Mau begins an open revolt against British rule.

DEC [**12**] On about this date Reg Christie murders his wife Ethel, because she suspects him of other murders, and puts her body under the floor at their home, 10 Rillington Place, London.

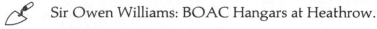

Sir Owen Williams: BOAC Hangars at Heathrow.

William Coldstream: *Seated Nude.*
Lucien Freud: *Francis Bacon.*
John Minton: *The Death of Nelson.*

Anthony Powell: *A Buyer's Market.*
Evelyn Waugh: *Men at Arms.*

Doris Lessing: *Martha Quest*.
Sir Angus Wilson: *Hemlock and After*.
Dylan Thomas: *Collected Poems*.

Benjamin Britten: *Abraham and Isaac*.
Vaughan Williams: *Sinfonia Antartica* (composed).
Sir Michael Tippett: *The Midsummer Marriage* (composed).

1953 Carvings of axes are noticed for the first time at Stonehenge.

JAN [**1**] 'Bomber' Harris, the ex-head of Bomber Command responsible for the bombing of Dresden, is knighted. [**22**] BOAC grounds all its Strato-cruisers after engine faults are discovered. [**25**] The liner *Empress of Canada* is gutted by fire at her moorings in Liverpool. [**27**] 200 MPs plead for Derek Bentley's controversial death sentence to be commuted but a reprieve is refused. [**28**] Bentley is hanged at Wandsworth Prison. [**31**] The car ferry *Princess Victoria* sinks off Stranraer in a storm: 128 people drown.

FEB [**3**] Gale-force winds accompanying high tides cause a major flood disaster on the east coast from Lincolnshire to Kent. 283 are drowned, thousands homeless. [**4**] Sweet rationing ends. [**16**] The new aircraft carrier *Hermes* is launched at Barrow. [**23**] An amnesty is granted to Second World War deserters. [**25**] An inquest is told that the *Princess Victoria's* stern doors were not properly closed and that water was allowed to sweep onto the car deck causing the ship to develop a sudden list.

MAR [**15**] Tito visits Britain. [**20**] The actress Vivien Leigh returns to Britain suffering from a serious nervous breakdown. [**24**] Queen Mary, the widow of George V, dies at Marlborough House in Pall Mall. [**25**] A hunt for the mass murderer Christie starts after bodies are discovered in a pantry by new tenants at 10 Rillington Place in London. [**26**] Police reveal that they have found the body of Christie's wife. [**31**] Queen Mary's funeral. Christie is arrested on the Thames Embankment and charged with murdering his wife.

APR [**15**] Christie is charged with the murder of three more women. [**16**] The Royal Yacht *Britannia* is launched by the Queen.

MAY [**2**] A BOAC Comet airliner crashes near Calcutta: all 43 on board are killed. Experts want to know why the wings came off in mid-air. [**18**] The bodies of Beryl Evans and her baby are exhumed as the suspicion grows that Timothy Evans, who was hanged for the crime, did not murder them. [**24**] The

Foreign Office advises British families to leave Egypt. An attempt on the south face of Everest fails. Chris Chataway runs two miles in 8 minutes 49.6 seconds, a new record. [**29**] Hillary and Tensing reach the summit of Everest at 11.30 am.

Jun [**1**] News of the conquest of Everest reaches Britain. [**2**] Coronation of Elizabeth II. [**11**] A report on the *Princess Victoria* sinking reprimands the ship-owners. [**22**] The Christie trial opens at the Old Bailey: he pleads insanity. [**23**] Churchill suffers a severe stroke, although the news is kept from the press for four days. [**25**] Christie is sentenced to death. Timothy Evans' family asks for his case to be reviewed, but there is no immediate response.

Jul [**1**] MPs reject a Bill to suspend the death penalty for five years. [**15**] Christie is hanged. [**16**] The writer Hilaire Belloc dies. Hillary and Hunt (the Everest expedition leader) are knighted: Tensing is awarded the George Medal.

Aug [**27**] The de Havilland Comet II makes its first test flight.

Sep [**3**] Florence Horsbrugh, Education Minister, becomes the first woman cabinet minister. [**23**] The Royal Commission on capital punishment says that the jury should be left to decide whether or not the death penalty is imposed. [**26**] Sugar rationing ends after nearly 14 years.

Oct [**3**] The composer Sir Arnold Bax dies. [**8**] The singer Kathleen Ferrier dies aged 41. [**14**] 147 soldiers arrive at Southampton from imprisonment in North Korea. [**15**] Churchill is awarded the Nobel Prize for Literature. [**31**] 30,000 new homes have been built this month.

Nov [**9**] The poet Dylan Thomas dies in New York aged 39. [**11**] MPs approve a Bill enabling Prince Philip to become regent if the need arises. [**17**] Sir Arthur Bliss becomes Master of the Queen's Musick. [**21**] The Piltdown skull, which Charles Dawson 'planted' in Sussex in 1912, is shown to be a hoax.

Dec [**1**] Harold Macmillan boasts that 301,000 new homes have been built during the Government's second year in office. [**10**] Churchill receives his Nobel Prize in Stockholm. [**31**] A British expedition arrives in India on its way to search for the Abominable Snowman.

 Francis Bacon: *Pope Innocent X.*

 Ian Fleming: *Casino Royale.*
Dylan Thomas: *Under Milk Wood.*
Samuel Beckett: *Waiting for Godot.*

Benjamin Britten: *Gloriana*.
Sir William Walton: *Orb and Sceptre*.
Sir Michael Tippett: *Fantasia Concertante on a Theme of Corelli*.

1954 JAN [**10**] A Comet airliner crashes into the sea off Elba, killing 35 people; all BOAC jets are grounded as some kind of structural failure is suspected.

FEB [**3**] The Queen and Duke of Edinburgh arrive in Australia on a tour of the Commonwealth. [**5**] The first 'breeder' nuclear reactor comes into operation at Harwell. [**12**] An Advisory Committee on cancer reports that it has established a link between lung cancer and smoking.

MAR [**1**] Parliamentary approval is given to the establishment of an Atomic Energy Authority. [**21**] The suspicion grows that spies Guy Burgess and Donald MacLean were helped by a third man; Kim Philby is recalled from Washington for interrogation. [**25**] Parliament approves the inauguration of commercial television; this leads to the formation of the Independent Television Authority, and Channels 3 and 4.

APR [**8**] Another Comet airliner falls into the sea near Stromboli: 21 people die; this is the third Comet crash. [**16**] Stock car racing is seen for the first time in Britain at the Old Kent Road Stadium in London. [**24**] 40,000 Mau Mau suspects are rounded up in Kenya.

MAY [**6**] Roger Bannister runs the first sub-four-minute mile on the Iffley Road track at Oxford. The Home Secretary says that the problem of Teddy Boys is not serious . [**15**] The Queen and Prince Philip return to Britain. [**22**] 180,000 people flock to Wembley for the last rally of Billy Graham's evangelical tour.

JUN [**30**] An eclipse of the sun is visible throughout Britain.

JUL [**2**] All food rationing comes to an end. [**27**] The British Government agrees with Colonel Nasser's request to pull British troops out of the Suez Canal zone. [**31**] The Television Act is passed, allowing independent televison transmissions.

AUG [**1**] The UK Atomic Energy Authority is founded, marking the beginning of the nuclear energy industry in Britain. [**4**] The Independent Television Authority is set up, under the chairmanship of Sir Kenneth Clark.

SEP [**3**] The National Trust buys Fair Isle. [**6**] The 'Flying Bedstead'; Rolls Royce announces that it has developed a prototype vertical take-off plane. [**14**] Kidbrooke School in London, London's first new comprehensive school, is opened. [**24**] The Roman temple of Mithras is discovered near the Mansion House in London during redevelopment of the site.

Oct [**19**] Metal fatigue, a newly identified technical problem, is blamed for the Elba Comet crash; investigators will now look at the possibility that other plane crashes may be due to metal fatigue. [**29**] The dockers end their month-long strike. [**29**] Sir Winston Churchill celebrates his 80th birthday. He is presented by both Houses of Parliament with a portrait by Graham Sutherland; he dislikes it intensely, and Lady Churchill later destroys it.

Dec [**19**] Viscount Stansgate (later to be known as Mr Anthony Wedgwood-Benn and eventually as Tony Benn) reveals that he wants to renounce his title. [**20**] The novelist James Hilton dies in California.

 Sir Giles Gilbert Scott: Waterloo Bridge (completed)..
Sir Basil Spence: Coventry Cathedral (building work begins).

 Graham Sutherland: *Portrait of Sir Winston Churchill.*

 Philip Larkin: *Church Going; I Remember, I Remember.*
C. P. Snow: *The New Men.*
Sir Kingsley Amis: *Lucky Jim.*
Sir William Golding: *Lord of the Flies.*
J. R. R. Tolkien: *Lord of the Rings.*
Dame Iris Murdoch: *Under the Net.*

Sir Lennox Berkeley: *Nelson.*
Benjamin Britten: *The Turn of the Screw.*
Thea Musgrave: *Cantata for a Summer's Day.*
Sir William Walton: *Troilus and Cressida.*

1955 Jan [**6**] The comedian Rowan Atkinson is born. [**9**] 400 Jamaicans arrive in London in search of work; this represents the beginning of an important demographic change in Britain, one that will have social, cultural and political reverberations. [**21**] Archaeologists confirm that Piltdown Man was a hoax. [**23**] 380 Jamaican immigrants disembark at Plymouth. [**27**] The premiere of Sir Michael Tippett's opera *The Midsummer Marriage.*

Feb [**10**] The Commons vote by a majority of 31 to retain the death penalty. [**15**] The Government announces its plan to built 12 nuclear power stations during the next 10 years. There is an unfounded belief that electricity generated in nuclear power stations will be much cheaper than that from coal-fired stations; problems such as safety and the disposal of radioactive waste are overlooked in these calculations.

[**17**] The Government announces that it will proceed with the manufacture of hydrogen bombs. [**18**] The House of Lords rejects Lord Stansgate's request to renounce his title and pursue his political career in the Commons. [**25**] Britain's largest ever aircraft carrier, HMS *Ark Royal*, is completed.

MAR [**4**] Equal salaries for women teachers, to be reached in stages, are recommended by the Burnham Committee; this is another step towards equal rights for women. [**11**] Sir Alexander Fleming, the discoverer of penicillin in 1928, dies.

APR [**5**] Sir Winston Churchill resigns as Prime Minister. [**6**] Sir Anthony Eden, later Lord Avon, succeeds as Prime Minister, with Harold Macmillan as Foreign Secretary and R. A. Butler as Chancellor of the Exchequer. [**28**] The trial of Ruth Ellis for murder begins. There seem to be mitigating circumstances (jealousy, extreme provocation) even though she is guilty of killing David Blakeley. Her case, coming hard on the heels of the 1953 Evans-Christie case, is influential in the abolition of the death penalty.

MAY [**26**] The Conservatives win the General Election with a majority of 59. [**28**] 16 Teddy Boys are arrested after a disturbance at a dance hall in Bath.

JUN [**21**] Ruth Ellis, found guilty of murder, is sentenced to death.

JUL [**1**] The dock strike ends. [**4**] Britain undertakes to transfer her Simonstown naval base to South Africa during the next two years. [**7**] A Hawker Hunter fighter crashes at the Farnborough Air Show. [**13**] Ruth Ellis is hanged at Holloway Prison after her appeal is refused; she claims, after her trial, that someone else put the gun into her hand, but it is too late. There is a significant level of sympathy for her in the popular press. [**23**] Donald Campbell breaks the world water speed record in *Bluebird* on Ullswater (202 mph).

AUG Jeans become fashionable in Britain. [**3**] Duncan Sandys, Housing Minister, instructs the local authorities to set up Green Belts similar to London's around other towns and cities. The intention is to stop urban areas extending across food-producing farmland, and to stop the unsightly ribbon development of the inter-war years. Where possible, most new urban development is to be 'infilling'.

SEP [**22**] The first transmission of commercial television. The first televised advertisement is for Gibbs SR toothpaste. The BBC offers as a counter-attraction the burning to death of Grace Archer, a leading character in 'The Archers' radio serial.

OCT [**1**] The City of London is declared a smokeless zone. The effects of this policy are to make the air cleaner in London, reduce the frequency and seriousness of smog, and make it worthwhile to clean London's blackened public buildings. [**27**] Princess Margaret visits the Archbishop of Canterbury. [**31**] It is announced that Princess Margaret has decided not to marry Group Captain Peter Townsend after all, because of the constitutional problems involved in her marrying a divorcee.

Nov [**11**] An MP withdraws the allegation that Kim Philby was the third man in the Burgess and MacLean affair. [**26**] British troops fight terrorists in Famagusta in Cyprus.

Dec [**7**] Clement Attlee announces his retirement and is created an earl. [**14**] Hugh Gaitskell is elected Labour Party leader.

John Bratby: *Three People at a Table.*
Jack Smith: *After a Spanish Feast.*
Pietro Annigoni: *Portrait of the Queen.*

Sir William Golding: *The Inheritors.*
Anthony Powell: *The Acceptance World.*
Elizabeth Bowen: *A World of Love.*
Graham Greene: *Loser Takes All; The Quiet American.*
Evelyn Waugh: *Officers and Gentlemen.*
Sir Kingsley Amis: *That Uncertain Feeling.*

Alan Bush: *Men of Blackmoor.*
Sir William Walton: Music for Olivier's film *Richard III.*
Tristram Cary: Music for the film *The Ladykillers.*
Sir Michael Tippett: *Piano Concerto.*
Vaughan Williams: *Eighth Symphony.*

1956 Third Class accommodation on British Railways is redesignated Second Class. The Clean Air Act comes into force. The Sudan becomes independent. The first Aldermaston march is organized by the Campaign for Nuclear Disarmament, in protest against nuclear weapons.

Jan [**1**] Sudan becomes an independent republic. [**2**] The Astronomer-Royal says the idea of space travel is 'bilge'. [**23**] The film producer Sir Alexander Korda dies in London. [**31**] A. A. Milne, the creator of Winnie-the-Pooh, dies at Hartfield.

Feb [**21**] The Duke of Edinburgh's Award Scheme is announced.

Mar [**10**] Riots break out in Cyprus after the British deport Archbishop Makarios. [**23**] Pakistan is proclaimed an Islamic republic within the Commonwealth. The Queen lays the foundation stone of the new Coventry Cathedral.

Apr [**1**] The first US U-2 spy planes arrive at RAF Lakenhurst. [**17**] The introduction of Premium Bonds is announced by Harold

Macmillan. [**18**] The Soviet leaders Kruschev and Bulganin arrive in Britain on an official visit. [**20**] Commander Lionel Crabbe, a frogman, goes missing while investigating the hull of the Soviet cruiser *Ordzhonikidze* in Portsmouth Harbour.

MAY [**20**] The writer and caricaturist Sir Max Beerbohm dies. [**23**] Calder Hall, the first nuclear power station in Britain and the first large-scale nuclear plant in the world, comes into operation.

JUN [**13**] The last British troops leave Suez. [**22**] The poet Walter de la Mare dies.

JUL [**26**] President Nasser of Egypt nationalizes the Suez Canal Company. [**30**] Eden tells Nasser that Egypt cannot have the Suez Canal and imposes an arms embargo on Egypt.

AUG [**1-2**] There are talks between UK, USA and France on the Suez problem. [**8**] Eden says in a broadcast about the Suez crisis that Nasser cannot be trusted. [**27**] The National Youth Theatre is founded. [**29**] There is a massive build-up of French and British forces in the Eastern Mediterranean, with the object of menacing Egypt.

SEP [**9**] Nasser rejects a US plan for international control over the Suez Canal. [**21**] A Suez Canal Conference in London ends with an agreement that a Canal Users Association should be formed.

OCT [**31**] An Anglo-French offensive is launched against military targets in Egypt.

NOV [**1**] Premium Savings Bonds go on sale for the first time. [**4**] Demonstrators in the streets of London call for Eden's resignation over his handling of the Suez Crisis. [**7**] Eden agrees to withdraw troops from Suez if a United Nations force goes in instead. [**16**] The Egyptians block the Suez Canal by scuttling 49 ships in it. [**19**] Eden is said to be suffering from 'severe overstrain'; in fact he is psychologically disorientated by the strength of world reaction to his action over Suez and by the Americans' failure to support him in the way he had understood they would. Hungarian refugees arrive in Britain. [**21**] A United Nations force takes over the Suez Canal from British and French troops; Britain withdraws under strong pressure from the US. [**23**] Eden flies to Jamaica to rest and recover.

DEC [**5**] British troops begin to leave Port Said. [**18**] Dr John Bodkin Adams is arrested, suspected of murdering Mrs Morrell in November 1950 and several other elderly patients in his care.

Richard Hamilton: *Just what is it that makes today's homes so different, so appealing?*
Edward Middleton: *Cow Parsley.*
The Arundel Screen, Chichester Cathedral (medieval, reinstated).

 Philip Larkin: *An Arundel Tomb.*
Sir William Golding: *Pincher Martin.*
Anthony Burgess: *Time for a Tiger.*
Rose Macaulay: *Towers of Trebizond.*
Sir Angus Wilson: *Anglo-Saxon Attitudes.*
Dame Iris Murdoch: *The Flight from the Enchanter.*
John Osborne: *Look Back in Anger.*

 Sir Lennox Berkeley: *A Dinner Engagement; Ruth.*
Christopher Headington: *Piano Sonata.*
Edmund Rubbra: *Piano Concerto.*

1957 The Rent Act (Conservative measure) abolishes rent control and allows rents to be increased. Wyndham Lewis, 'the most fascinating personality of our time', according to T. S. Eliot, dies. Sir Alexander Todd is awarded the Nobel Prize for Chemistry. Antarctica is crossed by Sir Vivian Fuchs (1957-8).

JAN [**4**] Salvage crews continue to clear the Suez Canal of sunken ships. [**9**] Sir Anthony Eden resigns as Prime Minister. [**10**] Harold Macmillan becomes Prime Minister. [**16**] The Royal Ballet is founded.

FEB [**16**] Sir Leslie Hore-Belisha, Minister of Transport responsible for introducing Belisha beacons, driving tests and the Highway Code, dies.

MAR [**6**] Ghana becomes the first British colony in Africa to achieve independence. [**8**] The Suez Canal is reopened for smaller vessels. [**11**] The first indications that radiation may have genetic effects are published by the World Health Organization.

APR [**3**] The Labour Party calls for H-bomb tests to be abolished.

MAY [**14**] Emergency petrol rationing, prompted by the Suez crisis, comes to an end. [**15**] The first British hydrogen bomb is detonated over Christmas Island.

JUN [**1**] The first Premium Bond prize winners are drawn by computer, a random number selector called ERNIE. [**9**] Commander Crabbe's body is found by fishermen in Chichester Harbour. [**30**] The British Lion is stamped on eggs for the first time; the practice ends December 31 1968.

Jul [**20**] Harold Macmillan makes his 'never had it so good' speech at Bradford. [**23**] Picket line violence breaks out during a national bus strike.

Aug [**6**] It is revealed that 2000 people a week are still emigrating to the Commonwealth. [**15**] The dock strike spreads; 12,000 dock workers are now out on strike. [**31**] Malaya becomes independent.

Sep [**1**] The horn player Dennis Braine dies in a road accident at Hatfield. [**4**] The Wolfenden Report is published, recommending that homosexual acts between adults in private should be legalized.

Oct [**11**] Jodrell Bank telescope, the largest radio telescope in the world, comes into operation. [**17**] Part of the Windscale atomic plant in Cumbria is closed down following a serious fire and a radioactivity leak; this is the most serious accident in nuclear energy history so far.

Dec [**4**] Lewisham train crash; 92 people are killed as two trains collide in fog. [**17**] Dorothy Sayers, creator of Lord Peter Wimsey, dies. [**19**] An air service opens between London and Moscow. [**25**] The Queen's Christmas broadcast is televised for the first time.

 Jodrell Bank radio telescope.

 Peter Blake: *On the Balcony.*

 Anthony Powell: *At Lady Molly's.*
Dame Ivy Compton-Burnett: *A Father and his Fate.*
John Braine: *Room at the Top.*
Lawrence Durrell: *Justine.*
Alan Sillitoe: *Saturday Night and Sunday Morning.*
Evelyn Waugh: *The Ordeal of Gilbert Pinfold.*
Dame Iris Murdoch: *The Sandcastle.*
Muriel Spark: *The Comforters.*

 Sir Michael Tippett: *Second Symphony.*
Vaughan Williams: *Ninth Symphony* (composed).

1958 There are serious racial disturbances at Nottingham and Notting Hill. At Stonehenge, trilithon 57-58 is re-erected and set in concrete. Frederick Sanger is awarded the Nobel Prize for Chemistry.

Jan [**20**] Vivian Fuchs, leading a Commonwealth expedition, reaches the South Pole.

Feb [**5**] First performance of Tippett's *Second Symphony*. [**6**] In a plane crash at Munich airport, eight Manchester United players, three club officials and eight journalists are killed. [**13**] The suffragette Dame Christabel Pankhurst dies.

MAR [**2**] Fuchs completes his crossing of Antarctica. [**6**] The TUC and the Labour Party call for H-bomb tests to stop. [**18**] The last presentation of debutantes. [**21**] The London Planetarium is opened. [**27**] Sir David Lean's film *Bridge on the River Kwai* wins three Oscars.

APR [**4**] An anti-nuclear protest march from London to Aldermaston begins. [**10**] A Roman mosaic is discovered at Fishbourne, the first indication that there was once a Roman palace there.

MAY [**23**] Christopher Cockerell patents his newly-invented hovercraft. [**24**] The Dounreay nuclear reactor begins working.

JUN [**1**] The Clean Air Act comes into force, banning emissions of dark smoke. [**4**] The first Duke of Edinburgh Awards are presented at Buckingham Palace. [**9**] Gatwick Airport is opened by the Queen. [**16**] Yellow 'no waiting' lines on roads are introduced. [**20**] The seven-week long London bus strike ends.

JUL [**10**] Parking meters are in operation for the first time, in Mayfair. [**23**] The first life barons and baronesses are named under the Life Peerages Act. [**26**] The Queen creates her son Charles Prince of Wales.

AUG [**17**] The Government announces plans to resume nuclear bomb testing on Christmas Island. [**26**] The composer Ralph Vaughan Williams dies aged 85. [**30**] The police clash with 500 Teddy Boys at Nottingham. [**31**] There is fighting in Notting Hill between white and black youths.

SEP [**1**] British trawlers defy the Icelandic 12-mile limit, which comes into force today. [**7**] British scientists successfully fire their first ballistic rocket, Black Knight, from Woomera. [**8**] Race riot in Notting Hill.

OCT [**21**] The first women peers take their seats in the House of Lords.

NOV [**21**] Work starts on the Forth Road Bridge, to be the longest suspension bridge in Europe.

DEC An epidemic of serious deformities in British babies is thought to be caused by the drug thalidomide. [**5**] The first section of motorway in Britain, the Preston by-pass section of the M6, is opened by the Prime Minister, Harold Macmillan; this is a landmark in the development of the communications network. [**8**] The last of four nuclear reactors at Calder Hall comes into operation.

Stevenage Town Centre.

 Hubert Dalwood: *Icon*.
Jacob Epstein: *St Michael and the Devil*.

 Keith Waterhouse: *Billy Liar*.
Sir Kingsley Amis: *I Like it Here*.
Sir Michael Tippett: *Moving into Aquarius*.
Graham Greene: *Our Man in Havana*.
Lawrence Durrell: *Balthazar; Mountolive*.
Philip Larkin: *The Whitsun Weddings*.
Harold Pinter: *The Birthday Party*.

 Sir Peter Maxwell Davies: *Prolation*.
Sir William Walton: *Partita for Orchestra*.
Benjamin Britten; *Nocturne; Noye's Fludde*.
Peter Racine Fricker: *A Vision of Judgment*.

1959 D. H. Lawrence's *Lady Chatterley's Lover* is prosecuted on an obscenity charge. Rock 'n roll music begins to dominate youth culture.

FEB [**15**] Archbishop Makarios arrives in London for talks on Cyprus with Macmillan. [**21**] Macmillan arrives in Moscow on an official visit.

MAR [**17**] The Government announces its scheme for a major expansion of the road network. [**31**] Sir Winston Churchill's home is burgled; he loses £10,000 worth of property.

MAY [**2**] The first Scottish nuclear power station opens at Chapelcross. [**23**] The Mermaid Theatre in the City of London opens. [**24**] Empire Day is renamed Commonwealth Day. [**30**] The first hovercraft flight takes place at Cowes.

JUN [**17**] The pianist Liberace wins £8,000 from the *Daily Mirror* after the Cassandra column implies that he is homosexual.

JUL [**7**] The Litter Act comes into force. [**25**] The hovercraft makes its first Channel crossing, from Dover to Calais, in just over two hours.

AUG [**10**] Violent storms. [**16**] Street Offences Act comes into force; prostitution must disappear from the streets. [**19**] The sculptor Jacob Epstein dies.

SEP [**26**] The jockey Manny Mercer is killed in an accident during a parade before a race at Ascot.

OCT [**3**] Post codes are used for the first time, at Norwich. [**8**] In the General Election the Conservatives win easily (Conservatives 365, Labour 258, Liberal 6); Macmillan remains Prime Minister. [**27**] London housing officials say that slum clearances and rehousing cause misery and distress to those who are moved; this is the beginning of a major reconsideration of old housing, and the destruction of Victorian and Edwardian houses slows down.

NOV [6] Two motorists are killed in the first fatal accident on the M1 motorway, which was opened this week. [14] The Dounreay fast breeder reactor goes into operation. [19] The Archbishop of Canterbury says that adultery should be a criminal offence. [20] Britain joins the European Free Trade Association (EFTA).

DEC [14] The painter Sir Stanley Spencer dies. [23] The Earl of Halifax, politician and Viceroy of India 1926-31, dies.

David Roberts: Corpus Christi boathouse, Cambridge.

William Turnbull: *No 7*.

Philip Larkin: *Letter to a Friend about Girls.*
Ian Fleming: *Goldfinger.*
Mervyn Peake: *Titus Alone.*
Sir William Golding: *Free Fall.*
Malcolm Bradbury: *Eating People is Wrong.*
Deryck Cooke: *The Language of Music.*

Thea Musgrave: *Triptych.*
Christopher Headington: *Violin Concerto.*
'Livin' Doll' (song).

1960 Sir Macfarlane Burnet (Australian) and Peter Medawar (British) are awarded the Nobel Prize for Physiology and Medicine.

JAN The novelist Nevil Shute dies. [25] The composer Rutland Boughton dies. [31] The composer George Benjamin is born.

FEB [3] Macmillan makes his 'wind of change' speech at Cape Town. [17] The Government agrees to allow a US missile early warning system to be built at Fylingdales Moor. [19] Prince Andrew, Queen Elizabeth II's third child, is born at Buckingham Palace.

MAR [25] Oliver Cromwell's head, severed from his body at the Restoration in 1660, is buried at Sydney Sussex College, Cambridge.

APR [6] Dr Richard Beeching is chosen to head the team to rationalize the rail network; this process results in the closure of a great many branch lines, with far-reaching social effects. [13] The Blue Streak missile is abandoned as a weapon.

May [6] Princess Margaret marries Antony Armstrong-Jones in Westminster Abbey.

Jun [2] Planners in London devise ways of limiting the number of new high-rise buildings. [10] The first British guided-missile destroyer, HMS *Devonshire*, is launched. The Government decides to slow down the nuclear programme.

Jul [1] Ghana becomes a republic. [6] Aneurin Bevan, the Labour Minister who introduced the National Health Service in 1948, dies.

Aug [16] British rule in Cyprus comes to an end. [22] *Beyond the Fringe*, the first and most influential satirical revue, opens at the Edinburgh Festival.

Sep [12] MOT tests on motor vehicles are introduced. [15] Traffic wardens are first seen in London. [27] The militant suffragette Sylvia Pankhurst dies.

Oct [1] Nigeria becomes independent within the Commonwealth. [9] Serious flooding in southern England. [20] 'Lady Chatterley' trial opens; Penguin Books are tried for publishing an obscene book (D. H. Lawrence's *Lady Chatterley's Lover*). [21] Britain's first nuclear-powered submarine, HMS *Dreadnought*, is launched at Barrow.

Nov [1] It is announced that US Polaris missile submarines are to have a base on the Firth of Clyde. [2] Penguin Books are acquitted of the obscenity charge. [3] Hugh Gaitskell fights off Harold Wilson's challenge to his leadership. [16] The broadcaster Gilbert Harding collapses and dies on the steps of the BBC Studios in London. [17] Anthony Wedgwood-Benn succeeds to the title Lord Stansgate on his father's death, obstructing his career in politics.

Dec [9] The first episode of the television soap 'Coronation Street' is broadcast. [31] Farthings cease to be legal tender. It is the last day of call-up for National Service; from today compulsory service in the armed forces is abolished.

Sir Robert Matthew, Johnson-Marshall & Partners: New Zealand House, London.
Sir Basil Spence: University of Sussex, Falmer (begun).

Alan Davie: *Entrance for a Red Temple*.
Robyn Denny: *Baby is Three*.
Henry Moore: *Two-Piece Reclining Figure No 2*.

Anthony Powell: *Casanova's Chinese Restaurant*.
C. P. Snow: *The Affair*.
Lawrence Durrell: *Clea*.

Sir Kingsley Amis: *Take a Girl Like You.*
Edna O'Brien: *The Country Girls.*
Harold Pinter: *The Caretaker.*
Muriel Spark: *The Ballad of Peckham Rye.*

Sir Arthur Bliss: *Tobias and the Angel.*
Tristram Cary: Electronic music for *Dr Who.*
Sir William Walton: *Second Symphony.*
Alun Hoddinott: *Second Piano Concerto.*
Derek Bourgeois: *First Symphony.*
Benjamin Britten: *A Midsummer Night's Dream.*
Sir Peter Maxwell Davies: *O Magnum Mysterium.*

1961 The Graduated Pensions Scheme is introduced, to supplement the Old Age Pension. The Factories Act consolidates the safety regulations in all industrial premises and construction sites.

JAN [**14**] There are prison mutinies at Maidstone and Shrewsbury. [**20**] The Queen meets Archbishop Makarios in Cyprus.

MAR The Geneva Conference (UK, USA and USSR) begins, to discuss discontinuing nuclear weapons testing. [**8**] Sir Thomas Beecham, conductor and founder of the London Philharmonic Orchestra, dies. The first American Polaris submarines arrive at Holy Loch. [**13**] The old black-and-white £5 notes cease to be legal tender. The Canadian Gordon Lonsdale and four others go on trial in London for espionage. [**18**] George Blake is charged with spying.

MAY [**1**] The first betting shops open as the Betting and Gaming Act comes into force. [**5**] The Queen and Duke of Edinburgh visit Pope John XXIII at the Vatican. [**8**] George Blake is given a record 42-year gaol sentence. Anthony Wedgwood-Benn is refused admission to the Commons on the grounds that he is still Viscount Stansgate. [**17**] The new Guildford Cathedral is consecrated. [**18**] It is announced that there will be new Universities at Canterbury, Colchester and Coventry. [**31**] South Africa becomes a republic and withdraws from the Commonwealth.

JUN [**27**] Dr Michael Ramsey is enthroned as Archbishop of Canterbury.

JUL [**1**] The Princess of Wales is born, as Lady Diana Spencer, at Park House, Sandringham. [**19**] A UK-US agreement is made to establish a Missile Defence Alarm Station at Kirkbride in Cumbria. [**28**] The High Court decides that Lord Stansgate's election victory was invalid because he is ineligible and that his defeated opponent is the new MP.

AUG [**10**] The UK formally applies to join the EEC. [**31**] Failure of the Geneva Conference; the USSR announces the resumption of nuclear weapons testing.

SEP [**5**] The USA announces that it will resume underground nuclear tests. [**10**] 86 people are killed in a plane crash at Shannon airport. [**12**] Bertrand Russell, the philosopher, is imprisoned for protesting against nuclear weapons, even though he is 89. [**17**] There is a large anti-nuclear bomb demonstration in London.

OCT [**3**] Princess Margaret's husband, Antony Armstrong-Jones, is created Earl of Snowdon. [**4**] The Labour Party Conference votes against having Polaris bases in Britain. [**10**] There is a large-scale volcanic eruption on Tristan da Cunha; as a result its entire population is evacuated to the UK. [**24**] Malta gains its independence. [**31**] The painter Augustus John dies at Fordingbridge.

DEC Tanganyika becomes independent. [**7**] The LCC approves the building of 300-foot-high blocks of flats in Hammersmith; they will be the highest in Britain.

Eero Saarinen: US Embassy.
Sir Edward Maufe: Guildford Cathedral (begun 1936; consecrated May 17).

Graham Sutherland: *Noli me tangere*.
Peter Blake: *Got a girl*.
David Hockney: *We two boys forever clinging*.
Michael Ayrton: *Icarus transformed I*.

Sir Angus Wilson: *The Old Men at the Zoo*.
Evelyn Waugh: *Unconditional Surrender*.
V. S. Naipaul: *A House for Mr Biswas*.
Muriel Spark: *The Prime of Miss Jean Brodie*.
New English Bible, New Testament (March 14).

Richard Rodney Bennett: *The Ledge*:
William Mathias: *Second Piano Concerto*.

1962 Commonwealth Immigration Act; uncontrolled entry into Britain by citizens of the Commonwealth is ended. Smog in London kills 750 people. Francis Crick and Maurice Wilkins (British) and James Watson (American) are awarded the Nobel Prize for Physiology and Medicine.

JAN [**22**] The A6 murder trial opens; James Hanratty pleads not guilty to murdering Michael Gregston.

FEB   [11] An Essex schoolboy dances the Twist for 33 hours. [17] Hanratty is sentenced to death after a long and controversial trial.

MAR   The Liberal Eric Lubbock wins the Orpington by-election; this is seen as a turning-point in the fortunes of the Liberal Party.

APR   [4] Hanratty is hanged while controversy still surrounds the question of his guilt. [26] Britain's first satellite, Ariel, is launched from Cape Canaveral.

MAY   [11] Prince Charles goes to Gordonstoun. [25] The new Coventry Cathedral is consecrated. [29] First performance of Tippett's opera *King Priam* at Coventry. [30] First performance of Britten's *War Requiem* at Coventry.

JUN   [2] The writer Vita Sackville-West dies. [12] The composer John Ireland dies. [15] The nuclear power station at Berkeley comes into operation.

JUL   The Prime Minister, Harold Macmillan, asks seven senior ministers to resign and reconstructs his Cabinet with Butler as deputy Prime Minister, Brooke as Home Secretary and Maudling as Chancellor of the Exchequer. [3] The Government and the LCC accept the plan for a national theatre and opera house. [20] The historian G. M. Trevelyan dies. The world's first passenger hovercraft service opens, across the River Dee from Rhyl to Wallasey. [31] Sir Oswald Mosley tries to address a meeting of the Union Movement, but is stopped by a punch on the jaw; the meeting is part of a resurgence of right-wing extremism.

AUG   [6] Jamaica becomes independent. [31] Trinidad and Tobago become independent.

SEP   [2] There is a fierce street battle between Fascists and East Enders.

OCT   [9] Uganda becomes independent. [22] William Vassall is sent to prison for 18 years for spying for the USSR.

NOV   [24] First broadcast of the satirical television programme 'That Was the Week That Was'.

DEC   [5] A British nuclear bomb is exploded underground in Nevada. [25] Britain is snow-bound. [30] Worst snowstorms in Britain since 1881. [31] British Rail Board is set up with Dr Richard Beeching as chairman.

Erno Goldfinger: Alexander Fleming House, Elephant and Castle.
Sir Basil Spence: Coventry Cathedral (completed).
Sir Frederick Gibberd: Roman Catholic Cathedral of Christ the King, Liverpool (begun). [Replacing Lutyens' design of 1929.]

Francis Bacon: *Three Studies for a Crucifixion.*
Graham Sutherland: *Christ in Glory.*

 Dame Iris Murdoch: *An Unofficial Rose.*
Anthony Burgess: *A Clockwork Orange.*
Anthony Powell: *The Kindly Ones.*
Private Eye (first issue).

 Benjamin Britten: *War Requiem.*
Sir Michael Tippett: *King Priam.*
'Stranger on the Shore' (song).

1963　The Crowther and Newsom Reports recommend raising the
school-leaving age to 16. The Offices, Shops and Railway Premises
Act sets out comprehensive safety regulations for the work-place.
Controversy rages over the radical theology outlined in the Bishop of
Woolwich's book *Honest to God.* One of the stones at Stonehenge
(stone 23) falls down in a gale. Alan Hodgkin and Andrew Huxley
(British) and Sir John Eccles (Australian) are awarded the Nobel Prize
for Physiology and Medicine.

Jan　[18] Hugh Gaitskell, leader of the Labour Party since 1955,
dies. [29] Britain is refused entry to the EEC.
Feb　[1] Nyasaland becomes independent. [14] Harold Wilson is
elected leader of the Labour Party, defeating George Brown
and James Callaghan.
Mar　The Beeching Report on the slimming-down of British
Railways (to be renamed British Rail) is published. [5-6] First
frost-free night since December 22. [15] John Profumo offers
to resign from the Government. [16] Lord Beveridge dies. [17]
The first of the Tristan islanders return home. [22] Profumo
assures his fellow MPs that there was no 'impropriety' with
Christine Keeler.
Apr　[5] The Bradwell nuclear power station opens. [17] The Royal
Navy's first nuclear-powered submarine, *Dreadnought*, is
commissioned.
Jun　[5] Profumo resigns, admitting that he lied to the House. [27]
President Kennedy visits his ancestors' home in County
Wexford. [31] The Peerage Act comes into force, opening the
way for Lord Hailsham and Lord Stansgate to present
themselves as candidates for premiership in their respective
parties.
Aug　[1] The Criminal Justice Act comes into force; the minimum
prison age is raised to 17. [3] Dr Stephen Ward, who exposed
Profumo, commits suicide. [8] The Glasgow-London mail train

robbery (the 'Great Train Robbery'): armed robbers attack a train near Leighton Buzzard and steal £2.5 million. [**22**] Lord Nuffield dies.

Sep [**17**] Fylingdales missile early-warning station comes into operation. [**19**] The cartoonist Sir David Low dies. [**20**] Princess Anne goes to Benenden. [**25**] The Denning Report on the Profumo affair is published.

Oct [**10**] Macmillan announces that he will resign as Prime Minister, believing, on his doctor's advice, that he is terminally ill. [**18**] Macmillan is succeeded by Lord Home of the Hirsel as Prime Minister. [**23**] Lord Home renounces his title, becoming Sir Alec Douglas-Home.

Nov [**18**] The Dartford Tunnel, linking Kent and Essex under the Thames estuary, is opened. [**20**] Lord Hailsham renounces his title, becoming Mr Quintin Hogg. [**22**] The novelist Aldous Huxley dies.

Dec [**10**] Zanzibar becomes independent. [**12**] Kenya becomes independent.

Arup Associates: Kingsgate footbridge, Durham.
Ronald Ward: Millbank Tower, London.
Lord Snowdon, Cedric Price, Frank Newby: Aviary, London Zoo.

David Hockney: *Picture Emphasizing Stillness.*
Joe Tilson: *A-Z box of Friends and Family.*
Richard Smith: *Staggerlee.*
Bridget Riley: *Fission.*

John Robinson: *Honest to God.*
Muriel Spark: *Girls of Slender Means.*
Margaret Drabble: *A Summer Birdcage.*
John Fowles: *The Collector.*
Anthony Burgess: *Inside Mr Enderby.*
Dame Iris Murdoch: *The Unicorn.*
Sir Kingsley Amis: *One Fat Englishman.*

John Taverner: *Piano Concerto.*
Richard Rodney Bennett: *The Mines of Sulphur.*
Benjamin Britten: *Cantata Misericordium.*
Sir Michael Tippett: *Concerto for Orchestra.*
The Beatles: 'She Loves You' (song)..

1964 Dorothy Crowfoot Hodgkin is awarded the Nobel Prize for Chemistry.

FEB [**6**] Britain and France agree to build a Channel Tunnel. [**10**] The novel *Fanny Hill* is declared obscene by a magistrate, who orders copies of the book to be confiscated.

MAR [**3**] The Government announces that many railway lines will be closed. [**10**] The Queen's third son, Prince Edward, is born at Buckingham Palace. [**20**] The playwright Brendan Behan dies in Dublin. [**28**] Radio Caroline begins transmission from the North Sea. [**30**] Rival groups of Mods and Rockers fight on the beach at Clacton.

APR [**10**] Macmillan declines an earldom and the Order of the Garter. [**16**] Heavy sentences are passed on 12 men found guilty of taking part in the Great Train Robbery. [**21**] The BBC's second television channel begins transmission.

MAY [**2**] Nancy, Lady Astor, the first woman to sit in the House of Commons in 1919, dies. [**18**] Mods and Rockers clash at several south coast resorts.

JUN [**5**] The first British space flight; the 'Blue Streak' rocket is launched from Woomera in Australia. [**9**] Lord Beaverbook, Canadian-born newspaper owner, dies aged 85.

JUL [**27**] Sir Winston Churchill's last appearance in the Commons.

AUG [**12**] Ian Fleming, creator of James Bond, dies. [**13**] The last hangings in Britain take place, the executions of Peter Allen (at Walton Gaol in Liverpool) and John Walby (at Strangeways Gaol in Manchester). [**21**] Three women in London are found guilty of indecency for wearing the fashionable topless dresses.

SEP [**4**] The Forth Road Bridge is opened by the Queen. [**6**] Ian Smith arrives in London for talks on independence for Rhodesia [**18**] The playwright Sean O'Casey dies at Torquay. [**21**] Malta becomes independent.

OCT [**16**] In the General Election there is a Labour majority of five (Labour 317, Conservatives 304, Liberals 9); Harold Wilson becomes Prime Minister, George Brown his deputy and Callaghan Chancellor of the Exchequer. [**23**] Northern Rhodesia becomes the Republic of Zambia. [**27**] Wilson warns Rhodesia that a Unilateral Declaration of Independence would be treason.

NOV [**17**] The Government imposes an arms embargo on South Africa, disapproving of its apartheid policy.

DEC The IMF lends Britain £500 million. [**6**] Martin Luther King preaches at St Paul's. [**9**] Dame Edith Sitwell dies.

Sir Leslie Martin and Colin Wilson: St Cross Library, Oxford. Sir Denys Lasdun: Royal College of Physicians, Regent's Park.

Stirling and Gowan: Engineering Faculty, Leicester University.
Richard Sheppard: Churchill College, Cambridge.

 Richard Hamilton:*Portrait of Hugh Gaitskell as a famous monster of filmland.*
David Hockney: *California Art Collector.*
Ben Nicholson: *Sirius.*

 Sir Angus Wilson: *Late Call.*
Anthony Powell: *The Valley of Bones.*
C.P. Snow: *Corridors of Power.*
Samuel Beckett: *How it is.*
Sir William Golding: *The Spire.*
J.L. Carr: *A Day in Summer.*

 Benjamin Britten: *Curlew River.*
Gordon Crosse: *Meet My Folks!*
Richard Rodney Bennett: *A Jazz Calendar.*
Kenneth Leighton: *First Symphony.*
Sir Harrison Birtwistle: *Entr'actes and Sappho Fragments.*

1965 Redundancy Payments Act, providing graduated payments proportional to length of service. A new Rent Act (Labour measure) reintroduces rent control. A prices and wages freeze is introduced. Mary Quant invents the mini-skirt, a delight to the eye which becomes a symbol for the permissiveness of the Sixties. Dennis Gabor develops holography (an idea he conceived in 1947 and subsequently developed using laser).

JAN [4] T.S. Eliot, poet and playwright, dies. [7] The Kray brothers are remanded in custody on a charge of demanding money with menaces. [24] Sir Winston Churchill dies aged 91, seventy years to the day after his father's death. [30] State funeral of Sir Winston Churchill.

FEB [16] British Rail publishes its plan, based on the Beeching Report, to halve the rail network. [18] The Gambia becomes independent. [25] Dr Heenan is created a Cardinal.

MAR [3] The remains of Roger Casement are taken from Pentonville Prison to be reburied in Dublin.

APR [6] The Kray brothers are cleared of running a protection racket. [23] The first long-distance footpath in Britain, the Pennine Way, is opened.

MAY [14] The Kennedy Memorial at Runnymede is opened.

JUL [22] Sir Alec Douglas Home resigns as Conservative Party Leader. [24] The boxer Freddie Mills is found shot dead in his car outside his soho club. [**26**] The Maldive Islands become independent [**28**] Edward Heath becomes the Conservative Party Leader. [**31**] Cigarette advertising on television is banned.

SEP [**21**] British Petroleum discovers oil in the North Sea.

OCT [**8**] The Post Office Tower is opened. Edward Heath says that if elected he will take the UK into the European Community. [**28**] Parliament abolishes the death penalty for murder for an experimental five-year period. Ian Brady and Myra Hindley are charged with the brutal and sadistic murder of a 10-year-old girl, Lesley Ann Downey.

NOV [**8**] The Abolition of the Death Penalty Act and the Race Relations Act receive the Royal Assent. [**11**] Ian Smith, Prime Minster of Rhodesia, announces his country's unilateral declaration of independence; UDI is denounced by the British Government. [**22**] A belated official inquiry into Timothy Evans' conviction for murder begins. [**25**] The pianist Dame Myra Hess dies in London.

DEC [**16**] The novelist W. Somerset Maugham dies. [**17**] An oil embargo is imposed on Rhodesia. [**22**] The 70 mph speed limit is introduced for all roads not restricted to lower speeds. The broadcaster Richard Dimbleby dies. [**27**] The North Sea oil rig 'Sea Gem' collapses. [**28**] Westminster Abbey's 900th anniversary is celebrated.

Roche and Dinkeloo: Cummins Engine Factory, Darlington.
Hugh Casson: Elephant House, London Zoo.
Post Office Tower, London (completed).

Dame Iris Murdoch: *The Red and the Green.*
David Lodge: *The British Museum is Falling Down.*

John Taverner: *Cain and Abel.*
Sir Harrison Birtwistle: *Ring a Dumb Clarion.*
Sir William Walton: *The Twelve.*
Christopher Headington: *Reflections of Summer.*
Sir Michael Tippett: *The Vision of St Augustine.*

1966 Havergal Brian hears the first of his 32 symphonies for the first time, at the age of 78.

FEB [**17**] The Government protests to South Africa about petrol supplies to Rhodesia.

MAR [**5**] The Nelson Monument in Dublin is blown up. [**23**] The Archbishop of Canterbury meets the Pope in Rome. [**31**] In the General Election, Labour is re-elected with an increased majority (Labour 363, Conservatives 253, Liberals 12).

APR [**2**] The novelist C.S. Forester dies. [**5**] Shell announces an important discovery of oil off Great Yarmouth. [**10**] The novelist Evelyn Waugh dies. British forces in the Middle East are ordered to stop ships bound for Beira with oil for Rhodesia. [**14**] The South Downs are designated an Area of Outstanding Natural Beauty. [**19**] The Moors Murders trial begins. [**21**] The opening of Parliament is televised for the first time. [**30**] The first regular cross-Channel hovercraft service begins.

MAY [**16**] Seamen's strike begins. [**26**] British Guiana becomes fully independent, changing its name to Guyana.

JUN [**2**] de Valera is re-elected President of the Irish Republic.

JUL [**3**] An anti-Vietnam War demonstration takes place in Grosvenor Square. [**30**] England wins the World Cup.

AUG [**4**] Sir Edmund Compton becomes the first Parliamentary Commissioner (or 'Ombudsman'). [**10**] George Brown becomes Foreign Secretary. [**23**] The Cotswolds are designated an Area of Outstanding Natural Beauty.[**27**] Francis Chichester leaves Plymouth on his single-handed round-the-world voyage.

SEP [**8**] The Severn Bridge, carrying the M4 over the Severn estuary, is opened by the Queen. [**30**] Bechuanaland becomes independent, changing its name to Botswana.

OCT [**4**] Basutoland becomes independent, changing its name to Lesotho. [**18**] The Queen grants a free pardon to Timothy Evans, hanged in 1950 for the murder of his wife and daughter, and now officially admitted to be 'probably innocent'. [**21**] The Aberfan disaster: an unstable slag heap slides onto a junior school killing 144 people, including 116 children. [**23**] BP announces the discovery of rich gas fields in the North Sea. [**30**] Barbados becomes independent.

Seifert and Partners: Centrepoint, St Giles' Circus, London.

David Hockney: *Peter Getting out of Nick's Pool.*
John Piper: Tapestry, Chichester Cathedral.
Francis Bacon: *Henrietta Moraes.*

Anthony Powell: *The Soldier's Art.*
Graham Greene: *The Comedians.*
Jean Rhys: *Wide Sargasso Sea.*
Paul Scott: *The Jewel in the Crown.*
John Fowles: *The Magus.*

Havergal Brian: *First Symphony 'The Gothic'* (written in 1919).
Sir William Walton: *Missa Brevis.*
John Taverner: *The Whale.*
David Bedford: *That White and Radiant Legend.*
Gordon Crosse: *Changes; Purgatory.*
Benjamin Britten: *The Burning Fiery Furnace.*
Sir Harrison Birtwistle: *Punch and Judy.*

1967 Anthony Hewish and Jocelyn Bell discover the first pulsar, a rotating neutron star. British troops withdraw from Aden. The Abortion Act provides for the legal termination of pregnancy under specified conditions. A 'sit-in' at the London School of Economics triggers a wave of similar demonstrations, though with varying motives, at other universities. Ronald Norrish, George Porter (British) and Manfred Eigen (German) are awarded the Nobel Prize for Chemistry.

JAN   [**4**] Donald Campbell is killed on Coniston Water while attempting to break the world water speed record. [**18**] Jeremy Thorpe is elected leader of the Liberal Party following Jo Grimond's resignation.

FEB   [**8**] Sir Victor Gollancz, writer and publisher, dies.

MAR   [**4**] The first North Sea gas is pumped ashore at Easington. [**18**] The Liberian oil tanker *Torrey Canyon* is wrecked on the Pollard Rock off Land's End, producing a disastrous oil slick almost 300 square miles in area. [**28**] The *Torrey Canyon* is bombed in an attempt to set fire to the leaking oil.

MAY   [**11**] Britain applies to join the EEC. [**12**] John Masefield, Poet Laureate since 1930, dies. [**14**] The Catholic Cathedral at Liverpool is consecrated. [**28**] Francis Chichester arrives back in Plymouth at the end of his round-the-world voyage.

JUL   [**1**] BBC2 begins televising in colour. [**7**] Francis Chichester is knighted at Greenwich: the Queen uses Sir Francis Drake's sword. Actress Vivien Leigh dies in London. [**14**] The Decimal Currency Act provides for decimal currency in 1971. [**28**] The steel industry is nationalized.

AUG   [**2**] The Dartford Tunnel is formally opened. The poet Siegfried Sassoon dies. [**3**] The Aberfan tribunal reports that the National Coal Board was to blame for the disaster. [**27**] Brian Epstein, the Beatles' manager, is found dead of an overdose of sleeping pills.

SEP   [**10**] The Gibraltarians vote overwhelmingly in favour of remaining British. [**18**] The nuclear physicist Sir John Cockcroft dies. [**20**] The passenger liner *Queen Elizabeth 2* is launched at Clydebank. [**27**] The *Queen Mary* arrives at

Southampton at the end of her last transatlantic voyage. [**30**]
Re-organization of BBC Radio; Radios 1, 2, 3 and 4 begin
transmission.

Oct [**3**] The conductor Sir Malcolm Sargent dies. [**8**] Lord Attlee,
Labour Prime Minister 1945-51, dies. [**9**] The first driver is
breathalyzed, in Somerset.

Dec [**19**] France vetoes Britain's entry to the EEC. The pound is
devalued; Harold Wilson makes his 'pound in your pocket'
television speech.

Arne Jacobsen: St Catherine's College, Oxford.
Sir Frederick Gibberd: Cathedral of Christ the King,
Liverpool (completed).
Owen Luder, Tricorn Centre, Portsmouth.
Arup Associates: The Maltings, Snape.
Wilson and Leaker: Cumbernauld Centre.

Mark Lancaster: *Zapruder*.
Patrick Caulfield: *Battlements*.

Tom Stoppard: *Rosencrantz and Guildenstern are Dead*.
Sir William Golding: *The Pyramid*.
Sir Angus Wilson: *No Laughing Matter*.

Sir Peter Maxwell Davies: *Antichrist*.
Sir William Walton: *The Bear*.
Richard Rodney Bennett: Music for the film *Far from the
Madding Crowd*.
Alexander Goehr: *Second String Quartet*.
The Beatles: 'Sergeant Pepper's Lonely Hearts Club Band'.

1968 Clean Air Act.

Jan [**1**] C. Day Lewis is appointed Poet Laureate. [**15**] 20 are killed
as a hurricane strikes Scotland. [**31**] Mauritius becomes
independent.

Feb [**17**] The actor Sir Donald Wolfit dies. [**21**] Lord Florey, who
made possible the large-scale production of penicillin, dies.

Apr [**21**] Enoch Powell makes his 'River Tiber foaming with much
blood' speech at Birmingham, warning of the problems that
may flow from unrestricted immigration. [**23**] The first decimal
coins in Britain (5p and 10p) are issued.

May [**6**] A Gallup Poll suggests that 74% of Britons support Enoch
Powell's views on immigration. [**16**] Part of the Ronan Point
tower block collapses after a gas explosion; three people are

killed. Many now start to question the wisdom of building high-rise blocks: building standards too are questioned.

JUN [8] James Earl Ray is arrested at Heathrow for the murder of Martin Luther King. [10] NHS prescription charges are reintroduced. [24] The comedian Tony Hancock commits suicide.

AUG [3] The Countryside Act allows local authorities to designate Country Parks.

SEP [1] The first section of the new Victoria Line is opened. [6] Swaziland becomes independent. [15] The worst floods in south-east England since 1953. [16] The two-tier postal service begins. [26] The Theatres Act comes into force, abolishing censorship. [27] The French once again veto Britain's entry into the EEC. 13 members of the cast of *Hair* face the audience naked, in celebration of the abolition of censorship.

OCT [5] Clashes between police and crowds in Londonderry mark the start of violent and long-continued disturbances in Northern Ireland. [9] The HMS *Fearless* talks on Rhodesia fail. [10] Powell warns that immigrants may 'change the character of England'. [27] Anti-Vietnam War demonstration outside the American Embassy in Grosvenor Square; there are violent clashes between mounted police and demonstrators.

NOV [15] The liner *Queen Elizabeth* ends her last passenger voyage. [28] Enid Blyton, writer of children's books, dies.

GLC Architects: Queen Elizabeth Hall and Purcell Room, South Bank, London.
Sir Robert Matthew, Johnson-Marshall & Partners: University of York.

Dame Iris Murdoch: *The Nice and the Good*.
Muriel Spark: *The Public Image*.
Brian Moore: *I am Mary Dunne*.
C.P. Snow: *The Sleep of Reason*.
Sir Kingsley Amis: *I Want it Now*.

John Taverner: *Concerto for Orchestra*.
Alun Hoddinott: *Third Symphony*.
Sir Peter Maxwell Davies: *Taverner*.
Benjamin Britten: *The Prodigal Son*.
Humphrey Searle: *Hamlet*.
Havergal Brian: *Thirty-second Symphony* (composed).

1969 The Open University is founded. The Divorce Act liberalizes the law, granting divorce on any ground showing 'irretrievable breakdown' of a marriage. The first fertilization of a human egg outside the human body is achieved by Robert Edwards at Cambridge. 'Monty Python's Flying Circus' represents a significant new departure in television comedy. Derek Barton (British) and Odd Hassel (Norwegian) are awarded the Nobel Prize for Chemistry; Samuel Beckett for Literature.

JAN   The People's Democracy march from Belfast to Londonderry is broken up; this is the start of escalating unrest in Northern Ireland centring on political parades. [4] 50 people die when an airliner crashes near Gatwick.

FEB   [3] The London School of Economics is closed after more student protests. [23] The first broadcast of Kenneth Clark's 'Civilization', popularizing art history.

MAR   [5] Ronald and Reginald Kray are sentenced to a minimum of 30 years each for murder. [11] The author John Wyndham dies. [19] British troops land unopposed on Anguilla.

APR   [9] The British Concorde makes its maiden flight from Bristol to Fairford. [17] All women over 18 are now allowed to vote. [20] Belfast post offices and the main bus station are attacked by fire bombers. [21] It is announced that the British army is to guard key points in Northern Ireland. [22] Robin Knox Johnston arrives back in Falmouth after completing the first non-stop solo circumnavigation of the world. The *QE2* starts her first commercial voyage.

MAY   [1] James Chichester-Clark becomes Prime Minister of Northern Ireland. [12] The voting age is reduced to 18.

JUN   [7] The Snape Maltings is destroyed by fire. [9] Enoch Powell proposes voluntary repatriation of immigrants, to storms of criticism. [16] Earl Alexander of Tunis, the army commander who led the invasion of Italy, dies. [20] High-grade oil is discovered in the British Sector of the North Sea.

JUL   [1] Prince Charles is invested as Prince of Wales at Caernarvon Castle.

AUG   [12] There is a three-day street battle in Londonderry after the Apprentice Boys' march. [19] The British army takes over security and policing in Northern Ireland.

SEP   [27] The author Dame Ivy Compton-Burnett dies.

OCT   [10] The Hunt Committee reports on Northern Ireland, recommending disarming the police and disbanding the 'B Specials'. [14] The 50p coin is issued.

NOV   [3] Work begins on the National Theatre. [11] The owners of the *Torrey Canyon* agree to pay £1.5 million compensation each to Britain and France. [13] Quintuplets are born to Mrs Irene Hanson of Rayleigh, Essex.

DEC [**18**] The death penalty for murder is formally abolished, at the end of a trial period. [**22**] Bernadette Devlin MP is sentenced to six months in prison for incitement to riot in Belfast.

 Derek Walker and Milton Keynes Development Corporation Architects, with Lord Richard Llewellyn-Davies (plan): Milton Keynes.
James Stirling: History Faculty Library, Cambridge.
Ralph Erskine: Clare Hall, Cambridge.
Buckminster Fuller: Samuel Beckett Theatre, Oxford.

 Gilbert Proesch and George Passmore: *Underneath the Arches*.

 Elizabeth Bowen: *Eva Trout*.
Graham Greene: *Travels with My Aunt*.
Sir Kingsley Amis: *The Green Man*.
John Fowles: *The French Lieutenant's Woman*.
Piers Paul Read: *Monk Dawson*.
Dame Iris Murdoch: *Bruno's Dream*.
P. H. Newby: *Something to Answer For* (Booker Prize).
Cameron Report: Disturbances in Northern Ireland.

John Taverner: *Celtic Requiem*.
Robin Holloway: *Concerto for Orchestra*.
Sir Harrison Birtwistle: *Down by the Greenwood Side*.
Sir Peter Maxwell Davies: *Eight Songs for a Mad King*.
Thea Musgrave: *The Beauty and the Beast*.

1970 The Equal Pay Act is an important step towards stamping out sex discrimination. Sir Bernard Katz (British), Ulf von Euler (Swedish) and Julius Axelrod (American) are awarded the Nobel Prize for Physiology and Medicine.

FEB [**2**] Bertrand Russell, mathematician, philosopher and peace campaigner, dies aged 97. [**11**] Prince Charles takes his seat in the House of Lords. [**15**] Lord Dowding, chief of Fighter Command in the Battle of Britain, dies aged 87.

MAR [**2**] Rhodesia is declared a republic. [**12**] The quarantine period for dogs and cats is extended to one year as a precaution against rabies. [**16**] The complete New English Bible is published; a million copies are sold on the first day.

APR [**9**] The Beatles split up.

MAY [**31**] The great racehorse Arkle dies.

JUN [**4**] Tonga becomes independent. [**7**] The novelist E. M. Forster dies aged 91. [**15**] Sir Laurence Olivier is created a Life Peer; he is the first actor to be made a peer. [**17**] Decimal postage stamps go on sale for the first time. [**18**] The Conservatives win the General Election (Conservatives 330, Labour 287, Liberals 6); Edward Heath becomes Prime Minister, Iain MacLeod Chancellor of the Exchequer, Reginald Maudling Home Secretary. George Brown loses his seat. [**23**] Brunel's *Great Britain*, the world's first all-metal liner, returns to Bristol from the Falklands where it has been left as a rusting wreck since 1886. [**27-8**] There are violent disturbances in Belfast and Londonderry. [**29**] Britain makes her third application to join the EEC. Caroline Thorpe, Jeremy Thorpe's first wife, dies in a car crash.

JUL [**7**] Sir Allen Lane, publisher and founder of Penguin paperbacks, dies. [**8**] The artist Dame Laura Knight dies. [**20**] The Chancellor of the Exchequer Iain MacLeod dies suddenly. [**29**] The conductor Sir John Barbirolli dies. [**30**] Damages are awarded to 28 child-victims of thalidomide.

AUG [**2**] The army fires rubber bullets for the first time during disturbances in Belfast.

SEP [**12**] Concorde lands at Heathrow for the first time; there are complaints from nearby residents about the noise.

OCT [**10**] Fiji becomes independent. [**19**] BP announces the discovery of a big oilfield in the British Sector of the North Sea, 110 miles east of Aberdeen.

NOV [**20**] The 10 shilling note goes out of circulation. [**26**] More working days have been lost as a result of strikes so far this year than in any other year since 1926.

DEC [**2**] The Commons reject a move to retain British Summer Time in the winter months.

 Denys Lasdun: University of East Anglia.

 C.P. Snow: *Last Things*.
New English Bible (completed).
Len Deighton: *Bomber*.
Bernice Rubens: *The Elected Member* (Booker Prize).
Jane Gaskell: *A Sweet, Sweet Summer*.
Nan Fairbrother: *New Lives, New Landscapes*.
Jasper Ridley: *Lord Palmerston*.
Lily Powell: *The Bird of Paradise*.
Richard Barker: *The Knight and Chivalry*.
Susan Hill: *I'm the King of the Castle*.
Michael Hastings: *Tussy is Me*.

Alan Bush: *Joe Hill*.
Richard Rodney Bennett: *Victory*.
Sir Michael Tippett: *The Knot Garden*.
Nicholas Maw: *The Rising of the Moon*.

David Bedford: *The Garden of Love.*
Simon Bainbridge: *Heterophony.*
Kenneth Tynan: *Oh! Calcutta!*

1971 Margaret Thatcher, as Education Minister, abolishes free milk for schoolchildren. The Family Income Supplement is introduced. Internment without trial is introduced for those suspected of being members of or giving assistance to the IRA. EMI-Scanner developed by Godfrey Hounsfield from his invention of computed tomography in 1967. Dennis Gabor is awarded the Nobel Prize for Physics.

JAN [**1**] The Divorce Reform Act comes into force. [**2**] The Ibrox football ground disaster; 66 people are crushed to death when a barrier collapses. [**3**] The Open University begins its television transmissions. [**14**] The Angry Brigade lets off time bombs outside the home of Robert Carr, Secretary of State for Employment. [**15**] More decimal coins are issued: ½p, 1p and 2p. [**19**] Postal workers go on strike for a 19.5% pay rise.

FEB [**4**] Troop reinforcements are sent to Belfast after further violence. Rolls Royce is declared bankrupt. [**15**] Decimal Day; the decimal currency system comes into operation. [**21**] 100,000 trade unionists march in London in protest against the Industrial Relations Bill. [**24**] The Immigration Bill is introduced; this measure will end the right of Commonwealth citizens to settle in Britain.

MAR [**1**] One-day strike by 1.5 million engineers against the Industrial Relations Bill. [**8**] The postal strike ends. [**18**] More troops are sent to Northern Ireland, bringing the total to 9,700. [**20**] Chichester-Clark resigns as Prime Minister of Northern Ireland; he is succeeded by Brian Faulkner.

JUN [**14**] Upper Clyde Shipbuilders are forced into liquidation; the Government refuses to help 'lame ducks'. [**25**] Lord Boyd-Orr dies.

JUL [**7**] The Government publishes its terms for entry into the EEC. [**30**] Workers at Upper Clyde Shipbuilders take control of the shipyard.

AUG [**9**] Internment without trial begins in Northern Ireland.

SEP [**9**] Parliament is recalled for a special debate on Northern Ireland. [**27**] Prime Ministers Heath, Lynch and Faulkner meet at Chequers for discussions about Northern Ireland.

OCT [**4**] The Labour Party Conference votes by a large majority against the proposed terms for entry into the EEC. [**13**] The Conservative Party Conference votes overwhelmingly in favour of the EEC entry terms. [**28**] The Commons vote in favour of joining the EEC on the terms presented by the Government (356 to 244); 69 Labour MPs vote with the Government. [**30**] An opinion poll shows that most of the British electorate oppose Britain's entry into the EEC.

Nov   [**16**] The Compton report on Interrogation in Northern Ireland finds 'some ill-treatment but no brutality'.

Dec   [**11**] Geoffrey Rippon agrees terms with the EEC for the protection of fishing limits after Britain's entry; these turn out not to protect the interests of British fishermen. [**20**] Edward Heath meets Richard Nixon in Bermuda for talks.

James Stirling: Florey Building, Queen's College, Oxford.

David Hockney: *Mr and Mrs Clark and Percy.*
Gerda Charles: *The Destiny Waltz.*

Philip Larkin: *This Be the Verse.*
Anthony Powell: *Books Do Furnish a Room.*
Sir Kingsley Amis: *Girl, 20.*
Dame Iris Murdoch: *An Accidental Man.*
V. S. Naipaul: *In a Free State* (Booker Prize).
Douglas Dunn: *Terry Street.*
Gillian Tindall: *Fly Away Home.*
Susan Hill: *The Albatross.*
Geoffrey Hill: *Mercian Hymns.*
Kathleen Raine: *The Lost Country.*

John McCabe: *Second Symphony.*
Tristram Cary: Film music for *A Christmas Carol.*
Benjamin Britten: *Owen Wingrave.*
John Buller: *Finnegan's Wake.*
Egon Wellesz: *Ninth Symphony.*
The Beatles: 'My Sweet Lord!'

1972 Rodney Porter (British) and Gerald Edelman (American) are awarded the Nobel Prize for Physiology and Medicine.

Jan   [**9**] The miners' strike begins, causing widespread powercuts and disruption to industrial production. After being converted to a floating marine university at Hong Kong, and renamed 'Seawise University', the liner *Queen Elizabeth* catches fire and sinks. [**18**] Britain's first plastic warship, the minehunter HMS *Wilton*, is launched at Southampton. [**20**] Unemployment in the UK passes the l million mark. [**22**] Britain joins the EEC;

the 'Six' become the 'Ten' by the Treaty of Accession (becoming effective next Jan). [**30**] 'Bloody Sunday' in Londonderry; 13 protest marchers are killed by British troops opening fire on an unarmed Catholic demonstration.

FEB [**9**] A state of emergency is declared in the power crisis; industry is now officially to work only three days a week to conserve coal supplies. [**15**] Over l.5 million workers are laid off at the peak of the power crisis. [**22**] An IRA bomb attack on Aldershot kills five cleaning women, a gardener and a Catholic priest. [**25**] The miners vote to return to work.

MAR [**4**] A hovercraft capsizes in the Solent, killing five people. [**20**] A bomb blast in Belfast kills six and injures 47. [**25**] Heath decides to impose Direct Rule on Ulster from Westminster, suspending rule from Stormont. [**29**] The Tutankhamun exhibition opens at the British Museum. [**30**] Direct Rule comes into force; William Whitelaw is appointed Secretary of State for Ireland.

APR [**11**] Roy Jenkins and David Owen resign from the Labour front bench in protest at Wilson's decision to support a call for a referendum on Britain's membership of the EEC. [**13**] There are 23 explosions in the worst day of violence in Ulster since Direct Rule was imposed. [**17**] A work-to-rule begins on British Rail in support of a pay claim. [**18**] The new state of Bangladesh (formerly East Pakistan) is admitted to the Commonwealth. [**19**] The Widgery Report on 'Bloody Sunday' is published.

MAY [**3**] A Church of England synod fails to reach the required majority in favour of a union with the Methodist Church. [**13**] The work-to-rule causes a complete weekend close-down on British Rail. [**18**] Bomb disposal experts parachute onto the QE2 in mid-Atlantic following a bomb threat. The Queen meets the Duke of Windsor in Paris. [**22**] Ceylon becomes the independent republic of Sri Lanka. C. Day Lewis, Poet Laureate since 1967, dies. [**28**] The Duke of Windsor, ex-King Edward VIII, dies in Paris aged 77.

JUN [**5**] The funeral of the Duke of Windsor takes place at Windsor. [**11**] Four people are killed and 115 injured in a train crash at Eltham. [**12**] The rail dispute is settled.

JUL Reginald Maudling resigns because of his association with the Poulson corruption case; Robert Carr replaces him as Home Secretary. [**5**] 30 patients die in a fire at Coldharbour Hospital, Sherborne.

AUG President Amin orders the expulsion of 40,000 Asians from Uganda; many of them come to Britain. [**26**] Sir Francis

Chichester dies at Plymouth. [**28**] Prince William of Gloucester is killed in a plane crash.

Sep [**1**] Iceland extends her fishing limit from 12 to 150 miles, in an attempt to exclude British and other foreign fishing. [**17**] The first Asians arrive in Britain from Uganda.

Oct [**5**] The Congregational Church (England and Wales) and the Presbyterian Church in England combine to form the United Reformed Church. [**10**] Sir John Betjeman is appointed Poet Laureate. [**12**] Students jostle and insult the Queen when she visits Stirling University.

Nov [**6**] The Government imposes a 3-month pay freeze. [**26**] The Race Relations Act comes into force; from now on employers may not discriminate on grounds of colour. [**30**] The Government cancels its planned £10 million loan to Uganda because of Amin's treatment of Asians. The writer Sir Compton MacKenzie dies.

Dec [**30**] The Tutankhamun exhibition closes; 1.6 million visitors have seen it.

 Duncan Grant: *The Sharaku Scarf.*

 J.L. Carr: *The Harpole Report.*
Susan Hill: *The Bird of Night.*
Richard Adams: *Watership Down.*
Quentin Bell: *Virginia Woolf.*
John Berger: *G* (Booker Prize).
James Pope-Hennessy: *Trollope.*
Brian Moore: *Catholics.*
Peter Prince: *Play Things.*
Paul Strathern: *A Season in Abyssinia.*
Jonathan Street: *Prudence Dictates.*

 Tim Rice and Andrew Lloyd Webber: *Joseph and the Amazing Technicolor Dreamcoat* [musical].
Alexander Goehr: *Piano Concerto.*
Sir Michael Tippett: *Third Symphony.*

1973 Brian Josephson (British), Ivar Giaever (American) and Leo Esake (Japanese) are awarded the Nobel Prize for Physics. Geoffrey Wilkinson (British) and Ernst Otto Fischer (German) receive the Nobel Prize for Chemistry.

Jan [**1**] Britain and the Irish Republic formally become members of the EEC. [**11**] The Open University awards its first 800 degrees.

FEB   [1] The Common Agricultural Policy of the EEC comes into operation. [5] The first Protestant Loyalists are detained without trial in Northern Ireland. [7] Widespread violence in Northern Ireland. [22] The writer Elizabeth Bowen dies.

MAR   [1] A Fine Gael and Labour Party Coalition wins the Irish General Election; Liam Cosgrave becomes Prime Minister. [8] Two bombs explode in London; one person is killed and 238 are injured. [9] The Northern Ireland referendum shows that 592,000 are in favour of retaining links with Britain, 6,000 for a union with the Irish Republic. [18] John Cartland, proprietor of a Brighton language school, is murdered in Provence; his son Jeremy is suspected, but after a lengthy inquiry by the French authorities he is found neither guilty nor innocent and released. [26] Sir Noel Coward, playwright, songwriter and entertainer, dies.

APR   [1] Value Added Tax is introduced in Britain.

MAY   [18] Frigates are sent to protect British trawlers inside the disputed waters round Iceland. [21] A British warship chases an Icelandic frigate in the first Royal Naval action of the 'Cod War'. [31] Erskine Childers succeeds de Valera as President of the Irish Republic.

JUN   [8] Enoch Powell hints that people should vote Labour to protest against Britain's membership of the EEC.

JUL   [4] Riot at Long Kesh Prison in Northern Ireland. [10] The Bahamas become independent. [11] 122 people die in the Paris air crash. [18] The film actor Jack Hawkins dies. [30] 18 miners die in a pit cage accident at Markham colliery in Derbyshire.

AUG   [2] The Summerland fire at Douglas, Isle of Man: 50 people die. [20] The first of a series of IRA bomb attacks in London.

SEP   [2] J.R.R. Tolkien, author of *The Lord of the Rings*, dies at Bournemouth. [7] Len Murray succeeds Vic Feather as TUC General Secretary. [10] IRA bomb explosions in London stations injure 13 people. [16] Tommy Herron, the vice-chairman of the UDA, is shot dead at Lisburn. [20] A bomb explodes at Chelsea barracks. [28] The poet W.H. Auden dies.

OCT   [1] Denis Healey promises that Labour will tax the rich 'until the pips squeak'. [31] Three Provisional IRA leaders are freed from Mountjoy Prison by a hi-jacked helicopter.

NOV   [8] The Cod War between Britain and Iceland ends. [13] A state of emergency is declared as miners and power workers go on strike. [14] Princess Anne marries Captain Mark Phillips at Westminster Abbey. [25] The 200th British soldier to die in Northern Ireland is killed.

DEC   [2] In a Cabinet reshuffle, Francis Pym is made Northern Ireland Secretary, Whitelaw Employment Secretary. [5] A 50 mph speed limit is imposed to conserve fuel. [13] A three-day working week is ordered by the Government because of the coal-miners' slow-down and the Arab oil embargo. [19] Nine people die in a train crash at Ealing. [31] The three-day week begins.

 New London Bridge.

 Sir Angus Wilson: *As if by Magic.*
Anthony Powell: *Temporary Kings.*
Graham Greene: *The Honorary Consul.*
Dame Iris Murdoch: *The Black Prince.*
Michael Frayn: *Sweet Dreams.*
J. C. Farrell: *The Siege of Krishnapur* (Booker Prize).
Martin Amis: *The Rachel Papers.*
Oliver Sacks: *Awakenings.*
Shiva Naipaul: *The Chip Chip Gatherers.*
John Wilson: *CB: A Life of Sir Henry Campbell-Bannerman.*
Anthony Powell: *Temporary Kings.*
Robin Lane Fox: *Alexander the Great.*

 Sir Harrison Birtwistle: *Grimethorpe Aria.*
Alun Hoddinott: *Fifth Symphony.*
Benjamin Britten: *Death in Venice.*
Thea Musgrave: *The Voice of Ariadne.*
Nicholas Maw: *Life Studies.*
Cornelius Cardew: *The Old and the New.*
John Taverner: *Requiem for Father Malachy.*

1974 Sir Martin Ryle and Antony Hewish are awarded the Nobel Prize for Physics.

JAN   [1] Direct Rule in Northern Ireland ends and a new Ulster Executive takes office (but Direct Rule is resumed later in the year).

FEB   [1] The escaped Great Train Robber Ronald Biggs is arrested in Brazil. [4] 12 men are killed in an army coach explosion on the M62. [7] Grenada becomes independent. [28] The General Election result is inconclusive. Edward Heath hoped for a fresh mandate after his confrontation with the miners, but there is a narrow Labour victory (Labour 301, Conservatives 297, Liberals 14, Scottish Nationalists 7). Heath tries to form a Conservative-Liberal Coalition.

MAR [**4**] Heath resigns after the Liberals reject the coalition idea; a minority Labour Government is formed by Harold Wilson. [**6**] The miners return to work after the Wilson Government offers a 35% pay increase. [**9**] Britain returns to a five-day working week. [**20**] An attempt is made to abduct Princess Anne in the Mall; the gunman fails but injures four people.

MAY [**8**] The nurses begin a series of strikes in protest against their low pay. [**17**] Car bombs in Dublin and Monaghan kill 28 people and injure over 100. [**19**] A state of emergency is declared in Northern Ireland. A car bomb explodes in a car park at Heathrow.

JUN [**1**] An explosion at the Flixborough chemical works kills 29 people. [**10**] Henry, Duke of Gloucester, son of George V, dies. [**17**] An IRA bomb explodes at Westminster Hall.

JUL [**10**] The Government announces that it has chosen a British-designed reactor for the next stage of its nuclear energy programme (= the 1980s). [**14**] IRA bombs explode in Birmingham and Manchester. [**17**] Bombs explode in the Tower of London. [**18**] The Maplin airport project, which could have combined a seaport rivalling Rotterdam, is scrapped. [**24**] Sir James Chadwick, physicist and discoverer of the neutron, dies. [**25**] The International Court of Justice at The Hague rules that the UK is not bound to observe Iceland's unilateral decision (in 1972) to extend its rights from 12 miles to 50 miles from the coast. [**26**] An IRA bomb explodes at Heathrow car park.

AUG [**15**] The collapse of the Court Line leaves many holiday-makers stranded in foreign resorts.

SEP [**3**] Two crew members are drowned when Edward Heath's yacht *Morning Cloud* is hit by huge waves in the Channel.

OCT [**1**] Britain's first McDonald's hamburger restaurant opens in South London. [**5**] IRA bomb explosions in two Guildford pubs kill five people. [**10**] In this year's second General Election, Harold Wilson hopes for a fresh mandate for his (numerically weak) Government, but it produces only a small overall majority (Labour 319, Conservatives 277, Liberals 13, Scottish Nationalists 11). [**15**] There is rioting in the Maze Prison. [**18**] A Whitehall Unit is set up to prepare for the devolution of power to Wales and Scotland.

NOV [**4**] Judith Ward is given 12 life sentences for causing the M62 bomb deaths. [**7**] Two people die in a pub bombing at Woolwich. [**8**] After 300 years, Covent Garden market moves out of central London to a new site at Nine Elms. Ronald Milhench is sent to prison for forging the Prime Minister's signature. [9] The composer Egon Wellesz dies. [11] Sandra Rivett, Lady Lucan's nanny, is murdered by an intruder. Lord Lucan, widely assumed to be the murderer, drives to Newhaven and mysteriously disappears, never to be seen again although alleged 'sightings' are reported from time to time. [12] Wolfson College, Oxford is opened. [15] Donald Coggan succeeds Michael Ramsey as Archbishop of Canterbury. [21] 21 people are killed and 120 injured in two Birmingham pub bombings. The MP John Stonehouse disappears on a Miami beach; it is assumed that he has drowned.

 Seifert and Partners: Grand Metropolitan Hotel, Knightsbridge, London.

 Howard Hodgkin: *Small Durand Gardens, London.*

 Beryl Bainbridge: *The Bottle Factory Outing.*
Muriel Spark: *The Abbess of Crewe.*
Sir Kingsley Amis: *Ending Up.*
Lawrence Durrell: *Monsieur, or the Prince of Darkness.*
Jacob Bronowski: *The Ascent of Man.*
John Le Carré: *Tinker, Taylor, Soldier, Spy.*
Nadine Gordimer: *The Conservationist* (Booker Prize – shared).
Stanley Middleton: *Holiday* (Booker Prize – shared).
Dame Iris Murdoch: *The Sacred and Profane Love Machine.*
John Wain: *Samuel Johnson.*
David Hare: *Knuckle.*
Tim Teal: *Cushing's Crusade.*

 Gordon Crosse: *The Story of Vasco.*
Iain Hamilton: *The Catiline Conspiracy.*
R14

1975 Press allegations about Jeremy Thorpe's private life become an increasing embarrassment to the Liberal Party. The Community Land Act brings development land within public control (repealed in 1979). Sex Discrimination Act.

JAN [10] Two workers at Windscale die of leukaemia. [14] Lesley Whittle, a young heiress, is abducted. [24] Dr Coggan is enthroned as Archbishop of Canterbury. [27] Five IRA bombs explode in London. [31] The Duke of Norfolk dies.

FEB [**11**] Margaret Thatcher becomes leader of the Conservative Party, after her successful challenge to Heath's leadership. [**14**] The novelist P.G. Wodehouse dies aged 93. Sir Julian Huxley dies. [**28**] The Moorgate tube station disaster; this is the worst underground train accident so far, in which 42 people are killed as a train travelling at speed crashes into a blind tunnel.

MAR [**4**] Charlie Chaplin is knighted. [**7**] Lesley Whittle's body is found in a drain shaft; she has been strangled with a wire noose by her kidnapper, nicknamed the Black Panther. [**21**] John Stonehouse, the disappearing MP, is arrested in Australia for theft, forgery and deception. [**25**] The QE2 becomes the largest liner to have passed through the Panama Canal. [**27**] Sir Arthur Bliss, composer and Master of the Queen's Musick since 1953, dies.

MAY [**20**] The sculptor Barbara Hepworth dies in a fire at her studio at St Ives in Cornwall. [**27**] A coach crash in Wharfedale kills 32 elderly people.

JUN [**1**] Snow falls in London for the first time since records began. [**5**] The National Referendum on Britain's membership of the EEC results in 17.4 million voting 'yes' and 8.5 million voting 'no'. [**11**] The first oil is pumped ashore from Britain's North Sea oilfields. The prosecution in the Birmingham bomb trial concedes that the six people accused have been beaten up while in custody.

AUG [**1**] Britain signs the Helsinki Agreement on security and co-operation in Europe. [**27**] Haile Selassie, the deposed Emperor of Ethiopia, dies in exile in England. [**29**] Eamon de Valera, three times Prime Minister of the Irish Republic and President 1959-73, dies aged 92.

SEP [**28**] The Spaghetti House siege; gunmen hold seven Italians hostage in a London restaurant.

OCT [**3**] The Spaghetti House siege ends and the hostages are freed unharmed. [**15**] Iceland unilaterally extends its fishing grounds from 50 to 200 miles; this leads to a resumption of the Cod War between Britain and Iceland. [**23**] Professor Fairley, a leading cancer expert, is killed by a car bomb intended for Hugh Fraser MP. [**30**] More than 16 million elm trees have so far been destroyed by Dutch Elm Disease.

NOV [**7**] Cardinal Heenan, Roman Catholic Archbishop of Westminster, dies. [**12**] An IRA bomb explodes at Scott's Restaurant in London, killing one man. [**18**] Two people are killed when another bomb goes off at Waltons Restaurant in London. [**25**] The Government authorizes the sending of three frigates to protect British trawlers fishing in the disputed waters off Iceland. [**27**] Ross McWhirter, compiler of the *Guinness Book of Records*, is shot dead at his home in London by two IRA gunmen.

DEC [**10**] The first shots are fired in the Cod War. [**11**] The end of the Balcombe Street siege in London; Mr and Mrs Matthews had been held hostage in their flat by IRA terrorists since December 6.

 Sir Denys Lasdun: The National Theatre, London (completed).

 David Hockney: Set and costumes for *The Rake's Progress*.

 Malcolm Bradbury: *The History Man.*
Anthony Powell: *Hearing Secret Harmonies.*
David Lodge: *Changing Places.*
Dame Iris Murdoch: *A Word Child.*
Tom Sharpe: *Blott on the Landscape.*
Martin Amis: *Dead Babies.*
Richard Adams: *Shardik.*
Frederick Forsyth: *The Dogs of War.*
Ruth Prawer Jhabvala: *Heat and Dust* (Booker prize).
William McIlvanney: *Docherty.*
Helen Corke: *In Our Infancy.*
Seamus Heaney: *North.*
Brian Moore: *The Great Victorian Collection.*
Dominic Cooper: *The Dead of Winter.*
Ian McEwan: *First Love, Last Rites.*

1976 The Agricultural Rent Act abolishes 'tied' farm cottages.

JAN [**2**] Winds up to 105 mph cause destruction and 22 deaths. [**4**] Five Catholics are killed in an ambush by Protestant terrorists. [**5**] Ten Protestants are machine-gunned at Whitecross by Catholic terrorists, in what is seen as the worst sectarian murder since 'the troubles' began in the 1960s. [**7**] The frigate HMS *Andromeda* is rammed by an Icelandic gunboat. The President of the Royal Academy, Sir Thomas Monnington, dies. [**12**] The novelist Agatha Christie dies. [**21**] Concorde enters passenger service with simultaneous take-offs from London and Paris. [**24**] Soviet commentators refer to Margaret Thatcher as 'The Iron Lady'.

FEB [**12**] Workmen discover a perfectly preserved rose that was cemented into a wall at Romsey Abbey in 1120. [**23**] The painter L.S. Lowry dies at Glossop. [**24**] Britain sends a fourth gunboat to Iceland.

MAR [**16**] Harold Wilson resigns as Prime Minister. Norman Scott tells a court of his relationship with Jeremy Thorpe. [**19**] It is announced that Princess Margaret and Lord Snowdon are to separate. [**23**] Ian Smith rejects Wilson's conditions for a Rhodesia settlement. [**24**] Viscount Montgomery of Alamein dies aged 88.

APR [**5**] James Callaghan succeeds as Prime Minister.
[**27**] Britain starts exporting North Sea Oil, from Forties field.

MAY [**10**] Thorpe resigns as leader of the Liberal Party. [**12**] Jo Grimond agrees to act as caretaker leader of the Liberal Party. [**26**] There is widespread condemnation of Wilson's resignation honours list, which includes knighthoods for James Goldsmith and Joseph Kagan as well as a peerage for the Political Secretary who helped draw up the list (Lady Falkender).

JUN [**1**] Interim agreement is reached in Oslo between Iceland and Britain, ending the Cod War. [**9**] The actress Dame Sybil Thorndike dies aged 93. [**28**] The Seychelles become an independent republic.

JUL [**1**] Donald Nielson is convicted of the murder of Lesley Whittle. [**7**] David Steel is elected Liberal Party leader. [**21**] Christopher Ewart-Biggs, British Ambassador to the Irish Republic, is assassinated. Donald Nielson is given five life sentences for murder. [**22**] The archaeologist who has done much to popularize archaeology, Sir Mortimer Wheeler, dies. [**30**] Richard Ingrams, editor of *Private Eye*, is tried on libel charges brought by Sir James Goldsmith.

AUG [**1**] Trinidad and Tobago become an independent republic. [**4**] Lord Thomson of Fleet, owner of *The Times*, dies. [**6**] John Stonehouse begins a seven-year prison sentence for fraud. [**14**] The Women's Peace Movement of Northern Ireland, led by Betty Williams and Mairaed Corrigan, holds its first big rally. [**22**] The drought is the worst in Britain for 500 years; it is also the hottest summer since at least 1727. [**25**] Unemployment passes the 1.5 million mark.

SEP [**2**] The European Commission on Human Rights reports on the Irish Government's charges against Britain; the British authorities are found guilty of torturing detainees in Ulster following the introduction of internment in 1971, but not guilty of discriminating between Protestant and Republican extremists. Percy Shaw, who invented cat's eyes, dies.
[**20**] EEC members sign a convention in Brussels, allowing a European Parliament to be set up. The minesweeper HMS *Fittleton* sinks after colliding with the frigate *Mermaid* off the

Dutch coast: 12 die. [**24**] Ian Smith accepts the idea of majority rule in Rhodesia within two years.

OCT [**14**] The actress Dame Edith Evans dies aged 88. [**21**] Michael Foot is elected deputy leader of the Labour Party. [**25**] The Queen opens the National Theatre. [**26**] Deryck Cooke, who completed Mahler's 10th Symphony, dies. [**29**] Mining begins on the newly-discovered coalfield at Selby. [**30**] EEC agrees on the introduction of a 200 mile EEC fishing zone (in force from January 1 1977).

NOV [**7**] Crosses are planted in Belfast for the lives lost in Northern Ireland since 1969 - 1,662 in all. [**19**] The architect Sir Basil Spence dies. [**28**] The composer Harold Darke dies.

DEC [**4**] The composer Benjamin Britten dies. [**16**] It is announced that Wales and Scotland are to have referenda on devolution (a greater measure of self-government).

Milton Keynes Development Corporation Architects: Cofferidge Close, Stony Stratford.
National Exhibition Centre, Birmingham.

David Hockney: *Gregory with Gym Socks.*
Carl André: *Bricks.*
Richard Long: *119 Stones.*
Lucien Freud: *Portrait of Frank Auerbach.*

Daphne du Maurier: *The Winding Stair.*
Sir Kingsley Amis: *The Alteration.*
David Storey: *Saville* (Booker Prize).
Beryl Bainbridge: *A Quiet Life.*
William Trevor: *The Children of Dynmouth.*
Penelope Lively: *A Stitch in Time.*
Ronald Lewin: *Slim: The Standardbearer.*
John Banville: *Doctor Copernicus.*
Robert Nye: *Falstaff.*
Richard Holmes: *Shelley: The Pursuit.*
Richard Cork: *Vorticism and Abstract Art in the First Machine Age.*

Andrew Lloyd Webber: *Evita.*
Michael Berkeley: *Meditations.*
David Bedford: *The Rime of the Ancient Mariner.*
Sir Peter Maxwell Davies: *The Martyrdom of St Magnus; First Symphony.*
Gordon Crosse: *Second Symphony.*

1977 Sir Nevill Mott (British), J. von Vleck and P. Andersen awarded the Nobel Prize for Physics.

JAN [5] Roy Jenkins resigns as MP to become the first President of the EEC Commission, but with the intention of eventually returning to form a 'third force' in British politics. [14] Lord Avon, Conservative Prime Minister 1955-57, dies. [24] The second round of Rhodesian talks fails; Ian Smith rejects British proposals for a transition to black majority rule. [29] Seven IRA bombs explode in central London without any casualties.

FEB [2] There is an important meeting of NEDC on industrial strategy to reduce strike action. [15] Statistics show that in 1976 deaths exceeded births for the first time since records began in 1837; this indicates an important trend towards demographic stability. [19] Anthony Crosland dies. [21] David Owen, aged 38, becomes Foreign Secretary. [22] The Government presses the UN to investigate reports of killings in Uganda.

MAR [3] Lord Faulkner, former Northern Ireland Prime Minister, dies. [7] The Queen arrives in Australia on her Silver Jubilee tour. [10] Callaghan arrives in Washington for talks with President Carter. [25] There is an EEC summit meeting in Rome, chaired by Callaghan. [28] The mountaineer Eric Shipton dies in Salisbury. [31] The Queen and Prince Philip arrive home at the end of their tour.

APR [2] Red Rum wins the Grand National for the third time. [7] Margaret Thatcher begins a visit to China. [12] A new British initiative on Rhodesia begins; David Owen arrives in Tanzania on a diplomatic tour of Southern Africa, in the hope of reaching a negotiated transfer of power in Rhodesia.

MAY [13] Peter Jay, the Prime Minister's son-in-law, is named as the next ambassador to Washington.

JUN [7] The Queen lights a bonfire in Windsor Great Park, starting a week of Silver Jubilee celebrations.

AUG [13] The writer Henry Williamson dies.

SEP David Owen presents Ian Smith with new Anglo-American proposals for a Rhodesian settlement. A National Front march in Manchester is banned. [13] The London-born conductor Leopold Stokowski dies in Hampshire aged 95.

OCT [28] Yorkshire police begin a hunt for a serial murderer, the Yorkshire Ripper, who is making apparently random attacks on young women.

NOV Firemen strike for a 30% pay rise. [14] The composer Richard Addinsell dies.

Dec [**12**] Lady Churchill, widow of Sir Winston Churchill, dies. [**25**] Charlie Chaplin dies.

 Colin St John Wilson: New British Library, London.

 David Hockney: *Model with Unfinished Self-Portrait; My Parents.*

 P.G. Wodehouse: *Sunset at Blandings.*
John Le Carré: *The Honourable Schoolboy.*
Paul Scott: *Staying On* (Booker Prize).
John Fowles: *Daniel Martin.*
Beryl Bainbridge: *Injury Time.*
Richard Adams: *The Plague Dogs.*
George Painter: *Chateaubriand, Vol 2: The Longed-for Tempests.*
Nigel Nicolson: *Mary Curzon.*
Patrick Leigh Fermor: *A Time of Gifts.*
Bruce Chatwin: *In Patagonia.*
A. N. Wilson: *The Sweets of Pimlico.*
Tom Paulin: *A State of Justice.*
Nigel Williams: *My Life Closed Twice.*

 Sir Michael Tippett: *Fourth Symphony: The Ice Break.*
Simon Bainbridge: *Viola Concerto.*
Frederick Delius: *The Magic Fountain.*
Iain Hamilton: *Tamburlaine.*

1978 Liverpool Cathedral is finally completed. To celebrate Henry Moore's 80th birthday an exhibition of his sculpture is held in Hyde Park. Peter Mitchell is awarded the Nobel Prize for Chemistry.

Jan The firemen's strike ends. The Government suffers a series of defeats on its Scottish Devolution Bill; it is amended so that devolution can only happen if a minimum of 40% of the whole electorate votes 'yes'. [**11**] It is revealed that Lady Churchill destroyed the Graham Sutherland portrait of her husband. [**30**] Margaret Thatcher says that many in Britain fear being 'swamped by people with a different culture'.

Feb [**13**] Heath criticizes Thatcher for causing an 'unnecessary row' over immigration.

Mar An internal agreement is reached in Rhodesia between Smith and three black leaders. [**30**] The Conservatives reveal that they have hired the services of an advertising agency, Saatchi and Saatchi.

May [**1**] The first May Day bank holiday is celebrated in Britain. [**24**] Princess Margaret and Lord Snowdon are divorced.

JUN [**3**] Jeremy Thorpe is interviewed by police investigating a plot to murder Norman Scott. [**27**] Evidence suggests that Britain will be self-sufficient in oil in two years' time.

JUL [**25**] The world's first test-tube baby is born: Louise Brown is born at Oldham General Hospital. [**31**] The Devolution Acts for Wales and Scotland receive the Royal Assent.

AUG [**4**] Jeremy Thorpe is on trial at Barnstaple for conspiracy to murder. [**30**] A case of smallpox is confirmed in Birmingham; Janet Parker dies on September ll.

SEP A series of strikes begins, lasting thorough the winter; people are turned away from hospitals, bodies are left unburied, and rubbish accumulates in the streets. [**10**] Police attribute two more murders to the Yorkshire Ripper, making a total of 10. [**11**] Georgi Markov, a Bulgarian defector, is stabbed in the thigh with a poisoned umbrella point at a bus stop on Waterloo Bridge. [**15**] Georgi Markov dies. [**30**] The Ellice Islands become the independent nation of Tuvalu.

OCT [**6**] The unveiling of the Chagall window in Chichester Cathedral, the last of Dean Walter Hussey's remarkable commissions. [**12**] The *Christos Bitas* is grounded off St David's Head: an oil slick threatens the Welsh Coast.

NOV [**11**] Committal proceedings begin against Thorpe. The TUC refuses to endorse the Government's 5% wage limit. [**30**] Publication of *The Times* is suspended because of an industrial dispute.

DEC The Government introduces a plan to impose sanctions on private firms awarding pay rises above 5%; the plan is defeated in the Commons. [**17**] There are IRA bomb explosions in Southampton, Bristol, Manchester and Coventry. [**18**] Further bombs explode or are discovered in London, Bristol and Southampton.

 Robert Matthew, Johnson-Marshall and Partners: Hillingdon Civic Centre, Uxbridge.

Edward Bawden: *Walled Garden.*
Marc Chagall: *The Arts to the Glory of God*, Chichester Cathedral.
David Hockney: *Le Plongeur*; Sets for *The Magic Flute.*

J.R.R. Tolkien: *The Silmarillion.*
Dame Iris Murdoch: *The Sea, The Sea* (Booker Prize).
Graham Greene: *The Human Factor.*
Barbara Pym: *The Sweet Dove Died.*
Sir Kingsley Amis: *Jake's Thing.*

Ian McEwen: *The Cement Garden.*
Mark Girouard: *Life in the English Country House.*
Harold Pinter: *Betrayal.*
John Grigg: *Lloyd George: The People's Champion.*
Robert Gittings: *The Older Hardy.*
Maurice Gee: *Plumb.*
David Cook: *Walter.*
Helen Hodgman: *Jack and Jill.*
Sara Maitland: *Daughter of Jerusalem.*
Peter Boardman: *The Shining Mountain.*
Humphry Carpenter: *The Inklings.*

Michael Berkeley: *The Wild Winds.*
Sir Michael Tippett: *Fourth String Quartet.*

1979 Sir Laurence Olivier receives a special Academy Award for his unrivalled contribution to theatre and cinema. Godfrey Newbold Hounsfield (British) and Allan McLeod Cormack (American) are awarded the Nobel Prize for Physiology and Medicine.

JAN   Secondary picketing in the road haulage strike creates increasing problems. 150,000 people are laid off because of the strike. [**8**] An oil tanker explodes in Bantry Bay killing 49 people. [**31**] Industrial disputes have led to accumulations of rubbish building up in the streets.

FEB   A 'concordat' between the TUC and the Government depends on the Government bringing inflation down to 5% within three years. [**22**] St Lucia becomes independent. [**26**] Tom Keating's trial for art forgery ends because of his failing health.

MAR   [**1**] 32.5% of Scots vote in favour of the devolution proposals, failing to reach the required 40%. The Welsh vote overwhelmingly against devolution. The Government is defeated in a confidence vote, necessitating a General Election. [**30**] The Conservative MP Airey Neave is assassinated in the car park at Westminster by the IRA. [**31**] The Royal Navy finally withdraws from Malta.

APR   [**4**] The eleventh victim of the Yorkshire Ripper dies. [**23**] A teacher is killed and 300 are arrested after clashes in Southall between supporters of the National Front and the Anti-Nazi League.

MAY   [**3**] Jeremy Thorpe loses his seat in the General Election, marking the conclusive end of his political career.
[**4**] Margaret Thatcher becomes the first woman Prime Minister; she leads a Conservative Government, with Lord

Carrington as Foreign Secretary, William Whitelaw as Home Secretary and Geoffrey Howe as Chancellor (Conservatives 339, Labour 269, Liberals ll). [**29**] Bishop Abel Muzorewa becomes Zimbabwe's (Rhodesia's) first black Prime Minister.

JUN   The first elections to the European Parliament are held. [**22**] Jeremy Thorpe is acquitted of the conspiracy to murder charge.

JUL   [**12**] The Gilbert Islands become the independent nation of Kiribati.

AUG   [**8**] Nicholas Montsarrat, author of *The Cruel Sea*, dies. [**14**] John Stonehouse is released from prison. Gale force winds cause havoc in the Fastnet yacht race: 17 people are drowned. [**18**] A heart transplant operation is attempted for the first time at Papworth Hospital. [**27**] Lord Mountbatten is assassinated by the IRA at Mullaghmore; his boat *Shadow V* explodes, killing him, his boatman and his grandson Nicholas; Dowager Lady Brabourne dies the next day.

SEP   [**2**] The 12th victim of the Yorkshire Ripper dies. [**5**] State funeral of Lord Mountbatten. [**14**] Plans are announced for the redevelopment of the London docklands. [**18**] Corporal punishment is abolished in all Inner London Schools. [**27**] The entertainer Dame Gracie Fields dies. [**29**] The Pope arrives in Ireland.

OCT   [**30**] The inventor Sir Barnes Wallis dies.

NOV   [**13**] *The Times* reappears after a year's absence. [**21**] The House of Commons hears that Sir Anthony Blunt was the 'fourth man' in the Burgess, MacLean and Philby spy affair; Buckingham Palace announces that Blunt has been stripped of his knighthood. [**23**] Thomas McMahon is sentenced to life imprisonment for the murder of Lord Mountbatten.

DEC   UDI in Rhodesia comes to an end with an agreement on free elections. [**5**] Jack Lynch resigns as Prime Minister of the Irish Republic. [**7**] Charles Haughey is elected leader of Ireland's governing party.

 Keith Garbett: Bar Hill Village Hall, Cambridge.

 David Hockney: *Divine*.

 Sir William Golding: *Darkness Visible*.
Beryl Bainbridge: *Another Part of the Wood*.
Angela Carter: *The Bloody Chamber*.
Penelope Fitzgerald: *Offshore* (Booker Prize).
Jennifer Johnston: *The Old Jest*.

Penelope Mortimer: *About Time.*
Peter Dickinson: *Tulku.*
Thom Gunn: *Selected Poems.*
Brian Finney: *Christopher Isherwood: A Critical Biography.*
P. S. Rushforth: *Kindergarten.*
Max Hastings: *Bomber Command.*
Christopher Reid: *Arcadia.*

 Alun Hoddinott: *The Rajah's Diamond.*
Alexander Goehr: *Babylon the Great is Fallen.*
Sir Michael Tippett: *Triple Concerto for Violin, Viola, Cello and Orchestra.*

1980 The socket of a second Heel Stone is discovered at Stonehenge by Michael Pitts. Frederick Sanger (British), Paul Berg and Walter Gilbert are awarded the Nobel Prize for Chemistry.

JAN [**18**] The photographer and designer Sir Cecil Beaton dies.

FEB [**17**] The painter Graham Sutherland dies. [**28**] The BBC announces that it will scrap five of its orchestras as an economy measure.

MAR [**25**] Robert Runcie is enthroned as Archbishop of Canterbury. [**27**] The residential North Sea oil platform *Alexander Kielland* collapses in a storm, killing 100 men.

APR [**2**] There is a riot in the St Pauls area of Bristol in which 19 police are injured. [**4**] Argentina is reported to be increasing her links with the Falkland Islands; this turns out to be a preliminary to an invasion. [**22**] Unemployment passes the 1.5 million mark. [**29**] The film director Alfred Hitchcock dies. [**30**] Armed men seize 20 hostages in the Iranian Embassy in London.

MAY [**5**] SAS troops storm the Iranian Embassy, freeing the hostages. [**30**] EC foreign ministers agree to reduce Britain's annual payment to the EC to about 25%.

JUN [**8**] There is a wave of bombings in Ulster. [**12**] The holiday camp owner Sir Billy Butlin dies in Jersey. [**30**] The sixpenny piece ceases to be legal tender today.

JUL [**10**] Alexandra Palace is badly damaged by fire. [**23**] The dispute between the BBC and its musicians is resolved: three orchestras are reprieved. [**24**] The entertainer Peter Sellers dies. [**31**] Shirley Williams, William Rodgers and David Owen urge Labour MPs to join forces with them against the far left.

AUG   [**4**] The Queen Mother's 80th birthday. [**15**] The wreck of the *Titanic*, which sank in 1912, is located on the seabed.

OCT   [**10**] Margaret Thatcher makes her 'the lady's not for turning' speech at the Conservative Party Conference. [**14**] ICI announces that it will make 4500 of its workers redundant. [**28**] The Director of Public Prosecutions decides not to prosecute the National Theatre over the Howard Brenton play *The Romans in Britain*.

NOV   [**17**] Peter Sutcliffe, the Yorkshire Ripper, murders student Jacqueline Hill.

DEC   [**3**] Sir Oswald Mosley dies in France. [**8**] John Lennon is murdered outside his Manhatten apartment by Mark Chapman. Unemployment passes the two million level for the first time since 1935. There is a summit meeting in Dublin between Mrs Thatcher and Irish Prime Minister Charles Haughey about closer co-operation between the UK and the Irish Republic. [**17**] Prof. Alan Walters is appointed as personal economic adviser to Mrs Thatcher.

 Ralph Erskine: Byker Development, Newcastle.

 Howard Brenton: *The Romans in Britain*.
John Le Carré: *Smiley's People*.
J.L. Carr: *A Month in the Country*.
Richard Adams: *The Girl in a Swing*.
Dame Iris Murdoch: *Nuns and Soldiers*.
Sir Angus Wilson: *Setting the World on Fire*.
Graham Greene: *Dr Fischer of Geneva*.
Sir William Golding: *Rites of Passage* (Booker Prize).
Barbara Pym: *A Few Green Leaves*.
Sir Kingsley Amis: *Russian Hide-and-Seek*.
Anthony Burgess: *Earthly Powers*.
A. N. Wilson: *The Laird of Abbotsford*.
Julian Barnes: *Metroland*.
David Lodge: *How Far Can You Go* (Whitbread 'Book of the Year').
David Newsome: *On the Edge of Paradise: A. C. Benson the Diarist*.
Isabel Colegate: *The Shooting Party*.
Robert Bernard Martin: *Tennyson: The Unquiet Heart*.

 William Mathias: *The Servants*.
Sir Harrison Birtwistle: *On the Sheer Threshold of the Night*.

Michael Berkeley: *At the Round Earth's Imagin'd Corners.*
George Benjamin: *Ringed by the Flat Horizon.*
Philip Cannon: *Lord of Light.*
Sir Peter Maxwell Davies: *The Lighthouse.*

1981 JAN [5] Peter Sutcliffe, a lorry driver, is charged with the final 'Yorkshire Ripper' murder; he has murdered 13 women over the last four years. Norman St John Stevas is replaced as Leader of the House of Commons by Francis Pym. [6] The novelist A.J. Cronin dies in Switzerland. [21] Sir Norman Stronge and his son, both former Stormont MPs, are killed by the IRA. [25] The Limehouse Declaration; William Rodgers, Roy Jenkins, Shirley Williams and David Owen form a Council for Social Democracy. The break-away 'Gang of Four' will form a new centre party, the SDP.

FEB [10] The National Coal Board plans to close 50 pits employing 30,000 miners; the miners press for a national miners' strike. [12] Rupert Murdoch buys *The Times.* Ian Paisley is suspended from the House of Commons for referring to the Northern Ireland Secretary in unparliamentary language. [14] 48 young people die in a disco fire in Dublin. [20] Peter Sutcliffe is charged with the murder of 13 women. [24] Prince Charles and Lady Diana Spencer announce their engagement.

MAR [9] John Lambe, the M5 Rapist, is given 12 life sentences for 16 rapes. [26] The inauguration of the Social Democratic Party is seen by many people as a refreshing development in British politics, possibly as the beginning of the end of the see-saw of two-party political debate.

APR [3] Race riot in Southall. [4] Race riot in Brixton. [11] Start of a weekend of serious violence in Brixton.

MAY [5] Bobby Sands dies at the end of a 66-day fast. [9] A bomb explodes at the Sullom Voe oil terminal while the Queen and King Olav are formally opening the complex. [12] The IRA hunger striker Francis Hughes dies. [15] Princess Anne gives birth to a daughter, Zara. [22] Sutcliffe is sentenced to life imprisonment for the Ripper murders.

JUN [10] Eight leading IRA prisoners escape from the Crumlin Road prison. [13] Blanks are fired at the Queen in the Mall on her way to the Trooping of the Colour. [16] An alliance is formed between the Liberals and the SDP, the first of a series of muddles over the centre's political identity. [24] The Humber Bridge is opened to traffic. [30] Garret Fitzgerald becomes Prime Minister of the Irish Republic.

JUL   [3] More riots in Southall. [4] Riots in Toxteth, Liverpool. [8] Riots in Moss Side (Manchester) and Wood Green (London). [15] There is another outbreak of violence in Brixton. [29] Prince Charles marries Lady Diana Spencer.

AUG   [8] There are riots in Northern Ireland following the death of the ninth hunger striker and ten years of internment.

SEP   [14] A 17-year-old youth is sent to prison for five years for firing blanks at the Queen. [17] The Royal Docks close, in readiness for redevelopment.

OCT   [4] The hunger strike at the Maze Prison ends: ten have died. [15] Norman Tebbitt's remark that his father 'got on his bike and looked for work' angers the unemployed. [17] Lt. Gen. Sir Steuart Pringle is badly injured by an IRA car bomb.

NOV   [14] Unionist MP Robert Bradford is shot dead in Belfast [25] Lord Scarman's Report on the summer race riots is published.

DEC   [8] There are sudden heavy falls of snow. Arthur Scargill becomes leader of the National Union of Mineworkers. [13] The composer Cornelius Cardew dies. [17] The Law Lords rule that the Greater London Council's cheap fares policy (fares in effect subsidized from rates) is illegal. [19] The Penlee Lifeboat Disaster; the lifeboat *Solomon Browne* is lost with her crew of eight while attempting to rescue the crew of the coaster *Union Star*.

 The Barbican, London (completed).

 Martin Amis: *Other People.*
George Clare: *Last Waltz in Vienna.*
Salman Rushdie: *Midnight's Children* (Booker Prize).
Victoria Glendinning: *Edith Sitwell: a Unicorn among Lions.*
Nigel Hamilton: *Monty: the Making of a General.*
William Boyd: *A Good Man in Africa.*
Douglas Dunn: *St Kilda's Parliament.*
Adam Mars Jones: *Lantern Lecture.*
A. N. Wilson: *The Healing Art.*

 Andrew Lloyd Webber and T.S. Eliot: *Cats* (musical).
Simon Bainbridge: *Landscape and Woods.*
Sir Peter Maxwell Davies: *Second Symphony.*

1982 Unemployment passes two million.

FEB   [5] Laker Airlines collapses with debts of more than £210 million. [**19**] In Belfast the De Lorean car company goes into liquidation.

MAR [**3**] The Queen formally opens the Barbican Centre. [**18**] An Argentinian scrap metal dealer raises the Argentine Flag in South Georgia — a signal of intention from Argentina that is not correctly interpreted by the British Foreign Office.

APR [**2**] The Falklands War begins; Argentine forces invade and capture the Falkland Islands. [**5**] The Foreign Secretary, Lord Carrington, resigns. A British Fleet sails from Portsmouth, bound for the Falklands. [**6**] The importation of Argentine products is banned. [**7**] The Defence Secretary announces a 200-mile radius naval blockade of the Falklands. [**25**] British forces recapture South Georgia.

MAY [**1**] British aircraft bomb Port Stanley in the Falklands. [**2**] The Argentine cruiser *General Belgrano* is torpedoed and sunk by the British submarine *Conqueror*, even though outside the 200-mile 'Exclusion Zone' and steaming away from it towards Argentina. [**4**] HMS *Sheffield* is destroyed by an Exocet missile from an Argentine plane; the *Sheffield* sinks with the loss of 21 lives. [**7**] Britain extends the total 'Exclusion Zone' to within 12 nautical miles of the coast of Argentina. [**15**] There is a British commando raid on the Argentine airstrip on Pebble Island. [**21**] The British Forces establish a bridgehead at San Carlos. HMS *Ardent* is sunk with the loss of 22 men. 21 men are killed when a Sea King helicopter crashes. [**24**] HMS *Antelope* is sunk after catching fire. [**25**] HMS *Coventry* and the *Atlantic Conveyor* are destroyed. [**28**] Goose Green and Darwin are captured by the British, which seems to mark a turning-point in the conflict. Pope John Paul arrives in Britain, landing at Gatwick.

JUN [**6**] The British take Bluff Cove and Fitzroy. [**7**] The Argentines raid *Sir Tristram* and *Sir Galahad* at Bluff Cove. [**14**] The Argentine forces formally surrender to troops of the British task force as British troops take Port Stanley; a ceasefire is agreed. Fighting ends in the Falklands. [**17**] The Argentine leader, General Galtieri, is deposed. [**21**] Prince Charles' son William is born in London.

JUL [**2**] Roy Jenkins is elected leader of the new SDP. [**7**] Michael Fagan intrudes into the Queen's bedroom, exposing alarmingly poor security at Buckingham Palace. [**13**] The film actor Kenneth More dies at Fulham. [**20**] IRA bombs explode in Hyde Park and Regent's Park killing 12 people, injuring 50, and killing 7 army horses. [**22**] Britain lifts the 200-mile Exclusion Zone round the Falklands.

Aug   [**29**] Ingrid Bergman, the film actress, dies in Chelsea.
Sep   [**5**] Sir Douglas Bader, pilot and leader of 'The Few' in the
       Battle of Britain, dies.
Oct   [**31**] The Thames Barrier, designed to prevent London from
       flooding, is raised for the first time.
Nov   [**1**] Channel 4 Television begins transmitting. [**7**] The police
       find the trousers stolen from Sir Geoffrey Howe on a train.
       [**10**] Geoffrey Prime is gaoled for 35 years for spying.
Dec   [**6**] A bomb in the Droppin Well bar in Ballykelly kills 16
       people and injures 66. [**12**] 30,000 women form a ring round
       the Greenham Common missile base in a protest against
       nuclear weapons.
Dec   [**15**] The border between Gibraltar and Spain is reopened after
       13 years.

    The Thames Barrier.

    A. N. Wilson: *Wise Virgin.*
       Thomas Keneally: *Schindler's Ark* (Booker Prize).
       Bruce Chatwin: *On the Black Hill.*
       John Fowles: *Mantissa.*
       Anthony Burgess: *The End of the World News.*
       Graham Greene: *Monsignor Quixote.*
       William Boyd: *An Ice-Cream War.*
       Tom Sharpe: *Vintage Stuff.*
       John Wain: *Young Shoulders.*
       Edward Crankshaw: *Bismarck.*
       Timothy Mo: *Sour Sweet.*
       Lisa St Aubin de Teran: *Keepers of the House.*

    Douglas Young: *The Hunting of the Snark.*
       David Bedford: *Sun Paints Rainbows on the Vast
       Waves.*
       George Benjamin: *At First Light.*
       Robin Holloway: *Serenata Notturna.*
       Kenneth Leighton: *Homage to Percy Grainger.*
       William Mathias: *Lux Eterna.*
       Paul Patterson: *Sinfonia.*

1983 The £1 coin comes into circulation. Sir William Golding receives the
       Nobel Prize for Literature.

Jan   [**17**] Breakfast television begins in Britain. [**31**] The wearing of
       seat belts in the front seats of cars becomes compulsory.

Feb [9] The 1981 Derby Winner 'Shergar' is stolen in County Kildare, never to be seen again. [23] Sir Adrian Boult, conductor, dies at Tunbridge Wells aged 93. [24] The composer Herbert Howells dies.

Mar [3] The writer Arthur Koestler and his wife commit suicide. [8] The composer Sir William Walton dies in Ischia. The spy Donald MacLean dies in Moscow. [15] The novelist Dame Rebecca West dies.

Apr [12] Sir Richard Attenborough wins eight Oscars for *Gandhi* .

May [16] London police begin using wheel clamps in an attempt to stop illegal parking. [21] Lord Clark, the art critic, dies. [24] A large bomb damages the Andersonstown police station in Belfast.

Jun [9] The Conservatives win the General Election with a landslide majority (Conservatives 397, Labour 209, Liberal/SDP Alliance 23); Margaret Thatcher remains Prime Minister. [12] Michael Foot resigns as leader of the Labour Party. [13] Roy Jenkins resigns as leader of the SDP, to be succeeded by David Owen.

Jul [3] The home of Gerry Fitt, former Ulster MP, is destroyed by fire. [13] Neil Kinnock escapes unhurt when his car overturns on the M4. [16] A helicopter crashes into the sea near the Scilly Isles, killing 20 people. [19] A new species of dinosaur is discovered in a Surrey clay pit.

Sep [18] St Kitts and Nevis become independent. [25] 38 IRA prisoners escape from the Maze Prison; a prison officer is stabbed to death during the escape.

Oct [2] Neil Kinnock is elected leader of the Labour Party, Roy Hattersley his deputy. [5] Cecil Parkinson MP admits having had a relationship with his secretary Sarah Keays. [10] Sir Ralph Richardson dies. [14] Cecil Parkinson resigns from the Cabinet. [19] Maurice Bishop, Prime Minister of Grenada, is shot by troops; General Austin takes control. [24] Dennis Nilsson confesses to 15 or 16 murders during his trial. [25] American troops invade Grenada, an action that is opposed by Britain. [27] Grenadan resistance to the American troops fails and Governor-General Sir Paul Scoon is reinstated.

Nov [4] Dennis Nilsson is sentenced to life imprisonment eight times over, although he boasts of killing 15 young men. [14] The first Cruise missiles arrive at Greenham Common from the USA. [18] John Habgood is enthroned as Archbishop of York. An official report accuses some police officers of being racists and bullies. [26] £26 million of gold bullion is stolen at Heathrow Airport.

Dec [**3**] Women peace campaigners break into the Greenham Common missile base. [**10**] There is a bomb explosion at the Woolwich RA barracks. [**17**] There is a massive IRA bomb explosion outside Harrods in London; six people are killed and many injured. [**25**] A bomb explodes in Oxford Street.

Terry Farrell: TV-am Studios.

Philip Larkin: *Required Writing.*
Malcolm Bradbury: *Rates of Exchange.*
Dame Iris Murdoch: *The Philosopher's Pupil.*
J. M. Coetzee: *Life and Times of Michael K* (Booker Prize).
William Trevor: *Fools of Fortune.*
Victoria Glendinning: *Vita.*
Kenneth Rose: *King George V.*
Alan Walker: *Franz Liszt: the Virtuoso Years.*
Jonathan Keates: *Allegro Postillions.*
Sean O'Brien: *The Indoor Park.*
Timothy Garton Ash: *The Polish Revolution; Solidarity.*
Peter Ackroyd: *The Last Testament of Oscar Wilde.*
Lisa St Aubin de Teran: *The Slow Train to Milan.*

Sir Peter Maxwell Davies: *Into the Labyrinth.*
Sir Harrison Birtwistle: *The Mask of Orpheus.*
John Butler: *Towards Aquarius.*
Wilfrid Josephs: *Rebecca.*

1984 There is a growing awareness of the dangers and causes of acid rain.

Jan [**9**] Sarah Tisdall, a Foreign Office clerk, is charged under the Official Secrets Act. [**11**] Two British lorry drivers are hi-jacked by French farmers as they drive through France in protest against foreign meat imports into France. [**13**] Six people die in hurricane-force winds. [**25**] The Government announces that workers at GCHQ may not belong to a trade union. [**26**] The Governor of the Maze Prison resigns after publication of a critical report on IRA prisoner escapes.

Feb [**3**] The Indian diplomat Ravindra Mhatre is abducted in Birmingham and later murdered. [**9**] Harold Macmillan accepts an earldom, becoming Lord Stockton, on his 90th birthday.

Mar [**6**] The National Coal Board says it will close 21 coal mines and lay off 20,000 employees. Scientists begin warning of the likelihood that burning fossil fuels will accentuate the greenhouse effect, and cause the atmosphere to become warmer. [**7**] Stephen Waldorf, an innocent passer-by who was shot in error by the police in 1982, is to receive £120,000 in compensation from the Metropolitan Police. [**12**] The miners begin their strike against the proposed pit closures, led by Arthur Scargill; mass picketing leads to violent confrontations between pickets and the police. [**14**] Gerry Adams, MP for West Belfast, is injured in an attempt to assassinate him. [**23**] Sarah Tisdall is sent to prison for six months for allegedly leaking documents to a newspaper; there are widespread protests at her sentence.

APR [**4**] Bailiffs evict women from Greenham Common. [**9**] There is more violence on the picket lines in the miners' strike. [**17**] WPC Yvonne Fletcher is shot dead outside the Libyan People's Bureau in St James's Square; the Bureau is besieged by the police for ten days. [**22**] The British Government breaks off diplomatic relations with Libya. [**27**] The St James's Square siege comes to an end; 30 Libyans from the bureau are deported. The British ambassador and other diplomats return from Tripoli.

MAY [**19**] The Poet Laureate Sir John Betjeman dies.

JUN [**3**] Levels of childhood leukaemia are reported to be abnormally high near the Sellafield nuclear re-processing plant in Cumbria, causing renewed anxiety about the safety of nuclear plants in general. [**14**] Four people are killed in explosions aboard an oil tanker at Milford Haven. [**28**] The last issue of *Tit-Bits* is published.

JUL [**5**] The abducted Nigerian exile Umaru Dikko is found in a crate at Stansted Airport and rescued. [**6**] David Jenkins is installed as Bishop of Durham. [**9**] The roof of one of the transepts of York Minster is struck by lightning and destroyed by fire. [**16**] The High Court rules that the Government's ban on union membership at GCHQ is illegal. The Lords vote to abolish the Greater London Council and other metropolitan authority elections.

AUG [**5**] The film actor Richard Burton dies. [**15**] The writer J.B. Priestley dies. [**18**] Clive Ponting, a civil servant, is charged with an offence under the Official Secrets Act, relating to information allegedly passed on to an MP about the circumstances surrounding the sinking of the *General Belgrano* in 1982. [**26**] An outbreak of salmonella poisoning at Stanley Royde Hospital in Wakefield leads to 26 deaths. [**27**] The actor James Mason dies in Switzerland.

SEP [**15**] Prince Charles' and Princess Diana's second son, Prince Henry, is born. [**22**] The Bishop of Durham calls the Coal Board chief, Ian MacGregor, an 'imported, elderly American'; Archbishop Runcie makes it known that he disapproves of the remark.

OCT [**12**] The Grand Hotel bombing; four people are killed and many injured when an IRA bomb explodes at the Grand Hotel, Brighton during the Conservative Party Conference. Mrs Thatcher, who is staying at the hotel, is unhurt but upset at the loss of her friends. [**31**] ACAS talks between the National Union of Mineworkers and the National Coal Board break down again.

NOV [**6**] The Government admits that the log of the submarine *Conqueror* relating to the sinking of the *General Belgrano* is missing. [**22**] The Law Lords uphold the Government's ban on union membership at GCHQ. [**30**] Two miners are charged with murdering a taxi-driver, David Wilkie, by dropping a concrete block on his car.

DEC [**11**] 11 die in a multiple crash on the M25 in fog. [**19**] Ted Hughes is appointed Poet Laureate.

J.G. Ballard: *Empire of the Sun.*
Sir William Golding: *The Paper Men.*
Sir Kingsley Amis: *Stanley and the Women.*
Angela Carter: *Nights at the Circus.*
Anita Brookner: *Hôtel du Lac* (Booker Prize).
David Lodge: *Small World.*
Fay Weldon: *The Life and Loves of a She-Devil.*
Peter Ackroyd: *T. S. Eliot.*
Christopher Hope: *Kruger's Alp.*
James Buchan: *A Parish of Rich Women.*
David Hughes: *The Pork Butcher.*
Lyndall Gordon: *Virginia Woolf: a Writer's Life.*
Blake Morrison: *Dark Glasses.*
Jeremy Read: *By the Fisheries.*
Jane Rogers: *Her Living Image.*
Andrew Motion: *Dangerous Play.*

Sir Michael Tippett: *The Mask of Time.*
Sir Peter Maxwell Davies: *The No. 11 Bus.*
Peter Racine Fricker: *Whispers at the Curtains.*
Iain Hamilton: *Lancelot.*
Andrew Lloyd Webber: *Starlight Express; Requiem.*

1985 Spain re-opens her frontier with Gibraltar after 16 years.

JAN [**14**] The musician and philanthropist Sir Robert Mayer dies. [**29**] Oxford University refuses to award Margaret Thatcher an honorary degree, because of her destructive education policies.

Feb [**11**] Clive Ponting is acquitted of breaching the Official Secrets Act. [**20**] The Irish Dail passes a Bill enabling shops to sell contraceptives. [**28**] Nine police are killed in an IRA bomb attack on Newry police station.

Apr [**11**] 24 people are killed by a Tamil bomb in Colombo shortly before Mrs Thatcher's arrival in Sri Lanka. [**27**] Lord Byron's publishers, John Murray, discover the manuscript of his only known short story. [**30**] Britain's first black bishop, the Ven. Wilfrid Wood, is appointed.

May [**3**] An epidemic in Stafford is identified as Legionnaire's Disease: 30 people die. [**6**] Four children are drowned by a freak wave during a school outing to Land's End. [**11**] The Bradford football stadium fire; 55 football supporters are trapped in or behind a burning stand and are burnt to death. [**12**] Prince Andrew opens the new Falklands airport, which has cost Britain £276 million. [**16**] The two miners who killed David Wilkie are sentenced to life imprisonment for murder; on appeal the charge is reduced to manslaughter. [**29**] The Heysel football stadium disaster; 41 Italian and Belgian supporters are killed in a riot before a Liverpool v Juventas match. As a result of the appalling behaviour of British football supporters, British teams are afterwards banned for an indefinite period from European competition.

Jun [**3**] Lord George Brown of Jevington, Labour politician, dies. [**5**] The Government gives its approval to the development of Stansted as London's third airport, ending a long period of uncertainty not only about Stansted but about all the alternative sites. [**6**] A worldwide ban on British football teams is imposed by FIFA. [**23**] An Air India Boeing crashes into the Irish Sea, killing all 329 people on board.

Jul [**2**] The Church of England's general synod approves the ordination of women, although many in the church strongly oppose it. [**8**] Britain lifts its ban on trading with Argentina. [**16**] The Local Government Act; the GLC is abolished.

Aug [**22**] 54 people are killed at Manchester Airport when a Boeing 737 bursts into flames while on the runway.

Sep [**9**] There are riots in the Handsworth area of Birmingham. [**28**] There are violent riots in Brixton, following the shooting of an innocent black woman, Mrs Cherry Groce, by a policeman.

Oct [**6**] A policeman is killed during riots in the Broadwater Farm Estate in Tottenham; these riots were a reaction to the collapse and death of a black woman while police searched her home. [**19**] Miners in Nottinghamshire and Derbyshire vote to set up a Union of Democratic Mineworkers. [**31**] The two miners sentenced to life imprisonment have their sentences changed to eight years for manslaughter.

DEC   [2] The poet Philip Larkin dies. [7] The poet and novelist Robert Graves dies.

John Fowles: *A Maggot.*
Anthony Burgess: *The Kingdom of the Wicked.*
Dame Iris Murdoch: *The Good Apprentice.*
Keri Hulme: *The Bone People* (Booker Prize).
Peter Ackroyd: *Hawksmoor.*
Douglas Dunn: *Elegies* (Whitbread 'Book of the Year' Award).
David Nokes: *A Hypocrite Revered.*
Robert Edric: *Winter Garden.*
Doris Lessing: *The Good Terrorist.*
John Milne: *Out of the Blue.*

Oliver Knussen: *Higglety, Pigglety, Pop!*
Sir Peter Maxwell Davies: *Third Symphony.*

1986   The Greater London Council is abolished. Corporal punishment is abolished in all state schools. The computerization of share transactions creates a 'big bang' of buoyant sales. Stanley Cohen (British) and Rita Levi-Montalcini (Italian) are awarded the Nobel Prize for Physiology and Medicine.

JAN   [7] Thatcher refuses to join Reagan in breaking economic and commercial links with Libya. [9] Michael Heseltine resigns from Thatcher's Cabinet, accusing the Prime Minister of stifling debate. [17] The Royal Yacht *Britannia* evacuates Britons and others from Aden. [20] Anglo-French agreement on a twin tunnel Channel rail link. [24] Leon Brittan resigns from the Cabinet.

FEB   [14] The composer Edmund Rubbra dies. [16] The police clash with pickets at Rupert Murdoch's printing plant at Wapping. [26] The European Court rules that retirement age should be the same for men and women, yet the British Government does nothing to equalize retirement age or pension rights.

MAR   [2] The Queen signs a proclamation which formally gives Australia legal independence. [18] Income tax is reduced to 29%. [31] A woman dies in a fire at Hampton Court Palace.

APR   [15] US planes bomb Benghazi and Tripoli in retaliation for Libyan terrorist acts; the planes used in this raid take off from British airfields, which causes widespread protests in Britain.

[**17**] Two British hostages are killed in Lebanon in retaliation for British connivance at the air attack on Libya. [**24**] The Duchess of Windsor, widow of ex-King Edward VIII, dies. [**26**] The Chernobyl nuclear reactor in the Soviet Union explodes; high levels of radiation affect north-west Europe, including Britain, causing people to think again about the wisdom of developing nuclear energy.

MAY [**3**] There are violent clashes between police and pickets at Wapping. [**16**] Ex-President Galtieri is gaoled for negligence in the conduct of the Falklands War.

JUN [**10**] Patrick Magee is found guilty of the Grand Hotel bombing. Bob Geldof is given an honorary knighthood for his work in raising money for the starving in Africa. [**20**] The movement of sheep is banned in Cumbria because of the build-up of radiation levels following the Chernobyl disaster.

JUL [**23**] Prince Andrew marries Sarah Ferguson and is created Duke of York. [**25**] The Appeal Court bans publications by former MI5 officer Peter Wright.

OCT [**26**] Jeffrey Archer resigns as deputy chairman of the Conservative Party after rumours of scandal. [**27**] 'Big Bang' day in the City; there is confusion as a computer fails. [**29**] The M25 is finally completed.

NOV [**6**] 45 men from an oil rig are killed in a helicopter crash in the Shetlands. [**21**] The Government's AIDS advertising campaign is launched. [**27**] It is revealed that George V's doctor hastened the King's death, so that it would appear in the morning rather than the evening papers.

DEC [**19**] John Stalker announces his intention to retire from the Greater Manchester Police Force. [**22**] David Penhaligon, MP for Truro, is killed in a road accident. [**29**] Harold Macmillan, Lord Stockton, Conservative Prime Minister, dies.

Richard Rodgers: Lloyd's, Leadenhall Street.

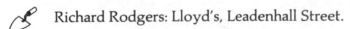

Sir Kingsley Amis: *The Old Devils* (Booker Prize).
John Le Carré: *A Perfect Spy*.
The Independent (first issue Oct 7).

Sir Harrison Birtwistle: *Yan Tan Tethera*.
Oliver Knussen: *Hells Angels*.
Sir Peter Maxwell Davies: *Violin Concerto*.
Michael Finnissey: *String Quartet*.
Robin Holloway: *Inquietus* (for Peter Pears).
Andrew Lloyd Webber: *The Phantom of the Opera* (musical).

1987 JAN [2] Golliwogs are banned from Enid Blyton's books by their publisher because of the offence caused to black people. [12] There are exceptionally low temperatures and heavy snowfall. Prince Edward resigns his commission in the Royal Marines. [19] Christopher Nolan, the paralyzed Irish writer, is awarded the Whitbread Prize. [20] Terry Waite, the Archbishop of Canterbury's special envoy, is abducted in Beirut while trying to negotiate the release of other hostages; now he becomes a hostage himself. [24] 300 people are injured in fierce clashes between police and pickets outside the Wapping print works.

MAR [6] The cross-channel ferry, *Herald of Free Enterprise*, capsizes outside Zeebrugge harbour because the crew leave the bow-doors open; about 200 people are drowned in the disaster. [10] Charles Haughey is elected Prime Minister of the Irish Republic on the Speaker's casting vote. [11] Dr Garret Fitzgerald resigns as leader of the Irish Fine Gael Party. [14] Roy Jenkins is elected Chancellor of Oxford University. [19] Three men are sentenced to life imprisonment for the vicious murder of PC Blakelock on the Broadwater Farm Estate. [27] 12 people are killed in violent storms.

APR [3] In an attempt to prove rehabilitation, Myra Hindley confesses to two more murders. [7] The *Herald of Free Enterprise* is righted. [8] 104 more bodies are found inside the ship. [25] Lord Justice Gibson and Lady Gibson are killed by a car bomb in Ireland.

MAY [3] Peter Wright's memoirs are published in the US and Canada [8] Nine IRA gunmen are killed in a battle with police and soldiers in County Armagh.

JUN [11] In the General Election the Conservatives are returned with a majority of 101, Margaret Thatcher is Prime Minister for her third consecutive term. [12] Princess Anne is created 'Princess Royal'. [27] There is mounting controversy over the treatment of alleged child abuse cases in Cleveland.

JUL [1] One of the Moors murderers' victims' bodies is found after a search on Saddleworth Moor assisted by Ian Brady. [13] Six children who were taken from their parents by social workers in the Cleveland child abuse case are returned to their parents. [18] Oxford University refuses Thatcher an honorary degree for the second time. [24] Jeffrey Archer wins a libel action against the *Daily Star*. In the Zeebrugge Inquiry's report three crew members are blamed for leaving the doors open, and the company is accused of sloppiness.

AUG [6] David Owen resigns as leader of the SDP after a majority vote to open discussions about a merger with the Liberals.

[**11**] The Cleveland child abuse inquiry begins. [**17**] Rudolf Hess dies mysteriously in prison, apparently by his own hand. [**19**] Michael Ryan massacres 16 in Hungerford. [**30**] Three people are arrested near Tom King's home; they are later charged with conspiracy to murder the Northern Ireland Secretary.

Sep [**22**] The Home Secretary prohibits the sale of semi-automatic rifles.

Oct [**8**] An inquest finds that the victims of the Zeebrugge disaster were unlawfully killed. [**15**] The Queen abdicates as monarch of Fiji. [**16**] The hurricane: the worst storm since 1703 strikes Britain in the middle of the night. 15 million trees are blown down, revealing the poor state of English woodlands, and 17 people are killed. Questions are raised about the Meteorological Office's failure to predict this major weather phenomenon. [**19**] There are floods in Wales and Cumbria; four are drowned near Llandeilo when a bridge collapses as a train crosses. The cellist Jacqueline du Pré dies. [**27**] Gilbert Mc Namee is sentenced to 25 years in prison for conspiring to cause bombings, including the 1982 Hyde Park bombing.

Nov [**8**] The Remembrance Day bombing at Enniskillen; there is widespread condemnation of this atrocity, in which 11 innocent people are indiscriminately killed. [**17**] The Government announces its plans to introduce the community charge in 1990 – a decision it will come to regret. [**18**] 31 people die in a fire on an escalator at the Kings Cross tube station. [**24**] A 'No Smoking' rule is in force throughout the London Underground system from today.

Dec [**2**] The Government announces stronger controls on firearms. [**7**] Dr Gareth Bennett commits suicide as it emerges that he is the author of a preface to *Crockford's* that is critical of Archbishop Runcie.

 The Boyle family: *Kerb study with metal edge.*

 Malcolm Bradbury: *Cuts.*
Dame Iris Murdoch: *The Book and the Brotherhood.*
Sir William Golding: *Close Quarters.*
Christopher Nolan: *Under the Eye of the Clock* (Whitbread Prize).
Penelope Lively: *Moon Tiger* (Booker Prize).
Bruce Chatwin: *The Songlines.*
Peter Ackroyd: *Chatterton.*
Peter Wright: *Spycatcher.*

🎼 Sir Harrison Birtwistle: *Endless Parade.*

1988 Sir James Black (British), Gertrude B. Elion and George H. Hitchings (American) are awarded the Nobel Prize for Physiology and Medicine.

JAN [**3**] Margaret Thatcher becomes the twentieth century's longest serving Prime Minister.

FEB [**7**] The novelist and critic Marghanita Laski, dies; so does the actor Trevor Howard. [**9**] Six people die in 100 mph winds. [**10**] Viscount Whitelaw resigns as leader of the House of Lords owing to ill-health. He is replaced by Lord Belstead. [**24**] An official report on the October hurricane criticizes the Meteorological Office.

MAR [**3**] The Liberals and the SDP join to form the Social and Liberal Democratic Party. [**6**] Three members of the IRA are shot dead in Gibraltar after a bombing conspiracy is uncovered; there is controversy over the way the shootings were carried out. [**10**] While ski-ing, the Prince of Wales narrowly escapes death in an avalanche; the Prince's friend Hugh Lindsay dies in the accident. [**16**] The Loyalist gunman Michael Stone shoots three mourners dead at an IRA funeral.

APR [**14**] John Stonehouse, the disappearing MP, dies. [**19**] Teachers are given a 4.75% pay rise. [**21**] Judges are given a 7.45% pay rise, nurses 15%. [**23**] Lord Ramsey, former Archbishop of Canterbury, dies.

MAY [**11**] The spy Kim Philby dies in Moscow.

JUN [**6**] Lester Piggott, the jockey, loses his OBE. [**8**] The broadcaster Russell Harty dies of hepatitis contracted while filming in Europe. [**17**] Viraj Mendis loses his appeal against deportation to Sri Lanka. [**18**] Mrs Marie Wilks is murdered on the M50.

JUL [**6**] An explosion on the North Sea oil rig Piper Alpha kills 150 men. A report on the Cleveland child abuse case is published. [**28**] Paddy Ashdown is elected leader of the SLD.

AUG [**11**] So far 6,000 seals have died in the North Sea; at first the high levels of pollution in the sea are suspected, but the cause of death is canine distemper. [**19**] Sir Frederick Ashton dies.

SEP [**26**] In a continuing muddle over names for the political centre, the SLD votes in favour of being called 'Democrats'. [**30**] A jury in Gibraltar rules that the three IRA terrorist suspects were 'lawfully killed'.

OCT [**31**] General Galtieri of Argentina is sentenced to 12 years imprisonment for his incompetent management of the Falklands War.

Nov [**8**] Salman Rushdie wins the Whitbread Prize with *The Satanic Verses.*

Dec [**4**] Edwina Currie rashly claims that most British egg production is infected by salmonella, which brings a storm of criticism from the egg producers and calls for her resignation. [**12**] The Clapham train crash; 34 people are killed as two trains collide. [**16**] Edwina Currie resigns after many protests about her salmonella comments. [**21**] The Lockerbie disaster: a Pan Am jumbo jet explodes in the air over southern Scotland and crashes onto Lockerbie; 270 people on board and 11 residents of Lockerbie are killed as a result of a terrorist bomb in the luggage.

Stephen Hawking: *A Brief History of Time.*
Sir Kingsley Amis: *Difficulties with Girls.*
Salman Rushdie: *The Satanic Verses* (Whitbread Prize).
Graham Greene: *The Captain and the Enemy.*
Paul Sayer: *The Comforts of Madness.*
Alan Bennett: *Talking Heads.*
Peter Carey: *Oscar and Lucinda* (Booker Prize).
John Stalker: *Stalker.*

1989 The introduction of the Community Charge (poll tax) as a substitute for rates meets widespread protest and defiance in Scotland, foreshadowing the problems the Government will encounter in 1990 when the charge is to be imposed in England and Wales.

Jan [**8**] A Boeing 737 crashes onto the Ml near Kegworth in Leicestershire; 47 people are killed. [**18**] A Manchester church is stormed to remove Viraj Mendis for deportation to Sri Lanka. [**20**] Field-Marshal Lord Harding dies. [**25**] Lord Basnett, former trade union leader, dies.

Feb [**12**] Five people die during riots in Pakistan over Rushdie's *Satanic Verses*, which is felt to be insulting to Islam. [**14**] Ayatollah Khomeini, the Iranian leader, orders Rushdie's execution for blasphemy; Rushdie goes into hiding. Khomeini is widely criticized for interfering in the internal affairs of another country and for assuming jurisdiction over a British subject. [**20**] Three terrorist bombs destroy a large area of the barracks at Tern Hill in Shropshire. [**28**] Hereford Cathedral drops its plans to sell the medieval *Mappa Mundi* in order to raise money.

Mar [**3**] Michael Stone is sentenced to life imprisonment in Belfast for the Milltown cemetery murders. [**4**] Five people die in a train crash in Purley. [**5**] The Ozone Layer Conference begins in London, an indication of growing awareness of environmental problems. [**6**] Two people die in a train crash in Glasgow. [**28**] The remains of Piper Alpha are sent to the seabed.

APR   [**5**] President Gorbachev arrives in Britain for a three-day visit. [**15**] The Hillsborough football stadium disaster; 95 Liverpool supporters are crushed to death in a pen due to poor crowd control. [**18**] An explosion on Cormorant Alpha leads to a shut-down of 25% of North Sea oil production. [**19**] The novelist Dame Daphne du Maurier dies. [**28**] 14 Liverpool supporters are sentenced to three years in prison for their part in the Heysel stadium riot.

MAY   [**1**] A riot starts at the Risley remand centre, in protest at the conditions at the centre; the riot ends three days later with a promise of an inquiry. [**14**] Actors make a more orderly protest over the developers' plan to bury the site and remains of the Elizabethan Rose Theatre in Southwark. [**25**] The Scottish Lord Chancellor is disciplined by his church, the Free Presbyterian Church, because he attended a Roman Catholic funeral. [**27**] There is a violent Muslim protest in Parliament Square against Salman Rushdie's book.

AUG   [**30**] Uppark House, a fine eighteenth-century mansion in Sussex, is gutted by fire. It is to be rebuilt.

OCT   [**19**] Britain and Argentina formally end hostilities.

DEC   [**19**] Stella Gibbons, author of *Cold Comfort Farm*, dies aged 86. [**26**] The composer Sir Lennox Berkeley dies.

 The Church of Scientology Castle, East Grinstead (completed).

 Anthony Burgess: *Any Old Iron.*
Sir William Golding: *Fire Down Below.*
Richard Adams: *Traveller.*
Anita Brookner: *Lewis Percy.*
Dame Iris Murdoch: *The Message to the Planet.*
Kazuo Ishiguro: *The Remains of the Day* (Booker Prize).

 Sir Michael Tippett: *New Year.*
Mark-Anthony Turnage: *Greek.*

1990 In the country, growing disquiet over the Government's apparent callousness culminates in furious demonstrations against the Community Charge. Similar disquiet in the Cabinet over Mrs Thatcher's unwillingness to accommodate her colleagues' views also simmers towards overt rebellion.

JAN [7] Terry Thomas, the film actor, and Lord Gardiner, the former Lord Chancellor, die. [9] Ruskin Spear, the portrait painter, dies. [19] The pianist Semprini dies. [25] A storm gusting to 110 mph sweeps across Southern England and Wales; 46 people are killed.

FEB [1] The composer Peter Racine Fricker dies. [7] Gales sweep across southern England again; two die and there is severe flooding in river valleys. [11] There is yet another storm. [26-28] There are more storms; Towyn in North Wales is flooded when sea defences give way.

MAR The residents of Towyn are evacuated. There are widespread demonstrations against the poll tax, especially in central London; demonstrations continue during the summer. Farzad Bazoft, a 31-year-old British journalist, is accused by the Iraqis of spying and hanged. [10] The Labour politician Lord Stewart of Fulham dies. [20] Lord Rothschild, banker and Government adviser, dies.

APR Strangeways Prison riot; the prison is taken over by the inmates for 25 days and wrecked. An earthquake centred on Wrexham registers 5.2 on the Richter scale. The Trade and Industry Secretary, Nicholas Ridley, confirms that steel cylinders detained by customs officers are, as suspected, parts of a huge 'super-gun' bound for Iraq.

MAY [5] Reginald Goodall, the great Wagnerian conductor, dies. [22] The actor and entertainer Max Wall dies aged 82.

JUN David Owen winds up the SDP: it is down to only two MPs. Captain Timothy Lancaster is sucked out of a broken aircraft windscreen four miles above Oxfordshire; he is held by his legs until the plane lands – and survives. [1] Actor and comedian Eric Barker dies. [2] Sir Rex Harrison, film and stage actor, dies. [9] Photographer Angus McBean dies. [14] Comedienne Elsie Walters dies. [16] Dame Eva Turner, opera singer, dies. [21] Elizabeth Harwood, opera singer, dies. [28] The Prince of Wales breaks his right arm in two places after a fall while playing polo in Gloucester.

JUL Tom King announces an 18% cut in the armed services, and a halving of the British Army of the Rhine over the next five years; these changes reflect changing relationships between East and West, and the end of the Cold War. [15] Margaret Lockwood, film actress, dies in London. [24] Ian Gow MP gives a message to the IRA on television: 'they will never, never win. We are never going to surrender'. A week later (July 30) he is killed by an IRA car bomb at his home in

Sussex. After accusing Kuwait of stealing Iraqi oil, the Iraqi government sends thousands of troops to the Kuwait border.

AUG [**2**] Iraqi forces invade Kuwait. [**4**] The European Community joins the world blockade by freezing Kuwaiti assets. [**8**] Iraq announces the annexation of Kuwait. [**19**] Iraq orders westerners in Kuwait to assemble at three hotels preparatory to being taken to key military installations as human shields. [**23**] President Saddam's propaganda blunder; he appears on television with a group of British hostages, stroking the hair of five-year-old Stuart Lockwood.

SEP [**6**] Margaret Thatcher tells the House of Commons that British troops will be sent to the Gulf as part of a 'Coalition' force to re-establish the independence of Kuwait. [**7**] Historian A. J. P. Taylor dies. [**12**] Actress Athene Seyler dies aged 101.

OCT [**2**] Two suspected terrorists are arrested at Stonehenge. [**21**] The former Prime Minister, Edward Heath, has a three-hour meeting with President Saddam in Baghdad, in an attempt to negotiate the release of the British hostages. [**24**] Heath returns with 33 released British hostages, steadfastly maintaining that negotiation and diplomacy are the key to the entire problem.

NOV [**7**] The author Lawrence Durrell dies. [**13**] Sir Geoffrey Howe makes a dramatic and outspoken Commons speech explaining his resignation as deputy Prime Minister; the speech is decisive in bringing Mrs Thatcher's term of office to an end. [**14**] The journalist and broadcaster Malcolm Muggeridge dies aged 87. Michael Heseltine announces that he will challenge the leadership of the Conservative Party. [**22**] Margaret Thatcher resigns as Prime Minister, saying 'It's a funny old world'. [**23**] The author Roald Dahl dies. [**28**] John Major becomes Prime Minister, defeating the other candidates, Michael Heseltine and Douglas Hurd.

DEC [**1**] 'Breakthrough': the two sides of the Channel Tunnel are joined and people are able to walk through for the first time. [**17**] The Government invokes Section 10 of the Reserve Forces Act, allowing the call-up of reservists, which has not been done since the Korean War; 1500 extra personnel, mainly medics, will be needed in the Gulf. [**22**] Prince Charles visits the British troops assembling in the Gulf. [**28**] Some army reservists express surprise at receiving call-up papers for the anticipated Gulf War. [**30**] British troops go on manoeuvres in the Saudi desert in readiness for war. [**31**] Dame Joan Sutherland gives her farewell performance at Covent Garden, with Pavarotti in *Die Fledermaus*. Archbishop Robert Runcie, also shortly to retire, delivers his New Year message, praying that Terry Waite, his special envoy held in captivity in the Lebanon now for almost four years, will be released in 1991.

Arup Associates: Sussex Grandstand, Goodwood.
Chapman Taylor: Bolton Market Place.
Fitzroy Robinson Partnership: St Martin-le-Grand, London.
Wells-Thorpe and Suppel: Porsche Showroom, Hove.

 Fernando Botero: *Venus*, Broadgate.

 Peter Ackroyd: *Dickens.*
Sir Kingsley Amis: *The Folks that Live on the Hill.*
Fay Weldon: *Darcy's Utopia.*
William Boyd: *Brazzaville Beach.*
Harold Pinter: *The Dwarfs.*
Paul Godfrey: *Once in a While the Odd Thing Happens.*
A. S. Byatt: *Possession* (Booker Prize).

 Robin Holloway: *Clarissa.*

1991 JAN [**5-6**] 27 people die in gales, including two visitors to Brighton who are overtaken by a huge wave. [**15**] The United Nations deadline for the Iraqi withdrawal from Kuwait passes: Iraq does not withdraw. [**16**] The UN 'Coalition' forces launch a ferocious air attack on Iraqi forces in Kuwait and Iraq to disable the Iraqi air force and weapons factories. 'Operation Desert Storm', the Gulf War, begins. [**31**] Archbishop Robert Runcie retires.

FEB [**7**] The IRA launch a mortar-bomb attack on 10 Downing Street when the War Cabinet is in session. John Major says it is a deliberate attempt to kill the Cabinet; windows are shattered but no one is hurt. The Queen reminds the IRA that 'they will not suceed' in destroying the democratic process. [**14**] The 'Birmingham Six' are released after their convictions are overturned by the Court of Appeal. [**27**] Kuwait City is liberated; the Iraqi army is effectively defeated on the ground by Coalition forces. [**28**] Ceasefire in the Gulf War follows the liberation of Kuwait.

MAR [**8**] The Liberal Democrats win the Ribble Valley by-election from the Conservatives. [**20**] Michael Heseltine announces the scrapping of the unpopular poll tax; it is to be replaced by a mainly property-based tax. [**26**] Peter Brooke, Northern Ireland Secretary, announces that inter-party talks on the future of the province are to take place later in 1991. Norman

Lamont raises VAT to 17.5% in order to lop £140 per head off the Poll Tax.

APR [**2**] British businessman Roger Coope is freed after spending five years in Iranian jails for alleged spying. The writer Grahame Greene dies in Vevey, Switzerland. [**4**] Prime Minister John Major announces humanitarian help for Kurdish refugees hours after former Prime Minister Margaret Thatcher appealed for aid on television, declaring 'this is not a time for legal niceties'. [**5**] Author and illustrator Eve Garnett dies aged 91. [**6**] Kurdish demonstrators storm the Iraqi Embassy in London. Police find weapons and a detonator in the Embassy. Britain joins Coalition forces in sending aid to the Kurds. [**9**] At an EC summit meeting in Luxembourg, John Major calls for a safe refuge for the Kurds in Northern Iraq. [**13**] Dame Peggy Ashcroft is given an award for her lifetime achievements by the Society of the West End Theatre (Laurence Olivier awards). Alec Ball is jailed for three years after driving his mechanical digger into the front of a house and causing £45,000 of damage, when the owner refused to heat his lunch in her microwave oven. Ralph Morris, head of Castle Hill School at Ludlow, is jailed for 12 years for sex offences against pupils. [**16**] Sir David Lean, film director, dies in London. [**19**] Dr George Carey is enthroned as Archbishop of Canterbury. The Allies warn Iraq as relief troops fly out: 'One shot and it's war again.' [**21**] Irish man of letters, Sean O'Faolain, dies aged 91. [**22**] In a speech at Stratford on Avon, Prince Charles condemns low educational standards and says: 'In following fashionable trends in education, we end up with an entire generation of culturally disinherited young people.' [**23**] President Walesa of Poland pays a State visit to Britain and is the guest of honour at a banquet given by the Queen at Windsor Castle. [**24**] Gerald Ratner, Managing Director of Britain's biggest chain of jewellers, declares that his goods are 'crap' and that his earrings are likely to last for a shorter time than a Marks & Spencer sandwich. He later says he was joking.

MAY [**2**] Missing undergraduate Rachel McLean, is found murdered under the floorboards at her Oxford lodgings. [**3**] Labour wins three marginal seats in local elections in Derbyshire. [**4**] The British Government increases its aid to Bangladesh where 100,000 people died in a cyclone on 1 May. [**6**] Actor Wilfrid Hyde White dies in Los Angeles aged 87. [**8**] In an article in *Vanity Fair* Mrs Thatcher speaks of her anguish at her abrupt departure from office, saying: 'The pattern of my life was fractured. It is like throwing a pane of glass with a complicated map upon it on the floor . . . You threw it on the floor and it shattered.' Frank Tempest is attacked by two pit bull terriers in Lincoln and receives appalling facial injuries. [13] Two-year-old Paula Holmes is attacked by a pit bull terrier in Bolton. [14] The Queen and Prince Philip are given a welcome at the White House at the start of a 10-day state visit to America during which the Queen will confer an honorary knighthood on General Schwarzkopf for his part in the Gulf War. [15] Tory MP Edwina Currie is awarded £5,000 libel damages against *The Observer* for a magazine article in which she was likened to a fictitious MP. [16] Former Royal Marine Captain Douglas Brand receives a life sentence in Baghdad for alleged spying. [17] Labour wins the Monmouth by-election, with a swing of 13% from the Conservatives. John Major complains that the voters have been misled by the Labour Party's alleged lies about the Government's proposed National Health Service reforms. [18] Muriel Box, film director, dies aged 85. [19] Britain's first woman astronaut, Helen Sharman, joins two Russian astronauts in the Soyuz TM 12 capsule and is blasted into space on an 8-day journey to the Soviet MIR space station 250 miles from Earth. Six-year-old Rucksana Khan is savaged by a pit bull terrier in Bradford, Yorkshire, receiving serious chest and facial injuries. Home Secretary Kenneth Baker imposes an immediate ban on the importation and breeding of pit bull terriers and the Japanese Tosas, with possible legislation being introduced to have them destroyed. [20] Justice Hollis allows a 12-year-old girl to have an abortion against her mother's wishes. A Government White Paper on education proposes giving polytechnics the same status as universities, increasing participation in education and training for 16-18 year olds by giving them vouchers towards further education, and creating new vocational qualifications equal in status to A-levels. [21] Teenager Patricia Cahill from Birmingham receives 18 years imprisonment in Thailand for alleged drug-smuggling. [23] Coral Browne, actress, dies. [24] Prince Charles and the Home Secretary attend the funeral of Rajiv Gandhi, assassinated in India on 21 May. Mrs Thatcher visits Russia as a guest of President Gorbachev. [31] Sir Angus Wilson, novelist and short story writer, dies in Suffolk aged 77. [31] The social worker who devised 'pin-down', an oppressive regime in Staffordshire childrens' homes, claims that the scheme was administered openly and with the approval of his superiors.

JUN [1] Three soldiers are killed and 18 people injured during an IRA attack on an Ulster Defence Regiment in Glennan, Co. Armagh. [3] Prince William has an operation for a fracture of the skull after being struck by a golf club at school. [3] The SAS shoot dead three IRA terrorists in the village of Coagh, County Tyrone. [6] Prince William leaves hospital. [7] Bill Morris becomes General Secretary of the Transport and General Workers' Union – the first black trade union leader. [10] The Duke of Edinburgh is 70 today. Britain bans a Soviet 'spyship' from carrying out research in UK waters. [11] The Maguire family's convictions for running an IRA bomb factory are quashed by the Court of Appeal. England triumph over the West Indies in the Test match at Headingley after 22 years of trying. Peter May, who kidnapped Simon Jones, aged four, and held him prisoner for eight weeks in his hostel room in Hemel Hempstead, Hertfordshire, receives a prison sentence of 11 years. [14] Actress Dame Peggy Ashcroft dies aged 83. Sir Bernard Miles, actor and director, dies also aged 83. [16] Gwen Ffrangcon-Davies, the actress, is made a Dame of the Order of the British Empire; she is believed to be the first centenarian to be so honoured. [18] In a speech in Chicago, Margaret Thatcher renews her campaign against a European super-state and says the result would be 'nothing less than a disaster'. The Prince of Wales is said to be suffering from 'serious degenerative disc problem.' The Prince cancels most of his engagements for the rest of the month. Foreign Secretary Douglas Hurd warns that the critical talks in Luxembourg on the future of Europe could collapse if Britain is pushed too hard: the British Government will not accept the idea of a federal Europe. [19] Mrs Thatcher speaks out on Europe again in New York and is verbally attacked by former Prime Minister Edward Heath. Colonel Gadaffi declares that Britain can 'go to hell' when his efforts to restore diplomatic relations collapse. He declares his support for the IRA as a 'just cause'. [20] Albert Dryden, who spent his redundancy money on building a bungalow in Co. Durham without first obtaining planning permission, shoots dead a Local Authority planning officer as he attempts to serve a demolition order on the building. [21] The Queen takes the salute at the Mansion House in the City of London during a victory parade for forces who served in the Gulf War. Douglas Brand arrives in Britain after nine months in an Iraqi jail for alleged spying. [26] David Farquhar, an RAF Wing Commander, is court-martialled for his negligence in leaving Gulf military secrets in an unguarded car last year. [**27**]An IRA bomb is found in a bag outside the Beck Theatre in Hayes, Middlesex, where the band of the Blues and Royals staged a concert the day before. The bomb is safely defused. Patrick Pottle and Michael Randle are acquitted by an Old Bailey jury of assisting the escape of spy George Blake from Wormwood Scrubs prison 25 years ago, because they acted from humanitarian motives. [**28**] At the Luxembourg summit, Jacques Delors, the European Commission president, backs down on federalism and says 'the language doesn't matter'. [**29**]The Queen visits Northern Ireland for the first time in 14 years to present colours to the Ulster Defence Regiment. She tells them, 'I admire your courage. Terrorism cannot be allowed to win.' Margaret Thatcher announces that she will resign as an MP for Finchley after the next General Election but that she will still play an active part in British politics, perhaps from the House of Lords. [**30**] An army bomb disposal squad blows up an IRA bomb left outside the Royal Air Force careers office in Fishergate, Preston, Lancs.

JUL   [**1**] Chairman Roy Watts, head of the newly privatised Thames Water, vigorously defends his huge pay rise and says, 'I am worth every penny'. Wearing rear seat belts in cars becomes compulsory. Thirty survivors of the Battle of the Somme gather at the Thiepval memorial for their last anniversary reunion. [**2**] Lorraine Voelcker, 27, and her children, 16-month-old Laura and two-and-a-half year old Galen are found dead in Forge Cottage in Kirtling, near Newmarket. Lorraine, the wife of a US serviceman, is believed to have been dead for 10 days and her children to have starved to death. [**3**] Stormont talks on the future of Northern Ireland collapse. [**7**] Two suspected IRA terrorists escape at gunpoint from Brixton top-security prison, London; they are now believed to be in a safe house in London. Home Secretary Kenneth Baker orders an inquiry into this 'grave lapse of security'. [**10**] The Queen opens the new Sainsbury Wing at the National Gallery.
[**15**] The G7 Economic Summit takes place in London.
[**17**] President Gorbachev visits London to seek economic aid for the Soviet Union. [**22**] John Major outlines his Citizen's Charter.

 Robert Venturi: National Gallery Extension (Sainsbury Wing) (completed).
Dartford Bridge over the Thames Estuary (completed).

Royal Academy, Burlington House, London (new Sackler Galleries opened).
Quinlan Terry: Cathedral of St Mary and St Helen, Brentwood, Essex.

 Susan Hill: *Air and Angels.*
Penelope Lively: *City of the Mind.*
William Trevor: *Two Lives.*
Fay Weldon: *Moon over Minneapolis.*
Margaret Forster: *The Battle for Christabel.*
Julian Barnes: *Talking It Over.*
Bernard Ingham: *My Style of Government: The Thatcher Years.*

 George Lloyd: *Twelfth Symphony.*
Mark-Antony Turnage: *Momentum.*
Sir Harrison Birtwistle: *Gawain.*
Sir Michael Tippett: *Byzantium.*

APPENDICES
of Key Dates

These snapshot summaries are not intended to be comprehensive. They are meant as a useful source of reference to direct readers to appropriate sections of the book where the events or persons are described in further detail.

Wars, Battles and Conquests

BC	
700-300	Celts settle in Britain
55	Julius Caesar's first expedition to Britain
AD	
43	Roman Conquest of Britain begins
123	Hadrian's Wall
c. 400	Saxon raids resumed
515	Battle of Mount Badon
577	Battle of Dyrham
599-900	Viking Raids
793	Sack of Lindisfarne by Vikings
825	Battle of Ellandun
878	Battle of Ethandun: Alfred defeats the Danes
1066	Battle of Hastings (Norman Conquest)
1075	Rise of the Norman barons
1099	First Crusade: Godfrey of Bouillon takes Jerusalem
1106	Battle of Tinchebrai
1148	Second Crusade
1189	Third Crusade
1191	Capture of Acre by Crusaders
1264	Battle of Lewes
1265	Battle of Evesham
1256	Battle of Dunbar
1258	Battle of Falkirk
1314	Battle of Bannockburn
1238	Beginning of the Hundred Years War
1400	Owen Glendower leads a revolt in Wales
1403	Battle of Shrewsbury
1415	Battle of Agincourt
1455	First Battle of St Albans (Wars of the Roses)
1461	Battle of Towton (Wars of the Roses)
1471	Battle of Tewkesbury (Wars of the Roses)
	Battle of Barnet (Wars of the Roses)
1485	Battle of Bosworth Field
1513	Battle of Flodden Field
	Battle of Guinegatte
1558	Calais lost to the French
1588	Defeat of the Spanish Armada
1639	First Bishops' War
1640	Second Bishops' War
1642-6	First English Civil War
1642	Battles of Edgehill and Chalgrove Field
	First Battle of Newbury
1644	Battle of Marston Moor
1645	Battles of Naseby and Philiphaugh
1648	Second Civil War
1651	Battle of Worcester
1685	Battle of Sedgemoor
1672-74	Third Anglo-Dutch War
1689-97	The War of the League of Augsburg
1689	Battle of Killiecrankie
1690	Battle of the Boyne
1691	Capitulation of Limerick
1692	Massacre of Glencoe
1692	Defeat of the French off La Hogue
1701-13	The War of the Spanish Succession
1704	Capture of Gibraltar

1704	Battle of Blenheim
1706	Battle of Ramillies
1708	Battle of Oudenarde
1709	Battle of Malplaquet
1715	The 'Fifteen' (Jacobite Rebellion)
	Battles at Preston and Sheriffmuir
1739	War of Jenkins' Ear
1740-48	War of the Austrian Succession
1743	George II defeats the French at Dettingen
1745	Battle of Fontenoy
1746	Battles of Culloden and Falkirk
1751	Clive seizes and defends Arcot in India
1756-63	The Seven Years War
1757	Battle of Plassy
1775	American War of Independence
1798	Rebellion under the United Irishmen is put down
1800	The English take Malta
1801	Nelson destroys the Danish fleet at Copenhagen
1803	England resumes war with France
1805	Battle of Trafalgar
1808-14	Peninsular War
1809	Battle of Corunna
1812	United States declares war on Britain
1814	British defeated at New Orleans
	War ends with United States
1815	Battle of Waterloo
1819	Peterloo Massacre
1839	First Afghan War
1854-56	The Crimean War
1854	Battles of Alma, Balaclava and Inkerman.
1857	The Indian Mutiny breaks out
1878	The Second Afghan War
1879	Zulu War
1885	General Gordon killed at Khartoum
1898	Battle of Omdurman
1899-03	Second Boer War (South Africa)
1900	Relief of Mafeking and Ladysmith
1914-18	First World War
1914	Battle of the Marne
	Battle of Mons
	First Battle of Ypres
	Second Battle of Ypres
1915	Gallipoli landings
1916	Battle of Jutland
1917	Third Battle of Ypres (22 Apr - 25 May)
	Battle of the Somme (21 Mar - 5 Apr)
	Battle of Passchendaele (26 Oct - 10 Nov)
1939-45	Second World War
1940	The evacuation of Dunkirk (29 May - 3 Jun)
	Battle of Britain (air)
1942	Battle of El Alamein (23 Oct)
1944	D-Day (6 Jun) - Allied landings in Normandy
1948	Emergency in Malaya
1952	Mau Mau emergency in Kenya
1956	Suez: Anglo-French attack on Egypt
1976	Cod War with Iceland
1985	Falklands War
1990-91	Gulf War

Constitutional, Legal and Religious

1086	The Domesday Survey	1662	Third Act of Uniformity
1100	Charter of Liberties	1664	Conventicle Act
1164	The Constitutions of Clarendon	1665	Five-Mile Act
1166	The Assize of Clarendon	1673	Test Act
1170	Thomas Becket, Archbishop of Canterbury, is murdered	1679	Habeas Corpus Act is passed
		1681	Oxford Parliament
1215	King John signs Magna Carta	1688	The 'Glorious Revolution'
1258	Provisions of Oxford	1689	Bill of Rights
1265	Simon de Montfort's Parliament		First Mutiny Bill
1279	Statute of Mortmain	1690	Locke's *Two Treatises on Government*
1294	'Model Parliament' of Edward I	1701	Act of Settlement
1297	Confirmatio Cartarum	1707	Union of Scotland and England is effected
1310	Lords Ordainers appointed	1711	Occasional Conformity Act
1351	Statute of Labourers	1714	Schism Act
	Statute of Provisors	1716	Septennial Act
1377	First introduction of Poll Tax	1721	Robert Walpole becomes the first Prime
1382	Wycliffe begins translating the Bible		Minister
1392	English becomes the official language in Parliament and the law courts	1727	First Indemnity Act for Nonconformists
		1752	Britain adopts New Style calendar
1393	Statute of Praemunire	1783	American independence internationally
1401	*De Haeretico Comburendo* – the burning of heretics – is made legal in England		recognized
		1787	The Society for the Abolition of the Slave
1476	William Caxton sets up the first English printing press at Westminster		Trade is founded
		1801	Parliamentary Union of Great Britain and
1494	Poynings' Law makes the Irish Parliament dependent on the English executive		Ireland is effected
		1807	The Slave Trade is abolished
1533	Act forbidding all appeals to Rome	1824	Repeal of Combination Acts in Britain
1534	Act forbidding the Payment of Annates to Rome	1829	Catholic Emancipation in Britain
		1832	First Reform Act
	Act abolishing the Pope's Authority	1833	Beginning of the 'Oxford Movement'
1535	First Act of Supremacy		First Government grant made to schools
	Coverdale's English Bible is printed	1834	Poor Law Amendment Act
	Sir Thomas More is executed for his refusal to recognize Henry VIII as head of the Church	1835	Poor Law Municipal Reform Act
		1846	Repeal of Corn Laws
		1869	John Stuart Mill's *The Subjection of Women*
1536-9	Dissolution of the Monasteries		is issued
1539	Six Articles	1870	Irish Land Act passed
1549	First English Book of Common Prayer		Forster's Education Act
1549	First Act of Uniformity	1884	Third Parliamentary Reform Act
1559	Second Act of Supremacy	1893	Home Rule Bill passes third reading in
	Second Act of Uniformity		Commons but is rejected by Lords
1563	Thirty-Nine Articles	1900	British Labour Party founded
1601	Elizabethan Poor Law	1906	Mrs Pankhurst begins militant agitation
1603	Union of the English and Scottish Crowns	1911	Parliament Act: power of Lords reduced
1605	Gunpowder Plot	1916	First Daylight Saving Act
1628	Petition of Right	1918	Representation of the People Act –
1628	Petition of Right		franchise extended to most women and all
1647	Charles I is handed over to Parliament		men
1649	Charles I is executed: England is governed as a Commonwealth	1928	Franchise extended to all women
		1972	Britain joins the EEC
1660	Restoration of the monarchy	1990	Community Charge (Poll Tax) introduced
1661	Corporation Act		in England and Wales

Science and Invention

1589 Harington's 'Ajax' flushing water closet
1589 William Lee invents the knitting machine
1614 John Napier: Logarithms
1628 William Harvey describes the circulation of the blood in *Concerning the Motion of the Heart and Blood*
1636 William Gascoigne invents the micrometer
1662 Robert Boyle discovers the relation between gas pressure and volume
1665 Robert Hooke publishes *Micrographia*
1666 Sir Isaac Newton: Calculus
1668 Sir Isaac Newton constructs a reflecting telescope
1672 Newton reads his *New Theory about Light and Colours* to the Royal Society
1682 Halley's Comet so named
1684 Robert Hooke invents heliography
1687 Sir Isaac Newton: Laws of gravitation and motion, set out in his *Philosophiae Naturalis Principia Mathematica* or *Mathematical Principles of Natural Philosophy* (allegedly written after watching an apple fall in his garden in 1665)
1698 Thomas Savery invents the first steam pump
1704 Sir Isaac Newton publishes *Opticks*
1712 Thomas Newcomen invents the first steam engine
1721 The compensator pendulum for clocks is invented by George Graham
1725 William Ged: Stereotyping
1729 The astronomer James Bradley detects stellar aberrations
1730 John Hadley invents the reflecting quadrant
1733 John Kay invents the flying shuttle
1735 John Harrison invents the chronometer
1740 Benjamin Huntsman invents the crucible method of making steel from scrap
1746 John Roebuck invents a process for manufacturing sulphuric acid
1754 Joseph Black discovers carbonic gas
1755 Joseph Black discovers magnesium
1756 Joseph Black discovers carbon dioxide
1757 John Bird invents the sextant
1758 Jedediah Strutt invents a ribbing machine (for stockings)
1764 James Hargreaves invents the spinning jenny
1765 James Watt invents the condensing steam engine
1766 Henry Cavendish discovers hydrogen
1769 Venetian blinds patented by Edward Bevan
1772 Daniel Rutherford discovers nitrogen
1774 Joseph Priestley discovers oxygen
1785 Edmund Cartwright invents the power loom
1796 Edward Jenner invents vaccination
1798 Henry Cavendish determines the mean density of the earth
1800 Henry Maudslay invents the metal lathe
Sir William Herschel discovers infra-red rays in sunlight
1804 Richard Trevithick invents the steam locomotive
1812 Bryan Donkin invents food canning
1813 Brewster's Law (Sir David Brewster)
1813 William Wollaston isolates palladium from platinum
1815 Sir Humphry Davy invents the miner's safety lamp
1817 Sir David Brewster invents the kaleidoscope
1823 Charles Babbage invents the digital calculating machine
1823 Charles Macintosh invents waterproof fabric
1823 Michael Faraday succeeds in liquefying chlorine
1824 Joseph Aspdin: Portland cement
1825 William Sturgeon: Electromagnet
1825 Michael Faraday isolates benzine

1827 John Walker: early friction match
1829 Thomas Graham formulates his law on the diffusion of gases
1831 Michael Faraday – the dynamo. Electromagnetic induction.
1835 Charles Babbage: early computer
1836 Screw propeller – Sir Francis Smith
1839 William Fox Talbot invents photography
1840 Sir William Grove invents incandescent electric light
MacMillan invents the first true bicycle
1845 Robert Thomson: Pneumatic tyre
1845 Self-raising flour is patented by Henry Jones of Bristol
1847 Dr James Simpson first makes use of chloroform as an anaesthetic
1852 Lord Kelvin and William Hankine invent refrigeration
1854 Sir John Elder invents the compound marine steam-engine
1855 Alexander Parkes: Celluloid
1855 Sir Henry Bessemer: Bessemer converter (steel production)
1855 Robert Bunsen: Bunsen burner
1856 Sir William Perkins creates mauve, the first artificial dye
1860 Baron Lister invents antiseptic surgery
1861 Frederick Walton: Linoleum
1864 James Clark Maxwell: electromagnetic theory of light
Sir Charles Parsons invents the turbine
1868 Sir William Ramsay discovers helium
1878 Edward Hughes invents the microphone
H. J. Lawson invents the modern safety bicycle
Sir Joseph Swan demonstrates the filament electric lamp
1883 Sir Joseph Swan produces the first synthetic fibre
1884 Sir Charles Parsons invents the turbine
1885 Sir James Dewar invents the vacuum flask
1888 John Boyd Dunlop invents an improved pneumatic tyre
1889 Sir Frederick Abel invents cordite
Friese-Green invents the cine camera
1892 Charles Cross and E. Bevan: Viscose
1894 Sir William Ramsay and Baron Rayleigh discover argon
1896 Sir William Ramsay discovers helium
1897 Sir Joseph Thomson discovers the electron
J. Langley demonstrates the effect of adrenalin in speeding up the heart rate
1898 John P. Holland invents the submarine
1901 Cecil Booth invents the vacuum cleaner
1904 Sir John Fleming: the Diode valve
1913 Hans Geiger: Geiger counter
1913 Henry Mosely: Atomic number
1914 Sir Ernest Swinton: the tank
1925 John Logie Baird discovers the proton
1928 Sir Alexander Fleming discovers penicillin
1930 Sir Frank Whittle invents the jet engine
1932 Sir James Chadwick discovers the neutron
1950 Sir Fred Hoyle: theory of continuous creation of matter
1964 Britain starts gas and oil exploration in North Sea
1965 T. Gabor: laser holography
1967 Radio Astronomy Group, Cambridge: Pulsars
1969 Concorde makes first flight
1971 Godfrey Hounsfield: EMI-Scanner (developed from his invention of computed tomography in 1967)
1979 Louise Brown, the first test tube baby, is born at Oldham, Lancs, through methods of transplanting ovum developed by R. Edwards and P. Steptoe

Exploration and Discovery

1497	John Cabot discovers Newfoundland.
1577	Francis Drake begins a voyage round the world (returns 1580).
1584	Sir Walter Raleigh discovers Virginia.
1585	John Davis makes three voyages past Greenland to Baffin Bay and discovers Davis Strait.
1600	The English East India Company is founded.
1607	Virginia is colonised by a London company: Jamestown is founded.
1610	Henry Hudson discovers Hudson Bay.
1620	The Pilgrim Fathers settle in New England.
1769	Captain James Cook visits New Zealand.
1770	Captain Cook discovers the east coast of Australia.
1773	Captain James Cook crosses the Antarctic Circle.
1789	Sir Alexander Mackenzie discovers the Mackenzie river in North America.
1796	Mungo Park explores the River Niger in Africa.
1828	Australian interior explored by Charles Sturt.
1831-6	Charles Darwin voyages round the world as a naturalist on the *Beagle*.
1841	James Ross discovers some of the coastline of Antarctica.
1848	The Franklin expedition to find the North-West Passage ends in disaster.
1851	David Livingstone discovers the River Zambezi in Africa.
1855	David Livingstone discovers the Victoria Falls in Africa.
1856	Richard Burton and John Speke discover Lake Tanganyika in Africa.
1860	Robert Burke and William Wills cross Australia (from south to north).
1877	Sir Henry Stanley traces the River Zaire (Congo) in Africa.
1912	Captain Scott reaches the South Pole (beaten by Amundsen).
1909	Sir Ernest Shackleton gets to within 100 miles of the South Pole. (He dies on his fourth Antarctic expedition in 1922.).
1935	Eric Shipton leads an expedition to survey the Everest region.
1953	E. P. Hillary and Sherpa Tenzing of the Everest Expedition led by Colonel John Hunt reach the summit of Everest.
1957-8	The Antarctic Continent is crossed by Sir Vivian Fuchs, leading the British Commonwealth Trans-Antarctic Expedition.

Monarchs – since the Conquest

House of Normandy
1066-1087   William I
1087-1100   William II
1100-1135   Henry I
1135-1154   Stephen

House of Plantagenet
1154-1189   Henry II
1189-1199   Richard I
1199-1216   John
1216-1272   Henry III
1272-1307   Edward I
1307-1327   Edward II
1327-1377   Edward III
1377-1399   Richard II

House of Lancaster
1399-1413   Henry IV
1413-1422   Henry V
1422-1461   Henry VI

House of York
1461-1483   Edward IV
1483   Edward V
1483-1485   Richard III

House of Tudor
1485-1509   Henry VII
1509-1547   Henry VIII
1547-1553   Edward VI
1553-1558   Mary I
1558-1603   Elizabeth I

House of Stuart
1603-1625   James I
1625-1649   Charles I
1649-1653   Commonwealth
1653-1658   Protectorate of Oliver Cromwell
1658-1659   Protectorate of Richard Cromwell
1660-1685   Charles II
1685-1688   James II
1689-1694   William and Mary (jointly)
1694-1702   William III (sole ruler)
1702-1714   Anne

House of Hanover
1714-1727   George I
1727-1760   George II
1760-1820   George III
1820-1830   George IV
1830-1837   William IV
1837-1901   Victoria

House of Saxe-Coburg
1901-1910   Edward VII

House of Windsor
1910-1936   George V
1936   Edward VIII
1936-1952   George VI
1952-   Elizabeth II

British Prime Ministers

Key to Party: (C) Conservative, (Cln) Coalition, (L) Liberal, (Lab) Labour, (N) National or National Coalition, (P) Peelite, (T) Tory, (W) Whig

1721-1742	Sir Robert Walpole (W)
1742-1743	Earl of Wilmington (W)
1743-1754	Henry Pelham (W)
1754-1756	Duke of Newcastle (W)
1756-1757	Duke of Devonshire (W)
1757-1762	Duke of Newcastle (W)
1762-1763	Earl of Bute (T)
1763-1765	George Grenville (W)
1765-1766	Marquess of Rockingham (W)
1766-1767	Earl of Chatham (W)
1767-1770	Duke of Grafton (W)
1770-1782	Lord North (T)
1782	Marquess of Rockingham (W)
1782-1783	Earl of Shelbourne (W)
1783	Duke of Portland (Cln)
1783-1801	William Pitt (T)
1801-1804	Henry Addington (T)
1804-1806	William Pitt (T)
1806-1807	Lord Grenville (W)
1807-1809	Duke of Portland (T)
1809-1812	Spencer Perceval (T)
1812-1827	Earl of Liverpool (T)
1827	George Canning (T)
1827-1828	Viscount Goderich (T)
1828-1830	Duke of Wellington (T)
1830-1834	Earl Grey (W)
1834	Viscount Melbourne (W)
1834-1835	Sir Robert Peel (T)
1835-1841	Viscount Melbourne (W)
1841-1846	Sir Robert Peel (T)
1846-1852	Lord John Russell (W)
1852	Earl of Derby (T)
1852-1855	Earl of Aberdeen (P)
1855-1858	Viscount Palmerston (L)
1858-1859	Earl of Derby (C)
1859-1865	Viscount Palmerston (L)
1865-1866	Earl Russell (L)
1866-1868	Earl of Derby (C)
1868	Benjamin Disraeli (C)
1868-1874	William Gladstone (L)
1874-1880	Benjamin Disraeli (C)
1880-1885	William Gladstone (C)
1885-1886	Marquess of Salisbury (C)
1886	William Gladstone (L)
1886-1892	Marquess of Salisbury (C)
1892-1894	William Gladstone (L)
1894-1895	Earl of Rosebery (L)
1895-1902	Marquess of Salisbury (C)
1902-1905	Arthur Balfour (C)
1905-1908	Sir Henry Campbell-Bannerman (L)
1908-1915	Herbert Asquith (L)
1915-1916	Herbert Asquith (Cln)
1916-1922	David Lloyd-George (Cln)
1922-1923	Andrew Bonar Law (C)
1923-1924	Stanley Baldwin (C)
1924	James Ramsay MacDonald (Lab)
1924-1929	Stanley Baldwin (C)
1929-1931	James Ramsay MacDonald (Lab)
1931--1935	James Ramsay MacDonald (N)
1935-1937	Stanley Baldwin (N)
1937-1940	Neville Chamberlain (N)
1940-1945	Winston Churchill (Cln)
1945	Winston Churchill (C)
1945-1951	Clement Attlee (Lab)
1951-1955	Sir Winston Churchill (C)
1955-1957	Sir Anthony Eden (C)
1957-1963	Harold Macmillan (C)
1963-1964	Sir Alec Douglas-Home (C)
1964-1970	Harold Wilson (Lab)
1970-1974	Edward Heath (C)
1974-1976	Harold Wilson (Lab)
1976-1979	James Callaghan (Lab)
1979-1990	Margaret Thatcher (C)
1990-	John Major (C)

Some British and Irish Writers

A selection only – all writers are listed in the Index.

Jane Austen (1775-1817)
Sir James Barrie (1860-1837)
Samuel Beckett (1906-1990)
William Blake (1757-1827)
George Henry Borrow (1803-1881)
James Boswell (1740-1795)
Elizabeth Bowen (1899-1973)
Rupert Brooke (1887-1915)
Anne Brontë (1820-1849)
Charlotte Brontë (1816-1855)
Emily Brontë (1818-1848)
Elizabeth Barrett Browning (1806-1861)
Robert Browning (1812-1889)
Edmund Burke (1729-1797)
Robert Burns (1759-1796)
Samuel Butler (1835-1902)
Lord George Byron (1788-1824)
Lewis Carroll (1832-1898)
Geoffrey Chaucer (c1345-1400)
Samuel Taylor Coleridge (1772-1834)
Wilkie Collins (1824-1889)
Dame Ivy Compton-Burnett (1892-1969)
William Congreve (1670-1729)
Joseph Conrad (1857-1924)
Sir Noël Coward (1899-1973)
William Cowper (1731-1800)
Daniel Defoe (1660-1731)
Charles Dickens (1812-1870)
Benjamin Disraeli (1804-1881)
Sir Arthur Conan Doyle (1832-1898)
John Dryden (1631-1700)
Daphne Du Maurier (1907-1989)
George Eliot (1819-1880)
T. S. Eliot (1888-1965)
Henry Fielding (1707-1754)
Ford Madox Ford (1873-1939)
E. M. Forster (1879-1970)
John Galsworthy (1867-1933)
Mrs Elizabeth Gaskell (1810-1865)
Edward Gibbon (1737-1794)
George Gissing (1857-1903)
Sir William Golding (1911-)
Oliver Goldsmith (1730-1774)
Kenneth Grahame (1859-1932)
Robert Graves (1895-1985)
Graham Greene (1904-1991)
Sir Rider Haggard (1856-1925)
Thomas Hardy (1840-1928)
Seamus Heaney (1939-)
Gerard Manley Hopkins (1844-1889)

Henry James (1843-1916)
Samuel Johnson (1709-1784)
Ben Jonson (1572-1637)
James Joyce (1882-1941)
John Keats (1795-1821)
Charles Kingsley (1819-1875)
Philip Larkin (1922-1985)
D. H. Lawrence (1885-1930)
Doris Lessing (1919-)
Christopher Marlowe (1564-1593)
Andrew Marvell (1620-1678)
Somerset Maugham (1874-1965)
A. A. Milne (1882-1956)
John Milton (1608-1674)
William Morris (1834-1896)
Dame Iris Murdoch (1919-)
Edith Nesbit (1858-1924)
Alexander Pope (1688-1744)
Beatrix Potter (1866-1943)
Anthony Powell (1905-)
J. B. Priestley (1894-1984)
John Ruskin (1819-1900)
Sir Walter Scott (1771-1832)
William Shakespeare (1564-1616)
George Bernard Shaw (1856-1950)
Mary Shelley (1797-1851)
Percy Bysshe Shelley (1792-1822)
Richard Sheridan (1751-1816)
Sir C. P. Snow (1905-1980)
Edmund Spenser (1552-1599)
Laurence Sterne (1713-1768)
Robert Louis Stevenson (1850-1894)
Jonathan Swift (1667-1745)
Algernon Swinburne (1837-1909)
Alfred Lord Tennyson (1809-1892)
William Thackeray (1811-1863)
Dylan Thomas (1914-1953)
J. R. R. Tolkien (1892-1973)
William Trevor (1928-)
Anthony Trollope (1815-1882)
Sir Edgar Wallace (1884-1941)
Evelyn Waugh (1903-1966)
Mary Webb (1881-1927)
Oscar Wilde (1854-1900)
Sir Angus Wilson (1913-1990)
P. G. Wodehouse (1881-1975)
Virginia Woolf (1882-1941)
William Wordsworth (1770-1850)
W. B. Yeats (1865-1939)

Index

Index of Persons

Index of Persons

Bromhead, Lieutenant, 256
Bronowski, Jacob, 381
Brontë, Anne, 212, 231, 232
Brontë, Charlotte, 209, 223, 230, 231, 233, 234, 236
Brontë, Emily, 210, 231, 232
Brooke, Henry, 185
Brooke, Peter, 361, 408, 411
Brooke, Rupert, 262, 290, 296, 297
Brookner, Anita, 396, 400, 408
Broughton, Jack, 168
Brown, Sir Arthur, 261, 340
Brown, Curtis, 313
Brown, Ford Madox, 234, 238, 245
Brown, Lord George, 364, 367, 373, 397, 401
Brown, Lancelot 'Capability', 189, 213
Brown, Louise, 388
Brown, Samuel, 212
Browne, Coral, 413
Browne, George, 87
Browne, Thomas, 124, 131
Browning, Elizabeth Barrett, 201, 221, 231, 237, 242
Browning, Robert, 201, 224, 227, 248, 249, 254, 263
Bruce, James, 181
Bruce, Robert, 48, 51, 52, 53, 54
Bruce, Sir William, 136
Brummell, George 'Beau', 186, 226
Brunel, Isambard Kingdom, 201, 219, 223, 224, 228, 229, 234, 236, 372
Brunel, Sir Marc Isambard, 228, 233
Brydges, Robert, 155
Buchan, James, 400
Buchan, John, 253, 288, 298, 299, 303, 329
Buchanan, President, 240
Buckingham, Edward Stafford, Duke of, 76, 84
Buckingham, George Villiers, 1st Duke of, 114, 115, 116, 117, 119
Buckingham, George Villiers, 2nd Duke of, 135
Buckingham, Henry, Duke of, 77
Buckler, C, 288
Bulganin, Nikolai, 352
Bull, John, 98, 113, 118
Buller, John, 375
Buller, Sir Redvers, 274
Bulwer-Lytton, Edward, 228
Bunning, James, 233
Bunsen, Robert, 237
Bunyan, John, 118, 131, 134, 138, 140, 141, 142, 143
Burdett, Thomas, 75
Burdon, Rowland, 219
Burges, William, 237, 238, 244, 245, 250, 253
Burgess, Anthony, 299, 352, 362, 363, 389, 392, 398, 408
Burgess, Guy, 344, 348, 390
Burghley, William Cecil, Lord, 95, 96, 97, 100, 108
Burgoyne, General, 185, 201, 209
Burgred, 22, 24
Burke, Edmund, 163, 181, 182, 187, 192, 196
Burke, Robert, 241
Burke, Thomas, 258, 299
Burlington, Lord, 161, 165
Burn, William, 233
Burn, W., 288
Burne-Jones, Edward, 220, 235, 259, 269, 271
Burnel, Robert, 47
Burnet, Gilbert, 140
Burnet, Sir John, 325
Burnet, Thomas, 142, 143
Burnett, Frances, 239, 246
Burney, Charles, 161, 185, 206
Burney, Fanny, 196, 210, 226
Burns, Robert, 174, 190
Burra, Edward, 321, 330, 332
Burrows, Sir John, 106
Burton, Decimus, 215, 218, 232
Burton, Isabel, 264
Burton, Richard (actor), 310, 399
Burton, Sir Richard, 213, 236, 240, 265
Burton, Robert, 111, 116, 122
Bury, Lady Charlotte, 217
Bush, Alan, 273, 338, 344, 351, 372
Bushnell, John, 136
Bute, Earl of, 201, 202
Butler, John, 374, 394
Butler R.A., 276, 334, 349, 360
Butler, Reg, 344
Butler, Samuel, 133, 140, 222, 251, 256, 271, 276, 278
Butlin, Sir Billy, 272, 388

Butterfield, William, 231, 236, 248, 251
Butterworth, 259
Butterworth, George, 292, 294, 299
Buxton, Anthony, 287
Byatt, A.S., 411
Byng, Admiral, 177, 182, 198
Byrd, William, 91, 98, 101, 105, 106, 113, 117
Byrhtnoth, 28
Byron, John, 203
Byron, Lord, 201, 202, 203, 204, 205, 206, 207, 208, 209, 210, 211, 215, 397, 401
Bywater, Percy, 307
Bywaters, Frederick, 306

Cabot, John, 79
Cabot, Sebastian, 81, 96
Cade, Jack, 71
Cadwallon, 12
Caedwalla, 15
Caernarvon, Lord, 307
Caesar, Julius, 3
Cahill, Patricia, 413
Caine, Michael, 320
Calgacus, 6
Callaghan, James (Lord), 291, 362, 364, 382, 384
Calvert, Raisley, 219
Camden, William, 105, 114, 117
Cameron, 140
Campbell, Colen, 156, 159, 160
Campbell, Sir Colin, 239
Campbell, Donald, 350, 368
Campbell, Sir Malcolm, 260, 312, 317, 322, 340
Campbell, Roy, 309
Campbell-Bannerman, Sir Henry, 284
Campion, Edmund, 90, 102, 103
Campion, Thomas, 99, 115
Canaletto, 169
Canning, George, 181, 203, 205, 208, 212, 213, 216, 222
Cannon, Philip, 393
Caractacus, 4, 5
Carausius, 7
Cardew, Cornelius, 379, 394
Cardigan, Earl of, 234, 237, 247
Carey, Dr George, 412
Carey, Henry, 163, 166, 168
Carey, Peter, 403
Cargill, 140
Carlile, Wilson, 231
Carlsen, Kurt, 344
Carlyle, Thomas, 219, 224, 226, 257
Caroline, Queen, 166, 176, 190, 212, 213, 219
Carpenter, Richard, 233, 235, 237
Carr, J.L., 365, 377
Carr, John, 181, 183, 186, 200, 205, 207, 210, 228
Carr, Robert, 113, 114, 374, 376
Carrington, Lord, 387, 390, 393
Carroll, Lewis (Dodgson), 220, 242, 246, 250, 271
Carson, Sir Edward, 288, 290, 292
Carter, Angela, 388, 390, 400
Carter, Howard, 252, 306, 327
Carter, President Jimmy, 384
Carteret, John, Lord, 167, 184, 191, 192
Cartimandua, 5
Cartland, Barbara, 274
Cartland, Jeremy, 378
Cartland, John, 376
Cartwright, Edmund, 168, 189, 192
Cartwright, Thomas, 100
Cary, John, 221
Cary, Joyce, 328, 336
Cary, Tristram, 309, 351, 358, 375
Casement, Sir Roger, 298, 299, 365
Cassivelaunus, 3
Casson, Hugh, 366
Castle, Barbara, 290
Castlereagh, Lord, 181, 203, 205, 206, 213
Catesby, Robert, 111
Catherine de Valois, Queen, 67, 69
Catherine of Aragon, 77, 80, 81, 83, 86, 87, 88
Caulfield, Patrick, 369
Cavell, Dame Edith, 245, 297
Cavendish, Lord Frederick, 257
Cavendish, Henry, 163, 179, 187, 203, 221
Cavendish, Michael, 119

Index of Persons

430

Index of Persons

Elric, 25
Elswitha, 23
Elwulf, 21, 22
Elyot, Sir Thomas, 87, 89, 90
Emberton, Joseph, 318
Emma, 28, 30
Emmet, Robert, 200
Empson, Richard, 82
Engels, Friedrich, 230
Eomer, 12
Eormenric, 10
Epillus, 3, 4
Epstein, Brian, 368
Epstein, Jacob, 257, 280, 292, 293, 310, 316, 333, 341, 355, 356
Erasmus, 81, 82, 83
Eric, 24
Eric Bloodaxe, 26
Eric II, 48
Eric IX, 92
Eric XIV of Sweden, 97
Ermengarde, 42
Ernest Augustus, Duke of Cumberland, 199, 223, 234
Ernest Augustus, Prince (Hanover), 198, 206, 222
Erskine, Ralph, 372, 389
Esake, Leo, 377
Espinasse, François, 287
Essex, Lady, 113, 114
Essex, Robert Devereux, Earl of, 108, 109
Ethefrith, 10
Ethelbald, King of Mercia, 16, 17
Ethelberht, Archbishop, 18
Ethelbert II, 17
Ethelbert, 9, 10, 18
Ethelbriht, 17
Ethelburg, 17
Ethelred I, 14, 15, 16, 18, 19, 23
Ethelred II, 22, 28, 30
Etheldreda, 14, 15
Ethelthryth, St, 14
Ethelwald, 13
Ethelwold, 13, 14
Ethelwold, Moll, 18
Ethelwulf, 20, 22
Etherege, Sir George, 134, 136, 139
Etty, William, 219
Eugene, Prince, 176
Euler, Ulf von, 372
Eustace of Boulogne, 32, 38
Evans, Sir Arthur, 273, 331
Evans, Beryl, 346
Evans, Dame Edith, 263, 385
Evans, Edith, 307
Evans, Marian – see Eliot, George
Evans, Merlyn, 330
Evans, Timothy, 346, 365, 367
Evelyn, John, 115, 124, 136, 176
Ewart-Biggs, Christopher, 384
Eworth, Hans, 93, 98

Fagan, Michael, 395
Fairbairn, William, 233
Fairbrother, Nan, 373
Fairfax, Thomas, 113, 125, 136
Fairhurst, Harry, 290
Fairless, Michael, 277
Fairley, Professor, 382
Falconer, William, 201
Falkender, Marcia Williams, Lady, 382
Faraday, Michael, 193, 213, 214, 215, 217, 219, 247
Farinmail, 10
Farnaby, Giles, 123
Farnol, Jeffery, 288
Farouk, King, 343
Farquhar, George, 149, 150, 153, 174, 175, 177
Farrar, Dean Frederick, 219, 241, 270, 277
Farrell, J.C., 377
Farrell, Terry, 394
Farriner, Thomas, 135
Fastolf, Sir John, 68
Faulkner, Brian (Lord), 374, 386
Fawkes, Guy, 111
Fayrfax, Robert, 74, 84
Feather, Vic, 377
Fenby, Eric, 282, 324

Fenton, Secretary, 104
Fenwick, Sir John, 148
Feologild, 21
Ferdinand of Aragon, 77, 78
Ferdinand, Duke of Brunswick, 199
Ferguson, Sarah (Duchess of York), 403
Fermor, Patrick Leigh, 387
Ferrers, Earl, 176
Ferrier, Kathleen, 291, 347
Ffrangcon-Davies, Dame Gwen, 414
Field, John, 207, 223
Field, Nathaniel, 115
Fielding, Henry, 153, 162, 163, 164, 165, 168, 171, 172, 173
Fielding, Sarah, 168
Fields, Gracie, 271, 390
Fildes, Luke, 252, 275
Filmer, Sir Robert, 141
Finch, Peter, 299
Finlay, Frank, 311
Finney, Albert, 323
Finney, Brian, 391
Finnissey, Michael, 403
Finzi, Gerald, 307, 342
Firbank, Ronald, 303, 309, 313
Firth, John, 84
Fischer, Ernst Otto, 377
Fisher, Geoffrey, 336
Fisher, John, 88
Fisher, John (1st Baron of Kilverstone), 295
Fitt, Gerry, 394
Fitzgerald, Edward, 203, 241, 259
Fitzgerald, Dr Garret, 393, 400
Fitzgerald, Michael, 304
Fitzgerald, Penelope, 390
Fitzherbert, Anthony, 85
Fitzroy, Henry, 84, 85, 89
Fitzsimmons, Bob, 270
Fitzurse, Reginald, 40
Flamsteed, John, 126, 158, 204
Flaxman, John, 173, 197, 204, 219
Flecker, James Elroy, 294
Fleming, Sir Alexander, 256, 278, 336, 349, 350
Fleming, Ian, 285, 347, 357, 364
Fleming, Sir John, 278
Fletcher, Francis, 111, 113, 115, 119, 127
Fletcher, John, 117, 127
Fletcher, Yvonne, 399
Flicke, Gerlach, 92
Flinders, Matthew, 207
Florey, Sir Howard, 271, 329, 339, 369
Fonteyn, Dame Margot, 302
Foch, Marshal, 301
Foot, Michael, 293, 385, 397
Foote, Samuel, 178
Forbes, 78
Forbes, General, 199
Forbes, S, 264
Ford, John, 104, 111, 116, 119, 120, 121, 122
Forde, Emanuel, 108
Forester, C.S., 272, 367
Formby, George, 279
Formosus, Pope, 25
Forster, E.M., 255, 281, 284, 285, 288, 295, 309, 372
Forster, Margaret, 410, 416
Forsyth, Bruce, 313
Forsyth, Frederick, 382
Fowler, Charles, 217
Fowler, Sir John, 265
Fowles, John, 363, 367, 371, 387, 393, 396, 398, 402
Fox, Charles James (1st Baron Holland), 171, 190, 195, 202
Fox, George, 128, 146
Fox, Henry, 173
Foxe, John, 98, 105
Francis I of France, 84
Francis I of Scotland, 89
Francis II of France, 96, 97
Francis, John, 227
Francis, Sir Philip, 181, 205, 215
Franco, 326
Frankau, Gilbert, 304
Franklin, Benjamin, 188
Franklin, Sir John, 231
Fraser, Hugh, 382
Fraser, Simon, 170

Index of Persons

Index of Persons

Index of Persons

Index of Persons

441

Index of Persons

Ross, James, 219
Ross, Sir James Clark, 219, 227
Ross, Pilot, 302, 303
Ross, Sir Ronald, 270, 275
Rosse, Earl of, 229
Rossetti, Christina, 218, 243, 246, 251
Rossetti, Dante Gabriel, 217, 234, 235, 239, 243, 244, 246, 248, 249, 261
Rothenstein, Sir William, 272, 275
Rothschild, Lord, 409
Roubiliac, 177
Rousseau, Jean Jacques, 179
Rowe, Nicholas, 150, 151, 152, 153, 156, 174, 175, 176, 177, 180, 181
Rowlandson, Thomas, 205
Rowley, Thomas, 209
Rowley, William, 120, 129, 133
Roy, Rob, 155, 179
Royce, Sir Frederick Henry, 237, 244, 279, 320
Rubbra, Edmund, 274, 337, 353, 398
Rubens, Bernice, 373
Rubens, Sir Peter Paul, 121, 119
Runcie, Robert, Archbishop, 305, 388, 391, 396, 405, 407, 410, 411
Runciman, Alexander, 180
Rundell, Maria, 202
Rupert, Prince, 124, 125
Rushdie, Salman, 394, 403, 404, 407, 408
Ruskin, John, 211, 228, 233, 234, 235, 236, 237, 238, 246, 253, 255, 273
Russell, Admiral, 148
Russell, Bertrand, 251, 278, 296, 338, 360, 372
Russell, Earl, 278
Russell, Lord John, 219, 230, 234, 238, 245
Russell, Lord, 93
Russell, Lord William, 142, 143, 149
Russell, William, 254
Rutherford, Daniel, 182, 206
Rutherford, Ernest, 1st Baron Rutherford of Nelson, 202, 271, 275, 289, 325
Rutherford, Margaret, 266
Ruthven, Earl of, 109
Rutland, Earl of, 63, 73
Ryan, Michael, 405
Ryle, Gilbert, 342
Ryle, Sir Martin, 379
Rymer, James, 229, 231

Saarinen, Eero, 360
Sacheverell, Dr Henry, 154
Sacks, Oliver, 379
Sackville, Thomas, 97
Sackville-West, Vita, 312, 318, 361
Saddam, President, 410
Sala, George, 244
Salisbury, Earl of, 63, 68, 72, 73
Salisbury, Robert Cecil (1st Earl of), 255, 259, 261, 266, 267, 268, 274, 277
Salt, Henry, 207
Salvin, Anthony, 222, 224, 238, 245
Samuel, Herbert, 1st Viscount, 344
Sancroft, William, 139, 146, 147
Sanders, George, 282
Sands, Bobby, 393
Sandys, Duncan, 350
Sanger, Frederick, 354
Sargent, John Singer, 276, 285
Sargent, Sir Malcolm, 268, 369
Sarsfield, Patrick, 147
Sassoon, Siegfied, 314, 369
Savage, James, 212, 217
Savery, Thomas, 149
Sawtre, William, 63
Saxe, Marshal, 169
Sayer, Paul, 407
Sayers, Dorothy L., 266, 267, 308, 314, 354
Scales, Lord, 71
Scargill, Arthur, 323, 394, 395
Scarman, Lord, 391
Schopenhauer, Arthur, 200
Schorne, John, 48, 52, 75, 104
Schreiner, Olive, 259
Schrodinger, Erwin, 319
Schubert, Franz, 246
Schwarzkopf, Norman, 413
Scoon, Sir Paul, 397
Scott, Elizabeth, 313, 319
Scott, Sir George Gilbert, 231, 243, 244, 245, 251

Scott, Sir Giles Gilbert, 227, 249, 275, 292, 309, 311, 315, 318, 320, 331, 333, 339, 349
Scott, Lieut-Col. H.Y.D., 247
Scott, Michael, 221
Scott, Norman, 382, 384, 388
Scott, Paul, 367, 387
Scott, Sir Peter, 286
Scott, Captain Robert, 281, 284, 291, 291, 292
Scott, Sir Walter, 199, 201, 204, 206, 207, 208, 209, 210, 211, 213, 214, 215, 216, 217, 220
Scotus, Duns, 51
Scrocmail, 11
Scroggs, Lord Chief Justice, 139
Scrope, Archbishop, 64
Scrope, Lord, 66, 99
Searle, Humphrey, 370
Seaxburg, 14
Secker, 204
Secker, Thomas, 175, 180, 199
Sedley, Sir Charles, 136
Seely, John, 291
Seger, William, 106
Segrave, Sir Henry, 312, 316
Seidl, Anton, 258
Selassie, Emperor Haile, 323, 330, 380
Selden, John, 116, 145
Selfridge, Harry Gordon, 285
Selkirk, Alexander, 151, 154, 175, 178
Sellar, 317
Sellers, Peter, 310, 389
Semprini, 409
Septimius Severus, 7
Sergius, Pope, 15
Serio, Sigeric, 28
Settle, Elkanah, 137
Severus, Septimius, 6
Sewell, Anna, 212, 254, 255
Sexburga, 16
Seyler, Athene, 410
Seymour, Edward, 91
Seymour, Queen Jane, 89
Seymour, Thomas, Lord, 92, 93
Seymour, William Earl of Hertford, 112
Shackleton, Sir Ernest, 252, 286, 287, 294, 296, 297, 298, 299, 306
Shadwell, Thomas, 122, 123, 135, 137, 138, 142, 144, 146
Shaftesbury, Lord, 140, 141, 155, 179, 199
Shah, Bahadur, 235
Shakespeare, William, 98, 103, 104, 106, 107, 108, 109, 110, 111, 112, 113, 114, 117
Sharman, Helen, 413
Sharp, Cecil, 241
Sharpe, Archbishop, 140
Sharpe, Mrs, 214
Sharpe, Tom, 383, 393
Sharpham, Edward, 111
Shaw, George Bernard, 238, 271, 278, 280, 283, 287, 288, 306, 308, 316, 326, 327, 343
Shaw, John, 238
Shaw, Norman, 251, 254, 260, 262, 265, 281
Shaw, Percy, 384
Shelburne, Lord, 180, 189
Sheldon, Gilbert, 133
Shelley, Mary Wollstonecroft (née Godwin), 196, 209, 210, 234
Shelley, Norman, 329
Shelley, Percy Bysshe, 193, 204, 206, 209, 211, 212, 213, 214, 215
Shenstone, William, 168
Shepherd, Edward, 164, 188
Sheppard, Jack, 184
Sheppard, Richard, 365
Sheraton, Thomas, 202
Sheridan, Frances, 177, 201
Sheridan, Richard Brinsley, 172, 178, 184, 185
Sheriff, Laurence, 99
Sherlock, William, 145
Sherriff, R.C., 315
Sherwin, William, 138
Shiel, Matthew, 275
Shillibeer, George, 218
Shipton, Eric, 322, 343, 386
Shirley, James, 122
Shore, John, 155
Shorthouse, Joseph, 257
Shovel, Sir Cloudesley, 152
Shrapnel, Lt Henry, 189, 213

442

Index of Persons

Index of Persons

446